John Wiley & Sons, Inc.

Hands-On Teaching Strategies for Using Math Manipulatives Kits from ETA/Cuisenaire®!

Grades K–8

SAVE OVER 30% off regular retail price on our most popular pre-service kit!

W9-AAD-191

Item No. WH-1003

Hands-On Teaching Strategies for Using Math Manipulatives Kits

Includes 20 Manipulatives, a 120-page Teacher's Resource Binder by Dr. Gail Thornton and Gail Lowe-Parrino, and a convenient shoulder bag.

Plastic Manipulatives: Angle Ruler, GeoReflector™ Mirror, Fraction Tower® Cubes, PopCubes®, Cuisenaire® Rods

ManipuLite® Manipulatives: Base Ten Blocks, Color Tiles, Factor Blocks™, Two-Color Counters, Number Cubes, Tangrams, Pattern Blocks

Overhead Sets: Base Ten Blocks, Coins, Color Tiles, Fraction Circles, Geoboard with Rubber Bands, Pattern Blocks, Spinners, Tangrams

www.etacuisenaire.com

College students and professors!

Do you use a Wiley/Jossey-Bass text for your Elementary Math Methods course?

Then you'll want to take advantage of our special offer for **Hands-On Teaching Strategies for Using Math Manipulatives Kits** at a spectacular savings of over 30% off the retail price.

To place your order, mail in this pre-printed order form or order online at www.etacuisenaire.com/wh

---

ETA/Cuisenaire Order Form

☐ I am a teacher/education student.   ☐ I am a college/university professor.

Name _____

Institution _____

Address _____

City _____ State _____ Zip _____

Phone _____ FAX _____ e-mail _____

Send me the following **Hands-On-Teaching for Using Math Manipulatives Kits**

_____ WJ-1003   Standard Kit $51.95

_____ WJ-1003NTG   Standard Kit *without Guide* $36.95

Subtotal _____

Applicable Sales Tax _____

10% Shipping and Handling, for a total of $ _____

TOTAL _____

(Please mention promotion code P0106WJ24 when ordering.)

Charge this order to (check one) ☐ VISA ☐ MasterCard

☐☐☐☐ ☐☐☐☐ ☐☐☐☐ ☐☐☐☐

Exp. Date _____ Phone ( ) _____

Signature _____

☐ My check for $ _____ is enclosed.

Make check payable to ETA/Cuisenaire.

Please mail this order form to: **ETA/Cuisenaire
500 Greenview Court
Vernon Hills, IL 60061-1862**

☐ Please send me a FREE Mathematics Catalog.

My permanent address, if different from above, is:

_____

_____

- Pricing expires December 31, 2007.
- Orders received after December 31, 2007, will receive a 30% discount off current list price.
- No P.O. Boxes allowed.

Hands-On Teaching Strategies for Using Math Manipulatives Kits from ETA/Cuisenaire® is an excellent resource for pre-service teacher training. The Kit builds teachers' confidence by providing new strategies for successful mathematics instruction. This Kit includes sets of commonly used manipulatives along with detailed, comprehensive, classroom-tested activities to help you explore math using manipulatives.

Available in two formats to meet every budget!

- Our **Standard Kit** includes the 120-page Teacher Resource Binder along with the collection of manipulatives shown on the previous page. All are packaged in a convenient shoulder bag.

- The **Standard Kit without Guide** includes all the manipulatives packaged in the shoulder bag of our Standard Kit but excludes the Teacher Resource Binder.

P0106WJ24

About the Authors

ROBERT E. REYS is Curators' Professor of Mathematics Education at the University of Missouri–Columbia. He is a former mathematics teacher and district mathematics coordinator. His research interests are in the areas of calculators, mental computation, estimation, and number sense. He has authored nearly 200 articles in professional journals, and was General Editor for five yearbooks of the National Council of Teachers of Mathematics.

MARY M. LINDQUIST is Fuller E. Callaway Professor of Mathematics Education, Emeritus at Columbus State University (Georgia). She worked with undergraduate and graduate students in early childhood, middle grades, and secondary mathematics education. Mary was president of the National Council of Teachers of Mathematics and chair of the Commission on the Future of the Standards, the oversight committee for *Principles and Standards of School Mathematics* (NCTM, 2000). She has served on many national and international committees, including those involved with the National Assessment of Education Progress (NAEP) and the Trends in International Mathematics and Science Study (TIMSS). She was awarded the prestigious Lifetime Achievement Award for her service, leadership, and research by the Mathematics Education Trust.

DIANA V. LAMBDIN is Armstrong Professor of Teacher Education and Professor of Mathematics Education at Indiana University in Bloomington, where she teaches courses for prospective elementary teachers, supervises students' field experience, works with masters and doctoral students in mathematics education, and also serves as Associate Dean for Teacher Education. Prior to entering the field of teacher education, she was a mathematics teacher in Massachusetts, Michigan, and Iowa. Diana has been active as an author, editor, project evaluator, and workshop leader and was a member of the writing team for *Principles and Standards for School Mathematics* (NCTM, 2000).

NANCY L. SMITH has been an educator for over twenty-five years. She taught elementary school and middle school mathematics for ten years in Richmond, Missouri. She is currently Professor in the Department of Early Childhood/Elementary Teacher Education at Emporia State University in Emporia, Kansas, where she teaches elementary mathematics education courses for preservice and inservice teachers, teaches general elementary education courses, and supervises student teachers in the Olathe Professional Development Schools.

Contents

Preface

This edition of *Helping Children Learn Mathematics* reflects the changing world of learning and teaching elementary school mathematics. Change is everywhere. It includes technology. It includes new and different elementary mathematics programs. It includes assessment, much of which is driven by the federal No Child Left Behind Act of 2001. It includes a landmark document that provides a vision for the future—*Principles and Standards for School Mathematics*, prepared by the National Council of Teachers of Mathematics. Teachers of mathematics in elementary school not only experience these changes but, more important, also have an opportunity to help lead the way.

This edition of *Helping Children Learn Mathematics* is built around three main themes:

- helping children make sense of mathematics
- incorporating practical experiences and research to guide teaching
- emphasizing major ideas discussed in detail in the *Principles and Standards for School Mathematics*

This book is intended for those of you who are or who will be teachers of mathematics in elementary school. It is designed to help you help children learn mathematical concepts and skills, as well as important problem-solving strategies. In the process it will challenge your thinking and, we hope, will further stimulate your interest in learning and teaching mathematics.

Helping Children Learn Mathematics is a unique resource that consists of two main parts.

The first part (Chapters 1–6) provides a basis for understanding the changing mathematics curriculum and how children learn mathematics. It offers some guidelines for planning and evaluating instruction. And it directs attention to problem solving and assessment, both of which have profound implications for mathematics teaching at all levels and the importance of which is reflected by their integration throughout the book.

The second part (Chapters 7–17) discusses teaching strategies and techniques, as well as learning activities, related to specific mathematical topics. The emphasis is on using models and materials to develop concepts and understanding, so that mathematics learning is indeed meaningful. We believe that meaning is most effectively established by helping students discuss mathematics as they move from concrete materials and examples to generalizations and abstractions.

Features of This Text

We have continued to revise this textbook in order to meet the changing needs of students preparing to become teachers, or teachers who are continuing to learn. This edition continues the rich history of this book—with a dash of new breath. It has been updated to reflect current recommendations, readings, and practices while maintaining the characteristics and features that have made it a popular choice of instructors. A useable text for instructors, it is also readable and understandable by students who are being introduced to teaching elementary mathematics. Yet, its depth also makes it appropriate for teachers to use as they continue to learn about teaching mathematics.

Updated coverage of NCTM Standards and Expectations

The Standards and Expectations from the *Principles and Standards for School Mathematics* are a valuable resource for you to use along with *Helping Children Learn Mathematics* during your teaching career. Excerpts of them have been highlighted throughout the book, and Appendix A reproduces them in their entirety. The five mathematical process standards identified in the *Principles and Standards*—problem solving, communication, connections, representations, and reasoning and proof—are addressed in Chapter 5. These processes are the foundation on which students make sense of mathematics. Chapter 6 takes a more in-depth look at problem solving and at how it can be used in teaching and learning mathematics. It discusses various problem-solving strategies and presents a wide variety of problems for which the strategies are useful.

NEW! "Snapshots of a Lesson" now include video clips

Each chapter-opener Snapshot is an excerpt from an actual mathematics lesson to show the vital role teachers play in helping students talk and learn about mathematics. Featuring student–teacher and student–student dialogue, they cover a wide range of grades (K to middle school) and mathematical topics, demonstrate many effective classroom practices, and provide a smooth, practical segue into the body of the chapter. In this edition, many Snapshots are video based, with the clips easily accessed online. You'll see them called out with this camera icon:

◀Updated & Expanded! Classroom Applications

In addition to strategies woven into the text, the following two sections will help you practice translating theory into practice as you guide and teach children in their study of mathematics.

- **In the Classroom" Activities.** Found throughout the text in special boxes, these activities provide a wealth of ideas and strategies for

teaching children the topics of each chapter. We often include suggestions for using these activities and for reflecting on what happens as children do them. Additional suggestions for using these activities are given in *Teaching Elementary Mathematics: A Resource for Field Teachers*. (See "Also Available" below.)

- **"Things to Do" Sections.** Found near the end of each chapter, these sections embody our active learning and teaching approach to mathematics. Divided into two parts, they are designed to engage you in inquiring and thinking about mathematics—to offer you experiences and introduce you to investigations that will help you achieve the understanding and insight you need to be a successful teacher. The first part, "From What You've Read," relates directly to this book. The second part, "Going Beyond This Book," offers four types of activities: *In the field, In your journal, With additional resources, and With technology*. These include some microteaching activities linked to *Teaching Elementary Mathematics: A Resource for Field Experiences*.

Updated & Expanded! Topics in Mathematics Education

- **Technology & Computational Alternatives.** Chapter 10 offers a balanced yet detailed discussion of technology, calculators, and computational alternatives—mental computation, estimation, and written techniques, along with the importance of students' making wise choices among these alternatives. Calculators are powerful tools, and we have included calculator activities throughout the book. We have also made a conscious effort to integrate a wide variety of other tools, such as spreadsheets, simulation packages, and the Internet, to enhance mathematics learning. The Math Links boxes within the chapters highlight additional technology resources. The Wiley web site (www.wiley.com/college/reys) connects to web resources, including virtual interactive manipulatives, video clips, lesson plans, and this text's instructor's manual.

- **Equity.** Equity means treating all students fairly and having equal expectations regarding all students' potential for learning and succeeding in mathematics, regardless of gender or of ethnic and cultural background. Equity is an important issue in mathematics classes and is highlighted in the NCTM's *Principles and Standards for School Mathematics*. Throughout the text, we discuss and illustrate many ways of providing for individual differences—from the wide range of student abilities portrayed in the "Snapshots of a Lesson" to the "In the Classroom" activities. Our book is intended to help you create an environment in your mathematics classroom that is positive and productive for everyone.

- **NEW! Cultural Connections.** Today's schools reflect our culturally diverse society, a diversity that is growing rapidly. A "Cultural Connections" section near the end of most chapters highlights differences in the mathematical experiences and mathematical performance of students from different cultures. As mathematics teachers, the more we learn about different cultures the more prepared we are to deal with diversity within our classrooms.

- **Assessment.** Completely updated to reflect today's emphasis on this important topic in Mathematics Education.

Additional features

Other hallmark features of the text have been enhanced in this edition. These include:

- **Focus Questions.** Focus questions point the way into each of the chapters. Think about these questions in advance, and use your readings and the activities in the chapter to help you form a response to each question.

- **Children's Literature.** Although often underused in mathematics education, literature can be a powerful ally in helping children learn. We have made a concerted effort to identify books that you can use effectively to stimulate children's interest in mathematics and to promote mathematics learning. We cite and discuss specific books at various points within the text, and we provide an annotated list of useful books in the **Book Nook section** at the end of each chapter (except Chapter 1).

- **Updated and streamlined research.** References to important research are found throughout the text. As a teacher, you are often called on to provide a rationale for curricular or instructional decisions, and we think you will find these references to relevant research useful; much of the research we cite has important implications for learning and teaching.

- **Updated resources.** We provide annotated lists of selected books and articles at the end of each chapter. The annotations should help you pursue these references in more depth. All the other references cited in our book are included in a single comprehensive bibliography at the back of the book.

- **Reproducible Masters in Appendix B.** In our teaching, we have frequently found certain materials to be useful in a variety of ways. Included in these masters are manipulatives, recording sheets, and organizing sheets; all are found in Appendix B. A favorite of past users of the text, these pages can be duplicated for your students or used to make transparencies for an overhead projector. We welcome your feedback on them, and ideas for other masters to include.

- **Manipulatives.** In addition to the print manipulatives described above, students have the option of purchasing at a discounted price a manipulative kit from Cuisenaire, the most popular manufacturer of manipulatives. Please refer to the flyer included with this text for ordering information or visit www.cuisenaire.com. Virtual manipulatives, available on the internet, are also referenced in the text.

Also available: **Teaching Elementary Mathematics: A Resource for Field Experiences, 3rd edition (ISBN 0-470-04516-7)**

Featuring a wealth of materials to use in observing, interviewing, teaching, and reflecting while students are in schools, this resource is designed for students to use when they participate in field experiences such as practicums, observations, and professional development school (PDS) experiences in K–8 classrooms. It is aligned with and designed to support *Helping Children Learn Mathematics* but may also be used alone. The activities in it engage preservice elementary teachers in collecting information about the school and school resources, observing and interviewing teachers and children, and doing mathematics with children in the form of games, technology activities, and mini-lessons.

Supplements

In addition to links to videos and virtual interactive manipulatives as described above, the eighth edition of *Helping Children Learn Mathematics* is accompanied by the following instructor and student supplements:

Online Instructor's Manual

The Instructor's Manual is a useful resource for both veteran and new elementary methods instructors. It is available on the Wiley web site at www.wiley.com/college/reys. Each chapter includes:

- Chapter overview, student objectives, and key vocabulary
- Supplemental lecture ideas, textbook extension ideas, and class and field activity suggestions
- Extensive resource list (both print and media)
- Extensive transparency masters highlighting key textbook ideas, NCTM Standards 2000 summaries, and children's work samples (available in Microsoft Word and PowerPoint formats).

Test Bank

Password protected in the instructor's section of www.wiley.com/college/reys, a test bank of over 500 items features both objective and open-ended questions with varying levels of complexity.

Helping Children Learn Mathematics is an idea book. We believe that you will learn much from reading it and from talking about what you have read. The NCTM's *Principles and Standards* highlights communication as an important part of mathematics learning, and this book is designed to encourage and facilitate communication.

It is not possible—or desirable—to specify the exact steps to follow in teaching mathematics. Too much depends on what is being taught, to whom, and at what levels. In your classroom, it is you who will ultimately decide what to teach, to whom to teach it, how to teach it, and the amount of time to spend. This book will not answer all of these questions for you, but we think you will find it very helpful in making wise decisions as you guide elementary school students in their learning of mathematics. We believe this book will be a valuable teaching resource that you can use again and again in your classroom long after the course has been completed.

◢ Acknowledgments

Over the years many people have contributed to the development and continued improvement of *Helping Children Learn Mathematics*. We thank Marilyn Suydam for her hard work and insights during the early years of this text's development. Marilyn is now retired, but her legacy of significant contributions remains a vital part of this book.

For this 8th edition, we are particularly grateful to Paula Stickles, Poloko Lecha, and Crystal Walcott, of Indiana University, for their help. Paula provided helpful suggestions for chapter revisions. Poloko did essential library research, helped update material, and took care of many time-consuming chores in helping us prepare the final manuscript. Crystal was instrumental in identifying videos and helping us prepare the excerpts for the Snapshots; she also made significant contributions to the reference lists. Rick Callan, a veteran Indiana classroom teacher and presidential awardee, deserves many thanks for providing extensive suggestions for Book Nook updates. Also thanks to Troy Regis, of the University of Missouri, for sharing his classroom teaching experiences as part of his many contributions to this edition.

Our thanks to a number of faculty who provided thoughtful reviews and offered suggestions for this edition. Specifically, we want to thank Lecretia Buckley, Purdue University; Jeff Frykholm, University of Colorado; Kelli Thomas, University of Kansas, and Tad Watanabe, Penn State University.

We also wish to acknowledge the many colleagues, friends, and students who have contributed in various ways to the development of this book over the years. In particular, we thank Barbara Reys, of the University of Missouri, Frank Lester, of Indiana University, and Paul Lindquist for their help and support.

We also wish to recognize the help of many reviewers and contributors of ideas and suggestions for prior editions, including: Roda Amaria, Salem State College; Peter Appelbaum, *Arcadia University*; Tom Bassarear, Keene State College; Jennifer Bay-Williams, *Kansas State University*, Martha Boedecker, *Northwestern Oklahoma State University*, Carol Bonilla Bowman, *Ramapo College*; Daniel Brahier, Bowling Green State University; Christine Browning, Western Michigan University; Grace Burton, University of North Carolina, Wilmington; Rick Callan, *Franklin College*, Richard Caulfield, *Indiana University*, Astrida Cirulis, *National-Louis University*; Bob Drake, University of Cincinnati; Dianne Erickson, Oregon State University; Skip Fennell, McDaniel College; Marvel Froemming, Moorhead State University; K. Gaddis, *Lewis & Clark College*; Lowell Gadberry, *Southwestern Oklahoma State University*; Enrique Galindo, *Indiana University*; Madeleine Gregg, *University of Alabama*; Elsa L. Geskus, Kutztown

University; Bob Glasgow, Southwest Baptist University; Claire Graham, Framingham State College; Janet Handler, Mount Mercy College; Kim Harris, University of North Carolina Charlotte; Kim Hartweg, *Western Illinois University*; Ruth M. Heaton, University of Nebraska, Lincoln; Karen Higgins, Oregon State University; Ellen Hines, Northern Illinois University; Robert Jackson, University of Minnesota; Gae Johnson, *Northern Arizona University*; Susan Johnson, Northwestern College; Todd Johnson, Eastern Washington University; Mary Kabiri, Lincoln University; Henry S. Kepner, *University of Wisconsin-Milwaukee*; Diane H. Klein, *Indiana University of Pennsylvania*; Rick Kruschinsky, University of St. Thomas; Vena Long, University of Tennessee; Margie Mason, *College of William and Mary*; Robert Matulis, Millersville University; Sueanne McKinney, *Old Dominion University*; William Merrill, Central Michigan University; Alice Mills, *Quincy University*; Jean Mitchell, *California State University, Monterey Bay*; Eula Ewing Monroe, Brigham Young University; Margaret (Maggie) Niess, Oregon State University; Jamar Pickreign, Rhode Island College; Don Ploger, Florida Atlantic University; Sara Powell, *University of Charleston (SC)*; Frank Powers, *University of Idaho*; Jacelyn Marie Rees, McNeese State University; Gay Ragan, *Southwest Missouri State University*; Denise M. Reboli, *King's College (PA)*; Andy Reeves, University of South Florida-Tampa; Candice L. Ridlon, *Towson University*; Tom Romberg, University of Wisconsin; Thomas E. Rowan, University of Maryland, College Park; Mary Ellen Schmidt, Ohio State University–Mansfield; Linda Sheeran, *Oklahoma State University*; Marian Smith, *Florida A&M University*; Marilyn Soucie, *University of Missouri*; Frances Stern, New York University; David L. Stout, University of West Florida; Gertrude R. Toher, *Hofstra University*; Frederick L. Uy, *California State University, Los Angeles*; Juan Vazquez, Missouri Southern State College; Kay Wall, *University of Central Oklahoma*; Pat Wall, *Northern Arizona University*; Judy Wells, *Indiana State University*; Dorothy Y. White, University of Georgia; Margaret Wyckoff, University of Maine–Farmington; and Bernard Yvon, University of Maine.

R.E.R.
M.M.L.
D.V.L.
N.L.S.

CHAPTER 1

School Mathematics in a Changing World

◀ Introduction

Soon you will be in your own classroom, responsible for helping children learn mathematics. What is your vision of the mathematics you will be teaching? What is your vision of the classroom? Many of you will remember your experiences in elementary school. Some of you will remember that math class was mainly about learning the multiplication tables, fractions, or long division. Others may remember exploring patterns, doing geometry projects, or solving problems. Mathematics in elementary school may have been a positive experience for some of you, but for others it was filled with anxiety and frustration. Why were you learning math and when would you use it? Teachers want students to learn mathematics and to learn that it is a useful subject. How can they make sure this happens?

This book is designed to expand your vision of mathematics teaching and learning and to help you help students learn mathematics. The book interweaves three main themes:

- *Theme 1.* The philosophy and recommendations of the *Principles and Standards for School Mathematics* (NCTM, 2000) are fundamental to helping children learn mathematics.
- *Theme 2.* Mathematics must make sense to children. Research has shown that if children make

sense of the mathematics they are learning, they can build on this understanding to learn more mathematics and use it to solve problems.
- *Theme 3.* Learning to teach mathematics requires practical experience. The chapter-opening Snapshots, the In the Classroom activities, and the end-of-chapter lists of resources will help you develop ways of helping children learn mathematics.

You cannot, however, just read this text. You must also listen to children learning mathematics, and you must reflect on the teaching of mathematics. This looking and reflecting may or may not be part of the class you are now taking, but throughout your education as a teacher and after you become a teacher, you must take advantage of opportunities to do these things. Learning to teach all students is a lifelong journey. During that journey, you, like all teachers, will often ask questions such as these:

- What mathematical knowledge and understanding does each student bring to the class?
- What mathematics do students need to learn?
- How can I teach each unique child so that he or she will learn?
- How important is my own attitude toward mathematics?

Your answers to these questions will influence what you do when you are teaching. No matter what age of children you teach, you will probably have several general *goals*:

* To help children make sense of specific mathematical content, including both procedures and concepts.
* To help children learn how to apply mathematical ideas to solve problems.
* To foster positive dispositions, such as persistence, flexibility, willingness to learn, and valuing mathematics.

Developing ways to help children learn mathematical content is considered in later chapters of this book. This first chapter focuses on an overall look at the mathematics program that has evolved (and will continue to change) as the world changes. Begin thinking about your own perceptions of mathematics and the role mathematics plays in elementary and middle schools. What influences the curriculum? How do your beliefs influence what you teach?

You are entering the teaching field at a time when accountability is a major focus. Mathematics programs are being adapted to the changing needs of our society, to changing knowledge about how children learn, and to changing viewpoints about mathematics. Before looking at these changes, think about mathematics itself. What is mathematics to you?

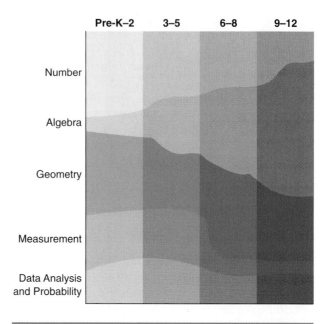

FIGURE 1-1 Vision of the mathematics content distribution through the grade levels. (Source: *Principles and Standards for School Mathematics*, p. 30, copyright 2000 by the National Council of Teachers of Mathematics. All rights reserved.)

throughout the grades pre-K to 12. Numbers are an important part of this vision, but algebra, geometry, measurement, and data analysis and probability are also important. As you can see, numbers, as well as geometry, are emphasized early and then receive progressively less instructional attention as algebra increases in importance.

FOCUS QUESTIONS

1. What is mathematics?
2. What determines the mathematics currently taught?
3. What are the NCTM's six principles for school mathematics?
4. What resources are available to help you continue developing your knowledge of mathematics and the learning and teaching of mathematics?

What Is Mathematics?

Frequently, people equate mathematics and arithmetic. In school mathematics, arithmetic is about numbers. At times, arithmetic, especially computation with numbers, has been the only focus in elementary school. Currently, however, this is far from the case. Figure 1-1 shows how the National Council of Teachers of Mathematics (NCTM) envisions the distribution of mathematics content

Math Links 1.1

You can find out more about the NCTM's *Principles and Standards for School Mathematics* by reading answers to Frequently Asked Questions. You can access these questions from http://www.nctm.org/standards/faq.htm or from this book's Web site.

www.wiley.com/college/reys

Although we can consider mathematics as a collection of separate areas such as geometry and algebra, this may not be the best way of looking at it. Unifying views of mathematics may be more useful. Do any or all of the following five views of mathematics come close to your view? How will your view of mathematics affect how you help children learn?

1. *Mathematics is a study of patterns and relationships.* Children need to become aware of recurring ideas and of relationships between mathematical ideas. These relationships and ideas provide a unifying thread throughout the curriculum. Children should come to see how one idea is like or unlike others already learned. For instance, children in first grade can consider how one basic fact (say, 3 + 2 = 5) is related to another basic fact (say, 5 − 3 = 2). Or older children can generalize a numerical pattern and describe it algebraically.

2. *Mathematics is a way of thinking.* Mathematics provides people with strategies for organizing, analyzing, and synthesizing information. People who are comfortable with mathematics use it to solve everyday problems. For example, some people write an equation to figure out how much something would really cost, and some construct tables to record their income and expenditures.

3. *Mathematics is an art, characterized by order and internal consistency.* Many children think of mathematics as a confusing set of discrete facts and skills that must be memorized. Teachers tend to focus on developing the skills required to "do" mathematics, and in doing so they may forget that children need guidance to recognize and appreciate the underlying orderliness and consistency as they construct their own understanding of mathematics.

4. *Mathematics is a language that uses carefully defined terms and symbols.* Learning these terms and symbols enhances our ability to communicate about science, real-life situations, and mathematics itself.

5. *Mathematics is a tool.* Not just mathematicians use mathematics, but everyone in the course of daily life uses it. Seeing this will help children appreciate why they are learning mathematics. They, too, will be able to use mathematics to solve both abstract and practical problems, just as mathematicians and other people do. Mathematics has become an essential part of our world, both in everyday life and in the workplace.

What Determines the Mathematics Being Taught?

Mathematics plays a prominent role in the elementary school program. It is second only to reading in the amount of time devoted to it and in the amount of money spent for curricular materials. Its importance is reflected in the degree of concern about it voiced by parents, politicians, arid other social groups.

The federal government has not specified a national curriculum for school mathematics, as is the practice in most other countries. At various times, different national professional organizations have made recommendations about curriculum. The NCTM, the largest professional organization of teachers of mathematics, developed standards for curriculum and for evaluation, teaching, and assessment (NCTM, 1989, 1991, 1995). Because states and localities in the United States have the right to determine their own school policies, these standards are not prescriptive, but they have provided vision and direction for schools in developing mathematics curricula.

In 2000, the NCTM published an update of the standards in a document titled *Principles and Standards for School Mathematics* (NCTM, 2000). The principles, shown in Figure 1-2, represent fundamental beliefs about the characteristics of a high-quality, equitable mathematics program. The standards, detailed in later chapters, describe the mathematical content and mathematical processes that should be taught in school mathematics. Combined, the principles and standards present a vision for mathematics education programs in a changing world.

As you begin to think about mathematics programs, you should give careful attention to three general factors: the needs of the subject, the needs of the child, and the needs of society. Consideration of these factors highlights the importance of the NCTM's principles. Each principle aids teachers in making decisions about the mathematics program they design and implement. The interaction of the principles with the needs of the subject, the child, and society can help shape a mathematics program that enables all children to become mathematically literate citizens.

Needs of the Subject

The nature of mathematics helps determine what is taught and when it is taught in elementary grades. For example, whole numbers are the basis for many mathematical ideas; moreover, experiences with whole numbers arise long before children come to school. Thus, lower grades emphasize whole-number work first, building on children's experiences. Work with rational numbers logically follows work with whole numbers. Such seemingly natural sequences are the result of long years of curricular evolution. This process has involved much analysis of what constitutes a

Principles	
• **Equity** Excellence in mathematics education requires equity—high expectations and strong support for all students.	• **Learning** Students must learn mathematics with understanding, actively building new knowledge from experience and prior knowledge.
• **Curriculum** A curriculum is more than a collection of activities: it must be coherent, focused on important mathematics, and well articulated across the grades.	• **Assessment** Assessment should support the learning of important mathematics and furnish useful information to both teachers and students.
• **Teaching** Effective mathematics teaching requires understanding what students know and need to learn and then challenging and supporting them to learn it well.	• **Technology** Technology is essential in teaching and learning mathematics; it influences the mathematics that is taught and enhances students' learning.
Content Standards*	**Process Standards***
• *Number and Operations*	• *Problem Solving*
• *Algebra*	• *Reasoning and Proof*
• *Geometry*	• *Communication*
• *Measurement*	• *Connections*
• *Data Analysis and Probability*	• *Representations*

FIGURE 1-2 • *Principles and Standards for School Mathematics.* (Source: NCTM, 2000, pp. 12, 14, 16, 20, 22, 24, Appendix.) *These are the areas of the Standards; see Appendix A for full statement of the standards and the related expectations for various grade levels.

progression from easy to difficult, based in part on what is deemed necessary at one level for the development of ideas at later levels. Once a curriculum is in place for a long time, however, people tend to consider it the only proper sequence. Thus, omitting a topic or changing the sequence of topics often involves a struggle for acceptance. However, research shows that all students do not always learn in the sequence that has been ingrained in our curriculum. You need to be open to change so that each child's needs are met.

Sometimes the process of change is aided by an event, such as when the Soviet Union sent the first Sputnik into orbit. The shock of this evidence of another country's technological superiority sped

curriculum change in the United States. The "new math" of the 1950s and 1960s was the result, and millions of dollars were channeled into mathematics and science education to strengthen school programs. Mathematicians became integrally involved in planning mathematics education, and because of their interests and the perceived weaknesses of previous curricula, they developed curricula based on the needs of the subject. The emphasis shifted from social usefulness to such unifying themes as the structure of mathematics, operations and their inverses, systems of notation, properties of numbers, and set language. New content was added at the elementary school level, and other topics were introduced at earlier grade levels.

Mathematics continues to change; new mathematics is created and new uses of mathematics are discovered. As part of this change, technology has made some mathematics obsolete and has opened the door for other mathematics. The influence of technology and the importance of a flexible approach to curriculum are emphasized in the NCTM's Technology Principle and Curriculum Principle.

The Technology Principle You will teach at a time when technology dominates activities both in and out of school. The Technology Principle (see Figure 1-2) acknowledges that technology will continue to be important in teaching and learning mathematics, as long as it enhances what is being learned and how it is being taught. As you teach your classes, you should keep asking three questions:

1. How can I help children use technology appropriately?
2. What mathematics do children need in order to use technology wisely?
3. That mathematics is no longer necessary because of technology?

Some parents continue to be concerned about the use of calculators in learning mathematics in elementary schools. A meta-analysis of 54 research studies on calculator use and attitudes (Ellington, 2003) suggests that using calculators does not hinder the development of mathematical skills and that students who used calculators had better attitudes toward mathematics than those who did not. Of course, children need to learn to use calculators appropriately, as they do any other tool (see Chapter 10).

The Curriculum Principle No one knows exactly what mathematics will be needed as the twenty-first century progresses, but it is clear that students will need to know how to reason mathematically and how to apply mathematical thinking to a wide range of situations. How you view mathematics will determine how you view teaching mathematics. If you view mathematics as a collection of facts to learn and procedures to practice, then you will teach that to your students. If you view mathematics as a logical body of knowledge, you will design a curriculum that lets you focus on guiding children to make sense of mathematics.

Children need a curriculum that does more than represent mathematics as a collection of isolated skills and fun activities. They need a curriculum that is focused, coherent, and well articulated:

- *Focused.* A curriculum that focuses on the important mathematics topics and ideas at each grade.
- *Coherent.* A curriculum that fits mathematical ideas together in a meaningful way.
- *Well articulated.* A curriculum that grows across the grades.

Throughout the remaining chapters of this text, you will investigate topics and strategies that you can incorporate into the mathematics curriculum for your students. The 10 content and process standards (see Appendix A) provide a framework to guide you in judging whether your curriculum is coherent, focused, and well articulated.

Needs of the Child

The mathematics curriculum has been influenced by beliefs about how children learn and, ultimately, about how they should be taught. Before the early years of the twentieth century, mathematics was taught to train "mental faculties" or provide "mental discipline." Struggling with mathematical procedures was thought to exercise the mind (like muscles are exercised), helping children's brains work more effectively. Around the turn of the twentieth century, "mental discipline" was replaced by *connectionism*, the belief that learning established bonds, or connections, between a stimuli and responses. This led teachers to the endless use of drills aimed at establishing important mathematical connections.

In the 1920s, the Progressive movement advocated *incidental learning*, reflecting the belief that children would learn as much arithmetic as they needed and would learn it better if it was not systematically taught. The teacher's role was to take advantage of situations as they occurred to teach arithmetic, as well as to create situations in which arithmetic would arise.

During the late 1920s, the Committee of Seven, a committee of school superintendents and principals from Midwestern cities, surveyed pupils to find out when they mastered various topics (Washburne, 1931). Based on that survey, the committee recommended teaching mathematics topics according to students' mental age. For example, subtraction facts under 10 were to be taught to children with a mental age of 6 years 7 months, and facts over 10 at 7 years 8 months; subtraction with borrowing or carrying was to be taught at 8 years 9 months. The recommendations of the Committee of Seven had a strong impact on the sequencing of the curriculum for years afterward.

Another change in thinking occurred in the mid-1930s, under the influence of *field theory*, or *Gestalt theory*. With William Brownell as a prominent spokesperson, this approach placed greater emphasis on a planned program to encourage the development of insight and the understanding of relationships, structures, patterns, interpretations, and principles. It contributed to an increased focus on learning as a process that led to *meaning and understanding*. The value of drill was acknowledged, but it was given less importance than understanding; drill was no longer the major means of providing instruction.

The relative importance of drill and understanding is still debated today. In this debate, people often treat understanding and learning skills as if they were opposites, but this is not the case. Clearly, drill is necessary to build speed and accuracy and to make skills automatic. But equally clearly, you need to know *why* as well as *how*. Both skills and understanding must be developed, and they can be developed together.

Changes in the field of psychology have continued to affect education. During the second half of the twentieth century, educators came to understand that the developmental level of the child is a major factor in determining the sequence of the curriculum. Topics cannot be taught until children are developmentally ready to learn them. Or, from another point of view, topics must be taught in such a way that children at a given developmental level are ready to learn them.

Additionally, educators' attention is being drawn to the increasing evidence that children *construct* their own knowledge. Thus, helping children learn mathematics means being aware of how children have constructed mathematics from their experiences both in and out of school. Such consider-

ations are now routinely taken into account in developing mathematics curricula.

The NCTM's Teaching Principle and Learning Principle are directed at helping teachers understand and use these ideas.

The Teaching Principle   To teach mathematics effectively, teachers must know more than just mathematics. They need to know their students as learners, and they must adjust their pedagogical strategies in response to students' varying experiences. Teachers must design lessons that reveal to them what students already know, that reveal students' misunderstandings, and that guide students to construct more complex understandings of mathematics. Teachers must create challenging and supportive classroom learning environments that help children make sense of mathematics. Teachers must also encourage students to think, question, solve problems, and discuss their ideas. In the NCTM *Standards* (2000), the Teaching Principle says, "Effective mathematics teaching requires understanding what students know and need to learn and then challenging and supporting them to learn it well" (p. 16). Teachers can help children make sense of mathematics in many ways. Chapter 3 initiates the discussion of teaching, and succeeding chapters focus on ways to teach and on useful types of activities.

The Learning Principle   What it means to learn mathematics has changed a great deal over the past century. Currently, the phrase *mathematical proficiency* is used to describe what it means to learn mathematics successfully. Figure 1-3 shows the

Mathematical Proficiency	
• *Conceptual Understanding*	Comprehension of mathematical concepts, operations, and relations
• *Procedural Fluency*	Skill in carrying out procedures flexibly, accurately, efficiently, and appropriately
• *Strategic Competence*	Ability to formulate, represent, and solve mathematical problems
• *Adaptive Reasoning*	Capacity for logical thought, reflection, explanation, and justification
• *Productive Disposition*	Habitual inclination to see mathematics as sensible, useful, and worthwhile, coupled with a belief in diligence and one's own efficacy

FIGURE 1-3 Mathematical proficiency in a changing world.

(Source: National Research Council, p. 5.)

National Research Council's (Kilpatrick, Swafford, and Findell, 2001) description of the five strands of mathematical proficiency. Their overriding recommendation is that "throughout the grades from pre-K through 8 *all students can and should be mathematically proficient*" (p. 10). They warn, however, that these strands are interdependent and must be appropriately interwoven by teachers.

In a changing world, learning mathematics with understanding is essential in order to meet this goal of mathematical proficiency. As stated in the NCTM's Learning Principle, students must actively build knowledge of mathematics from their personal experiences and prior knowledge. Research has shown that if children are able to make sense of the mathematics they are learning, they can build on this understanding to learn more mathematics and use that mathematics to solve problems in order to become mathematically proficient.

Ideas about developing mathematical proficiency are considered in more depth in Chapter 2, but the Teaching Principle and the Learning Principle (see Figure 1-2) should lead you to consider some initial questions: What does it mean to learn mathematics with understanding? How did you learn mathematics? How can you learn to understand what children know? Where can you turn to find out what mathematics children need to learn and how you can challenge and support them in learning that mathematics?

Needs of Society

The usefulness of mathematics in everyday life and in many vocations has also affected what is taught and when it is taught. In early America, mathematics was considered necessary primarily for clerks and bookkeepers. The curriculum was limited to counting, the simpler procedures for addition, subtraction, and multiplication, and some facts about measures and fractions. By the late nineteenth century, business and commerce had advanced to the point that mathematics was considered important for everyone. The arithmetic curriculum expanded to include such topics as percentage, ratio and proportion, powers, roots, and series.

This emphasis on *social utility*, on teaching what was needed for use in occupations, continued into the twentieth century. One of the most vocal advocates of social utility was Guy Wilson. He and his students conducted numerous surveys to determine what arithmetic was actually used by carpenters, shopkeepers, and other workers. He believed that the "dominating" aim of the school mathematics program should be to teach those skills and *only* those skills.

The outburst of public concern in the 1950s over the "space race" resulted in a wave of research and development in mathematics curricula. Much of this effort was focused on teaching the mathematically talented student. By the mid-1960s, however, concern was also being expressed for the disadvantaged student, as U.S. society renewed its commitment to equality of opportunity. With each of these changes, more and better mathematical achievement was promised.

In the 1970s, when it became apparent that the promise of greater achievement had not fully materialized, another swing occurred in curriculum development. Emphasis was again placed on the skills needed for success in the real world. The minimal-competency movement stressed the basics. As embodied in sets of objectives and in tests, the basics were considered to be primarily addition, subtraction, multiplication, and division with whole numbers and fractions. Thus, the skills needed in colonial times were again being considered by many to be the sole necessities, even though children were now living in a world with calculators, computers, and other features of a much more technological society.

By the 1980s, it was acknowledged that no one knew exactly what skills were needed for the future but that everyone needed to be able to solve problems. The emphasis on problem solving matured through the last 20 years of the century to the point where problem solving was not seen as a separate topic but as a way to learn and to use mathematics (see Chapter 6). In the 1990s, the standards movement became a major focus. All subject areas developed standards, and almost all states developed standards for mathematics. The NCTM's standards gave guidance to states and localities. Along with standards came an emphasis on assessment, accountability, and equity.

The Assessment Principle People often think of assessment as testing to see what students have learned. The Assessment Principle (see Figure 1-2) presents a much broader view of assessment. Helping all students learn mathematics requires that assessment be an integral part of the instructional program. But assessment should not be something that is done to students; rather, a mathematics program must include assessments that are done *for* students, to guide and enhance their learning (NCTM, 2000). In order to develop a program that provides for the strengths and needs of individual students, teachers must continue to gather information about their students' progress. Useful and effective assessment is more than a test at the end of a unit. Asking students questions during lessons helps them describe their thinking and understanding, and their responses help teachers make the decisions they must make to meet students' needs. Observing students as they solve problems or build ideas provides a different look at student understanding. Ultimately, as the Assessment Principle directs, "Assessment should become a routine part of the ongoing classroom activity rather than an interruption" (NCTM, 2000, p. 23). (The Assessment Principle is considered in more detail in Chapter 4.)

Today's society seems focused on assessments in the form of tests that are used to compare students' performance across schools, states, and nations. But if these tests are not aligned with school and community goals for mathematics education, will your students be able to demonstrate what they know and are able to do in mathematics? Will these tests provide information about the mathematical proficiency of your students? Society needs a citizenry and a workforce that can solve problems, reason mathematically, process and interpret data, and communicate in a technological world. Will performance tests measure these things? Will these tests help schools focus on improving mathematics programs in order to prepare students for life in today's society? The answer to all such questions will be negative if these tests are not aligned with school and community goals and with the notion of mathematical proficiency.

Accountability A serious effort to hold schools accountable for student learning began with the new century. Accountability is one of the pillars of the No Child Left Behind Act (NCLB, 2001), which requires states to show that each school is making yearly progress in academic subjects and that all students are becoming mathematically proficient. However, it is left to the states to decide what is meant by mathematically proficient. Most states' mathematics standards emphasize the type of proficiency described in Figure 1-3, but their assessments often undercut this by emphasizing procedural fluency.

Along with its focus on accountability, the NCLB called for supporting supplementary services and professional development for teachers. Unfortunately, the majority of the available funds have gone into testing for accountability. Poor-performing schools are still struggling and are still in need of well-prepared teachers to meet the challenge of helping all students become mathematically proficient. One of the strengths of NCLB is its focus on closing the achievement gap—that is, on bringing all students, including the disadvantaged, to a proficient level. This laudable goal is well expressed in the NCTM's Equity Principle.

The equity principle The Equity Principle (see Figure 1-2) states clearly that excellence in mathematics education means ensuring that all students learn mathematics. This vision can be realized only if each person involved in education firmly believes that all children can learn mathematics and that each child should be expected to do so. Every child must be given the opportunity to learn worthwhile mathematics. This means designing instructional programs that can encompass all the different interests, strengths, needs, cultures, and mathematical backgrounds of students. Plenty of evidence supports the idea that all students can learn mathematics. High-quality instructional programs are needed that let well-prepared teachers and other school personnel respond to students' varied strengths and needs.

Our schools are characterized by diversity-students from many different cultures and languages, from many different economic and home backgrounds, with many different strengths, ways of learning mathematics, and past experiences with mathematics. Equity *does* mean that all children must learn worthwhile mathematics, but it *does not* mean that all should have the same instruction. In fact, it means that children can reach the high expectations set for them only if we meet the individual needs of each child. Your repertoire of ways to reach children will grow as you teach and learn. At this point, you can begin by challenging the popular belief that only some children can learn mathematics. This is an important first step in becoming a teacher who can help every child learn.

Your Role

Before reading this section, you might have responded with a blank look to the question, "What determines the mathematics being taught?" Hopefully, this discussion has helped you see that answering this question leads us to consider the needs of the subject, the child, and society. These needs have always been considered, but the relative importance assigned to them has changed over time. If your goal is to help each child become mathematically proficient, you will have to consider many factors, some of which you can control and some of which you cannot. Certainly, you can hold high expectations for each child, in the belief that every child can learn mathematics. Equally certainly, you cannot control whether your students will have to take mandated state tests. This book focuses on the things you can control, the things that you can do in the classroom to provide a worthwhile mathematics program for each child.

Where Can You Turn?

There are many places you can turn for help with the curriculum, with helping students learn, and with continuing to develop your knowledge of mathematics and of mathematics learning and teaching. There are many resources available to support you. In this section, we discuss a few of the resources that we reference throughout this book.

National Guidelines for School Mathematics

We frequently refer to the latest update of *Principles and Standards for School Mathematics* (NCTM, 2000). In this chapter, we have briefly discussed the principles. The five process standards form the framework for Chapter 5 and the background for a more extensive look at problem solving in Chapter 6. The five content standards give structure to Chapters 7–17. Appendix A provides a complete version of the NCTM's expectations for pre-K through grade 8, giving a quick overview of what children at different grades are expected to know and be able to do. The *Principles and Standards* document itself explains the standards at each of the grade bands (pre-K–2, 3–5, 6–8, and 9–12). While you are a student, you can access the entire document on the Web without charge for 3 months.

Math Links 1.2

The entire NCTM *Standards* document is available, both in print and electronically, from NCTM. The electronic version also provides interactive activities to help you better understand the intent of each standard. You can access this from http://www.nctm.org/standards/ (if you have NCTM membership) or from this book's Web site.

www.wiley.com/college/reys

State and Local Guidelines

Almost every state has a document with standards, guidelines, or frameworks for school mathematics. Most are more detailed than the NCTM's standards, specifying content grade by grade. Many localities have their own versions of the state document. State assessment programs should be aligned with the recommendations of the state document. You need to become familiar with the state document, and use it to plan your year when you are teaching. Links to state mathematics curriculum frameworks are available at the Web site of the Center for the Study of Mathematics Curriculum: http://www.mathcurriculumcenter.org.

Research

There is a substantial body of research in mathematics education, both about children's learning and about teaching. *The Research Companion to Principles and Standards for School Mathematics* (Kilpatrick, Martin, and Schifter, 2003) provides support for the recommendations and approaches in the NCTM document. Research is referenced throughout this book, not only to acquaint you with research in mathematics education, but also to illustrate or support discussions in the text. You should also become familiar with several references in addition to the *Research Companion*.

The National Assessment of Educational Progress (NAEP, pronounced "nape") is the nation's measure of students' achievement and trends in achievement in the academic subjects. With the passage of the NCLB in 2001; NAEP has become more prominent. The framework for NAEP mathematics is closely aligned with the NCTM's standards. The NAEP assessment contains a variety of types of items (multiple choice, short response, and open-ended response). The mathematics assessment is given to a sample of students at grades 4 and 8 in every state. Results are reported by states as well as by race, gender, and socioeconomic status. Figure 1-4 shows the overall, national results for the years 1990 through 2003. Note that both grades improved their results over this period. More information about NAEP, including sample items, may be found at http://nces.ed.gov/nationsreportcard.

Research reports appear in many journals. We often use articles from the research journal of the NCTM, *Journal for Research in Mathematics Education* (JRME), to guide our recommendations in this book. JRME articles often lead directly to the classroom ideas and recommendations found in other NCTM journals, such as *Teaching Children Mathematics*.

Cultural and International Resources

The Trends in Mathematics and Science Study (TIMSS), an international study also given at grades 4 and 8, clearly shows that U.S. students could do better in mathematics. The results of the most recent TIMSS study, in 2003, showed that

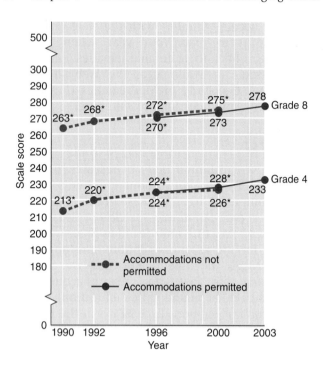

FIGURE 1-4   Trends in student performance: NAEP. (Source: U.S. Department of Education, Institute of Educational Sciences, National Center for Education Statistics (NCES). National Assessment of Education Progress (NAEP, 1990, 1992, 1996, 2000, 2003 Mathematics Assessments.) *Significantly different from 2003.

U.S. fourth-grade students were above the international average but had improved little since the previous assessment, in 1995. Eighth-grade U.S. students were also above the international average and did show significant improvement since 1995. Performance varies greatly within the United States and is closely linked to economic status.

The TIMSS study also collects information about curriculum, teaching, and teachers. Video studies of classrooms suggest that Japanese teaching in grade 8 more closely resembles the recommendations of the NCTM's standards than does teaching in the United States. These results suggest that U.S. educators can learn much from analyzing how other countries teach mathematics. You can find more information, including sample items from TIMSS, at http://nces.ed.gov/timss.

Many of the other chapters in this book suggest resources that will help you understand how mathematics is taught and learned in other cultures and that show you ways to use culturally oriented activities as you strive to reach each child.

History

Before 1900, arithmetic was taught in college, and it then became a high school subject. You can gain some historical perspective on mathematics education, and have an enjoyable experience at the same time, by looking at mathematics textbooks from the 1800s and early 1900s. Read the prefaces of the books, note the book's length, and look at the exercises and the activities. Are the activities relevant for today's children in learning mathematics? If you are a student of history, you may want to examine the trends in mathematics education over the decades. How has the emphasis changed and how has it remained the same? Did students spend more time on learning procedures or on problem solving? Were students provided with manipulatives to help them grasp the ideas?

For a quick summary of trends in mathematics education over the past few decades and the events these trends were responding to, see Figure 1-5. *A History of School Mathematics, Volumes 1 and 2* (Stanic and Kilpatrick, 2003), is a rich source of writings and references.

Textbooks and Other Materials

Most teachers use a textbook when teaching elementary and middle school mathematics. Today's textbooks provide supplementary materials such as assessments, problems to solve, and extra practice. Teachers' manuals also provide a wealth of materials and teaching suggestions.

There are many different types of textbooks. Some provide a lot of drill and practice but offer little help in developing understanding and using mathematics. Others may do the opposite, providing a great deal of help in developing students' understanding but falling short on practice of

Decade	Event	Trend
1960	Sputnik	New Math
1970	Poor skills	Back to Basics
1980	Poor problem solving	Problem Solving
1990	Poor achievement	Standards and Assessment
2000	No Child Left Behind Act	Accountability for All

FIGURE 1-5 Major trends in school mathematics by decades.

necessary skills. As you gain experience, you will be better able to judge the quality of a textbook and better able to depart from it as appropriate. If you have not had much experience, you may want to stick with the textbook until you become more comfortable with teaching. But be sure always to ask why you need to teach a given lesson. Does it help children develop the mathematics they need? Does it achieve this goal in a way that makes sense to children? Does it help children make sense of the mathematics?

Electronic Materials

The kind and amount of materials available at teachers' fingertips are increasing every day. The Web provides immediate access to lesson plans, help with the mathematics itself, assessment items, and information that can be used in teaching mathematics. Additionally, many sites have videos of mathematics classes. Each of the remaining chapters of this book begins with a Snapshot of a lesson. Most of these snapshots are excerpts from videos that illustrate teaching related to the topic of the chapter. We recommend that you view each video in full, and we provide information on how to access the video on the Web.

The Math Links included in each chapter recommend some stable sites that are worth investigating. A simple search of the Internet for information about mathematics for elementary or middle school students and teachers will lead you to many other Web sites. Here, however, a caution is in order: Availability on the Web is no guarantee of quality. Recently, a prospective teacher brought to class an activity that she had found on the Web in which young children would find the capacity of their mouths by filling them with marshmallows! The mathematics is questionable because the unit of measurement could change as the marshmallows are squashed. Perhaps more importantly, children could easily choke on a mouthful of marshmallows. Teaching involves making good judgments on many fronts.

Math Links 1.3

*T*o see an example of a helpful site for teachers, visit the Math Forum. This Web site includes a mathematics library, a discussion board for teachers, lesson plans and activities created and submitted by teachers, Problems of the Week for students, and answers to math problems from Ask Dr. Math. You can access this Web site at http://www.mathforum.org/ or from this book's Web site.

www.wiley.com/college/reys

Professional Organizations

Being a part of a profession opens many opportunities and responsibilities. Professional association with others and the support you can find from being a part of a professional organization will enhance your teaching career. Journals, conferences, and other materials of a professional organization are often available through schools and even to individuals who are not members of the organization.

The NCTM offers many publications, including a journal for elementary teachers of mathematics (*Teaching Children Mathematics*, formerly the *Arithmetic Teacher*) and one for middle school teachers (*Mathematics Teaching in the Middle School*). You will find many references in this book to these journals. The NCTM also sponsors conferences, workshops, and other support activities. There are many affiliated groups, both state and local, that offer support and programs.

Math Links 1.4

*T*he NCTM provides many resources for teachers at its Web site. You can access these from http://nctm.org/eresources or from this book's Web site.

www.wiley.com/college/reys

Professional Development

Start taking advantage of professional development opportunities. Some of these will be formal, such as workshops, college courses, and conferences; others will include informal study groups. Your school, district, or state will provide some opportunities for you. Others will be commercially sponsored or sponsored by a professional organization. An increasing number of opportunities on the Web are designed so you can participate as your schedule permits.

Often, schools or districts have funds set aside for professional development that are available on request. Some districts have teachers design their own professional development plans and support them in carrying out those plans.

Other Teachers

Teachers learn from each other. You will learn from your school experiences, but do not let learning stop there. Look for schools where sharing ideas about helping students learn mathematics and sharing teaching tips and materials are the norm. Look for teachers in other schools, either near you or far away but connected electronically, who are willing to discuss and to share. A good teacher who is willing to work with you is an invaluable resource.

What Is Your Role Now?

As you prepare for teaching mathematics, be sure to think about the broader context of your work and carefully consider these three challenges:

- *Examine your own disposition toward mathematics and your beliefs about who can learn mathematics.* Be ready to question your beliefs, to evaluate proposed changes, and to make a difference in helping children learn mathematics.

- *Take seriously the title of this book. Teaching means helping students learn, not merely giving out information.* As you begin working with children, stop and listen to them, individually and collectively. Reflect on what you are hearing, and learn with and from the children.

- *Realize that doing mathematics and teaching mathematics are different.* Teaching mathematics requires a depth of understanding about mathematics (Ma, 1999), about students, about

schools, about curriculum, and about pedagogy. If you come to this realization and actively seek knowledge and experiences that integrate these areas, you are well on your way to becoming a good teacher.

A Glance at Where We've Been

Teaching mathematics in a changing world means that the curriculum and instruction must change to reflect the needs of the subject, the child, and society. In this chapter you have been challenged to consider your view of mathematics as a subject. You have seen a glimpse of the changes through the past as well as recommendations for teaching mathematics in the twenty-first century. The six principles put forth by the NCTM underpin many of the recommendations for today. Resources have been identified to support your study through the rest of this book and, more important, as you teach. The challenge is to keep an open mind and continue your own learning about teaching children mathematics. Prepare to help your students make sense of mathematics.

Things to Do: From What You've Read

1. What are the three general goals mentioned in the introduction? Which do you think is the most important? Explain why.

2. Give an illustration (different from those in this chapter) of how mathematics is a study of patterns and relationships, a way of thinking, an art, and a language.

3. Which of the resources discussed in this chapter have you already used? Which ones do you think will be most helpful to you?

4. Explain in your own words the six principles that underpin *Principles and Standards for School Mathematics*.

5. Mathematical proficiency is described through five strands. Describe the five strands using specific examples from your personal experience and background. Explain how these strands are interwoven and interdependent.

Things to Do: Going Beyond This Book

IN THE FIELD

1. *As you observe in a school, look for signs of the role that mathematics plays in that school. Does it differ from class to class?

2. *Interview teachers or prospective teachers about their belief that all children can learn mathematics and what it would take to make this happen.

3. *Examine a copy of your state or district curriculum guide. How does the scope and sequence of topics align with the expectations for pre-K–2, grades 3–5, or grades 6–8 in the *Principles and Standards for School Mathematics* (see Appendix A)?

IN YOUR JOURNAL

4. The Technology Principle recommends that technology supports effective mathematics teaching. Write a statement of your experience using calculators and describe your philosophy regarding calculators in learning elementary mathematics.

5. Several educators have noted that the curriculum is in a continuous process of change in order to maintain balance as the needs of the subject, the child, and society pull it first one way and then another. Discuss this comment.

6. React to the three challenges presented in the close of the chapter.

WITH ADDITIONAL RESOURCES

7. Read Chapter 2 of *Principles and Standards for School Mathematics*. Choose the principle that you think is the most important; critique the discussion of that principle.

8. Read the Executive Summary of *Adding It Up: Helping Children Learn Mathematics*. Describe the five strands of mathematical proficiency and how they are intertwined and interdependent. What recommendations are provided for policies and practices needed if all children are to become mathematically proficient?

---

*Additional activities, suggestions, and questions are provided in *Teaching Elementary Mathematics: A Resource for Field Experiences* (Wiley, 2007).

9. Examine the role of drill and practice for learning mathematics over the past century. Begin by reading one of the articles or books listed in the resources or by examining old textbooks. How is drill and practice viewed today in helping students learn mathematics? Has it changed over the past century?

10. Find a recent issue of *Teaching Children Mathematics* or *Teaching Mathematics in Middle Grades*. Select an article that describes a classroom application. Describe the principle(s) and/or the standard(s) that are considered in the recommendations for this classroom application.

11. Read the article by Bishop (2001) that is annotated at the end of this chapter. Briefly describe the six values; choose one and describe how your experiences learning mathematics relates to it.

WITH TECHNOLOGY

12. Conduct a Web search for the National Assessment of Educational Progress (NAEP), The Nation's Report Card Web site. Select the subject of Mathematics. Three achievement levels (Basic, Proficient, and Advanced) are described in detail for 1990–2000. What are the results of these three levels for grade 4 and grade 8 across the decade? What are the results for your state?

13. NCTM has created a Web site that "Illuminates *Principles and Standards*." Your task is to visit the site (illuminations.nctm.org) and select the button called "i-math investigations." You need to select a particular grade level, pre-K–2, 3–5, 6–8, or 9–12. Select one of the elementary levels. Explore at least one of the ready-to-use, online, interactive, multimedia math investigations that illuminate the Standards. Think about how you might use one of these investigations when you teach.

14. Conduct a Web search for the "Ask Dr. Math" Web site. Review the questions that elementary teachers and students send for Dr. Math to answer. Find a question and answer what you feel is particularly useful and explain why it is useful for you as you prepare to teach mathematics in the elementary level. Send a question to Dr. Math. How long is it before your question is answered? Was the answer helpful?

15. Check the information for your state provided at the "Link to State Mathematics Content Standards" at the Center for the Study of

Mathematics Curriculum: http://www.mathcur-riculumcenter.org. Identify the content areas for a state (either your state or one that your instructor assigns). How do these areas compare to the five content standards of the NCTM?

Note to Instructors: You can find additional resources, learning activities, and black-line masters in this text's accompanying Instructor's Manual, at www.wiley.com/college/reys.

Annotated Resources

Bishop, A. J. "What values do you teach when you teach mathematics?" *Teaching Children Mathematics*, 7(6) (February 2001), pp. 346–370.

This article uses educational research to support a connection between mathematics and culture and focuses on the values that teachers convey when teaching mathematics.

Kilpatrick, J., Swafford, J., and Findell, B. (Eds.). *Adding It Up: Helping Children Learn Mathematics*. Washington, DC: National Academy Press, 2001.

What does research indicate about teaching and learning mathematics? The conclusions and recommendations drawn from research provide targets for improving the nation's teaching and learning of mathematics. After identifying what children know about numbers by the time they

arrive in school, this book explores how students learn mathematics in elementary and middle grades.

Kilpatrick, J., Martin, G., and Schifter, D. *Research Companion to Principles and Standards for School Mathematics*. Reston, VA: NCTM, 2003.

The majority of this book surveys the research literature associated with the 10 standards and the remainder includes various perspectives on teaching and learning and the role of standards.

Ma, L. *Knowing and Teaching Elementary Mathematics: Teachers' Understanding of Fundamental Mathematics in China and the United States*. Mahwah, NJ: Lawrence Erlbaum, 1999.

This book describes the nature and development of the "profound understanding of fundamental mathematics" elementary teachers need to become accomplished mathematics teachers; the book suggests why such teaching knowledge is much more common in China than in the United States, despite the fact that Chinese teachers have less formal education than their U.S. counterparts.

National Council of Teachers of Mathematics (NCTM). *Principles and Standards for School Mathematics*. Reston, VA: NCTM, 2000.

A resource and guide for all who make decisions that affect the mathematics education of students in prekindergarten through grade 12. The recommendations are grounded in the belief that all students should learn important mathematical concepts and processes with understanding.

Stanic, G. M. A., and Kilpatrick, J. (Eds). *A History of School Mathematics, Volumes 1 and 2*. Reston, VA: NCTM, 2003.

These volumes contain the history of mathematics education in the United States and Canada during the nineteenth and twentieth centuries with emphasis on the period from after World War II.

CHAPTER 2

Helping Children Learn Mathematics with Understanding

◆ Snapshot of a Lesson

Key Ideas

1. Using an array as a model for multiplication
2. Using skip counting to count arrays
3. Relating multiplication notation to arrays

Background

This lesson snapshot, excerpts pp. 24-25, is from *Investigations in Number, Data, and Space: Arrays and Shares*, a fourth-grade lesson in the elementary mathematics curriculum by Karen Economopoulos, Cornelia Tierney, and Susan Jo Russell, copyright © 2004 by Pearson Education, Inc. Reprinted by permission. In this investigation, students use arrays as models for multiplication. In session 1 of the investigation, students worked together to identify everyday items that come in arrays. They determined the total number of items by skip counting, recorded the dimensions and multiplication notation, and drew a picture of the array. As homework for session 1, students looked for arrays at home, recorded them, and brought in the arrays to show the class. Students are discussing the new arrays they found for homework.

TEACHER: I want to show you what Sara brought in. [*The teacher holds up an egg carton.*] What can you tell me about this?

NICK: It's an egg carton.

MARCI: It's a 3 by 6.

PINSUBA: It can hold 18 eggs.

B.J.: You could say it has 6 rows of 3 or 3 rows of 6.

TEACHER: I have another egg carton over there on the table. How would you describe that one?

KENYANA: A 2 by 6.

TEACHER: What else can you say about it?

KYLE: Or a 6 by 2.

IRENA: It holds 12.

LESLEY ANN: It's like a dozen.

TEACHER: What do you mean by a dozen?

LESLEY ANN: It's 12. A dozen is the same as 12.

ALEX: My dad says a baker's dozen is 13.

TEACHER: How can you compare these two arrays?

JOEY: Both hold eggs.

SARAH: Both count by 6s.

KIM: One's bigger.

REBECCA: One just has 6 and 6. The other one has 6 and 6 and 6.

TEACHER: What if I do this? [*The teacher tears the egg carton for a dozen in half.*]

NICK: That's a 2 by 3.

TEACHER: How many eggs does it hold?

JESSE: Six.

RIKKI: Half a dozen.

TEACHER: David, want to share your album? What's it for?

DAVID: Basketball cards. Each page is a 3 by 3.

TEACHER: How many cards will it hold?

DAVID: Nine to a page, and I have almost 5 pages full.

EMILIO: He'll have 45 if he gets 5 pages, because 9, 18, 27, 36, 45—that's five 9s.

TEACHER: Did anyone else find a different array?

NHAT: An ice tray.

TEACHER: Tell us about the ice tray.

NHAT: It's a 7 by 3. It has 21 holes.

TEACHER: That's an unusual ice tray with three rows. Any other arrays? [*Many students call out and the sharing continues.*]

Introduction

How do children learn mathematics? This important question has no simple answer. Each elementary classroom is filled with children who have different backgrounds, interests, strengths, and needs. It is important for teachers to not only know the children in their classroom well but to answer the question, "How will my students best learn mathematics?" Teachers provide their answers through classroom practices. In fact, every instructional activity within the classroom expresses the teacher's view of learning. The way in which you plan lessons, present topics, and handle questions reflects how you perceive learning and influences what happens in the classroom. Because teachers' beliefs about the learning process make such a difference in the classroom, a thoughtful study and understanding of how mathematics is learned should have high priority for every elementary teacher. The purpose of this chapter is to build on your previous knowledge from educational psychology and stimulate your thinking about how to help all children learn mathematics.

FOCUS QUESTIONS

1. How can we create a supportive classroom climate for the diverse learners in our classroom?

2. What is procedural knowledge and how is it different from conceptual knowledge?

3. How do behaviorist approaches to learning differ from constructivist approaches to learning?

4. What are four recommendations for helping children make sense of mathematics based on what is known about how children learn mathematics?

How Can We Support the Diverse Learners in Our Classrooms?

When starting a school year, teachers look forward to meeting their new class of students. Each year brings a new mix of children with varying personalities, strengths, and needs. Elementary classrooms are becoming increasingly more diverse. Nationwide, the last decade has seen large increases in the number of students who are members of ethnic minorities, are English language learners, and receive services for disabilities. Data from the National Center for Educational Statistics (http://nces.ed.gov) indicate that a typical classroom of 25 students includes approximately

- 10 students who are members of a minority group
- 4 students who speak a language other than English at home
- 10 students who qualify for free or reduced-cost lunches
- 4 students who live in poverty
- 3 students with disabilities who receive services, half of whom spend more than 80% of their school day in a regular classroom

The students in our classrooms are diverse in many additional ways. They vary in their cognitive, physical, and social development and abilities. They come from different cultures and family structures. They have different background experiences, interests, levels of motivation, and styles of learning. In the end, every child in every class is unique. As teachers, we are charged with helping each and every one of these children learn mathematics and develop to their maximum potential. The current national focus on accountability in education reinforces that responsibility.

NCTM's vision, described in the Equity Principle, is that "All students, regardless of their personal characteristics, backgrounds, or physical challenges, must have opportunities to study—and support to learn—mathematics. Equity does not mean that every student should receive identical instruction; instead, it demands that reasonable and appropriate accommodations be made as needed to promote access and attainment for all students" (NCTM, 2000, p. 12). You can help make that vision a reality by taking the attitude that providing for all the children in your mathematics classroom is not an overwhelming task but an exciting challenge. In Chapter 3 we will examine how you can adapt lessons to meet the needs of individual students. There are many other strategies you can use to support all students without having to individualize instruction for each one. In the following sections, we describe six of these strategies.

Creating a Positive Learning Environment

Creating a positive learning environment means being concerned both with the physical setting and with other factors: "If we want students to learn to make conjectures, experiment with alternative approaches to solving problems, and construct and respond to others' mathematical arguments, then creating an environment that fosters these kinds of activities is essential" (NCTM, 1991, p. 56). The teacher is largely responsible for creating an appropriate environment. Here are some of the things you should do.

- Make sure the classroom arrangement is safe and comfortable and that it supports the lesson's learning activities. When you do a demonstration, be sure all students can see you, the board, or the screen. If students will spend most of their time working in small groups, arrange their desks in clusters before the lesson begins. If they need to use manipulatives or other supplies, have them packaged and available for easy access or distribution. Consider a room arrangement that lets both you and the students move around the room easily.

- Make sure the classroom atmosphere is intellectually stimulating for learning mathematics. Encourage intellectual risk-taking, and help children feel safe about taking risks. Help children understand that confusion, partial understanding, incorrect answers, conceptual errors, and some frustration are natural as they construct their mathematical knowledge. Children who do not inhibit their intuitive responses and are not overly concerned about giving wrong answers are more likely to observe patterns accurately, feel free to make conjectures, engage in discussions, and take risks when doing mathematics.

- Communicate the fact that confusion, partial understanding, and some frustration are a natural part of the process of learning mathematics. Make sure students understand that they will not all learn the same things at the same time and that they will not all be equally proficient, but that everyone can indeed become proficient. Tell them that learning mathematics is a long-term process. Sometimes progress will be slow; and sometimes learning will jump ahead in moments of aha and insight, when they will say, "I've got it!" or, "Now I understand!"

- Reward students for critical thinking and creative problem solving, so students learn to value and respect those approaches. Students who experience a problem-solving approach to mathematics consistently perform higher than those who experience a focus on skills and procedures (Sutton and Krueger, 2002). Table 2-1 shows some additional recommendations from NCTM for shifting the classroom learning environment so it better supports all students.

Table 2-1 • Five Shifts in Classroom Environment

Mathematics Instruction Should Shift:	
Toward	Away from
Classrooms as mathematics communities	Classrooms as collections of individuals
Logic and mathematical evidence as verification	The teacher as the sole authority for right answers
Mathematical reasoning	Mere memorizing of procedures
Conjecturing, inventing, and problem solving	Finding answers mechanistically
Connecting mathematics, its ideas, and its applications	Treating mathematics as a body of isolated concepts and procedures

Adapted from *Professional Standards for Teaching Mathematics* (NCTM, 1991).

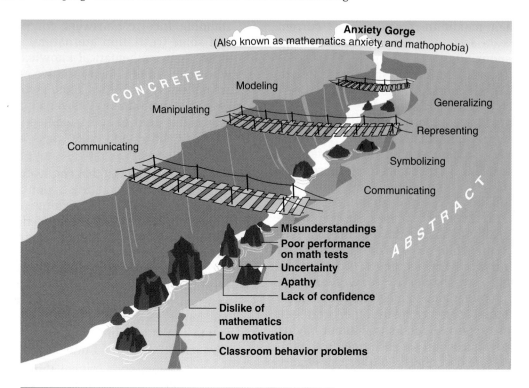

FIGURE 2-1   Bridges linking meaning to mathematics.

Avoiding Negative Experiences That Increase Anxiety

Many children experience some degree of mathematics anxiety, or "mathophobia"—a fear of mathematics or other negative attitudes toward mathematics. Mathematics anxiety can be expressed as poor performance, more than the usual number of misunderstandings, lack of confidence about doing mathematics, and so on (see Figure 2-1). Data from the National Assessment of Educational Progress (NAEP) suggest that primary-grade children generally express positive attitudes about mathematics, but attitudes toward mathematics tend to become progressively more negative as children move into middle school and high school (Lubienski, McGraw, and Strutchens, 2004). Students who experience mathematics anxiety tend to take less mathematics during secondary school, thereby blocking their access to many careers.

What can be done about mathematics anxiety? Here are some suggestions for ways you can help students cope with this problem:

- Emphasize meaning and understanding rather than memorization. Children do not easily learn isolated facts, things that are not logical, or things that have no meaning (Caine and Caine, 1995). Mathematics learning must be characterized by sense making (i.e., the mathematics learned must make sense to the learner). Chil-

dren attempting to memorize mathematics without understanding are likely to fall into the "anxiety gorge" in Figure 2-1. Helping students make connections between the concrete (e.g., models and manipulatives) and the abstract (e.g., generalizations and symbolic representations) facilitates understanding, promotes success at learning, and helps relieve mathematics anxiety, as illustrated in Figure 2-1.

- Model problem-solving strategies rather than presenting finished solutions. Encourage students to offer suggestions and to try their ideas and see what happens. Help students realize that using incorrect strategies and taking unnecessary steps are a natural part of developing problem-solving skills. Remind students that, in the long run, mastering the process of problem solving is more important than finding the right answer to one particular problem. Focusing on the process rather than the answer helps reduce the anxiety associated with getting "wrong" answers.

- Show a positive attitude toward mathematics. If you have math anxiety, do all you can to overcome it. Students' attitudes are greatly influenced by the attitudes of their teachers. Teachers who enjoy teaching mathematics and who share their interest and enthusiasm for the subject tend to produce students who like mathematics (Fennema et al., 1990).

- Give students mathematical experiences that they will enjoy and that will interest and challenge them while allowing them to be successful. Successful experiences in learning mathematics result in self-confidence.

- Show a positive attitude toward students at all times. Encourage, support, and praise all students, and help all students appreciate the power, usefulness, and importance of mathematics.

- Encourage students to tell you how they feel about mathematics. What do they like, and why do they like it? This self-reflective (or metacognitive) diagnosis can help you detect symptoms of mathematics anxiety.

- Be careful not to overemphasize speed tests or drills in your classroom. Some children may enjoy the challenge of competition, but others are uncomfortable with it—for these students, timed races breed apprehension and fear of mathematics.

- Use diagnostic techniques to identify students who are experiencing particular difficulty or need special help, and provide this help quickly to get them back on track. Research indicates that unless action is taken or help provided, the level of anxiety does not lessen on its own (Hart and Walker, 1993). The best strategy is prevention, and the second best is early detection followed by some of the specific actions listed above.

Establishing Clear Expectations

Clear expectations for student behavior and achievement are necessary in a well-run elementary classroom. Students tend to do what they think the teacher means rather than what the teacher says. To make their expectations clear, "teachers must think through what they really expect from their students and then ensure that their own behavior is consistent with those expectations" (Good and Brophy, 2003, p. 127). Ways to establish clear expectations include the following:

- Make it clear that you respect and value student ideas and ways of thinking; also make it clear that you expect your students to respect and value each other.

- Establish a mathematics class motto for your students: "Do only what makes sense to you." This motto encourages students to question, reflect, and seek explanations that make sense to them. It also paves the way for constructing knowledge that students find meaningful and that they understand.

- Another class motto might be: "Maybe one answer—certainly many paths." This motto will help your students realize that the process is just as important as the answer. Focusing on answers places too much emphasis on the end result. Ask students to explain their thinking, so you can see what path they took to get to their answers. A focus on process requires this kind of communication, which may take the form of talk in the classroom or explanatory notes in students' journals.

- Encourage children to reflect on their learning—not just on what they have learned, but also on how they learned it, their thought process. Metacognition is an important part of learning. Individual reflection or interaction with others (both teachers and peers) encourages students to communicate and explain their thinking.

Treating All Students as Equally Likely to Have Aptitude for Mathematics

Do not let your words or actions suggest that some students—for example, boys or students of Asian background—are more likely than others to excel in mathematics. Doing so sends a message to those other students that you expect them not to succeed. Make it clear that you expect students to succeed in mathematics regardless of their gender, race, or cultural and ethnic background. Expecting high achievement from everyone sends a powerful message that mathematics is for everyone. Research consistently confirms that teacher expectations greatly affect student performance (Koehler and Grouws, 1992).

A complex assortment of social forces produces or influences inequities related to mathematics. For example, parents of young children may indicate that they expect their sons to be better at mathematics than their daughters. School counselors may subtly discourage students from particular ethnic or socioeconomic backgrounds from studying mathematics or pursuing careers where mathematics is important.

Research has shown that teachers can do a lot to help minority students succeed in mathematics. Unfortunately, however, the quality of instruction in schools with high concentrations of minorities is often below average in quality, incorporating less rigor and sense making (Weiss and Pasley, 2004). To be an effective teacher, you must have high expectations for all students, and you must challenge all students equally. You must also consider minority students' languages, cultures, and community backgrounds as assets, not as liabilities. If you develop flexible assignments and assessments that help you identify and use student strengths, you can increase the cognitive level of interactions of minority students. You should also provide immediate and effective remediation when needed (Holloway, 2004).

Research suggests that teachers may actually treat girls and boys differently in the mathematics classroom. For example, teachers may tend to call on boys more and may be less likely to praise girls for correct responses and less willing to prompt girls who give wrong answers (Ansel and Doerr, 2000). Teachers also tend to attribute boys' failure at mathematics to a lack of motivation, whereas they tend to attribute girls' failure to a lack of talent. Girls may take such criticism to heart and think that it truly indicates their mathematical abilities.

The willingness of students to take risks—to take a chance on answering a question when they are not certain of the answer—may be a factor behind gender differences on tests. Numerous studies have reported that boys gamble more than girls in choosing answers to questions on multiple-choice tests when they are not sure, and this may be rewarded by higher scores (Ramos and Lambating, 1996).

Gender differences also arise with respect to *learned helplessness*—the belief that the individual cannot control outcomes and is destined to fail without the existence of a strong safety net. Learned helplessness includes feelings of incompetence, lack of motivation, and low self-esteem. It usually develops from what is perceived as failure or lack of success in learning, and it is often associated with mathematics. Students feel there is little sense in trying because the opportunity for success is beyond their control. Both boys and girls experience *learned helplessness*, but girls are particularly susceptible to this syndrome.

Within the NCTM's *Principles and Standards,* the Equity Principle (see Figure 1-2) should lead teachers to make strong efforts to confront and eliminate biases. Actions you can take to address inequities include the following:

- Dispelling myths (such as "mathematicians work in complete isolation" or "only white males do mathematics") that discourage women and some minorities from pursuing careers in mathematics (Henrion, 1998).

- Having equally high expectations for all students, and clearly communicating those expectations to both students and their parents.

- Engaging both boys and girls in solving difficult problems, raising questions, and communicating their mathematical thinking—that is, making sure boys and girls participate equally in the class discussion and receive equal shares of your time and attention.

- Calling attention to role models of both genders and the widest range of racial, cultural, and ethnic backgrounds, in both mathematics and science; also, helping students increase their awareness of career opportunities for people with strong mathematics backgrounds. (The Resources section at the end of this chapter includes books that will help you find biographies and stories about mathematicians and scientists of varied backgrounds.)

- Communicating to parents the importance of encouraging all their children—both girls and boys—to aspire to success in mathematics.

- Discussing learned helplessness with students having problems and developing ways to prevent learned helplessness or to remedy it (Renga and Dalla, 1993).

- Using a variety of ways to assess student performance (e.g., a range of test formats, interviews, and portfolios).

Helping Students Improve Their Ability to Retain Mathematical Knowledge and Skills

Retention reflects the degree to which students can hold onto and use what they have learned. For example, if students can read a clock in class but have forgotten how to do so by the time they get home, we would say that their retention of this skill is very limited. Clearly, retention of knowledge and skills is an important aspect of learning.

Forgetting is a problem in all disciplines, but the cumulative nature of mathematics increases its importance. Forgetting occurs over a summer, a spring vacation, a weekend, a day, or even shorter periods. It can make the retention of skills and specific knowledge decrease dramatically from the peak during instruction. For instance, the knowledge that lets students answer questions like the following is quickly forgotten if it is not used regularly:

What is a prime number?

What is the transitive property?

How many pints are in a gallon?

Skills, too, are quickly lost if not used regularly. For example, students may have trouble doing exercises like these:

What is the quotient of 2/3 and 1/5?

Use the formula to find the area of a trapezoid.

Thus, classroom and achievement tests of mathematical skills and knowledge often report very changeable levels of performance.

Performance at problem solving, in contrast, is more stable over time and less susceptible to big declines. One reason is that problem solving is a complex behavior supported by several higher-level thinking processes. Such processes take time to develop, but once established, they are retained longer than other skills and often improve as time goes by.

Retention is an important goal in mathematics education. You must recognize its importance and gear your instruction to maximize it. Research suggests several ways you can help children improve their retention:

- *Meaningful learning is the best way to increase retention.* All phases of mathematics (knowledge, skills, and problem solving) that have been developed with meaning and learned with understanding are retained longer.

- *The manner in which a concept was learned can aid long-term retention* (National Research Council, 1999). For example, physically measuring the diameter and circumference of many different circles, observing patterns, and recording them helps students remember that the ratio of the diameter and circumference is constant more than simply being told by the teacher.

- *Establishing connections aids long-term retention.* Connections help children see how mathematical ideas are related to each other and to the real world. Mathematical topics must not be taught in isolation, but in conjunction with problem solving and with applications in meaningful, real-world contexts. For example, in the Snapshot of a Lesson at the beginning of this chapter, having the students bring examples of arrays from home strengthened their understanding of the concept of multiplication. Research documents the value of establishing connections, not only to gain better understanding but also to promote retention.

- *Periodically reviewing key ideas helps anchor knowledge and can contribute substantially to retention.* The spiral development of high-quality mathematics programs reflects the importance of periodic reviews of mathematical topics for children at every age. These reviews may be explicit or implicit. Some teachers spend the first few minutes of each math lesson explicitly reviewing previously learned concepts; others implicitly incorporate reviews of previous topics in discussions of new topics. In either case, reviews help remove rustiness, reinforce and refresh knowledge in ways that improve immediate performance, and contribute to higher achievement and greater retention.

How Can We Help Children Acquire Both Procedural Knowledge and Conceptual Knowledge?

The overriding goal for mathematics education is for students to become mathematically proficient. According to the National Research Council (2001), mathematical proficiency incorporates five important strands: conceptual understanding, procedural fluency, strategic competence, adaptive reasoning, and productive disposition. In this section, we will elaborate on conceptual understanding and procedural fluency. In mathematics education, the relative importance of teaching students procedural knowledge or fluency versus conceptual knowledge or understanding has long been debated. But this debate involves a false dichotomy. Clearly, not only are both procedures and concepts necessary for expertise in mathematics but they are intertwined. As a teacher, you need to understand what constitutes procedural knowledge and conceptual knowledge and the importance of helping students make meaningful connections between them. Both types of knowledge are essential in order for students to be able to learn mathematics with understanding.

Procedural knowledge is reflected in skillful use of mathematical rules or algorithms. A student with procedural knowledge can successfully and efficiently use a rule or complete a process, a sequence of actions. For example, a student who has procedural knowledge of two-digit division can perform the steps in the long-division algorithm quickly and accurately. *Conceptual knowledge* involves understanding what mathematical concepts mean. For example, one aspect of conceptual knowledge for division is that one meaning of division means forming equal groups. Students with conceptual knowledge link ideas in networks of connected meanings, can incorporate new information into those networks, and see relationships among different pieces of information (Hiebert and Carpenter, 1992). The students in the Snapshot of a Lesson are developing conceptual knowledge of multiplication by using models in a way that makes sense to them. As they learn more challenging multiplication procedures, their conceptual knowledge of what it means to multiply should help them learn more easily.

Procedural knowledge alone helps students answer specific questions, but it lacks important

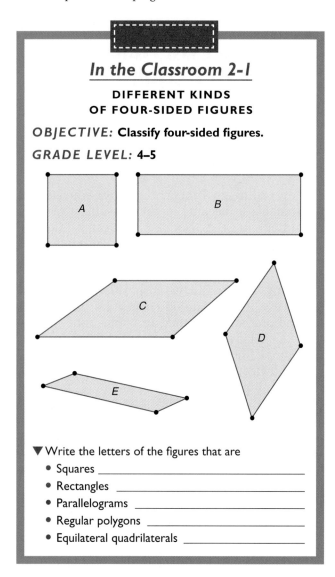

In the Classroom 2-1

DIFFERENT KINDS OF FOUR-SIDED FIGURES

OBJECTIVE: Classify four-sided figures.

GRADE LEVEL: 4–5

▼ Write the letters of the figures that are

- Squares _____
- Rectangles _____
- Parallelograms _____
- Regular polygons _____
- Equilateral quadrilaterals _____

connections. Conceptual knowledge requires that the learner actively think about relationships and make connections, while also making adjustments to fit the new learning into existing mental structures. Research shows that conceptual knowledge not only doesn't diminish skills but may even help students recall and use skills (Hiebert, 2003a). For example, in response to the question "What is a square?" procedural knowledge might lead a student to respond, "A square is a figure with four congruent sides and four right angles." Procedural knowledge would not, however, help the student understand other relationships—for example, that a square is a rectangle, a parallelogram, a regular polygon, and an equilateral quadrilateral. In the Classroom 2-1 requires that students demonstrate conceptual knowledge—that is, a deeper understanding of four-sided figures.

There is a negative consequence of teaching procedural knowledge without conceptual knowledge. If teachers indicate that the only important thing is to get the right answer, then students will have no motivation to learn why algorithms work. The addition algorithm for 23 + 49 could be memorized as "add the 3 and the 9 to get 12. Bring down the 2 and carry the 1. . . ." Rote learning (memorization without meaning) has no place in school mathematics, but it highlights one of the ever-present dangers associated with teaching algorithms. Research suggests that students with highly developed rules or procedures for manipulating symbols are reluctant to make the effort to connect these rules to other representations that might help them understand the mathematical meaning of the algorithms (Hiebert et al., 1997a). In addition, a student who learns a procedure without meaning will have difficulty knowing when to use it, remembering how to do it, applying it in new situations, and judging if the results are reasonable.

As a teacher of mathematics, you will need to help students establish connections and see relationships between conceptual and procedural knowledge. They may not be able to do it automatically. Keep in mind, however, that research suggests that understanding (conceptual knowledge) should come before proficiency in skills (procedural knowledge) (Hiebert and Carpenter, 1992). Your challenge is to construct learning experiences that help your students build connections between mathematical ideas as they explore and learn mathematics. A closer look at what we know about how children learn mathematics will help you meet this challenge.

◢ How Do Children Learn Mathematics?

The vision for mathematics education promoted by the National Council of Teachers of Mathematics (NCTM, 2000) is for all children to learn mathematics with understanding.

The discussion of the Learning Principle in the *Principles and Standards for School Mathematics* includes this statement: "Learning with understanding is essential to enable students to solve the new kinds of problems they will inevitably face in the future" (NCTM, 2000, p. 21). The National Research Council concurs: "All young Americans must learn to think mathematically, and they must think mathematically to learn" (2001, p. 16).

The premise that mathematics must be learned with understanding is based on research that has been accumulating for many years and reflects advances in mathematics education, psychology, and other areas of science. At the elementary level, teachers must deal with the fact that children's ability to learn mathematics depends on their reading ability; however, once children have basically learned to read, they build their reading skills while learning other subjects, including mathematics. Mathematics, in contrast, builds on itself, becoming more abstract as the ideas build (e.g., from arithmetic to algebra). Evidence from science suggests that learning changes the physical structure of the brain, and different parts of the brain may be ready to learn different things at different times (National Research Council, 1999). Ultimately, to learn more abstract mathematical concepts, children need to have developed both physically and psychologically enough to handle the abstraction.

Early in the twentieth century, John Dewey asserted that learning comes from experience and active involvement by the learner. Much has been discovered since then about how children learn mathematics, but the importance of meaningful experience remains unchallenged. Later, Jean Piaget argued that learners actively construct their own knowledge. This view of learning, known as *constructivism*, suggests that rather than simply accepting new information, students interpret what they see, hear, or do in relation to what they already know. As the Learning Principle indicates, students learn mathematics with understanding by actively building new knowledge from their personal experiences and prior knowledge. In this chapter's Snapshot of a Lesson, students used everyday objects, from their own homes or cultures, arranged in arrays to help them make sense of multiplication.

Teachers develop their lessons based on how they believe children learn. There are currently two prevailing theories of learning, behaviorism and constructivism. *Behaviorism* focuses on observable behaviors and is based on the idea that learning means producing a particular response (behavior) to a particular stimulus (something in the external world). From this perspective, students learn specific skills (behaviors) by observing teachers demonstrating those skills in relation to specific stimuli (e.g., a mathematics problem). For example, a teacher demonstrates how to find the mean of a set of numbers, and students learn to produce that type of response (finding the mean) when given that type of stimulus (a second set of numbers). Behaviorism's focus on behaviors excludes consideration of any thought processes students may use to arrive at their answers.

Constructivism has a different focus: it concentrates on what happens between the stimulus and the response. That is, the focus is on the thinking students do. From this perspective, learning depends not only on what the teacher does but also on the students themselves—how they integrate new ideas with their experiences and with what they already know.

Both views of learning hold implications for teaching mathematics. Both are key to a further understanding of how children learn mathematics.

Building Behavior

Behaviorism focuses on external actions and observable behaviors—on stimuli and responses. The main advocates of the behaviorist perspective over the years include Edward L. Thorndike, B. F. Skinner, and Robert Gagné; today, few learning theorists argue for an exclusively behaviorist approach to mathematics learning. Behaviorism has had a significant impact on mathematics programs, and teachers must consider behaviorist psychology when developing instructional goals and planning lessons. Nevertheless, strict adherence to a behaviorist approach to mathematics learning in elementary school is inappropriate because of its lack of consideration of the child's own thinking. Thus, as a teacher, you can draw on behaviorist ideas, but you must do so wisely and with an awareness of their limitations. Keeping this point in mind, we will examine behaviorism a bit more closely.

A major tenet of behaviorism is that behavior can be shaped through reinforcement—that is, through rewards and punishments. Teachers can use reinforcement (e.g., feedback on a student's performance, praise or criticism in class) to get students to practice desired behaviors (e.g., written algorithms). It is well documented that meaningful practice has great value and power in mathematics learning, but excessive practice, premature practice, or practice without understanding is associated with negative effects (Koehler and Grouws, 1992). Such practice often leads to a fear or dislike of mathematics and an attitude that mathematics does not need to make sense, despite the fact that making sense of mathematics should be a major goal of mathematics learning.

A behaviorist approach can be useful in helping children learn a fixed set of skills in a fixed order—that is, to help children acquire procedural knowledge. Many behaviorists think of mathematics as being sequenced in a linear fashion, where one idea builds on another and where proficiency in one skill is used to develop proficiency in the next skill. For example, the concept of multiplication as repeated addition suggests that students need to master addition before moving to the concept of multiplication. This hierarchical view of mathematics learning makes it a popular candidate for a behaviorist approach.

The first consideration in planning a lesson from a behaviorist perspective is to state precisely the objectives, or goals, of instruction. Such statements give the teacher direction in planning lessons and give the students clear expectations—both valuable outcomes that are consistently supported by research. Then, once an objective has been clearly stated, the teacher should identify the prerequisites for achieving that goal and use those prerequisites as building blocks in planning instruction. For example, suppose you have stated this objective: Use the formula $A = 1/2\, ba$ to find the area of a triangle. Some prerequisite questions would be

What is area?

What is a triangle?

What is a triangle's base?

What is a triangle's altitude?

Clear answers to these prerequisite questions are necessary in order to reach the objective; however, the following questions could also be considered prerequisites:

How do you multiply by a fraction?

How do you multiply two whole numbers?

This indicates the difficulty in constructing a complete set of prerequisites for any objective in mathematics, no matter how simple the objective may seem. Of course, you have to consider prerequisites when preparing lessons, but you must be guided by common sense, not by zeal to state every last prerequisite.

From the behaviorist perspective, clarifying the goals for instruction focuses the instruction on the desired learning outcomes. What behavior do you want the students to exhibit at the end of instruction? That outcome provides the focus of the lesson. This process of forming behaviorally oriented objectives may be useful, but it ignores a more important goal—learning mathematics with meaning. Students may be able to demonstrate a desired behavior without understanding of what that behavior means. If the objective of the lesson is to use the formula correctly to find the area of a triangle, the lesson's focus is on lower-level cognitive outcomes, where the students are only expected to correctly identify and use the base and altitude of the triangle to calculate the area. If, on the other hand, the objective of the lesson is to explain how the area of the triangle is half the area of a specific rectangle (see Figure 2-2), the students are directed toward a higher cognitive level of understanding of the area of the triangle. From this higher-level perspective, the prerequisite questions for the lesson must include the question of understanding the area of a rectangle. The lesson must then focus the students on identifying the rectangle that is formed

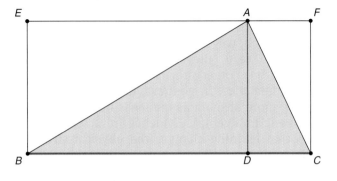

FIGURE 2-2   The area of triangle *ABC* is half the area of rectangle *BEFC*. The length of the rectangle equals the base of the triangle and the width of the rectangle equals the altitude of the triangle.

by the base and altitude of the triangle (rectangle *BEFC* in Figure 2-2).

This example shows how emphasizing behavioral outcomes for a lesson may result in lower-level cognitive procedures. Unfortunately, many mathematics programs include a hefty proportion of such outcomes, probably because they are easily measured. The result is programs where students are "shown" algorithms and mathematical relationships are "illustrated" on the textbook pages, but where learning with understanding is sadly underemphasized.

The attractive features of the behaviorist approach are that it provides instructional guidelines, allows for short-term progress, and lends itself well to the current focus on accountability. Knowing what outcomes will be assessed in state or standardized tests gives teachers specific direction for designing their lessons; however, a real and constant danger in using a behaviorist approach is that it leads to a focus on simple, short-term objectives that are easily measured. These simple objectives, in turn, lead to mastery of specific skills, rather than to higher-level understandings and the development of connections that make knowledge meaningful and useful. The emphasis on short-term objectives often results in a de-emphasis of long-term goals and higher-level cognitive processes such as problem solving.

Nevertheless, careful use of a behaviorist approach can result in more learner involvement and can even promote higher-level thinking in mathematics. Lesson outcomes can be identified that encourage children to develop concepts and use critical thinking. This possibility is illustrated by the use of behaviorally oriented verbs in stating outcomes, verbs such as *explore, justify, represent, solve, construct, discuss, use, investigate, describe, develop,* and *predict.* In sum, the behaviorist approach does lead to some useful ideas in teaching mathematics:

- Behavior can be shaped by reinforcement of drill and practice.
- Students can be helped to learn specific skills in a fixed order.
- Clear statements of objectives help teachers design lessons directed at specific learning outcomes.
- Clear statements of objectives and learning outcomes give students a clear idea of expectations.

Although identifying specific outcomes is an important part of mathematics instruction, the constructivist perspective helps teachers focus more directly on helping students understand and make sense of mathematics.

Constructing Understanding

During the first half of the twentieth century, William Brownell advanced a notion of meaningful learning that was a forerunner of constructivism.

Brownell conceived of mathematics as a closely knit system of ideas, principles, and processes—a structure that should be the cornerstone for learning mathematics. Connections among concepts should be established so that "arithmetic is less a challenge to the pupil's memory and more a challenge to his [or her] intelligence" (Brownell, 1935, p. 32).

In recent years, research has consistently confirmed that isolated "learnings" are not retained (Hiebert, 2003a). Mathematics can and should make sense to learners. If it does, it will have meaning to learners and will be understood as a discipline with order, structure, and numerous relationships—and will be likely to be called on in a variety of problem-solving situations. Meaningful learning provides the basis for mathematical connections and is an integral part of the constructivist perspective.

In addition to Brownell, Jean Piaget, Jerome Bruner, and Zoltan Dienes have each contributed to the growth of constructivism. Figure 2-3 summarizes their frameworks of the learning process. Many of the major recommendations for teaching

Levels of Thinking by Elementary School Children as Characterized by Piaget	Levels of Developmental Learning as Characterized by Bruner	Levels of Mathematical Learning as Characterized by Dienes
Formal Operational: Considers the possible rather than being restricted to concrete reality. Capable of logical thinking that allows children to reflect on their own thought processes.	**Symbolic:** Manipulation of symbols. Child manipulates and/or uses symbols irrespective of their enactive or iconic counterparts.	**Formalization:** Provides an ordering of the mathematics. Fundamental rules and properties are recognized as structure of the system evolves.
		Symbolization: Describes the representation in language and/or mathematical symbols.
		Representation: Provides a peg on which to hang what has been abstracted. Images and pictures are used to provide a representation.
Concrete Operational: Thinking may be logical but is perceptually oriented and limited to physical reality.	**Iconic:** Representational thinking based on pictures, images, or other representations. Child is involved with pictorial and/or verbal information based on the real world.	**Generalization:** Patterns, regularities, and commonalities are observed and abstracted across different models. These structural relationships are independent of the embodiments.
		Free Play: Interacts directly with physical materials within the environment. Different embodiments provide exposure to the same basic concepts, but at this stage few commonalities are observed.
Preoperational: Represents action through thought and language but is prelogical in development.	**Enactive:** Firsthand manipulating, constructing, or arranging of real-world objects. Child is interacting directly with the physical world.	

Left axis: Advanced ↑ / Early —
Right axis: Abstractions ↑ / Introductory —

FIGURE 2-3 Frameworks of the learning process.

mathematics advocated by the *Professional Standards for Teaching Mathematics* (NCTM, 1991) and more recently in the NCTM's *Principles and Standards for School Mathematics* (2000) are based on their theories of how children learn mathematics. Both of these documents provide strong support for changing from the traditional behaviorist approach to a constructivist approach. In fact, "educational research offers compelling evidence that students learn mathematics well only when they *construct their own mathematical understanding*" (National Research Council, 1989, p. 58).

Some of the myths associated with constructivism, such as "constructivist learners work alone" or "cooperative learning is constructivist," continue to linger (Clements, 1997). What, then, does it really mean for students to construct their own mathematical understanding? It means different things to different people, but three basic tenets of constructivism help us answer this question:

1. *Knowledge is not passively received; rather, knowledge is actively created or invented (constructed) by students.* Piaget (1972) suggested that mathematics understanding is made (constructed) by children, not found like a rock or received from others as a gift.

2. *Students create (construct) new mathematical knowledge by reflecting on their physical and mental actions.* They observe relationships, recognize patterns, and make generalizations and abstractions as they integrate new knowledge into their existing mental structure (Dienes, 1960).

3. *Learning reflects a social process in which children engage in dialogue and discussion with themselves as well as with others (including teachers) as they develop intellectually* (Bruner, 1986). This tenet suggests that students are involved not only in manipulating materials, discovering patterns, inventing their own algorithms, and generating different solutions, but also in sharing their observations, describing their relationships, explaining their procedures, and defending the processes they followed.

Consider these three tenants and apply them to your own learning of the material in the previous section on procedural and conceptual knowledge. As you read about these ideas, were you able to make any connections to things you already knew? To assist in your understanding of this new information, it may be useful to create some examples of the two types of knowledge. You may want to think about what makes sense and where you are still unsure. Perhaps you will write a journal entry. Then discuss your examples and ideas with other

students or the teacher. By actively working with the material, reflecting on it, and discussing it with others, you will be more likely to add this new information to your personal knowledge bank than if you just memorize definitions.

These tenets have significant implications for learning and teaching mathematics. They also suggest that, from the constructivist perspective, learning is a process that takes time and reflects a passage through several developmental stages. Research has established that each stage of children's cognitive development provides a window of opportunity for a range of learning activities in mathematics. At each stage, the lower limit of what children can learn is determined by the concepts and skills that they have already learned. The upper limit is determined by tasks that they can successfully complete only with scaffolding or support from someone more skilled or knowledgeable. The Russian psychologist Lev Vygotsky referred to the child's *zone of proximal development* to describe this range of learning activities and experiences (Steele, 1999).

Research suggests that learning activities that fall within a child's zone of proximal development have a high probability of success, whereas activities outside the zone have much less likelihood of success. While we want to provide children with tasks that will help them move to a higher level of thinking or to mastery of a higher-level skill, we do not want the tasks to be so far beyond their reach that they cannot succeed and give up. Vygotsky's notion of a child's zone of proximal development challenges you to know your students well and to have a reasonably good understanding of the limits of their zones.

Learning is active and internally monitored; it is a process of acquiring, discovering, and constructing meaning from experience. In this context, teaching math with the use of concrete models and making connections with the children's experiences helps them make sense of mathematics. The process results in learning that is filtered through the student's unique knowledge base, thoughts, perceptions, and feelings.

Piaget, Bruner, and Dienes characterize children's levels of development somewhat differently (see Figure 2-3), but overall, their proposed frameworks are remarkably similar. A careful examination of these frameworks reveals four important observations about how children learn:

- Several characteristic and identifiable stages of thinking exist, and children progress through these stages as they grow and mature.

- Learners are actively involved in the learning process.

- Learning proceeds from the concrete to the abstract.
- Learners need opportunities for talking about or otherwise communicating their ideas with others.

How Can We Help Children Make Sense of Mathematics?

Teaching occurs only to the extent that learning occurs. Therefore, effective teaching of mathematics rests heavily on considerations about how children learn. The process of building bridges from the concrete to the abstract and helping children cross them is at the heart of good teaching—and it is a continual challenge.

A blend of learning theory, research, teaching experience, and thinking about how children learn mathematics leads to practical recommendations for teaching mathematics in a manner consistent with the NCTM's Learning Principle—the principle that emphasizes the importance of personal experiences and prior knowledge in actively building new mathematical knowledge. What follows are four recommendations for helping children make sense of mathematics, based on the four observations listed above, derived from the frameworks of Piaget, Bruner, and Dienes. These recommendations provide a strong foundation for mathematics instruction, and we extend and apply them throughout this book. No priority of importance is suggested by the order in which they are listed.

Recommendation 1: Teach to the Developmental Characteristics of Students

As children grow, they progress through identifiable stages of development (see Figure 2-3), and children learn best when mathematical topics are appropriate for their developmental level. Topics should be presented in enjoyable and interesting ways that challenge children's thinking and allow them to add new concepts and skills to existing ones. Effective and efficient learning of mathematics depends on this type of teaching—it doesn't just happen.

The learners in our classrooms have many diverse characteristics—each child is different from every other child. Nevertheless, there are common characteristics that are typical of children in a particular age group and that is useful for teachers to know about. In this section, we focus on three types of development that influence mathematics instruction: cognitive development, physical development, and social development. *Cognitive development* has to do with how a child thinks and reasons. It also influences how the child learns new information. As educators, we probably pay more attention to our students' cognitive development than to any other type. The knowledge and skills we want children to learn are mainly cognitive in nature. *Physical development* has to do with the child's muscles and motor skills. If we want children to participate actively in mathematics, then a child's physical development must also be considered when planning lessons. *Social development* has to do with how children interact with others. It also helps describe their self-concept, how they feel about themselves. If you design lessons that require students to interact with you and other students, you must consider their social development.

Children aged 4–7 are in the primary elementary grades (preschool through grade 2). Children in this age range are developing rapidly cognitively, physically, and socially. They are active learners. With each year of growth, their cognitive ability to understand concrete and abstract ideas increases. Their physical abilities to focus, control muscle movements, and demonstrate motor skills also increase during these years. And socially, they are learning to understand and express themselves and to understand and interact with others. Table 2-2 summarizes some key ideas to keep in mind when teaching mathematics to children in the primary grades (Kostelnik, et al., 2004).

Children aged 8–11 are in the intermediate elementary grades (grades 3–6). Children in this age range are becoming more independent learners. Their thinking is becoming increasingly sophisticated, as is their physical and social development. These children are also active learners who enjoy the challenges of working independently and with others. Table 2-3 summarizes some key ideas to keep in mind when teaching mathematics to children in the intermediate grades (Kostelnik, et al., 2004).

It is useful to consider the general developmental characteristics of children in the primary and intermediate grades that may impact your mathematics instruction. Keep in mind, however, that there is a big difference in development between children at the beginning of these age ranges and those at the end. Note that Tables 2-2 and 2-3 include some suggestions to get you started thinking about how you can plan lessons that support learners at particular developmental levels.

Table 2-2 • Characteristics of Learners in the Primary Grades (Ages 4–7)

Cognitive Characteristics (thinking and ways of learning)	Suggestions for Teachers
• Piaget's preoperational stage • Centration—able to focus on only one idea or stimulus at a time • Irreversibility—unable to recognize the reversibility of changes to actions or objects • Begins to understand ideas beyond firsthand concrete experiences	• Use everyday experiences to connect mathematics concepts to children's life experiences • Break tasks into manageable parts • Encourage informal exploration, choice, and experimentation with concrete materials • Use questions to stimulate thinking and challenge misconceptions • Begin using pictures and symbols to represent concrete actions
Physical Characteristics (muscle and motor skills)	**Suggestions for Teachers**
• Developing control of large and small muscles, fine-motor skills • Short attention span	• Provide short, hands-on activities with choice and opportunity for movement • Focus more on process than product • Provide materials that can be easily handled or manipulated
Social Characteristics (self-concept and interpersonal skills)	**Suggestions for Teachers**
• Egocentric—focuses more on self than others, talks at rather than with others • Developing sense of self and abilities • May have a best friend and exclude others • Learning to express oneself and make decisions	• Encourage friendship skills, sharing, taking turns, and working with another person • Provide positive support, challenge, and feedback • Allow children to make their own plans for manipulating things in the environment and solving problems

Table 2-3 • Characteristics of Learners in the Intermediate Grades (Ages 8–11)

Cognitive Characteristics (thinking and ways of learning)	Suggestions for Teachers
• Piaget's concrete operational stage • Able to decenter, can focus on part/whole • Understands reversibility of actions or objects • Able to classify and sequence by attribute • Can use logic and concrete objects to solve problems	• Use concrete materials and link to symbols • Provide opportunities to manipulate, classify, and sequence both objects and numbers • Explore multiple representations and strategies • Have students regularly explain thinking
Physical Characteristics (muscle and motor skills)	**Suggestions for Teachers**
• Able to complete more complex physical skills	• Provide experiences that promote active, physical involvement • Provide opportunities for children to use real tools and materials, make models and diagrams, and conduct experiments
Social Characteristics (self-concept and interpersonal skills)	**Suggestions for Teachers**
• Growing more independent • Small groups of friends have major influence • Hard to accept failure or criticism	• Provide opportunities for problem solving and projects • Provide opportunities for group work • Provide positive support, challenge, and feedback

Recommendation 2: Actively Involve Students

Actively involving students in the learning process encourages them to make sense out of what they are doing and thereby develop greater understanding of mathematics. There is an ancient Chinese proverb that emphasizes the importance of active involvement for students as they construct their own mathematical meaning:

> I hear and I forget; I see and I remember; I do and I understand.

Active involvement may require physical activity but always demands mental activity. One of the daily challenges of teaching is to do the things that encourage and reward active involvement. These include directly interacting with the children, offering them hands-on experience with manipulatives, having them interact with learning materials such as textbooks and technology-based materials, and having them reflect on what they have done, thought, and experienced in class. Broadly speaking, we can classify such methods of actively involving students into two categories: exploration and sense making, and reflection and use of metacognition.

Encouraging Student Exploration and Sense Making One way to actively involve students is to encourage physical involvement. Suppose, for example, you were developing a lesson on volume. A traditional approach might include giving students the formula for finding the volume of a right prism: $V = bhl$. You could then show students drawings of various right prisms and ask them to use the formula to compute the volume of each.

A more active, developmentally appropriate approach would help children understand volume through an activity such as In the Classroom 2-2, where children are given blocks and asked to build different boxes (right prisms). As they build the boxes, they begin to relate the dimensions of the boxes to their volumes. Finding the volume of boxes is a primary objective for this activity; however, as students find the volumes of the boxes, they also learn that different boxes can have the same volume. Furthermore, they come to understand why they need to multiply the dimensions of a box to

In the Classroom 2-2

PATTERNS WITH BLOCKS

OBJECTIVE: **Find the volume of rectangular prisms and explore how a prism's volume relates to its dimensions.**

GRADE LEVEL: **3–4**

▼ Each of these boxes holds 16 blocks. Record the length, width, height, and volume (number of blocks) in the table.

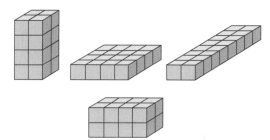

Length	Width	Height	Volume

▼ Take 24 blocks. Estimate how many different boxes you can make. _____

▼ Make as many different boxes as you can. Record the length, width, height, and volume in the table. How many different boxes did you make? _____

Length	Width	Height	Volume

▼ You have four piles of blocks. You must use all the blocks in a pile to make boxes.

    Pile A has 16 blocks.   Pile B has 25 blocks.
    Pile C has 36 blocks.   Pile D has 50 blocks.

- Which pile of blocks would let you build the most different boxes? Why?
- Which pile would let you build the fewest different boxes? Why?

▼ Build the boxes, fill in a table, and see if you are right. What did you find out?

▼ What patterns do you see in your tables?

find the volume, so the formula for the volume of a box evolves naturally from this active involvement.

An activity like this involves children in using models, making decisions, and thinking about mathematics, rather than just methodically applying a formula. It also lets them physically experience important mathematical properties. For example, using 16 blocks they build a $4 \times (2 \times 2)$ box and they build a $(4 \times 2) \times 2$ box. Because both boxes have 16 blocks and the same dimensions, they are demonstrating that $(4 \times 2) \times 2 = 4 \times (2 \times 2)$. The boxes are the same, just oriented differently. Similarly, as they continue to build boxes with 16 blocks, they construct models that show $(2 \times 2) \times 4 = (2 \times 8 \times 1)$ and, more important, they practice arithmetic and develop algebraic thinking. If you compare the "teacher telling" approach with the "children discovering" approach, you can see that the "children discovering" approach, which actively involves children in discovering the formula, will probably result in greater understanding and retention. We are more likely to remember something we've figured out for ourselves than something we have just been told.

Encouraging Student Reflection and the Use of Metacognition You can also actively involve students mentally, by helping them develop their metacognitive skills. *Metacognition* refers to thinking about one's own thinking (i.e., cognition about cognition). It includes what one knows or believes about oneself as a learner and how one regulates and adjusts one's own behavior. Children need to become aware of their own strengths, weaknesses, and typical behaviors and of the repertoire of procedures and strategies they use to learn and do mathematics and, more specifically, solve problems.

In a sense, metacognition means looking over your own shoulder—observing what you do as you work and thinking about what you are thinking. Students who monitor their mathematical thinking search for understanding and strive to make sense of the mathematics being learned. Competent problem solvers are efficient at keeping track of what they know and of how well or poorly their attempt to solve a problem is proceeding. They continuously ask

What am I doing?

Why am I doing it?

How will it help me?

More and more research suggests that what students know or believe about themselves as mathematics learners not only greatly affects their performance but also influences their behavior as they do mathematics (National Research Council, 2001).

Children who are skillful at metacognition can learn, for example, that practice improves their performance on particular tasks, that drawing a picture often helps them understand a problem, and that "I get scared when I see a word problem." This type of metacognitive knowledge often helps students control and adjust their behavior. For instance, if Sheena knows that she frequently makes keystroking errors with her calculator, she is more likely to work slowly and to check on the reasonableness of her calculator's answers.

The development of metacognitive skills requires that children observe what they know and what they do and that they reflect on what they observe. Encouraging students to think about their thinking is an important aspect of mathematics teaching. Here are a few things you can do to help students develop metacognitive awareness:

1. Help students be explicit about how they work when solving problems. For example, consider asking questions like these:
   - Why did you do that?
   - How did you know not to use that information?
   Teachers routinely consider such questions themselves when solving problems, but if they then go on to present complete, polished solutions to students, they may inhibit students from discussing their own decisions. There is value in helping children be aware of your behind-the-scenes decision making. When teachers share their own thinking, they provide a model for students.

2. Prepare students to accept and be aware of common problem-solving experiences by pointing out various aspects of problem solving:
   - Some problems take a long time to solve.
   - Some problems can be solved in several different ways.

3. Encourage students to become more aware of and to think about their own mathematical thinking. For example, you might ask students to discuss the following questions:
   - What mathematics problems do you like best? Why?
   - What mathematics problems are most difficult?

Some educators recommend that teachers have students with special needs brainstorm how they learn best and then help them to use those strengths (Diezmann, Thornton, and Watters, 2003). This may include helping them use specific learning approaches or styles, helping them use specific methods for communicating their thinking and their approaches to problem solving, and encouraging them to rephrase tasks or problems in their own words.

Recommendation 3: Move Learning from Concrete to Abstract

When you think about how learning should move from the concrete to the abstract, it is important to keep in mind that *concrete* is a relative term. To one child, joining two blocks and four blocks is concrete, but 2 + 4 is not; another child may view 2 + 4 as concrete and $x + y$ as abstract. Symbols and formal representations of mathematical ideas follow naturally from the concrete level, but only after conceptualization and meaningful understanding have been established. Without such understanding, children do not feel comfortable working with mathematical symbols, and the mathematics does not make sense to them. As Bruner noted in his framework, children need opportunities to work with objects in the physical world before they will be ready to work with pictures and other representations. Then, after working with pictures and other representations, they will be ready to work with symbols.

Using Manipulatives and Models Manipulative materials and models have a critical role throughout elementary school in helping students learn mathematics. Mathematical ideas are abstract by their very nature, so any model that embodies them is imperfect and has limitations. But even though the model is not the mathematics, models provide a context for the mathematical concept under consideration. Research shows that learning occurs best when students have a meaningful context for the mathematical knowledge and understand fundamental relationships associated with the knowledge (National Research Council, 1999). The children in the Snapshot of a Lesson used everyday objects to make the concept of multiplication meaningful to them. Helping children establish meaningful connections between the model (context) and the mathematics is a challenge, but it is a rewarding struggle.

Suppose you were developing the concept of a circle. You might use a plate to illustrate this concept, but it would also illustrate many other mathematical concepts: area, boundary, circumference, and diameter, to name but a few. Moreover, when a concept is first being formed, the learner has no way of knowing which attributes characterize it. Thus, the learner may think that irrelevant attributes matter (e.g., the design on the plate, its attractive finish, or a chip or crack) and may even fail to take in the relevant attributes. The learner may end up not being at all clear about what characterizes a circle.

You could introduce a model such as a coin, but students might still focus on the interior rather than the boundary. In contrast, models such as a bike tire and a ring would reinforce the roundness associated with a circle but would also make it clear that a circle is associated with the outer edge or boundary of the models (see Figure 2-4). Research has shown that lightly directing children's attention to the important attributes enhances learning, so you might take a piece of chalk or a water-soluble pen and trace around the outer part of the coin or plate to highlight the circle.

The use of perceptually different models, such as those shown in Figure 2-4, is called *multiple embodiment*, or *multiembodiment*. Research has shown that transfer across contexts is difficult if children have experienced the concept in only a single context rather than in multiple contexts (National Research Council, 1999). The more different the models or contexts, the more likely the students are to focus only on the common characteristics and make the correct abstractions. You cannot expect children to abstract correctly from a single model in mathematics. Multiembodiment helps students abstract or generalize appropriately. It also decreases the likelihood that children will associate a mathematical concept with a particular model, which is a danger whenever a single model is used to illustrate the concept.

Mathematical learning depends heavily on abstraction and generalization. Multiembodiment

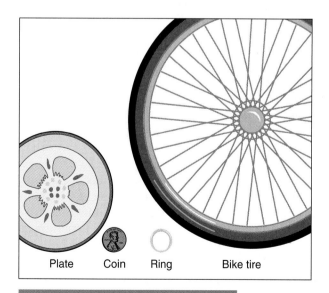

Plate Coin Ring Bike tire

FIGURE 2-4 Some models of a circle.

rests on the value of experiencing a mathematical concept in a variety of different physical contexts. Each embodiment has many different attributes. Children need to experience many different embodiments (along with models that do not embody the concept) before they can recognize which attributes all the embodiments share, allowing them to make the correct generalizations.

Students also need to recognize that even embodiments of the same kind have variable characteristics. For instance, consider again the plate shown in Figure 2-4 as an embodiment used to develop the concept of a circle. To help children realize that they should ignore such features as size, design, and chips, you could show them several different kinds of plates. By pointing out how these features vary, you can encourage children to focus their attention on a feature that does not vary—the plate's roundness. By using varied examples of a single type of model, you can increase the likelihood that learners will focus on only the mathematically significant attributes.

Similarly, you could use rings of different designs, styles, and materials to show children that these attributes don't matter and help them recognize that the rings model a circle. You should also point out that some rings don't model a circle—for example, this "adjustable ring":

This ring does not model a circle because it is not a closed figure. If you were using plates to model a circle, you could use an oval serving platter as a nonexample. Such *nonexamples* (models that don't embody the concept) play an important role in concept formulation. Research confirms that students learn more when presented with a combination of examples and nonexamples of a mathematical concept than with examples alone (Hiebert and Carpenter, 1992).

Making Formal Representations Follow Conceptualization   Children need many experiences with concrete models before they can work meaningfully with abstract symbols. Those initial experiences with models should help children develop conceptual knowledge about the topic, as can talking about the topic and looking at pictorial representations. Finally, you can show children how symbols can be used to record what has been expressed orally about the concrete models or pictures.

How long should a model be used? That depends on both the student and the mathematical content. In general, too little time is spent with models. That is, students are rushed (or dragged) too quickly through firsthand experiences with models and then confronted with symbolic representations. Students need to feel comfortable with a model and both observe and talk about the key mathematical features it embodies. It is a good idea to keep models available for students. They will know when they no longer need a model and will stop using it for a faster method. Even at this stage, leaving the model doesn't mean that they will never use it again. The same model may be used at various levels throughout elementary school to help children develop new or more sophisticated concepts.

Recommendation 4: Use Communication to Encourage Understanding

The use of models, manipulatives, and real-world examples provides many opportunities for thinking, talking, and listening. The importance of communication in mathematics learning is demonstrated by the fact that communication is one of the key process standards in the NCTM's *Principles and Standards* (2000). You will learn more about these important standards in Chapter 5. When children explain their approaches, talk about mathematics, make conjectures, and defend their thinking orally, as well as in writing, their understanding deepens. Talking and writing about mathematics are essential in learning mathematics.

Using Oral Communication to Encourage Sense Making   Lev Vygotsky, who originated the concept of the zone of proximal development, is also well known for his ideas about the role of language in learning. Vygotsky believed that learning is a social experience—that is, interactions with others challenge learners to make sense of new ideas (Kostelnik, Soderman, and Whiren, 2004). This theory supports the idea that we should provide children with many opportunities to talk about their thinking. Often, communicating our thoughts to others can clarify them for ourselves as well.

Students at all levels should talk about mathematics before being asked to communicate about mathematics symbolically. Just as speaking precedes writing for children, so should the talking about mathematics precede writing about it using symbolic representations. Both student-to-student communication and student-to-teacher communication are important in the learning process.

Also, in talking about mathematics, students are likely to give you valuable insights into their thinking and understanding. This talk may take different forms. For example, by listening to the discussion in the Snapshot of a Lesson, we know that Emilio has made a connection and can use the 3×3 array to count by 9's and figure out how many baseball cards there are on five pages. Others in the class may learn from his insight.

This kind of talking between students is natural and gives them many opportunities to explain what they did, justify their thinking, and share their methods. You should do all you can to stimulate and encourage this kind of student-to-student communication, even if much of it takes place outside your hearing.

Now consider an example of student–teacher interaction as a fourth-grade class is exploring primes and composite numbers by building rectangles with tiles.

BOB: So every even number is composite.

TEACHER: Every even number? What about two?

This question stimulates additional thinking and encourages Bob to try justifying his overgeneralization or to modify it. Questions are a vital element in the learning process. Students should ask each other questions and ask teachers questions, and teachers should ask students questions. Such interactions give students opportunities to talk about their ideas, get feedback on their thinking, and hear other points of view. Thus, students learn from one another as well as from teachers.

Using Written Communication to Convey Thinking
In writing about mathematics, students provide insight into what they are thinking and what they understand. Just like talking, putting our thoughts in writing forces us to think more deeply or helps us clarify our thoughts. Young children who are still developing their writing skills can communicate in writing by drawing pictures or dictating their thoughts to a more skilled writer. You can write prompts to help students get started. For example,

I think the answer is. . .because. . . .

Another way to do it is. . . .

The thing I liked best was. . .because. . . .

I still don't understand. . . .

In addition, after students have had experience with a concept through the use of models and oral language they should begin to learn the mathematical notation to communicate those same ideas.

Using conventional symbols to represent mathematical concepts is a valuable part of being able to communicate mathematically.

Talking and writing about mathematics makes it more alive and more personal, and it keeps student interest high. Reading students' writing carefully and listening carefully to what students say, as well as noticing what they do *not* say, help you tailor your teaching to all the unique individuals in your class.

A Glance at Where We've Been

The children in classrooms today are increasingly more diverse. Teachers must create a classroom climate to support their diverse learners. This includes setting a positive learning environment, avoiding negative experiences, establishing clear expectations, showing positive attitudes toward math, treating aptitudes as equal, and working to improve student retention.

Mathematics learning can and must have meaning. This statement is the cornerstone of all instructional planning and teaching. Conceptual and procedural knowledge are essential elements of mathematics learning. Mathematics learning is a slow process that requires years of development. Many individual differences exist, and the rate of learning varies greatly among children. Given these variables, the essential role of teachers is to help children construct mathematical knowledge that is meaningful to them. In performing this role, teachers use behaviorist and constructivist learning theory to make countless decisions to plan appropriate learning activities, establish an inviting classroom environment, and organize the classroom to ensure that all children are actively participating in experiencing, learning, abstracting, and constructing mathematics that is meaningful to them.

Research and learning theory suggest that as children move through distinct stages of development, there is significant value in children being actively involved constructing their own knowledge, learning moves from concrete to abstract, and that communication plays an important role in facilitating construction of new knowledge. In addition to hands-on experiences, children learn from telling, explaining, clarifying, making conjectures, and reflecting on what they have done. They also learn from watching, listening, reading, following directions, imitating, and practicing. All of these experiences contribute to learning mathematics; teachers have the responsibility of deciding the proper balance of these experiences.

Things to Do: From What You've Read

1. Select one of the methods for creating a classroom climate supportive of diverse learners. Explain how you plan to carry this out in your classroom.

2. Provide some mathematics examples to help distinguish between procedural and conceptual knowledge.

3. Defend the statement in Figure 2-2 that triangle *ABC* has an area that is half the area of rectangle *BEFC* using the different regions in the diagram.

4. Examine the learning frameworks in Figure 2-3. Tell how the models proposed by Piaget, Bruner, and Dienes are alike. How are they different?

5. Identify the three tenets on which constructivism is based. From the Snapshot of a Lesson, identify evidence of these tenets.

6. Select Table 2-2 or 2-3. Then describe how this information will influence your math instruction.

7. State in your own words what the zone of proximal development is. Do you think it is important? Tell why.

8. What is metacognition? Examine the activity described In the Classroom 2-1. Describe how metacognition might be used to think about your thinking during that activity.

9. List some characteristics of mathematics anxiety. Discuss how the use of learning bridges can save victims from the "anxiety gorge."

10. What are some specific actions an elementary teacher can take to better treat aptitudes among students as equal?

11. Describe some specific steps that teachers can take to improve retention of mathematics learning.

12. React to one of the recommendations for helping children make sense of mathematics.

Things to Do: Going Beyond This Book

IN THE FIELD

1. *Patterns with Blocks.* Use In the Classroom 2-2 with a child. Did the child realize that two of the pictured boxes are the same box, just in a different position? Would it make sense to try this activity with children if blocks were not available? Why?

2. *Classroom Manipulatives.* Identify models and manipulatives that are available to use in a mathematics classroom that you visit. Did you see them being used? If so, what models and manipulatives were being used and how?

3. *Equity in Whole-Class Lessons.* Observe a mathematics class and be sensitive to the verbal and physical clues that suggest boys are treated differently from girls. If you see evidence that boys are treated differently from girls, discuss some examples.

4. *Student Attitudes.* Ask a child some questions to learn about their attitudes and perceptions about mathematics. For example:

   If I say, "Let's do some mathematics," what would you do?

   What school subject do you like most? Are you good at it?

   Do you think knowing mathematics will help you when you grow up? Tell why.

   Do you think your teacher liked to teach mathematics? Tell why.

   Summarize what you learned about this child's feelings about mathematics.

IN YOUR JOURNAL

5. Reflect on your own experiences learning mathematics. Describe how you learned mathematics.

6. Consider the two learning theories, behaviorism and constructivism. Describe personal experiences that suggest the influence of these theories on your learning of mathematics.

---

*Additional activities, suggestions, and questions are provided in *Teaching Elementary Mathematics: A Resource for Field Experiences* (Wiley, 2007).

WITH ADDITIONAL RESOURCES

7. Examine an article discussing gender/race/culture as related to learning mathematics. Describe significant issues raised and implications for you as a teacher.

8. Examine one of the vignettes from the *Professional Standards for Teaching Mathematics* (NCTM, 1991). Present this vignette to your classmates, and discuss its value in helping you help children learn mathematics.

9. Obtain a publication from the Math/Science Network (Lawrence Hall of Science, University of California, Berkeley, CA 94720), such as *Math for Girls and Other Problem Solvers* or *Use Equals to Promote the Participation of Women in Mathematics*. Review one of their publications and share your reactions.

10. Examine the Learning Principle in the *Principles and Standards for School Mathematics* (NCTM, 2000). Describe some specific ideas that would be useful in planning instruction and helping children learn mathematics.

11. Examine the book *Gender Equity: Sources and Resources for Education* by Sanders, Koch, and Urso 1997. Describe some things you can do in your teaching to help encourage girls to study mathematics.

12. Examine the NCTM Yearbook *Multicultural and Gender Equity in the Mathematics Classroom* (Trentacosta and Kenney, 1997). Read one of the articles, and then identify and discuss several specific implications for mathematics teaching.

13. Examine the book by Reimer and Reimer in *Book Nook for Children* and report how you might use this resource. Do you think this personalization helps promote more interest in learning mathematics? Do you think helping children learn more about women's contributions in mathematics is an important instructional goal? Tell why.

WITH TECHNOLOGY

14. Check the Women's Educational Equity Act (WEEA) at the Equity Resource Center Web site, www.edu.org/womensequity/ for a history of Title IX, a list of publications, current articles, and other Web links. Report on something related to equity and mathematics that you find at this site.

15. Conduct a Web search for the Ask Dr. Math Web site. Review the questions that elementary teachers and students send for Dr. Math to answer. Do you find any evidence of mathematics anxiety in the questions that you see? Do you see a difference in the questions submitted by girls and by boys?

Note to Instructors: You can find additional resources, learning activities, and black-line masters in this text's accompanying Instructor's Manual, at www.wiley.com/college/reys.

Book Nook for Children

Hopkins, L. B., and Barbour, K. *Marvelous Math: A Book of Poems*. New York: Aladdin, 1998.

Sixteen poems cover different mathematical topics that include division, multiplication, fractions, counting, and measurement. All of these poems will relate to everyday living in our world. The book will let children see how mathematics plays important roles in our everyday living. This book will be a good springboard for introducing different topics in mathematics.

A Day with No Math. Orlando, FL: Harcourt Brace Jovanovich, 1992.

This book will let children see how we use mathematics in our everyday living. Children will see many topics in mathematics in the story line. Addition, measuring, estimating, geometry, statistics, probability are just some of the topics presented in this story about a boy who does not like to do math. As he falls asleep, he dreams what it would be like with no math in our daily living, and then realizes through his dream just how important mathematics is in our daily living.

Reimer, L., and Reimer, W. *Mathematicians Are People, Too: Stories from the Lives of Great Mathematicians* (2 volumes). New York: Pearson, 1997.

Share moments of mathematical discovery experienced by famous mathematicians with your students. Use these stories to demonstrate that both males and females are mathematicians, that mathematicians come from a variety of cultures, and that the work of mathematicians is applied to many diverse fields. Use this book with children in grades 3–7 to experience the stories of great mathematics, including Pythagoras, Galileo, Pascal, Albert Einstein, and Ada Lovelace.

(continues)

Scieszka, J., and Smith, L. *Math Curse*. New York: Viking, 1995

This book will let children see that if you let math become an anxiety, it will become a curse. Many core topics are presented in this book such as fractions, counting, dividing, Fibonacci numbers, physical education, problem solving, measurement, to name just a few topics. This book will let children appreciate mathematics in a new way. This book can be used at all levels of mathematical learning.

Annotated Resources

Boling, A. N. "They don't like math? Well, let's do something." *Arithmetic Teacher*, 38 (March 1991), pp. 17–19.
Students in grade 4 say math is their favorite subject. Then what happens in grades 6 and beyond that causes students to be more likely to say that math is their least favorite subject? This article contains current ideas about the causes and what can be done to overcome the problems.

Burke, M., and Curcio, F. (eds.) *Learning Mathematics for a New Century: 2000 Yearbook*. Reston, VA: NCTM, 2000.
This yearbook provides a variety of articles responding to important questions as we enter the twenty-first century: Where have we been? Why is mathematics education important in the twenty-first century? What is the role of technology? Where shall we go?

Ginsburg, H. P., and Baron, J. "Cognition: Young children's construction of mathematics." In *Research Ideas for the Classroom: Early Childhood Mathematics* (ed. R. J. Jensen). Reston, VA: NCTM, and New York: Macmillan, 1993.
Explore issues of how children learn and how to implement effective arithmetic instruction in the primary grades. Research on children's cognitive development as well as studies on the formation of early numerical concepts are examined. Ideas for establishing learning environments that are conducive to the development of a conceptual understanding of mathematics are explored.

Harrington, A. "Understanding then doing: Doing then understanding." *Mathematics Teaching*, 177 (December 2001), pp. 10–12.
Consider the tension between doing and understanding through the discussion of the author's problems with teaching mathematics to a group of students who are objecting to not being shown how to do the problems.

Hiebert, J., Carpenter, T. P., and Fennema, E. *Making Sense: Teaching and Learning Mathematics with Understanding*. Portsmouth, NH: Heinemann, 1997.
Consider elements necessary in a classroom in order for children to learn mathematics with understanding. Explore examples of different and diverse classrooms that help clarify ways of teaching for understanding.

Kazemi, E., and Stipek, D. "Promoting conceptual thinking in four upper-elementary mathematics classrooms." *Elementary School Journal* 102(1) (September 2001), pp. 59–80.
Investigate classroom practices that promote conceptual mathematical thinking and how teachers can promote student participation in a classroom community where conceptual understandings are valued and developed.

Stigler, J. W., and Hiebert, J. *The Teaching Gap: Best Ideas from the World's Teachers for Improving Education in the Classroom*. New York: Free Press, 1999.
Authors describe the teaching practices of three countries (Japan, Germany, and the United States) gathered through the TIMSS video study and make recommendations to improve American classroom education.

CHAPTER 3

Planning and Teaching

◀ Snapshot of a Lesson

Lesson Snapshot: Working with Two Rules

This lesson snapshot, excerpts pp. 21-22, is from *Investigations in Number, Data, and Space: Does it Walk, Crawl, or Swim?*, a second-grade lesson in the mathematics curriculum, by Susan Jo Russell, Rebecca B. Corwin, and Karen Economopoulos. Copyright © 2004 by Pearson Education, Inc. Reprinted by permission.

Key Ideas

1. Collecting information about a group of people
2. Sorting and classifying information
3. Counting and comparing sets of data

The following discussion takes place during an activity called Guess My Rule: Two-Rule Version. The class is trying to guess the two rules their teacher is using to group students.

TEACHER: I'm thinking of one rule for students standing by the chalkboard [*for example, WEARING GLASSES*] and a different rule for students standing by the windows [*WEARING GREEN*]. I'll start out with Jeffrey and Ebony by the chalkboard, and I'm going to put Phoebe and Trini by the windows. Any ideas about who else might fit?

AYAZ: I think Chen goes by the chalkboard.

TEACHER: Yes, he does fit there.

LAURA: Does Paul go by the windows?

TEACHER: No, he doesn't fit there.

LAURA: How about by the chalkboard?

TEACHER: Yes, Paul fits the rule I have for the group by the chalkboard. Who thinks he or she might know where Simon goes?

HARRIS: I don't think he goes in either place.

TEACHER: You're right. So what should Simon do?

HARRIS: He should just stay in his seat.

TEACHER: OK, Harris is suggesting that Simon stay in his seat because he doesn't fit either rule. Does everyone agree?

JUANITA: Well, he should stand up.

TEACHER: Why should he do that?

JUANITA: Because then we'll remember that we already tried Simon and he didn't fit anywhere.

TEACHER: OK, so that's how we'll tell who doesn't fit. [*Later in the game*]

TEACHER: I think you're ready to guess the rule for the people by the windows.

LINDA: It's GREEN.

TEACHER: Yes, my rule was WEARING GREEN. OK, everyone who is wearing green move over to the windows. [*Several students from the "chalkboard group" start moving over to the windows*].

TEACHER: But you're in the chalkboard group!

[*They look confused. One of the students starts moving back*].

TEACHER: But you're in the GREEN group!

SEVERAL STUDENTS TALKING AT ONCE: Wait a minute. I'm in both. Jess has green and he's in the chalkboard group. Yes, and Chen has a green shirt, and he's in the chalkboard group, too.

TEACHER: You're right. But Chen and Jess do fit my rule for the chalkboard group and they're wearing green. Let's see if we can get the rule for the chalkboard group and then we'll have to figure out what to do about students who fit both my rules. Does anyone think he or she knows who else goes in the chalkboard group?
[*Later*]

TEACHER: OK, you guessed that the chalkboard group all are wearing glasses. Now we have all these students who are wearing glasses over here, and all these students who are wearing green over there. But what can we do about the students who are wearing both glasses and green? They can't just keep running back and forth!

EBONY: Well, all the students who are wearing both could go to a different place.

GRAHAM: They could stand over by the door.

LAURA: They could go in the middle, like kind of touching both groups.

TEACHER: How would that work? [*Eventually all the students have been assigned to the chalkboard group (WEARING GLASSES), the window group (WEARING GREEN), the middle group (WEARING GLASSES AND GREEN), or are standing up at their seats (NOT WEARING GLASSES OR GREEN).*]

TEACHER: Now, who can tell me why some of you moved to the middle?

ROSIE: Some kids wearing green also are wearing glasses.

TIM: If you have both things, you stand in the middle. If you have one thing, you stand at the side.

TEACHER: Who can pick one of the groups and say exactly what the rule is for that group? And don't forget the group that is standing near their seats. They're an important group, too!

JUANITA: Well, the chalkboard group is wearing glasses.

TEACHER: It's true. I see glasses on everyone in the chalkboard group. But that's not the only place I see glasses. Can anyone add to Juanita's description?

SIMON: The middle group has glasses too.

TEACHER: Hmm, so how do I tell the difference?

JUANITA: The middle group is wearing green and they're wearing glasses.

TRINI: And the chalkboard group is wearing glasses and isn't wearing green!

TEACHER: What a clear way of putting it, Juanita and Trini. Can anyone else describe one of the groups? How about the group standing near their seats? That's a real challenge.

◆ Introduction

Teachers may play many different roles in the classroom, including counselor, gardener, police officer, parent, actor, architect, friend, guide, cheerleader, and others that you can probably think of. Which roles will you play? To some extent, that depends on your personality, your school, the students in your class, and many other factors, but all teachers must play the role of instructor.

The instructor role involves four basic functions: planning, teaching, assessing, and analyzing. Consider how the teacher in the Snapshot of a Lesson performed these functions: first, she made plans—deciding on the focus of the lesson (the objective) and then figuring out how to carry out the lesson from the textbook. Then she taught the lesson (as illustrated in the Snapshot discussion)—

presenting the problem, giving directions, asking questions; and listening to, observing, and providing feedback to the students. During and after the lesson, she assessed the students' understanding. Finally, she reflected on the lesson and analyzed what went on.

In this chapter, we focus on the planning and teaching functions. First, we discuss the kinds of general questions a teacher must ask and answer before beginning to make specific plans—questions that address such topics as what the teacher and students already know and how to get students talking and questioning. We then discuss levels of planning (for the year, for units, for lessons), planning for different types of lessons, and planning to meet the needs of all students. Throughout these discussions, we show how asking questions and making plans can translate into actual teaching practices in the classroom. This chapter also briefly touches on assessment and analysis (covered in detail in Chapter 4). In later chapters, we explain how to help children learn specific mathematics concepts and skills and we elaborate on each of these instructional functions. Thus, this chapter serves as an organizer for much of what you will learn throughout the rest of this text.

This chapter also makes general recommendations for mathematics teaching in today's technological and global society and provides concrete suggestions for teaching mathematics in that context. And, like every other chapter in this book, this chapter reflects our acceptance of the idea that children actively construct their own new understandings as they build on what they already know.

FOCUS QUESTIONS

1. What questions must an elementary mathematics teacher answer before beginning to plan?

2. Why does the teacher plan mathematics lessons so carefully?

3. What levels of planning does the teacher create? What are three types of lessons used to teach mathematics, and what is the purpose of each?

4. How can the teacher meet the needs of all students?

5. How does the teacher integrate planning with assessing and analysis?

Preparing to Teach: Questions to Ask Before Planning Begins

Teaching children mathematics is a complex task. As a teacher, you will have to make many on-the-spot decisions during instruction. But there is much you can do beforehand to increase the chance that the year, each unit, and each individual lesson will succeed for all the diverse learners in your classroom. Making this happen means asking and answering several important questions before lessons begin, even before you begin writing lesson plans. We discuss these questions and answers in the following sections.

Do I Understand the Mathematics I Am Teaching?

Teachers today are being asked not only to teach mathematics in ways different from how they were taught in elementary school, but also to teach topics and concepts they did not learn in school.

When this happens to you—when you have to teach something you don't know much about—your first job will be to learn all you can about it. This point is made in NCTM's *Principles and Standards*, which states, "Students' understanding of mathematics, their ability to use it to solve problems, and their confidence in, and disposition toward, mathematics are all shaped by the teaching they encounter in school. . . . *Teachers must know and understand deeply the mathematics they are teaching and be able to draw on that knowledge with flexibility in their teaching tasks. . .*" (NCTM, 2000, pp. 16–17; emphasis added). Similarly, the National Research Council (2002) notes that teachers must be proficient at a much deeper level than their students in order to teach mathematics well. We know from a variety of research that teachers with strong content knowledge are better able to develop their students' conceptual understanding of mathematics by providing multiple representations of the same concept. They are more likely to encourage student questions and comments (because they feel more confident in their own ability to deal with them) and they are better at analyzing student errors and misunderstandings. They are also more likely to connect the mathematics being taught to daily life and to other content areas (Sutton and Krueger, 2002). Doing these things can lead to higher student achievement in mathematics.

There are many ways you can improve your subject matter knowledge, and doing so will not only make you more skilled but will increase your confidence too! Educators have emphasized how important it is for you to work through lesson problems and activities before presenting them to students, because by working through the lesson and taking the role of the learner, you deepen your understanding of the mathematics and you experience firsthand what your students will be doing (Brodesky et al., 2004). These same educators suggest that teachers identify the mathematical goals of each lesson and what is most important for all students to learn, in order to avoid teaching in ways that do not meet those goals or that even conflict with them. And this process, too, requires that teachers understand the mathematical content at a deep level. Even if the lesson topic is familiar to you, you need to review the mathematics you will be teaching, in order to experience it in the same way the students will, so you can focus on students' conceptual understanding (Mewborn, 2003).

In other words, *be sure you understand the material well*. Chapter 1 gives several suggestions about where you can turn for help in case you don't; one of the best of these resources is the teacher's guide for your school's textbook. Many of these guides not only help you undertand the mathematics being taught, but also alert you to common student misconceptions and describe effective methods and materials you can use to teach the topic.

What Are the Developmental Characteristics of My Students?

Understanding your students' characteristics, especially their levels of development, can help you plan lessons that are appropriate for everyone in your classroom. For example, a teacher planning a first-grade lesson should realize that his students need to manipulate concrete objects to solve addition problems and are just beginning to use symbols to represent those objects. Also, remembering that first graders are still egocentric in their thinking could give the teacher the idea of making up story situations, with the students themselves as characters. Experts suggest that teachers are making developmentally appropriate decisions when they use what they know about the following topics (Bredekamp and Copple, 1997):

- how children develop and learn
- the strengths, needs, and interests of the individual children in their class
- the social and cultural contexts in which the children live

Before planning mathematics lessons, you should review the general developmental characteristics of the children in your classroom, as well as the characteristics of individual learners. In Chapter 2, we discussed some of the developmental characteristics of students in elementary school, and these overall trends provide a good starting point as you begin planning mathematics experiences for your students. Remember, however, that children do not all progress through developmental stages at exactly the same time and that they may, therefore, vary greatly in their readiness for learning. Thus, some first graders will understand addition and develop fluency with basic facts before some third graders. Likewise, some intermediate-grade students may have difficulty visualizing the blocks shown in In the Classroom 2-2; they may need to "build" these boxes before the task becomes meaningful. Children at the concrete operations stage must root their ideas in concrete objects; they have little ability to manipulate abstract relationships. These children would find it difficult (if not impossible) to learn how to find the volume of a cube by looking at a two-dimensional drawing.

You should also focus on your students' strengths as well as on their weaknesses. This will lead you to ways of using areas of strength to help students compensate for their weaknesses. It will also help you identify parts of a lesson that may give students problems and think of ways to make those parts more accessible. For example, a student who has trouble focusing but loves to talk and read might be paired with a student who focuses well but has reading difficulties. What is a strength for one student, may be a weakness for another (Brodesky et al., 2004).

Finally, considering your students' social and cultural experiences when planning can make your lessons more relevant and meaningful. Children may find it easier to learn and be more motivated to learn if they can see connections to their lives. For example, when planning a lesson on patterns, one teacher had the children bring in small, countable food items from home to create the patterns. Students' learning styles and preferences also are a reflection of their social and cultural experiences so if you can be aware of and teach with these things in mind, the lesson will be more likely to succeed.

What Do My Students Already Know?

As a teacher, you must identify and build on what your students already know. Instructional time is precious, not to be wasted on lessons that are too easy or difficult for your students. Of course, if students in your classroom are at different academic levels or if they have learning problems or disabilities, providing equitable treatment may mean adapting instruction to meet their particular needs. To meet the needs of all of the children in your class, you have to assess them. Paper-and-pencil tests are useful tools in assessment, especially if you go beyond looking at final scores and analyze how children reached their answers. Also, you can learn a lot about your students simply by observing and talking with them; this can reveal much that would not be noticeable from tests. You should use the results of assessment to help select instructional materials and approaches, group students for instruction, adapt materials, and decide what needs to be taught or retaught to individuals and to the class as a whole.

After assessing your students, you must organize the mathematics so you teach it in a way that is appropriate and understandable to them. Mathematics includes both conceptual and procedural knowledge; thus, you face two challenges—helping students to develop both types of knowledge and helping them understand the relations between them. In no other discipline is previous knowledge more critical—for example, it would clearly be pointless to ask students to estimate a distance in kilometers if they didn't already have some sense of the length of a kilometer.

The importance of children's previous knowledge is clear from the way that quality mathematics programs are organized, both to provide continuous development and to help students understand the basic structure of mathematics. Scope-and-sequence charts give an overview of how particular topics are developed across grade levels. A careful examination of such a chart reveals how the sequence of activities related to a particular topic is organized in a *spiral approach*, giving students repeated opportunities to develop and broaden concepts. The spiral approach incorporates and builds on earlier learning to help guide the child through the increasingly intricate study of a topic. For example, angle measurement is informally introduced in primary grades and returned to many times in later grades, each time at a higher level of sophistication. Figure 3-1 shows how the spiral approach uses previous experience to develop the concept of "angle."

The description we just gave of the spiral approach represents an ideal; the reality, however, may be somewhat different. In theory the spiral mathematics curriculum provides for continuous growth and development, but in practice many topics are revisited without appreciable change in the level of treatment from one year to the next. Consequently, much valuable time may be spent each year treading water, merely reviewing topics rather than building on prior learning or introducing new topics. Of course, a certain amount of review is

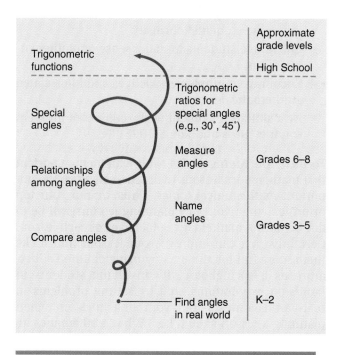

FIGURE 3-1 Spiral approach toward developing the "angle" concept.

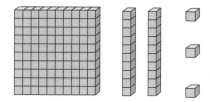

In the Classroom 3-1

PLACE VALUE

OBJECTIVE: Identify students' growing levels of understanding about place value.

GRADE LEVEL: 4

MATERIALS: Base-ten blocks

▼ At the beginning of the school year, interview children individually to assess their understanding of place value. For each student, record the results on a card with the student's name. Then, quarterly, interview the children again to see how their understanding of place value has grown. Be sure to record your observations on the cards to maintain an ongoing record of the development of each student's understanding and of any misunderstandings that may become evident in the interviews.

▼ Conduct the interviews at a table with a piece of paper that you can write numbers on in large print and with the base-ten blocks in a tub for the children to use.

▼ With each student:
1. Write a two-digit number on the paper, such as 48. Ask the student to read the number to you.
2. Point to an individual digit in the number and ask the student to explain what it means. For example, point at the 4 and ask "What does this four mean?" Repeat this question for each digit.
3. Ask the student to use the base-ten blocks to represent the number, and ask the student to explain why the blocks represent the number.
4. Repeat the process with a three-digit number (such as 137) and, perhaps, with a four-digit number.

probably necessary, for reasons like those discussed in the next paragraph. But the Trends in International Mathematics and Science Study (TIMSS) reported that mathematics programs in the United States reflect more review of topics from year to year than do mathematics programs in other countries such as Germany and Japan (TIMSS, 1996). Unnecessary repetition is detrimental because it turns students off. It robs both teachers and students of the excitement inherent in exploring new topics. It also uses up time that would otherwise be available for new learning, which means that fewer new ideas can be experienced each year.

The spiral approach holds profound implications for learning and teaching. For example, when planning a lesson, you must consider what prerequisites students must have to succeed in the lesson, and you must check to see if students have them. Often, you will find students who have never learned, incorrectly learned, or simply forgotten such prerequisites. Detecting these weaknesses early and quickly will let you plan the right kind and amount of review, so you can properly prepare students for later lessons without wasting time. In the Classroom 3-1 describes a way of gathering information about students' growing understanding of place value. Early in the second grade, students may be able to do no more than read two- and three-digit numbers, but as the year progresses, their understanding of place value will grow and they will gain the ability to explain the digits by representing them with base-ten blocks. Maintaining a record of their growth is important in order to identify gaps or misunderstandings.

Besides knowing what students learned in earlier grades, teachers must look ahead to see what their students will need to know tomorrow, next month, and next year. Third-grade teachers must know what their students learned in kindergarten, first grade, and second grade, as well as what their students will have to know in fourth grade and beyond. This broad perspective helps teachers appreciate the importance of their role. It also helps them detect gaps in their students' mathematics learning, so they can fill in any gaps as quickly and effectively as possible.

Of course, a gap for one student may not be a gap for another. If an individual student has a gap in understanding that most students do not have, you will need to work with that student to fill in the gap. It is not appropriate to force the whole class to review something that only one or two students do not understand. As a teacher, you will need to make many instructional decisions directed at helping individual students while continuing to challenge *all* your students, extending their experiences and their levels of understandings, as illus-

trated by the spiral approach in Figure 3-1. In addition, you should maintain records of how individual children's understandings develop (e.g., as indicated by In the Classroom 3-1) and pass this information on to teachers in the following grade. This will help those teachers continue to extend the learning of individual students.

What Kinds of Tasks Will I Give My Students?

What are the appropriate kinds of tasks for your students? This is another key question you must answer before you begin planning lessons. Appropriate tasks might be "projects, questions, problems, constructions, applications, and exercises" (NCTM, 1991, p. 20). Tasks must encourage students "to reason about mathematical ideas, to make connections, and to formulate, grapple with, and solve problems" (p. 32). One educator states,

> No other decision that teachers make has a greater impact on students' opportunity to learn and on their perceptions about what mathematics is than the selection or creation of the tasks with which the teacher engages the students in studying mathematics. Here the teacher is the architect, the designer of the curriculum. (Lappan, 1993, p. 524)

Expanding on this idea, other educators suggest that good tasks:

- Are often authentic in that they come from the students' environment
- Are challenging yet within students' reach
- Pique the students' curiosity
- Encourage students to make sense of mathematical ideas
- Encourage multiple perspectives and interrelated mathematical ideas
- Nest skill development in the context of problem solving (Reys and Long, 1995)

Focus on the Mathematics It is extremely important that mathematics lessons maintain a focus on the important mathematical topics. Thus, one of your top priorities when you start planning lessons will be to decide on the mathematics objectives of each lesson. Certainly, you can improve your lessons and make them more fun for students by using children's literature as a springboard, by involving students in hands-on explorations, and by setting problems in real-world contexts. But your first question when planning a lesson should be, "What mathematics do I want the children to learn from this?" It is not appropriate to use manipulative materials just as toys, to engage students in talking and writing only about their feelings and not about the mathematics, or to do lessons that are just fun for fun's sake.

As a teacher, you will be responsible and held accountable for helping children meet district and state standards, and you can do this only if your mathematics lessons involve students in tasks that are mathematically rich. When children are genuinely engaged in solving mathematical problems that make sense to them, the learning they take away from that experience is likely to be deep and lasting. The Snapshot of a Lesson at the beginning of this chapter shows children engaged in important mathematical processes such as those recommended by the *Principles and Standards for School Mathematics* (NCTM, 2000).

Provide Necessary Practice   Part of deciding about appropriate tasks is considering how to provide necessary practice. Clearly, students need practice in order to acquire fluency with a mathematical idea or procedure. Just as we must practice learning to walk or driving a car, we must practice basic addition facts or how to make patterns. The choice is not if, but when. Research has long indicated that drill and practice should follow, not precede, the development of meaning (Brownell and Chazal, 1935). Research also indicates that drill and practice should not consume as much time as developmental work that helps children to understand the idea or procedure (Suydam and Weaver, 1981). Whenever possible, practice should be meaningful—it should be much more focused on reinforcing conceptual understandings than on going over rote procedures. Finally, practice should help children apply their knowledge in new contexts.

Many textbook series provide practice on the content presented, lesson by lesson. Your decision whether to assign this practice material (in addition to all the other practice that students get—for instance, in the course of problem solving) must be based on your students' needs. You have to strike a balance between two conditions: one is that children must understand the mathematics before practicing it; the other is that practicing a skill that has already been mastered is boring and thus can be harmful. Therefore, you should include practice on previously learned topics as a small but regular component of each lesson. Keep in mind that completing a meaningful task will often provide just as much practice as completing textbook exercises, if not more.

Use the Strategic Moment   No matter how carefully you plan your lessons, you will still have to make many moment-to-moment decisions during instruction. Situations frequently arise in class that give you an opportunity to teach a topic in an especially effective way (see Figure 3-2). Taking advantage of these *strategic moments* is imperative, so you need to be ready for them, not thrown off your stride when they come up. Often, these moments let you connect to

Several first-grade children come into the room all excited by the parade they saw yesterday, with "hundreds" and "thousands" of marchers. You've planned a lesson on measurement for that day. What do you do?

All the traffic lights in town are off. Why? The computer has failed. You've planned a lesson on multiplication with two-digit numbers. Do you discuss the computer's role in society instead?

You are teaching a lesson on estimation. You have the class use calculators to find 3762.5 × 795.6 quickly. A child asks, "Why is there no zero after the decimal point in the answer?" How do you continue the lesson on estimation?

FIGURE 3-2   Some strategic moments.

your students' lives and interests, helping them see the relevance of particular mathematics topics.

To some extent, you can arrange the classroom environment (e.g., by bringing in something new and interesting) to increase the likelihood that strategic moments will arise. Knowing what concepts you want to teach and how these develop for the children in your class will help you recognize and take advantage of the strategic moment when it comes.

Experience will also help you make the many on-the-spot decisions that are part of teaching. You will learn what works and what doesn't. Try to define for yourself the goals you want to attain and how to attain them, and then try to work within that framework. Consider how children develop and learn. Observe the children in your class as individuals, and watch for their errors and their successes. These observations will help you assess their needs and plan their instruction. The better you know your children, the more ready you will be to see and grasp strategic moments and make good decisions.

How Will I Encourage My Students to Talk, What Kinds of Questions Will I Ask, and How Will I Group My Students?

You can help your students learn mathematics better by encouraging them to communicate their thoughts to you and to each other, by asking them the right questions at the right times, and by grouping students in ways that are appropriate to their characteristics and to the mathematics being taught.

Talking   You can use classroom talk, or discourse, to make certain that the classroom discussion helps students make sense of the mathematics you are teaching. Classroom discourse also helps children who are learning English develop and practice their language skills. As a teacher, your role will be to orchestrate mathematical discourse and to use language in a variety of situations for a variety of purposes (Copley, 1999). You will be the organizer, cheerleader, and conductor of the entire process of discourse, making appropriate tools available and finding ways to help children assume responsibility for their own learning. A flow of ideas—not only from teacher to student but also from student to teacher and from student to student helps every child learn mathematics (NCTM, 1991). Here are some ways you can help create effective classroom talk.

- Show your students that you expect them to communicate their thinking, to you and to other students. In addition, model ways in which your students can question and be questioned by their peers, and show them that you expect them to do this. Students must explain and justify their thinking.

- Make your mathematics class a safe place for students to conjecture and to make mistakes. Students often learn a great deal by listening to others and analyzing mistakes. Be certain to give students the opportunity to change their minds about conjectures and possible solutions.

- Pose questions and assign tasks that encourage children to talk about their mathematical thinking as well as to listen and respond to other students' ideas. Interactions among children give them opportunities to talk about their ideas, get feedback, and see things from other points of view. Students can learn from one another as well as from the teacher.

Notice how the teacher in the Snapshot of a Lesson at the beginning of this chapter was able to implement all three of these ways. The children were engaged in the activity and willingly communicated their thinking. Notice also how the teacher used questioning to lead them to draw some conclusions about their sorting activity.

Questioning   In Chapter 2 we discussed the importance of good questions in facilitating learning. Questions that are aimed at checking children's knowledge of a fact or their ability to perform a skill are relatively low level and are the easiest to create during a lesson. Higher-level questions require children to analyze or synthesize information, as when we ask students to explain why a procedure works or how they decided an answer is correct. In mathematics lessons, teachers tend to use questions of the first type much more frequently than those of the second type (Evertson et al., 1980). Children's ability to answer lower-level questions may correlate with high scores on some achievement tests, but such questions give children the wrong picture of mathematics by implying that mathematics involves only simple answers and that there is only one correct answer per question. So plan on being a teacher who asks plenty of higher-level questions that encourage children to do more talking about mathematics, talking that explores why a procedure works, what would happen if something were changed in the problem, and how mathematics could be applied in real-life situations.

To be this type of teacher, you will need to consider the types of questions you want to ask and write them in your lesson plans. Try to prepare a range of questions, but focus on questions that require children to think rather than merely supply a fact from memory or perform a learned procedure. (See the list of questions in Chapter 2.) If you ask only lower-level questions, students may come to believe that the main goal in mathematics is to memorize facts rather than to understand and make sense of mathematical ideas. Remember, however, that creating higher-level questions can be challenging—you'll have much more success if you develop such questions before the lesson begins.

The NCTM *Professional Standards* (NCTM, 1991, pp. 3–4) includes five categories of higher-level questions teachers should ask:

1. *Questions that help students work together to make sense of mathematics:* "What do others think about what Janine said?" and "Can you convince the rest of us that that makes sense?"

2. *Questions that help students rely more on themselves to determine whether something is mathematically correct:* "Why is that true?" and "How did you reach that conclusion?"

3. *Questions that seek to help students learn to reason mathematically:* "How could you prove that?" and "What assumptions are you making?"

4. *Questions that help students learn to conjecture, invent, and solve problems:* "What would happen if. . .?" and "Do you see a pattern?"

5. *Questions that relate to helping students connect mathematics, its ideas, and its applications:* "How does this relate to. . .?" and "Have we ever solved a problem like this one before?"

Math Links 3.1

*T*o see a teacher and students communicating, view the video "Developing Estimation Strategies by Making Connections Among Number, Geometry, Measurement, and Data Concepts: Estimating Scoops," at the NCTM Standards Web site: http://standards.nctm.org/document/eexamples/chap4/4.6/index.htm

www.wiley.com/college/reys

Grouping   One way to increase student communication in your mathematics class is to use a variety of grouping patterns. There are three basic patterns of grouping for mathematical instruction:

- Whole class, with teacher guidance
- Small group, either with teacher guidance or with student leaders
- Individuals working independently

Many teachers use whole-class instruction too extensively. You should keep in mind that small-group work can help children develop their reasoning abilities through active involvement, can ensure that children work on content focused on their particular needs, and can at the same time help them learn to work together to solve problems. Having individuals work alone can also serve important purposes. Here are some guidelines to help you decide when to use which grouping pattern:

1. Use large-group instruction:
   - If the topic can be presented to all students at approximately the same point in time (i.e., if all students have the prerequisites for understanding the initial presentation).
   - If students need continuous guidance or modeling from the teacher to master the topic.
2. Use small-group instruction:
   - If students can profit from student-to-student interaction with less teacher guidance.
   - If you are trying to encourage exploration and communication about mathematics.
   - If you are trying to help students benefit from the acquisition of cooperative learning skills.
3. Use individual instruction:
   - If students can follow a sequence or conduct an activity on their own.
   - If the focus is individual practice to attain mastery.

Most effective teachers use a combination of grouping patterns. For example, a teacher might develop new material with the whole class and then have children work individually or in small groups for one or more activities designed to help them consolidate the new learning. Communication with one another is especially valuable because the students help each other master mathematical ideas. The teacher moves from group to group, providing assistance by asking thought-provoking questions as needed (Davidson, 1990). The whole class is then brought together again for a teacher-mediated discussion so that children can hear ideas from students in other groups. The teacher ends the discussion by providing closure on the lesson for the day. This method of integrating whole-class and small-group work has proved more effective than whole-class instruction alone for developing higher-level thinking skills (Thornton and Wilson, 1993, p. 275).

A variation on small-group learning involves just two children working together on a task. This is particularly appropriate for young children who may not be developmentally ready to work in larger groups. The process of working together promotes the learning of both children.

Educators have pointed out that "Simply putting students in small groups will not guarantee that they will interact in ways that are beneficial to learning" (Farivar and Webb, 1994, p. 521). You will need to teach students skills in communication, team building, small-group socialization, and helping, so they can "use one another" as resources for doing mathematics.

Before you place children in groups, carefully consider their individual abilities and personalities. For example, you might think that placing low, middle, and high achievers in separate groups would better meet their needs, but research has found that homogeneous (similar ability) groups do not help increase overall student achievement and may promote inequity—that is, this type of grouping has not been found to narrow achievement gaps. In fact, low-achieving students actually perform worse when placed in homogeneous groups than they do in heterogeneous (mixed ability) groups. Middle- and high-achieving students do show some gain when placed in homogeneous groups, and there may be times this is helpful but grouping them heterogeneously holds even more promise (Marzano et al., 2001).

Small-group learning requires more planning and class time than whole-class instruction, but this is more than outweighed by the positive results: increased mathematical communication, social support for learning mathematics, opportunities for all students to experience success in mathematics, increased likelihood that children will see more than one approach to solving a problem, and opportunities to deal with mathematics through discussion of meaningful problems (Fitzgerald and Bouck, 1993, pp. 251–252).

What Materials Will My Students and I Use?

Planning for instruction also involves selecting materials. Teachers have varying levels of freedom when selecting materials to support their lesson objectives. Some can start with the textbook lessons and supplement them creatively, finding ways to adapt the textbook to the learners in their classroom. Others may be required by the school to use particular curriculum materials or textbooks and not to make more than the minimum adaptations needed for the students in their class. Either way, you will need to make the best use of the available materials, given your goals for the lesson and the children in your class. Whatever curriculum materials you use, sometimes you will want to locate additional resources. Educational publishers and the Internet provide lots of options, and you can also consider resources such as children's literature, manipulatives, and technology.

Textbook Lessons   Beginning teachers often wonder how much to depend on a textbook for lesson planning. To what extent can you use textbook lessons "as is"? How and why should you adapt them for your individual use? Obviously, answers to these questions depend on the textbook, on how closely its goals and methods align with your district and state standards, and on your own teaching preferences. It certainly does not make sense to develop your own original lesson plans if you have a textbook that provides an appropriate outline for each lesson. If you determine that the lessons are developmentally appropriate for your students, that they engage the students in genuine problem solving, and that they promote conceptual development, there is no reason not to use them, adapting them as seems necessary. Teachers' guides to textbooks can give you a variety of ideas for teaching lessons using the textbook. Guides also often provide suggestions for follow-up activities, such as written work and games. And many guides offer suggestions for remediation, enrichment, and alternative tasks for children with learning disabilities and other special needs.

If you are required to teach from a textbook with a more traditional approach, you can consider-

ably enhance the lessons by embedding them in a motivating theme or problem-solving-context. Such a context will give you and your students an organizing framework for teaching and learning and will help tie the lesson (or several lessons) together. Contexts for lessons may be taken from real-life situations (e.g., from current events or from special days such as holidays noted on a calendar) or may be developed from integrative themes tied to other subjects such as science, social studies, or children's literature. To get a sense of what a context is, look at Table 3-1, which shows some examples of how you can use contexts to enhance mathematics lessons.

Make sure you give students open-ended tasks that allow for multiple solution paths or multiple solutions. This allows students at different levels to participate and learn where they are. It also lets students select the approach that best fits their learning preferences. For example, one student may prefer to draw a picture to solve a problem while another needs to use blocks. It is relatively easy to start with traditional textbook tasks and make them more open ended (Kabiri and Smith, 2003), as illustrated in Figure 3-3. Notice that not only does the open-ended problem in Figure 3-3 encourage critical thinking more than the traditional problem does, but it also gives students the opportunity to practice using the formula for volume many times rather than just once.

Table 3-1 • Using Contexts in Mathematics Lessons

This Is a Context	This Is Not a Context
Sorting M&Ms for party favors gives a reason for using this manipulative.	M&Ms (alone) are a manipulative, not a context.
Planning a schedule for a class field trip involves telling time.	Time is a math topic, not a context.
Ordering carpet for classrooms in the school is a context. We need to know the area of the room to find out how much to order.	Area of rectangles is a math concept, not a context.
Measuring classroom objects to decide how to fit them into storage containers gives purpose to a lesson.	Measuring classroom objects is a mathematics procedure, not a context.

Traditional Problem: A rectangular aquarium is 12 in. wide by 14 in. long by 12 in. high. What is the volume of water needed to fill the aquarium? (Houghton Mifflin 2002, p. 475).

Open-ended Problem: You have been asked to design an aquarium in the shape of a rectangular prism for the school visitor's lounge. Because of the type of fish being purchased, the pet store recommends that the aquarium should hold 24 cubic feet of water. Find as many different dimensions for the aquarium as possible. Then decide which aquarium you would recommend for the lounge and explain why you made that choice.

FIGURE 3-3 A measurement problem shown in both a traditional and an open-ended form. Reprinted with permission from *Mathematics Teaching in the Middle School*, 2003 by the National Council of Teachers of Mathematics. All rights reserved.

You may also need to supplement lessons in order to increase the focus on problem solving and conceptual development. For example, if your text does not provide enough meaningful experiences or hands-on practice with manipulatives for the students in your class, you may need to find other ways of providing such experiences and practice. Ultimately, you will be the one who best knows your students and their needs. Treat your textbook as one of many available resources to help you teach mathematics to your students. Adapting textbook lessons can be challenging but also very rewarding. If you have the freedom to do so, another option is to select curriculum materials that already incorporate the kind of instruction recommended by NCTM.

Standards-Based Curricula Research tells us that implementing NCTM's standards recommendations for instruction can improve student achievement on both traditional objectives like computation and reform objectives like problem solving (Ross et al., 2003). Research has also shown that curriculum materials (textbooks) have a powerful impact on what is taught and how it is taught. In the 1990s, the National Science Foundation began funding several mathematics curriculum development projects aimed at designing and implementing curriculum materials that more closely aligned with NCTM's standards (Reys et al., 2003). To date, around 15% of schools have adopted these programs, and research is showing that students using standards-based curricula score at least as well as and often better than students using more traditional curriculum materials (Reys, Reys, and Chavez, 2004).

In this chapter, we provide sample lessons from two of the standards-based elementary programs: *Investigations in Number, Data, and Space* (for grades K–5), and *Math Trailblazers* (for grades K–5). These programs challenge students to understand the mathematics, to use higher-level thinking, and to learn mathematics through problem solving. The Snapshot of a Lesson, at the beginning of this chapter, is from the *Investigations in Number, Data, and Space* curriculum. Many traditional programs report they have incorporated NCTM's standards in their texts, but this often means they have incorporated the content standards without fully implementing the instructional approaches recommended by NCTM. This particular program, as illustrated in the Snapshot, engages children to use higher level thinking and be actively involved in their mathematics learning.

Teachers find it challenging to teach mathematics in the ways recommended in the standards. Often, they must significantly change their approach to mathematics instruction. At first they may need to spend more time preparing and planning for lessons. Sometimes, teachers seeking to give their students additional support in these challenging standards-based curricula end up eliminating essential components of the program. If you use these curricula, you must be careful to include classroom discourse, allow students to learn the mathematics concepts through problem solving, and apply the mathematics in real situations (Sutton and Krueger, 2002).

You should also realize that new ways of teaching and learning mathematics are not only challenging for teachers, but may also be confusing for parents. So it is important to keep communication lines with parents open. Some schools invite parents for math nights where teachers can explain the rationale for new instructional methods. Math nights can also give parents opportunities to directly experience these new types of math lessons, while giving teachers opportunities to suggest ways for parents to help their children at home. Some teachers send children home with letters for parents at the start of each unit, so parents know what is happening in math class. Remember that parents and teachers are partners in educating children. Anything you can do to help parents understand your goals should help you reach those goals.

Children's Literature Teachers often use children's trade books to enhance lessons in language arts, social studies, science, music, art, dance, and drama, but it is also easy, effective, and appropriate to use children's literature in mathematics lessons. Fiction and nonfiction books can provide "rich, authentic explorations of time and place and human experiences that make the concepts children are exploring vivid, relevant, and involving" (Whitin and Wilde, 1992, p. xi). Stories can provide children with a common starting point from which to share and discuss mathematical ideas. Mathematics and language skills develop hand-in-hand as children talk about problems and read and write about mathematical ideas. In addition, you can incorporate multicultural children's literature in your mathematics lessons as a way of making cultural connections for your students.

Use of children's literature in mathematics lessons can enhance learning in many ways. Children's literature:

- Integrates mathematics into other curriculum areas.
- Provides a meaningful context for mathematics.
- Supports the art of posing problems.
- Demonstrates that mathematics develops out of human experience.
- Fosters the development of number sense.
- Addresses humanistic, affective elements of mathematics.
- Celebrates mathematics as a language.
- Restores an aesthetic dimension to mathematical learning (Whitin and Wilde, 1992).

Many reference books for teachers can help you identify stories that work well for integrating children's literature with lessons on particular mathematics topics. The Book Nook for Children at the end of each chapter in this book includes numerous such suggestions.

Manipulatives Effective teachers use manipulatives when appropriate to explore problems and provide experiences that help children make sense of mathematics and build their mathematical thinking. The use of manipulatives is also an effective way to meet your students' diverse learning needs. Manipulatives let teachers represent mathematical ideas in multiple ways using a variety of different models. The time children take to become familiar with the materials is time well spent—during this process, children construct knowledge as they make connections between the models and the mathematical ideas.

All through this book, we stress the importance of having children use manipulatives to model mathematical ideas. Commonly used materials in elementary school include chips or tiles, interlocking cubes, pattern blocks, attribute blocks, tangrams, base-ten blocks, fraction models, geoboards, measuring instruments, spinners and dice, and play money. (Appendix B shows patterns for many of the better-known manipulatives.) Research indicates that lessons using manipulatives are more likely to help children achieve mathematically than are lessons without manipulatives (Sowell, 1989). Also, handling the manipulatives appears to help children construct mathematical ideas and retain them better than merely seeing someone else demonstrate a concept with manipulatives—though even this seems more beneficial than not using manipulatives at all. One researcher points out that some discrepant findings in this area stem from the fact that "concrete materials do not automatically carry meaning for students" (Thompson, 1994, p. 557). Like many others, this researcher suggests that the focus must continually be on *understanding*. Other researchers are concerned with what *concrete* means—evidence indicates, that children may find manipulatives represented on a computer monitor as concrete as actual manipulatives (Clements and McMillen, 1996). Research also indicates that students learn when they connect real-world situations, manipulatives, pictures, and spoken and written symbols. Clearly, it is helpful for students to "see" concepts by experiencing them through models.

Math Links 3.2

*G*o to the National Library of Virtual Manipulatives for Interactive Mathematics Web site to try out a variety of electronic manipulatives that could be used with children. This site includes several common manipulatives, such as base-ten blocks and fraction pies, as well as graph tools, puzzles, and games: http://matti.usu.edu/nlvm/nav/vlibrary.html

www.wiley.com/college/reys

Experts suggest that when planning a lesson involving manipulatives, teachers should be certain that:

- They choose manipulatives that support the lesson's objectives.
- They carefully plan to orient students to the manipulatives and to the corresponding classroom procedures.
- The lesson involves the active participation of each student.
- The lesson plan includes evaluation procedures that reflect an emphasis on the development of reasoning skills (Ross and Kurtz, 1993, p. 256).

One practical challenge you will face as a teacher is how to store materials so they can be found and used easily (Suydam, 1990). Shelves and small plastic boxes (or dishpans) are helpful in this regard. Children should be able to reach and remove things easily themselves without your assistance. You should also do the following:

- Color code or label the materials, and put a matching code or label on the storage space.
- Package manipulatives into sets for one student, two students, or a small group.
- Package sets of materials in durable individual containers, such as heavy plastic bags or transparent containers.
- Store individual sets of materials in trays, such as box lids, shallow pans, or stackable bins.
- Put extra pieces into a spare parts container.

Remember that young children, whose fine-motor skills aren't fully developed, may have difficulty if manipulatives are too small or too difficult to connect. To help children who have special needs, you might use materials with built-in organization (such as an abacus) or materials that fit together (such as connecting cubes), rather than separate objects such as base-ten blocks. Or you can use containers that keep counters separated, such as egg cartons, or mats with clearly separated sections. Finally, remember to have the children pass out and collect the materials as much as possible. You don't have to do it all!

Technology   The increased availability of technology in today's homes and classrooms is having a profound effect on teaching and learning. There are several compelling reasons for incorporating technology in our mathematics instruction. One is to prepare students to function in our technological world. Another is given by NCTM's Technology Principle: "Electronic technologies . . . furnish visual images of mathematical ideas, they facilitate organizing and analyzing data, and they compute efficiently and accurately. They can support investigation by students in every area of mathematics. . . . When technological tools are available, students can focus on decision making, reflection, reasoning, and problem solving" (NCTM, 2000, p. 24).

Computers have become essential tools in our larger society and are one of the most common forms of technology used in elementary classrooms. Many students today have access to desktop, laptop, and handheld computers. According to a recent report, 99% of public schools were connected to the Internet in 2002, compared with only 35% just 6 years before (US Department of Education, 2005). Until recently, school access to the Internet was typically available only in computer labs. But between 1994 and 2000, the percentage of classrooms that had computers with Internet access skyrocketed from 3% to 77%. However, just the availability of computers is not enough to impact instruction. The 2000 NAEP teacher questionnaire found that "one-fourth of fourth graders and two-thirds of eighth graders had teachers who reported they never or hardly ever used computers in connection with mathematics instruction" (Grouws, et al., 2004, p. 253).

The way we choose to use technology also can impact student achievement. For example, the 1996 NAEP mathematics assessment examined how computers were used in grades 4 and 8 and found that the use of computers to develop lower-level skills was negatively related to academic achievement. In contrast, for both fourth- and eighth-grade students, using computers to develop higher-level thinking skills was associated with higher student achievement (Wenglinsky, 1998).

Research shows that even preschool children benefit from using computers, especially from programs that are open-ended, encourage discussing and solving problems, and support the development of conceptual knowledge (Clements, 1996). Unfortunately, many teachers are unsure how to use computers to do these things and often opt for lower-level uses. For example, of the teachers in the NAEP questionnaire who reported using computers, the primary use in grade 4 was for mathematics games, followed by drill and practice activities.

There are basically six types of computer software available. Students use each type of computer software in a slightly different way, and the different types of software also offer different benefits to children. One educator describes each software type in terms of its potential for developing problem-solving and higher-level thinking skills (Crown, 2003).

- *Drill-and-practice software* provides practice for a skill that has been previously taught. The computer presents a problem to the student, waits for an answer, and indicates whether the student is right or wrong. Some drill-and-practice programs keep records and provide a score, or they may even adjust the difficulty level of problems based on student responses (e.g., number and type of errors). The primary focus of drill-and-practice software is on mastery of lower-level skills and basic facts.
- *Tutorial software* provides instruction on new skills. It may introduce information, present

examples, and provide practice. Depending on whether the student grasps the concept easily or has difficulty, the program will move to a more difficult lesson or provide additional instruction. Some tutorials are quite effective in presenting new information, but they give students little opportunity to think creatively. Also, tutorial software might encourage children to focus on procedures or rules prematurely, before they have solidified their conceptual knowledge of the topic.

- *Simulation software* allows students to experience events and explore environments that might be too expensive, messy, dangerous, or time-consuming to experience and explore in reality in the classroom. For example, through computer simulation, students can run a business or go on an expedition, or they can conduct a probability experiment (such as flipping coins or drawing randomly from a collection) with many more trials than would be feasible to conduct by hand. Simulation software has the potential to support problem solving and critical thinking, but teachers have to carefully plan related discussions and activities to help students gain these benefits.

- *Educational game software* engages students in fun activities that address specific educational skills or may aid in the development of logical thinking or problem-solving skills. Games usually include randomized events, offer an opportunity to "win," and present some obstacles to winning that the child must overcome. Often these games provide drill-and-practice opportunities. In addition, they can help children improve their higher-level thinking skills by analyzing game situations and developing strategies. However, games do not typically develop key mathematical content knowledge.

- *Problem-solving software* is designed to aid in the development of higher-order problem-solving strategies. Problem-solving programs are similar to simulation programs, where students are placed in a situation in which they can manipulate variables and receive feedback, but problem-solving programs do not necessarily model real-life situations. One type of problem-solving software involves programming. Students write programs in a computer language such as Logo to instruct the computer to operate in a particular way; in the process, the students develop logical thinking and problem-solving skills. Problem-solving software can improve students' performance on problem-solving tasks but may not develop their mathematics skills or concepts unless the teacher can help students look beyond the task itself and focus on the mathematics.

- *Tool software* can enhance both teaching and learning and may be the most effective type of software for developing mathematics through problem solving. Tools help efficiently and effortlessly with graphing, visualizing, and computing. Useful classroom tool software includes word processors, databases, spreadsheets, graphing programs, hypermedia, dynamic geometry software, computer microworlds, and applets (electronic versions of manipulatives, also called *virtual manipulatives*).

Today, many software programs of the types described above are available on the Internet, which gives teachers and students access to people, information, and resources that have never before been so accessible. Throughout this text, look for Math Links that will direct you to a wide variety of Internet resources that can enhance the teaching and learning of mathematics.

Math Links 3.3

*Y*ou can not only locate resources for students on the Web, but you can also find resources to support your teaching. For example, MarcoPolo is a teacher site that provides standards-based Internet materials for K–12 teachers: http://www.marcopolo-education.org

www.wiley.com/college/reys

Calculators are another important technology tool in elementary mathematics classrooms. According to NCTM, "Calculators should be available at appropriate times as computational tools, particularly when many or cumbersome computations are needed to solve problems. However, when teachers are working with students on developing computational algorithms, the calculator should be set aside to allow this focus. Today the calculator is a commonly used computational tool outside the classroom, and the environment inside the classroom should reflect this reality" (NCTM, 2000, pp. 32–33). In NCTM's Number and Operation standard, students in grades pre-K-2 are expected to "use a variety of methods and tools to compute, including objects, mental computation, estimation, paper and pencil, and calculators" (NCTM, 2000, p. 78). Students in grades 3–5 should be able to "select appropriate methods and tools for computing with whole numbers from mental computation, estimation, calculators, and paper and pencil. . ." (NCTM, 2000, p. 148).

Calculators not only let students compute quickly and accurately, but they also let them examine patterns, solve problems, develop mathematical concepts, and perform other higher-level tasks. Research has shown that students who used calculators in a variety of ways had higher achievement than students who used only paper-and-pencil methods. They were better at mental computation, had better attitudes toward mathematics, and did not become overly reliant on the calculators. Their problem-solving abilities were also enhanced (Sutton and Krueger, 2002). In the 2000 NAEP, eighth graders who were allowed regular access to calculators scored substantially higher in mathematics than those who never or hardly ever used calculators in mathematics class. It was also found that only 48% of eighth graders had teachers who reported that their students used calculators almost every day (Strutchens et al., 2004). (See Chapter 10 for more about calculators and how they can be used to develop higher-level thinking.)

Today, more and more students have access in school to technology that goes beyond calculators and desktop computers, including handheld computers or data collection devices, classroom networks, interactive whiteboards, digital cameras, video cameras, calculator-based laboratory systems, and CDs, videos, and DVDs. As a teacher, you must not only learn to be comfortable using these technologies, but must also consider how they might be integrated into your mathematics lessons. Do not bring in technology simply to impress or motivate your students. Remember that technology will improve student achievement only if it is used to develop the higher-level thinking skills involved in collecting and analyzing data, investigating patterns, and solving problems.

Finally, teachers must ensure equitable access to technology. Make sure not to use technology only as a reward for early finishers; rather, plan opportunities for all children to use technology during the lesson. If there is not enough technology available for all to use it at the same time, design a schedule that gives each student an opportunity to use it on a regular basis.

Planning for Effective Teaching

Planning lies at the heart of good teaching. Children learn best from lessons that are interesting and carefully organized, directed by thoughtful questions, and enriched by activities and materials that give them the opportunity to develop ideas about mathematics. Careful development of ideas, based on clear explanations, careful questioning, and good use of manipulatives and technology, is particularly important in helping children learn mathematics. Teachers make many of the decisions related to these factors during the preparations just discussed. Once those decisions have been made, it is time to organize them in plans for the year as a whole, for units, and for individual lessons.

Teachers plan in a variety of ways. Some just list the objectives they want children to attain or at least take a step toward attaining. Some jot down key questions they want to ask. Some lay out materials for children to use or run off worksheets for them. And some read the comments in the teacher's guide to the textbook. All of these approaches require teachers to think through what they plan to do and how they will do it.

Few experienced teachers take the time to write out a complete, detailed plan for every mathematics lesson they teach. Some do it occasionally, when they know that the idea they want to teach must be developed especially carefully or when the lesson is one they haven't taught before. Experienced teachers often have detailed mental plans, although they may not write more than a page of sketchy notes. They may have taught a similar lesson many times before and therefore have a good sense of appropriate sequencing, timing, and questioning and of potential pitfalls. Beginning teachers, however, lack that experience, and so it is particularly important for them to write detailed lesson plans (Leinhardt et al., 1991). Careful planning helps make initial teaching experiences good ones, for both the children and the teacher.

The Importance of Planning

Good plans give you the security of knowing what you will do and say, of having interesting activities and materials ready for the children's use, and of anticipating what the children might do. A good, detailed lesson plan gives you a way to judge how well the lesson went. Even though you might not be able to follow your plan precisely, it will help you evaluate your teaching and assess your students' learning. A written plan can also be shared with other teachers, who can provide helpful comments and suggestions. Moreover, writing detailed plans helps you learn how to plan in your head. The following quote summarizes why planning for mathematics instruction is so important:

> By planning for instruction that promotes the development of children's thinking and reasoning about mathematics, you will not only help them make sense of the content they are studying but also help them learn ways of thinking that later will enable them to make sense of *new* content. (Rathmell, 1994, p. 290)

Levels of Planning

Planning for your mathematics class is done at three levels. You start at the broadest level with a plan that sets out your goals and objectives for the year. Then, moving down a level, you plan how to achieve those goals and objectives by organizing the mathematics content into units. Finally, at the narrowest level, you plan daily lessons for teaching specific parts of that content. Each level of planning is important in ensuring that you meet all your grade-level requirements in a logical fashion.

Planning for the Year Before the school year begins, you need to consider what you want to have the children in your class accomplish during that year. Of course, you do not need to develop these goals on your own. Most schools prepare scope-and-sequence charts or curriculum guides, or they rely on those provided with the textbook series they use. Your district or state may provide a curriculum framework for your grade level, and the NCTM's *Principles and Standards for School Mathematics* (NCTM, 2000) indicates, in broad terms, the mathematical content and processes appropriate for students at each of the grade bands (pre-K–2, 3–5, 6–8, and 9–12). (See Appendix A for these content expectations.) You should be familiar with the NCTM standards, your state education requirements, and your school's scope-and-sequence guide or curriculum before you do any planning. Such materials are designed to ensure that children are taught the desired range of content across grade levels. You should also check with your principal and other teachers to determine whether any changes have been made to meet the needs of the children in your school and to learn how much flexibility you have in making changes for your class.

After determining the goals of mathematics instruction for the year and the order in which topics are to be taught, you need to consider the approximate amount of time you want to spend on each phase of the curriculum, based on the relative importance of each. Doing this helps you be sure that you can fit in all the mathematics content you want to include. The goals for the year can be organized by textbook chapters or units. The NCTM standards, your state education requirements, and your school's curriculum guide or the textbook's planning chart can help you with this and with the decision about how much time to assign to teaching each topic. Most mathematics textbooks contain 130 to 150 lessons. Given the typical 180-day school year, you may have the flexibility to spend extra time on some topics or to teach topics that are not in the textbook. Prepare a brief outline listing each unit, its objectives, and the estimated number of days and dates you will teach it.

Planning for Units Once you have outlined your year, you can begin planning your units. Begin by outlining, in sequence, the topics that are to be taught and how much time you will spend on each. Then decide on supplemental materials, instructional strategies, and assessments. Next, outline what you want to accomplish each week—that will make the process of developing daily lesson plans much easier. Some schools require teachers to maintain a lesson plan book in which they note the objectives (and sometimes other details as well) for each day's lessons for a week. Even if this is not required, it is a good idea because it keeps you aware of progress toward meeting your goals for the year and it gives you a guide to follow each day. You cannot expect to follow this guide exactly, but as you plan each week or unit, you can review the progress of the children in your class and then vary or pace the content to be taught to meet their individual needs. Or you can plan to teach different content to small groups or individuals.

Planning for Daily Lessons Finally, once you have outlined the units, you are ready to write daily lesson plans. Putting your lesson plan into writing will help you clarify many of your ideas, give you a "road map" to follow while teaching, and give you a record that you can use to evaluate each lesson and to plan subsequent lessons. Consider the questions discussed at the beginning of this chapter and use the process of writing the plan to help you think deeply about the lesson, the steps involved in teaching it, and the time you will need for each step. Then, if you diverge from the plan, you will be able to pinpoint where you diverged and return later to pick up where you left off. Your plan should be concise yet complete. Since it is just for your use, you may reach the point where you can write just short sentences or phrases to cue your memory. Use a format that lets you refer easily to the plan while you are teaching.

Planning Different Types of Lessons

When writing daily lesson plans, you must also consider the format of the lesson. The most familiar format for mathematics lessons, review-teach-practice, may also be one of the least effective, especially when it is used to introduce new content. In this lesson format, the teacher begins by reviewing homework or problems worked during a previous lesson; then the teacher briefly explains a new concept or demonstrates a new skill, using sample problems; finally, the teacher assigns exercises (of the same type as the sample problems) for student practice. Typically, for the remainder of the lesson, students practice solving similar problems on their own while the teacher assists individual students.

According to the Trends in International Mathematics and Science Study (TIMSS), this mathematics lesson format is commonly used in the United States and Germany (*Pursuing Excellence*, 1996), and students from both countries have not performed particularly well on tests of mathematics achievement. Many educators attribute much of this poor performance to the ineffectiveness of the review-teach-practice lesson format. By contrast, the typical lesson format in Japan (whose students were top TIMSS scorers) is similar to the investigative lesson (described below): the teacher poses a challenging problem that students then think about; individual students present ideas for solutions to the class, which then discusses these ideas. The teacher uses the discussion to highlight the key mathematical concepts, and then the students practice similar problems.

Review-teach-practice lessons in the United States and Germany focus on skill acquisition, on teaching students to do something; in Japan, the typical lesson focus is on understanding mathematical concepts. In U.S. and German classrooms, students spend more than twice as much time practicing routine procedures as students in Japanese classrooms (although many Japanese students practice skills in paid tutoring sessions after school). Japanese students spend most of their class time inventing new solutions and thinking about mathematical concepts. Analysis of TIMSS data suggests that what occurs in lessons is critical to students' learning. The specific topics taught and how these topics are presented and developed shape what students learn and are able to do. In the United States, lessons often consist of episodic encounters between students and curricular content, rather than ensuring that students stay focused on the content, as is done in other countries. Topics and concepts are presented in a fragmented and disjointed manner, and underlying themes and principles are either not identified or merely stated but not developed.

Instead of the traditional review-teach-practice format, we suggest using three different lesson formats: investigative lessons, direct instruction lessons, and explorations. These formats can provide structure for most of the situations you will encounter during mathematics lessons. You will probably choose to use different types of lessons on different days, depending on your goals and your students' previous experiences with the content.

But no matter which format you are using, be sure to keep in mind the overarching goals of ensuring student understanding and maintaining active student involvement.

You will probably design many lessons that use aspects of more than one of these formats. In other words, the three lesson formats should not be seen as entirely distinct. Nevertheless, it is useful to outline the general characteristics of each form, as we do in the sections below.

No matter what lesson format you select, the beginning of a lesson plan usually shows basic information, such as the lesson objective(s), how you will assess students, what adaptations you might make (i.e., gearing up and gearing down), and what materials you will need. The lesson itself generally consists of three phases: (1) launch (how you will begin the lesson); (2) investigate, instruct, or explore (depending on the lesson format); and (3) summarize (how you will bring the lesson to a close). In the lesson plan, the lesson outline details these phases of the lesson. Figure 3-4 shows a generalized lesson plan covering all three formats; in this figure, you can see how the lesson outline differs among the formats. The descriptions below should help you learn how to write lesson plans using each format; we also provide a sample lesson plan using each format, which you could try out with children.

The kind of teaching envisioned by the NCTM *Standards* (NCTM, 1991, 2000) is probably very different from the kind of teaching you experienced when you were in elementary school. The emphasis is shifting from a teacher-directed classroom to one in which students are actively involved in learning. Though still in control, of course, the teacher involves the students through discussions and activities, usually by incorporating much small-group work. Direct instruction and discussions with the whole class have not disappeared, but children learn much more effectively when they work with materials to solve problems and talk about their results with each other.

Regardless of the lesson format, the teacher orchestrates the classroom discourse by "deciding when to provide information, when to clarify an issue, when to model, when to lead, and when to let students struggle with a difficulty" (NCTM, 1991, p. 35). You learn to make these decisions through planning and through experience. No one mode of instruction can be considered best. You should learn many instructional modes and use them as appropriate. The NCTM *Standards* (2000) urges teachers to consider the goal, the task, and the students (i.e., to ask what will best help them learn).

Generalized Lesson Plan for All Three Formats

Introductory Information

Grade Level _____   **Date** _____

Topic/Title _____

Objective(s) Determine what you want your students to know or do. Align with district and state standards.

Assessment What types of information will you collect to help you determine how well individual children achieved the objective(s) of your lesson and where they had trouble? Assessment information may come from a variety of sources—for example, classroom observations, written class work (either individual or group), homework. Your dual goals in planning for assessment are to be able to make appropriate follow-up instructional decisions and to be able to report on students' progress (e.g., by assigning grades or writing a narrative report). Be sure to describe the criteria you will use to decide who "got it" and how you might translate your assessment to a grade.

Gearing Down What will you do if your lesson, as planned, turns out to be too advanced for some or all students? How can the lesson be modified (on the spot) for slower students?

Gearing Up What will you do if your lesson, as planned, turns out to be too easy for some or all students? How can the lesson be modified (on the spot) for faster students?

Materials List all materials needed:
• math manipulatives, technology (and how many of each)
• books, including page numbers (and how many of each)
• other supplies (scissors, markers, posters, etc., and how many of each)
• handouts (attach a copy of each)
• references (include bibliographic information for books or resources used in planning the lesson)

Lesson Outline (include approximate times for each segment of your lesson)

LAUNCH (setting the stage)
Describe briefly how you will begin the lesson. Your aim is to motivate students to get involved in the lesson activities and to ensure that all the children understand what they are to do. Include questions you might ask. Introduce the context you will use (e.g., real-life examples, manipulatives, problems, or puzzles).

INVESTIGATE (for investigative format)
This part of the lesson could consist of one continuous problem-solving activity (whole class, small group, or individual), or it could be divided into several segments, each involving different activities or groupings. For each segment, give a step-by-step description of what you (the teacher) will be doing and what the students will be doing. In particular, provide examples of the types of questions you might ask and of any products that the students will create. If your lesson is divided into segments, give an approximate time for each segment; also, describe how you plan to make transitions from each segment to the next.
  OR
INSTRUCT (for direct instruction format)
Whole-Class Teacher Instruction and Modeling What concepts, definitions, formulas, algorithms, etc., will you explain and model? List all the examples you will use, and order them appropriately. Include directions for the activities that will follow.
Activities Activities may be done by individuals or small groups. Students work with you on problems or exercises that follow rather closely from what they learned during your whole-class instruction and modeling. Then, when they are ready to practice independently from you, circulate, assisting individual students, answering questions, and, for students who finish early, providing tasks that let them extend their learning. Make a list of the questions you will ask as you circulate. Include a copy of any written materials that students will work on, such as a worksheet. Include several simpler problems that you could use in helping students who have trouble. Include several more challenging problems that you could assign to early finishers.
  OR
EXPLORE (for exploration format)
For each exploration, give a step-by-step description of what you will be doing and what the students will be doing. In particular, give examples of the types of questions you might ask and of any products that the students will create. If you plan to rotate students through several activities, include the approximate time for each and describe how you plan to make transitions from each segment to the next.

SUMMARIZE (closure)
Describe how you will bring the lesson to a close. Find a way that motivates the students to reflect on their activities and what they learned. Include questions you might ask yourself and/or your students to help you determine whether the lesson was a success.

FIGURE 3-4   Generalized lesson plan.

Investigative Lessons Investigative, or problem-based, lessons are most appropriate for helping children develop problem-solving skills, learn new concepts, or apply and deepen their understanding of previously learned topics. In an investigative lesson, students try to solve a problem or conduct an investigation on their own. The problem or investigation may have been brought up by the teacher or by one or more of the students, but the lesson itself revolves around ideas that the students generate through their own investigations. Obviously, the teacher is responsible for guiding the lesson, but the students are expected to come up with their own approaches, strategies, and solutions.

In the *launch phase* of an investigative lesson, you make sure that the students are motivated to do the lesson and that the problem at hand is explained. The launch might come from a student presenting a problem that he or she has been struggling with and asking classmates to work on, too. Or you might provide motivation by reading a children's story or a newspaper clipping, playing a game, presenting a puzzle, or using some other context that involves the problem to be worked on.

Once all the students understand the challenge, the *investigate phase* of the lesson begins. In this phase, the students work on the problem. This might involve learning stations, individual work, paired problem solving, or small groups, and students might use models, manipulatives, computers, calculators, or other tools. In an investigative lesson, the problem should truly challenge the students, so it is important that you do not explain up front how to approach the problem. The students should not simply mimic strategies or skills that you have just shown them. Instead, they should decide for themselves how to get started and what to try. Your role as teacher is to let them go. You should circulate around the room, listening in on conversations, observing what individuals or groups are doing, and occasionally interjecting questions or comments to help students recognize where they may be going wrong or to suggest a different approach.

During the *summarize phase* of the lesson, the class talks together about its findings. Using information you gathered from observing the children at work, you orchestrate a discussion in which various groups or individuals report what they tried and what they discovered. It is important to be neither too negative nor too positive about student ideas and responses. Encourage students to challenge each other's ideas. They need practice in learning how to judge when mathematical ideas are valid and when they are not. Also be sure not to finalize the solution to the problem prematurely.

Students learn a lot from listening to each other and from hearing about alternative approaches. Your job is to encourage the students to share their ideas while maintaining control of the discussion and trying to guide it in ways that advance your curricular agenda. During the final portion of the summarize phase, it may be important to help students be explicit in stating what they have learned from the investigation. This is time for stating generalizations or rules that have been formulated. It may be tempting to cut short this phase, but do not do so. Talking together and sharing ideas are critical to meaningful learning of mathematics.

Figure 3-5 shows an investigative-format lesson plan for second grade created from a lesson from the *Math Trailblazers* textbook series. In the lesson outline portion of this plan, the teacher details how he or she wants to conduct the lesson. Read the outline to get a sense of what the teacher intends to do. Notice that the launch phase of the lesson includes background information and discussion that students need before they start their investigation. Now look at the outline of the investigate phase and note that the teacher has considered how the students will be organized, moving the children back and forth between small-group and whole-group discussion as needed. Finally, the outline of the summarize phase includes additional questions to be asked at the end of the lesson.

Direct Instruction Lessons In direct instruction lessons the teacher plays a more central role in directing the instruction than in investigative lessons. Direct instruction lessons are appropriate when the teacher wants to communicate specific knowledge, to introduce new vocabulary, or to teach specific procedures. In a direct instruction lesson, the teacher exercises more control than in an investigative lesson, and the lesson generally has a tighter focus. The three phases of a plan for a direct instruction lesson are usually (1) launch, (2) instruct, and (3) summarize (see Figure 3-4) and each phase may be subdivided into smaller segments of various types, depending on the content of the lesson.

As with investigative lessons, in the *launch phase* of the lesson, the teacher provides a motivating introduction and introduces the students to the problem; led by the teacher, the class talks together about how to approach the problem and what previously learned concepts and skills might be useful. In the *instruct phase*, the teacher shows the students how to proceed but also elicits ideas from the students while helping them move toward the concept or skill that is the goal of the lesson. Guided practice is included during the instruct

Sample Investigative Lesson Plan

Introductory Information

Grade Level _2_   **Date** _March 15, 16_

Topic/Title _Measurement/When Close Is Good Enough_

Objective(s)	The students will: 1. Estimate length and distance with nonstandard units. 2. Measure length and distance with nonstandard units. State standards: The student estimates and measures using standard and nonstandard units of measure with concrete objects in a variety of situations.
Assessment	Objective 1: Answers to questions 1 and 4 on p. 40 and questions 1–6 on p. 41 should be reasonable estimates. 6/8 correct shows mastery. Objective 2: Observe while measuring, jot down notes. Questions 2, 5, and 6a,b on p. 40—3/4 correct shows mastery.
Gearing Down	Do the first hand span and cubit measure together. Assign partners if needed.
Gearing Up	Encourage students to measure additional items with hand spans and cubits, or have students estimate and then use a different nonstandard unit of their choosing.
Materials	Overhead projector; Discovery book p. 41, Hand Spans and Cubits activity pages; pp. 39–41 for each students Reference: *Math Trailblazers: 2nd Grade*, Unit 4, Lesson 4, by Wagreich et al., 1997, Kendall/Hunt Publishing Company.

Lesson Outline

LAUNCH—Day 1 (15 minutes)

- Who remembers measuring length? What tools have you used? Today we're going to use two nonstandard tools.
- Hand span—With your fingers spread wide, the distance from tip of thumb to tip of little finger. Everyone show the length of their hand span. Compare with your neighbor. Are they all the same length? That is why we call it a nonstandard unit.
- Cubit—The distance between your elbow and the tip of your longest finger. Everyone show your cubit. Compare. Are they all the same? Also a nonstandard unit.
- Hand spans and cubits let us make approximate, not exact, measurements. Think of some examples when an approximate measurement with nonstandard units would be OK.
- Demonstrate how to measure the length of the dry erase board with hand spans, then cubits. Show how to use free hand to mark place before moving.

INVESTIGATE—Day 1 (30 minutes), Day 2 (30 minutes to finish charts and do pp. 40, 41)

- Assign students to groups of 4 and send to one of the locations on p. 39. Each is to measure with hand spans. If time permits, measure other objects and record on the sheet. Students write their measures in the table on the overhead transparency. (15 minutes)
- Whole-class discussion: Discuss why there are differences. Discuss how to handle partial hand spans or cubits. Decide on a rule for the future. (10 minutes)
- Do you think it will take more or fewer cubits to measure the dry erase board? About how many?
- Groups finish p. 39 with cubits. Record results on transparency. (15 minutes)
- Now let's estimate how many hand spans and cubits for the width and height of the door. Explain how you estimated. Did you use the information on our chart to help you?
- Individually, students complete pp. 40, 41. Send p. 41 in Discovery book as homework.

SUMMARIZE—Day 2 (15 minutes)

- Why did we get so many different measurements on our chart? Why are these approximate measurements?
- What is the difference between a standard unit and a nonstandard unit?
- What other tools could be used as nonstandard measures? Does your family use any nonstandard tools?

FIGURE 3-5   Sample investigative lesson plan.

phase—students actively practice using the concept or skill, with guidance and feedback from the teacher. Afterward, the students have a chance to work with the ideas presented earlier in the lesson and to make them their own, working independently from the teacher. The task during this phase should be closely related to the original task but not so similar that the students are simply copying what the teacher has just shown them. Finally, during the *summarize phase*, the teacher and students summarize what was learned.

Figure 3-6 shows a direct instruction lesson for fourth grade created from a lesson from the *Investigations in Number, Data, and Space* textbook series. Notice the role of the teacher during the instruct phase of the lesson. The teacher provides important information, models the procedure, guides the students to practice the procedure, and gives them opportunities to practice. During the summarize phase, students not only have an opportunity to reflect on their learning but also share the products they created.

Explorations   Sometimes teachers want to provide a series of learning activities, or *explorations* for students to simultaneously work on either independently or in small groups around the room. These activities are often called learning centers or learning stations; they are commonly used in early childhood classrooms with very young children who are not ready to participate in more formal lessons, but they can also be appropriate for older elementary and middle school students. An exploration should be structured so the children can complete them without teacher assistance and allow for more individual choice, while working with assigned materials, than in an investigative lesson. Explorations are not just free time. They provide opportunities for students to work independently on important mathematical tasks. Students can work at their own pace and make decisions about their learning. The learning activities can all be related to a particular topic and provide various levels of difficulty or complexity. They can also provide a variety of opportunities to practice a skill and may encourage the development of conceptual knowledge or of problem-solving skills. In addition, explorations can provide remedial or enrichment activities for students who need them. A set of explorations can be made available on particular days of the week, over the course of a unit, or over a period of days in place of whole-class lessons.

Explorations don't necessarily resemble a typical whole-class lesson, but you still need to identify the student objectives and carefully plan the activities. You need to consider how the activities will be managed and think about how you can package the necessary materials for easy access and cleanup.

Explorations let you plan to meet the needs of students with varied learning styles and interests. Some students may prefer to work with technology, while others may want to use manipulatives. Planning a variety of activities will give students choices. Also, by considering how you can make particular activities less difficult or more challenging, you can plan to meet individual needs.

Consider your class size and how many children you want to work with each activity at the same time. You might plan for 5 or 6 stations and have groups of children rotate through all of them, spending a predetermined amount of time at each location. Or you could provide several sets of materials for each activity so several groups or individuals can be working on the same activity at the same time. One educator calls these types of experiences *menus* and suggests providing a menu of activities related to a particular unit or topic (Burns, 2000). You can require that all students complete certain explorations on the menu, while others could be optional. Once again, this is also an effective way for you to meet students' individual learning needs. You could assign students who are struggling to complete particular activities, while assigning those who are more advanced to complete more challenging activities. Alternatively, the students could decide in what order they would like to complete the activities and how much time they will spend on them. Once students are familiar with the routine of completing these types of activities and are able to work fairly independently, explorations can also give you time to assess individual students or small groups.

An exploration generally involves three phases: (1) launch, (2) explore, and (3) summarize (see Figure 3-4). The *launch phase* of an exploration will probably involve telling the students about the available activities, what you expect from them for each activity, how they should manage materials, how they will move from one activity to another, and what products they will create and you will check. You can give older students written instructions for each activity, but young children will need you to model the activities and provide oral instructions. Often, you will do best to gradually introduce the activities involved in an exploration to the whole class over several class periods. Then when students are sent to work independently, they have previous experience with the activities and are more likely to be successful when working on their own.

Sample Direct Instruction Lesson Plan

Introductory Information

Grade Level _4_   **Date** _November 15_

Topic/Title _Multiplication / Things That Come in Arrays_

Objective(s)	The students will: 1. Use arrays as models for multiplication.
	2. Use skip counting to count arrays.
	State standard: The student identifies multiplication and division fact families.
Assessment	Objective 1: Check Student Sheet 3 for accuracy, 5 in class items and 3 homework items.
	Need to get 6/8 correct to show mastery.
	Objective 2: Observe and question students while they are working in class.
	Check off those who can skip count to find the total.
Gearing Down	If students are having trouble drawing the array, they can draw it on grid paper.
Gearing Up	Challenge students to think of and record some larger arrays.
Materials	Color tiles, grid paper, overhead projector
	six-pack of juice cans, egg carton, four-pack of yogurt
	Student Sheet 3, 2–3 copies for each student and a transparency
	References: _Second Grade Investigations in Number, Data, and Space: Arrays and Shares_ Investigation 2, Session 1, by Karen Economopoulos, Cornella Tierney, and Susan Jo Russell, 2004 Pearson Education Inc. _Amanda Bean's Amazing Dream,_ by Andy Neuschwander, Scholastic, NY, 1998.

Lesson Outline

LAUNCH (15 minutes)

- Read _Amanda Bean's Amazing Dream._
- Display juice cans, egg carton, and yogurt containers.
- What do you notice about these and the pictures in the book? How can we describe their arrangement?

INSTRUCT (35 minutes)

- These items are all arranged in rectangular arrays. For each, how many rows and how many in each row?
- Is there more than one way to describe these arrays? Example: 3 rows of 2 or 2 rows of 3.
- Go back to the story and find other things arranged in arrays, such as. . . .
- What other things come in rectangular arrays? Any things in this room? List on the board.
- I'll show how to fill in the chart with the first item, the six-pack of juice. (Student Sheet 3 on transparency.) Show two arrays with tiles or grid paper. I can skip count each row 2, 4, 6 or 3, 6. Total number of cans is 6. The dimensions could be 2 rows of 3, written as 2×3, or 3 rows of 2, written as 3×2. Draw both arrays in the last column.
- Hand out Student Sheet 3. Let's do the egg carton together. . . .
- In pairs, fill in the chart for the yogurt containers. I'll come around to see what you get.
- Hand out another copy of Student Sheet 3. Partners may fill in at least 5 more items that come in arrays. You may use examples you think of, that are listed on the board, or were in the book. You may use color tiles or grid paper to make the array before drawing it. Try to skip count to find the total in the array.
- Students work on the task.

SUMMARIZE (10 minutes)

- Give students opportunities to share items from their lists and the dimensions.
- Which items are packaged in the same types of arrays? Which items seem most popular? Which arrays have the same number of items on each side? How are these arrays different from the others?
- Your assignment tonight is to find at least 3 more arrays at home. You may also bring in some examples tomorrow.

FIGURE 3-6   Sample direct instruction lesson plan.

During the *exploration phase*, students work independently for a specified amount of time. Be sure you have planned the step-by-step procedures for each activity. Be sure students understand what to do when they have completed one activity and are ready for another. Also consider your role. Will you be circulating? What questions will you ask about particular activities? You might carry a clipboard and make notes about student learning as you observe or keep a list so you can check products that particular groups have created and can mark groups off if the products look satisfactory.

In the *summarize phase*, find time to talk with the students, letting them share strategies or products they created. You may want to instruct everyone to complete one particular activity and make that the focus of the discussion for that day.

Figure 3-7 shows a kindergarten exploration plan from *Investigations in Number, Data, and Space* textbook materials. Notice that in the launch phase, the teacher provides instructions so the children can work independently while completing their activities. In the explore phase, the teacher lists organizational details, in the summarize phase, the teacher uses questions to get the children to talk about their experiences.

Meeting the Needs of All Students

Once you have created a lesson plan, one more step remains before you are ready to teach it. Be sure to review the special needs of your students and make adaptations to your plan so all students can have the opportunity for success and challenge. Equity of educational opportunity is one of the NCTM's fundamental principles. Similarly, the *Professional Standards for Teaching Mathematics* call for every child to have equal opportunities to learn mathematics. According to these standards, "every child" includes

- Students who have been denied access in any way to educational opportunities as well as those who have not.
- Students who are African American, Hispanic, Native American, and other minorities as well as those who are considered to be a part of the majority.
- Students who are female as well as those who are male.
- Students who have not been successful in school and in mathematics as well as those who have been successful (NCTM, 1991, p. 4).

Throughout this book, we discuss ways of promoting equity. It is important to note that providing equal opportunities to learn does not necessarily mean providing exactly the same instruction to every child. *Equity* implies fairness and justice. What is fair and just for one student may be different from what is fair and just for another. Providing equitable instruction means adapting instruction appropriately for the needs of each student.

Teachers are often concerned that planning to meet the needs of each student in their classroom will be an overwhelming task. However, rather than create a different lesson plan for each student, you should create a single lesson plan and then consider how you can adapt it to make it more accessible for the different learners in your class. To help in planning, think of three students from your class: a student who is ready for the lesson, a student who will require help with the lesson, and a student who is ready to work beyond the lesson. Keep the different needs of these three students in mind while you plan. In addition, if you have any students who are learning English, keep their needs in mind too. Next, think of some supportive or enrichment strategies that you can use to meet students' individual needs while helping all the children meet the mathematical goal of the lesson. In this text, we refer to adaptations for students who need help with a lesson as strategies for *gearing down* the lesson and adaptations for students who are ready to work beyond the lesson as strategies for *gearing up* the lesson. Be careful not to go too far and "lose the integrity of the mathematics content and pedagogy or set expectations too low for students" (Brodesky, 2004, p. 150).

Some educators believe that a teacher must ask three questions while planning to individualize instruction for students who need extra help (Karp and Howell, 2004):

1. What organizational, behavioral, and cognitive skills are necessary for students with special needs to derive meaning from this activity?
2. Which students have important weaknesses in any of these skills?
3. How can I provide additional support in these areas of weakness so that students with special needs can focus on the conceptual task in the activity? (p. 119)

It is useful to begin collecting ideas and approaches for adapting lessons. Currently, much is being written about how teachers can provide equitable instruction for students from different cultures, students who are English language learners, and students with identified special needs. Knowing some of these recommendations will give you a head start at becoming an effective teacher.

Teaching Students from Other Cultures As the United States becomes more culturally diverse, the

Sample Exploration Lesson Plan

Introductory Information

Grade Level _K_ **Date** _October 15_

Topic/Title _Algebra/Making Patterns_

Objective(s)	The students will: 1. Use concrete objects to create linear, repeating patterns. 2. Differentiate between a pattern and a nonpattern. State standard: The student uses objects to generate repeating patterns, and identifies and continues patterns.
Assessment	Objective 1: Check place mats for patterns. Should be 100% accurate. Objective 2: Show each child 4 premade place mats and ask the child to tell which are patterns. Should get 3 out of 4 correct to show mastery.
Gearing Down	Just use 2 different shapes/objects to create patterns. (Station 1)
Gearing Up	Use 3 or more objects. Allow students to label their patterns orally—AB, ABC, etc.
Materials	12″ × 18″ construction paper with 2-inch squares marked along each 18-inch side. Station 1: orange and yellow leaf stickers. Station 2: fall rubber stamps and stamp pad. Station 3: markers and fruit stencils. Reference: *Kindergarten, Investigations in Number, Data, and Space*, Investigation 1: Exploring Patterns, by Susan Jo Russell, 2004, Pearson Education, Inc.

Lesson Outline

LAUNCH (10 minutes)

- What have we been doing at our math centers this week? (Making patterns with pattern blocks, connecting cubes, and buttons.) What are we having at school next week? (PTA Fall Harvest Party)
- Today we're going to decorate place mats for the party. (Show blank mat with squares marked.) We're going to make patterns by putting one object in each square. We want to be sure the objects make a pattern. How do we know if it is a pattern? (Repeating element)
- Demonstrate using each material, discussing how to apply to place mats. Show one pattern and one nonpattern. Ask children to tell if an arrangement is a pattern or not with thumbs up or down. Review how patterns can be described with AB, ABC, etc.
- When you get to your center, you may make your place mat. Show it to me when you are finished. Then you can make more patterns with manipulatives in the tubs.

INVESTIGATE (20 minutes)

- Children move to their preassigned center groups. When they finish their place mat, they'll tell me about it and I'll check it off. They may make more patterns on blank paper or using manipulatives such as pattern blocks.
- While circulating, I'll show 4 premade place mats and ask each child to tell me which are patterns and which are not.
- Other notes I can record: Who is making patterns and who is making random arrangements? What kinds of patterns are they making? How are they describing their pattern?

SUMMARIZE

- Children move back together as a whole class and show a partner their place mat. They should also tell why it is a pattern.
- Select 5 place mats. Final questions: How can we tell this is a pattern? How could we describe this pattern?

FIGURE 3-7 Sample exploration lesson plan.

task of making mathematics relevant for all students both becomes more challenging and offers more opportunities. One educator suggests, "Integrating the mathematics of world cultures into K–12 instruction can be a key step in increasing the engagement and mathematical empowerment of students, regardless of their backgrounds:

- Classroom engagement can increase when students see mathematical connections to their cultural roots.

- Students can gain a new respect for the cultures of others when they understand how mathematics was developed by people from many countries and backgrounds.
- Tying mathematics to other aspects of life, including art, literature, technology, and games, helps students see its relevance" (Spicer, 2005, p. 10). Excerpted from Spicer, Judith (2004). Mathematics of World Cultures-A World of Possibilities, ENC Focus (12) 32. Retrieved from http://enc.org/features/focus/archive/math-roots1/document.shtm?input = FOC-003606-index. Reproduced with permission of Eisenhower National Clearinghouse.

It is important to plan lessons and activities that take into account the realities of students' daily lives, as well as to ensure that students' cultural backgrounds are reflected in the mathematics curriculum and materials. Doing this allows the teacher to model interest in learning about cultures different from their own. The Cultural Connections throughout this book can help you learn more about mathematics in various cultures. Even if you do not have students from those cultures in your classes, they are interesting topics for all children to explore.

Another educator has suggested that students' cultures may affect their learning preferences (Copley, 1999). While being careful not to stereotype students from a particular culture, you may benefit from learning more about the general learning preferences of children from that culture. Keep in mind, too, that ethnicity is not the only cultural factor to be considered. Cultural differences can also be recognized among students from families of low, middle, and high socioeconomic status (Payne, 1996). For example, students from low socioeconomic status families may lack important background knowledge or may not have mastered certain cognitive strategies; of course, such deficits can be identified and remedied.

You should also understand cultural norms and how they will show themselves in your classroom. For example, you should be aware that some students from other countries may need help adapting to new teaching and testing styles (Abrams and Ferguson, 2005). Students whose previous instruction focused on memorization and repetition, may become frustrated in a classroom where the teacher uses a more open-ended approach. In addition, some behaviors considered acceptable in the students' home culture may not be as well received in their new location. For example, in some cultures students do not look their teachers in the eye when speaking with them. That behavior may be viewed as disrespectful if we do not understand the reason it occurs. With support, students can maintain their own cultural identity and still learn to function successfully in class in the new culture. Teachers must communicate instructions and expectations clearly and help students adjust to the new culture. Be aware that some of your students may feel and act in ways that could make it difficult for them to succeed in class without your help and understanding: "In many countries, students are not to speak unless the teacher asks them a question directly. To volunteer answers might be considered boastful or conceited. Many students will not question what the teacher says, even if they know it to be wrong" (Miller and Endo, 2004, p. 789).

Teaching English Language Learners Students who are learning English have special needs in our classrooms. According to one expert, there are five basic principles of instruction that teachers must adhere to in order to meet the needs of English language learners (Herrell, 2000, p. xiv).

- *Give students **comprehensible input** (i.e., language they will understand)*. This may involve using clear and concise language and avoiding slang. Emphasize and repeat key vocabulary and concepts and accompany these key points with explanatory visuals, models, or physical actions.
- *Give students opportunities to **increase verbal interaction** during class activities (i.e., to talk more with you and with the other children)*. This will help English language learners practice their language skills. Be aware, however, that some children may need to listen to and make sense of a new language for an extended period of time before they will try to speak it in class. Be sure to respect this silent period. Also, match questions to the child's proficiency level. For children who are not yet using the language, allow them to respond with actions (e.g., by demonstrating a skill). For children who are able to speak only in single-word sentences, phrase your questions so one-word answers will suffice, or provide choices of answers from which they may select. Respond to the students' intent, not to their pronunciation, grammar, or choice of words. In addition, you may need to wait longer for English language learners to respond to questions, giving them time to translate the question, think about it, and then translate the answer. Finally, remember that not all cultures value verbal communication as much as ours does.
- *Teach in a way that **contextualizes language**. A manipulative or graphic organizer may help

students connect old and new knowledge and make your instruction more meaningful. Approach new ideas by beginning with students' current knowledge and by connecting to their lives to provide context. If you can, use both English words and words from students' native languages.

- *Use teaching strategies and groupings that **reduce the anxiety** of the students.* Look for ways to give English language learners additional support. Involve as many of their senses as possible. Give students ways to respond besides writing or speaking in English. Allow them to interact with a partner or in a small group, as this is less stressful than having to speak in front of the entire class. Often, working with a peer who speaks the same language can make a student more comfortable.

- *Assign activities in the classroom that offer students opportunities for **active involvement**.* Using manipulatives and everyday objects can bring meaning to a concept. Some students will be more proficient demonstrating with objects than explaining with words.

Math Links 3.4

*F*or more information on and resources for teaching English language learners, look under Resources for Teachers or Practice on the home page of the Web site for the National Clearinghouse for English Language Acquisition: http://www.ncela.gwu.edu

www.wiley.com/college/reys

Teaching Students with Identified Special Needs
Students with identified special needs are those students who have been tested, have been admitted into special education services, and have an individual education plan. These students can include gifted children, children with physical handicaps, and children with learning disabilities. There are two common myths about teaching students with learning disabilities (Karp and Howell, 2004, p. 119):

- Myth 1: *"Students with special needs are vastly different from the regular school population and must be spoon-fed information or they will not be able to learn it."* If you teach based on this belief, the result may be passive students who rely on others to tell them how to approach a problem. Since the goal is to develop independent learners, you must find ways to provide support

to these students while encouraging them to develop self-reliance and confidence.

- Myth 2: *"Students with special needs are just like all other children in the class, and "good teaching" is good teaching for all students."* In order to be successful, students with identified special needs require different learning conditions and depend on different learning strategies than the other students in the class. They often possess a significant deficit in one or more areas, and these deficits can be barriers to their learning (see Figure 3-8).

Memory: visual memory, verbal/auditory memory, working memory

Self-regulation: excitement/relaxation, attention, inhibition of impulses

Visual processing: visual memory, visual discrimination, visual/spatial organization, visual-motor coordination

Language processing: expressive language, vocabulary development, receptive language, auditory processing

Related academic skills: reading, writing, study skills

Motor skills: writing legibly, aligning columns, working with small manipulatives, using one-to-one correspondence, writing numerals

Reprinted with permission from *Teaching Children Mathematics*, 2004 by the National Council of Teachers of Mathematics. All rights reserved.

FIGURE 3-8 Potential barriers for students with special needs. (Source: Korp and Howell, 2004, p. 120.)

To teach children with special needs of any kind (gifted, physically handicapped, or learning disabled), you will need to make adaptations in the curriculum and in your instruction. Figure 3-9 shows nine ways to make such adaptations (Ebeling, Deschenes, and Sprague, 1994). To decide which adaptations are appropriate for which students, you must be familiar with three things: (1) individual students and their special needs, (2) the activity and its subject-content demands (what is required to successfully complete the assignment), and (3) the options available for making adaptations. The adaptation categories in Figure 3-9 can be useful when planning for all kinds of learners in your classroom.

Assessment and Analysis in Planning

Assessment should be an integral aspect of mathematics instruction. You need to ascertain whether you taught what you think you have taught and whether each child has learned what you think he or she has learned.

Nine Types of Adaptation

Size
Adapt the number of items that the student is expected to learn or complete.

For example:
Reduce the number of social studies terms a learner must complete at any one time.

Time
Adapt the time allowed for learning, task completion, or testing.

For example:
Individualize a timeline for completing a task; pace learning differently (increase or decrease) for some learners.

Level of Support
Increase the amount of personal assistance with a specific learner.

For example:
Assign peer buddies, teaching assistants, peer tutors, or cross-age tutors.

Input
Adapt the way instruction is delivered to the learner.

For example:
Use different visual aids; plan more concrete examples; provide hands-on activities; place students in cooperative groups.

Difficulty
Adapt the skill level, the problem type, or the rules on how the learner may approach the work.

For example:
Allow the use of a calculator to figure out math problems; simplify task directions; change rules to accommodate learner needs.

Output
Adapt how the learner can respond to instruction.

For example:
Instead of answering questions in writing, allow a verbal response; use a journal for some students; allow students to show knowledge with hands-on materials.

Participation
Adapt the extent to which a learner is actively involved in the task.

For example:
In geography, have a student hold the globe while others point out locations

Alternate Goals
Adapt the goals or outcome expectations while using the same materials.

For example:
In social studies, expect one student to be able to locate just the states while others learn to locate capitals as well.

Substitute Curriculum
Provide different instruction and materials to meet a learner's individual goals.

For example:
During a language test, one student is learning computer skills in the computer lab.

FIGURE 3-9 Nine types of curriculum and instruction adaptations. (Source: Reproduced with permission from Ebeling, D., Deschenes, C., and Sprague, J. *Adapting Curriculum and Instruction in Inclusive Classrooms: Staff Development Kit*. Bloomington, IN: Institute for the Study of Developmental Disabilities, 1994.)

All the assessment information teachers collect is useful as they plan lessons. They know more about the achievement and progress of each child, as well as what his or her individual needs are.

Many teachers also find it helpful to keep an evaluative record of the effectiveness of their lessons. They jot down notes in their plan books or their teacher's guides about the things that went well and the things that didn't during each lesson (see Figure 3-10). They keep records of activities tried, articles read, ideas they want to try, and other anecdotal records. These notes help them to plan the following year. You may think you will remember what happened, but you will probably forget.

Finally, the *Professional Teaching Standards* (NCTM, 1991) considers *analysis:* "the systematic reflection in which teachers engage. It entails the ongoing monitoring of classroom life—how well the tasks, discourse, and environment foster the development of every student's mathematical literacy and power" (p. 20). Such analyses are a primary source of information for planning and im-proving instruction during the course of a lesson and as lessons build during the year.

A Glance at Where We've Been

Effective elementary mathematics teachers must understand the mathematics being taught; be aware of their students' developmental characteristics; consider what their students already know; think about the kinds of tasks they will give their students in order to maintain a focus on the mathematics, provide necessary practice, and take advantage of strategic moments; think about how they will encourage students to talk, what kinds of questions they will ask, and how they will group students; and consider the kinds of materials they will use in class, including curriculum materials, children's literature, manipulatives, and technology.

FIGURE 3-10   A sampling of stick-on notes from a fifth-grade teacher's textbook.

Planning lies at the heart of good teaching. Planning helps ensure that all essential content is included, permits scheduling the work in feasible periods of time and in a sensible sequence, helps control the pace of a lesson, aids in holding children's attention, helps avoid unnecessary repetition while ensuring necessary review and practice, and helps the teacher feel confident. Planning must be done for the year, the unit, and the lesson. Lesson plans should include clearly stated objectives, procedures, time allotments, and assessment. The review-teach-practice lesson format, though widely used, is not very effective. Different types of lessons (investigative, direct instruction, and exploration) can be more effective when used appropriately. When planning, a teacher must also consider equity—how to meet the needs of all their students, including students from other cultures, English language learners, and students with identified special needs.

Finally, teachers' plans must provide for assessment and analysis.

Things to Do: From What You've Read

1. From the questions to ask before planning, select one and discuss why it is important to you.

2. Discuss one way you plan to supplement your math textbook materials when you teach.

3. Name a specific special need that students in your class may have. How can you adapt lessons for those students?

4. Why is lesson planning important? Why is it important to plan for the year and unit in addition to making daily lesson plans?

5. What must you consider as you plan a lesson? What should you include in a daily lesson plan?

6. Briefly describe the most important differences among the three different types of lessons described in this chapter. When and why would you choose to use each type?

7. Describe the five varieties of questions that teachers should be prepared to incorporate into their daily teaching activities so students can make sense of mathematics. Write at least one question for each variety.

8. Use the lesson plan outline to write a lesson plan for a lesson that you might teach.

9. Plan a follow-up activity to assess learning resulting from the lesson in the Snapshot of a Lesson at the beginning of this chapter.

Things to Do: Going Beyond This Book

IN THE FIELD

1. Interview several second and third graders using the directions from In the Classroom 3-1. Were all the children able to use the base-ten blocks to explain the place values? Describe the different levels of understanding that you found. Did you find that any of the children had misunderstandings about place value? Compare your results with those of others in your class and then compile a summary of the children's different understandings.

2. *Analyzing Classroom Discourse.* Observe in a classroom, keeping a record that lets you answer the following questions. What proportion of time does the teacher talk? What types of questions does the teacher ask? What evidence do you see that children have learned some mathematics? How many of the children have an opportunity to talk? Make a list of what they say (either to the class or to each other). In your opinion, is the classroom discourse about significant mathematics? Why?

3. *Locate an article that suggests using small groups in math. Talk over these suggestions with a classroom teacher, and write a summary of the ideas you want to try in your classroom.

4. *Equity for Students with Special Needs.* Observe in a mathematics class where students identified for special education services are included in the room. What types of adaptations are made for them? If you were this teacher, what else would you do for these children?

IN YOUR JOURNAL

5. Reflect on your skill and confidence related to lesson planning. What areas are strengths? What areas do you hope to improve? What do you plan to do to increase your skill and confidence?

6. Describe a lesson you think would lend itself to working with children in cooperative learning groups. How would cooperative learning groups support children in this lesson?

*Additional activities, suggestions, and questions are provided in *Teaching Elementary Mathematics: A Resource for Field Experiences* (Wiley, 2007).

WITH ADDITIONAL RESOURCES

7. Select a topic to teach. Locate resources such as literature, manipulatives, or technology to enhance your teaching of the topic.

8. Select a content topic. Compare the way it is taught in a standards-based text versus a more traditional text.

9. Select a content topic. Follow its development through three grade levels in a textbook series. Trace what is review and what is new development of mathematical content.

10. Examine a textbook and the supplemental materials that accompany it to see what assistance is provided for adapting instruction for various levels of students. Are suggestions for modifying lessons included? Are there extra-challenge ideas? Are there review activities for students who need extra practice? How would you use these materials if your class included students with widely varying levels of understanding and skill?

11. Read the article by De La Cruz (1999). Prepare to describe to others what you learned about specific classroom-tested ways of addressing issues of diversity in the classroom.

12. Select a topic and plan a week's work for it for a particular grade level. What strategies would you use in teaching this topic and why?

WITH TECHNOLOGY

13. Explore NCTM's Electronic Examples at http://standards.nctm.org/document/eexamples/. Select one of the examples and develop a lesson plan that integrates the example in the children's activities. Describe any special preparation needed in order for the lesson to be effective.

14. Collect five resources with ideas for incorporating different technologies in teaching mathematics in the elementary grades. For each, describe the technology. Write a lesson plan that describes how you would incorporate one of the ideas in a particular class.

15. Search the Internet for teacher resource Web sites. Find a lesson plan that you could use with your grade level of interest. Modify the lesson plan to fit a specific classroom situation with which you have had experience.

Note to Instructors: You can find additional resources, learning activities, and black-line masters in this text's accompanying Instructor's Manual, at www.wiley.com/college/reys.

Book Nook for Children

Bresser, R. *Math and Literature (Grades 4–6).* White Plains, NY: Cuisenaire, 1995.

This resource gives intermediate-grade teachers 20 lessons based on popular children's books, including *Counting on Frank, The Giraffe That Walked to Paris,* and *Jumanji.*

Crawford, S. A., Sanders, N., and Girouard, P. *15 Easy & Irresistible Math Mini books,* New York: Scholastic, 2002.

Easy-to-read stories and activities that invite kids to add, subtract, measure, tell time, and practice other important early math skills.

Simmons, K., and Guinn, C. *Math, Manipulatives & Magic Wands: Manipulatives, Literature Ideas, and Hands-On Math Activities for the K–5 Classroom.* Gainesville, FL: Maupin House, 2001.

Students learn national math standard skills as part of literature-based hands-on projects. Projects, ideas, literature links, and blackline masters make this a good resource that enriches the language-arts block and helps you teach the language of math to all your students.

Thiessen, D., and Matthais, M. *The Wonderful World of Mathematics: A Critically Annotated List of Children's Books in Mathematics.* Reston, VA: NCTM, 1998.

This book reviews approximately 500 books in mathematics for preschool through grade 6. The reviews describe each book's content and accuracy and discuss whether activities for the reader are included. Each book is rated in terms of its usefulness in teaching mathematics. The grade level of each book is included in the bibliographical entry.

Welchman-Tischler, R. *How to Use Children's Literature to Teach Mathematics.* Reston, VA: NCTM, 1992.

This book promotes the connection between mathematics and children's literature. The first seven chapters present activities organized according to the following themes: (1) providing a context; (2) introducing manipulatives; (3) modeling a creative experience; (4) posing an interesting problem; (5) preparing for a concept or skill; (6) developing a concept or skill; and (7) providing a context for review. The eighth chapter provides a discussion of how mathematical thinking can be applied using children's literature. Twenty books for teachers and 81 books for children are listed.

Whitin, D., and Wilde, S. *Read Any Good Math Lately?* Portsmouth, NH: Heinemann, 1992.

Stories are good ways for learners to explore the mathematics of their own lives and the lives of others. Each chapter of the book explores books on a given mathematics topic. The book ends by giving a series of mini-essays on the best of the new mathematical books for young readers and includes a "Top Twenty-Five."

Annotated Resources

Artzt, A. F., and Newman, C. M. *How to Use Cooperative Learning in the Mathematics Class.* Reston, VA: NCTM, 1990.
This book introduces new ideas and updates older methods for incorporating a cooperative learning approach into the K–12 mathematics classroom. Information on cooperative learning is provided with research results and strategies for using cooperative learning groups effectively in the mathematics classroom. Sample mathematics activities using cooperative groups are presented.

Bright, G. W. "Understanding children's reasoning." *Teaching Children Mathematics*, 3 (September 1996), pp. 18–22.
Think about ways to gain information about children's thinking in a mathematics lesson. A distinction is made between probing and harassing; solution strategies of children; planning instruction on the basis of children's thinking.

Burns, M. "What I learned from teaching second grade." *Teaching Children Mathematics*, 3 (November 1996), pp. 127–134.
A second-grade mathematics teacher discusses how she created a structure for classroom learning; use of homework as a medium to inform parents about their children's mathematics learning; and tactics that support learning.

De La Cruz, Y. "Reversing the trend: Latino families in real partnerships with schools." *Teaching Children Mathematics*, 5(5) (January 1999), pp. 296–300.
Discusses parental participation in the mathematics education of Hispanic American children under the Children's MathWorlds Family Connection (CMWFC) program. Obstacles to mathematics learning are resolved by parental involvement.

Hiebert, J., Carpenter, T. P., and Fennema, E.. *Making Sense: Teaching and Learning Mathematics with Understanding.* Portsmouth, NH: Heinemann, 1997.
What elements are necessary to teach for understanding in mathematics? This book describes successful diverse classrooms and ideas that make sense.

Koontz, T. *Multicultural and Gender Equity in the Mathematics Classroom: The Gift of Diversity.* Reston, VA: NCTM, 1997.
A multicultural vision of research and practice can reinforce cultural and gender equity to ensure a powerful mathematics program for all students. A variety of perspectives and diverse voices are addressed, suggesting various possible classroom models.

Lampert, M. *Teaching Problems and the Problems of Teaching.* New Haven, CT: Yale University Press, 2001.
An experienced classroom teacher and noted researcher on teaching describes her fifth-grade math class through the course of a year, showing how classroom dynamics—the complex relationship of teacher, student, and content—are critical in the process of bringing each student to a deeper understanding of mathematics, or any other subject.

Lindquist, M. M. "Assessing through questioning." *Arithmetic Teacher*, 35 (January 1988), pp. 16–18.
Four different techniques for questioning are given to assess students' understanding: silent questions, oral questions, written questions, and students' questions.

Scheibelhut, C. "I do and I understand, I reflect and I improve." *Teaching Children Mathematics*, 1 (December 1994), pp. 242–246.
Integration of writing in the study and teaching of mathematics in elementary school is discussed along with the importance of reflecting and the advantages of using writing in the teaching of mathematics.

Vacc, N. N. "Planning for instruction: Barriers to mathematics discussion." *Arithmetic Teacher*, 41 (February 1994), pp. 339–341.
Students can communicate mathematically if given the opportunity. Read about the barriers and how you can overcome them as you plan for instruction that includes discussion.

CHAPTER 4

Assessment: Enhanced Learning and Teaching

Snapshot of a Lesson

Key Ideas

1. Documenting student understanding is complex.

2. Students' classroom responses provide incomplete evidence of their understanding.

3. Multiple assessement methods are needed to get a more complete picture of students' understanding.

4. Individual task-based interviews can provide useful insights.

Background

Portions of the classroom and individual interview episodes below are available on the NCTM Illuminations Web site (see Math Links 4.6, p. 80, for details). The entire interviews are captured on the video in *Mathematics: Assessing Understanding, Grades K–6* by Marilyn Burns, available from ETA/Cuisenaire Company. In the excerpts below, we first see two second graders, Cena and Jonathan, counting and answering questions about place value during a whole-class discussion. We also gain additional insights into their thinking by hearing how each of them responds to questions posed during an individual, task-based interview. Their teacher will, no doubt, also examine their written work to assess

their understanding. Teachers gain deeper insights into their students' understanding when they use multiple methods of assessment.

The camera zooms in on Cena, a $7\frac{1}{2}$-year-old student, waving her hand, eager to respond, during a whole-class lesson. The teacher has drawn many stars on the chalkboard. In order to count the stars, the children have instructed the teacher to count one-by-one, pausing to put a circle around each group of ten stars. After the teacher has circled 4 groups of ten stars, and has counted the 9 stars that are left, she calls on Cena to tell how many stars there are altogether.

49 stars

CENA: [*Pointing at the board as she explains*] Look, you got, um, 1, 2, 3, 4 tens and you, like, put 4. . .4 right there. And put. . .yeah. . .put 4. [*The teacher* *writes a 4.*] And then if you have 9, um, stars leftover, then you put 9 right there. [*The teacher writes a 9 next to the 4.*]

CENA: Yeah, you have 49.

Cena seems confident in counting using tens and ones, and she also appears to understand how to write the numeral associated with the total number of stars.

Next we see Cena on her own, on a different day, during an individual task-based interview conducted by mathematics educator Marilyn Burns. Cena's first task is to count a pile of tiles into groups of ten. Cena counts aloud as she separates the tiles into 2 piles of ten with 4 tiles left over. Ms. Burns then asks Cena how many tiles she has altogether. Although Cena has successfully grouped the tiles by tens, she looks confused. She hesitates. She is unable to say how many tiles there are in all. She chooses to count all of the tiles, one by one, and then gives the answer of 24.

Ms. Burns poses several other tile-counting tasks. At one point, Cena counts out 18 tiles, one by one. Ms. Burns asks Cena to write the number 18 on paper and she does this correctly, with ease.

MS. BURNS: Great! That's how you write 18. Cena, can you tell me…can you show me with the tiles what the 8 means?

CENA: Um, 8. um.

MS. BURNS: Put them [*waving her hand over some of the tiles*] right up here next to the 8. [*There's a pause. Cena is not sure what to do.*]

MS. BURNS: So, I just want to see just the 8. You can count out loud.

CENA: 1, 2, 3, 4, 5, 6, 7, 8 [*as she pulls 8 of the 18 tiles aside, and puts them near the numeral 8 on her paper*].

MS. BURNS: 8, So, this is just 8 tiles. When you wrote the number 18 you wrote a 1 and an 8. Can you show me what the 1 means? [*Cena moves 1 tile forward.*]

MS. BURNS: And when you counted 18 there were all these tiles together [*motioning toward the entire group of 18*]. So if this is the 8 [*motioning toward the 8 tiles now pushed near the numeral 8*] and this is the 1 [*motioning toward the 1 tile now pushed near the numeral 1*], where do those fit [*motioning toward the rest of the 18 tiles*]?

CENA: Um, over here? [*Cena discards the remaining tiles and does not seem bothered that although she was asked to represent 18 with the tiles, only 9 tiles remain on her paper.*]

In another video clip of the same whole-class star-counting lesson, we see Jonathan, one of Cena's $7\frac{1}{2}$-year-old classmates. Jonathan appears to demonstrate a firm understanding of place value by counting a large number of stars drawn on the chalkboard by first grouping them in tens. The teacher calls on Jonathan to count the stars.

MS. BURNS: What shall we do?

JONATHAN: Um, count by tens!

MS. BURNS: Okay and how will we do that?

JONATHAN: Just circle [*each*] 10. And then say 10, 20, 30, 40, 50, 60. [*Then Jonathan indicates how to find the total number of stars by counting on: reciting 61, 62, 63, 64, and so on.*]

Later, in an individual interview, after Jonathan has counted out a group of 16 tiles, and has successfully written the numeral "16," Ms. Burns asks him to show her, using the tiles, what the 6 means. At first, he has difficulty with understanding the task.

JONATHAN: Okay. Okay, what do you mean?

MS. BURNS: Well, I am interested in how you knew how to write a 1 and a 6 to mean 16. So, I thought maybe you would start by telling me what does the 6 mean and what does the 1 mean and how together that means 16.

JONATHAN: Well, sometimes, in my reason, in like that star thing—

MS. BURNS: Uh huh.

JONATHAN: Um, my reason is, you count and put it in tens. And then, and then you count the tens. And then there is some left over. So, like, um, there probably would be…. The right side of the thing means the ones that are left over, and the other side means how many tens.

MS. BURNS: Let's try it and see. So how many are left over in there [*motioning toward the numeral 16*]?

JONATHAN: Left over? Here? or…? [*He waves his hand around the table, confused.*]

MS. BURNS: No, left over in the number, on the right side. If you put this into tens [*motioning toward the pile of 16 tiles*], do you have any leftovers with 16?

JONATHAN: Probably. [*Said with a questioning tone. He seems quite skeptical.*]

MS. BURNS: What do you think? How many leftovers do you think you'd have?

JONATHAN: Um. Well. Um. Maybe 3 or so.

MS. BURNS: Try it.

JONATHAN: Around 3.

MS. BURNS: Try it and see.

JONATHAN: [*Reaches over to the pile of 16 tiles and counts out*] 1, 2, 3, 4, 5, 6, 7, 8, 9, 10.

MS. BURNS: And how many leftovers?

JONATHAN: [*Counts the leftovers silently*] 6. [*He seems rather surprised.*]

In the whole-class lesson, Jonathan appeared confident in counting the stars by forming circles of 10 and counting the extras to state how many altogether. However, during the individual interview, the fragility of his understanding was revealed. Amazingly, Jonathan was unable to predict how many groups of 10s and how many extra tiles there would be in a pile of 16 tiles, even immediately after counting out the 16 tiles (one by one) and writing the numeral 16. Even though he can say and write that there are 16, he can only guess (by inspection) that there will be just one pile of 10, and he has to rely on counting to find the number of leftovers (6).

Introduction

The Assessment Principle

Assessment should support the learning of important mathematics and provide useful information to teachers and students.

(NCTM, 2000, p. 22)

What comes to mind when you think of assessment? Grading? Exams? Quizzes? Homework? Projects? Individual teacher–student interviews? Standardized tests? According to NCTM's *Assessment Standards for School Mathematics* (NCTM, 1995), assessment is "the process of gathering evidence about a student's knowledge of, ability to use, and disposition toward mathematics and of making inferences from that evidence for a variety of purposes" (p. 3). In this chapter, we contrast two rather different types of assessment: "assessment *of* learning" and "assessment *for* learning" (Stiggins, 2002). As a classroom teacher, you will need to be familiar with both. In brief, assessments *of* learning (sometimes called summative assessments) primarily provide evidence of student achievement for purposes of public reporting and accountability. Common examples are end-of-year exams or standardized tests. Assessments *for* learning (sometimes called formative assessments) should serve

not only to document students' achievement, but also to help students learn more. Common examples include homework, in-class assignments, performance assessments, teacher observations, or even classroom tests. As a classroom teacher, you will be involved with both sorts of assessments (and in many cases, the distinction between them may become blurred).

Math Links 4.1

*Y*ou can read more about these ideas in a full text view of NCTM's Assessment Standards on the NCTM Web site. It may be accessed from http://standards.nctm.org (requires NCTM membership) or from this book's Web site.

www.wiley.com/college/reys

FOCUS QUESTIONS

1. What similarities and differences are there in the uses and characterisitics of assessments *of* learning (summative assessment) and assessments *for* learning (formative assessment)?

2. How do the four phases of classroom assessment help teachers use the assessment process to inform their instruction?

3. What different methods can teachers use to gather information about their students' abilities, dispositions, and interests, and what do each of these methods communicate to students about what is valued in teaching and learning mathematics?

4. What different methods are useful for teachers to keep track of assessment records and to communicate the results of those assessments to others?

Assessment *of* Learning: Summative Assessment

We begin this chapter with information about "assessment *of* learning" or assessment that is primarily designed to document what students know and are able to do. For example, tests are sometimes given (or other sorts of evidence collected) to decide which class to place students in, whether to move them from one group to another, what grade to record on their report card, or whether to promote them to the next grade. When assessments have serious consequences such as these, we call them "high-stakes assessments." In the situations just described, high-stakes decisions about the students themselves are being made as a result of the assessments.

However, more and more frequently these days, it is not just the individual students who are affected by the consequences of high-stakes assessments. For example, tests may be administered in order to document the achievement of a group of students, or to compare one group of students with another. Individual teachers, or schools, or districts may be held accountable for their students' test scores, taken as a group. Many schools, districts, and states now use student test results to make funding decisions. Indeed, the No Child Left Behind (NCLB) legislation from the Bush administration, which calls for annual testing in reading and mathematics each year in grades 3–8 and once in grades 10–12, provides "an example of federal funding that is linked, at least in part, to the results of standardized achievement tests at the state level.... Every state has now instituted some sort of statewide testing program, partly in response to this legislation" (Wilson, in press, p. 1). (Note: The history below was informed by Wilson, in press, and Stiggins, 2002.)

Testing as an industry in the United States began with the development of intelligence tests during World War I, prompted by the realization that many soldiers were not performing to expectations. The government wanted to find ways to classify people according to "innate" ability. Over the years, testing in the United States has grown into a multimillion dollar business, as demand for tests and testing services has rapidly expanded. Standardized college admissions tests also were developed early in the twentieth century; they have been used not only to help colleges decide which individuals to admit, but also to rank colleges (according to selectivity) and also to profile states (e.g., according to average SAT scores).

Throughout the twentieth century, high-stakes testing continued to expand and grow. In response to calls for public school accountability around the middle of the century, many districtwide testing programs were initiated. In the 1970s, statewide testing programs were developed in nearly every state. In 1972, the National Assessment for Educational Progress (NAEP) began testing samples of students nationwide (in various subjects including mathematics, and at various age or grade levels) in an effort to establish a sort of "census" for national student performance that could be documented and tracked over time.

Early standardized tests established models for the sorts of tests (mostly paper-and-pencil and multiple choice) that were used in schools for decades, until the "standards movement" began in the late 1980s. When NCTM'S *Curriculum and Evaluation Standards for School Mathematics* (NCTM, 1989) were published, they were the first large-scale attempt at defining content standards for school curricula; other content areas (e.g., science, English, social studies) were prompted to follow suit in defining content standards. NCTM's standards not only defined specific goals for what students should know and be able to do, but also called for reform in how students were assessed. The assessment recommendations were extended and amplified in 1995 with the publication of *Assessment Standards for School Mathematics* (NCTM, 1995). Both NCTM documents called for moving away from a "bits and pieces" mentality of discrete objectives and away from the sole use of "objective" items (primarily multiple choice). Instead, they recommended moving toward the use of more problems set in context and more tasks that would ask students to produce their own answers and explain their reasoning, rather than simply selecting answers from a list of choices.

In the mid-1990s some states, reacting to the atmosphere of assessment reform across the country, modified their testing systems. For example, Vermont instituted a portfolio system of assessment in mathematics, and Kentucky became involved in similar reforms. Many states revised their tests to include constructed-response items (items where students write in their own answers and explanations) as well as machine-scored, mainly multiple-choice questions. Even today, the standardized tests used by many states continue to include some emphasis on non-multiple-choice tasks. During the past 10–15 years, nearly every state has developed its own content standards in mathematics, as well as in other content areas.

Math Links 4.2

*T*o find web links to all the state mathematics standards, you can click on "resources" and then on "state standards" after going to http://mathcurriculumcenter.org or you can link to that site from this book's Web site.

www.wiley.com/college/reys

As content standards were being developed, educators, test developers, and politicians all became interested in looking at the alignment of standards with assessments (e.g., Romberg and Wilson, 1992; Romberg, 1995). In other words, it became important to think about the extent to which items on a state's tests were appropriately matched with expectations from the state's list of standards. At the classroom level, teachers frequently engage in similar alignment activities when they do "curriculum mapping" to ensure that their plans for units and lessons are appropriately connected with state or district standards, and when they work to ensure that their classroom assessments are similarly well focused.

As mentioned above, in January 2002 the No Child Left Behind Act was enacted by the Bush administration, and it has had "far-reaching consequences for high-stakes testing in mathematics across the country. The law requires that states develop content standards in mathematics, create annual assessments aligned with those standards, and administer those tests to nearly all students annually in grades 3–8, and at least once in grades 10–12. Further, states must show that all groups of students, disaggregated by poverty, race and ethnicity, disability, and limited English proficiency, reach proficiency in mathematics by 2013–2014" (Wilson, in press, p. 7). Between now and then, schools must show evidence of "adequate yearly progress" toward specific annual measurable objectives; if they don't, they are threatened with a variety of mandates ranging from changing their instructional practices or curricula to allowing their students to transfer to other schools, firing their teachers and administrators, or even closing the underperforming schools entirely.

The NCLB Act has also had an immediate impact on the role of the National Assessment of Educational Progress (NAEP). Since 1972, the mathematics tests known as "main" NAEP have been administered approximately every 4 years to a nationally representative sample of students in grades 4, 8, and 12. In addition, states were given the opportunity—starting in 1990—to have additional schools participate in main NAEP voluntarily in order to be able to obtain state-by-state comparisons of their students' performance. Now, under NCLB, states are required to participate in NAEP and achievement on these tests will provide the federal government with a mechanism for documenting state-level progress toward NCLB goals.

Math Links 4.3

*Y*ou can view hundreds of released items from the National Assessment of Educational Progress (NAEP), along with data on student performance, by visiting the "nation's reportcard" website maintained by the National Center for Education Statistics (NCES). It may be accessed from nces.ed.gov/nationsreportcard/ or from this book's Web site.

www.wiley.com/college/reys

In 2001, the government unveiled a Web site (see Math Links 4.3) through which the general public can see examples of many of the questions used on the National Asssessment of Educational Progress, as well as data about how students across the nation have performed, over the years, on these questions and on the NAEP tests more generally. From the National Center for Education Statistics (NCES) Web site, you can click on SAMPLE QUESTIONS to access the "questions tool" which permits you to look at any test items released by NCES.

Using this tool, you can also access performance results for every question in the database—as calculated for the nation as a whole, by state, or by region, or in relation to various background questions given to participating students, teachers, and schools. So, for example, you can use the questions tool to look for interesting fourth-grade math assessment tasks on geometry, you can print them out for use with your own students, and then—for comparison purposes—you can also find out how other students have performed on these tasks during NAEP testing. For these same tasks, you can obtain results about the performance of students from the nation as a whole, or from your state, or among groups of students with similar characteristics to yours (because test results can be sorted by gender, ethnicity, socioeconomic status, etc.).

NCTM has been producing "interpretative reports" of the NAEP mathematics results ever since 1972. The most recent of these reports was published by NCTM in 2004 (Kloosterman and Lester, 2004). From these reports, you can learn about national trends in student performance in specific content areas, such as Number or Geometry. You can also read about performance on different sorts of items (multiple choice or open-ended) and about performance by various subgroups of students. Additionally, the reports include analyses of survey data on attitudes, beliefs, and instructional contexts collected from students and classroom teachers involved in the assessment. Here are some examples of statements from the most recent interpretive report:

- "In 2000, performance by fourth-grade students increased to the highest level ever recorded by National Assessment. . . . [Results] indicate that upper-elementary-grade students may now be performing about two grade levels higher than their counterparts 20 years ago" (Kloosterman et al., 2004, pp. 71–72).

- "In 2000, no significant gender differences were noted among fourth graders. . . . [However] the long-standing trend of differences in performance among ethnic groups continued. White students scored significantly higher than each of the other reported groups. No significant differences were observed between the scores of Hispanic students and those of American Indian and Alaska Native students. Both of those groups scored higher than black students and the sample of Asian American and Pacific Islanders was too small to warrant drawing any conclusions (Kloosterman et al., 2004, p. 73).

Assessment *for* Learning: Formative Assessment

There is no doubt that you will be impacted, as a classroom teacher, by many mandates for "assessment *of* learning" such as those described above. However, much more of your effort and time will need to be focused on classroom assessment—"assessment *for* learning." Infrequent, high-stakes tests may be important, but they cannot provide you with the information about student achievement that you will need, moment-by-moment, day-by-day in order to make crucial instructional decisions.

Phases of Assessment

NCTM's *Assessment Standards* identify four phases for the classroom assessment process: planning, gathering, interpreting, and using. Let's consider an actual classroom example (from Moskal, 2000) as we explore these phases.

While planning for an upcoming unit on decimals with her sixth-grade class, Ms. Lee decided it would be important to gather information about what her students already understood about place value, ordering, and density of decimals. So, she posed the following question in class: "Write all the numbers between 3.4 and 3.5 on the board."

One of the students, Dana, wrote: 3.41 3.42 3.43 3.44 3.45 3.46 3.47 3.48 3.49.

Nakisha disagreed, asserting there were more numbers between 3.4 and 3.5. Ms. Lee asked the class, "Who is correct? Dana or Nakisha?" She assigned them to use paper and pencil to take a stance and explain their reasoning.

Figure 4-1 shows the response of three students from Ms. Lee's class. Jim thought Nakisha was right. To support his claim, he offered examples of more numbers between 3.4 and 3.5. Afwandi also agreed; but instead of offering specific examples of other numbers, she simply claimed, "There are infinitely many numbers between 3.4 and 3.5." Juan offered an example of how to find additional numbers between any pair of decimals.

Ms. Lee reviewed all of her students' papers. Juan appeared to have some rudimentary knowledge of the concept of infinity. Jim's response concerned her because he seemed to be (incorrectly) claiming that 3.410 was missing from Dana's list. Dana had listed 3.41, but maybe Jim didn't realize that the trailing zero on 3.410 didn't change the value of the number. It wasn't clear from Afwandi's response what she understood about the density of decimal numbers. It seemed possible that her answer about "infinitely many numbers" was merely a phrase she had heard before, and echoed without really understanding.

FIGURE 4-1 Responses from three of Ms. Lee's students (Moskal, 2000, p. 192).

Ms. Lee decided more instruction was needed, particularly regarding zeros in decimal numerals. She decided to try—by posing another task—to help her students think about zeros in decimals at the same time that she would gather more information about their thinking. So she assigned this task: "Identify the numbers below that are equal: 02.3 20.3 20.03 20.030 2.3. Explain how you know which numbers are equal" (Moskal, 2000, p. 193).

Ms. Lee's approach to teaching about decimals provides an example of the planning, gathering, interpreting, and using phases of the asssssment process. She began by *planning* a task (write all the numbers between 3.4 and 3.5). After her students had completed the task, she *gathered* their responses and *interpreted* them. Finally, she *used* the information she had gathered to plan another assignment for her students. Of course, the events in each phase of this model may vary, depending on the type of assessment you use, the mathematical topic, and your students' responses. However, making instructional decisions is one of the primary ways that teachers use information gained through the classroom assessment process. For example, Ms. Lee might also decide to talk with Afwandi, or to engage her in a task-based interview, to gain more insights into her understanding of "infinitely many." Note that it was Jim's response, and similar responses from other students, that convinced Ms. Lee to assign another task to help students reconsider the role that zero plays in decimals.

Now that we have examined a specific example, let's think, more generally, about the four phases of classroom assessment.

When you are *planning an assessment*, it is important to think about the purpose of the assessment, the methods you will use to collect data, how you will interpret the evidence you collect (e.g., how you will award points for students' written problem-solving work), and how you will summarize and use your findings. Will the outcome of your assessment be to change your lesson plans for the next week? Or will you use the information when explaining to parents what their children's strengths and weaknesses are? How you answer these questions may affect the sorts of data you decide to collect.

When you are *gathering evidence*, think about the variety of tasks or activities you might use and try to choose appropriately. For example, if you want to find out what your students understand about decimals, you could have them complete some worksheets on addition and subtraction of decimals. But that task might not provide you with as much information as having them show you

how they could use base-ten blocks to represent an addition or subtraction problem with decimals or having them write about using base-ten blocks and draw pictures to accompany their writing.

When you are *interpreting evidence*, it is important to think ahead of time about the criteria you will use to judge the adequacy of responses. You should think about how you *hope* your students respond to a task or question and what sorts of difficulties or misconceptions they *might* have. What sorts of responses will you consider exemplary, adequate, or flawed? What will you consider adequate evidence of understanding?

Finally, when *using results* from assessments, think about how you will communicate your judgments and how they will affect future instructional decisions. For example, how well will a numeric or letter grade help your students understand where they went wrong and what they need to do differently? Can you supplement the grade with written comments? Can you find time for brief individual conferences with some of your students? How will you use what you've learned about your class, as a whole, in planning for future instruction?

Making Instructional Decisions

As a teacher, you will be making many instructional decisions. As with any decision, the better informed you are, the wiser are the choices you usually make. The NCTM *Assessment Standards* suggest ways that you may use assessment information differently in making instructional decisions than teachers did years ago (see Table 4-1).

One shift in assessment practices is a move toward gathering assessment data continuously rather than periodically or at the end of a chapter, when it is too late to modify your instruction. Another trend is toward using a wide variety of sources of information (rather than tests primarily). The third change is related to keeping the needs and progress of students in mind when making long-range teaching plans (rather than following a set plan of study regardless of how well students are doing).

Monitoring Student Progress

Several shifts in monitoring student progress are also called for by the NCTM *Assessment Standards* (Table 4-1). These include assessing a wide range of student abilities rather than focusing just on testing students' factual knowledge and skills; providing more extensive and elaborated feedback to students on their progress; using a wider variety of methods for gathering information (rather than re-

Table 4-1 • Major Shifts in Assessment Practices

Toward	Away from
Shifts in Assessing to Make Instructional Decisions	
Integrating assessment with instruction	Depending on scheduled testing
Using evidence from a variety of assessment formats and contexts	Relying on any one source of information
Using evidence of every students' progress toward long-range planning goals	Planning primarily for content coverage
Shifts in Assessing to Monitor Students' Progress	
Assessing progress toward mathematical power	Assessing knowledge of specific facts and isolated skills
Communicating with students about performance in a continuous, comprehensive manner	Simply indicating right or wrong answers
Using multiple and complex assessment tools	Primary reliance on answers to brief questions on quizzes and tests
Students learning to assess their own progress	Teachers and external agencies as the sole judges of progress
Shifts in Assessing to Evaluate Students' Achievement	
Comparing students' performance with performance criteria	Comparing student with student
Assessing progress toward mathematical power	Assessing knowledge of specific facts and isolated skills
Certification based on balanced, multiple sources of information	Relying on only a few, narrowly conceived sources of evidence
Profiles of achievement based on public criteria	Single letter grades based on variable or nonpublic criteria

Adapted with permission from *Assessment Standards for School Mathematics,* copyright 1995 by the National Council of Teachers of Mathematics. All rights reserved.

lying primarily on tests and quizzes); and involving students more in the assessment process.

Evaluating Student Achievement

Teachers today are also doing several things differently in terms of grading and certifying students' achievement (Table 4-1). One change is a move toward judging students' performance against stated criteria (standards or expectations) rather than by comparing students with one another. The second and third shifts were mentioned earlier: assessing a broad range of components of mathematical power rather than isolated skills and knowledge, and using a variety of sources for gathering assessment information. Finally, there are trends toward making achievement criteria more open and public.

The number of shifts listed in this opening section is an indication of the need for change in many of our assessment practices. This change will come through time and open minds. This chapter is an opportunity for you to begin asking yourself questions about how you will assess students in order to make decisions, monitor progress, and evaluate achievement.

Math Links 4.4

*A*s you can see, there is much to consider when you assess your students. However, there are many helpful Web sites that can assist you, such as the site of the Balanced Assessment in Mathematics Program, which offers a free on-line library of over 300 mathematics assessment tasks. It may be accessed from http://balancedassessment.concord.org/ or from this book's Web site.

www.wiley.com/college/reys

Ways to Assess Students' Abilities and Dispositions

There are many different ways to gather information about the abilities, dispositions, and interests of students. What type of information to collect and how to obtain it depend on the purpose for which it will be used. You first need to ask yourself what you want to assess.

For example, if you want to assess the principle discussed in Chapter 2—that mathematics learning should make sense to students—then you want to observe students and ask them questions that elicit their level of understanding, to find out whether they have attached meaning to what they are doing. If you want your students to be persistent and willing to approach problems in a variety of ways, then you need to assess these characteristics through problems of a challenging nature. If you want your students to be able to communicate well and to work well with others, as discussed in Chapter 2, then you should make those characteristics part of your assessment.

Once you have engaged your students in activities likely to elicit the behaviors that you want to judge, you need some sort of guidelines or framework to use in looking at the data you collect. For example, if you want to see how well your students can communicate about the notions of area and perimeter, you might ask them to write a letter to a younger child comparing and contrasting these two ideas and providing an example of a real-world problem using each measure. But how will you judge which student letters are better than others? You may choose to use a rubric or scoring guide.

A *rubric* or *scoring guide* is a rating scale that can be designed or adapted for use with a certain class of students or a particular task. Generally, a scoring guide is used to assign anywhere from 0 to 10 points to student work to provide a rating of performance. This is different from awarding points when grading a quiz or test, where you generally count the number of correct answers to arrive at a score. Instead, with a rubric you look at performance on the task and rate that performance along a continuum.

Rubrics or scoring guides can be either holistic or analytic. Holistic criteria assign a single score based on the overall quality of the student's work. The simplest type of holistic scoring guide may have just two or three levels, and general descriptors of the achievement necessary to attain them. For example, you might award points for a student's problem-solving work as shown in the scoring guide in Figure 4-2. On the other hand, when it seems important to score various dimensions or traits of student work separately, analytic scoring rather than holistic scoring is appropriate. (See Figure 4-10 later in the chapter for an example of an analytic scoring guide for assessing open-ended questions.)

4	Exemplary work	Goes well beyond expectations of the task (e.g., problem solved in more than one way, or student has extended the problem and completed a more difficult version).
3	Excellent work	Task as stated is completed with no errors, work is clear and complete.
2	Good work	Task is completed with only a few minor errors. Work shows understanding of the problem and uses anticipated approaches.
1	Needs more instruction	Student work may include evidence that the problem was not understood completely; may use inappropriate methods or faulty reasoning; may make significant errors.

FIGURE 4-2 General holistic scoring guide for math problem solving.

One very straightforward way of constructing a scoring guide is to think about sorting students' work into three piles:

1. does not understand the outcome (concept or process),
2. developing understanding (but not quite there), and
3. understands the idea and can apply and communicate about it.

For any specific task, you can develop *performance indicators* to help you judge which student work to put in which categories. Ultimately, these performance indicators provide descriptions of how well the students are making sense of the mathematics.

For example, you might design a task for students to show what they know about the meaning of decimals by using base-ten blocks to build specified decimal numbers (e.g., 3 tenths, or 1 and 5 hundredths) and to demonstrate decimal relationships (e.g., build 2 tenths and build 22 hundredths and explain which one is larger). Each flat block could represent a whole number, each rod a tenth, and each little cube a hundredth. In this example the student has displayed 2.46.

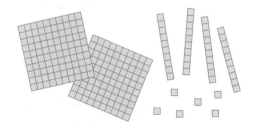

Sample Performance Indicators for a Student Who:

Does not understand	Is developing understanding	Understands
• When told to use one flat to represent a whole, cannot use blocks to show how many tenths would be equivalent to that one whole • When told to use one flat to represent a whole, cannot use blocks to show how many hundredths would be equivalent to that one whole • Has difficulty understanding that the same blocks can be used to represent different powers of 10 in different problems (may think a flat must represent 100 if earlier experiences assigned a value of 1 to each small cube)	• When told to use one flat to represent a whole, can state which block would represent one tenth (rod) and which block would represent one hundredth (little cube) • Can use blocks to show why 10 tenths and 100 hundredths are each equivalent to one whole • May interchange value of blocks when building decimals • May have difficulty building decimals with blocks, especially when the decimal includes zeros (e.g., 3.04). • May have difficulty stating what number is represented by a given collection of blocks (e.g., 5 flats, 2 rods, and 3 little cubes)	• Understands that the same blocks can be used to represent different powers of 10 in different problems • When told which block represents one, can state what number is represented by any collection of blocks • Can build, order, and compare decimal using blocks to illustrate • Can build alternative models for the same decimal (e.g., can represent 3.45 either with 3 flats, 4 rods, and 5 little cubes or with 3 flats and 45 little cubes)

FIGURE 4-3   Scoring guide with performance indicators for base-ten block task on decimals.

Figure 4-3 shows a three-category rubric or scoring guide with performance indicators for this task. This type of scoring guide is often called an annotated holistic rubric.

Observation

Observing students as they work and making judgments about their performance from observation is probably one of the most commonly used assessment methods in the classroom. Yet many teachers never go one important step further: to make notes about their observations or think carefully about what they want to look for and why. Watching and listening may seem easy and commonplace, but it takes practice and planning to hone your observation skills. For example, it is helpful to plan what you will observe on a given day.

Suppose you are teaching first grade and your students are solving problems involving addition facts. You may want to observe and record which students are using physical materials, which are doing most of the problems mentally, which are using thinking strategies to determine basic facts (which will be discussed in Chapter 9), and which are relying on memorized facts. At times, you may plan to observe only one student in a cooperative group setting:

Does José jump right in or wait for others to begin?

Does he know his doubles facts? Does he know the facts that make 10?

Is he able to use known facts to figure out unknown facts? If so, what strategies does he use? What sense does he make of the mathematics? Does he accept or challenge the ideas of others?

From such observations, you can gain insight into a student's attitude and disposition toward mathematics. This knowledge, in turn, can help you plan ways to encourage strengths and work on weaknesses.

Your notes about what you have observed will certainly be useful for anecdotal records that you can use for individual assessment, for future planning, and for reporting to parents. Your observations can also help you decide what to do immediately in the classroom, while you are leading a discussion or presenting a new concept.

Some practical tips are helpful in organizing yourself for classroom observations (Beyer, 1993). Some teachers find it helpful to set aside a page in a notebook for each student or to use individual notecards in a file. But it can be clumsy to page through the notebook or fumble through the cards when you are walking around the room. To make observation notes easier to handle, some teachers like to tape an index card for each student in the class on a single page of heavy cardboard, with the cards overlapping as shown in Figure 4-4.

When you want to write notes about a particular individual, you just flip to his or her card. When a card is full, you can file it away in that student's file and replace it with a fresh card. Another handy idea is to carry a page of computer labels or a packet of stick-on notes on your clipboard as you

FIGURE 4-4 Flip cards for recording classroom observations. Cards can be arranged alphabetically or by classroom seat assignments, whatever will help you find the right card quickly.

circulate around the class. Make notes about individual students on separate labels or notes (putting name and date on each). Later you can paste these notes into the individual students' folders or pages in your observation notebook. If you want to remember to collect data on certain students on a given day, you can write their names on labels or stick-on notes in advance as a reminder. Whichever form or process you use, it is extremely important to remember to date your observations.

You can read more about assessing via classroom observation in Beyer (1993), Bush (2001), Chambers (1995), Cross and Hynes (1994), Glanfield, Stenmark, and Bush (2001), Sgroi et al. (1995), and Stenmark and Bush (2001).

Questioning

In Chapters 2 and 3, we discussed the value of asking questions of students to help direct their mathematical thinking. Good questioning techniques can also complement and enlighten your assessment observations. Asking good questions is an art that needs to be developed and practiced. When you teach through questioning, you actively involve students and know more about what they are thinking. In planning your lessons, you should think of questions that will help you gauge whether students are

- making sense of the mathematics
- approaching a problem in different ways
- clearly explaining their thinking
- showing evidence of generalizing

Limit the number of questions that can be answered yes or no or with one-word responses. For example, instead of asking "Should we add, subtract, multiply, or divide to solve this problem?" ask, "What could we do to understand this problem better?" or "What sort of picture can we draw to help decide what operation to use?" As a teacher, you should also work to develop more high-level and open-response questioning, asking students to explain or defend their answers or to describe another way to solve the problem. Remember that students need time to think about their answers to such questions. Practice waiting silently.

Finally, recognize that you can involve many more of your students in thinking deeply about mathematics if you think of ways to get everyone involved in asking and answering questions. For example, you can pose a question to the class and ask everyone to "think-pair-share." The students should first think about their own answers, then pair up with a partner to talk about their ideas, and finally be ready to offer suggestions to the entire class. (For even more opportunities for small-group discussion, you can have the pairs join up for discussion in groups of four or six before you bring the whole class together to talk about the question.) With this questioning model, everyone is encouraged to think and talk about the question. The conversation in the classroom is no longer "ping-pong" from teacher to individual student and back.

Some useful references on questioning include Burns (1985), Mumme and Shepherd (1990), Spangler (1992), Sullivan and Clarke (1991), and Vaac (1993).

Math Links 4.5

*T*o view some on-line lesson videos, with accompanying guidelines for thinking about teacher questioning, visit NCTM's Reflections website at http://my.nctm.org/eresources/reflections or link from this book's Web site. Choose "Discourse" from the options under "Reflect by Topic."

www.wiley.com/college/reys

Interviewing

As illustrated in the snapshot that opened this chapter, interviewing is a combination of questioning and observing, usually done with one student in a quiet place. It is a powerful way to learn about a student's thinking and to give her or him some special attention. Key factors in a successful interview are establishing rapport with the child, accepting responses without judging, and encouraging the child to talk and explain.

For example, at the beginning of the school year, Ms. Morihara decided to conduct short interviews with her new fourth graders to assess their understanding of odd and even numbers. Here is what Tonya said during that interview:

MS. MORIHARA: Tonya, is 9 an odd or even number?

TONYA: It's odd...unless you go by 3s, then it's even.

MS. MORIHARA: Oh, that's interesting. Can you show me what you mean with tiles?

[Ms. Morihara gave Tonya 9 tiles to explain her thinking. Tonya stacked the tiles into 4 groups of 2 and showed her the 1 that was left over.]

TONYA: See, if we divide evenly by 2s, there is 1 left over so it is odd.

[Tonya then divided the 9 tiles into three groups of 3.]

TONYA: But, if we divide it into groups of 3, there aren't any left over, so it is even. That is why 9 is both odd and even.

MS. MORIHARA: Thank you very much, Tonya, for explaining your thinking to me.

This interview with Tonya shows how just a short interview can provide a wealth of information regarding a student's understanding of mathematics. Tonya is doing some interesting thinking about number relationships, particularly what it means to separate various numbers of tiles into even-sized piles. She seems to recognize that there may be different numbers of tiles left over depending on what sized piles the tiles are sorted into, and she is interested in focusing not just on the number of piles, but also on the number of leftovers. Though she is confused about the definitions of "odd" and "even," she actually seems on the verge of understanding the more complex notions of "factor" and "multiple." If you had a chance to probe Tonya's thinking even further, what questions would you ask her? How would you attempt to change her misconceptions?

Although you will certainly not have time to ask in-depth questions of each of your students each day or even every week, it can be enlightening to choose a few children to interview each week until you have had a chance to talk with each one individually. Teachers are often surprised at how students value private time with them and

how much they learn in a short time about the individual student. You may be able to squeeze in an interview or two each day during whole-class silent reading time, work-station time (when other students are circulating from station to station), or seatwork time.

Before interviewing a student, you need a basic plan of what concepts or skills you want to assess, what materials you will need, what questions you will ask, and when and how you will record the information. You may want to have alternative paths to take if the interview proceeds in different ways.

The interview itself generally has three parts: initiation, questioning/hypothesis formulation, and questioning/hypothesis testing (Long and Ben-Hur, 1991). During the initiation phase, the interviewer puts the student at ease by chatting informally, asking nonthreatening personal interest questions, showing the child the materials that will be used and ensuring that he or she is familiar with them, and explaining the purpose of the interview.

Next, the interviewer begins posing tasks, always making certain to rephrase questions in the student's own language when necessary and to encourage the student to explain, elaborate, and show what he or she knows. Students often understand more than it appears at first glance.

It is the interviewer's responsibility to ask questions in a variety of ways in order to formulate hypotheses about how the child is thinking about the task and what the child does and does not understand. It is critical that the interviewer remain nonjudgmental about student responses, even though students often look for subtle clues about the correctness of their answers. Some noncommittal phrases that are helpful in prompting children to explain their thinking further (without indicating whether previous responses have been right or wrong) include the following:

- I am interested in knowing more about your thinking. Talk to me about it.
- Pretend you are the teacher and I am your student. Please help me understand.
- Can you explain that in a different way?
- I like it when you take the time to explain your thinking.
- I think I understand now, but what if. . .?

As the second phase of the interview proceeds, the interviewer begins to formulate hypotheses about what the child knows and where the child has trouble.

The third phase of the interview is the time to ask questions specifically designed to test hypotheses, to see if the difficulties really are what they

In the Classroom 4-1

PRIMARY INTERVIEW ON PLACE VALUE

OBJECTIVE: **To determine students' understanding of place value.**

GRADE LEVEL: **1-3**

MATERIALS: **Unifix cubes, paper and pencil, base-ten blocks**

TASKS:

1. Can you show me 24 Unifix cubes? Observe if child counts accurately (says numbers in proper order, uses one-to-one correspondence, has a method for keeping track of which cubes have been counted).

2. Now let's suppose we want 34 cubes. Can you show me that? Does child count out 10 more or count over from beginning?

3. Can you write the number 34 here?

4. Let's put the 34 cubes into groups of ten. How many tens do you think we can make? Do you think you'll have any cubes left over? Shall we count out the 34 cubes into piles to make sure?

5. Let's look at 34, the number you wrote. Can you show me with the cubes what the 3 means? Can you show me what the 4 means?

6. Now let's make four piles of 10 cubes each. And let's have five leftover. Do you know how many cubes we have here altogether? How can you tell? (Does student know to count the piles by 10 and add the leftovers? Or does he or she count all?)

7. a. If the child has trouble with the questions above, check further by asking him or her again to count out several different numbers of cubes (e.g., 17, 26, or 30) and to predict how many tens and how many left over. Ask the reverse question. For example, if we have 2 tens and 7 left over, how many cubes would that be?

   b. If the child has no trouble with the questions above, probe for understanding of place value of larger numbers such as 123 or 347 using base-ten blocks and asking how many piles of 100 could be made and how may piles of 10 and how many ones. Also ask the reverse question: If we have three flats and six sticks and two units, how many cubes would that be altogether? Extension: Check to see how many different ways the child can show 136.

INTERVIEW REMINDERS:

Listen and watch carefully! Let them do it! Don't teach!

Be flexible. Ask for more examples, if needed.

Ask: How would you show a friend? How would you explain it to a little kid?

---

seem to be. A big temptation for many teachers is to slide into teaching during an interview. It is important to resist the temptation to fix errors or misconceptions on the spot. If there is lots of time, teaching may be appropriate, but reteaching or tutoring is often better reserved for another time or another day. The focus of a classroom interview should be to figure out what a student knows, not to help him or her on the spot. In the Classroom 4-1 is a plan for interviewing third-grade students about their understanding of place value.

A classic, and very useful chapter about classroom interviews is "Listening to Children: The Interview Method" (Labinowicz, 1985). Additional sources of information on interviews include Bush, (2001), Chambers (1995), Cross and Hynes (1994),

Glanfield et al., (2001), Kamii and Lewis (1991), Long and Ben-Hur (1991), and Stenmark and Bush (2001).

Math Links 4.6

It is also interesting to see the kind of insight into a child's thinking a teacher can gain from an interview. You can do this by viewing video clips at the NCTM Illuminations Web site. They may be accessed from http://illuminations.nctm.org/index.asp or from this book's Web site. Choose "Standards," then scroll down to "Video Reflections for Grades Pre-K–2" and click on "Understanding a Child's Development of Number Sense."

www.wiley.com/college/reys

Performance Tasks

In a class that is alive with problem solving and investigations, many valuable opportunities arise to observe students working on performance tasks. In fact, the only way to assess some skills is through performance tasks. For example, if one objective is for children to know how to measure with a ruler, then they need to be assessed doing such measuring. Questions on written tests that present a picture of a ruler perfectly lined up next to a picture of some other object to be measured do not reveal much about the actual skill of measuring. From this task you can judge whether the child can read measurements from the ruler, but you have no idea whether he or she would actually be able to use a ruler effectively.

Performance tasks generally mirror the real world, are open-ended, and require time for grappling with a problem. It is often helpful to pair children when observing performance of such tasks, so that you can hear their conversation as they work. In planning, you should list some of the areas you want to observe as the pairs work on appropriate tasks.

As an example of a performance task, look back at In the Classroom 2-2 (Chapter 2). In that activity, children are asked to build different boxes (right prisms) with some blocks. As they build boxes of various dimensions and various volumes, the formula for the volume of a box evolves naturally. The children are involved in using models, making decisions, and thinking mathematically, rather than just applying a formula. Figure 4-5 lists

	Jason	Amy	Lawanda	Tyler	Zaria	Kristin	Becca	Drew
Strategy								
Used trial and error								
Organized by length (or height or width)								
Found and used patterns								
Made other comparisons								
Used a combination of strategies								
Result								
Found few or all combinations								
Found the connection to factors of the number								
Found/did not find the formula								
Able/unable to describe the procedure								
Attitude								
Worked well with others								
Curious, explored other shapes, other numbers								
Enthusiastic								
Remained engaged								

FIGURE 4-5 Observation guide for block-building activity.

three areas you might plan to observe and examples of the notes you might make while observing the performance task from In the Classroom 2-2.

As indicated in Chapter 3, the *Professional Standards for Teaching Mathematics* (NCTM, 1991) emphasize worthwhile mathematical tasks as a core dimension. You may want to begin with simple tasks and then build up to longer, more complicated ones. Often, you will be surprised at the tenacity of very young children on a task that is engaging them; you should not rule out richer tasks for this age. Badger (1992), Moon (1993), and Sanford (1993) provide additional interesting reading about performance assessment in the elementary math classroom, as do Bush (2001), Glanfield et al., (2001), and Stenmark and Bush (2001).

Self-Assessment and Peer Assessment

Self-assessment is an activity that engages many people. For example, actors, athletes, and musicians often study videotapes of their performances in order to figure out how to improve. In a similar way, when math students engage in activities that promote self-awareness and self-evaluation, they can eliminate weaknesses and become better problem solvers. Students are often the best assessors of their own work and feelings. When students evaluate their own work, the responsibility for learning is theirs.

You can begin the self-assessment process by having students validate their own thinking or their answers to selected exercises. For example, in a nonthreatening way, you could ask Dwayne to show you how he arrived at the answers to each of the problems below:

$$
\begin{array}{r@{\qquad}r}
28 & 24 \\
\times\,46 & \times\,39 \\
\hline
168 & 216 \\
112 & 72 \\
\hline
280 & 936 \\
\end{array}
$$

It is important to ask questions about correct answers as well as incorrect ones, and to ask about standard approaches as well as nonstandard, so that children do not think they are questioned only when something is wrong. Asking only about incorrect answers does not help build their self-esteem or establish the feeling that they have control of the mathematics.

It is helpful for students to learn to ask themselves a variety of mental self-assessment questions while they are engaged in problem solving. You can help students develop the habit of self-assessment by prompting them with questions such as

"What are you doing now?" "Why are you doing that?" "How will it help you find the solution?" (Kenney and Silver, 1993). Eventually, these questions will become second nature to the students, and you will no longer need to prompt them. Being able to think about one's own thinking and to monitor one's own problem-solving efforts (*metacognition*) is one of the goals of problem-solving instruction.

Engaging students in self-assessment of their problem-solving efforts after they have finished solving problems is another useful way to improve their monitoring abilities. For example, you might ask students to write a sentence or two in response to prompts like those in Figure 4-6 after they have finished a problem-solving activity.

Students can also analyze each others' strategies for solving problems. As they listen to and discuss how another student or group of students solved a problem, they begin to see different ways to proceed and to make judgments about which way makes the most sense to them, which seems easier or different, and which leads to stumbling blocks. Not only will they learn from such discussions and self-assessments, but you will also learn a lot about the students.

Sometimes knowing about students' attitudes, beliefs, and feelings about mathematics and mathematical tasks helps you, as a teacher, know how to design lessons more effectively. No one is better at assessing how a student feels about a given task than the student who is doing it. You may want to give a simple attitude inventory (see Figure 4-7). How would you plan a lesson that involves problem solving if you find from the survey that most of your students have a negative attitude toward problem solving? How could this information help you in grouping students in the lesson?

You might assign students to write math journals or letters to themselves or to others. One teacher had her students write letters to themselves about their strengths and weaknesses at the beginning of each grading period. Months later, they read back over their letters to see if they had made progress in any of the areas they had previously self-identified as weaknesses (see Figure 4-8). This information can be shared with parents during conference time.

You may learn more from children by asking them questions such as the following (Spangler, 1992):

What are you really good at in math? What things do you need to improve on?

If you were telling a friend about the favorite thing you do in mathematics class, what would

Think about the problem you just worked on. Then answer these questions by circling what you think:

1. How sure are you that your answer is right?

ABSOLUTELY   PRETTY   SORT OF   NOT SO   I KNOW I GOT
SURE   SURE   SURE   SURE   IT WRONG

Why are you sure (or not sure) about your answer?

2. How hard was this problem for you?

VERY, VERY   PRETTY   SORT OF   NOT SO   REALLY
HARD   HARD   HARD   HARD   EASY

Why was this problem at this difficulty level for you?

3. Have you ever solved a problem like this one before?

YES,   YES, ONCE   NOT   DON'T   NO,
MANY TIMES   OR TWICE   SURE   THINK SO   DEFINITELY
                                                             NOT

If so, describe the other problems and tell why they were like this one. If not, what was different about this problem from the others you've seen?

FIGURE 4-6   Self-assessment questions for problem solving.

Attitude Inventory Items

Pretend your class has been given some math story problems to solve. Mark true or false depending on how the statement describes you. There are no right or wrong answers for this part.

_____ 1. I will put down any answer just to finish a problem.
_____ 2. It is no fun to try to solve problems.
_____ 3. I will try almost any problem.
_____ 4. When I do not get the right answer right away I give up.
_____ 5. I like to try hard problems.
_____ 6. My ideas about how to solve problems are not as good as other students' ideas.
_____ 7. I can only do problems everyone else can do.
_____ 8. I will not stop working on a problem until I get an answer.
_____ 9. I am sure I can solve most problems.
_____ 10. I will work a long time on a problem.

_____ 11. I am better than many students at solving problems.
_____ 12. I need someone to help me work on problems.
_____ 13. I can solve most hard problems.
_____ 14. There are some problems I will just not try.
_____ 15. I do not like to try problems that are hard to understand.
_____ 16. I will keep working on a problem until I get it right.
_____ 17. I like to try to solve problems.
_____ 18. I give up on problems right away.
_____ 19. Most problems are too hard for me to solve.
_____ 20. I am a good problem solver.

FIGURE 4-7   A problem-solving attitude survey for elementary students. (Source: Reprinted with permission from "How to Evaluate Progress in Solving Problems," copyright 1987 by the National Council of Teachers of Mathematics. All rights reserved.)

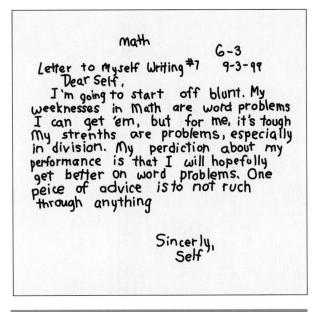

FIGURE 4-8 Sample student self-assessment "letter to myself" written at the beginning of the year. Students can compare this letter with a letter written at the end of the year to show their growth over the school year.

you tell him or her? What other things about math class might you tell your friend? Why?

If you and a friend got different answers to the same problem, what would you do?

How do you know when you have solved a problem correctly?

Student self-assessment instruments for mathematics can be found in a variety of sources (e.g., Charles, Lester, and O'Daffer, 1987; Stenmark, 1991). Other useful resources on self- and peer-assessment include Clarke (1992), Collinson (1992), Garafalo and Bryant (1992), and Kenney and Silver (1993).

Work Samples

Work samples can include written assignments, projects, and other student work that you collect and evaluate. Figure 4-9 reproduces the work of four children on the following problem:

> A carpenter makes only 3-legged and 4-legged tables. At the end of one day, he had used 31 legs. How many stools and tables did he make?

Figure 4-10 provides a typical analytic scoring scale for assessing children's work in problem solving on three measures (understanding the problem, planning a solution, and getting an answer).

Table 4-2 shows one teacher's scores for each of the four children on the three measures in Figure 4-10. There are, in fact, many different schemes for scoring problem solving, and each involves judgment. For example, try scoring the papers in Figure 4-9 using the same analytic scoring scale to see whether you agree with the scorer in Table 4-2. (You may well disagree, but you should be able to justify your position.)

Perhaps more important than scoring children's work is analyzing it to see what you can learn about the students. Looking again at the work of the four students in Figure 4-9, for example, you might conclude that only Suzy searched for more than one answer to the problem.

Portfolios

Portfolios have long been used to evaluate works of art, but in recent years this technique has also been used for assessment in mathematics education, and for other school subjects. A portfolio is a "purposeful collection of student work that exhibits the student's efforts, progress, and achievement in one or more areas. The collection must include student participation in selecting the contents, the criteria for selection, and criteria for judging merit, and evidence of student self-reflection" (Paulson,

Table 4-2 • Scoring for Children's Work in Figure 4-12 Using the Scale in Figure 4-13

	Understanding the Problem	Planning a Solution	Getting an Answer	Total
Suzy	2	2	1	5
Toby	1	1	0	2
Katie	2	2	1	5
Ralph	2	2	1	5

FIGURE 4-9 Samples of children's problem-solving work.

Paulson, and Meyer, 1991, p. 60). A student's mathematics portfolio might include such things as special problem-solving tasks, writings, investigations, projects, and reports. These samples could be presented through a variety of media, including paper and pencil, audio or videotapes, and computer disks. Some teachers keep both classroom working portfolios, in which students keep the majority of their work, and assessment portfolios, which contain selected samples of their work for purposes of making judgments about students' attitudes, abilities, and dispositions in mathematics.

If you have your students keep portfolios, you will need to answer the following questions:

What is the purpose of the portfolio? Who will be the audience? (The students themselves? You as teacher? Parents?)

What will be included and who selects? (Problem-solving work? Tests and quizzes? Writing about math? Only best efforts or a collection of representative work?) See Figure 4-11 for a list of the items one teacher chose to require.

Analytic Scoring Scale

Understanding the Problem
0: Complete misunderstanding of the problem
1: Part of the problem misunderstood or misinterpreted
2: Complete understanding of the problem

Planning a Solution
0: No attempt or totally inappropriate plan
1: Partially correct plan based on part of the problem being interpreted correctly
2: Plan could have led to a correct solution if implemented properly

Getting an Answer
0: No answer, or wrong answer based on an inappropriate plan
1: Copying error, computational error, partial answer for a problem with multiple answers
2: Correct answer and correct label for the answer

FIGURE 4-10   A scale for scoring problem solving.
(Source: Reprinted with permission from "How to Evaluate Progress in Problem Solving," copyright 1987 by the National Council of Teachers of Mathematics. All rights reserved.)

Where will the portfolios be kept? (In notebooks? In folders? In the classroom? In student desks or lockers or at home?)

Will you grade the portfolios? If so, how? (Will the portfolio include already graded items, and if so, is a student graded twice on the same material? Is the portfolio graded on the basis of completeness, comprehensiveness, insight, etc.? Can a well-compiled portfolio that contains many poor papers receive a high grade? Can a messy, incomplete portfolio belonging to an excellent math student—and containing all A papers—receive a low grade?)

How often will you give feedback? (Monthly, quarterly, at the end of each grading period?)

Minimum requirements for inclusion in your portfolio at the end of each grading period:

1. 3 homework assignments
2. 3 writing samples
3. 2 quizzes
4. 2 examples of class notes
5. 1 example of special project work
6. 1 example of cooperative group work

Your portfolio is not limited to the above. At the end of each grading period, you will choose five pieces of work to remain in your portfolio to represent the grading period's work.

FIGURE 4-11   One teacher's specifications for portfolio contents.

These are only representative questions; there are many more to be considered. Once you have decided these things for yourself, portfolios can be a rich source of information for you and your students.

A particular benefit of portfolios is their value as a self-assessment tool for students. It is important for students to date the entries so that they (and others) can see their growth over time. It is also helpful if they describe each task and reflect on it. Figure 4-12 provides some advice for getting started with math learning portfolios.

Some useful references on the subject include Clarke (1992), Kuhs (1997), Lambdin and Walker (1994), and Mumme (1990).

Writings

The NCTM *Standards* call for more emphasis on communication in mathematics. As stated in Figure 4-13, numeracy and literacy go hand in hand. Student writings as a form of communication can provide another source for assessment. You may want students to keep a journal or to add writing to other assignments.

Getting Started with Portfolios

Start small and simple.
• Especially if you have many students, portfolios are a lot of work.

Developing a rationale is important.
• Why do you want your students to keep portfolios?
• What will you say to students and parents about your goals?

Portfolios need to be accessible.
• Establish a central place in your classroom for keeping portfolios.

Class time allocated for portfolio work is time well spent.
• Students need guidance in labeling and choosing.
• Sharing samples of student work in class is important.
• Students need guidance in being reflective.

A table of contents is essential.

The criteria you identify for judging students' portfolios reflect your goals and values.
• What categories of mathematical tasks will you require be included?
• Will you require examples of both draft and revised work?
• Will you require written reflections?
• Will you put grades on the portfolios? If so, how?

FIGURE 4-12   Tips for getting started with portfolios.

Words and numbers are of equal value,
for, in the cloak of knowledge,
one is warp and the other woof.
It is no more important to count the sands
Then it is to name the stars.

FIGURE 4-13   An idea to engage students in writing about numbers. (Source: From *The Phantom Tollbooth* by Norton Juster. Text copyright © 1961 by Norton Juster. Text copyright renewed 1989 by Norton Juster. Reprinted by permission of Random House Children's Books, a division of Random House, Inc.)

A simple way to begin is to ask students to write about what they did or did not understand for one assignment, how they felt about an activity, what they learned today in class, or what they like about mathematics. Your creativity in providing suggestions will help spark theirs. For example, you might ask them to write a letter to a friend about math class or to write a poem about triangles. As writing becomes a part of math class, you can use it to assess children's knowledge of and attitudes toward mathematics. Figure 4-14 provides some sample ideas for writing prompts.

Teacher-Designed Written Tests

Tests can inform and guide your instruction, rather than simply determine grades. Students learn from tests, but too often the lessons they learn may not be those intended. When too much emphasis is placed on written tests, students can learn that they do not have to know why some procedure

Describe an activity our class might do to help us understand how big one million really is.

Let's play teacher! You want to teach some first graders how to subtract two-digit numbers. Give examples of the problems and materials you will use. Tell what you will say and what you will have the children do.

Audrey claims that her teacher could improve the average test score in the class by 10 points if she just added 10 points to everyone's score. Kelly doesn't believe that would work. What do you think? Explain your thinking.

Which decimal is closer to one-half, 0.307 or 0.32? How do you know? Explain how you could show or prove it.

What connections are there between fractions and decimals? Explain and use examples in your explanation.

FIGURE 4-14   Sample writing prompts for having children explain their understanding of mathematical concepts.

works, to explain how they solved a problem, or to be able to solve word problems because a passing grade may be obtained without ever doing these things.

Carefully constructed and correctly analyzed tests can tell us a lot about students. For example, the children's papers in Figure 4-15 are for a simple test on subtraction of two-digit numbers, but they reveal a lot about the students. Notice how many of them missed the problems with zeros. If the first or seventh item had not been on the test, the teacher might not have realized that Jim regroups—and then ignores—even when regrouping is not necessary. (Try analyzing the kinds of errors the other students made and what characterizes each student.)

Most paper-and-pencil tests do not give you the opportunity to learn how a student arrived at an answer. One way to gain more insight is to ask the students to explain in writing what they did. If children are accustomed to explaining orally in class, then this task will be easier for them, and you will receive more meaningful explanations. Ask for explanations on a few items, and accept them in the children's language. Otherwise, they will soon learn to parrot explanations that are meaningless to them.

There is no reason why paper-and-pencil tests cannot include estimation items and require manipulatives and calculators. Tests can also permit the use of textbooks or notebooks, ask thought-provoking questions, and require students to connect new learnings to previous ones. They need not be races against time in which the students

FIGURE 4-15 Samples of children's papers for a written test of subtraction.

regurgitate all they remember from the week or about the procedure last taught.

Thoughtful, well-constructed tests are one way—often a very efficient way—to gather information. Alone, they do not give a complete assessment of students' knowledge, but they can add one more piece to the puzzle.

Standardized Achievement Tests

At some point you will undoubtedly be asked to administer standardized or statewide tests. The results of these tests may be used to take a look at your students' achievements in general. For exam-

ple, if you see that your students did poorly in measurement, then you need to rethink what you are doing in that area. If student test results come back late in the year at your school, you might ask to see the results from the previous year for students in your class. Sometimes this information can provide valuable insight into what areas of study need extra work this year.

Remember that norm-referenced tests are designed to spread children across the whole normal distribution. There will always be 50 percent of the students below average and 50 percent above average. Thus some items on such tests are not intended for everyone at a grade level to answer correctly. The fact that an item on multiplying fractions appears on a fourth-grade test does not necessarily mean that this is a recommended skill for all students at this level. Refer to your school, district, or state curriculum framework or standards for expectations for your grade level.

As mentioned earlier in this chapter, standardized tests are changing. Some allow the use of calculators; some ask questions in an open format rather than multiple-choice format; some ask for explanations; and some include problem-solving situations. Be sure your students are familiar with the format of whatever standardized tests they are required to take. In addition, you should strive to help your students learn mathematics in ways that are meaningful to them and that help build their confidence and the attitude that they can do mathematics. These are some of the best ways to ensure that your students will be able to show what they know on standardized achievement tests.

Keeping Records and Communicating about Assessments

It is important to keep both informal and formal records of students' learning and their disposition toward mathematics. Certain types of recordkeeping may be required by your school system, but you can always keep additional records of your own.

A word of caution: Do not become burdened with a multitude of records, but keep enough that you can reflect on your students' progress and can justify any major decisions about them or what to teach. The type of records you keep also will depend on the ways you report information to students, parents, and the school administration.

Recording the Information

Teachers are aware of many things about their students and keep many informal records about them. For example, you may know from daily interactions that Treena is always willing to answer in math class, that Joshua does not work well with Katrina, that Yong knows how to compute but seems to lack understanding about when and why certain operations are used, and that Cary is often absent on math test days. But maybe you need to jog your memory about Rachel before her parents come for the next parent conference. Or maybe you are thinking about changing the composition of cooperative groups and wondering if Jerry and Richard worked well together in the past.

Because of the volume of information about students that may be useful, it is often helpful as well as necessary to record some of it. Several techniques for recording information are described here. You may find others or modify these to suit your needs.

Checklists Checklists may be used in a variety of ways to record individualized information about students' understandings, attitudes, or content achievement. They may be simply lists that are marked in different ways, rating scales, or annotated checklists (see Figures 4-16 through 4-19). The beauty of checklists is that they can be adapted to your situation and, in fact, may help you think about your goals and the needs of each child you are teaching.

MATH CLASS PARTICIPATION									
	Center A	Center B	Center C	Group Leader	Group Recorder	Group Reporter	Bulletin Board	Materials	Other
NAME DATE: March									
Atkins, Willie	2	4	6	5	13	10	✓	✓	mCounts
Bero, Chuck	9	10	11	10	5			March	
Connel, Brenda	2	3	5			10		✓	
Coroi, Troy	11	10	9	5		13	✓	March	mCounts
Cosby, Kim	11			5		13	✓		

FIGURE 4-16 Checklist of student participation: useful for tracking which children need to be encouraged to participate, and in which activities or roles. For example, Brenda has worked at math centers and has been responsible for materials. She may need encouragement to become a group leader or group recorder.

CLASS OBSERVATION Class 5th period		Week Feb. 6-10/13-17		
NAMES	COMMENTS		ACTION NEEDED	TAKEN
Atkins, Willie			
Bero, Chuck	Needs a challenge	*	Yes
Connel, Brenda			
Coroi, Troy			
Cosby, Kim	No homework for 3 days	*	Called

FIGURE 4-17   Annotated class observation checklist: provides teacher with reminders of points to discuss when communicating with parents and students.

You cannot spend all your time keeping records, so select a few significant aspects of students' learning and attitudes and target a few children each day. For example, you may want to observe and keep records about children working in cooperative groups one week and the next week focus on individual children's understanding of a new topic.

If you use a checklist, you will want to keep it handy so that you can make quick entries as children are engaged in tasks. If you wait until the end of the day, you may forget some of the day's gems or be too preoccupied with other tasks to jot them down.

If you are recording information that is meant only for you, keep the checklist away from the eyes of your students. Be especially sensitive to children's feelings. A public checklist that shows the progress of each class member's skill attainment may be a great boost for those at the top but detrimental to those at the bottom, who often need the most encouragement.

Student Files   Many teachers keep a record of students' learning in the form of a file of work samples from each child. If children are keeping their own portfolios, those may suffice, and you will not need to keep additional samples of their work in your own student files. In either case, you may want to keep a summary profile for each child, like the one shown in Figure 4-19. Sometimes the school's format for reporting to parents requires that you keep such a record.

Class Records   Often, the only class record is the grade book. Although it may be necessary to keep such a record, you must realize the limitations of a grade book. Alternatively, you could modify it with shorthand entries of your choosing to tell you more than attendance; grades on assignments, quizzes, and tests; and cumulative grades.

You could also supplement the grade book with a cumulative checklist made from your daily or weekly checklists. You can determine which items to include by reviewing the usefulness and fre-

STUDENT DISPOSITIONS	Helen	Art	Whit	Beverly	Anita	Jim
CLASS: 3rd Grade Math MONTH: October						
Confidence Is sure of answer Knows how to proceed	✓ ✓			✓ ✓		
Flexibility Will change direction Tries several ways	If prodded ✓		✓ ✓		✓	
Perseverance Stays with task Enjoys involved problems	✓	✓		✓		
Curiosity Wants to find out why Challenges		✓	✓ ✓			✓
Sharing Works well with others Shows leadership		✓		✓		✓

FIGURE 4-18   Checklist of students' dispositions. The checklist is helpful in deciding which students might need special activities or encouragement, or as information to inform conferences with parents or students.

```
┌─────────────────────────────────────────────────────────────────────────┐
│                    Student Profile in Mathematics K–4                     │
│  Date_Feb.___                                                             │
│  Student_Jeremy Gelder_____   Teacher_Matt Bell_____   Grade_2___  │
│                                                                           │
│  Content Areas                                                            │
│     Number Sense & Numeration  Still sees numbers as ones – needs to      │
│                                develop place value                        │
│     Estimation    Good feel for numbers – size of quantities             │
│     Concepts of Operations Good problem solver                            │
│     Computation                                                           │
│     Geometry & Spatial Sense Geometry he loves                            │
│     Measurement                                                           │
│     Statistics & Probability                                              │
│     Fractions & Decimals                                                  │
│     Patterns & Relationships  Better at spatial patterns                  │
│  Math Power                                                               │
│     Problem Solving    Likes to think in creative ways                   │
│     Reasoning                                                             │
│     Communication    Explains well                                        │
│     Connections                                                           │
│     Concepts    Developing                                                │
│     Procedures  Doesn't like to follow procedures – invents his own       │
│  Dispositions                                                             │
│     Confidence    Growing                                                 │
│     Flexibility                                                           │
│     Perseverance  On many tasks                                           │
│     Curiosity    Great                                                    │
│     Reflection                                                            │
│  Other Comments                                                           │
│                                                                           │
└─────────────────────────────────────────────────────────────────────────┘
```

FIGURE 4-19   Sample student profile.

quency of your entries in these earlier checklists. The cumulative checklist will then give you a picture of the class as a whole and help you plan.

Communicating the Information

Most teachers have three main audiences to whom the information they have gathered will be communicated: students, parents or guardians, and administration. Each group will receive different amounts of information in different ways.

To Students   Much of your communication of information to students will be done orally or through actions, but also you will be writing comments on work samples, portfolios, tests, journals, or other forms of assessment materials. You may give a letter or number grade. All of these communications influence children's feelings about the value of different aspects of mathematics, their expectations of what they can accomplish, and their sense of their own worth.

Be positive and fair. Use information from your checklists or from student portfolios when letting each student know whether he or she is meeting expectations, and look for ways to demonstrate to each that he or she can do what is expected. Finally, remember that it is important that children grow in their ability to self-assess. One of your goals should be to help children become independent learners. If they always have to rely on you to validate their work and their thinking, they will not reach this goal.

To Parents or Guardians   You will be reporting to parents or guardians both in written form and orally. The format of these reports is often determined by the school system, but you are responsible for the quality. You will grow in your ability to communicate with parents, but it is important from the beginning that you keep records and use them to illustrate or justify your oral and written comments. Phone calls can be useful for immediate feedback to parents not only when there is a problem, but also to applaud good behavior or outstanding achievement. Parents and children are often surprised and gratified when a teacher calls home to report something good. Some teachers try to make good calls

Dear Parents,

Your child will be developing a "portfolio" in math class this year. One of the primary purposes of this project is to allow students the opportunity to reflect on their work, including exemplary work, work that is considered a "personal best," or work that they feel is in some way memorable. Through this project, students can begin to develop critical self-evaluative tools that will be extremely valuable in the years ahead.

A second purpose of the portfolio project is to allow students to share some of their work with you. Please take some time this week to discuss your child's portfolio with him or her. Your child has been given written guidelines for the portfolio project. Please review the guidelines together.

Please help your child this week as he or she finalizes selections for the portfolio. There is no set number of pieces required, but a selection of 5 or 6 pieces is suggested. Help your child select pieces that best meet the guidelines and that are *most* representative of the major math content areas that we have covered during this grading period. The attached "News Bulletin" from this grading period may provide you with a better idea of the topics your child has studied and the activities he or she has participated in. Students have been asked to provide written accounts about *why* they chose particular pieces for their portfolios, so be sure to talk with your child about why he or she is choosing each piece for inclusion in the portfolio. (If you wish, you too may include some written comments about the pieces selected or the selection process.)

After you have read the "News Bulletin" and have helped your child with his or her portfolio selections, please sign and detach the form below. Your child is to return the signed form, along with his or her portfolio, by Friday, November 15.

Thank you for helping to make your child's mathematical experience a memorable one!

Sincerely,

_____

I have read and discussed the "News Bulletin" with my child and have helped him or her select choice pieces for his or her portfolio. _____

FIGURE 4-20   Letter to parents about math portfolios.

home to all students early in the year. This practice can set up good relationships with parents and establish the expectation that a teacher phone call need not necessarily mean bad news. Some teachers use regular newsletters to keep parents informed about classroom activities and goals or letters to parents to tell them about special events or request their help. With today's broad access to e-mail, many teachers use that form of communication to maintain contact with parents. (Figure 4-20 shows a letter one teacher sent to parents to enlist their assistance in developing and maintaining their children's math portfolios.)

At parent conferences, you have an opportunity to explain goals for your instruction and to enlist parents' aid in helping their child meet those goals. It is helpful if you have collected a wide variety of samples of student work to share with the parents as you talk about their child's progress. Parent conferences are also times for gathering information. Parents often provide insights about their children that may not be evident to you in the classroom. The information you glean from them should be included in notes in your student files.

To the School Administration   When you begin teaching, you will need to find out what types of records and grades are required in your school and how they are used:

- What sort of report card format is used? A/B/C letter grades? S/I/N (satisfactory, improving, needs improvement) progress indicators? Numeric grades? Narrative reports?

- Does the administration expect written reports on each child?

- Is there an official checklist?

- Is the class grade record sufficient?

- Is information on students passed to the next teacher, kept in a permanent file, or used to make tracking decisions?

- Is the information used in teacher evaluations?

The type and use of records vary from school to school, so it is necessary to find out about your own situation. When you know how the records are to be used, you will be better able to provide information that is suitable for particular uses.

Cultural Connections

Ever since the early 1970s, when the U.S. government began documenting the mathematics achievement of American children through the National Assessment of Educational Progress (NAEP), certain groups of students have consistently been shown to lag behind other groups. In particular, black and Hispanic students generally have lower NAEP scores than white students. Socioeconomic status (SES) has generally been a reasonable predictor of achievement as well (Strutchens et al., 2004). It is well known that, on average, students in poverty tend to have lower test scores than students who come from affluent backgrounds.

One way that each student's performance on the NAEP mathematics assessment is reported is by assigning it an achievement level (either basic, proficient, or advanced). In 2000, most students were judged basic. In fact, only slightly more than 25% of all students at the fourth- or eighth-grade levels were judged either proficient or advanced. However, the performance of black and Hispanic students was markedly weaker, with only 5–6% of the blacks, and only 10% of the Hispanics receiving scores judged proficient or higher.

Both students who take the NAEP tests, and their teachers, complete questionnaires about classroom practices that offer us glimpses into what goes on in our nation's schools. In many cases, the NAEP questionnaire data indicate that students of all racial, cultural, and socioeconomic status have similar school experiences across the nation. However, the data also reveal certain interesting (and rather disturbing) differences.

In particular, NAEP questionnaire data, combined with NAEP assessment data, can offer insights into how mathematics assessments and instruction often differs in American classrooms depending on the race, ethnicity, or social class of that classroom's students. For example, from the 2000 NAEP we discover that multiple-choice testing has been increasing in American classrooms over the past decade, and that it is increasing more for students of color and of poverty.

> The percentage of students whose teachers reported using multiple-choice assessments once or twice a month increased between 1992 and 2000 from 49 to 60 for 4th graders and 34 to 44 for 8th graders. This increase could be a result of teachers preparing their students to take state-mandated multiple-choice tests. However, the percentages vary widely by race. In 2000, more teachers of black (70%) and Hispanic (69%) 4th graders than white (56%) 4th graders reported assessing their students with multiple-choice tests at least monthly. The disparities were even larger at the 8th-grade level, where 63% of black students, 53% of Hispanic students, and 38% of white students were assessed with multiple-choice tests at least once monthly. Students who qualified for free or reduced-price lunch were more likely to be assessed with multiple-choice tests than their higher SES counterparts within each race/ethnicity group. However, an analysis of race/ethnicity and SES together reveals that even high-SES black and Hispanic students were assessed with multiple-choice tests more than average white students. . . . Hence SES differences between black and white students do not account for the black–white disparities in multiple-choice testing. (Strutchens et al., 2004, pp. 286–287)

If certain portions of the school population are being tested with multiple-choice assessments more frequently in recent years than others, what effect does this have on their ability to think, reason, and perform on higher-level assessments? NAEP can also help us answer this question, because NAEP includes not only multiple-choice tasks, but also short constructed-response tasks (where students must write in their own answers), and extended constructed-response tasks (where students must not only write answers, but also must provide an explanation of their reasoning). In 2000, white students performed considerably better than black or Hispanic students on each of the three NAEP item types; however, "score differences related to the extended constructed-response items were most dramatic" (Strutchens et al., 2004, p. 300). Similar score differences were found when comparing students by economic condition. These findings have led some researchers to hypothesize that schools enrolling large numbers of students of color or students in poverty may be "plagued by a 'pedagogy of poverty,' which is characterized by instruction that is very directive, controlling, and debilitating for students (Haberman, 1991). The pedagogy of poverty often does not lead to students' developing critical-thinking or problem-solving skills" (Strutchens et al., p. 301).

Your goal, as a teacher, must be to help ALL students develop high levels of problem-solving ability and conceptual understanding, as well as robust procedural skills. The findings cited above from the National Assessment of Educational Progress help us gain appreciation for the inequities that can result when teachers treat students differently according to their racial, ethnic, cultural, or socioeconomic backgrounds.

A Glance at Where We've Been

Assessment is an integral part of teaching. It should "support the learning of important mathematics and provide useful information to teachers and students" (NCTM, 2000, p. 22). Assessments *of* learning (summative assessments) are primarily designed to document what students know and are able to do. Final exams, and state and national standardized tests are familiar examples of assessments *of* learning.

Assessments *for* learning (formative assessments) help teachers make informed decisions about the varied aspects of their day-to-day work: planning instruction, making instructional decisions, monitoring student progress, and evaluating student achievement. The assessment process itself has four phases: planning the assessment, gathering data, interpreting the data, and using the results to plan further instruction.

There are many methods used to gather, analyze, and present the information from assessments, whether the assessments are focused on student learning or on students' dispositions (attitudes and beliefs) toward mathematics. In the classroom, these methods include informal observations, interviewing, peer assessments, portfolios, writing, testing, and many other methods. For many forms of assessment, rubrics or scoring guidelines provide a framework for examing the information collected.

Assessment information needs to be recorded in ways that make it easy to analyze and use. There are numerous techniques for recording and communicating information. Portfolios, in particular, can provide a broad and useful picture of student progress and show growth over time.

Assessment can make a difference in how you help your students learn mathematics. You can use it in a positive way to encourage the children to become independent learners, to modify your instruction, and to communicate with parents and others with an interest in students' achievement.

Things to Do: From What You've Read

1. Make a list of as many assessment-related concepts and terms as you can think of (e.g., *achievement, portfolio, observation, conference, test*). Draw a concept map to show how these ideas are related to one another in your mind.

2. Explain the difference between assessment *of* learning (summative assessment) and assessment *for* learning (formative assessment), and give two examples of each.

3. Identify, and briefly describe, each of the four phases of assessment.

4. Which of the recommendations for shifts in assessment (Table 4-1) have you experienced in your own years as a student? Briefly describe when and how. Which of the shifts are most closely connected to the classroom? How are they connected?

5. A narrow view is that assessment in mathematics focuses on how well students can carry out procedures in a limited amount of time. Describe a broader view of mathematics assessment.

6. Write a "letter to self" similar to that shown in Figure 4-8. In your letter you should reflect on your current strengths and weaknesses, as well as your future goals as a teacher of elementary school mathematics.

7. Try scoring the papers in Figure 4-9 using the analytic scoring scheme shown in Figure 4-10. Compare your scores with those shown in Table 4-2. Be prepared to justify the scores you give.

8. List three ideas for keeping records of your observations of students as they work during class.

9. What sorts of assessment records would be good to keep to assist with a parent–teacher conference? What other ways can you communicate with parents about their children's progress?

Things to Do: Going Beyond This Book

IN THE FIELD

1. * *Analytic/Holistic Problem Solving Scoring.* Collect a set of problem-solving papers from students. Analyze and score them using the analytic scale in Figure 4-10.

---

* Additional activities, suggestions, and questions are provided in *Teaching Elementary Mathematics: A Resource for Field Experiences* (Wiley, 2007).

2. *Observing Students in Class.* Observe one or two students during a mathematics class. Describe what you observed. If you were to work with these students in mathematics, what course of action would you take?

3. *Performance Task.* Try a performance task with a couple of students. Make a list of observations and use it as the basis for your description of the children's performance. You may find samples in *Measuring Up: Prototypes for Mathematics Assessment* (Mathematical Sciences Education Board, 1993) or *Mathematics Assessment: A Practical Handbook for Grades 3–5* (Stenmark and Bush, 2001).

4. Talk to one or more classroom teachers about how they grade their students in math. Ask what sorts of tasks are figured into the grade and how they are weighted. Ask to see the teacher's gradebook so you can understand what sorts of records it includes. Find out what other records the teacher keeps (e.g., folders, portfolios, notes).

IN YOUR JOURNAL

5. Defend your position on this statement: Students' work on tests provides the most accurate assessment of their mathematical understanding.

6. Will student use of calculators interfere with assessing their understanding of mathematics? Explain your decision on this issue.

7. Which assessment practices do you think provide the best evidence of children's understanding of mathematics? Explain why you like these particular practices.

WITH ADDITIONAL RESOURCES

8. Read a teacher-authored article about assessment from one of these books listed in the Annotated Resources section (Bush, 2001, or Lambdin et al., 1996, or Webb, 1993). Write a brief summary of the article, followed by your own reflection about two good points in the article and one point that you disagree with or that you think could have been improved.

9. Analyze a test in an elementary mathematics textbook. Would it make a difference if the students used calculators? What items would you need to change?

10. Analyze a test in an elementary mathematics textbook to determine whether it requires writing about mathematics. If not, what changes could you make so that it would do so? What other changes could you make to the test so that it would be more authentic?

11. Examine a standardized test. Does it allow use of calculators? Identify examples of good and poor questions, and explain your opinions.

12. Many teachers use cooperative learning methods during instruction but face the problem of aligning assessment techniques with that instruction. Read the article by Kroll, Masingila, and Mau (1992), which describes methods to include cooperative problem solving in assessment and offers suggestions for choosing appropriate problems and incorporating aspects of both individual and group grading. Identify a math problem that you think would be useful as a group problem-solving assessment and design a scoring guide for assessing student work on it, adapting Kroll et al.'s suggestions.

WITH TECHNOLOGY

13. Visit the Web site of the Nation's Reportcard (nces.ed.gov/nationsreportcard/), which offers public access to test items from the National Assessment for Educational Progress (NAEP), as well as state and national performance data from years of administration of this test. Search for fourth-grade mathematics test items in a content area of your choice (e.g., number or algebra or geometry). Identify an item that was easy for most students, and another item that was difficult for many students. Write a paragraph about each item, offering your reasoning about why the difficulty level of these items was different.

14. Design an assessment that you could give to students to assess their understanding regarding order of operations using a calculator.

15. Create problems that you might ask on a test where the capabilities of the calculator do not simply give the students the answer.

16. Many state departments of education post sample items from their statewide assessments on their Web sites. Check the web site for your state and obtain an example of an open-ended item. Then examine and discuss the rubric that is provided.

Note to Instructors: You can find additional resources, learning activities, and black-line masters in this text's accompanying Instructor's Manual at www.wiley.com/college/reys.

Book Nook for Children

Cohen, M. *First Grade Takes a Test.* New York: Dell Publishing, 1980.

This is the story of a first grade class that takes a special test. When the teacher gives the test,

Sammy, Jim, and George can't find the correct answers to some of the questions. Classmate Anna Marie has no trouble finding the answers and she is eventually moved to a special class. The first grade class is sad without Anna Marie. Eventually, Anna Marie returns and tells the class she has missed them. But is getting the highest score that important? This book prompts teachers to consider how children think when given a test.

Finchler, J. *Testing Miss Malarkey*. New York: Scholastic, 2000.

This is the story of a class and how upset everyone is—including the teacher and principal—over The Instructional Performance Through Understanding test. See how things change as teacher and students prepare for the test.

Murphy, S. *Pepper's Journal*. New York: Harper-Collins, 2000.

Joey and Lisa keep a journal on their new cat, Pepper, for 1 year. This book will help provide students insights into how a journal is kept and may offer them a good introduction to journal writing. There are activities in the back of the book for teachers and parents.

Prelutsky, J., and Smith, L. *Dr. Seuss Hooray for Diffendoofer Day!* New York: Random House, 1998.

This is the story of a school with a very diverse faculty, who teach in a wide variety of ways. Then, one day, the principal brings in a test for everyone to take. The students are worried, but the teacher reminds them that they know everything that is on the test, plus more. The principal tells them that all students from miles and miles around will be taking this test to see who is learning and what school is the best. If the school doesn't do well, the school will be torn down and they will have to attend a school that only teaches and behaves in one way for all students. At the end, the school does very well and everyone passes the test. Readers see that everyone learns differently and people can learn by doing things differently.

◀ Annotated Resources

Bush, W. S. *Mathematics Asssessment: Cases and Discussion Questions for Grades K–5*. Reston, VA: NCTM, 2001.
One of the best ways to learn about assessment and make changes in practices is through work with other teachers.

This book provides a glimpse into the assessment experiences of 13 elementary school teachers of mathematics around the continent and offers helpful hints to lead groups of teachers in discussions about the cases.

Cooney, T. J., Sanchez, W. B., and Ice, N. F. "Interpreting teacher's movement toward reform in mathematics assessment." *Mathematics Educator*, 11(1) (Winter 2001), pp. 10–14.
Discusses calls for change in educational reform in mathematics education. Describes one approach to systemic assessment reform in a large suburban county. Presents teacher reactions toward the projects.

Glanfield, F., Stenmark, J. K., and Bush, W. S. *Mathematics Assessment: A Practical Handbook for Grades K–2*. Reston, VA: NCTM, 2001.
The ideas in this book are great starting points for thinking about assessment. Readers will find advice about getting started with assessment, selecting, developing and managing assessment tools, and using the results. Samples of good assessment tasks, scoring rubrics, checklists, observation forms, and sources for tasks and more literature are also included.

Kloosterman, P. W., and Lester, F. K. (eds.). *Results and Interpretations of the 1990 through 2000 Mathematics Assessment of the National Assessment of Educational Progress*. Reston, VA: NCTM, 2004.
Often referred to as "The Nation's Report Card," the mathematics assessments of the National Assessment of Educational Progress (NAEP) have come to be regarded by many policy makers as the primary yardstick by which to judge American schools' success in meeting national expectations. This monograph reports and interprets trends in NAEP mathematics data collected between 1990 and 2000.

Lambdin, D. V., Kehle, P. E., and Preston, R. V. (eds.). *Emphasis on Assessment: Readings from NCTM's School-Based Journals*. Reston, VA: NCTM, 1996.
This collection of 30 articles on assessment selected from NCTM's journals is organized into four sections: rationale for change, testing and grading, alternative assessment options, and evaluation of teacher effectiveness. The book also includes annotated bibliographies on assessment for elementary and middle school teachers, for secondary teachers, and from the *Journal for Research in Mathematics Education*.

Moon, J., and Schulman, L. *Finding the Connections: Linking Assessment, Instruction, and Curriculum in Elementary Mathematics*. Portsmouth, NH: Heinemann, 1995.
Classroom practices in grades K–6 provide a model for integrating assessment with instruction, ideas for communicating with parents, students, and administrators, and guided opportunities to practice and reflect on the assessment process.

Stenmark, J. K., and Bush, W. S. *Mathematics Assessment: A Practical Handbook for Grades 3–5*. Reston, VA: NCTM, 2001.
A rich collection of examples, reflections, explanations, and "Tips from Teachers" helps teachers explore the role of assessment in reshaping mathematics teaching and learning. The book includes advice about getting started with assessment, selecting, developing, and managing assessment tools, and using the results. It also includes samples of good assessment tasks, scoring rubrics, checklists, and observation forms that may be copied for classroom use.

Webb, N. L. *Assessment in the Mathematics Classroom* (1993 Yearbook). Reston, VA: NCTM, 1993.
A collection of 27 articles on assessment, all of which have clear implications for classroom practices.

CHAPTER 5

Processes of Doing Mathematics

Snapshot of a Lesson

Key Ideas

Doing mathematics involves

1. Posing and solving problems, both purely mathematical and from the real world

2. Looking for patterns, formulating conjectures, and gathering data to prove or disprove them

3. Talking about mathematical ideas and using a variety of representations

Background

This lesson is adapted from a true classroom story described in more detail in the book *Mathematics in the Making* by Heidi Mills, Timothy O'Keefe, and David Whitin, 1996.

Janelle is a second grader in a colorful, lively, classroom. The desks are arranged in groups of four, although the children typically spend a good portion of each day working at various learning centers around the classroom—an art center, a pet center, and a reading corner with a cozy rug and comfy pillows. A significant amount of time is also spent on mathematical problem solving. Janelle and her classmates are often actively engaged in interactive, investigative activities, many of which grow out of questions they bring up themselves.

One day Janelle was proudly showing her new size 2 sport shoes to everyone. When she was chatting with Elizabeth, she noticed that they were approximately the same height. "You're just about the same size as me," she observed, "What size shoe do you wear?" "Two," Elizabeth responded. "So do I!" said Janelle, "I wonder if people who are the same size always have the same shoe size?"

Janelle and Elizabeth shared this thought with their teacher, Mrs. Lester. They were familiar with posing questions and figuring out how to investigate them. They were eager to poll their classmates to see whether their idea about shoes and heights was right. Janelle designed a recording sheet by borrowing a class list from the teacher and copying everyone's name onto the page. She drew two boxes next to each name—one for height and the other for shoe size.

Elizabeth and Janelle recruited Alex to help them go around the classroom asking people about their shoe sizes and their heights. Janelle was the recorder. It wasn't hard to figure out shoe sizes because if their classmates didn't know, they just took off their shoe and looked inside. But very few of the children knew how tall they were, so most of the boxes for height had to be left blank.

Janelle, Elizabeth, and Alex sat on the floor by the reading corner and looked at their data. "Hey, you know what? I just thought of something," said

Alex. "I was thinking about who is big and who is small in our class, even if we don't really know exactly how big they are. Some of the biggest kids in the class have shoe sizes that are smaller than some of the smaller kids. Something doesn't make sense here!"

"Who do you mean?" asked Elizabeth.

"Well, Mac is one of the biggest kids, but he only wears size $3\frac{1}{2}$. Chantal wears size 12, but she's smaller than Mac," said Alex.

"Maybe boys' and girls' shoes come in different sizes," Janelle suggested.

Even Mrs. Lester didn't know for sure if that was true, but this idea led Janelle, Elizabeth, and Alex to try comparing the heights and shoe sizes of girls and boys separately.

Elizabeth made a new recording sheet (Figure 5-1). She wrote boys' names on the left and girls' names on the right and put shoe sizes next to the names. She and Janelle looked on the list for two girls or two boys with the same shoe sizes. She

Photo: David Young-Wolff/Photo Edit

planned to ask them to stand back to back to see whether they were the same height. The students had decided that they didn't have to bother with finding a way to measure heights because they could just compare people directly. (Note that they were now investigating a new statement: If you have the same shoe size, then you are the same height—rather than the converse—if you're the same height, you have the same shoe size, which they had started out with.)

James and Nicky had the same shoe size on the chart, so Janelle drew a line to connect those two names. But when James and Nicky stood back to back, they were not the same size. Janelle decided to note this by scribbling over the line connecting their names. Janelle also connected Brian's and Nick's names with a scribbly line because they were different heights, even though they wore the same size shoes. She used smooth lines to mark pairs of students who matched both in shoe size and in height (e.g., Janelle and Elizabeth). Figure 5-1 shows what Elizabeth's recording sheet might have looked like when she was only partway through her analysis—after having compared the heights of some of the boys with same-sized shoes, and some of girls with same-sized shoes, but before comparing the heights and shoe sizes of boys with girls. Elizabeth's recording sheet may look confusing at first glance, but it provides an accurate picture of how Elizabeth and Janelle were actually thinking about their data and the problem they had chosen to explore.

Janelle, Elizabeth, and Alex were *doing mathematics*. They were involved in observing apparent patterns and regularities, formulating conjectures,

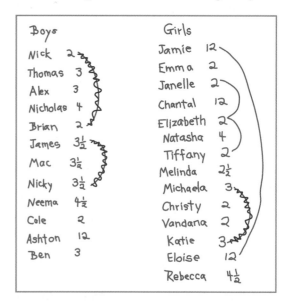

FIGURE 5-1   Elizabeth's recording sheet.

gathering data, talking with their peers and with their teacher about their ideas, and inventing ways to represent their findings. Their work involved the fundamental mathematical processes that this chapter is all about: problem solving, reasoning and proof, communication, connections, and representations.

Introduction

As we have seen in earlier chapters, school mathematics is moving in new directions. Now, in many mathematics classrooms, it is rare for a lesson to be taught to rows of children studiously bent over worksheets, practicing computations, rules, and formulas. Instead, it is more common to observe children first working in small groups while talking and using tiles or blocks to model a problem, then moving to their desks to write individually about what they have discovered, and finally engaging in a whole-class discussion about what has been learned. Students are encouraged to share their ideas, observations, and problem-solving processes. They listen carefully to each other, and they challenge and question each other.

In doing mathematics, students are actively involved in a wide variety of physical and mental actions—actions that can be described by verbs such as *exploring, investigating, patterning, experimenting, modeling, conjecturing,* and *verifying.* Doing mathematics is learning mathematics.

The *Principles and Standards for School Mathematics* (NCTM, 2000) highlight this active vision of learning and doing mathematics by identifying the five process standards listed in Table 5-1 (problem solving, reasoning and proof, communication, connections, and representations). These process standards share equal billing with the five content standards (i.e., number, algebra, geometry, measurement, and data). The NCTM *Standards* make it clear that doing mathematics means engaging in these fundamental processes. This chapter provides a brief introduction to these five important processes for doing and making sense of matheamtics. (In Chapter 6, we give additional attention to problem solving as a foundation on which the entire mathematics curriculum can be organized.)

FOCUS QUESTIONS

1. What five processes are identified in *Principles and Standards for School Mathematics* as key to an active vision of learning and doing mathematics?

2. How is teaching mathematics through problem solving different from simply teaching students to solve problems?

3. For young children, what does mathematical reasoning involve and how does it help them make sense of mathematical knowledge and relationships?

4. How can elementary children be encouraged to communicate their mathematical thinking?

5. What connections are important to aid elementary children in learning mathematics?

6. What are three major goals for representation as a process in elementary school mathematics?

Math Links 5.1

*R*ead more about the five process standards by choosing from the left-hand menu of NCTM's index to *Principles and Standards for School Mathematics* on the web at http://standards.nctm.org/document/chapter3/index.htm or link from this book's Web site.

Math Links 5.2

A variety of Web resources for each Process Standard that may be used by teachers and children may be found at NCTM's Illuminations Web site. It may be accessed from http://illuminations.nctm.org/swr/index.asp or from this book's Web site.

www.wiley.com/college/reys

Problem Solving

What comes to mind when you think of problem solving? Some people think of challenging situations they may have encountered in real life, such as when their car got stuck in a snow bank, and they were unable to get it out until they put floor mats under the wheels to provide greater traction. Similarly, when you think of problem solving in the mathematics classroom, you may think of challenging situations involving numbers or shapes or patterns. For example, a state official may need to figure out how many distinct license plates can be produced if each must be printed with a unique identifier consisting of exactly six characters. Perhaps the characters may be chosen only from among the 10 numeric digits (0–9) and 25 of the 26 letters of the alphabet (with the letter *O*

Table 5-1 • Process Standards for School Mathematics (NCTM, 2000)

Problem Solving	Instructional programs from pre-K through grade 12 should enable all students to: • Build new mathematical knowledge through problem solving. • Solve problems that arise in mathematics and in other contexts. • Apply and adapt a variety of appropriate strategies to solve problems. • Monitor and reflect on the process of mathematical problem solving.
Reasoning and Proof	Instructional programs from pre-K through grade 12 should enable all students to: • Recognize reasoning and proof as fundamental aspects of mathematics. • Make and investigate mathematical conjectures. • Develop and evaluate mathematical arguments and proofs. • Select and use various types of reasoning and methods of proof.
Communication	Instructional programs from pre-K through grade 12 should enable all students to: • Organize and consolidate their mathematical thinking through communication. • Communicate their mathematical thinking coherently and clearly to peers, teachers, and others. • Analyze and evaluate the mathematical thinking and strategies of others. • Use the language of mathematics to express mathematical ideas precisely.
Connections	Instructional programs from pre-K through grade 12 should enable all students to: • Recognize and use connections among mathematical ideas. • Understand how mathematical ideas interconnect and build on one another to produce a coherent whole. • Recognize and apply mathematics in contexts outside of mathematics.
Representation	Instructional programs from pre-K through grade 12 should enable all students to: • Create and use representation to organize, record, and communicate mathematical ideas. • Select, apply, and translate among mathematical representations to solve problems. • Use representations to model and interpret physical, social, and mathematical phenomena.

excluded because it can be confused with the numeral zero). How many different license plates are possible? That's a problem! In the opening snapshot, Elizabeth, Janelle, and Alex tried to figure out how shoe size and height are related. That's a problem too!

Alternately, when you think of mathematical problem solving you may remember the story problems or word problems that often came at the end of each chapter of the mathematics text when

you were in elementary school. After you had learned to perform certain computations (say, multiplication of fractions), your text may have provided problems in context that used those same skills. In many cases, these may not have been genuine problems for you because the techniques to use had been clearly outlined in the preceding pages.

Problem solving, as envisioned by the NCTM *Standards*, is much more than just finding answers to lists of exercises. Problem solving is a "major means of developing mathematical knowledge" (NCTM, 2000, p. 116). By general agreement, a problem is a situation in which a person wants something and does not know immediately what to do to get it. Problem solving is the foundation of all mathematical activity. As such, problem solving should play a prominent role in the elementary school mathematics curriculum. The children in the Snapshot of a Lesson identified a problem in which they were interested—whether children who are the same height wear the same shoe size. They probably also were, implicitly, thinking that taller children would wear larger shoes. Yet as they collected data, they discovered that Chantal with a shoe size of 12 was shorter than Mac, who wore a size $3\frac{1}{2}$ shoe. Typical of young children, they exhibited flexibility with their problem statement, shifting their problem to whether children with the same shoe size were the same height. This new problem caused them to adapt their data collection strategy for solving the problem. Although there

was no computing involved, these children were certainly "doing mathematics."

Consider a different type of problem, actually a game that can be played by children in upper elementary grades. To investigate this particular problem, you will need to play the game with one or more opponents. You'll need two dice, 12 small chips or tiles or markers each, and a piece of paper on which to make a game board for each person (see In the Classroom 5-1).

Place your chips on the game board, putting as many or as few as you like on each of the 12 numbered spaces. (For example, you might choose to put all your chips on your favorite number, 4. Or you could put one chip on each space. Or you might put two chips on each of the even spaces and leave all the odd spaces empty. It's your decision.) Roll the dice. Say you get 3 and 5. Find the sum $(3 + 5 = 8)$. If you have any chips on the 8 space, you may remove one of them. When anyone rolls, everyone plays, so your opponents should also be removing a chip from the 8 space on their

---

In the Classroom 5-1

ROLLING THE DICE

OBJECTIVE: Using a dice game to investigate experimental and theoretical probabilities and to develop analytical reasoning skills.

GRADE LEVEL: 3–6

MATERIALS: Twelve counters or chips for each player, one pair of dice for each four players.

RULES OF THE GAME

Up to four players can play together with one pair of dice. Each player has his/her own game board. You begin by placing all 12 of your counters on your game board. The game board has 12 spaces numbered 1–12. You may place as many counters as you choose (from 0 to 12) on each space. You may leave spaces blank, and you may put one or more than one counter on any space.

Players take turns rolling the dice. The fist player rolls the two dice and finds their sum. (For example, if 2 and 3 are rolled, the sum is 5.) Each player may remove one counter from his or her 5 space. Even if there is more than one counter on that space, only one may be removed. If there are no counters on that space, no counters may be removed from any space. The next player rolls the two dice and finds their sum (e.g., $4 + 4 = 8$). Each player now removes one counter from his/her 8 space, and so on. The goal of the game is to empty your board. The first player with no counters left on his/her board is the winner.

ANALYZING THE GAME

When you have played several times, talk with each other about these questions:

- Which sums were rolled most often?
- Which sums were never rolled, or not rolled very often?
- Why do you think some sums came up more often than others?
- Can you prove which sums are most likely to occur?
- What do you think is a good strategy for placing your counters on the game board? Why?

WRITING ABOUT THE GAME

Write advice to a friend who is new to the game. Tell him or her your favorite strategy for placing counters on the game board, and explain why you believe this strategy is a good one.

ROLLING THE DICE GAME BOARD

boards, if they can. Roll the dice again, sum the results, and remove another chip. The goal of the game is to be the first person to remove all your chips from your board. Try the entire game a couple of times before reading on.

Here's the problem: Find a good strategy for placing your chips at the start of this game, so that you are more likely to be able to clear your board quickly. Which squares are good to avoid? Are there certain sums that rarely (or never) came up when you rolled the pair of dice? Why? Which squares are good to put chips on? Are there certain sums that came up rather often? Why? Can you explain why some sums are more likely than others?

A fourth-grade class played this game several times, worked on the problem of finding a useful game strategy, talked about what they discovered, and then wrote about their findings. See Figure 5-2 for what some of the children wrote.

What I learned was that when playing with two dice your best odds are with seven. And when you see a pattern, go with it sometimes, not all the time.

If you bett on something you allways bett on a seven. Never on a one, tow, three, four, five, six, eight, nine ten, elven, or trelv.

That number seven is the best number to beat on not to [two] or twelve if you go to a cuceno [casino] you should no [know] that.

FIGURE 5-2 Fourth-grade student's writing about playing the dice game.

In a classroom where mathematics is taught through problem solving, students given the challenge of the dice game might already have had previous experiences with making organized lists or making tables. Nevertheless, their teacher would *not* have provided them with advice about exactly how to solve the problem if he or she wanted this to be a true problem-solving challenge. A reasonable approach is to begin experimenting by playing a few games. It is helpful to keep a list of the sums obtained when the dice are rolled. If you don't keep a list, it may be hard to be sure which sums come up more often than others. Haphazard experimentation is not likely to produce a good, well-justified solution. Solving this problem requires students to think logically and to make some important decisions, particularly about how to keep track in a systematic way of the sums that come up. (Perhaps even better is keeping track of the pairs of dice that lead to those sums; writing down $5 + 2 = 7$ is more informative than just writing 7, since 7 could be obtained in several different ways.) A skill such as making an organized list or a table can be useful in a wide variety of problem situations.

When you roll two dice, you are much more likely to roll a sum of 7 than a sum of 3, since there are only two ways to get 3 ($1 + 2$ and $2 + 1$), but there are many more ways to get 7. As this problem helps develop general problem-solving expertise, it also deepens students' understanding of probability (helping them to recognize that we can compare the likelihood of rolling various sums by seeing how many ways those sums can be formed). The probability of rolling a 7 is actually $\frac{6}{36}$, whereas the probability of rolling a 3 is only $\frac{2}{36}$ (refer to Figure 5-3 to see two ways of representing the 36 different possible sums: $1 + 1$, $1 + 2$, ..., all the way up to $6 + 6$). Students who work on this problem are learning about probability *through* problem solving. They are also developing and using a strategy for playing a game that can be used to solve other problems in mathematics, as well as in other contexts.

What kinds of problems are appropriate for elementary school students? In the early grades, most school mathematics problems are related in some way to the children's own experiences, as in the Snapshot of a Lesson, because their world is relatively circumscribed and children relate best to concrete situations. By upper elementary, however, the universe of problem contexts should diversify. Increasingly, problems can grow out of situations in the world at large or from the investigation of mathematical ideas. Mathematics instruction in the upper grades can take advantage of the increasing

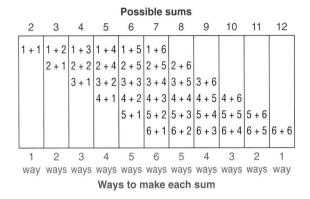

Possible sums

2	3	4	5	6	7	8	9	10	11	12
1 + 1	1 + 2	1 + 3	1 + 4	1 + 5	1 + 6					
	2 + 1	2 + 2	2 + 4	2 + 5	2 + 5	2 + 6				
		3 + 1	3 + 2	3 + 3	3 + 4	3 + 5	3 + 6			
			4 + 1	4 + 2	4 + 3	4 + 4	4 + 5	4 + 6		
				5 + 1	5 + 2	5 + 3	5 + 4	5 + 5	5 + 6	
					6 + 1	6 + 2	6 + 3	6 + 4	6 + 5	6 + 6
1 way	2 ways	3 ways	4 ways	5 ways	6 ways	5 ways	4 ways	3 ways	2 ways	1 way

Ways to make each sum

+	1	2	3	4	5	6
1	2	3	4	5	6	7
2	3	4	5	6	7	8
3	4	5	6	7	8	9
4	5	6	7	8	9	10
5	6	7	8	9	10	11
6	7	8	9	10	11	12

FIGURE 5-3 Two tables show the number of ways to get each possible sum when rolling the dice.

sophistication of students and their growing knowledge of such topics as probability, statistics, and geometry.

Upper elementary students can deal with messier and more complex problems than primary children can, not only because they are more capable and confident in working with mathematical ideas than younger children, but also because they can use technology to alleviate much of the drudgery that—until recently—often constrained school mathematics to considering problems with "nice numbers." Computers, calculators, and electronic data-gathering devices such as calculator-based laboratories (CBLs) and calculator-based rangers (CBRs) provide simpler methods for gathering and analyzing data that in years past might have been considered too much trouble. Similarly, classroom Internet connections make it possible for students to look up facts and figures quickly and easily for use in posing and solving a wide variety of real-world problems. Graphing calculators and easy-to-use computer software enable students to move effortlessly between different representations of problem data. They can also compute with large quantities of data and with "messy" numbers, both large and small, with relative ease. As a result, problems in the elementary school can and should be responsive to student questions and interests.

This discussion about problem solving as one of the five fundamental processes for school mathe-matics has described the general nature of problem solving and briefly considered the types of problems that may be appropriate for elementary school students. However, the most important point is that problem solving can serve as a foundation for all mathematics teaching because problem solving also involves students in work with all the other fundamental processes of doing mathematics (reasoning, communicating, connecting, and representing). Problem solving is a way of teaching and learning. This means it involves more than the presentation of word problems; it involves the way you encourage children to approach mathematical learning. A situation is posed, as in a word problem, and then there is a search for a resolution. But the situation that is posed often has a mathematical basis beyond the application of some procedures. Students or the teacher may pose the problem. In either case, using problems as a jumping-off point for mathematics instruction involves the teacher in posing questions that provoke student thought and also in encouraging students to pose their own questions. Using problem solving as a foundation for mathematics instruction requires students to engage in a search for a reasonable solution or solutions.

One group of researchers proposes that

> Students should be allowed to make the subject problematic . . . allowing students to wonder why things are, to inquire, to search for solutions, and to resolve incongruities. It means that both curriculum and instruction should begin with problems, dilemmas, and questions for students. (Hiebert et al., 1997a)

Franke and Carey (1997) are among those who have begun the process of documenting the changes in children's perceptions about mathematics when they are taught in an environment reflecting the spirit of the NCTM *Standards*. They write about students who have been involved in the Cognitively Guided Instruction (CGI) program. In the CGI model of instruction, the teacher poses a rich mathematical task. Students take time to work individually or in small groups to solve the problem and then share their approaches with each other. Students are encouraged to listen carefully to each other and to question each other about processes and strategies. The teacher's role is to choose appropriate tasks and to orchestrate the classroom discourse, using what he or she knows about the students' developmental level. A key aspect of CGI is the teacher's ability to analyze the children's thinking and to guide classroom problem solving accordingly. The CGI first graders studied by Franke and Carey (1997) "perceived of mathematics as a problem-solving endeavor in which many different strategies are considered viable and communicating mathematical thinking is an integral part of the task" (p. 8). In a study of another problem-centered mathematics program, after 2 years in the program third graders scored significantly higher on standardized measures of computational proficiency and conceptual understanding and held stronger beliefs about the importance of finding their own or different ways to solve problems than those in "textbook classes" (Wood and Sellers, 1996).

Problem solving has been the focus of numerous books, collections of materials, and research studies in recent years (e.g., Lester and Charles, 2003). Because it is so fundamental to teaching and learning mathematics, we have devoted another entire chapter to it in this textbook. Chapter 6 focuses on helping you probe deeper into questions such as the following:

- What is really involved in teaching mathematics through problem solving?

- What problem-solving strategies should be taught?

- How can problem solving be evaluated?

Reasoning and Proof

From their earliest experiences with mathematical challenges and problems, children should understand that they are expected to supply reasons for their arguments. The question "Why do you think so?" should be commonplace in the classroom. Teachers should not be the only ones asking, "Why?" Asking why comes naturally to small children. They should be encouraged to sustain their natural curiosity for justification as they share their mathematical ideas with each other. When children observe a pattern (e.g., whenever you add two odd numbers, the answer is even), they should be encouraged to ask why. One second grader used square tiles to represent and sort various numbers (see Figure 5-4) and then explained his reasoning as follows:

> All the even numbers are just rectangles because you can make them go two by two. But all the odd numbers can't. Odd numbers make rectangles with chimneys. If you put two rectangles with chimneys together, the new one doesn't have a chimney. So two odds makes an even.

If students are consistently expected to explore, question, conjecture, and justify their ideas, they learn that mathematics should make sense, rather than believing that mathematics is a set of arbitrary rules and formulas. This notion underlies NCTM's Reasoning and Proof process standard.

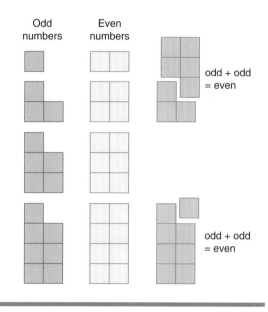

FIGURE 5-4   Pictures of odds and evens can help students justify why the sum of two odd numbers is always even.

Being able to reason mathematically is essential to making sense of mathematics and, ultimately, to justifying mathematical conjectures. Proof is often interpreted as a formal process, reserved for students in advanced mathematics. On the contrary, in the elementary classroom, clear articulation of one's reasoning is the goal because this serves as an important precursor to formal proof. Young children have limited experience with what constitutes a reasonable argument. To help them develop their reasoning powers, NCTM advocates posing problems that encourage children to examine, explain, and justify their own thinking—and the thinking of their peers. Children learn to reason by being encouraged to detect fallacies and to critique their own thinking and the thinking of others (NCTM, 2000).

Figure 5-5 shows two related problems used with a third-grade class to engage the children in logicial thinking, and in critiquing one another's reasoning (McGivney-Burelle, 2004/2005).

As soon as their teacher introduced the Playground Problem: Version A, children immediately raised their hands and began guessing how many boys and girls were on the playground. A variety of answers were proposed, but the most common suggestion was that there were probably an equal number of boys and girls on the playground. As one student explained, "Well, it has to be fair!" (Mc-Givney-Burelle, 2004/2005, p. 273). After further

Playground Problem, Version A

There are 10 children on a playground. Some of them are brothers and sisters. The oval represents the playground and the dots represent the children. The letters next to each dot represent the children's names.

Which of the children are brothers and sisters?

How many of the children are boys and how many of them are girls?

How many families are on the playground?

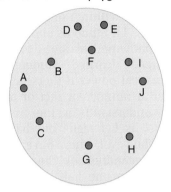

Playground Problem, Version B

There are 10 children on a playground. Some of them are brothers and sisters. The oval represents the playground and the dots represent the children. The letters next to each dot represent the children's names.

To help us out, each child on the playground will point to his or her sister. On paper, we will draw a red arrow to represent this. For example, if there is a red arrow leaving from C and pointing to B, then we know that B is a sister of C.

Which of the children are brothers and sisters?

How many of the children are boys and how many of them are girls?

How many families are on the playground?

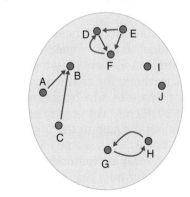

FIGURE 5-5 Two logical reasoning problems. [Source: Adapted from Jean M. McGivney-Burelle's "Connecting the Dots: Network Problems That Foster Mathematical Reasoning." *Teaching Children Mathematics* (December 2004/January 2005), pp.272–277. Reprinted with permission from *Teaching Children Mathematics*, copyright © 2004 by the National Council of Teachers of Mathematics]

discussion, however, some children recognized that there was not enough information given in Version A to determine how many boys and girls would be on the playground. Eventually the children convinced each other that, "it could be anything that adds to 10. There could be ten girls and no boys or 10 boys and no girls and anything in between" (McGivney-Burelle, 2004/2005, p. 273).

Their teacher then posed Playground Problem: Version B, which includes additional information. She helped them understand the new situation by examining a simpler problem first—asking two children to come forward to act as brother and sister. Marcus pointed to Jessica (pretending she was his sister), while Jessica left her arms by her sides. When Rosie joined them, representing another sister, the students figured out that Marcus should point to both girls, and the girls should point to each other. The children then broke into groups to discuss what could be concluded from the Playground Problem network with red arrows showing sister relationships. After some thought, they noted the following:

- Arrows from both A and C to B mean B must be a sister to both A and C. Because there are no arrows pointing to A or C, they must be brothers. So B must be a girl, while A and C must be boys.
- Arrows from E to D and from E to F mean D and F must be sisters of E, so D and F are girls. No arrows pointing toward E mean that E must be a boy.
- Mutual arrows between G and H mean they are sisters to each other, therefore both girls.

What about I and J? The children suggested it was impossible to determine their gender and thought they must be "only children."

"But why couldn't I and J be brothers?" a student wondered aloud. "I mean, since kids are only pointing to their sisters, couldn't it be that I and J are brothers and so there are no arrows between them?" After some discussion along these lines, the students concluded that it was impossible to infer the relationship between I and J. . . . The most definitive answers that the class could come to were that there were "*at least* five girls (B, D, F, G, H), *at least* three boys (A, C, E), and *at least* four families (ABC, DEF, GH, with I and J from either the same family or different families). Beyond that it was purely speculation. (McGivney-Burelle, 2004/2005, p. 275)

Reasoning and proof cannot be taught in a single unit or lesson; they must be consistent expectations throughout all units and lessons in all grades. "By developing ideas, exploring phenomena, justifying results, and using mathematical conjectures in all content areas and—with different expectations of sophistication—at all grade levels, students should see and expect that mathematics makes sense" (NCTM, 2000, p. 56).

But what must elementary teachers consider in order to promote an environment where children are nurtured and encouraged to make sense of mathematical ideas and thus develop their abilities to reason mathematically, providing proofs of mathematical conjectures? Russell (1999) identifies four important points about active mathematical reasoning in elementary school classrooms: (1) reasoning is about making generalizations, (2) reasoning leads to a web of generalizations, (3) reasoning leads to mathematical memory built on relationships, (4) learning through reasoning requires making mistakes and learning from them.

Reasoning Is About Making Generalizations

Mathematics is much more than just finding answers to specific problems or computations. Indeed, in today's world, machines can do much of the computational drudgery. Reasoning mathematically involves observing patterns, thinking about them, and justifying why they should be true in more than just individual instances. A simple example of mathematical reasoning occurs when a kindergartner, proud of his new-found ability to think about big numbers, eagerly challenges his mother by asking, "Do you know how much 2 trillion plus 3 trillion is? It's 5 trillion!" There is no doubt that this boy has never seen a trillion of anything, nor is he able to write numbers in the trillions. But he is familiar with the pattern in smaller cases (2 apples + 3 apples = 5 apples; 2 hundred + 3 hundred = 5 hundred), so he is able to generalize to adding trillions.

Russell (1999) offers another example of making generalizations in the story of Katie, a third grader who was working with a partner to find factor pairs for 120. Katie and her partner believed at first that 3×42 might be such a factor pair (a result obtained by incorrectly counting squares on a rectangular array on graph paper); however, Katie reasoned that answer must be incorrect because she remembered that 6×20 was a valid factor pair for 120, and from previous experience in finding factor pairs, she had figured out that if you halve one factor, you should double the other factor to keep the product the same. This is a powerful and useful generalization. Using this line of reasoning, Katie reported that the correct factor pair must be 3×40, not 3×42 because—thinking about 6×20—if 6 is halved to get 3, then 20 should be

doubled to get 40 to keep the product the same: $6 \times 20 = 3 \times 40$. When children go beyond specific instances of mathematical ideas to consider general cases, they are reasoning mathematically.

Reasoning Leads to a Web of Generalizations

A second point about mathematical reasoning is that it "leads to an interconnected web of mathematical knowledge within a mathematical domain" (Russell, 1999, p. 1). Students should expect newly encountered mathematical ideas to fit with ideas they have already learned. Students have much more mathematical power if they have many ways to think about a number or fact or assertion. Students might understand in the first grade that "three-quarters" is between "one-half dollar" and "one dollar"; however, they have a much more extensive understanding of the fact that three-quarters is between one half and one when they also understand this relationship in terms of fractions ($\frac{1}{2}, \frac{3}{4}, 1$), in terms of equivalent fractions ($\frac{2}{4}, \frac{3}{4}, \frac{4}{4}$), in terms of decimals (0.5, 0.75, and 1.00), and by visualizing pieces of a pie or portions of a collection of trading cards. When students incorrectly claim that 0.25 must be larger than 0.5 because 25 is more than 5, they apparently have not developed this robust web of connections for these ideas. They are unable to reason about the other meanings they may know for these two numbers, and are thereby unable to recognize the contradiction in their thinking.

Reasoning Leads to Mathematical Memory Built on Relationships

A third point about mathematical reasoning is that the development of a web of mathematical understandings is the foundation of what Russell calls *mathematical memory* (or mathematical sense), a capability that provides the basis for insight into mathematical problems. For example, consider the problem of finding the sum of the first 100 counting numbers: $1 + 2 + 3 + \ldots + 100$. Some time during your years of studying mathematics, you probably encountered a formula that would allow you to calculate the sum of any arithmetic series (a list of numbers where the difference between consecutive numbers is always the same—here, the difference is always just one). If you are like most people, you have long since forgotten that formula because it is not something that you use every day. On the other hand, if you have ever seen a geometric illustration of that formula, your web of mathematical understanding may be strong enough to help you reconstruct the formula with little trouble.

Picture the sum from 1 to 100 as a set of stairs. Picture another identical set of stairs. Turn the second set of stairs upside down on the first, and you have a rectangle (100 wide, 101 high). (See Figure 5-6 for a picture of a related, simpler problem: a 10-by-11 rectangle built from two staircases from 1 to 10.) It's easy to find the area of the 100-by-101 rectangle ($100 \times 101 = 10{,}100$). The sum you want is half of this (100×101 divided by 2, or 5,050) because the rectangle is made of two staircases instead of just the one original staircase. So $1 + 2 + 3 + \ldots + 100 = 100(101)/2$.

Using the same idea, you can figure out how to find the sum, S, from 1 to any number, n. It's just $S = n(n + 1)/2$. A similar line of reasoning can be used to find the sums for various other arithmetic series (such as $1 + 3 + 5 + \ldots + 175$ or $12 + 15 + 18 + \ldots + 639$). In other words, if you can connect the idea of summing numbers in a series with the geometric illustration of the dual staircases, you'll never again need to worry about forgetting the formula for the sum of an arithmetic series. (See an interesting article about second-graders' responses to the challenge of finding the sum of 1 through 10 after reading the story *Ten Black Dots* in Weinberg, 1996.)

Learning through Reasoning Requires Making Mistakes and Learning from Them

A final, important point about mathematical reasoning and proof is that one of the best ways to develop stronger reasoning and proof abilities is to study flawed or incorrect reasoning. There will be many times when your students think they've figured something out, but their reasoning just isn't quite right. That's just human nature. For example, a student might observe that you can make the problem $29 + 95$ easier to do mentally by adding 29 and 100, then subtracting 5 (obtaining the correct sum, 124). Can this same shortcut be used to make the problem 29×95 easier to do mentally (i.e., can you multiply 29 times 100, and then subtract 5)? It turns out that just isn't correct! Why? Rather than just tell your students that this doesn't work, it would be much better to help them investigate why the shortcut works for addition and why it does not work for multiplication. Some possible approaches would be to try adding and multiplying a wide variety of examples to try to figure out what is going on. Or it might help to represent the problems geometrically (using a 29-by-95 array to represent the multiplication and comparing it with a 29-by-100 array may offer some insights; see Figure 5-7).

Your role as a teacher is to encourage students constantly to examine their own thinking and the thinking of others, and to help them uncover and understand flawed reasoning when it occurs. For a collection of readings all focused on reasoning and proof in school mathematics, see Stiff (1999).

◆ Communication

Because language is a powerful tool for organizing thinking about mathematical ideas, it is extremely important for students to have many experiences with talking and writing about mathematics, describing and explaining their ideas. Conversely, it is also important that students often be on the receiving end of communications: hearing about, reading about, and listening to the descriptions and

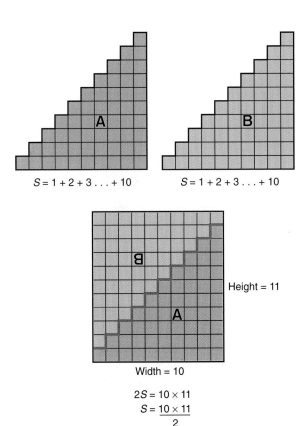

$S = 1 + 2 + 3 \ldots + 10$

$S = 1 + 2 + 3 \ldots + 10$

Height = 11

Width = 10

$2S = 10 \times 11$

$S = \dfrac{10 \times 11}{2}$

FIGURE 5-6 A 10-by-11 rectangle built with two staircases from 1 to 10 can help you remember the formula for the sum of a series of numbers.

FIGURE 5-7   Visualizing 29 × 95 and 29 × 100 helps students think about why
29 × 95 ≠ (29 × 100) − 5.

explanations of others. Two-way communication about mathematical ideas helps students identify, clarify, organize, articulate, and extend their thinking. Have you ever noticed how struggling to explain an idea helped you figure out what you were really thinking? Reflection and communication are intertwined. Sharing your ideas with others through talking or writing forces you to think more deeply about those ideas. Also, in thinking about your ideas, you often deepen your understanding and, consequently, are able to communicate even more clearly. Communication is obviously a process rather than an end in itself.

Students should be encouraged to communicate their mathematical thinking in a variety of modes: through pictures, gestures, graphs, charts, and symbols, as well as through words (both spoken and written). Figures 5-4, 5-5, 5-6, and 5-7 clearly illustrate the power of visuals in communicating about mathematics. Such nonverbal communication is often useful in promoting learning.

Math Links 5.3

*I*f you would like the opportunity to see a teacher facilitating children's communication, you can view the video clips *Teaching, Learning, and Communicating About Fractions* at the NCTM Illuminations Web site. At this site, reflection questions are also provided to help you focus your viewing. The videos may be accessed from http://illuminations.nctm.org/info/standards.asp (or from this book's Web site), by scrolling down to Grades 3-5 and selecting *Teaching, Learning, and Communicating About Fractions*.

Especially at first, students' efforts at communicating about mathematical ideas may be idiosyncratic (they may use symbols, expressions, or notations that they make up on their own), as Elizabeth did in the opening Snapshot of a Lesson. Angela Andrews, a teacher who has written a fascinating book about the problem-solving experiences of her kindergarteners, shares several examples of their naive uses of language and notation. For example, she reports that a student used the notation shown in Figure 5-8 to represent the number of scoops of rice needed to fill a certain bottle at the rice table. When she questioned him about his writing, he confidently reported, "Oh, that jar held $10\frac{1}{2}$ scoops, Teacher." His symbol for $10\frac{1}{2}$ was certainly not the standard representation, but it was effective in communicating his idea" (Andrews and Trafton, 2002, p. 94).

Over time, with more experience and practice, students learn to use conventional and more precise language to express their ideas. Indeed, mathematics as a language has a vocabulary, syntax, and symbolism all its own (cf. Perry and Adkins, 2002). Sometimes words or phrases used in everyday conversation may be used in mathematics with different, more precise, meanings. The symbolism of mathematics (particularly equations and graphs) often helps clarify concepts and promote understanding. Throughout their elementary school years, students should have daily opportunities for communicating about mathematical ideas. Gradually, they should be expected to incorporate more precise mathematical terms in their explanations.

Making writing a regular part of the mathematics curriculum provides students with opportunities to review, reiterate, and consolidate their thinking about mathematical ideas. One of the simplest yet most effective modes of writing about mathematics is open-ended writing as follow-up to a lesson. In response to the prompt "What did you learn today?" children will describe their activities and their understanding in a variety of ways. Wilde (1991) shares writing about a fraction lesson by Vilavanh, a fifth grader who was trying to explain her thoughts on comparing $\frac{1}{2}$ with $\frac{1}{8}$:

> When you do fractions you have to think what number is higher or lower that can equal a whole pizza. When you are splitting a pizza you have to think how many pieces will each person get. When you

have a number like this—$\frac{1}{2}$, $\frac{1}{8}$—the number that is higher has to give eight pieces to a person. You'll only have a little piece [with $\frac{1}{8}$]. The person who gets $\frac{1}{2}$ gets a bigger piece, gets a lot, because $\frac{1}{2}$ is bigger than $\frac{1}{8}$.

Vilavanh apparently is beginning to understand that a fraction with a larger denominator represents division into more pieces, and thus the pieces are smaller.

Mathematics journals can be used to prompt students to write about mathematics. The regularity of writing in a journal can help students monitor their own understanding of mathematical concepts. Students can be encouraged to write about such questions as "What am I puzzled about?" and "What mistakes do I make and why?" When teachers take time to respond to student journals on a regular basis, however briefly, the journals can become a regular chain of communication between student and teacher. Also, teachers can use students' writing diagnostically. When the writings of many students in a group or class reveal similar confusions or misconceptions, the teacher can more appropriately plan future lessons.

Other forms of writing in math class include having students write their own word problems, having them describe their solutions to problem-solving activities, having them describe a procedure or process, and writing about connections between and among ideas. Young children can be encouraged to use their own invented spelling, and all students can benefit by accompanying words with pictures and symbols so they can express themselves as fully and completely as possible.

Some useful references on writing and communication in mathematics classes include Azzolino (1990), Ciochine and Polivka (1997), Countryman (1992), Ford (1990), Van Zoest and Enyart (1998), and Wilde (1991). For a collection of readings all focused on communication in school mathematics, see Elliott (1996).

◆▷ Connections

Although mathematics is often represented as a list of topics or a collection of skills, this is a shallow view. Mathematics is actually a well-integrated domain of study. The ideas of school mathematics are richly connected. It is important for the elementary school curriculum to provide children with ongoing opportunities to experience and appreciate the connectedness of the subject.

FIGURE 5-8   Child's representation of $10\frac{1}{2}$ from Andrews and Trafton, 2002, p. 94.

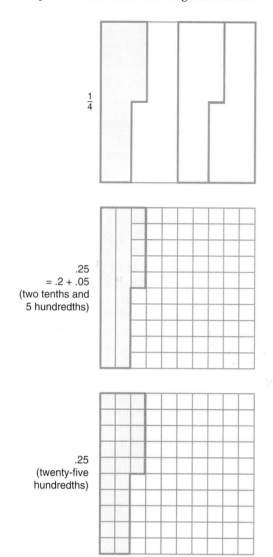

FIGURE 5-9 Some representations for one-fourth, ($\frac{1}{4}$,) 25 hundredths (0.25), and 2 tenths plus 5 hundredths (0.25 = 0.2 + 0.05) show that they are equivalent.

At least three types of connections are important in learning mathematics. First, ideas within mathematics itself are richly connected with one another. Students who learn about fractions, decimals, and percentages in isolation from one another miss an important opportunity to see the connections among these ideas. For example, in Figure 5-9, we can see why $\frac{1}{4}$, .25, and 2 tenths + 5 hundredths are actually all names for the same quantity.

A second important type of connection is between the symbols and procedures of mathematics and the conceptual ideas that the symbolism represents. For example, why do we refer to 3^2 as "3 squared"? 3^2 is 3×3, or 9. A drawing of 9 dots, arranged in a 3-by-3 array, forms a square. Simi-

larly, any array of *x*-by-*x* dots would form a square; thus students can recognize why x^2 is read as "*x* squared." The area of any geometric figure is generally reported in square units (e.g., square feet, square centimeters, square miles). Why? Because measuring area is actually just measuring how many "squares" it would take to cover a surface. If the squares are 1 inch on each side, then you are measuring in square inches. In fact, you can write "in.^{2}" instead of "square inches" for the same reason. So here we can *see* connections between number theory (the "square numbers" 4, 9, 16, etc., as shown in Figure 5-10), algebraic language (*x* squared), and measurement (square inches).

A third type of connection is between mathematics and the real world or between mathematics and other school subjects. For example, engaging students in problems as they occur naturally in the classroom or in the lives of the children often provides a totally natural connection to mathematics. For example, *our class has 24 students. Today 4 desks are empty. Tony, Melissa, and Gaby brought their lunches from home. Everyone else who is here today wants to buy the school lunch. How many orders for lunch should be sent to the office?* As children encounter problems from real-world contexts where mathematics is a significant part of the solution, students come to recognize and value the utility and relevance of the subject. Classroom instruction should also provide many opportunities for children to experience mathematics as found in domains such as science, business, home economics,

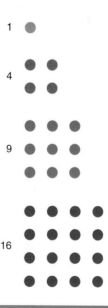

FIGURE 5-10 Arranging dots in square patterns connects the numbers 1, 4, 9, and 16 to their reference as square numbers.

social studies, literature, and art. Mathematical connections can be highlighted through integrated or thematic curricula, and through mathematics lessons motivated by situations in children's literature. The famous poet, Carl Sandburg (1960), wrote a poem entitled "Arithmetic" which included images such as "arithmetic is where numbers fly like pigeons in and out of your head" and "arithmetic is numbers you squeeze from your head to your hand to your pencil to your paper till you get the answer." After reading and discussing Sandburg's poem, children might write about their reactions, or brainstorm other aspects of mathematics (with examples), or they could even be prompted to write their own poems about mathematics after the style of Sandburg (focusing on their own views of arithmetic, or their own thoughts about other aspects of mathematics).

For a collection of readings all focused on connections in school mathematics, see House (1995).

Math Links 5.4

*T*o find many resources for connecting mathematics and other school subjects, visit the Education-World site, which can be accessed from http://www.education-world.com/a_curr/curr146.shtml or from this book's Web site.

www.wiley.com/college/reys

Representations

When most people think of mathematics, they may think of numbers such as 2, 29, or 5280, or of numeric or symbolic expressions such as 5×2, $(a + b)(a - b)$, or $5798 \div 13$, or of equations such as $x^2 + y^2 = r^2$ or $2x + 7 = 13$. Alternatively, they may think of tables of numbers or graphs or geometric figures. All are commonly used representations for mathematical ideas. Interestingly, it often is possible to use a variety of these different representations to illustrate the same mathematical ideas. Different representations for an idea can lead us to different ways of understanding and using that idea. This is the power of representation. Lesh and Landau (1983) identify five ways that many mathematical ideas can be represented—see Figure 5-11—and they emphasize that helping students become comfortable moving among these representations is an important goal of school mathematics.

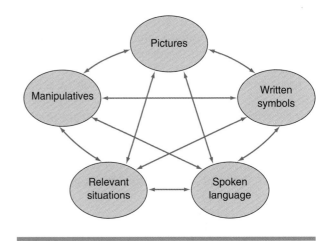

FIGURE 5-11   Five representations for mathematical ideas.   (Source: Adapted from Lesh and Landau, 1983, p. 271.)

The school mathematics curriculum has traditionally involved children in learning about a variety of representations for mathematical ideas; unfortunately, however, different representations have sometimes been learned in isolation from one another. Consider the following scenario (Clement, 2004, p. 97).

TEACHER: I will tell you a number, and you write it. Please write for me the number *one-half.*

STUDENT: [Writes $1\frac{1}{2}$.]

TEACHER: Please write for me the number *one and one-half.*

STUDENT: [Writes $1\frac{1}{2}$.] It is the same thing.

TEACHER: [Writes $\frac{1}{2}$ and points to it] What would you call this?

STUDENT: Half.

Lisa Clement (2004), who reported this scenario, suggests that even children who have a reasonable understanding of fractions as encountered in their everyday lives may not have made connections between those ideas and the language or symbolism traditionally used to represent them. "The connections children make between language and written symbols may be different from the connections adults make" (Clement, 2004, p. 97). Children often use the word "half" not "one-half" when they share in real life, for example, asking "can I have half your brownie?" As a result, when the teacher asks them to write "one-half," they may write "$1\frac{1}{2}$"— writing "1" to represent the "one" in "one-half" and writing "$\frac{1}{2}$" to represent the "half."

Similarly, students might learn about fractions in one chapter and decimals in another, but they also should be provided with opportunities to connect these two different representations for the same numbers. It is important to challenge students to connect, compare, and contrast the utility and power of different representations.

The NCTM *Standards* (2000) discuss three major goals for representation as a process in school mathematics: (1) creating and using representations to organize, record, and communicate mathematical ideas; (2) selecting, applying, and translating among representations to solve problems; and (3) using representations to model and interpret physical, social, and mathematical phenomena.

Creating and Using Representations

In the snapshot that opened this chapter, children were developing their own individual representations for organizing, recording, and communicating data about the heights and shoe sizes of their classmates. When they discovered that their initial recording sheet wasn't helpful in showing how heights and shoe sizes were related (or not related) and didn't help with sorting out boy–girl differences, they devised a new representation. It is important for young children to have repeated opportunities both to invent their own ways of recording and communicating mathematical ideas and to work with conventional representations. The mathematical symbols and representations that are used every day (e.g., base-ten notation, equations, graphs of various types) have been polished and refined over many centuries. When students come to understand them in deep ways, they have a set of tools that expands their capacity to think mathematically.

Selecting, Applying, and Translating Among Representations

As mentioned earlier, mathematical ideas can often be represented in different ways. Each of these representations may be appropriate for different purposes. For example, a student who can think flexibly about numbers is probably able to think about the number 24 in many different ways: 2 tens and 4 ones, 1 ten and 14 ones, a little less than 25, double 12, the perimeter of a square with side 6, the area of rectangles with sides 2 × 12 or 4 × 6, and so on. Depending on the problem at hand, some of these representations may be more useful than others. Technology now offers students many opportunities for experiences with translating among representations. Data analysis software can help students easily compare and contrast various graphical representations. It is important that students consider the kinds of data and questions for which the graphical representation is appropriate.

For example, Figure 5-12 shows the results when a class was asked to describe the heights of the students in the class.

The children recorded their heights in the appropriate rows in a spreadsheet and prepared three graphs: a bar graph, a circle graph, and a line graph. Which graph best represents the data collected? Children are used to being lined up by height. However, the circle graph does not order

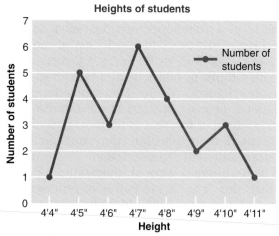

FIGURE 5-12   Which graph best represents the height of students in the class?

the heights as clearly as either the bar or line graph. The line graph incorrectly gives the impression that there are children of heights between the measurement points. On the other hand, the bar graph shows that the most common height of the children is 4 feet 7 inches and that the second most common height is 4 feet 5 inches.

Using Representations to Model and Interpret Phenomena

Much of mathematics involves simplifying problems—stripping away context and excess information to reduce the problem to symbols or representations that are easier to work with. This is mathematical modeling. For example, to solve the following word problem, you might reduce it to a picture or to a table of numbers:

> Alice is stacking soup cans for display on a shelf at the end of a supermarket aisle. She wants the display to look like a pyramid. On the top row she wants to put just one can, on the next-to-top row 3 cans, on the next row down 5 cans, and so on. Alice decides the display can be 6 rows high. How many cans should she start with on the bottom row?

Once you've made a picture or a table of numbers, the fact that the problem is about stacking soup cans is no longer really important. You've modeled the problem and used the power of mathematics to solve it. Similarly, when students ask, when solving word problems, "Do I add or do I subtract?" they are asking for advice about modeling the situation at hand. It is important to encourage students not to move too quickly and unthinkingly from real-world situations to abstract models. The best answer to the question about adding or subtracting is to ask, "What's going on in the problem?" or "Can you draw a picture or can you act it out to help you decide which operation to use?"

It is also important to check back at the end of solving a problem to ensure that the solution obtained from the mathematical model fits the original situation. A classic example is a problem where students are asked to determine how many buses are needed to take a group of children on a field trip. The problem tells how many students need to be transported (e.g., 130) and how many can fit in each bus (perhaps 40). Many students correctly pick out the numbers in the problem and divide ($130 \div 40$), but when the division doesn't come out evenly, they may offer decontextualized answers such as $3\frac{1}{4}$ or 3.25. They have forgotten to check back with the context of the problem, to see that a realistic answer would be 4 buses or perhaps 3 buses and a large van.

Math Links 5.5

Children can use electronic "virtual manipulatives" to model and solve problems. Visit the website of the National Library of Virtual Manipulatives (NLVM) to see a wide variety of such tools. For example, click on Virtual Library, then Algebra, and then the Towers of Hanoi to experiment with using a virtual manipulative to solve that problem. The NLVM is at http://nlvm.usu.edu/en/nav/index.html or can be accessed from this book's Web site.

www.wiley.com/college/reys

In sum, representations are ways of thinking about ideas. Individuals develop their own idiosyncratic ways of thinking, but mathematics offers a broad repertoire of conventional representations that are helpful in problem solving and in communicating about mathematical ideas (Lubinski and Otto, 2002; NCTM, 2001). One of the most important goals of mathematics instruction should be to help students build bridges from their own ways of thinking to the conventional, so that they come to understand, value, and use these powerful mathematical tools. For a collection of readings all focused on the roles of representation in school mathematics, see Cuoco (2001).

Cultural Connections

As we have seen in this chapter, NCTM's *Principles and Standards for School Mathematics* (2000) recommends classroom instruction that focuses on engaging students in learning mathematics through problem solving, communicating, reasoning, connecting, and using a variety of representations. While there can be no doubt that all students benefit from these sorts of experiences, special attention may be necessary to ensure that students whose first language is not English are genuinely included in classroom conversations and problem-solving activities. These students are sometimes referred to as learners of English as a second language (ESL) or learners of English as a new language (ENL).

Teachers involved in Project IMPACT (Increasing the Mathematical Power of All Children and Teachers)—an effort which focused on schoolwide reform in elementary schools in predominantly minority urban schools outside Washington D.C.—focused on establishing a mathematics culture in each classroom that encouraged "language, communication, mathematical content, mathematical connections, decision making, and equity"

(Campbell and Rowan, 1997, p. 60). In the Project IMPACT schools, an extremely high proportion of the student population either spoke some language other than English as their native tongue or came from a different cultural heritage. Prior to the start of Project IMPACT, teachers' response to this language and cultural diversity had been to strip away as much of the language and context from the mathematics curriculum as possible, in an effort to help make math lessons more accessible to the language minority students. This is a common first reaction to the challenge of teaching ENL or ESL learners. However, while this approach may help these learners acquire proficiency with computation and symbol manipulation, it unfortunately narrows their mathematics education to arithmetic only, stripping much of the challenge, beauty, and relevance from the mathematics curriculum and removing any focus on the process standards that we have discussed in this chapter.

Instead, the Project IMPACT teachers supported their students in using problem solving, reasoning, connections, and representations in their mathematics lessons by implementing a variety of helping strategies. They used mixed ability groups so that children could help each other with language challenges. They ensured that everyone understood problem contexts by encouraging students to talk through the word problems during whole-class sharing before going off to work individually, in pairs, or in small groups. They assigned buddies to help each other with language

FIGURE 5-13 Teacher Tips for Interactions in Diverse Classrooms, from Rubenstein, 1997, p. 220. Reprinted with permission from *Multicultural and Gender Equity in the Mathematic Classroom: The Gift of Diversity*, copyright 1997 by The National Council of Teachers of Mathematics

1. Use tools to help you communicate with students.
   a. Use manipulatives, pictures, contexts, stories, and drama.
   b. Write directions, key questions, terms, or ideas on chart paper, the chalkboard, or the overhead projector.
   c. Demonstrate (show, don't just tell) what you want students to do.
   d. If you use handouts, have students read the directions. Have them repeat them in their own words before following them. Check for understanding.
2. Listen to students. Don't assume you know what they will say.
3. Watch for clues that students are understanding.
   a. Use eye contact.
   b. Watch their facial expressions and other body language.
   c. Notice if they are asking one another to explain what you are saying.
   d. Ask them to say back to you what you have explained (directions, new ideas, etc.).
4. When students respond and you don't understand, try one of the following:
   a. Ask them to speak slower or use different words.
   b. Ask another student to explain what the first student said.
   c. Ask them to show what they mean by coming to the chalkboard, drawing a diagram, or using concrete materials.
   d. If appropriate, promise to speak personally with them later, then do so.
   e. Identify what you think you *do* understand and say it back to the student: "What I heard you say was that you have another method you'd like to use. But I'm not following your method. Please explain it again slower or show us at the board."
5. Use lesson openings and closings to your advantage (and your students'!).
   a. Begin by asking them where you left off yesterday or ask key questions to review what they should have learned. Ask more than one student to say what was learned in a different way. Listen to how they phrase things. Ask other students for corrections or modifications.
   b. Include a summary at the end of your lesson. Have students tell what they have learned. Listen to how they say it. As above, ask for other ways to express the new ideas.
6. Use guided practice in your lessons, as appropriate, for example, for skill development. "We'll do number 1 together." Then develop it with them. "Now, you do number 2." Give them an item just like the first, monitor them, and see how they do. In this way you get evidence of their learning, and you see which students understand and can be resources for explaining to others. Continue alternating between examples done together and those done by students individually or in pairs.

translation or with using concrete diagrams or materials to show their thinking. Figure 5-13 provides several additional teacher tips that are useful for all students, but particularly helpful when your class includes students with different language or cultural backgrounds.

Additionally, the Project IMPACT teachers worked together in grade-level teams to help and support each other with helping their ESL learners. The result of Project IMPACT was instruction that took account of "diversity in the children's racial-ethnic heritage and primary languages" at the same time that it supported mathematics instruction aligned with NCTM's process standards (Campbell and Rowan, 1997, p. 60).

◀◆ A Glance at Where We've Been

Learning and doing mathematics involves engaging in five key processes: problem solving, reasoning and proof, communication, connections, and representations. These processes are inextricably linked with each other and with the mathematics content that students learn (number, algebra, geometry, data, and measurement). Through these processes, students engage actively in making sense of the mathematics they are learning.

Problem solving requires that students be engaged in questions where the solution is not known, nor is easily identified. Good problems give students an opportunity to extend what they know, building their understanding of mathematical ideas. An important role for teachers is to select challenging problems, mathematics tasks, or opportunities that engage their students in the process of problem solving. Careful attention to establishing this environment will support students in enhancing their mathematical understanding.

Being able to reason mathematically is essential in order to make sense of mathematics and, ultimately, to justify or prove mathematical conjectures. To meet this challenge, children must be expected to supply reasons for their arguments from their earliest experiences with challenges and problems. Reasoning is about making generalizations and connecting new ideas with old to develop a web of mathematical understandings. Beginners' reasoning is often faulty, but that's OK. One of the best ways to help students develop stronger reasoning abilities is to encourage them to examine flawed arguments and to figure out where the thinking went wrong.

Communication provides a way for children to share their ideas with others. Their knowledge deepens as they help others understand their mathematical ideas and conjectures. Listening to the explanations of other children is equally important in the communication process. Two-way communication about mathematical ideas helps children identify, clarify, organize, articulate, and extend their thinking. Children need to be encouraged to present their ideas in a variety of modes (e.g., pictures, gestures, graphs, charts, and symbols) in addition to spoken and written words.

Connecting mathematical ideas helps children expand their understanding. At least three types of connections are important in learning mathematics: mathematics connected with other mathematical ideas; symbols connected to mathematical procedures; and mathematics extended and connected to contexts outside of mathematics. Teachers need to emphasize mathematical connections to encourage their students to routinely seek connections and to enjoy that search.

A variety of representations can be used to express the same mathematical idea: pictures, manipulatives, written symbols, relevant situations, and spoken language. The different representations lead to different ways of understanding and using that idea. Children should be encouraged to (1) create and use a variety of representations; (2) select, apply, and translate among representations to solve problems; and (3) use representations to model and interpret physical, social, and mathematical phenomena.

◀◆ Things to Do: From What You've Read

1. What are the five key mathematical processes described in this chapter? For each process, briefly describe how the classroom snapshot that opens this chapter shows children engaging in that process.

2. a. Solve this problem and clearly write up your solution: A programmer designed a new program that required the user to enter a three-character password in order to be recognized as a legal user. The first character must be a W or K. The second character must be a number: 1, 2, 3, 4, 5. The third character must be a symbol selected from $, %, *. How many possible passwords can be created for this program? What is the probability of guessing the password on the first try?

b. Describe your work on this problem considering each of the following:

- Problem Solving: Do you consider this task a problem? Why or why not?
- Reasoning and Proof: Did your solution provide proof that your solution is correct?
- Communication: How did you communicate your solution? Did you use multiple ways to explain your solution? Listen or read another student's solution to the problem. Was it communicated in the manner you communicated your solution?
- Connections: Connect this problem with another mathematical idea. Connect this problem with another problem outside of mathematics.
- Representations: Show a solution to the problem in more than one way. Describe how you used different representations in these ways.

3. Make a list of as many different representations for the number 75 as you can think of. Compare your list with the lists of others. You might use equivalent expressions, models, words, pictures, and so on. It is a sign of flexibility in thinking to be able to represent numbers and other mathematical ideas in many different ways.

4. What are the three distinct types of connections that are important in school mathematics? Give two examples of each type of connection.

5. Be prepared to name and discuss NCTM's Five Process Standards. Can you give an example of what each might involve in the classroom? Which of these processes are familiar from your own study of mathematics? Which of these have not been a part of your experiences in learning math?

Things to Do: Going Beyond This Book

IN THE FIELD

1. *Mathematical Processes.* Observe an elementary school classroom while children are engaged in a math lesson or investigation. Make a list of instances in which the children show evidence of using one or more of the five mathematical processes. Tell what the children were doing or saying and what tasks were involved. What role did the teacher play?

2. Plan a bulletin board focused on describing the five mathematical processes.

3. Check a textbook for evidence that students are encouraged to make connections.

4. *"Doing Math"?* Talk to one or more elementary teachers about their vision of what it means to "do mathematics." Ask whether they connect math to other areas of their curriculum and, if so, how. Write a reflection about how teachers' views of mathematics fit (or do not fit) with a view involving the five mathematical processes discussed in this chapter.

IN YOUR JOURNAL

5. Select a problem from a mathematics problem-solving text. Solve the problem. As you solve the problem, keep track of what you are doing in your journal. After you have finished solving the problem and recording your activities, summarize your actions in solving the problem.

6. Explain in your journal how you would plan to engage students in the five mathematical processes as you planned a unit.

WITH ADDITIONAL RESOURCES

7. Identify a journal article or book chapter about writing and communication in mathematics classes (e.g., you could choose Ciochine and Polivka, 1997, from the Annotated Resources list, or find a different article from one of the NCTM's teacher journals, *Teaching Children Mathematics* or *Mathematics Teaching in the Middle School*). Summarize the main ideas for supporting communication in the classroom.

8. Begin a resource folder for yourself that contains sections for each of the five mathematical processes. Collect and review recent articles in journals, such as *Teaching Children Mathematics*, to locate ideas that support the five mathematical processes.

WITH TECHNOLOGY

9. Obtain catalogs from software companies; select promising software to promote the five mathematical processes.

10. Write a review of a current mathematics software program that is used by children in a local elementary school. Explain how children are encouraged to incorporate the mathematical processes.

*Additional activities, suggestions, and questions are provided in *Teaching Elementary Mathematics: A Resource for Field Experiences* (Wiley 2007).

11. NCTM has created a Web site that "illuminates the new principles and standards." Your task is to visit the site (illuminations.nctm.org) and select the button called "i-math investigations." You need to select a particular grade level, pre-K-2, 3-5, 6-8, or 9-12. Select one of the elementary levels. Explore at least one of the ready-to-use, online, interactive, multimedia math investigations that illuminate the standards. Explain how they support children to engage in the five mathematical processes.

12. Collect some numerical data about children (e.g., height, arm span, hand span). Record the data in a spreadsheet and create at least three different charts. Describe which chart best represents the data.

Note to Instructors: You can find additional resources, learning activities, and black-line masters in this text's accompanying Instructor's Manual, at www.wiley.com/college/reys.

Book Nook for Children

Harness, C. *Ghosts of the White House.* New York: Scholastic, 1998.

This is the story of a class that takes a field trip to the White House. One girl, Sara, wishes that she could meet many of the presidents from the past. As Sara continues walking through the White House, many ghosts of the presidents come out and talk to Sara giving her information about the White House and themselves. This book is good for connecting graphs and time lines of historical data.

Nagda, A.W., and Bickel, C. *Tiger Math: Learning to Graph From a Baby Tiger.* New York: Scholastic, 2000.

This is the story of TJ, a Siberian tiger cub, who was born in the Denver Zoo. The book shows readers how TJ grew in inches and weight using four different types of graphs: picture graphs, circle graphs, bar graphs, and line graphs. This is a good book about representation. Readers will learn about the Siberian tigers too.

Schmandt-Besserat, D. *The History of Counting.* New York: Morrow Junior Books, 1999.

This resource book for students and teachers informs readers about how our number system was invented and how other cultures and societies invented their own number systems so they could be precise in counting. The author shows many different cultures in this book and also focuses on our modern decimal system and tells how it, too, evolved. The book was written by an archaeologist who took 20 years in authoring it.

Sciedzka, J. *Math Curse.* New York: Viking, 1995.

Mrs. Fibonacci has told her class, "You know, you can think of almost everything as a math problem." The Math Curse has begun. Suddenly the book's hero cannot look anywhere without thinking of math problem after math problem—in the closet, at the dinner table, on the bus. He is agitated until he realizes he can solve all the problems he sees. Encourage your students to solve the problems and then challenge them to find more math problems in their world.

Turner, P. *Among the Odds and Evens. A Tale of Adventure.* New York: Scholastic, 1999.

The Kingdom of Wontoo is visited by X and Y, two Adventurers that soon learn that there are two types of numbers: the Odds, which are eccentric, and the Evens, orderly and predictable. As the story unfolds, the reader will see how odd and even numbers are represented in a variety of pictures. The reader will also learn that adding two Evens or two Odds always result in an Even number. This book is a great start for algebraic reasoning for young students.

Annotated Resources

Andrews, A. G., and Trafton, P. R. *Little Kids—Powerful Problem Solvers: Math Stories from a Kindergarten Classroom.* Portsmouth, NH: Heinemann, 2002.
Arranged by months of the year, this collection of real-life stories of kindergartners investigating mathematical ideas shows how creative, thoughtful, and insightful young children can be. Angela Andrews' students truly focus on making sense of the problems they encounter, and in the process they estimate, predict, hypothesize, analyze, and apply a wide variety of mathematical concepts.

Ciochine, J. G., and Polivka, G. "The missing link? Writing in mathematics class!" *Mathematics Teaching in the Middle School*, 2 (March–April 1997), pp. 316–320.
Develop reasoning and communication skills through writing activities in your mathematics class. Children learn mathematics best by arguing about strategies and express-

ing opinions in a carefully written form. The forms of the writing include formal essays about mathematical problems, writing to prompts, or focused journal writing. Students learn to clarify, refine, and consolidate thinking.

Ducolon, C. K. "Quality literature as a springboard to problem solving." *Teaching Children Mathematics*, 6(7) (March 2000), pp. 442–447.

How can literature boost the processing skills and knowledge of elementary students? The book considers the importance of problem-solving skills in understanding mathematics, the creation of different levels of mathematical problem-solving questions by students, and the use of literature in the development of integrated curriculum in mathematics.

Mokros, J., Russell, S. J., and Economopoulos, K. *Beyond Arithmetic: Changing Mathematics in the Elementary Classroom*. Palo Alto, CA: NCTM, 1995.

Using examples from a wide variety of elementary classrooms, these authors describe their vision for school mathematics instruction that focuses on helping children make sense of problem-based lessons through reasoning, connec-

tions, communication, and representations (the NCTM process standards). Down-to-earth, readable, and practical, this book includes attention to teaching, curriculum, and assessment.

Schifter, D. *What's Happening in Math Class? Envisioning New Practices through Teacher Narratives*. New York: Teachers College Press, 1996.

Thirteen teacher-authors share their struggles and successes in attempting to reshape their teaching of mathematics along the lines of NCTM's recommendations. "Good teaching . . . is part art, part science. All too often in our writing we focus more on the skill and science, less on the sensory and art. These narratives help us redress that imbalance" (from the foreword by Suzanne Wilson).

Weinberg, S. "Going beyond ten black dots." *Teaching Children Mathematics*, 2 (March 1996), pp. 432–435.

Second graders' responses to finding the sum of the numbers from 1 through 10 after reading the book, *Ten Black Dots*. Includes student work that demonstrates their problem solving.

CHAPTER 6

Helping Children with Problem Solving

◆ Snapshot of a Lesson

Key Ideas

1. Working collaboratively to solve an unfamiliar problem
2. Looking for patterns and using representations in problem solving

Background

This lesson is based on the video *Valentine Exchange*, from Teaching Math: A Video Library, K-4 from Annenberg Media. Produced by WGBH Educational Foundation © 1995 WGBH. All rights reserved. To view the video, go to http://www.learner.org/resources/series32.html (video #42). Lilia Olivas is a fourth-grade bilingual teacher at an elementary school in Tucson, Arizona. The day after students exchange Valentine's Day cards in her classroom, Ms. Olivas poses a problem involving patterns and functions.

Ms. Olivas models a valentine exchange between herself and a student, Gina, at the front of the class. She asks the students how many valentines are exchanged if she gives Gina one valentine and, in turn, Gina gives Ms. Olivas one valentine. Another student, Chelsea, offers an explanation as to why the exchange involved two valentines.

MS. OLIVAS: What if I had three people exchange valentines?

STUDENT: You'll have six exchanges [*actually six valentines exchanged, from three exchanges*].

MS. OLIVAS: We'll have six exchanges? Will you show us how you came to that number, six?

In both English and Spanish, the class discusses whether or not there would indeed be a total of six valentines exhanged. One student asks why the number of valentines exchanged has to be six. To help students understand, Ms. Olivas models the exchange of valentines with two other students at the front of the class and finds there are six valentines exchanged. Ms. Olivas calls a third student to the front of the class and asks how many valentines are involved when four people exchange valentines with each other. They find that there are twelve.

In Spanish, Ms. Olivas poses a problem to the class: Figure out how many valentines would be exchanged in their class of 24 students if everyone gave everyone else a valentine. She asks the students to investigate this problem by working on their own, with a partner, or in small groups.

Ms. Olivas encourages students to use manipulative materials in solving this problem. One pair of students chooses to use cubes of different sizes to represent people and valentines. Another group uses stacks of pattern blocks. Students draw figures and tables on paper to keep track of the exchanges.

MS. OLIVAS: [*To camera*] The benefit is that you don't have a controlled situation. I'm not controlling their thinking. I'm allowing them to explore freely, to develop new ideas, to share, to reason, and that's what I want out of my students. I want them to be confident mathematical learners.

Ms. Olivas circulates around the classroom, listening to students, observing their work, and occasionally asking questions.

MS. OLIVAS: I'm looking at what Winston has here. What does this "24" mean?

WINSTON: [*Working in a group of three students*] 24 valentines.

MS. OLIVAS: And you each had a valentine? Twenty-four people? If you started making exchanges, would there be 24 exchanges?

SECOND STUDENT: [*In the same group of three*] This is how I did it. Two, four, six, eight, . . . twenty-four. [*The student counts by twos the number of cubes he has arranged to represent the valentines.*] Like, if you and Winston exchange, that's two. [*Points to the first two cubes and continues to explain that the two students in each pair exchange with each other. He then explains that you add them up to get 48 valentines exchanged. It seems he is thinking that the number of valentines exchanged will always be double the number of people involved, which is actually not true.*]

THIRD STUDENT: [*In the same group, questioning his teammate's solution*] Forty-eight is probably not the answer. I think it's much larger. [*He describes valentine exchanges that his teammate has left out.*]

MS. OLIVAS: [*To camera*] The questions that I concentrate on are questions that help them to think about what they are doing. I would ask something like, "Can you explain what these mean?" "Tell me your thinking." "Tell me how you're doing these things."

Ms. Olivas speaks with groups of students to discuss their thinking and the meaning of the manipulatives they are using. Students talk within their group and with the teacher about the mathematical meaning of the strategies they choose.

One student in the class develops his own approach to the problem. Instead of finding the number of valentines exchanged by 24 students, he works on a simpler problem first, focusing on 12 people making exchanges.

MS. OLIVAS: [*To camera*] There was a student that understood what was expected, then decided that he was going to do half of the problem. And even though the answer was not right, he knew where he was going. He knew there was a strategy involved. It was making sense to him.

Ms. Olivas calls the class back together to discuss their experiences as they worked on the valentine exchange problem. Many students offer their thoughts about the day's activity, including issues that confused or frustrated them and strategies they employed for solving the problem.

MS. OLIVAS: [*To camera*] The whole focus is, "How were you thinking about the problem? How are you making sense of the information you have on the table? How was it making a connection in your mind? What are you looking at as far as strategy building and problem solving?"

Introduction

Mathematical problem solving is a skill people need throughout their lives. In school, students must solve problems in order to understand mathematical concepts, discover new mathematical relationships, and make sense of connections between mathematics and other subjects. Both children and adults confront mathematical problems in their daily lives—as consumers, citizens, and workers.

A problem-solving approach can pervade the mathematics curriculum. Teachers can use problems to introduce new topics, to form threads that connect topics throughout instruction, and to ascertain whether children can apply what they have learned to new situations (Midgett and Trafton, 2001). The *Principles and Standards for School Mathematics* (NCTM, 2000) recommends that "instructional programs from prekindergarten through grade 12 should enable all students to

• build new mathematical knowledge through problem solving;

- solve problems that arise in mathematics and in other contexts;
- apply and adapt a variety of appropriate strategies to solve problems;
- monitor and reflect on the process of mathematical problem solving."

This chapter describes how elementary school teachers can support children's mathematical growth through problem solving. For example, children can build new mathematical knowledge by having concepts introduced through problems set in familiar contexts (e.g., sports, games, and everyday activities) or through problems involving a variety of representations (e.g., hundreds charts, fraction bars, and counting cubes). A strong mathematics program builds on the natural, informal problem-solving methods that the child has before entering school. Many of the best problems involve everyday situations—for example, first graders will relate to problems such as "How many more chairs will we need if we're having five visitors and two children are absent?" and "How many cookies will we need if everyone is to have two?" while fifth graders might be more interested in problems such as "Who has the higher batting average, Benny or Marianne?" or "Which of these dice games is a fair game?"

No matter what type of problem is involved, children who are effective problem solvers plan ahead when given the problem, ask themselves if what they are doing makes sense, adjust their problem-solving strategies when necessary, and look back afterwards to reflect on the reasonableness of their solution and their approach.

FOCUS QUESTIONS

1. What is the difference between solving problems and practicing exercises?

2. What does it mean to teach math through problem solving? What "signposts" for teaching guide this approach?

3. What types of problems can be used in teaching through problem solving?

4. What strategies for problem solving are helpful for elementary students?

5. Why is looking back such an important phase in problem solving? What questions should students learn to ask themselves when they are solving problems and reflecting on their solutions?

What Is a Problem and What Is Problem Solving?

A *problem* is something a person needs to figure out, something where the solution is not immediately obvious. Solving problems requires creative effort and higher-level thinking. If a child immediately sees how to get the answer to a problem, then it is not really a problem for that child.

Skill in solving problems comes through experiences with solving many problems of many different kinds. Children who have worked on many problems score higher on problem-solving tests than children who have worked on few. This chapter offers many suggestions for helping children become more proficient in mathematics through problem-solving experiences in the mathematics classroom.

As a teacher, you must be sure not to shield children from problem-solving challenges by assigning "problems" that really are just exercises. For example, a page in a traditional children's textbook (after children have been taught how to add large numbers) might begin with exercises such as

3194	5479	6754
5346	3477	8968
+8877	+6399	+7629

Next, there might be a story problem such as this one*:

(A) 7809 people watched television on Monday.

9060 people watched on Tuesday.

9924 people watched on Wednesday.

How many people watched in the 3 days?

But this story problem is merely an exercise with words around it, not a true problem. The only challenge is doing the computation. Sometimes tasks like this—which can be solved by applying a mathematical procedure in much the same way as it was learned—are called *routine problems* or exercises. Looked at this way, many traditional textbook word problems are routine problems. If the past week's work has been on addition, a textbook's routine word problems are typically solved by adding; if the topic has been division, then

---

*Solutions for the problems presented in this chapter may be found in the *Helping Children Learn Mathematics Instructor's Manual* (available at the Wiley Book Companion Web site, www.wiley.com/college/reys).

students can simply look for two numbers in the routine problems and divide. It is little wonder that children taught in this way flounder on tests or in the real world, where problems are not conveniently grouped by operation. By contrast, *nonroutine problems*—that is, true problems—generally require thinking because the mathematical procedures that children must use to solve them are not obvious. In the remainder of this chapter, when we refer to problems, we usually mean nonroutine problems.

Try the following nonroutine problem:

(B) Begin with the digits

1   2   3   4   5   6   7   8   9

Use each digit at least once, and form three four-digit numbers with the sum of 9636.

While solving this problem, children will get considerable practice in addition, but they will also have to try many possibilities. If they are thoughtful about applying previously learned mathematical ideas, they may be able to take a more efficient approach. For instance, 9636 has a 6 in the ones place, so students who know something about sums of odd numbers and sums of even numbers might realize that the numbers being added cannot all have an odd number in the ones place and cannot have just one odd number in the ones place, since these choices would result in an odd sum. The digits in the ones place could be all even or could be one even and two odd, since these choices would result in an even sum. Children who can add four-digit numbers have the knowledge required to solve this problem, but it is still a genuine problem because the solution is not immediately apparent.

Whether a problem is truly a problem or merely an exercise also depends on the person trying to solve it. For example, figuring out how to share 75¢ equally among three people is probably not a problem for you, but it probably would be a good problem for a second grader. What is a problem for Ann now may not be a problem for her in three weeks, and it may not be a problem now for Armando. The problems that you select for children must truly be problems for them in order to give them appropriate experiences in problem solving. Children who think they should always be able to solve problems immediately and easily are likely to view as impossible any problem where the solution is not immediately apparent, and they are unlikely to persist in working toward a solution. Finding the right level of challenge for students is not easy, but you can do it by trying out a range of problems, providing time, and encouraging students to explore many ways around obstacles.

Math Links 6.1

*T*he internet provides access to a wealth of problems. For example, take a look at the UMass-Dartmouth Math Contest site. It offers an Elementary Brain Teaser Contest for elementary and middle grade students. Archives of previous brain teasers are available, as well as a link to more problems via the White House Math Challenge. See http://www.umassd.edu/mathcontest/ or link from this book's Web site.

www.wiley.com/college/reys

You shouldn't underestimate children's abilities, as is illustrated by the following anecdote. Ms. Chewning, a teacher in Virginia, had been using a problem-solving approach to mathematics instruction with her second graders. She read in a newspaper about a problem that 40% of the nation's eighth graders had not been able to answer at even a basic level on a recent national mathematics test. She wondered how well her second graders could do with the following problem:

Jill needs to earn $45 for a class trip. She earns $2 each day on Mondays, Tuesdays, and Wednesdays. She earnes $3 each day on Thursdays, Fridays, and Saturdays. She does not work on Sundays. How many weeks will it take her to earn $45?

Ms. Chewning was delighted to find that

every single student attempted the problem, which was presented as optional. Such risk-takers they have become. Two students, using mental math only, presented me with the correct answer by the time I had completed writing the number story on the board. A total of 82% of the students, using a variety of strategies, successfully solved the problem in less than five minutes. Of the three students who struggled, two were right on track, making only minor computational errors, and the third achieved success after extensive trial and error. Needless to say, I was astounded. While I had expected them to be successful to some extent, I had not anticipated the speed and comfort with which they approached the task. (The University of Chicago School Mathematics Project, 2001, pp. 204–205)

Results from national assessments have shown that many American students have difficulty with problems that require analysis or thinking, though scores have been rising in recent years. Findings from the 2000 National Assessment of Educational Progress (NAEP)—which is administered at grades 4, 8, and 12—show an increase in the percentage of students performing at the proficient level in both fourth and eighth grade over the 10-year period from 1990–2000 (Kloosterman et al., 2004).

Fourth-grade students who perform at the proficient level are expected to consistently apply integrated procedural knowledge and conceptual understanding to problem solving in the five NAEP content strands.

Math Links 6.2

*Y*ou can view hundreds of released items from The National Assessment of Educational Progress (NAEP), along with data on student performance, by visiting The "nations reportcard" website maintained by The National Center for Education Statistics (NCES). It may be accessed from nces.ed.gov/nationsreportcard/ or from this book's Web site.

www.wiley.com/college/reys

American students have generally been found to be successful in solving routine one-step problems like those found in most textbooks, but to have more difficulty in solving multistep or nonroutine problems, particularly those that involve application of more than one arithmetic operation. The NAEP test includes some "extended-constructed-response" (ECR) items for which students must construct their own answers and provide an explanation of their solution. Students at all grade levels tend to have more difficulties with these ECR items than with multiple-choice items or "short-constructed-response" (SCR) items (where students must provide their own answers, but are not required to explain their solution). However, "with respect to SCR items administered in both 1992 and 2000, the percentages of 4th-grade students responding correctly increased significantly for 20 of the 25 common items, with no significant differences for the other 5 common items" (Arbaugh et al., 2004). American fourth graders' skill in solving routine word problems in subtraction has also improved since 1992, according to findings from the 2000 NAEP. Fourth graders' performance on word problems in multiplication was stable over the decade, but their performance on division-with-remainder word problems improved (Kloosterman et al., 2004).

Teaching Mathematics through Problem Solving

The primary goal of school mathematics instruction should be to ensure that students make sense of the mathematics they are learning, and we em-phasize this goal throughout this text. It is certainly important for students to learn—for example—how to subtract three-digit numbers or how to add fractions or how to compute the area of a circle, but this is not enough. Students must also learn to make sense of mathematical procedures and concepts, so that they will be able to remember them and to use them flexibly and appropriately in unfamiliar situations both during their school years and afterwards.

It may seem efficient to teach by telling students how to do things and then to have them practice until they are able to perform confidently, but this approach is actually not very effective. When children are told things, rather than figuring things out for themselves, they are less likely to remember them or to be able to apply the ideas in the future. Mathematical sense making is best supported by a teaching approach in which students are confronted with problems, supported in their efforts to solve those problems, and helped to discuss and consolidate the learning that results.

Here are some "signposts" to guide you in teaching mathematics through problem solving (Hiebert, 2003a):

- *Signpost 1: Allow Mathematics to Be Problematic for Students*. This signpost means it is important to give students problems that challenge them, to allow them to struggle, and to help them examine and make sense of the approaches that they use. All students can benefit from problem-solving experiences. This teaching approach is probably unfamiliar to many teachers, and many may even find it questionable. They may think that good teachers should explain things clearly and completely, so that students do not need to struggle at all. But it is precisely through the experience of solving challenging problems that students grow in their mathematical understanding.

    Allowing mathematics to be problematic does not mean you must search for lots of extra problems to assign. Instead, it means allowing students to grapple with the everyday mathematical challenges that the school curriculum includes, rather than immediately stepping in to tell students what to do. Imagine, for example, that a group of primary students had no experience with subtracting multidigit numbers, though they understand the concept of subtraction. A problem-based approach to teaching multidigit subtraction would not have the teacher begin by showing children how to subtract when no regrouping is required (as in 579 − 342) and later explaining how to regroup (as in 523 − 279); rather, it would have the teacher encourage the students themselves to think about how subtraction is the same and different in the two cases and to try figuring out how to solve the second type of problem in a way that makes sense.

- *Signpost 2: Focus on the Methods Used to Solve Problems.* When students are challenged to solve an unfamiliar problem, they should be encouraged to talk with one another about their methods, to compare them, and to think about their advantages and disadvantages. Given the problem $523 - 279$, some students might think about adding up to get from 279 to 523 ($279 + 1 = 280$, $280 + 20 = 300$, $300 + 223 = 523$, so the difference between 279 and 523 is $1 + 20 + 223$, or 244). Another student might think, "$523 - 279$ is hard to find, but I know it's the same as $524 - 280$ (adding 1 to each number), and that's the same as $544 - 300$ (adding 20 to each number). $544 - 300$ is easy to do! It's 244. So I know that $523 - 279$ is 244 too!" Still other students might choose to represent 523 with base-ten blocks and to think about trading in certain larger blocks for smaller blocks to make it possible to take away 279 blocks. This method most closely resembles the traditional paper-and-pencil approach.

  Learning begins when the students are challenged to make sense of the problem. Learning continues when they search for ways to solve it. And learning is extended when they share their approaches with one another. Students deepen their mathematical understanding by thinking about which approaches are easier and harder and by questioning each other about why various approaches make sense.

- *Signpost 3: Tell the Right Things at the Right Time.* Teachers who use a problem-solving approach to mathematics instruction must decide when to share information and when to let children figure things out for themselves. Speaking up too soon can eliminate the challenge and much of the learning, but it is also important not to leave students floundering when you can see they aren't making progress.

  Here are some suggestions for telling the right things at the right time. First, it's OK (indeed, important) to show students the written symbols of mathematics (e.g., notation for fractions, decimals, percents, operations, and equations) and to define technical language for them (e.g., the meaning of words such as difference, quotient, quadrilateral, and median). Words and symbols are all just social conventions, so there is no way that students will "discover" these things for themselves. However,

the best time to tell students about these things is when they arise naturally during the course of students' mathematical endeavors.

Second, it's also OK to tell students about alternative strategies for solving problems, if these strategies have not been suggested by class members. The important thing is to encourage students to compare their own methods with those of their peers and with those that you might suggest.

Finally, you should highlight the big mathematical ideas that come up during discussions of problem solving. In the course of solving a problem, children will uncover many important mathematical ideas. It is your job to guide the class in recognizing and talking about these discoveries.

Factors for Success in Problem Solving

Problem solving can be difficult to teach and to learn. Research on the characteristics of children who are successful or unsuccessful at solving problems, on the characteristics of problems, and on teaching strategies and classroom conditions that may help children be more successful at problem solving has led to some broad generalizations (McClain and Cobb, 2001):

- Young children enter school able to solve many problems. Instruction should build on what children already know.
- Children can begin solving problems in the earliest grades. They do *not* need to become skillful at computation before engaging in problem solving.
- Children's problem-solving abilities are related to their developmental level. They need to be given problems at appropriate levels of difficulty.
- Children should be taught a variety of problem-solving strategies to draw from as they meet a variety of problems. They should be encouraged to try solving a range of problems using the very same strategy, and try solving a single problem with more than one strategy. These efforts will help them recognize why some strategies are more appropriate for certain problems than for others. They can also be encouraged to adapt strategies to suit new types of problems.

Major factors that impact students' problem-solving skills are knowledge, beliefs and affects, control, and sociocultural factors. At all levels, teachers should be aware of the importance of all these factors when they teach problem solving:

- *Knowledge.* Students must learn to make connections between new problems and problems they have solved in the past. They must learn to recognize underlying structural similarities among problems and to choose the appropriate approach for solving each type of problem. That is, they should choose an approach based on a clear understanding of the problem rather than relying on surface features such as key words— for instance, the fact that the statement of a problem includes the words *in all* doesn't always mean that addition is the right approach, and *how many left* doesn't always indicate that subtraction is required.

- *Beliefs and affects.* Students' problem-solving abilities often correlate strongly with their attitudes, their level of self-confidence, and their beliefs about themselves as problem solvers. Teachers must show students that they believe *all* students can be good problem solvers. Teachers must also encourage students to develop their own strategies for and approaches to problem solving. Teachers who believe there is only one way to solve a problem prevent students from truly experiencing what it means to be a problem solver and to do mathematics.

- *Control.* It is extremely important for students to learn to monitor and control their own thinking about problem solving. Research indicates that good problem solvers often spend a considerable amount of time up front, making sure they understand a problem, and at the end, looking back to see what they did, analyze how their solution might be modified or improved, and think about how the problem is similar to and different from other problems. By contrast, weaker problem solvers tend to be impulsive, often jumping right in and crunching numbers with little regard for what they mean, without stopping to think about what approach might be most productive. Teachers must give students tasks and activities that encourage them to monitor, reflect on, and control their own thinking.

- *Sociocultural factors.* The atmosphere of the classroom should encourage students to use and further develop the problem-solving strategies that they have already developed naturally through experiences outside the classroom. Furthermore, the classroom climate itself (with its opportunities for discussion, collaboration, sharing, and mutual encouragement among students) plays an important role in helping students become more skillful problem solvers. To use problems effectively, teachers need to consider the time involved, planning aids, needed resources, the role of technology, and how to manage the class.

Choosing Appropriate Problems

Teaching through problem solving requires planning and coordinating the problems that you assign so that students have the chance to use a variety of problem-solving strategies and to analyze, write about, and discuss their solutions. When you teach mathematics, you will probably be expected to use a textbook, so you need to consider how to use it most effectively. Begin by thinking about the big mathematical ideas that are involved in each chapter or unit. Then look at the problems provided in the text and think about how you can use them to prompt your students to get actively involved with the big mathematical ideas. Try to think of or find additional problems you could assign to accomplish this goal, and remember the *signposts* we discussed above as you select problems to assign. The problems you assign do not need to be extremely clever or original. Most good problems are quite simple. Sometimes an effective approach is to assign a problem that involves exactly the mathematical ideas you want to emphasize, *before* students get to those ideas in the textbook. For example, if your students will soon be learning about multiplication, consider assigning a problem like this: how many colored pencils would be needed if there are 18 children and each child needs 3 pencils? Their approaches will give you insight into what they already know and the strategies they already have, and trying to solve the problem will help them begin to think about the important idea of equal-sized groups.

The following list describes a wide variety of problem types, with examples of each type:

- Problems that ask students to represent a mathematical idea in various ways.

  (C) Think about the number 10 separated into two parts. Draw a picture to show ways that 10 things could be put in two parts. Make up a story to go along with your picture. Write a number sentence to go along with your picture.

  (D) Make up a story and draw a picture about marbles for this number sentence: $18 \div 6 = 3$. (Figure 6-1 shows the responses of two third graders to this problem.)

- Problems that ask students to investigate a numeric or geometric concept.

  (E) Begin with a square that measures 6 cm by 6 cm. The area of the square is 36 cm². How many different shapes can you think of that have this same area? For each shape, explain your thinking. For example, how many different rectangles can you find with an area of 36 cm²? How many different triangles? Can you think of

Story:

six robber plan to steel 18 marbels from a toy shop. If they steel all 18 and devide them evinly between them selfs how meany marbles whould each robber get?

Picture of marbles:

Story: 18÷6 is kind a like 6×3

Picture of marbles:

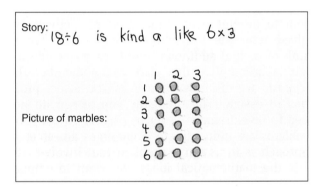

FIGURE 6-1   Stories about 18 ÷ 6 = 3 written by two third graders.

trapezoids or parallelograms with an area of 36 cm²? What other shapes can you think of with that area? (Tayeh and Britton, 2005).

- Problems that ask students to estimate or to decide on the degree of accuracy required or to apply mathematics to practical situations (e.g., buying something or building something):

(F) Kurt has 75¢. Does he have enough money to buy a candy bar costing 35¢ and a notebook costing 49¢?

(G) Erica is helping her father build a pen for her rabbit. She finds four pieces of lumber in the garage that they can use for corner stakes, and 36 feet of chicken-wire fencing. She recognizes that she can use these materials to make a variety of rectangular-shaped pens. Name three different sizes of rectangular pens they could build. What are the dimensions of the rectangular pen with the largest area?

(H) Which is the better buy, a 6-ounce jar of jelly for $1.79 or a 9-ounce jar for $2.79?

- Problems that ask students to conceptualize very large or very small numbers:

(I) Have you lived one million hours?

(J) How thick is a piece of paper?

- Problems that ask students to use logic, to reason, to strategize, to test conjectures, or to gauge the reasonableness of information:

(K) Three children guessed how many jelly beans were in a jar. Their guesses were 80, 75, and 76. One child missed by 1. Another missed by 4. The other child guessed right. How many jelly beans were in the jar?

Math Links 6.3

Visit the library of virtual manipulatives to see what's available for help with problem solving. For example, you can use a virtual balance scale and a collection of virtual coins to figure out which coin weighs less than the others in the Counterfeit Coin problem. See if, with practice, you can use logic and reasoning to solve the problem in fewer moves. Visit http://matti.usu.edu (or connect from this book's Web site), then select Virtual Library, Algebra, Coin Problem (listed under grades 6–8).

www.wiley.com/college/reys

(L) You and a friend have two dice to play a game. You can choose whether you will add or multiply the two numbers on the dice after you throw them. If you choose to multiply, you will multiply on all your turns, and your friend will add on all turns. If you choose to add, your friend will multiply. You get to go first. The winner will be the first person whose dice give an answer of 12. Would you choose to add or multiply? Explain your thinking (Stenmark and Bush, 2001).

- Problems that ask students to perform multiple steps or use more than one strategy:

(M) Ellie has $10.00 in her pocket. She spends $5.50 for a movie ticket. The theater offers a popcorn and drink special for $3.79. If Ellie buys the popcorn and drink, does she have enough money for a $1.45 candy bar, too?

(N) How many days have you come to school so far this school year?

In addition to giving students problems like these, you should sometimes give them open-ended problems—that is, problems that can have more than one correct answer. With open-ended problems, the answer depends on the approach taken (of course, the answer must be reasonable). Different students approach open-ended problems in very different ways, so such problems are ideal for ensuring that students at all levels can experience some measure of success. Open-ended problems are especially appropriate for cooperative group work, in which case they should be followed with a class discussion in which the mathematical ideas and planning skills involved are explored and students get a chance to clarify their thinking and validate their decisions. Traditional textbook problems are rarely open ended, but you can often make them open ended by modifying them in minor ways (Kabiri and Smith, 2003). Figures 6-2 and 6-3 each show a traditional problem and its transformation into an open-ended problem.

(O) Figure 6-2 shows the traditional and open-ended form of a problem based on buying from a restaurant menu. Such problems are familiar to most students and teachers (adapted from Kibiri and Smith, 2003, p. 187).

MENU

Side Dishes

Taco Salad	$3.50
Quesadillas	$2.25
Cheese Nachos	$1.50
Baked Potato	$1.75
Cole Slaw	$1.00

Main Dishes

Chicken and Rice	$6.95
Beef Fajitas	$8.95
Chicken Fingers	$4.50
Chimichangas	$5.95
Beef Burritos	$4.95

Desserts

Flan	$3.25
Baked Apples	$2.45
Empanadas	$3.15

Traditional form: Randy, Becky, CJ, Lauren, and Ty go to eat dinner at their favorite restaurant. Ty orders quesadillas, beef fajitas, and flan. CJ has chicken fingers and does not order a side dish or dessert. How much do these two meals cost? (Houghton Mifflin 2002, p. 54).

Open-ended form: Randy has $13.00 to spend at his favorite restaurant. He wants to order one main dish, two side dishes, and one dessert. He knows he will spend $1.50 on video games while he waits for his order. Find three different meals that Randy could choose. Show your calculations and explain how you thought about the problem.

FIGURE 6-2 A menu problem in two forms: traditional and open ended. (Source: Kibiri and Smith, 2003, p. 187. Reprinted with permission from *Mathematics Teaching in the Middle School*, copyright 2003 by the National Council of Teachers of Mathematics.)

(P) Figure 6-3 shows the traditional and open-ended form of a measurement problem (adapted from Kibiri and Smith, 2003, p. 190).

Traditional form: A rectangular aquarium is 12 in. wide by 14 in. long by 12 in. high. What is the volume of water needed to fill the aquarium? (Houghton Mifflin 2002, p. 475).

Open-ended form: You have been asked to design an aquarium in the shape of a rectangular prism for the school visitor's lounge. Because of the type of fish being purchased, the pet store recommends that the aquarium should hold 24 cubic feet of water. Find as many different dimensions for the aquarium as possible. Then decide which aquarium you would recommend for the lounge and explain why you made that choice.

FIGURE 6-3 A measurement problem in two forms: traditional and open ended. (Source: Kibiri and Smith, 2003, p. 190. Reprinted with permission from *Mathematics Teaching in the Middle School*, copyright 2003 by the National Council of Teachers of Mathematics.)

Math Links 6.4

*F*or another realistic, open-ended problem examine the Internet plan, Data Does It: Planning a Trip, found at the NCTM Illuminations Web site. Students use a variety of resources, including the Internet to plan short and long trips. It may be accessed from http://Illuminations.nctm.org/index_d.aspx?id = 359 or from this book's Web site.

www.wiley.com/college/reys

An open-ended problem such as the one in Figure 6-2 (O) is much more effective when constraints ensure that students must do mathematics at a high level to solve the problem and that the focus stays on the mathematics. Of course, it is also important that the constraints seem reasonable or realistic, not arbitrary. In problem (O), the constraints are that Randy is limited to $13, must spend $1.50 on video games, and must order a main dish, two sides, and a dessert. In a problem that involves buying things from a catalog, the constraints might be that the students have to buy between 5 and 10 items, that no item can cost less than $1 or more than $50, and that the total cost of the items must be between $175 and $200. Without enough constraints, students are likely to spend most of their time simply debating what to buy, with very little time spent estimating or computing how to spend their money. This can be fun for the children, but it involves little or no mathematics.

In the Classroom 6-1 shows an open-ended problem (Q) adapted from a problem-oriented elementary curriculum, *Investigations in Number, Data, and Space*. The children cut out seven rectangles and are instructed to arrange them in order from biggest to smallest. A third-grade teacher reports using this problem with her class of bilingual third graders, with good success in encouraging them to think about length and area. The problem allowed for multiple entry points and a variety of approaches for that diverse group of students. Her account of her students' conversations about their thinking is fascinating (Dwyer, 2003).

Problems (R) and (S), shown in Figures 6-4 and 6-5, represent a different sort of open-ended problem. In both problems, the numeric answer is not at all difficult to determine (and everyone should get the same answer). The challenge is to see how many different and interesting ways there are to find that answer.

In the Classroom 6-1

WHICH RECTANGLE IS BIGGEST?

OBJECTIVE: **Ordering rectangles, defining "biggest" in different ways, finding the number of tiles that cover rectangles**

GRADE LEVEL: **2–3**

MATERIALS: **Color tiles (1 tub per 6–8 students). For each student: scissors, glue, and some blank paper, and worksheet that pictures 7–10 rectangles of various sizes and shapes (skinny, fat, a few with the same length or width, etc.). Choose rectangle sizes so that color tiles will fit on top perfectly, since Part III of the activity involves covering the rectangles with color tiles to find areas. Do not arrange the rectangles in any particular order by size. Label rectangles with letters, A, B, C, etc.**

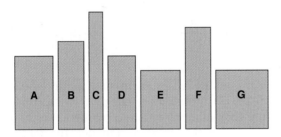

Part I: Ordering Rectangles

A. Paired Work

Have the students work with partners to arrange the rectangles from smallest to biggest on their paper, and to glue them in place after they have decided. (Teacher should observe what students are saying and doing. Different orderings and disagreements are expected. The question is purposely ambiguous. What's important is to observe how students justify their reasoning.)

B. Class Discussion

Bring the group together, with their papers. Ask one pair to show how they ordered the rectangles. (For example, a common ordering is to arrange the rectangles "standing up"—with their longer sides vertical—and to order them from tallest to shortest, with the wider one first whenever two have the same height.) Ask the students to explain why they chose their own particular order. Ask pairs who ordered the rectangles differently to show their paper, and explain their thinking. For example, a pair may have chosen to arrange the rectangles "lying down," or they may have tried to order by area rather than by height.

Encourage students to talk about the different ways they decided what was "big" and what was "small."

Part II: Covering Rectangles

While all the rectangles are still visible, tell the children to imagine they are chocolate bars. Which would have the most chocolate? Which would have the least? How can you figure it out? Students may suggest different approaches. One possibility is covering them with color tiles. Each color tile can represent one square of chocolate.

A. Paired work

Distribute a new sheet of paper showing all the orginal rectangles. Have students work in pairs to find how many color tiles it takes to cover each rectangle. They should write the corresponding number inside each rectangle.

B. Class Discussion

Bring students together to compare findings. Were they surprised about any results? Were any rectangles covered by the same number of tiles? Encourage students to discuss whether they think these rectangles are the same size or different sizes. (If they think different, which is "bigger" and why?) Were there any rectangles that were considered "big" in the first activity (ordering rectangles) but not as big in the second activity (covering rectangles)? [Note: Students may need numerous experiences before understanding that what we consider "big" may change, depending on the attribute we are considering—e.g., ordering by height rather than by area.]

Activity adapted from: Akers; J.; Battista, M., Godrow, A., Clements, H.D., & Sarama, J. "Shapes, Halves, and Symmetry," from *Investigations in Number, Data, and Space: Grade 2.* Menlo Park, CA: Dale Seymour Publications, 1996, pp. 52–54.

(R) Figure 6-4a shows that a pentomino is an arrangement of five square tiles where each tile has at least one side adjoining a side of another tile. Using graph paper and scissors, how many different pentominos can you make? How can you know that you have identified all the possible pentominos? Figure 6-4b shows one pentomino that will fold into a box and one that will not. How many of the possible pentominos will fold into an open box?

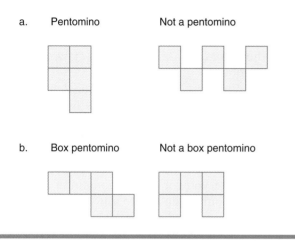

a.   Pentomino   Not a pentomino

b.   Box pentomino   Not a box pentomino

FIGURE 6-4 How many box pentominos can you make?

(S) Figure 6-5 shows marbles arranged in a pattern. How many marbles are there? Find the answer by counting or computing in as many different ways as you can.

FIGURE 6-5 How many different ways can you find the number of marbles in the picture?

Finding Problems

Where can you find problems to challenge your students? Most textbooks include a wide range of problems, and we have seen that textbook problems in traditional form can often be converted easily to open-ended problems. In addition, there are many resources for problems that will stimulate and challenge your students. Such resources include:

- Articles and books referenced in this chapter.
- A variety of Web sites.
- Writing problems yourself (possibly using ideas from newspapers or from events in your community). See, for example, a description of a broad assortment of problems drawn from a single newspaper circular describing activities related to Washington, D.C.'s annual cherry-blossom festival (Silbey, 1999).
- Using situations that arise spontaneously, particularly children's questions or conjectures. For example, after reading a story about a robbery, children might wonder, "If a bank robber stole a million dollars, how heavy and bulky would the money be? Could he run down the street with it in his pocket? In a shopping bag?" For another example, read Phyllis Whitin's account of her fourth-graders' surprise when, while working on the pentomino problem (R), they noticed that some of the pentominos had perimeter 10, while others had perimeter 12, even though all the pentomino shapes were made from exactly 5 square tiles. This led Whitin's students to make and explore a variety of conjectures as they wrestled with this unexpected observation (P. Whitin, 2004).
- Attending problem-solving sessions at professional meetings. Share problems with other teachers.
- Having children write problems to share with each other.
- Using children's literature as a context for solving mathematical problems embedded in or related to the story (Ameis, 2002; Thiessen, Matthias, and Smith, 1998; Whitin and Wilde, 1992).

Math Links 6.5

Collect problems from professional journals such as *Teaching Children Mathematics*, newspapers, magazines, resource books such as the Addenda and Navigations Series from National Council of Teachers of Mathematics, and web sites such as: http://www.figurethis.org/challenges/toc.htm or this book's Web site.

www.wiley.com/college/reys

It is never too soon to start a problem file, with problems categorized so you can locate them readily. Categorize them by mathematical content, by strategies, or by how you are going to use the idea. Laminating the cards permits them to be used repeatedly by students for individual or small-group problem solving.

Math Links 6.6

*O*n the Web, teachers and students can find a wealth of challenging and interesting mathematics problems, search for data for real-world problem-solving investigations, and seek answers to mathematical queries and conundrums. Some examples of sites to consider include http://mathforum.org/pow/, http://www.pbs.org/teacher source/math.htm, and http://www.sitesforteachers.com/ or this book's Web site.

www.wiley.com/college/reys

Having Students Pose Problems

Encouraging students to write, share, and solve their own problems is a good way to help them develop their problem-solving skills. By posing problems, students learn how problems are structured, they develop critical-thinking and reasoning abilities, and they learn to express their ideas clearly (Brown and Walter, 1990).

It is often helpful to begin by having students modify familiar problems. For example, third-grade students may have read the classic story *The Doorbell Rang* (Hutchins, 1986) and considered problems like this one: Suppose Mama baked 12 cookies. If she has 2 children (or 4 or 6 or 12) and each child gets the same number of cookies, how many cookies does each child get? This problem can be rewritten in various ways. As indicated, a simple modification would be to change the numbers. Some changes in number don't really affect the difficulty of the problem (e.g., 18 cookies and 6 children is hardly more difficult than 12 cookies and 2 children). But other changes in number might make a big difference (e.g., 12 cookies shared by 8 children or 12 cookies shared by 5 children are harder because they involve remainders). This could be turned into a more open-ended problem. By leaving the number of children unspecified, there can be more than one answer: Mama baked 18 cookies. She can share them equally among her children without breaking any cookies. How many different numbers of children can she have? Another interesting way to reformulate a problem is to exchange the known and unknown information—here, for example, making the number of cookies unknown: Mama baked a lot of cookies. If she has 2 children (or 4 or 6 or 12) and each child got 3, how many cookies did Mama bake?"

Here are four principles for helping students as they learn to pose problems (Moses, Bjork, and Goldenberg, 1990):

- Focus students' attention on the various kinds of information in problems: the information a problem gives them (the *known*), the information they are supposed to find (the *unknown*), and the *restrictions* that are placed on the answer. Encourage students to ask "what if" questions. For example, what if you make the known information different? What if you switch what is known in the problem and what is unknown? What if you change the restrictions?
- Begin with mathematical topics or concepts that are familiar.
- Encourage students to use *ambiguity* (what they are not sure about or what they want to know) as they work toward composing new questions and problems.
- Teach students about the idea of *domain* (the numbers they are allowed to use in a particular problem). Extending or restricting the domain of a problem is an interesting way to change it. For example, the problem "Name three numbers whose product is 24" is very different depending on whether you consider a domain of all whole numbers, only even whole numbers, all integers (both positive and negative), or perhaps even fractions and decimals.

The teacher plays a key role in establishing a classroom environment where students are encouraged to think deeply about how problems can be changed or rewritten. The teacher can model an inquiring mind by frequently asking "What if?" when discussing problems and by encouraging students to make conjectures and to reformulate problems.

Having students write their own problems (rather than modify problems already at hand) is also useful. Generally, this is best done after students have had considerable experience with modifying familiar problems. When you ask students to compose problems on their own, it is often important that you specify certain goals or constraints; otherwise, the assignment may become nothing more than an exercise in creativity. (Students may write fantastic stories with no discernible mathematics content or pose problems that are so complicated that no solution is possible.) You could specify goals or constraints, for example, by assigning students to write a word problem that matches a given mathematical expression or a given figure:

- Write a word problem for $250 \div 5 = 50$.
- Write a comparison word problem for $12 - 8 = 4$. (If you are not familiar with "comparison" subtraction problems, see Chapter 9 where they are defined along with "separation" subtraction problems and "part-whole" subtraction problems.")

- Write a multiplication word problem for the tree diagram shown below (e.g., two kinds of ice cream and three possible toppings for each gives six different types of sundaes).

Situations or information in magazine advertisements, newspaper articles, books of world records, sales flyers, and so on can also be effective in prompting students to pose problems. An approach used by a sixth-grade teacher was to challenge her students to write and illustrate problems that involved multiplication or division and that included extraneous information. Students responded with creative problems such as this:

At midnight, the wind over Jamaica started to increase as Hurricane Lucas came closer. Every 10 minutes from then on, the wind doubled, and five trees were pulled from the ground. At 12:30, the wind speed was 120 miles per hour. At what speed was the wind blowing at 12:00 midnight?

Students need help learning to write problems, and it is easy to integrate such lessons with language arts instruction. You could use a writing workshop approach, consisting of stages such as brainstorming and prewriting, writing, several rounds of peer critiquing followed by rewriting, and, finally, editing and publication. Student problems may be published on bulletin boards, on cards (to be made available for other students to solve), or in a class book of problems. The sixth-grade teacher mentioned above obtained a small classroom grant to produce enough copies of her class's illustrated book of problems to distribute one to each sixth-grade class in the school district. Her students proudly went on a field trip that took them from school to school delivering their books to sixth-grade classrooms, where they shared problem-solving experiences with other students their own age. A third-grade teacher in another state engaged her students in taking "the mathematician's

chair" as they challenged their peers with problems they had written themselves (Hildebrand, Ludeman, and Mullin, 1999). The teacher assessed their writing by considering three aspects of each problem on a scale of 1–4: the attributes of the problem, the structure of the problem, and the student's use of language conventions.

Using Calculators and Computers

The calculator's potential for helping children become more proficient at problem solving has been recognized since handheld calculators became widely available more than 30 years ago. Of course, if the focus of a lesson is on practicing paper-and-pencil computation or mental computation, students will not be using calculators, but when the focus is on problem solving or concept development, then calculators can often be an important aid, as we discuss in more detail in Chapter 10. You should consider having students use calculators whenever:

- They let children solve more complex problems or problems with realistic, rather than contrived, data.
- They eliminate tedious and time-consuming computations and help reduce children's anxiety about being able to do computations correctly.
- Their special functions can help children explore mathematical objects, concepts, and operations.

Because calculators present answers in decimal form, what comes up when students use a calculator while solving problems may surprise and challenge them. For example, consider this problem: "If one bus can transport 34 students, how many buses will be required to take 489 students." A student working on this problem keyed in 489 ÷ 34 and was surprised when her calculator showed 3.456138. How should this answer be interpreted? In this case, the calculator's answer presents an excellent opportunity for talking about division, remainders, and fraction-decimal equivalents.

One educator reports the story of a fifth grader named Jonathan who enjoyed using calculators to explore mathematical problems (Battista, 2003). Jonathan overheard a third grader working on finding pairs of whole numbers whose product was 9. Jonathan knew quite well that 9×1, 1×9, and 3×3 were the answers to the question. But it prompted him to think about a related problem: Are there more numbers that multiply to make 9, if you can use decimals or fractions? Jonathan was able to come up with quite a few number pairs mentally $(4\frac{1}{2} \times 2$, 6×1.5, $8 \times 1\frac{1}{8}$, $4 \times 2\frac{1}{4}$, etc.). He spent the next 30 minutes brainstorming a long list of other possibilities and checking them with a calculator. Eventually, an adult asked Jonathan, "How many pairs do you think there are?"

> Jonathan: "Billions." (Short pause.) "There's one for every number. Like a googolplex times 9 googolplex-ths [sic]" (To Jonathan, a googolplex was an unimaginably large number; he had encountered the term in his reading.) (Battista, p. 273)

Jonathan tends to use his calculator as a tool that helps him explore challenging mathematical problems—problems that he certainly could not easily explore without a calculator.

A popular type of problem-solving activity involving calculators is the "broken key" activity. The children are assigned a series of problems and are told they may use a calculator but must pretend that certain keys on the calculator are broken. (The specified "broken keys" can be number keys, operation keys, or a combination of the two. It may be helpful to give the children a small piece of masking tape to stick on the "broken keys" as a reminder.) Suppose one of the problems is: Compute 5×39 when the "3" key is broken. The children may suggest various ways to work around the broken key—for example, $40 - 1 + 40 - 1 + 40 - 1 + 40 - 1 + 40 - 1$, or $(5 \times 29) + (5 \times 10)$, or $(5 \times 40) - 5$. The teacher should ensure that students talk about and compare their approaches and the various operations they used.

Computers can also be important problem-solving tools. Like calculators, computers allow students to work on problems with realistic data. But computers also let students experience problems of different types, such as problems involving graphics and graphing. For example, students could collect data from classmates on their favorite types of music, enter the data into a spreadsheet, and then generate circle graphs or histograms to represent the data. Students could also try to determine whether musical preferences differ among children of different grade levels or between boys and girls—they could separate the data by grade level or gender and draw a histogram that compares the preferences of one group with those of the other.

Many fine software programs provide a variety of problem-solving experiences. Some, such as *Numbers Undercover*, involve computation. Others, such as The *Factory Deluxe*, address spatial visualization. Still others, such as *Math Shop*, provide direct experiences with problem solving. *The Cruncher* teaches spreadsheet skills for solving such real-life problems as how many weeks of allowance equal a new CD player.

Logo and *BASIC*, still available to students in some schools, can also provide rich problem-solving experiences. Working with these computer languages encourages students to make conjectures about what will happen, see what actually occurs, and then try something else. Other tools, such as *Geometer's Sketchpad*, let students create geometric figures, make conjectures, and explore relationships. For example, students can explore the sum of the angles of triangles, quadrilaterals, and other polygons and try to predict the sum for 10-sided polygons.

In recent years, the World Wide Web has become an extremely rich resource for mathematics education. On the Web, teachers and students can find a wealth of challenging and interesting mathematics problems, search for data for real-world problem solving, and seek answers to mathematical queries and conundrums (see the Math Links throughout this book).

Strategies for Problem Solving

The Hungarian-born mathematician George Polya proposed a now-classic four-stage model of problem solving (Polya, 1973):

1. *Understand* the problem.
2. *Devise* a plan for solving it.
3. *Carry out* your plan.
4. *Look back* to examine your solution.

This model forms the basis for the problem-solving approach used in problem-solving lessons in most elementary school mathematics textbooks. However, Polya's model can be less than helpful if taken too literally. Except for simple problems, it is rarely possible to go through the steps in lockstep sequence. Moreover, the steps are not discrete, and it is not always necessary to perform every step. For instance, while trying to understand a problem, students may move into the planning stage without realizing they have done so. Or simply understanding a problem may enable students to see a solution without any planning. In addition, going through the steps does not always help students find a solution. Many children become trapped in an endless process of reading, thinking, rereading—and rereading and rereading—until they give up.

Children need specific strategies that will help them move through the steps in a productive way.

Polya himself delineated many of these strategies, and many textbooks provide lists of the strategies geared to various grade levels. It is important, however, to distinguish between Polya's model itself and these strategies. Polya's four-stage model provides a general picture of how to move through the process of solving a problem, whereas strategies are tools that may be useful at various points in the problem-solving process.

In this section, we discuss seven strategies that can help children solve a wide variety of problems (see Table 6-1). Many textbooks introduce problem-solving strategies in a systematic way. If you are using a textbook that does not cover some of the strategies we discuss here, you can probably devise a plan for fitting them in by referring to the textbook's scope and sequence.

For additional guidance in helping children with problem-solving strategies, you can look at supplemental texts (e.g., Charles, Lester, and Lambdin, 2005). Of course, you should not limit students to using only the strategies that you have discussed in class. Rather, you should always encourage students to generate their own ideas about how to approach a new situation. If you see some students successfully using a strategy that you haven't discussed, you should encourage them to share their ideas with the rest of the class. You might also help the children think of a label for that new strategy so it can be referenced easily in future class discussions. You could list problem-solving strategies on a bulletin board for quick reference by students. For example, Jessica might discover that a good way to get started on a problem involving large numbers is to solve a similar but simpler problem with smaller numbers. When she shares her idea during whole-class discussion, you might suggest naming this the "make-it-simpler strategy"; this would give you the option of beginning future problem-solving discussions by asking whether the make-it-simpler strategy might be useful in attacking the problem at hand.

The following discussions of specific problem-solving strategies include illustrative problems, covering a range of mathematical topics and grade levels, that could be used to develop each strategy. Most problems can be solved with any of a variety of strategies. But even so, for a given problem it is often the case that some strategies are more effective than others. For this reason, children should have a repertoire of strategies that they feel comfortable using. And sometimes, students will have to use more than one strategy to solve a problem. Being able to draw on a repertoire that includes a wide variety of strategies allows students to attack many different types of problems. Moreover, when one strategy fails, the children have others to turn to, and this can help them develop confidence in their ability to find a path to a solution.

As you read, do stop and try to solve the problems!

Act It Out

Acting out a problem helps children visualize what is involved in the problem. In using this strategy, either the children themselves perform the actions described in the problem or they manipulate objects. When teaching the strategy, you should stress that the objects used do not have to be the real thing—for example, real money is obviously not needed to act out a problem involving coins, only something labeled "5¢" or "25¢." Children are adept at pretending, so they will probably suggest substitute objects themselves, but make sure they focus their attention on the actions, not on the objects.

In the early grades, you can develop the act-it-out strategy using simple real-life problems:

(1) Six children are standing at the teacher's desk. Five children join them. Now how many children are at the teacher's desk?

In later grades, when the problems are more challenging, it is probably unrealistic for students actually to act them out. But they might find it valuable to act out simpler variations of the problem to see if they can identify patterns of actions. Or they simply <u>think</u> about the actions involved, and keep notes of what would happen at each step of acting out the problem, if the problem situation involves multiple steps.

(2) There are 24 children in a class. Each child gives a valentine to each of the other children in the class. How many valentines are exchanged? (This is the problem discussed in the Snapshot of a Lesson at the beginning of this chapter. Thinking about acting this out requires thinking

Table 6-1 • A List of Useful Problem-Solving Strategies

Act it out	Guess and check
Make a drawing or diagram	Work backward
Look for a pattern	Solve a simpler or similar problem
Construct a table	

about how many valentines each child will need to bring to class. We can envision the first child giving a valentine to each other child—that's 23, and the second child doing the same—that's 23 more, and so on.)

(3) A man buys a horse for $60, sells it for $70, buys it back for $80, and sells it for $90. How much does the man make or lose in the horse-trading business?

Make a Drawing or Diagram

Within the past week or so you have probably used the drawing or diagramming strategy to help solve a real-life problem. Perhaps you had to find someone's house by following a complicated set of directions, so you drew a sketch of the route. Or maybe you wanted to rearrange a room and drew diagrams to see how the furniture could be placed. This strategy of making a drawing or diagram lets you depict the relationships among the different pieces of information in a problem in a way that makes those more apparent.

When teaching this strategy, stress to the children that there is no need to draw detailed pictures. Rather, encourage the children to draw only what is essential to represent the problem. For example, if the problem is about children in a classroom, stick figures (or even just circles) can represent the children and a square can represent the classroom—it is not necessary to draw the children's clothing or the walls of the classroom.

Here are two problems where students could apply the drawing or diagramming strategy:

(4) Aunt Katrina wants to hang six decorative plates on her dining room wall, in a straight line and spaced evenly apart (from each other and from the edges of the wall). Each plate is 8 inches in diameter and the wall is 104 inches long. How far apart should the plates be hung? (Hartweg, 2004/2005). See Figure 6-6 for two fourth-graders' attempts at this problem.

(5) A snail is at the bottom of a jar that is 15 cm high. Each day the snail crawls up 5 cm, but each night it slides back down 3 cm. How many days will it take the snail to reach the top of the jar? (Note: the answer is not $7\frac{1}{2}$ days. Draw a picture to see why not!)

At times you can use this strategy as the basis for an activity, by presenting a picture or diagram for which the children have to make up a problem. For instance, you could show children the following picture, which could prompt them to pose the

---

Aunt Katrina wants to hang six decorative plates on her dining room wall, in a straight line and evenly spaced apart. Each plate is 8 inches in diameter and the wall is 104 inches long. How far apart should the plates be hung? (Hartweg, 2004/2005).

A fourth-grader named Kelly attempted to solve this problem without drawing a picture. She understood that she needed to divide up the wall distance to figure out how far apart to space the plates. Her work shows that she tried dividing 104 by 6 and also by 8.

Kelly explained her thinking as follows: "I knew dividing by 6 wouldn't work because there was some left over, so I divided by 8 and got 13. Then I checked my work by multiplying 13 by 8 and got 104." When pressed about why she chose 6 and 8 as divisors, she replied that there were 6 plates with a diameter of 8. She believed that her answer was 13, but was unable to explain what the 13 represented. Without a drawing to help her see relationships, she was unable to solve the problem.

Lizzie was a classmate of Kelly's. Her solution is shown below.

Lizzie taped pennies onto a piece of paper to represent the 6 plates and determined that the plates took up 48 inches because they were each 8 inches across ("plates = 48 in."). She subtracted this amount from 104 to determine that the empty spaces totaled 56 in. ("not plates = 56 in."). She numbered the "7 spaces that don't have plates" on the wall (before, between, and after the 6 plates), and then divided the 56 by 7 to arrive at 8 inches for each of these spaces.

FIGURE 6-6 Two fourth graders attempt the plate-hanging problem. (Source: From Harweg, 2004/2005, pp. 280 and 282. Reprinted with permission from *Teaching Children Mathematics*, copyright 2004/5 by The National Council of Teachers of Mathematics.)

problem of how far each car goes before they crash or how long it takes them to crash:

(6)

60 miles per hour

50 miles per hour

Austin   1210 miles   Bloomington

Look for a Pattern

Understanding "patterns, relations, and functions" is one of the major goals of the Algebra Standard (across all grades K–12) in NCTM's *Principles and Standards for School Mathematics*. Recognizing, describing, extending, and generalizing patterns are important components of algebraic thinking. In many early learning activities, children have to identify a pattern in pictures or numbers. In problem solving, children look for patterns in more active ways—for example, by constructing a table that might help them see a pattern.

Here is a problem that appeared on the 1992 National Assessment of Educational Progress (NAEP) for mathematics:

(7) A pattern of dots is shown below. At each step, more dots are added to the pattern. The number of dots added at each step is more than the number added in the previous step. The pattern continues indefinitely.

Marcy has to determine the number of dots in the 20th step, but she does not want to draw all 20 pictures and then count the dots. Explain or show how she could do this and give the answer that Marcy should get for the number of dots.

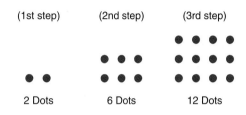

(1st step)   (2nd step)   (3rd step)

2 Dots   6 Dots   12 Dots

Figure 6-7 shows how four different children used the strategy of looking for a pattern to find the correct number of dots.

FIGURE 6-7 Examples of strategies used for finding the corrent number of Marcy's dots. (Source: From Stylianou et al., 2000, p. 138. Reprinted with permission from *Mathematics Teaching in the Middle School*, copyright 2000 by the National Council of Teachers of Mathematics.)

Here is another problem where finding a pattern is useful.

(8) In a town of 90,000 people, one person starts a rumor by telling it to three other people. If each person who hears the rumor tells it to 3 new people every 15 minutes, how long would it take to spread the rumor to every person in town?

Construct a Table

Organizing information into a table often helps children discover a pattern and identify missing information. Constructing a table is an efficient way to classify and order large amounts of information; also, it provides a record of what's been tried, so that children need not retrace nonproductive paths or repeatedly do the same computations. The following two problems lend themselves to the strategy of construcitng a table:

(9) Can you make change for a quarter using exactly 9 coins? 17 coins? 8 coins? How many different ways can you make change for a quarter?

(10) Your teacher agrees to let you have 1 minute of recess on the first day of school, 2 minutes on the second day, 4 minutes on the third day, and so on. How long will your recess be at the end of 2 weeks?

The mathematical idea involved in Problem (10) can be stated in terms of other situations, and such reformulations can alter the difficulty level of the problem. Reformulation can also give children practice in recognizing similarities in the structure of different problems—an ability that appears to be closely allied to good problem-solving skills. Here is a reformulation of Problem (10):

(11) Suppose someone offers you a job for 15 days. They offer you your choice of how you will be paid. You can start at 1¢ a day, get 2¢ the next day, 4¢ the next day, and continue doubling the amount every day. Or you can start at $1 the first day, get $2 the next day, $3 the next day, and continue adding $1 to the amount every day. Which would you choose? Why?

Textbooks frequently teach part of the table-construction strategy by having students read a table or complete a table that is already structured. However, it is vital that children also learn how to construct a table from scratch. They need to determine for themselves what form the table should have (e.g., how many rows and columns are needed), what the columns or rows should be labeled, and

Table 6-2 • A Spreadsheet Beginning to Solve Problem 11

Day Number	Double the Amount Each Day		Add $1 Each Day	
	Day's Pay	Total Paid	Day's Pay	Total Paid
1	.01	.01	1.00	1.00
2	.02	.03	2.00	3.00
3	.04	.07	3.00	6.00
4	.08	.15	4.00	10.00
5	.16	.31	5.00	15.00

so on. To teach children these skills, you can present problems that require children to collect information and then organize it into a table in order to report it. A spreadsheet can be helpful with this task, as it would be with Problems (10) and (11). Table 6-2 shows the beginning of a spreadsheet that children could use to solve Problem (11).

Guess and Check

For years, children have been discouraged from guessing. Of course, random guessing is not good problem solving, but guessing can be a useful strategy if students incorporate what they know into their guesses—that is, if their guesses are educated guesses rather than wild guesses. Educated guesses are based on careful attention to pertinent aspects of the problem, and on knowledge gained from previous work on similar problems. *The guess-and-check strategy involves making repeated educated guesses, using what has been learned from earlier guesses to make subsequent guesses better and better.* Too often, children just check a guess and, on finding that it is wrong, make another guess that may be even more off the mark. But when this happens, instead of saying "you're only guessing" in a derisive tone, you must help your students learn how to refine their guesses efficiently. Consider the following problem:

(14) Suppose it costs 23¢ to mail a postcard and 37¢ for a letter. Bill wrote to 12 friends and spent $3.46 for postage. How many letters and how many postcards did he send?

Suppose Roberto begins by making a guess of 6 letters and 6 postcards—total postage $3.60 (too much). It is your job not to let him just make another guess randomly; instead, you must help him understand that his next guess should be fewer letters than 6. Maybe he guesses 4 letters, so there must be 8 postcards—total postage $3.32 (too little). Now you must make sure he sees that there have to be more letters than 4 but still fewer than 6. That is, the only possibility is 5, and when he tries 5 letters and 7 postcards, he experiences the reward of having discovered the solution after only two wrong guesses—much better than he is likely to have done with random guessing.

Here are three more problems that you could use to teach children the guess-and-check strategy:

(15) A restaurant advertises combination milkshakes—that's 2 flavors of milkshake poured side-by-side into a glass. They brag that they offer 28 different twin-flavor combinations. How many different single flavors of milkshake must be available?

(16) Maggie hit the dartboard with 4 darts. Each dart hit a different number. Her total score was 25. Which numbers might she have hit to make that score?

(17) Use the numbers 1 through 6 to fill the 6 circles. Use each number only once. Each side of the triangle must add up to 9.

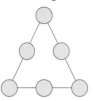

Work Backward

Children must work backward to solve a problem if the problem states a result or an endpoint and the children have to figure out the initial conditions or the beginning (many mazes are solved by working backward from the end to the beginning). Here are two problems that require children to work backward from given results:

(18) Complete the following addition table:

+			3			
	12		11	15		
6		6			7	
2			5	9		
						13
5						14

(19) Sue baked some cookies. She put half of them away for the next day. Then she divided the remaining cookies evenly among her two sisters and herself, so each got 4 cookies. How many cookies did she bake?

Solve a Similar but Simpler Problem

Children who know how to solve a given problem can usually solve a second problem that is somewhat similar, even if the second problem is also somewhat more difficult. The insight and understanding they gain from solving easier problems, where relationships are more apparent, carry through and let them solve harder problems. When given a problem that seems too hard, children can apply this strategy by setting the problem aside for a moment and solving a similar but simpler problem. Then they can try using the same method to solve the original problem.

Some problems are difficult just because they involve large numbers or complicated patterns, which make it hard for children to see how to solve them. Solving a similar, but simpler, problem first may help children figure out how to approach the original problem. In the Classroom 6-2 shows how to use this similar-but-simpler strategy to solve the following problem, which is difficult because of the large number 64:

(20) Sixty-four students play in pairs in a Checkers tournament. Losers are out of the tournament. Winners play until only one winner is left. How many games must be played before there is one winner left? (See In the Classroom

In the Classroom 6-2

SOLVE A SIMILAR BUT SIMPLER PROBLEM

OBJECTIVE: **Solve difficult problems by first identifying and solving a related, simpler problem.**

GRADE LEVEL: **4–5**

DIRECTIONS TO TEACHER **Work with the entire class to solve the first problem together, as an example of using the "solve a similar, but simpler" problem-solving strategy. Then have children work on the later problems alone, in pairs, or in small groups.**

PROBLEM **Sixty-four people enter a checkers tournament. They play individually against each other. Losers are out of the tournament. Winners play another game against a different player, until just one winner is left. That person wins the tournament. How many games must be played until there is a winner?**

UNDERSTAND **How many games will be played in the first round of the tournament? (32 games, 64 people in pairs) What do you need to figure out? (The total number of games before there is a winner.)**

PLAN **Is there a simpler problem you could solve first? (How many games would be played if there were only 2 players? 3 players? 4 players?)**

Can you find a pattern in the simpler problems that can be extended to the original problem?

SOLVE

Number of Players	Games to Play	Total Number of Games
2 (A and B)	A vs B	I
3 (A, B, and C)	A vs B, C vs winner of AB	2
4 (A, B, C, and D)	A vs B, C vs D, winners of AB and CD play each other	3
5 (A, B, C, D, and E)	A vs B, C vs D, E plays winner of AB, winner of that game plays winner of CD	4
Any number		The number of games to play is always one less than the number of players

Note to Teacher: students may find it helpful to draw stick pictures of players, labeling them A, B (or even with names) and connecting with lines to show who wins, and who plays whom next. Making a table is not necessary, but helps in displaying the information discovered.

LOOK BACK **How did solving a simpler problem help with solving the original problem? (The smaller numbers were easier to work with, and made it possible to see the pattern.)**

TRY THESE!

1. Jason and his 5 friends each gave one sticker to the 5 others. How many stickers were given out altogether?

2. Boxes of colored markers are labeled with their color on the top and on every side of the box except the bottom. Ten boxes are lined up against the wall on a shelf. How many labels can you see without moving any of the boxes?

3. After school at clown club, there were 8 kids. Every afternoon, each kid made a new funny face for each of the other clowns. They took pictures of all the faces for their clown scrapbook. How many pictures did the clowns add to their scrapbook each afternoon?

Adapted from p. 62-63 from SILVER BURDETT GINN MATHEMATICS Grade 4 by Francis Fennell, et al. (1999).

6-2, where this problem is used to introduce an entire lesson on solving a simpler problem.)

In the next problem, the difficulty arises from the "complicated" number 32.7. Students who are unsure how to solve this problem could try substituting simpler numbers, such as 30 miles per gallon and a 15-gallon tank; doing this might help them recognize that it makes sense to multiply the two numbers.

(21) We get 32.7 miles per gallon of gas in our car. If the tank holds 14 gallons and we fill it up, about how far can we go without filling up again?

When solving a problem requires a series of steps, children may need help in recognizing that they have to answer an intermediate, "hidden" question before they can answer the final question. Answering a hidden question is another form of solving a simpler problem first, as shown in the following problem:

(22) Fred bought 6 of the fish-flavored cat nibbles on sale. How much did he pay for all 6 nibbles? (Hidden question: What is the sale price of a fish-flavored cat nibble?)

SALE 3¢ Off Regular Price

CAT NIBBLES

Flavor	Regular Price for 1
Beef	8¢
Liver	5¢
Chicken	15¢
Fish	12¢

Students might find the following problem difficult because it involves so many numbers:

(23) Place the numbers 1 to 19 into the 19 circles so that the center number plus any two numbers on opposite sides of the center always make the same sum.

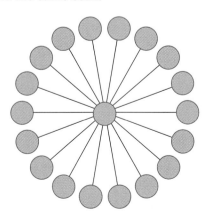

Students might tackle this problem by first trying simpler problems such as placing the numbers 1 to 5 or 1 to 7 or 1 to 9 in a similar pattern of circles.

When children do not understand a problem, you can try asking them to restate the problem in their own words. Hearing how they restate the problem can sometimes help you identify what it is that the children do not understand. At other times, restating the problem helps the children themselves figure out what the problem is asking. As a teacher, you yourself might try restating a problem as a way of eliminating unimportant words or using words that are more easily understood. Try rewording each of the following problems so that children will understand them:

(26) Find three different integers such that the sum of their reciprocals is an integer.

(27) I bought some items at the store. All were the same price. I bought as many items as the number of cents in the cost of each item. My bill was $2.25. How many items did I buy?

The Importance of Looking Back

Some of the most important learning that results from problem solving occurs after the problem has been solved, when students look back at the problem, at the solution, and at how they found the solution. Even more important may be the learning that results from looking back at their own thought process as they worked on the problem. In fact, research indicates that helping children discuss their own thinking with you and with each other may be the best way to help them become better problem solvers. In Chapter 2, you read about the importance of metacognition—thinking about one's own thinking. You should regularly schedule looking-back time after classroom problem solving to help children develop their metacognitive abilities and thereby improve their mathematical competencies.

Looking Back at the Problem

It is important to help students generalize after solving a problem. Generalizing involves relating the problem to other problems. Every problem-solver should get in the habit of asking himself or herself this important question: How is this problem similar to and different from other problems I've seen or solved before? Problems that are very different in context or detail can be very similar in their structure. Focusing on how a problem is structurally similar to other problems often results in more significant insights than does focusing on the details of the problem or on the answer.

Looking Back at the Answer

When teachers tell their students, "Be sure to check your work!" they usually mean that the students should go through the problem-solving process again to be sure they did not make any careless errors. But a more important type of checking is to look back at the answer to make sure it is reasonable. Problem solvers must learn to step back and ask themselves whether their answers make sense. Estimating the answer before solving the problem can help, as can thinking about whether the problem could have more than one answer. Healthy skepticism about answers is important for good problem solving.

Looking Back at the Solution Process

Too often, children are given problems with only one right way to solve. Many textbook exercises are like that. However, in real-life situations, two or more approaches are often quite possible, and the same is true of most interesting mathematics problems. Moreover, approaching a problem in different ways helps students understand the problem better. For example, think about the problems we have presented in this chapter. Maybe you do not agree with how we classified a particular problem under a particular strategy—you might have used a different strategy to solve that problem. But even for the problems where you felt the classification was satisfactory, there are probably other strategies that could be used to solve them. (Try and see!)

Also, beyond thinking about different ways of approaching problems, it's also important for students to look back and put the solution process into perspective. They should consider what they did at each stage of the process—what facts they uncovered, what strategies they used, and what was productive and unproductive. Sometimes, you can help children look back in this way by giving them a similar problem without numbers. This lets them focus on the relationships in the problem rather than on the specific details. As they think about how they would find the answer, no matter what numbers were involved, they must focus more clearly on the solution process. You can ask different students to talk about how they proceeded, so everyone can see that there are different ways of reaching the same answer.

Other techniques you can use to help children increase their understanding of the problem-solving process include having them write about how they solved a problem and encouraging them to evaluate their solution process, to see what was successesful and what was not.

Looking Back at One's Own Thinking

People who are good problem solvers are generally good at thinking about their own thinking—that is, they are good at metacognition. They monitor the skills they have and the things they already know, they think about how they can use their skills and knowledge to solve new problems, and they make judgments about what they are doing. Older children are better at these things than younger children, but by regularly teaching this type of looking back and thereby giving children experience with it, you can help all your students develop their metacognitive abilities.

An effective teaching technique is to model the sorts of questions students should ask themselves when thinking about their own thinking, both during problem solving and while looking back afterwards. You could even post a set of questions so students can refer to them—for example:

Was this problem like any I had ever seen before? If so, how were they similar and how were they different?

Was this problem easier (or harder) than I expected it to be? Why?

Did it take me more time (or less time) to solve this problem than I expected? If so, why?

What stumbling blocks did I come up against? How did I handle them? Are there other ways I could have done it?

How confident am I about my solution? Why?

Helping All Students with Problem Solving

As we have seen, giving students problems that are just within their reach, that challenge them to reach solutions, helps them make sense of mathematics. You must think carefully about how you organize and manage classroom instruction to ensure that all students have worthwhile problem-solving experiences. This includes paying careful attention to helping students with special needs—those with learning difficulties as well as those who are gifted in mathematics. Figuring out how to structure problem-solving sessions for a full class of diverse students will always be a challenge. Important considerations are how to manage time, classroom routines, and the needs of individual students.

Managing Time

Teaching mathematics effectively through problem solving requires time. Students need time to think about the problems, to mull over the relationships, and to explore methods of finding solutions. They need to be encouraged to keep working and not to give up prematurely. It takes more time to tackle a problem that you do not know how to solve than to complete an exercise where you know how to proceed. Consider tasks (A) (p. 121) and (B) (p. 122) in this chapter. Didn't (B) take you a lot more time than (A)? This is because (B) was probably an actual problem for you, whereas (A) was merely an exercise. You also need time for helping students to share and compare their solutions and to learn from one another. You can gain time for problem solving by reorganizing instructional activities so that some of the time previously allotted for practicing computational and other skills is redirected toward problem solving. This makes sense because students will be using and practicing such skills as they solve problems.

Managing Classroom Routines

When you teach problem solving, you will sometimes find it useful to teach the whole class, sometimes to divide the class into small groups, and sometimes to have children work in pairs or individually.

Large-group instruction (teaching the whole class) is effective for presenting and developing a new problem-solving strategy and for examining how different strategies can be used for solving the same problem. You can focus children's attention on a problem's structure, pose questions to help them use one strategy or find one solution, lead them to use other strategies or find other solutions, and encourage them to generalize from one problem to other problems. However, if you try to have the whole class actually solve a problem together, some students will come up with an answer before others have finished considering the problem carefully; in that case, the slower children will not benefit much. Moreover, what may be an appropriately challenging problem to some students may be a trivial exercise or an impossibly difficult task for others. Discussions about problem solving are feasible with large groups, but the actual process of solving problems should be practiced in small groups as well as individually and in pairs.

Small-group instruction makes it possible to group students by problem-solving ability and interests. Students in small groups have the opportunity to work cooperatively and at an appropriate level of difficulty for everyone in the group. Children feel less anxiety when everyone in a group is working together, discussing problems, sharing ideas, debating alternatives, and verifying solutions. Also, small groups of students can generally solve a wider range of problems than students working alone, although the groups may take longer on each problem. In addition, research indicates that when groups discuss what a problem means and how it might be solved, they achieve better results than when they are simply told how to solve it. Groups are clearly a means of promoting communication about mathematics.

Having children work in pairs is useful because they can teach each other, and this can happen no matter if you pair children of comparable abilities or of slightly different abilities. Peer teaching—with each child learning from the other—can occur in both situations.

Having children solve problems individually is also necessary, so children can progress at their own pace and use the strategies they find most comfortable. You may want to have problems available in the classroom that individual children can work on in their free time; a bulletin board, a problem corner, or a file of problems can be useful for this.

Managing Student Needs

In any given classroom, students are likely to vary widely in their ability to learn mathematics through problem solving and in the amount and kind of help they need to increase that ability. There are a variety of ways in which you can allow for different ability levels by challenging different students differently during problem-solving sessions (Diezmann, Thornton, and Watters, 2003).

Compensatory strategies are specific strategies that individual students can use to deal with their own specific learning needs. These strategies can be as different as the students' needs, but certain strategies can benefit almost all students. These strategies, which are particularly important when students are expected to tackle challenging problems, include:

- Using an approach that fits their way of learning. For example, students who tend to learn visually can try representing a problem and a solution method by making a drawing; other students can try talking through problems or using manipulatives.

- Using their strengths to communicating their thinking and keep a record of how they solved a problem—for example, using actions, symbols, words, or manipulatives. Sometimes a learning buddy can help bridge the gap between what a student is able to do or say while solving a problem and what needs to be in a written record of the solution.

- Rephrasing a problem in their own words in order to understand the problem better. (As we discussed above, this is a variant of the strategy of solving a similar but simpler problem.)

For students with specific needs, it may be important to:

- Help them get started by reading the problem aloud or having another student explain the problem. Also consider posing a simpler problem to get a student started or having hint cards prepared ahead of time for students to consult if they wish.

- Help them create a journal or card file of "types of math problems I can solve."

- Allow extra time for students with abstract reasoning or reading difficulties to break down problems by making notes summarizing "what I know" and "what I need to find out." Alternatively, you or another student could help them do this. Students with these types of difficulties are more likely to be successful at understanding and solving a problem if they can break it down in this way. (It is important to recognize that helping students understand a problem more clearly should not involve telling them how to do it; rather, you should help them figure out what is expected and what approaches they can use.)

There are a variety ways you can modify your instruction to help all children with problem solving, but these modifications are especially important for students with special learning difficulties.

- Assign problems that different students can approach in different ways.

- Routinely call on individual students to rephrase problems; this will help all the students understand the problem better.

- Ask pairs or small groups of students to share their solutions with the rest of the class; then ask one student from the group (sometimes, a student with special needs) to talk about what was discussed in the group as they worked on the problem.

- Allow students to write on the chalkboard or on a lap-size whiteboard, rather than on paper (especially students with vision or spatial-motor difficulties).

- Allow students to work on problems in quiet places (especially students with attention deficits).

Many students with learning disabilities are accustomed to instruction that focuses on learning through imitation, rather than learning through solving problems, so they may need time to adjust to this new approach. Your goal is to supply just the right amount of support and help, while still ensuring that each child is challenged by problems at the appropriate level of difficulty. For gifted students, you should prepare problem extensions ahead of time, so they can move on to thinking about a problem extension if they successfully complete the problem before the rest of the class. The extension might be a more general problem, a problem with larger numbers, or a problem with different constraints. For example:

> (28) Andrew has 20 cookies. How many will he have left over, if he shares them equally (without breaking any) with himself and 1 friend? Himself and 2 friends? Himself and 3 friends? Himself and 4 friends?

> (29) Andrew has some cookies, but we're not sure how many. He can share his cookies equally without any left over (and without breaking any) with one or two or three or four or five friends. What is the smallest number of cookies that Andrew could have?

Problem (28) might be appropriate for a third-grade class just being introduced to division, and Problem (29) could be an extension for students who need more challenge.

Cultural Connections

Problem solving is used in different ways in mathematics instruction in different countries around the world. In the Trends in International Mathematics and Science Study (TIMSS), Japanese students attained some of the highest overall test scores, while American students' scores were among the lowest. Interestingly, the TIMSS study also gathered videotapes of actual classroom instruction in different countries, and these give us a glimpse of how Japanese and American lessons tend to be structured differently (Shimizu, 2003; Stigler and Hiebert, 1999).

American lessons videotaped for the TIMSS study generally had two phases and involved students doing many "problems" (but the problems were often really just exercises, rather than true problems):

1. The teacher demonstrated or explained how to do sample problems.

2. The students worked on numerous problems (really exercises) on their own while the teacher helped individual students who were having trouble.

By contrast, a typical Japanese mathematics lessons—which lasts 45 minutes in elementary school—consisted of four (or sometimes five) phases, but typically focused on just one (or at most two) genuine problems:

1. The teacher posed a complex problem (something challenging that the students had not seen before).

2. The students worked on the problem on their own or in pairs.

3. The whole class discussed different students' approaches to the problem, orchestrated by the teacher.

4. The teacher summed up.

5. Optionally, depending on the time available and on students' facility at solving the original problem, students worked on extensions of the original problem.

A key difference between American and Japanese teaching is the role of the teacher while children are working on the initial problem (Shimizu, 2003). The Japanese teacher moves around the classroom not only to give guidance and assistance, but also to take note of the different ways in which students are approaching the problem. The Japanese teacher is planning which students to call on during the upcoming class discussion. In contrast, the American teacher is likely to call on whichever students raise their hands or on the students who seem likely to give a correct response or on students whose minds are wandering. The American teacher is less likely to think about what approach the student used to solve the problem and which approaches to discuss in which order during the class discussion.

Before Japanese teachers even assign a problem, they think about what approaches students are likely to take to the problem (and what errors are likely), and they decide on the order for talking about these approaches during the class discussion. As they circulate around the room, they look for particular approaches, and they plan to call on particular students to present their thinking. For example, a teacher might first call on a student who has solved the problem using a correct but very laborious method. Then the teacher might call on students with various incorrect solutions, so the class can debate whether the answers are correct and discuss and understand common errors. Later the teacher might call on students with elegant but nonobvious solutions.

As one researcher notes (Shimizu, 2003, p. 207):

> For Japanese teachers, a lesson is regarded as a drama, which leads up to at least one climax, or *yamaba*. In fact, a central characteristic of Japanese teachers' lesson planning is their deliberate structuring of their lessons around the yamaba. Thus, when a whole-class discussion begins, students listen carefully to the solutions proposed by their classmates and present their own ideas, because during this discussion, the lesson highlights, or yamaba, appear.

This same researcher offers five practical suggestions from Japanese teachers (Shimizu, 2003, p. 213):

- *Suggestion 1: Label students' methods* . . . during the whole-class discussion to ensure student ownership of the presented method and to make the discussion more interesting for the class.

- *Suggestion 2: Use the chalkboard effectively.* Whenever possible, record everything discussed during the lesson on the board in an organized fashion, and do not erase. This helps everyone compare different solution methods, and—at the end—offers a written bird's-eye view of the entire lesson.

- *Suggestion 3: Use the whole-class discussion to polish the students' ideas.* The Japanese word *neriage*—which translates as "polishing up"—

describes what should happen during the collaborative class discussion, as everyone involved participates in pulling all the various students' ideas together into one coherent mathematical idea.

- *Suggestion 4: Choose the numbers in, and the context of, the problem carefully.* The teacher must think about the variety of responses that he/she hopes the students will present and choose the problem accordingly.

- *Suggestion 5: Consider how to encourage a variety of solution methods.* If the teacher anticipates four different approaches, but her class comes up with only two of those four, she must be ready with pre-planned questions that can be asked to lead students to thinking about the problem in other ways, if these alternative approaches are important to the goal of the lesson.

Japanese teachers understand the importance of thinking deeply about the relationship between the mathematical content to be taught and the problems they assign, and they realize that anticipating student responses is a crucial aspect of lesson planning when teaching through problem solving.

A Glance at Where We've Been

Problem solving is one of the most important skills in mathematics; it should pervade the mathematics curriculum. Children need many experiences with genuine problems, not just with exercises. American students tend to have difficulty with nonroutine problems but have shown improving performance on routine problems. Problem solving helps students make sense of mathematics.

Signposts for teaching mathematics through problem solving include (1) allowing mathematics to be problematic for students, (2) focusing on the methods used to solve problems, and (3) telling students the right things at the right time. Factors that impact children's problem-solving skills include knowledge (making connections between what they know and new problems), beliefs and affects (self-confidence and a good attitude), control (the ability to monitor and direct their own thinking), and sociocultural factors (using non-school experience to solve problems; also, the classroom atmosphere). Effective teaching through problems means choosing appropriate types of problems (problems that test the right skills and

that are at the right difficulty level), finding good problems, having students pose problems, and using calculators and computers appropriately.

Children should be encouraged to use a variety of problem-solving strategies. Important strategies that can help children develop their problem-solving skills include acting out the problem, making a drawing or diagram, looking for a pattern, constructing a table, guessing and checking, working backward, and solving a similar but simpler problem. It is extremely important that children learn to look back after engaging in problem solving. They should look back at the problem to see how it is the same as and different from other problems, look back at the answer to make sure it is reasonable, look back at the solution process to assess whether they used the right strategy, and most important, look back at their own thinking, at how they thought about the problem and why.

Teachers can ensure that they help all children with problem solving, including children with special needs, by managing their time appropriately, managing the classroom routines (using large-group instruction and small-group instruction as appropriate, as well as having students work in pairs and individually), and managing student needs by using compensatory strategies to adjust instruction to the needs of individual students.

Cross-cultural studies of instruction in problem solving reveals that Japanese teachers tend to be more thoughtful and organized than American teachers, with better results.

Things to Do: From What You've Read

1. Provide a sample problem corresponding to each of the NCTM *Standards* (2000) problem-solving standards listed in the introduction to this chapter.

2. Solving problems is considered a key route to learning with understanding. What is the difference between a genuine problem and a mere exercise?

3. What does teaching mathematics through problem solving mean? What "signposts" for teaching guide this approach?

4. Give an example of a problem for each of the following: (a) children must represent mathemati-

cal ideas, (b) children must investigate, (c) children must estimate, (d) children must reason logically, and (e) children must use multiple steps or multiple strategies.

5. Give an example of a traditional mathematical story problem, and show how you might change the problem to make it open ended.

6. Describe why Polya's four-step plan is inadequate for helping students become good problem solvers. Why is it useful?

7. Solve the problems presented in this chapter; then say what level each is appropriate for (e.g., primary or intermediate).

8. Identify problems in this chapter for which calculators or spreadsheets would be useful. Are there problems for which using a calculator or a spreadsheet would take away all of the challenge? (These are important considerations when you are choosing problems for your class and deciding when students may and may not use calculators or spreadsheets.)

9. Choose a content topic for a particular grade level (e.g., number, geometry, data). Make up at least one interesting problem for that topic that can be solved by each of these strategies: look for a pattern, make a drawing or diagram, and construct a table.

10. Why isn't finding the answer the final step in solving a problem?

◀ Things to Do: Going Beyond This Book

IN THE FIELD

1. Choose a problem from this chapter and pose it to two children. Identify the strategies each child uses. Based on what you learn about the children from their solutions, identify a problem that you might use next with them and explain why you chose it.

2. *Mathematical processes.* Observe an elementary school classroom while children are engaged in a math lesson or investigation. Make a list of instances in which the children show evidence of using problem-solving strategies. Tell what the children were doing or saying and what tasks were involved. What role did the teacher play?

IN YOUR JOURNAL

3. *Solve the following problem (for 10 people) in at least two different ways and write up your solutions. Then build on your work to write a solution for the second and the third versions of the problem (for 15 people and for p people).*

There were 10 people at a party. Each person shook hands with each other person exactly once. How many handshakes took place? What if there were 15 people at the party? Write a formula for the number of handshakes if there were any number of people (p) at the party?

Optional problem extension (challenging).

A woman and her husband hosted a party for four other couples. The hostess asked everyone to shake hands with and introduce himself or herself to everyone else. Of course, no one shook hands with his or her spouse. At some point, the hostess stopped them and asked each person how many hands he or she had shaken. Each person gave a different response. What was the response of her husband?

(This problem appeared in the August 29, 2004, issue of *Parade*, the Sunday supplement to many newspapers. For a step-by-step solution, visit www.parade.com, click on "Ask Marilyn," and then search the archive for the key phrase "shake hands.")

WITH ADDITIONAL RESOURCES

4. Start a file with problems from this chapter, and then add other problems, especially nonroutine and open-ended problems. Many math education Web sites offer long lists of interesting problems. Solve your problems and identify the strategies that you found useful. Categorize the problems in the way you find most useful.

5. Search textbooks for a particular grade level. Find at least one problem that could be solved by using the following strategies: make a drawing or diagram, act it out, and solve a similar but simpler problem.

6. Plan an interactive bulletin board focused on problem solving.

---

*Additional activities, suggestions, and questions are provided in *Teaching Elementary Mathematics: A Resource for Field Experiences* (Wiley, 2007).

7. Pick a textbook and make a list of the problem-solving strategies it teaches. Compare that list to the list of strategies in this text. Note other ways that problem-related instruction is evident in this textbook. Write an evaluation of the book based on your strategy comparison, your additional notes, and the problem-solving standard from NCTM's *Principles and Standards for School Mathematics.*

8. Read one of the chapters from Lester and Charles (2003), an edited book for teachers about teaching mathematics through problem solving. Write a brief summary and a critique.

9. Read *Counting on Frank* (Clement, 1991). Write a lesson plan where this book would be read aloud to grade 4–6 students as a motivator for a problem-solving lesson.

10. Read O'Brien and Moss (1999). Choose your own context and problems similar to those used by these authors with fifth graders (problems with consistent data and with inconsistent data). If possible, try these problems with students of a similar age and analyze how they approach them.

11. Read Dwyer (2003), where a teacher reports about teaching problem solving to her class of bilingual third graders. Solve the problem the children solved and write about the features of this problem that allow for multiple entry points and a variety of approaches for that diverse group of students.

12. Obtain catalogs from software companies; select software that you think would help children develop their problem-solving skills.

13. Make up problems using newspaper or magazine articles or information from reference books (e.g., *Guiness Book of World Records*) or Web sites. Add the problems to your file.

WITH TECHNOLOGY

14. *Spreadsheet.* Use a spreadsheet to help solve Problems (10) and (11) of this chapter.

15. *Calculator.* Identify several problems in this chapter for which you would recommend that students be encouraged to use a calculator. Explain your reason for choosing these particular problems, and tell how you would use a calculator for each.

16. *Logo.* Use *Logo* programming to create a procedure that can be used to draw any regular polygon depending on the values input to the procedure.

17. *Geometer's Sketchpad.* Make a conjecture about the sum of the angles for regular polygons, and then use the *Sketchpad* to support that conjecture.

18. Make a file of ideas for using computer software and/or calculators in solving problems. Find problems for different grade levels.

Note to Instructors: You can find additional resources, learning activities, and black-line masters in this text's accompanying Instructor's Manual, at www.wiley.com/college/reys.

Book Nook for Children

Briggs, R. *Jim and the Beanstalk.* New York: Penguin Putnam Books for Young Readers, 1997.

One morning, Jim wakes up and sees a giant plant outside his window. He decides to climb the plant to see how high the plant grows. At the top, he finds a castle and a giant. He meets the giant and soon realizes that the giant has problems. Jim decides to help the giant with his problems.

Chwast, S. *The Twelve Circus Rings.* San Diego, CA: Gulliver Books, Harcourt Brace Jovanovich, 1993.

Lots of performers are active if there are 12 circus rings. The performers accumulate with "six acrobats, five dogs a barking. . ." reminiscent of the Twelve of Days of Christmas. At the end of the book, students are asked to reason through and find totals such as "How many monkeys are playing?" in all 12 rings.

Clement, R. *Counting on Frank.* Milwaukee, WI: Garth Stevens, 1991.

This story is about a boy who likes to ask questions. The best questions begin with "What if?" For example, "What if I drew with this ballpoint pen until it ran out, how long would the line be?" The story encourages readers to think about how to answer the wide variety of questions suggested in the book, and promotes seeing mathematical problems in everyday happenings. Problem solving, estimation, probability are just a few of the mathematical explorations in this book.

Murphy, S. J. *The Penny Pot.* New York: Harper Collins, 1998.

Jesse decides she wants her face painted at the school fair, but realizes that she doesn't have enough money. At the face painting booth, there is a penny pot. People place their extra pennies in the pot after having their face painted. Soon, there are enough pennies in the pot for Jessie to have her face painted. Different combinations of money are used to let the reader see how much money Jessie needs to have her face painted. There are also activities and games in the back of the book for teachers and parents.

Zaccaro, E. *Challenge Math for the Elementary and Middle School Student.* Bellevue, IA: Hickory Grove Press, 2000.

Challenge children in grades 4–8 using some of more than 1000 problems (presented with three levels of difficulty) in areas such as algebra, astronomy, trigonometry, probability, and more.

Annotated Resources

Andrews, A., and Trafton, P. R. *Little Kids—Powerful Problem Solvers: Math Stories from a Kindergarten Classroom.* Portsmouth NH: Heinemann, 2002.
Kindergarteners can do great math, especially if they are engaged and challenged from the start. This collection of stories from Angela's classroom is arranged by month of the school year. Each story provides inspiration for a classroom lesson. Making sense of math is the focus of the teaching, respecting children's thinking makes it possible. The collection shows how children can make sense of experience and observations, how they can estimate, predict, hypothesize, analyze, and apply mathematical concepts in practical and visible ways, how they can help, and occasionally hinder, but ultimately challenge each other, and the ability of even very young children to persist until they have resolved problems.

Burns, M. *50 Problem-Solving Lessons: Grade 1–6.* Sausalito, CA: Marilyn Burns Education Associates, 1996.
For many years, Marilyn Burns has produced a newsletter for teachers. Each newsletter contains classroom-tested activities from teachers across the country that are featured in this compilation of newsletters. The lessons span the strands of the math curriculum and are illustrated with children's work.

Charles, R. I., Lester, F. K., and Lambdin, D. V. *Problem-Solving Experiences in Mathematics: Making Sense of Mathematics.* Parsippany, NJ: Dale Seymour, 2005.
A series of six student books of problems (grades 3–8) and six teacher guides to help teachers infuse problem solving into their school mathematics curriculum. Designed to supplement any math textbook, the materials for each grade level provide skill-building activities that include one-step, multiple-step, concept, and strategy math problems.

Desoete, A., Roeyers, H., and Buysse, A. "Metacognition and mathematical problem solving in grade 3." *Journal of Learning Disabilities,* 34(5) (September–October 2001), pp. 435–439.
This overview of two studies examines the relationship between metacognition and mathematical problem solving in 165 children with average intelligence in grade 3 in order to help teachers and therapists gain a better understanding of contributors to successful mathematical performance. The analysis reveals three metacognitive components connected with mathematical problem solving.

Hartweg, K. "Solutions to the decorative plate hanging problem." *Teaching Children Mathematics,* 11(5) (December 2004/January 2005), pp. 280–284.
Fifth-grade students were given a problem in which they were to draw a diagram to show the placement and spacing for hanging six decorative plates along a 104-inch wall. Their teacher discussed the different approaches which four children used, the frustrations they experienced, and the sorts of questions the teacher posed to help them through their difficulties.

Hiebert, J., Carpenter, T. P., Fennema, E., Fuson, K., Wearne, D., Murray, H., Olivier, A., and Human, P. *Making Sense: Teaching and Learning Mathematics with Understanding.* Portsmouth, NH: Heinemann, 1997.
One of the clearest and most readable books on the market today about the essential features of classrooms that help students make sense of the mathematics they are learning by working from problem-based tasks. Based on the authors' work in four separate research projects, all of which investigated the effects of specific instructional approaches, this book offers real-world examples of classrooms that support students' learning with understanding.

Jitendra, A. "Teaching students math problem-solving through graphic representations." *Teaching Exceptional Children,* 34(4) (March–April 2002), pp. 34–39.
This study examines the usefulness of graphic representations in teaching students with learning disabilities for problem solving in mathematics. Cases of students with phobia for mathematics are examined. Assessment on the performance of students in problem-solving activities is provided. The use of schematic diagrams in teaching is explained.

Lester, F. K., and Charles, R. I. *Teaching Mathematics through Problem Solving: Prekindergarten–Grade 6.* Reston, VA: NCTM, 2003.
The primary goal of "teaching mathematics through problem solving" is to help students develop a deep understanding of mathematical concepts and methods by engaging them in making sense of problematic tasks in which the mathematics is embedded. This book offers a collection of 17 articles chosen to provide a vision of what it looks like to "teach through problem solving" and discussion of the

important issues that arise. Topics include "Benefits of Teaching through Problem Solving," "Mathematical Habits of Mind for Young Children," "Designing and Selecting Problem-Based Tasks," "Listening to Children," and "Problem Posing." Interspersed throughout the volume are nine "teacher stories," which provide personal reflections from actual classroom teachers on their efforts to infuse problem solving into all aspects of their own mathematics instruction.

Whitin, P. "Promoting problem-posing explorations." *Teaching Children Mathematics*, 11(4) (November 2004), pp. 180–186.

Working with a fourth-grade class to explore perimeter and area, this teacher made charts to help students track the regularities they observed and to encourage them to pose questions for further investigation. Though their questions originated from investigations of perimeter and area, they soon found themselves exploring other mathematical ideas such as factors and multiples, odd and even numbers, mathematical patterns, properties of rectangles, and calculation skills. The open-ended nature of the problem exploration gave students of varying abilities the opportunity to be challenged by pursuing what was most intriguing to them.

CHAPTER 7

Counting and Number Sense in Early Childhood and Primary Grades

Snapshot of a Lesson

Key Ideas

1. Engage students in oral counting
2. Provide a number of different contexts for counting practice

Background

This lesson is based on the video *Math Buddies,* from Teaching Math: A Video Library, K–4 from Annenberg Media. Produced by WGBH Educational Foundation. © 1995 WGBH. All rights reserved. To view video, go to http://www.learner.org/resources/series32.html (video #3). Mr. Chuck Walker teaches kindergarten at the Eissler Elementary School in Bakersfield, California. In a lesson he calls Math Buddies, Mr. Walker pairs kindergarteners with sixth graders in an effort to both support the kindergartener's mathematical understanding of number and to orient them into the school environment. The lesson is composed of 20 stations, both inside and outside of the classroom, where students investigate the numbers 1–50 through hands-on manipulative-based counting activities.

MR. WALKER: Now, the little buddies would like to welcome all of their big buddies to their classroom. Today, boys and girls, we're going to be exploring numbers. Numbers from 1 to 50.

MR. WALKER: [*To camera*] I use buddies to teach math to reinforce a lot of the skills that we teach in the classroom. The buddies know that they are to try to pull information from them, not to give them answers. That they are to try to help them discover and that's the whole idea.

Mr. Walker's intention is to show students how numbers occur naturally in our lives and environments. By exposing students to a variety of contexts, Mr. Walker underscores the power of numbers.

The video shows kindergartners and sixth graders working at a variety of counting stations. At one station, students glue objects onto a number grid. At another station, students count portions of snack food and place them into plastic storage bags. Outside, students count the number of times they swing back and forth on the swing set and the number of steps they take on a balance beam. In some of the instances pictured in the video, the older students intercede in the kindergartner's counting process. This is in conflict with Mr. Walker's instructions to the older children in which they were told not to supply answers to the kindergartners, but to help pull information from the younger buddies.

Toward the end of the class, Mr. Walker calls the younger and older buddies back together to discuss the work done at the stations.

MR. WALKER: [*To camera*] I like to pull all of the children together and talk about what we have accomplished throughout the day and try to put a little bit of closure to what has happened. And, I want them also to have that warmth of the buddies to make contact with one another as a group, to sing a few songs together, to bring us even closer together. And then to send them off with good feelings and knowing that they're going to return and continue to build upon the foundations we've already established the following week.

As Mr. Walker and the children sit in a circle, the teacher plays the guitar and asks students to sing along using the rules of a mathematics game.

MR. WALKER: You tell me what comes after . . . 0.

Mr. Walker continues to play the guitar and requests for students to sing the counting numbers that follow the numbers he sings. The students respond enthusiastically to his request, by singing the succeeding counting numbers.

Once Mr. Walker works his way through the counting numbers to 10, he changes the rules of the game.

MR. WALKER: Alright, I'm going to get a little more difficult for you. You ready? Tell me what comes before . . . 1.

Just as they had done before, the students sing counting numbers back to Mr. Walker. This time, they sing the counting number preceding Mr. Walkers' number.

Mr. Walker plays the guitar while he and his class sing a song to the big buddies as they leave the classroom.

MR. WALKER: I saw today exactly what I hoped would happen. I watched both the big buddy and the little buddy working together, interacting with one another. I saw them discovering. And you look for that little spark to see if something has happened, if something has clicked.

Number Sense

This chapter begins the second part of *Helping Children Learn Mathematics,* in that it discusses teaching strategies, techniques, and learning activities related to specific mathematical topics—in this case, beginning number sense. Number sense, like common sense, is difficult to define, but here are some characteristics. Number sense includes

- an understanding of number concepts and operations on these numbers
- the development of useful strategies for handling numbers and operations
- the facility to compute accurately and efficiently, to detect errors, and to recognize results as reasonable
- the ability and inclination to use this understanding in flexible ways to make mathematical judgments
- an expectation that numbers are useful and that work with numbers is meaningful and makes sense

These characteristics suggest that people with number sense are able to understand numbers and use them effectively in everyday living. Elementary school mathematics programs play a critical role in children's development of number sense.

These ideas regarding number sense are reminiscent of Brownell's ideas about meaningful learning (see Chapter 2). Students need to develop concepts meaningfully so that numbers are used effectively both in and out of school. Helping students to develop such number sense requires appropriate modeling, posing process questions, encouraging thinking about numbers, and in general creating a classroom environment that nurtures number sense.

Number sense is not a finite entity that a student either has or does not have. Its development is a lifelong process, and in early childhood and elementary school number sense development involves several stages:

1. Prenumber development
   - Classification
   - Patterning
2. Early number development
   - One-to-one correspondence
   - Comparisons
3. Number development
   - Connecting groups with number names, including oral and written cardinal and ordinal numbers
   - Group recognition
   - Counting forward and backward

- Skip counting
- Establishing benchmarks of quantities, such as 5 or 10
- Place value

The stages form the basis of whole-number development and provide the underpinnings for developing basic facts as well as mental and written computation involving addition, subtraction, multiplication, and division of whole numbers. Computations arising from meaningful problem-solving situations will promote children's development of number sense, establish solution strategies, and encourage them to reflect on the reasonableness of their results to make sure their answers make sense to them. Facility with whole numbers provides the foundation for work with fractions and decimals, topics that reflect the continuing development of number sense.

Two organizations, the National Council of Teachers of Mathematics (NCTM) and the National Association for the Education of Young Children (NAEYC) have identified early number concepts and skills that need to be established by all children. Their recommendations are remarkably consistent as shown by Figures 7-1 and 7-2. Figure 7-1 highlights typical learning paths related to number

development for young children along with some sample teaching strategies that are proposed by the NAEYC. Figure 7-2 presents part of the standard for prekindergarten through grade 2 that is in the *Principles and Standards for School Mathematics*. (See Appendix A for a full list of expectations.)

Math Links 7.1

*Y*ou will find detailed recommendations and suggestions for the early mathematics development of young children are available at the Web sites of National Association for the Education of Young Children at www.naeyc.org and the National Council of Teachers of Mathematics at www.nctm.org.

Let's explore several examples of number sense in action. What does the number 5 mean to young children? It can mean many things. It might be their current age or their age next year. It might be how old they were when they started kindergarten. Figure 7-3 illustrates a few uses and interpretations of the number 5 suggested by young children.

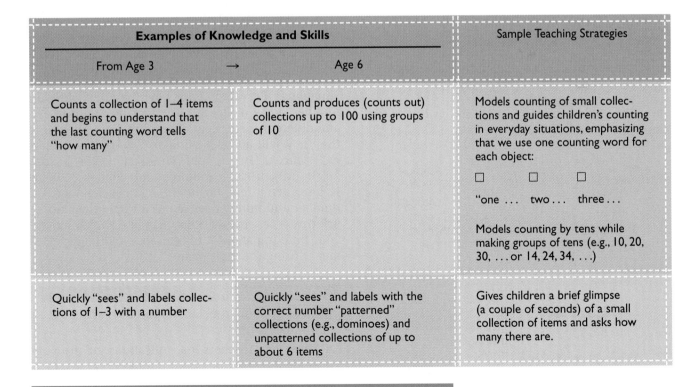

Examples of Knowledge and Skills		Sample Teaching Strategies
From Age 3 →	Age 6	
Counts a collection of 1–4 items and begins to understand that the last counting word tells "how many"	Counts and produces (counts out) collections up to 100 using groups of 10	Models counting of small collections and guides children's counting in everyday situations, emphasizing that we use one counting word for each object: ☐ ☐ ☐ "one … two … three … Models counting by tens while making groups of tens (e.g., 10, 20, 30, … or 14, 24, 34, …)
Quickly "sees" and labels collections of 1–3 with a number	Quickly "sees" and labels with the correct number "patterned" collections (e.g., dominoes) and unpatterned collections of up to about 6 items	Gives children a brief glimpse (a couple of seconds) of a small collection of items and asks how many there are.

FIGURE 7-1   Examples of number-related knowledge and skills and some teaching suggestions from the National Association for the Education of Young Children (www.naeyc.org).

Instructional programs from prekindergarten through grade 2 should enable all students to:	Pre-K–2 Expectations: All students should:
Understand numbers, ways of representing numbers, relationships among numbers, and number systems.	• Count with understanding and recognize "how many" in sets of objects • Develop understanding of the relative position and magnitude of whole numbers and of ordinal and cardinal numbers and their connections • Connect number words and numerals to the quantities they represent, using various physical models and representations

FIGURE 7-2 Number and Operation Standard for grades pre-K–2 from the National Council of Teachers of Mathematics (www.nctm.org).

Other children would provide different examples. These examples might be different for the same children tomorrow because children's concepts of numbers continuously grow and change.

Children begin to develop some sense about numbers long before they begin to count. For example, young children can answer these kinds of questions:

How old are you? [two]

What channel should we watch? [thirteen]

On what floor is your doctor's office? [four]

How many sisters do you have? [one]

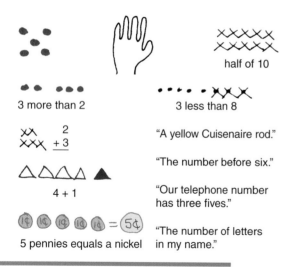

FIGURE 7-3 The meanings of the number 5 suggested by young children.

Such early experiences introduce the number names as well as their symbols—13 on the channel indicator or 4 on the elevator. These names and symbols are memorized through sound and sight recognition and provide an important beginning, but a child's knowledge of these concepts alone does not indicate the child's grasp of number.

For one thing, these experiences underscore a very important characteristic of number. It is an abstraction. It can't be adequately illustrated in just one situation. The multiple meanings of 5 illustrated in Figure 7-3 demonstrates how quickly the concept of *five* becomes associated with different situations. Research into how children develop number sense makes it clear that the more varied and different their experiences, the more likely it is that they will abstract number concepts from their experiences (Payne and Huinker, 1993; Fuson, 2003; Kilpatrick, Swafford and Findell, 2001). Helping children further their development of number and number sense has a high instructional priority. The goal of this chapter is to stimulate your thinking about number sense and its development during the early years.

FOCUS QUESTIONS

1. Why is subitizing an important early step in number sense?

2. How can teachers use questions to promote students' thinking about numbers?

3. What characteristics are associated with the different counting stages?

4. How can technology help children develop number sense?

Prenumber Concepts

Numbers are everywhere, and thus even young children have a vast amount of early number experience, as shown in Figure 7-3. Many of these experiences do not rely on numbers per se but provide the basis for building early number concepts and the foundation for later skills. Such experiences are called *prenumber experiences.* As a teacher, you need to help children take advantage of them. Different steps are involved in developing prenumber concepts that lead eventually to meaningful counting skills and number sense. Prenumber work is not all done before children do anything with numbers in school, but typically occurs simultaneously with activities involving number. Although the learning paths that children take are bound to differ greatly, they all begin with classifying whatever is to be counted.

Classification

Classification is fundamental to learning about the real world, and it can be done with or without numbers. For example, children can be separated into groups of boys and girls (which is classification) without considering number. Yet classification skills are prerequisite to any meaningful number work. If children want to know how many girls are in the class, they must be able to recognize (i.e., classify) the girls. Thus, before children can count, they must know what to count, and classification helps identify what is to be counted.

Classification is naturally integrated in other subjects, such as reading, science, and social studies. For example, recognizing consonant and vowel letters from the alphabet, requires classification, as does separating flowers from weeds or distinguishing between a leaf and stem in plants. In social studies, listing the states whose names begin with the letter M or naming the presidents in the twenty-first century are classification activities. Young children learn to distinguish between dogs and cats, reptiles and mammals, and toys they enjoy and those they never use. These are all examples of classification in action. Classification not only helps children make some sense of things around them, but also helps them become flexible thinkers. Classifying objects in different ways fosters the development of thinking skills.

As children classify, or sort materials, they must decide whether each object has the given characteristic. If children disagree on how an object should be classified, it forces them to defend their answers and clarify how the classification process was done. This type of argumentation is the beginning of helping children see the need for explaining their thoughts in mathematics, one of the goals of the NCTM *Standards.* At this point, there may be no counting as materials are classified, although words such as *more, few, many, most,* and *none* will likely be used in describing the resulting collections.

Classification allows people to reach general agreement on what is to be counted. For example, consider a pile of buttons and the following question: How many plastic buttons have two holes? The answer is a number that tells *how many.* When a number is used in this way, it is called a *cardinal number.* Before finding the specific cardinal number, however, you must first decide which buttons are plastic and how many of them have exactly two holes. Once this classification is done, the members to be counted are well defined, and ready to be counted.

Stories provide opportunities for classification. Books such as *Dave's Down-to-Earth Rock Shop* (Murphy, 2000) provide practice in visual discrimination as well as in classification.

Attribute blocks, sometimes called *logic blocks,* provide an excellent model for classification activities and help develop logical thinking. These blocks can be made from cardboard (see Appendix B for an attribute block master), but they are also commercially available in wood or plastic. They differ in several attributes, including color, shape, and size. Consider, for example, the 24 pieces shown in Appendix B and In the Classroom 7-1. These pieces illustrate three attributes:

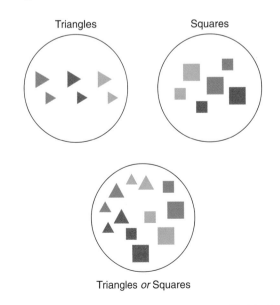

FIGURE 7-4 The union of two sets illustrates the mathematical meaning of "or."

In the Classroom 7-1

WHO AM I?

OBJECTIVE: **Using attribute pieces to develop classification and reasoning.**

GRADE LEVEL: 2–4

LBS	SBS	LBT	SBT
LRS	SRS	LRT	SRT
LGS	SGS	LGT	SGT
LBP	SBP	LBC	SBC
LRP	SRP	LRC	SRC
LGP	SGP	LGC	SGC

▼ Match me with the attribute blocks shown here:

A. I have three sides.
   I am blue.
   I am large.
   Who am I? _____

B. I am blue or red.
   I have three sides.
   I am not large.
   Who am I? _____

C. I am not blue.
   I am not red.
   I have five sides.
   I am small.
   Who am I? _____

D. I am not large.
   I have more than four sides.
   I am green.
   Who am I? _____

   • Which clues describe more than one piece? _____
   • Which clues describe only one piece? _____

▼ Your turn:
   Play "Who Am I?" with a partner.

Size: large, small (L, S)

Color: blue, red, green (B, R, G)

Shape: square, triangle, pentagon, circle (S, T, P, C)

The first block can be described in words as the "large blue square." Later in primary and upper elementary school, symbols, such as LBS, can be meaningfully attached to the attribute pieces, but

at this stage a clear verbal description of the pieces by young children is the goal. As children manipulate the blocks and describe them, they begin to make natural connections between the concrete model and different ways of representation. Many of the 24 pieces are alike in some attributes, but no two pieces are alike in all attributes, which provides opportunities for "Who am I?" games, as presented in In the Classroom 7-1. Such activities encourage children to think logically and develop communication skills. In the process, children informally explore fundamental notions, including matching, comparison, shape, sets, subsets, and disjoint sets as well as set operations.

Communication and language can be further developed as the set operations of union and intersection are encountered. The combining, or union, of *disjoint sets* (sets with no members in common) is a natural model for addition. The logical connection *or* can be used to develop the union of two or more sets. For example, as Figure 7-4 shows, the union of triangles and squares produces a set that contains all attribute blocks that are either triangles *or* squares.

The intersection of sets can be used to explore the logical connective *and.* Using the attribute blocks, you could examine the pieces that are pentagons *and* blue. Children might place these in yarn loops as shown in Figure 7-5. This arrangement also allows children to identify other subsets, such as pieces that are blue and not pentagons. Using *not* to describe a relationship is an important step in development.

The logical connectives *and, or,* and *not* can be used to help children classify pieces according to their attributes. For example, the "alike-and-difference trains" shown in In the Classroom 7-2 provide opportunities for students to use attribute blocks to classify and to search for patterns and

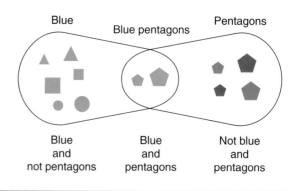

FIGURE 7-5 The intersection of two sets illustrates the mathematical meaning of "and."

In the Classroom 7-2

ALIKE-AND-DIFFERENCE TRAINS

OBJECTIVE: Using attribute pieces to recognize patterns and identify relationships.

GRADE LEVEL: 2–4

Each car in a train is like the car it follows in one or two ways, or it is different from the car it follows in one or two ways.

▼ Find the alike-and-difference pattern in each train, and describe the missing car:

Train A ▲ ▲ ▲ ▼ ▲ ____

Train B ▲ ⬠ ⬠ ● ● ____

Train C ● ● ____ ▽ ● ⬠

Train D ● ▲ ⬠ ● ● ____

- Which of these are one-difference trains? _____
- Which of these are two-difference trains? _____

▼ Your turn:
- Begin with ■. Make a train (with at least six cars) in which each car has exactly one attribute different from the car if follows. Compare your train with someone's train. Are they the same?
- Begin with ■. Make a train (with at least six cars) in which each car has exactly one attribute the same as the car it follows. Compare your train with a classmate's train. Tell how they are alike.

ferent attributes in mind simultaneously. Carefully observing and questioning children as they are using these materials will help you better understand what they are thinking, which in turn will help you design more appropriate learning activities.

Many different experiences are needed to sharpen children's observation skills and provide them with the basis on which to build the notion of numbers. Consider another example, in which children are asked to count money:

1¢   1¢   5¢

How much money is this?

Three, if coins are counted.

Seven, if cents are counted.

This example provides a reminder that a number name alone, such as three or seven, is rarely reported. In this case, "three coins" describes both *cardinality* (i.e., how many) and what was actually counted. This example also provides another reminder that what is to be counted must be well defined or clearly understood. If there is any confusion about what is being counted, then counting discrepancies are certain to happen.

Such discrepancies occur in many different forms but are particularly troublesome with a number line. Two children standing on a number line that has been made from a roll of adding machine tape and fastened to the floor provide an example:

Barb   Scott

You can ask,

How far is it from Barb to Scott?

Is it 4? or 3? or 5?

The solution depends on what is to be counted:

Should the intervals between the dots be counted?

Should the dots be counted?

All of the dots?

use logical thinking as well. Children at all grade levels can benefit from structured activities with these materials.

Attribute blocks almost guarantee student involvement, but they also require teachers to assume an active role. When children are engaged in activities with attribute blocks, directed questions and probes can provide clues about their thinking processes. Observing children's actions reveals much about their maturity. For example, when asked to choose a piece that is blue and a triangle, one child might choose a blue piece but not a triangle. Another might select a triangle that is not blue. These responses may only reflect poor listening skills; however, additional questioning may show that the two children don't understand what the word *and* means or are unable to keep two dif-

On the number line above, what number goes in the box?

Number in □ = _____

FIGURE 7-6   Fourth-grade item from the Third International Mathematics and Science Study.

Research confirms that confusion between dots and intervals often contributes to later misunderstanding with a number line (Kloosterman and Lester, 2004). For example, about one-third of fourth graders were able to correctly answer the item on the Third International Mathematics and Science Study shown in Figure 7-6. Confusion over what should be counted is a classification problem that must be solved before counting can be meaningful. Thus classification is a very important step in developing number sense and early counting skills.

Patterns

Mathematics is the study of patterns. Creating, constructing, and describing patterns require problem-solving skills and constitute an important part of mathematics learning. Patterns can be based on geometric attributes (shape, symmetry), relational attributes (sequence, function), physical attributes (color, length, number), or affective attributes (like, happiness). Sometimes patterns combine several attributes. For example, a child's list of favorite colors provides a pattern involving physical attributes (color) and affective attributes (like).

Paper, cubes, attribute blocks, pattern blocks, and other manipulatives (objects) provide opportunities for children to stack, arrange, and order objects in various ways. Number sense and mathematical exploration grow from such patterning. In the early grades, patterns help children develop number sense, ordering, counting, and sequencing (Coburn et al., 1992). Later, patterns are helpful in developing thinking strategies for basic facts, discussed in Chapter 9, and in developing algebraic thinking, considered in Chapter 14. In addition, as children grow older, their experiences with patterns accelerate as they explore graphing, number theory, and geometry. Patterns, as with puzzles, are usually intellectually inviting and stimulating for people of all ages.

Exploring patterns requires active mental involvement and often physical involvement. The opportunities to do patterning are limitless. Here are four different ways that patterns might be used in developing mathematical ideas.

Copying a Pattern   Children are shown a pattern and then asked to make one "just like it." The original pattern might take many different forms. For example, children might be given a string with beads and asked to make the same pattern:

Or pattern blocks (see Appendix B for a pattern block master) could be laid out for children to copy:

This experience requires students to choose the same pieces and arrange them in the same order. Or one could model a figure on a geoboard (see Appendix B for a geoboard master) and ask children to copy the figure on an empty geoboard.

Finding the Next One   The trains in In the Classroom 7-2 illustrate problems where children "find the next one." In that case, "the next one" is the next car in the train. Consider a somewhat easier pattern suggested by "stairs" of Cuisenaire rods:

Children might be asked to find the next rod for the staircase. This find-the-next activity naturally leads to continuing or extending the pattern.

Extending a Pattern   Children are shown a pattern and asked to continue it. For example, an initial pattern can be made with blocks, and children can be asked to continue the pattern:

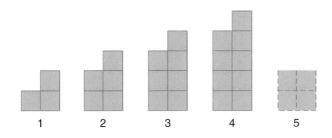

Notice how this visual pattern might serve as the foundation for exploring several important mathematical ideas. It could lead to classifying odd numbers. It could be used to observe something common about the representations—that they are all a rectangle plus one. This latter observation might lead to the algebraic generalization $2N + 1$ to describe odd numbers.

Making their own patterns   Children need opportunities to create their own patterns and are eager to do so. Sometimes the patterns they make are highly creative and reveal insight into their mathematical thinking.

Language and communication are important elements of patterning activities. You should encourage children to "think out loud" as they search for patterns. Ask them to explain why they selected a certain piece or why they did what they did. Sometimes children "see" different patterns than you anticipate. As teachers, you must try to learn and understand children's patterns and encourage them to share their thinking.

Comparisons

Comparison of quantities is another important part of learning to count and is also essential in developing number awareness. Comparisons are plentiful in classrooms as children use materials. Teacher-led activities frequently provide opportunities for comparisons, with questions such as:

Does everyone have a piece of paper?

Are there more pencils or desks?

These questions either directly or indirectly involve comparisons that may lead to the important and powerful mathematical notion of one-to-one correspondence. Look at Figure 7-7a and consider this question: Are there more hearts or gingerbread cookies? Counting provides a solution, particularly with the cookies scattered on a plate; however,

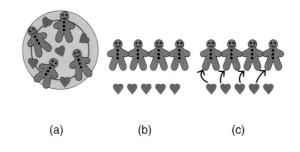

(a)   (b)   (c)

FIGURE 7-7   Models for making comparisons by (a) counting; (b) physically comparing without counting; and (c) one-to-one correspondence.

the cookies are arranged in an orderly fashion (Figure 7-7b), you can make direct comparisons and answer the question without counting. Sometimes placing connectors (laying string or yarn; drawing lines or arrows) provides a visual reminder of the one-to-one correspondence that underlies many comparisons, as in Figure 7-7c. In this case the one-to-one correspondence confirms that there is one more heart than cookies. The process of recording tallies to keep track of the number of objects (see Chapter 17) rests on the notion of one-to-one correspondence.

When making comparisons, students must be able to discriminate between important and irrelevant attributes. In Figure 7-8a, for example, who has more leaves—Bonnie or Sammy? The leaves are very different; their sizes, shapes, and colors vary. Still, the procedure for setting up a correspondence is the same.

To ensure that members of two sets are arranged in an orderly fashion for comparison, a method that is sometimes helpful involves using

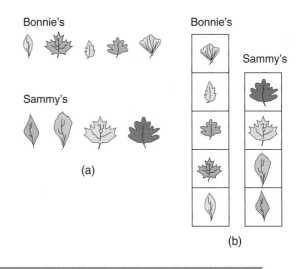

FIGURE 7-8   A framework for comparison that facilitates a one-to-one correspondence.

pieces of square paper or index cards. In this case, placing each leaf on a card and then stacking the cards on a common base, as in Figure 7-8b, provides a helpful framework. This method provides a graphical representation of the information, allowing quick and accurate visual comparisons.

Several different but equally valid verbal descriptions may be used for the example given in Figure 7-8:

> Bonnie has more leaves than Sammy.
>
> Sammy has fewer leaves than Bonnie.

Children need to become familiar with descriptions of relationships such as *more than, less (fewer) than,* and *as many as.* A grasp of these terms can be followed by more explicit characterization:

> Bonnie has one more leaf than Sammy.
>
> Sammy has one less leaf than Bonnie.

In these cases, the notion of order and succession are being developed. Children must come to realize that 4 is the number between 5 and 3 as well as one more than 3 and one less than 5. Understanding of such relationships can evolve naturally as comparisons are made and discussed.

When comparisons are made among several different things, ordering is involved. For example, children can print their first names on some grid paper:

Then they can physically compare their names with others' names to answer questions such as these:

> Who has the longest name?
>
> Who has the shortest name?
>
> Can you find someone with a name the same length as yours?
>
> Can you find someone whose name has one more (less) letter than your name?

Ordering often requires several comparisons, and graphs help organize information. The graph in Figure 7-9 was constructed by classifying children's names according to length. It summarizes much information and presents it in an organized form. The graph could be used to answer the previous questions and additional questions such as these:

> Which length name is most popular?
>
> Greg wasn't here today. Where should his name go on our graph?
>
> Can you think of anyone you know who has a shorter name than Tim?

FIGURE 7-9 Classification of children's names on a graph for comparison.

As more things are ordered, the ordering process becomes more complicated, and most children need some guidance to be able to order things efficiently. That's why organizational techniques, such as graphing (see Chapter 17), are particularly helpful and will contribute to the early development of numbers.

Early Number Development

Making comparisons and recognizing more and less of quantities may be done without counting, yet may also provide opportunities for counting. Visual comparisons help develop the recognition of small quantities, yet research by Piaget and others shows that for young children this number recognition may be unstable (Kilpatrick, Swafford, and Findell, 2001). This leads to important stages of number development.

Conservation

The phenomenon of *conservation of number*—that a given number does not vary—reflects how children think. You need to be aware of the symptoms of the lack of conservation of number in children and its implications for early number development and counting. This idea occurs in different forms, but let's look at an example involving counting and numbers.

Two rows of blocks are arranged side by side, and a teacher and a 5- or 6-year-old child look at them together. The teacher asks the child to make a comparison to decide whether there are more orange blocks or more purple blocks, and initiates the following dialogue:

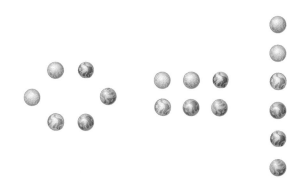

TEACHER: How many purple blocks?

STUDENT: [*Counting them*] Nine.

TEACHER: How many orange blocks?

STUDENT: [*Counting again*] Nine.

TEACHER: Are there more purple blocks or orange blocks?

STUDENT: They are the same.

Now the teacher spreads out the orange blocks as follows:

TEACHER: How many purple blocks now?

STUDENT: Nine.

TEACHER: How many orange blocks now?

STUDENT: Nine.

TEACHER: Are there more purple blocks or orange blocks?

STUDENT: More orange blocks.

TEACHER: I thought you said there were nine purple and nine orange.

STUDENT: I did, but this nine [*pointing to row of orange blocks*] is bigger.

This example illustrates a typical case where a young child thinks a number varies and depends on arrangement or configuration. Here the child believes that stretching out the row of blocks changes the number of blocks, and verbalizes this by saying "one nine is bigger than another nine" and sees no flaw in his or her reasoning. Thus at this stage children believe the number in a quantity may change depending on its arrangement.

Look at the following grouping of marbles.

Some children count six marbles in each of these groups but report one group has more. For adults it seems inconceivable that "this six" could be more than "that six," but as this and other

examples in this book show, children's logic and adults' logic can be very different.

Conservation was described by Jean Piaget and has been the subject of much research. Rarely do children conserve number before 5 or 6 years of age. Children up to this age don't realize that moving the objects in a set has no effect on the number of the objects. Thus many children in kindergarten and some in first and second grade are nonconservers. A child can be adept at counting and remain naive about conservation. Whenever this happens, instructional activities should be used to increase the child's awareness of the invariance of number.

Group Recognition

The patterns encountered in classifying and making comparisons provide many number-sense experiences. In fact, before actually counting, children are aware of small numbers of things: one nose, two hands, three wheels on a tricycle. Research shows that most children entering school can identify quantities of three things or less by inspection alone without the use of counting techniques (Clements, 1999a).

The skill to "instantly see how many" in a group is called *subitizing,* from a Latin word meaning "suddenly." It is an important skill to develop. In fact, one instructional goal for first-grade students is to develop immediate recognition of groups of up to five or six. Sight recognition of quantities up to five or six is important for several reasons:

1. *It saves time.* Recognizing the number in a small group is much faster than counting each individual member of that group.

2. *It is the forerunner of some powerful number ideas.* Children who can name small groups give evidence of knowing early order relations, such as 3 is more than 2 and 3 is 1 less than 4. Some may also realize that 3 contains a group of 2 and a group of 1.

3. *It helps develop more sophisticated counting skills.* Children who recognize the number in a small group will more quickly begin counting from that point.

4. *It accelerates the development of addition and subtraction.* Early work with these operations involves manipulation with objects. Being able to recognize the quantity in a small group frees children of the burden of counting small quantities to be joined or removed and allows them to concentrate on the action of the operation.

Sight recognition is evidenced by children's skills in reading the number of dots on the face of a die or on a domino. In fact, both of these materials provide natural as well as interesting models for developing and practicing this skill. As children grow older, their ability to recognize quantities continues to improve, but it is still limited. Certain arrangements are more easily recognized or subitized. For example, look at these arrangements:

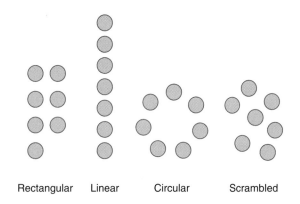

Rectangular   Linear   Circular   Scrambled

Children usually find rectangular arrangements easiest, followed by linear, and then circular, whereas scrambled arrangements are usually the most difficult. If the arrangement does not lend itself to some grouping, people of any age have more difficulty with larger quantities. Few adults can recognize by inspection groups of more than 6 or 8, and even these groups must be in common patterns such as those found on playing cards or dominoes. For example, look at these pictures of birds:

How many birds do you see? Each picture shows 12 birds, but you probably used different processes to count them. The picture at the left provides no clear groups, so you could either count every bird

or perhaps immediately identify the numbers in some subset of the birds and then count the rest. In the other two pictures, some natural groupings are suggested: four groups of 3 and two groups of 6. It is even more difficult to recognize larger groupings without counting or forming some subsets of numbers. Nevertheless, small-group recognition or subitizing is a powerful ally in counting larger groups.

Counting

Patterns facilitate the counting process; however, there are no sound patterns within the first 12 number names. Children learn these number names by imitating adults and older children. As young children practice counting, they often say nonconventional sequences of number names. It is not unusual to hear a young child count "one, two, five, eight, fifteen, twenty, six, hundred." This counting may sound strange, but it is perfectly natural. It reflects the child's struggle to remember both the number names and their order, both of which are necessary in order to count.

Eventually children may count apples, blocks, cards, rocks, stones, twigs, even petals on a flower. Try counting the petals on the flowers shown in Figure 7-10. They provide a very interesting setting for practicing counting and remind you that numbers are everywhere in nature.

Items such as blocks or petals are *discrete objects* (i.e., materials that lend themselves well to handling and counting). *Continuous quantities,* such as the amount of water in a glass or the weight of a person, are measured rather than counted.

What is counting? It is a surprisingly intricate process by which children call number values by name. A close look at the counting process shows that finding how many objects are present involves two distinct actions. A child must say the number-name series, beginning with one, and point to a different object as each number name is spoken. Children exhibit several different but distinct stages of counting, which we discuss as follows.

Counting Principles

How do children count? Look at an actual counting situation. Suppose seven shells are to be counted. A child who is what is called a "rational counter" says each number name as the shells are counted, as indicated in Figure 7-11. A rational counter also realizes that the last number named,

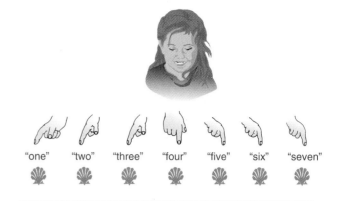

FIGURE 7-11 Rational counting: Correct sequence, with correct correspondence.

The child in the figure started with "one" and counted "two, three, . . ., seven," in a specific order. This is known as the *stable order rule*.

- *The order in which the objects are counted doesn't matter.* This is known as the *order irrelevance rule*. Thus the child can start with any object and count them in any order.

- *The last number name used gives the number of objects.* This principle is a statement of the *cardinality rule,* which connects counting with *how many*. Regardless of which block is counted first or the order in which they are counted, the last block named always tells the cardinal number of the objects being counted.

Knowing these principles will help you recognize the levels of children's counting skills. Careful observation of children, coupled with a good understanding of these principles, can pinpoint counting errors. Once the trouble is diagnosed, instruction can focus on the specific problem.

Counting Stages

There are several identifiable counting stages, and each reflects one or more of the counting principles. For example, some children may count the objects correctly and still not know how many objects have been counted. In response to the question "How many shells are on the table?" a child might correctly count "one, two, three, four, five, six, seven," as shown in Figure 7-11, and yet be unable to answer the question. This child does not realize that the last number named tells how many.

The shells in Figure 7-12 are shown in a linear arrangement because this configuration is easier to count than objects in rectangular or a scattered formulation. Sometimes it is helpful to encourage children to organize their objects prior to counting

FIGURE 7-10 Models from nature for counting practice. (Source: Top photo, PhotoDisc/Getty Images; bottom photo, Digital Vision/Getty Images.)

"seven," reports the total, or the cardinality of the set of shells that is being counted.

As adults, you probably cannot recall your own struggle with counting. Yet observing young children can remind you how counting strategies vary and are developed sequentially over a period of years (Fuson, 2003). Here are four important principles on which the counting process rests:

- *Each object to be counted must be assigned one and only one number name.* As shown in Figure 7-11, a *one-to-one* correspondence between each shell and the number name was established.

- *The number-name list must be used in a fixed order every time a group of objects is counted.*

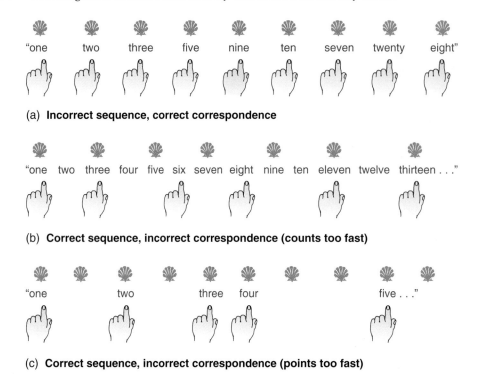

FIGURE 7-12 Rote counting errors.

to decrease the likelihood of counting errors that result in double counting or omiting objects.

Rote counting   A child using rote counting knows some number names, but not necessarily the proper sequence, as shown in Figure 7-12a. In this case, the child provides number names, but these names are not in correct counting sequence. These children may "count" the same objects several times and use a different counting sequence each time. Children who exhibit this error need to spend more time on the *stable order rule* as described in the second counting principle.

Rote counters may know the proper counting sequence, but they may not always be able to maintain a correct correspondence between the objects being counted and the number names. Figure 7-12b shows an example in which the rote counter is saying the number names faster than pointing, so that number names are not coordinated with the shells being counted. Rote counters may say the number names until they perceive all the objects as being counted. It is also possible that the rote counter points faster than saying the words, as illustrated in Figure 7-12c. This rote counter is pointing to the objects but is not providing a name for each of them. Asking children to slow down their counting and stressing the importance of one-to-one correspondence helps children with these types of rote counting errors.

It is important that children demonstrate all four counting principles. Otherwise, children may not have their number names in the proper sequence, or they may not consistently provide a number name for each object being counted. A one-to-one correspondence may not be shown, which is a critical distinction between rote and rational counting. Using a one-to-one correspondence in counting represents significant progress and establishes one of the prerequisites to rational counting.

Rational counting   In rational counting, the child gives a correct number name as objects are counted in succession; however, in rational counting the child not only uses one-to-one correspondence but also is able to answer the question about the number of objects being counted. Rational counters exhibit all four counting principles.

Rational counting is an important skill for every primary-grade child. Children notice their own progress in developing this skill and become proud of their accomplishments. Early in first grade, some children will count to 10, others to 20, some to 50, and a few to over 100 (Fuson, 2003). No upper limit should be imposed, although a goal of rational counting to 100 is clearly reasonable for most children by the end of first grade. Instruction should provide regular practice and encourage each child to count as far as he or she can.

Counting Strategies

Once mastery of rational counting to 10 or 20 has been reached, more efficient and sophisticated counting strategies should be encouraged.

Counting on   In counting on, the child gives correct number names as counting proceeds and can start at any number and begin counting. For example, a child may count a pile of 8 pennies and when 3 more pennies are added to the pile, count "nine, ten, eleven"; or begin with 78 pennies and count "seventy-nine, eighty, eighty-one"; or begin with 98 pennies and count "ninety-nine, one hundred, one hundred one." Counting on is preceded by counting all, where a child when the 3 pennies are added to the 8 pennies that had been counted would count all of them again by beginning to count from one and then end with eleven. Counting-on practice leads children to the discovery of many valuable patterns. Counting on is also an essential strategy for developing addition.

Being able to count on or back requires that children recognize the starting number and the nested inclusion of previous numbers. Thus if we start counting on from 8, a child must know the numbers that come immediately before and after 8 as well as the sequence of numbers preceding or "nested" within the number 8. Research suggests that even children reflecting all the counting principles show confusion or uncertainty about the nested inclusion of previous numbers (Fuson, 2003).

Counting back   When children count back, they give correct number names as they count backward from a particular point. For example, to count back to solve the problem, "Bobbie had 22 rabbits and 3 were lost," a child might count "twenty-one, twenty, nineteen" and conclude there were 19 left. At an early stage, counting back can be related to rockets blasting off (counting down—five, four, three, two, one, blast off); later, it becomes helpful in developing subtraction.

Many children find it difficult to count backward, just as many adults find it difficult to recite the alphabet backward. The calculator provides a valuable instructional tool to help children improve their ability to count backward. Many children are surprised to learn that it is as easy to count backward on a calculator as it is to count forward.

Instruction in counting should include practice counting backward as well as forward. Counting backward, "Five, four, three, two, one," helps children establish sequences and relate each number to another in a different way. In the Classroom 7-3 provides an activity that uses a calendar to practice counting forward and backward.

As shown earlier in Figure 7-6, children need to understand what is to be counted on the number line. Once the number line is clearly understood, the number line is a powerful model for counting on from any starting point A and counting to the right to B

In the Classroom 7-3

NUMBERS ON A CALENDAR

OBJECTIVE: **Using a calendar to count forward and backward.**

GRADE LEVEL: **2–3**

▼ Look at the calendar pictured below.

1. A calendar has many patterns. Tell a pattern you see.
2. What day and date is 7 days after the 7th?
3. What day and date is 1 week after the 5th?
4. If you start on Monday and count on 7 days, what is the day?
5. If you start on Sunday and count back 4 days, what is the day?
6. What day and date is 5 days before the 30th?
7. What day and date is 5 days after the 21st?
8. Count on 7 days after the 11th. What is the date? The day?
9. Count back 7 days from the 27th. What is the date? The day?
10. Make up some counting problems on your own that use the calendar. Give them to a friend to solve.

and counting back to the left starting from B and counting to A.

Just as counting on models addition, counting back models subtraction. For example, use the counting line below to start at B on the number line and count 5 steps back. This action models $7 - 5 = 2$.

If the counting line is replaced with the number line below, then counting back 5 from B would model $3 - 5 = -2$ and illustrates how the number line provides a natural entry into integers.

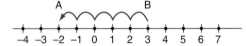

A number line never ends, so if a different part of the number line is shown, then counting back 5 from B would model a different computation. For example, in the number line below B denotes -1 so $-1 - 5$ is -6.

This demonstrates the importance of labeling a number line accurately and reminding children that since we can't show all the numbers, we are only looking at a piece of a number line. The piece of the number line shown is usually chosen to focus on certain numbers. Figure 7–13 shows how number lines might be shown different with number strings, and then children can use the patterns shown to name more of the marks.

In the Classroom 7-4 uses the calculator to count forward and back, and In the Classroom 7-5 shows how counting backwards with a calculator introduces negative integers.

You might ask, why introduce zero and negative numbers when counting? Since both counting on and back are important skills, children will encounter zero and negative numbers so it makes sense to introduce them. Furthermore, most young children already have an intuitive knowledge of nonpositive numbers and counting back on a calculator provides one tool for representing them on a number line. Other models include thermometers, losses and gains, pebbles in a bag, and elevators. Research suggests that young students are more

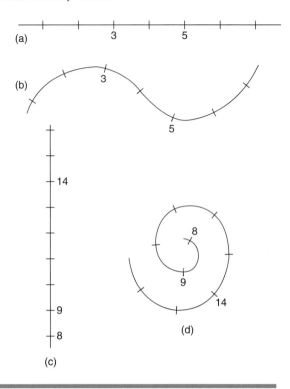

FIGURE 7-13 Examples of different number strings.

capable of understanding negative numbers far earlier than was once thought (Kilpatrick et al., 2001).

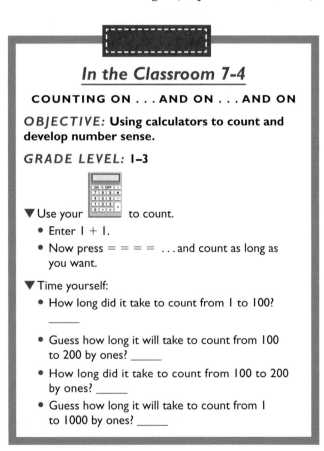

In the Classroom 7-4

COUNTING ON . . . AND ON . . . AND ON

OBJECTIVE: **Using calculators to count and develop number sense.**

GRADE LEVEL: **1–3**

▼ Use your calculator to count.
  ● Enter 1 + 1.
  ● Now press = = = = . . . and count as long as you want.

▼ Time yourself:
  ● How long did it take to count from 1 to 100? _____

  ● Guess how long it will take to count from 100 to 200 by ones? _____

  ● How long did it take to count from 100 to 200 by ones? _____

  ● Guess how long it will take to count from 1 to 1000 by ones? _____

In the Classroom 7-5

COUNTING ON AND BACK

OBJECTIVE: **Using calculators to count and develop number sense.**

GRADE LEVEL: **1–3**

▼ Enter 1 + 1 in your . Then Press = = = = . . .

- Stop when you get to 8. Predict the next number.
- Count to 15. Cover your display. Press the equal button 4 times. What number do you think is hidden? Check your display to see if you are fight.

▼ Try these:

4 + 1: _____, _____, _____, _____, _____, _____, _____

4 − 1: _____, _____, _____, _____, _____, _____, _____

0 + 4: _____, _____, _____, _____, _____, _____, _____

0 − 4: _____, _____, _____, _____, _____, _____, _____

Math Links 7.2

*T*here are a number of excellent Web sites that provide opportunities for children to make patterns, practice counting, and develop a better sense about numbers. Here are several:

Go the Math Forum Web site at http://math-forum.org/mathtools and then go to Math Topics. There you will find a number of K–2 virtual resources related to early number development, including those designed to help children practice counting, develop sight recognition of quantities, and practice with a five-frame.

Go to the Forum Web site at http://mathforum.org/mathtools and then go to Math Topics. Under Kindergarten, Math 1 and 2 you will find a number of K–2 virtual resources related to early number development, including those designed to help children practice counting, such as Sorting, Counting, Patterns, and Writing Numbers.

Go to the NCTM Illuminations Web site at http://illuminations.nctm.org/tools/index.aspx. There you will find a wide range of tools, several of which are related to early number development. Among those tools are the Five-frame and Bobbie Bear-Counting Strategies.

Go to the National Library of Virtual Manipulatives at http://www.matti.usu.edu. There you will find Color Patterns in the K–2 resources. It provides a range of patterns for children to explore. The Number Line Arithmetic and Number Line Bounce engage children in operations on the number line.

www.wiley.com/college/reys

Skip counting   In skip counting, the child gives correct names, but instead of counting by ones, counts by twos, fives, tens, or other values. The starting point and direction are optional. In addition to providing many patterns, skip counting as shown in In the Classroom 7-6 and 7-7 provides readiness for multiplication and division.

Skip counting, coupled with counting on and counting back, provides excellent preparation for counting change in a monetary transaction. Thus, given the coins shown, children would be encouraged to choose the largest-valued coin and then begin counting on—"twenty-five, thirty, thirty-five, forty."

In the Classroom 7-6

HUNTING FOR NUMBERS

OBJECTIVE: **Using a hundred chart to identify patterns and develop number sense.**

GRADE LEVEL: **2–3**

▼ Look at this chart:

1	2	3	4	5	6	7	8	9	10
11	12	13	14	15	16	17	18	19	20
21	22	23	24	25	26	27	28	29	30
31	32	33	34	35	36	37	38	39	40
41	42		44	45	46	47	48	49	50
51	52	53	54	55	56	57	58	59	60
61	62	63	64	65	66	67	68	69	70
71	72	73	74	75	76	77	78	79	80
81	82	83	84	85	86	87	88	89	90
91	92	93	94	95	96	97	98	99	100

- What is hidden by the ■?
- What number is after ■?
- What number is before the ■?

▼ Put a ● on any number.
- Begin at ●: Count forward five.
- Begin at ● again: Count backward five.

▼ Put a ▲ on a different number.
- Begin at ▲: Count forward five.
- Begin at ▲ again: Count backward five.

▼ Tell about any patterns you see.

In the Classroom 7-7

SKIP COUNTING

OBJECTIVE: Using a hundred chart to skip count and identify resulting patterns.

GRADE LEVEL: 1–3

▼ Use your calculator and a hundred chart to count.

1	2	3	4	5	6	7	8	9	10
11	12	13	14	15	16	17	18	19	20
21	22	23	24	25	26	27	28	29	30
31	32	33	34	35	36	37	38	39	40
41	42	43	44	45	46	47	48	49	50
51	52	53	54	55	56	57	58	59	60
61	62	63	64	65	66	67	68	69	70
71	72	73	74	75	76	77	78	79	80
81	82	83	84	85	86	87	88	89	90
91	92	93	94	95	96	97	98	99	100

- Start at 3 and count by 3s.
- Circle every number you counted.
- Describe a pattern.

▼ Which of these numbers would be counted?

13, 51, 61, 62, 63, 100, 113

Counting change is a very important skill whose usefulness children recognize. It holds great appeal for them. It should be introduced and extended as far as possible in the primary grades. Interestingly enough, most of the difficulties associated with counting change can be traced to weaknesses in counting. As teachers you should take advantage of every opportunity to encourage accurate and rapid skip counting.

Counting Practice

Counting practice should include counting on and counting back. Books such as *Anno's Counting Book* by Mitsumasa Anno and *I Can Count the Petals of a Flower* by John and Stacy Wahl provide a variety of rich and stimulating contexts for counting. These books engage children in counting and provide insight into how children count. Other books, such as *How Many Snails? A Counting Book* by Paul Giganti and *Count on Your Fingers African Style* by Claudia Zaslavsky, focus on numerical

relationships. Such books are useful for counting-based discussions between children and adults. For example, *Anno's Counting Book* provides a sequence of pictures of different scenes of the house where little people move from one house to another. Initially the teacher or parent can ask questions such as

How many children are in the house?

How many are boys?

How many are girls?

How many are wearing hats?

How many are on the second floor?

Starter questions are provided to encourage active participation and maintain a high level of interest. After students start counting, many new things to count are identified as the story unfolds.

Practice in skip counting from 1 and other start numbers, including 0, contributes to developing good counting skills and greater number sense. The hundred chart is an ideal model for practicing counting and skip counting, as in In the Classroom 7-6 and 7-7.

Research has shown some predictable trouble spots for children when counting. For example, children often slow down, hesitate, or stop when they reach certain numbers, such as 29; however, as soon as they establish the next number as 30, their counting pace quickens, until they are ready to enter the next decade (set of 10 numbers). Bridging the next century (set of 100 numbers) poses a similar challenge. As children count " . . . one hundred ninety-eight, one hundred ninety-nine," they may pause and be uncertain how to name the next number. Bridging to the next 10 or 100 are among the common transitional points of counting difficulty:

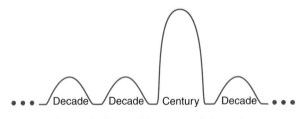

Bumps in the road for successful counters

Not only is the calculator a valuable instructional tool that helps improve children's ability to count, but it is also a powerful counting tool that they love to explore. Early counting with the calculator should emphasize the physical link between pressing the keys and watching the display.

Because the display changes constantly, the students begin to recognize patterns. Calculator counting involves a physical activity (pressing a key each time a number is counted), through which students can relate the size of a number to the amount of time needed to count it.

Children are usually surprised to find that it is as easy to count by any number on the calculator as to count by ones. A calculator can start at zero and count by ones (In the Classroom 7-4). Calculators can also begin at any starting point and skip count either forward or backward by any number (In the Classroom 7-5).

Calculator counting opens exciting mathematical explorations and promotes both critical thinking and problem solving. According to Huinker (2002), "using calculators as learning tools can empower young children with the capacity to investigate number ideas in ways that were previously inaccessible to them" (p. 316).

Developing Number Benchmarks

Number benchmarks are perceptual anchors that become internalized from many concrete experiences, often accumulated over many years. For example, the numbers 5 and 10 (the number of fingers on one and two hands) provide two early number benchmarks. Children recognize four fingers as being one less than five and eight as being three more than five or two less than ten:

"one less than five"   "three more than five"
"two less than ten"

The five-frame (5 × 1 array) and the ten-frame (5 × 2 array) (Appendix B) use these early benchmarks:

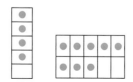

In Japan, the early benchmarks of 5 and 10 are later used with the ten-frame and the Japanese *soroban* (which is similar to an abacus) to promote counting, quick recognition of quantities, and mental computation (Shigematsu, Iwasaki, and Koyama, 1994).

Making Connections

Development of the numbers 1 through 5 is principally done through sight recognition of patterns, coupled with immediate association with the oral name and then the written symbol. For example, as Figure 7-14 illustrates, a picture of a tricycle and the question, "How many wheels?" can be used to develop the number 3. It is important that the number of wheels be linked to both oral name and written symbol. It is also important to provide different configurations of dots, blocks, and other objects, as well as different forms of the numerals, such as **3** and 3, to broaden their experiences.

How many wheels?

Three

Name (oral representation)

Model (visual representation)

Symbol (written representation)

FIGURE 7-14   A number development model linking visual, oral, and written representations.

Many valuable relationships are established as the numbers 1 through 5 are developed, but none are more useful than the notions of *one more* and *one less*. These connections are fundamental in early counting and also in learning place value with larger numbers. The notions *one more* and *one less* evolve from many different real-world experiences, such as these:

David has one less cookie than Jean-Paul.

Mira has one more apple than Beth.

They have one less player on their team.

Their group has one more girl than our group.

The concepts of *one more* and *one less* can be modeled in different ways. Figure 7-15 shows three such models. These arrangements provide a basis for developing the concept of 5 as well as discussing *one more* or *one less*. Using these models for discussion can help children establish important connections that link numbers such as 4 and 5. For example, children might say

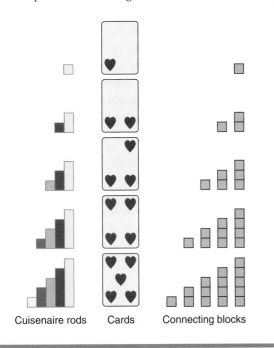

FIGURE 7-15   Three models for *one more* or *one less*.

The yellow rod is one step longer than the purple rod.

The five card is just like the four card except it has an extra heart in the middle.

Having many experiences with such models and patterns helps children abstract numbers and establish useful connections between them.

The hearts on the cards and the trains of blocks in Figure 7-16 provide clear reminders of the numbers represented and the notion of *one more* or *one less*. Both the staircase of rods and the trains of blocks vividly illustrate not only these concepts but also an important, yet subtle, difference between the models. The staircase of rods illustrates the concept of *more,* but it is not absolutely clear how much more until the length of the rods has been made clear. If you used a single rod without identifying a unit rod, it would not be possible to associate the rod with a unique number. Thus the rods are a different model for developing numbers than the cards or trains of blocks.

Some models illustrate zero more clearly than others. For example, a rod of length zero is more difficult to grasp than a card with zero hearts. Care should be taken to introduce zero as soon as it becomes natural to do so, using models appropriate for the purpose, including the number line. Help children distinguish between zero and nothing by encouraging the use of zero to report the absence of something. For example, when reporting the score of a game, it is better to say "Cardinals three, Bears zero" than to say "three to nothing."

As the numbers through 10 are developed, it is important that various patterns among them be discovered, recognized, used, and discussed. Many patterns suggesting many different relationships are shown in this number chart:

For example, the number 7 is shown by 5 dots and 2 more dots. The number 10 is composed of two groups of 5 dots. It is also useful to explore other patterns.

On the number chart, 6 is shown as 5 dots and 1 dot, but other representations are possible, as shown in Figure 7-16, and they should be explored and discussed with students. Part (b) of Figure 7-16, for example, shows that 6 can be represented as one group of 3, one group of 2, and one group of 1. It can also be shown as two groups of 3, as in parts (a) and (d), or three groups of 2, as in part (c). No mention is made of addition or multiplication in this context, but such observations provide helpful connections when these operations are developed.

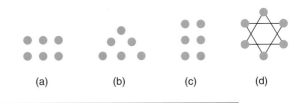

FIGURE 7-16   Some representations of 6.

Similar illustrations and applications of the numbers 7 through 10 should be presented. For example, 7 days in a week may suggest a natural grouping; 8 vertices (corners) of a cube suggest two groups of 4; and the number of boxes in a tic-tac-toe grid suggest three groups of 3.

Most children realize very early that 10 is a special number. At the early stage of number development, the most unusual thing about 10 is that it is the first number represented by two digits, 1 and 0. In addition to having 10 fingers and toes, children encounter the number 10 in many situations, such as in playing games and changing money. These experiences can be extended to include discussion about different representations of 10:

Can you find two groups of 5?

Can you find five groups of 2?

Does the group of 4, 3, 2, and 1 remind you of bowling?

The number 10 provides the cornerstone for our number system, and its significance is developed further in Chapter 8.

A ten-frame is certainly one of the most effective models for facilitating patterns, developing group recognition of numbers, and building an understanding of place value. The ten-frame can be made from an egg carton shortened to contain 10 boxes, or it may simply be outlined on paper or tagboard (see ten-frame in Appendix B). This frame is a powerful organizer and helps provide the base for many thinking strategies and mental computations. Initially, children might use counters to make different representations of the same number in the ten-frame, as illustrated in Figure 7-17. Encountering a variety of groupings on the ten-frame should stimulate discussion about different patterns.

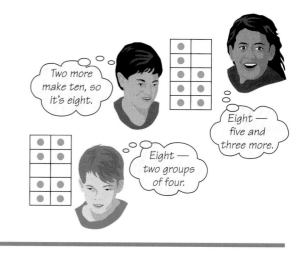

FIGURE 7-17 Representations of 8 on a ten-frame.

Figure 7-18 shows some of the connections that might be constructed as children examine different representations on the ten-frame. These relationships encourage children to think flexibly about numbers, thereby promoting greater number sense. Experiences with the ten-frame also facilitate the development of addition, subtraction, multiplication, and division, as well as place value.

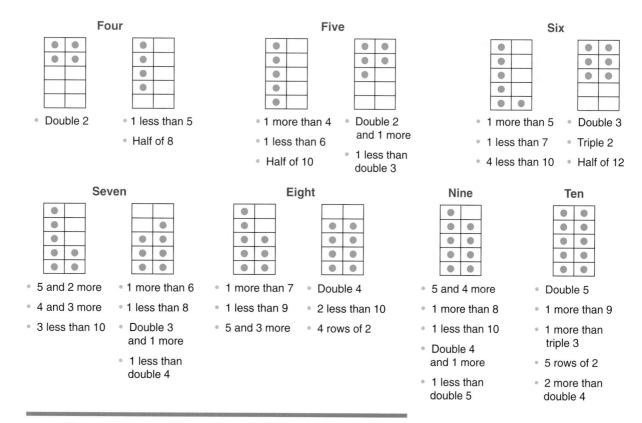

FIGURE 7-18 Connections from representations on the ten-frame.

Math Links 7.3

You will find Learning about Number Relationships and Properties of Numbers using Calculators and Hundreds Boards at the NCTM Standards Web site at http://standards.nctm.org/document/eexamples/. These virtual tools provide an opportunity to count with a calculator that is synchronized with a hundred board. Together they provide connections between calculator counting and a wide range of patterns that can be explored on the hundred board.

www.wiley.com/college/reys

Cardinal, Ordinal, and Nominal Numbers

Thus far we have discussed some important considerations in number development. A major goal has been counting and then finding a correct number name for a given group. This aspect of number provides a *cardinal number,* which answers the question "How many?" Another important aspect of number emphasizes arranging things in an order and is known as *ordinal number;* it answers the question "Which one?"

An emphasis on ordering or arranging things in a given sequence leads to ordinal numbers. The order may be based on any criterion, such as size, time of day, age, or position in a race. Once an order is established, however, the counting process not only produces a set of number names but also names each object according to its position. Thus, in counting the rungs on the ladder in Figure 7-19, number 1 is first, 2 is second, 3 is third, and so on.

Many children know some ordinal numbers such as first, second, and third before they begin school. Encounters with statements such as the following provide early and valuable experience with ordinal numbers:

The first letter of the alphabet is A.

Bob is second in line.

Cary was third in the race.

It is important that the development of early number concepts provides children with opportunities to learn both ordinal and cardinal numbers. Don't worry about which to teach first; just be sure both are given attention.

A knowledge of ordinal relationships, along with logical thinking, leads to more challenging experiences, such as those suggested in Figure 7-20. These questions are guaranteed to generate much discussion as they help children further clarify notions of ordinal numbers.

Another aspect of number provides a label or classification and is known as *nominal.* Examples are the number on a player's uniform, the license plate of a car, a postal zip code, and a telephone number. Nominal numbers provide essential information for identification but do not necessarily use the ordinal or cardinal aspects of the number.

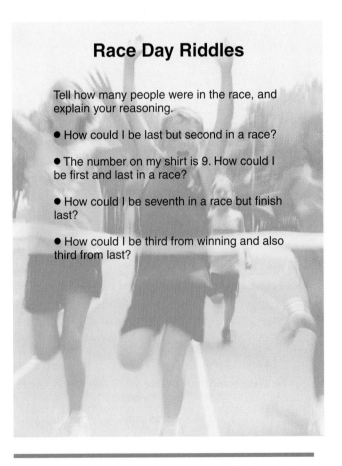

Race Day Riddles

Tell how many people were in the race, and explain your reasoning.

● How could I be last but second in a race?

● The number on my shirt is 9. How could I be first and last in a race?

● How could I be seventh in a race but finish last?

● How could I be third from winning and also third from last?

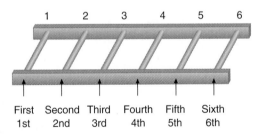

1	2	3	4	5	6
First	Second	Third	Fourth	Fifth	Sixth
1st	2nd	3rd	4th	5th	6th

FIGURE 7-19   A counting model for ordinal numbers.

FIGURE 7-20   Thinking about ordinal relationships.

(Source: Julia Fishkin/The Image Bank/Getty Images).

When using cardinal, ordinal, and nominal numbers, children do not need to distinguish between the terms. Distinctions can be made informally by asking questions within problem situations such as:

How many pieces are on the chessboard?

Which runner is third?

What is your phone number?

These questions not only help children think about numbers but also illustrate that numbers have different uses.

Writing Numerals

Young children should focus their attention on number development and relationships among numbers. Because young children typically have difficulty writing numerals as well as letters, they should spend less time writing numerals. The lack of development of the small muscles needed to write presents one problem, and the limited eye–hand coordination of many young children constitutes another difficulty. Both of these make it difficult or impossible for young children to write numerals. If children are pressured into premature symbolization, it can create unnecessary frustrations and anxieties.

First graders can usually recognize a number symbol and say it correctly long before they write it. Many young children initiate early writing of numerals on their own, and they get a feeling of great accomplishment from it; however, children's writing skills develop much more quickly as second graders than as kindergartners.

Children should begin by tracing the digits and here is a recommended stroke sequence:

(0) 1 2 3 4 5 6 7 8 9

Textbooks provide guidance to children in different forms. Usually a starting point is indicated as well as the direction:

| 2 | 2 | 2 | ⌒ | ⌒ | | |

Encourage children to draw the appropriate number of objects beside the numeral being written to help them connect the number concept with its symbolic representation. When children are learning to write numerals, have them work on

this writing skill aside from "mathematics." Thus children can master this skill and use it freely before applying it in written computational situations; otherwise, the writing task consumes all their concentration, and they forget about the mathematics being done.

Many children develop the necessary writing skills on their own. Even then, these youngsters need monitoring and maybe some occasional guidance. Others, however, need systematic step-by-step procedures to help them. Although there is no one best way to form a numeral, some patterns may help. Guiding a child's hand until the child takes the initiative in writing helps him or her get started. Later, outlines of numerals for children to trace are helpful. Here are some additional suggestions; these will not be necessary in all cases, but some children will profit from them:

- *Cut out shapes of numerals.* Use the overhead projector to project a numeral on the chalkboard or wall and have a child trace the numeral's silhouette.

- *As one child is tracing the projected numeral, have class members trace it in the air.* As the tracing is being done, describe it verbally such as "go to the right and then down." This activity can be extended to using only dots to form the outline or pattern for the children to follow.

- *Have a child who can make numerals stand behind someone who cannot.* Ask the skilled child to use a finger and gently "write" a numeral on the other child's back. The child in front should identify the numeral and write it on the chalkboard, trace it on a poster, or write it in the air. This approach calls on the tactile sense and helps some children better develop their writing skills.

- *Use numerals that have been cut from sandpaper and pasted to cards, or take some cord and glue it in the shape of numerals.* Place a mark on each numeral to show the child where to begin tracing it with his or her finger. This approach is particularly helpful with children who persist in reversing numerals.

- *Cover numerals to be traced with a transparency.* Then give the child a water-soluble pen and have him or her practice tracing the numerals.
- *For children having difficulty writing numerals, a calculator is helpful.* The calculator display provides a visual reminder of a number's symbol and removes the burden of writing complicated numerals.

The fact that numerals take different forms also should be mentioned but not belabored.

Some familiarity with these forms will help avoid confusion when a 4 appears as a printed number or as a digital display on a clock or calculator. The wide use of digital numbers in everyday living demands planned instruction to make children familiar with them.

Cultural Connections

Children enjoy learning words and symbols from other countries. This expands their world view and may cast a new light on their native system. Good teachers show an interest in the cultures of their students, and the diversity of cultures in classrooms provide many opportunities for sharing and learning.

Counting and early number development occurs in every culture. While in some countries the symbolism is similar to that used in the United States (Mexico and Germany), in others countries, such as Asia, it is different. Figure 7-21 shows how the numbers 0–10 are represented and named in several different countries. A look at this figure shows some connections, such as *quatro* in Spanish meaning four in English and connected with a quadrilateral meaning a polygon with four sides. Likewise, *null*

in German is used in English to reflect the cardinal number of an empty set. Although three in Japan and China both use the number name *san*, the symbols are different and in general connections between terms in Asian countries are not possible because of the dramatic differences in the languages.

Yet children in all of these countries learn to count, applying the same counting principles that were discussed earlier. In Asian countries, such as China, Japan, and Taiwan, students learn their own system for counting and communicating their results. In addition, the international availability of technology, including calculators, means that students in these countries must also become familiar with Hindu-Arabic notation. Thus Asian students must learn to recognize and use both Hindu-Arabic numerals and those used in their own country as well as the proper vocabulary with each of them.

The Japanese counting system is complex to us. Figure 7-21 shows the number symbols and two different number names used in Japan for the numbers four and seven. These numbers have alternate number names (e.g., 4 may be *shi* or *yon*) and although either is fine, there are preferred uses. For example, July or the seventh month is *Shichi-gatsu*, whereas 7 yen is *nana* yen. Figure 7-21 also shows two different columns with number names up to ten, which means Japan has two counting systems for the first 10 numbers. Figure 7-21 has a blank for the name of zero in Japan for the counting numbers. Counting begins with one, so there is no Japanese name for zero when counting. After 10 only one system is used, and we will explore it a bit more in the next chapter.

Ordinal numbers in English require students to memorize new words, such as first, third, and sixth. In China making ordinal numbers is easier. It is accomplished by simply adding *di* to the front of a number. So to make "one" become "the first," *yi* becomes *di yi* and to make "six" become "the sixth," *liu* becomes *di liu*. These examples of how culture influences counting provide a vivid reminder of the challenges of helping children from different backgrounds learn to count.

A Glance at Where We've Been

Good number sense is a prerequisite for all later computational development. Young children need to recognize small groups of objects (up to 5 or 6) by sight (*subitizing*) and name them properly. Subitizing saves time, helps develop more sophisticated

Number	English	Spanish	German	Japanese Symbol	Japanese	Japanese	Chinese Symbol	Chinese
0	Zero	Cero	Null	◯	Rei		零	Ling
1	One	Uno	Eins	一	Ichi	Hitotsu	一	Yi
2	Two	Dos	Zwei	二	Ni	Futatsu	二	Er
3	Three	Tres	Drei	三	San	Mittsu	三	San
4	Four	Quatro	Vier	四	Yon, Shi	Yottsu	四	Si
5	Five	Cinco	Funf	五	Go	Itsutsu	五	Wu
6	Six	Seis	Sechs	六	Roku	Muttsu	六	Liu
7	Seven	Siete	Sieben	七	Nana, Shichi	Nanatsu	七	Gi
8	Eight	Ocho	Auht	八	Hachi	Yattsu	八	Ba
9	Nine	Nueve	Neun	九	Kyuu	Kokonotsu	九	Jiu
10	Ten	Diez	Zehn	十	Jun or Ju	To	十	Shi

FIGURE 7-21   Symbols and number names for 0 to 10 in several different countries.

counting skills, and accelerates the later development of addition and subtraction. Activities involving sight recognition of the numbers of objects in small groups provide many opportunities to introduce and use key terms such as *more, less, after, before, one more,* and *one less.* To foster a better number sense, instruction on the numbers through 5 should focus on patterns and develop recognition skills. Models such as the five- and ten-frame, number line, hundred chart, and calculators provide a powerful tool for helping children explore and construct relationships for numbers to 10 and beyond.

Counting skills usually start before children begin school but must be developed by careful and systematic instruction before written work is appropriate. Rational counting is a goal for all young children and is characterized by several principles, including using a fixed number-name list, assigning one and only one name to each object counted, and realizing that the last object counted represents the number in the group.

Counting processes reflect various levels of sophistication, beginning with rote counting and eventually leading to rapid skip counting forward and backward. Counting skills are extended in the intermediate grades and often are further refined throughout our lives. Oral counting leads to ways of writing and representing cardinal, ordinal, and nominal numbers.

Competence with and understanding of the numbers 0 through 10 are essential for meaningful later development of larger numbers. The relationship of the sets of objects, the number names, the written symbols, and the order between numbers must be well understood. This knowledge is the basis for the successful study of elementary mathematics, and it prepares children for the necessary understanding of large numbers and place value.

◀ Things to Do: From What You've Read

1. Provide two activities to illustrate each expectation related to number sense from the NCTM's *Standard:* Numbers and Operations.

2. Suppose you send a note home to parents encouraging them to help their children improve sight-recognition skills. One parent responds, "Why should my child learn to recognize a group of 5? After all, you can just count them." How would you respond?

3. Four fundamental principles of counting were identified in this chapter.
   a. Describe in your own words what each of the principles means.
   b. Tell why that principle is essential to becoming a rational counter.
   c. Choose one of the principles and describe an activity that would help a child progress toward developing that principle.

4. Distinguish between rote and rational counting.

5. What is meant by conservation of number? Why is its development an important part of number sense?

6. Describe how counting could be used to answer these questions:

   a. How many floors are between the seventh and fifteenth floors?

   b. If Alfinio has read to the bottom of page 16, how many pages must he read to reach the top of page 21?

7. Describe how the ten-frame serves as a useful model for early number development.

8. What is subitizing? Tell why it is an important skill to help children develop.

9. A number line is a model useful in counting. Identify a strength and weakness of using the number line with young children.

10. Examine the number strings in Figure 7-13.

   a. Describe some patterns that might result from these number strings.

   b. How would you use these number strings to promote counting forward? Backward?

   c. Describe how you would ramp the number strings up or down to adapt to children with different levels of counting skills.

Note to Instructors: You can find additional resources, learning activities, and black-line masters in this text's accompanying Instructor's Manual, at www.wiley.com/college/reys.

Things to Do: Going Beyond This Book

IN THE FIELD

1. *Observing Counting.* Observe a young child counting in your classroom. Identify any counting errors and where they took place, such as bridging to the next decade. Also identify any counting principles that were exhibited.

2. *Counting Resources.* Find the instructor's guidebook or teacher's edition being used in a K–2 mathematics classroom in your school. Describe how resources, such as calculators and children's books, are used to support counting.

3. *Using Attribute Pieces.* In the Classroom 7-1 and 7-2 provide several patterning and logical reasoning activities using attribute pieces with children. Explore these trains with several children. How many different correct solutions did children find for Train A? Did your children find one-difference trains to be the same difficulty as two-difference trains? Did students feel comfortable knowing that more than one correct answer exists?

IN YOUR JOURNAL

4. Observe children counting on the playground. How do children demonstrate their counting abilities? In your journal, describe their counting activities and the strategies they appear to use.

5. There are controversies related to teaching counting in the classroom. In your journal, respond to this statement: "Counting is an immature habit that teachers need to help students break."

WITH ADDITIONAL RESOURCES

6. Examine *Number Sense and Operations* (Burton et al., 1993), *Developing Number Sense in Middle Grades* (Reys et al., 1991), *Navigating through Number and Operations in Prekindergarten–Grade 2* (Cavanagh et al., 2004) or the *SENSE* series (McIntosh et al., 1997). How do these books characterize number sense? Select and report on an instructional activity designed to foster number sense.

7. Read the article about zero by Anthony and Walsh (2004). Describe some of the misconceptions children have and share some of the suggestions made to help children gain a better understanding of zero.

8. Compare two current textbook series:

   a. Find how far each series expects children to be able to count when they begin first grade and when they complete first grade.

   b. Find examples of activities designed to develop number sense. Describe the activities and identify the grade level. Do you think these activities would be effective? Tell why.

   c. Find an example of a visual pattern that connects numbers to geometry.

9. Review *The Wonderful World of Mathematics: A Critically Annotated List of Children's Books in Mathematics* (Thiessen, Matthias, and Smith, 1998). Find three multicultural books related to counting that are highly recommended.

10. Read the book *How Many Snails? A Counting Book* (Giganti, 1988). Then read the article by Whitin, Mills, and O'Keefe (1994) to see how this

---

*Additional activities, suggestions, and questions are provided in *Teaching Elementary Mathematics: A Resource for Field Experiences* (Wiley, 2007).

book was used to explore mathematical problem solving. Discuss how the project was done and how the examples of children's work provides insight into their development of number sense.

WITH TECHNOLOGY

11. *Counting with Calculators.* In the Classroom 7-4 and 7-5 provide structured calculator counting activities. Try one or more of them with some children in a classroom that has calculators available. Were the children experienced at using the calculators or were they viewed as a novelty? Were the children comfortable making estimates for the counts? Describe some patterns that emerged.

12. *Virtual Calculators.* Investigate the NCTM Web site at http://standards.nctm.org/document/eexamples/ and try the Calculator and Hundreds Boards activity. Explore this resource by entering 5 + and then repeatedly enter the = symbol on the calculator. How does the hundred board change? Describe how this virtual tool can be used as an instructional tool. Identify advantages of using this tool over the handheld calculator and the paper hundred board.

13. View the *Math Buddies* video from the opening Snapshot, then answer these questions:

How many different counting stations did you see?

Which stations do you think children found most interesting?

Did you notice the children make any counting errors? Explain.

What are some advantages and disadvantages of the buddy system?

Book Nook for Children

Anno, M. *Anno's Counting Book.* New York: Thomas Y. Crowell, 1977.

How would you describe a picture that refers to zero? This book begins with a barren winter landscape—a hazy, blue sky above a hazy, white hill. On the next page the scene brightens: one tree, one bird, one house. Turn the page again and the snow has started to melt and you find two buildings, two trucks, two trees, two children, two dogs, and two adults. Suddenly there is almost more than you can count on each page! And the numbers continue to increase.

Giganti, P. *How Many Snails? A Counting Book.* New York: Greenwillow Books (Pearson K–12), 1998.

Use these many opportunities to help children practice their counting. A series of simple questions directs them to determine the differences between seemingly similar objects, encouraging them to develop powers of observation, discrimination, and visual analysis.

Murphy, S. *Dave's Down-to-Earth Rock Shop.* New York: Harper Collins, 2000.

Josh and Amy have a rock collection. They learn that they can sort their collections by many different ways such as color, size, type, and hardness. Josh and Amy also learn that the same objects can be organized in many different ways. A great book for students to learn about attributes. There are activities and games in the back of this book for parents and teachers to use.

Murphy, S. *Just Enough Carrots.* New York. Harper Collins, 1997.

This is the story of a bunny and his mother and how they shop in a grocery store for their lunch guests that are coming to their house. As they get the items they need, the bunny learns about counting and comparing different amounts from their cart of items to the other shoppers and their carts. A great introduction to comparing different amounts. There are activities and games in the back of this book for teachers and parents to use.

Schlein, M. *More Than One.* New York. Greenwillow Books, 1996.

This book will let the reader see how the number one can be more than one. This will depend on how the number one is attached to another number. For example: 1 basketball team, 1 month, 1 week, 1 year, etc. This is a great book to introduce number sense.

Wahl, J., and Wahl, S. *I Can Count the Petals of a Flower.* Reston, VA: NCTM, 1976.

This book provides a variety of rich and stimulating context teaching children to count using the petals of a flower.

Zaslavsky, C. *Count on Your Fingers African Style.* New York: Crowell, 1980.

Focus on numerical relationships in the African marketplace where people buy and trade using many different languages, including various methods of finger counting. This book explores the practicality of math within the context of African culture and helps children see that math can be fun and creative.

Annotated Resources

Baratta-Lorton, M. *Mathematics Their Way.* Palo Alto, CA: Addison-Wesley, 1976.

This is an activity-centered mathematics program for early childhood education. The goal of the activities in the book is to develop understanding and insight of the patterns of mathematics through the use of concrete materials. Relationships and interconnections in mathematics are stressed, so young children can deal flexibly with mathematical ideas and concepts.

Burton, G., Mills, A., Lennon, C., and Parker, C. *Number Sense and Operations.* Reston, VA: NCTM, 1993.

This book is part of the *Curriculum and Evaluation Standards for School Mathematics* Addenda Series, Grades K–6. This series was designed to illustrate the *Standards* and to help teachers translate them into classroom practice. Both traditional and new topics are explored in this book. Familiar activities have been redesigned and infused with an investigative flavor.

Cavanagh, M., Dacey, L., Findell, C., Greenes, C., Jensen-Sheffield, L., and Small, M. *Navigating through Number and Operations in Prekindergarten–Grade 2*, Reston, VA: NCTM, 2004.

This book provides a host of activities to facilitate children's early development of counting and number sense leading to operations of addition and subtraction. It is accompanied with a CD that provides interactive electronic activities.

Gallenstein, N. "Creative discovery through classification." *Teaching Children Mathematics*, 11 (September 2004) pp. 103–108.

This article is directed toward early childhood. Specific activities fostering classification skills are illustrated along with ways to use them.

Losq, C. "Number concepts and special needs students: The power of ten-frame tiles." *Teaching Children Mathematics*, 11(6) (February 2005), pp. 310–314.

Provides a careful examination of counting, subitizing, and mental computation within the context of ten-frames. Connections to missing addends and algebra are also made.

McIntosh, A., Reys, B., and Reys, R. *Number Sense: Simple Effective Number Sense Experiences Grade 1–2.* Palo Alto, CA: Dale Seymour, 1997.

These 10-minute activities help students develop a sense of what numbers represent and how to use them by exploring relationships and patterns, encouraging mental computation, recognizing equivalent representations of a number, establishing benchmarks, improving estimation skills, and exploring the idea of reasonableness. Includes activity masters, teacher's notes, and ideas for extending the activity.

Wickett, M. "Serving Up Number Sense and Problem Solving: Dinner at the Panda Palace." *Teaching Children Mathematics*, 3(9) (May 1997), pp. 476–480.

This article provides strategies for using literature to teach number sense and problem solving that help you develop class discussions that reflect students' thinking, give students opportunities to share their approaches and understandings, and give the teacher additional insights into students' thinking.

Zaslavsky, C. "Developing number sense: What can other cultures tell us?" *Teaching Children Mathematics*, 7(6) (February 2001), pp. 312–319.

This article presents ways to introduce number systems from finger counting to number words, to concrete materials, to the numerals invented by various societies to enhance students' number sense by learning about the systems of other cultures.

CHAPTER 8

Extending Number Sense: Place Value

Snapshot of a Lesson

Key Ideas

1. Illustrate power and importance of grouping by ten

2. Demonstrate the place-value concept with different models

3. Provide concrete representations of two-digit numbers and their corresponding symbolization

Background

This snapshot is from the video *Place Value Centers*, from Teaching Math: A Video Library, K–4 from Annenberg Media. Produced by WGBH Educational Foundation. © 1995 WGBH. All rights reserved. To view the video, go to http://www.learner.org/resources/series32.html (video #4). Shaylene Vickstrom is a first-grade teacher. Today she introduces the concept of place value through a familiar daily task, updating the counting center that keeps track of the number of days they have been in school so far this year. Ms. Vickstrom has placed pockets on the bulletin board to hold straws. At the beginning of the school day, she adds a straw to the "ones" pocket. Once they have 10 ones they bundle them and place bundles of 10 in the tens pocket. Ms. Vickstrom asks her students to explain what happens when they find 10 ones in the ones pocket.

MS. VICKSTROM: Amanda, what do we do to them?

AMANDA: Put them in a bundle of ten.

MS. VICKSTROM: Put them in a bundle of ten. That's right. And then, do they get to stay on the ones side?

AMANDA: No.

MS. VICKSTROM: Where do we have to move them to?

AMANDA: In the tens side.

MS. VICKSTROM: On to the tens side. That's right. So all of these over here are a bundle of ten. Aren't they? That's why they're on the tens side. But we have the single ones over here on the ones side.

Ms. Vickstrom transitions the students' attention from the calendar to the place-value mat by pointing out their similarities.

MS. VICKSTROM: I have something up here for you guys. This is my giant place-value mat. And guess what? This is an awful lot like the thing that's over there on the calendar that holds our ones and our tens. This is my ones side and it says "ones" right here. This is my tens side.

Ms. Vickstrom displays a large place-value mat and shares to the camera that the overall goal of today's lesson is to allow students to become familiar with place value. In particular, she wants to concentrate on the exchange of ones and tens so that students are prepared to move into addition and subtraction with double-digit numbers.

Ms. Vickstrom asks the age of two students in her class. She uses the place-value mat to model the age with unit tiles. She places six unit tiles on the ones area of the mat to represent the first student's age and then places seven additional unit tiles in the ones area to represent the second student's age. The class works together to find the sum of the students' ages. They bundle ten unit tiles into one tens rod and transfer the rod to the tens area of the mat.

MS. VICKSTROM: There's my bundle of ten. Now, if we wanted to add Racillia's age to Javier's age, do you think you know how much it is altogether if we are adding six plus seven. Kayla, what do you think?

KAYLA: 10, 11, 12, 13.

MS. VICKSTROM: Why did you start off on 10?

KAYLA: Because there's a bundle of ten.

MS. VICKSTROM: Because there's a bundle of 10 right there [*as she points to tens rod*]. So you counted, you said I already know there's 10 there, right? So you went 10....

AMANDA: 11, 12, 13.

Ms. Vickstrom explains how to write the numeral 13 by counting the number of tens rods and unit tiles from the place-value mat. She writes the numeral 1 under the tens area and the numeral 3 under the ones area.

MS. VICKSTROM: So, one special rule that we need to remember today is that on your ones side, once you get up to 10, you have to transfer them over here to your tens side.

Ms. Vickstrom explains the four activity centers. The first is a measuring center where children measure several items by linking together unifix cubes to form a train. Children then break down the trains into ones and tens on their place-value mats. Children record their results on a recording sheet.

At the second center, using cups and place-value mats, students take inventory of piles of beans, buttons, and stones.

At the third center, Mr. Montez, a student teacher in Ms. Vickstrom's class, works with students to model numbers from a hundred chart.

In the last center, students compete to see who can make the longest train of unifix cubes. Once all of the cubes in a pile are used, students break down the train into tens and ones using their place-value mats.

After students visit the centers, Ms. Vickstrom pulls the class back together to discuss what they have learned. As a class, they discuss the measuring center and the hundred board center.

MS. VICKSTROM: Now if Mr. Montez has 95 in his little mystery box, can somebody tell me what you would show on your place-value boards for 95 [*as she displays a place-value mat to the class*]? What would you show? Matthew?

MATTHEW: 95.

MS. VICKSTROM: 95. Okay, where would all of the cubes be? Would you have 95 cubes right here [*as she motions to the ones area of the place-value mat*]? Just all in a pile? What would you have?

MATTHEW: You'd have nine tens there.

MS. VICKSTROM: You'd have nine tens here [*as she motions to tens area of place-value mat*]? Okay, nine bundles of 10.

MATTHEW: And you'd have five ones there.

MS. VICKSTROM: Five ones. So what does... when we're looking at a number, Matthew, what does the number on the right-hand side stand for? This number [*points to the five*]. Right now the 5 is right there.

MATTHEW: The ones.

MS. VICKSTROM: That stands for the ones. What does the number on the left-hand side stand for?

MATTHEW: The tens.

MS. VICKSTROM: The tens.

In Ms. Vickstrom's reflection on the day's lesson, she shares the idea of providing multiple problem-solving activities in order to reach different types of learners. She also stresses the importance of hands-on activities and providing a culminating class discussion at the end of free exploration activities to share the group findings.

Math Links 8.1

You will find the full-text version of the Number and Operation Standard along with electronic examples at the NCTM Web site www.nctm.org.

www.wiley.com/college/reys

Introduction

Children must make sense of numbers and the ways in which numbers are used in and out of school. This sense making of numbers is a hallmark of NCTM *Standards* (2000), which include several concepts and skills related to extending number sense to place value. Place value is critical to this understanding or sense making and is one of the cornerstones of our number system. Figure 8-1 presents this emphasis in the *Standards* for prekindergarten through grade 2 and grades 3–5.

The snapshot shows children counting and how place value provides an organizational structure for counting. The same principles are involved as larger numbers are counted. Representations of larger numbers are based on learning operations with numbers in a sense making or meaningful way. So in counting from 9 to 10, or 99 to 100, or 999 to 1000, place value is an important part of the symbols and language. In a similar manner, adding 1 to 9 to get 10, or 1 to 99 to get 100, or 1 to 999 to get 1000 the changes in place value are again experienced. These transitions from one- to two-, two- to three-, or three- to four-digit numbers are fundamental to place-value work. And we use place value throughout all of our work with whole numbers and later with decimals.

FOCUS QUESTIONS

1. What are some instructional models that can help develop children's understanding of our number system?
2. Why is composing and decomposing numbers important in developing place value?
3. How can you help children bridge the gap between the concrete and symbolic representations of numbers?
4. How can calculators help children develop place-value concepts?
5. How do number names differ from country to country?

Our Numeration System

Although we say "our" numeration system, it is multicultural, and it is "ours" only to the extent that it is a part of our cultural heritage. History tells us that "our numeration system" is really the result of continuous development and refinement over many centuries (Zaslavsky, 2003). The number system we use, called the Hindu-Arabic system, was probably

Instructional programs from prekindergarten through grade 2 should enable all students to:	Pre-K–2 Expectations All students should:	Grades 3–5 Expectations All students should:
Understand numbers, ways of representing numbers, and number systems	• Use multiple models to develop initial understandings of place value and the base-ten number system • Develop a sense of whole numbers and represent and use them in flexible ways, including relating, composing, and decomposing numbers • Connect number words and numerals to the quantities they represent, using various physical models and representations	• Understand the place-value structure of the base-ten number system and be able to represent and compare whole numbers and decimals • Recognize equivalent representations for the same number and generate them by decomposing and composing numbers

FIGURE 8-1 Number and Operation Standard for grades pre-K–2 and 3–5 from the National Council of Teachers of Mathematics (www.nctm.org).

invented in India by the Hindus and transmitted to Europe by the Arabs, but many different countries and cultures contributed to its development.

The Hindu-Arabic numeration system has four important characteristics:

1. *Place value:* The position of a digit represents its value; for example, the 2 in $23 names "two tens" or "twenty" and has a different mathematical meaning from the 2 in $32, which names "two ones."

2. *Base of ten:* The term *base* simply means a collection. Thus, in our system, ten is the value that determines a new collection and is represented by 10. The system has 10 digits, 0 through 9.

3. *Use of zero:* A symbol for zero exists and allows us to represent symbolically the absence of something. For example, 309 shows the absence of tens in a number containing hundreds and ones.

4. *Additive property:* Numbers can be summed with respect to place value. For example, 123 names the number that is the sum of $100 + 20 + 3$.

These properties make the system efficient and contribute to the development of number sense. That is, once children understand these characteristics, the formation and interpretation of numbers—either large or small—is a natural development.

Roman numerals are still in use today in our society, but not for computation. Roman numerals are different from the Hindu-Arabic system in that they lack place value, have no symbol for zero, and no base. As a result, computation with Roman numerals is a difficult and cumbersome process.

Nature of Place Value

A thorough understanding of place value is necessary if computational algorithms for addition, subtraction, multiplication, and division are to be learned and used in a meaningful way. Place value develops from many various experiences, such as counting and mental computation (e.g., $1 plus $0.25 to get $1.25). Development of place value promotes number sense and rests on two key ideas:

• *Explicit grouping or trading rules are defined and consistently followed.* These ideas are illustrated in the opening snapshot as different models are used, and are also implicit in the bulletin board display shown in Figure 8-2. Such a display provides a constant reminder of the importance of grouping by tens to place value. Our base-ten system is characterized by trading 10 ones for 1 ten (or 1 ten for 10 ones), 10 tens for 1 hundred, 10 hundreds for 1 thousand, and so on. The two-way direction of these trades (e.g., 10 tens for 1 hundred or 1 hundred for 10 tens) should be stressed because there are times when each type of trade must be used. These equivalent trades illustrate composing and decomposing numbers mentioned in Figure 8-1. It also should be noted that similar trades are followed with numbers less than one—decimals. Thus, 1 can be traded for 10 tenths (or 10 tenths for 1), 10 hundredths for 1 tenth (or 1 tenth for 10 hundredths), and so on.

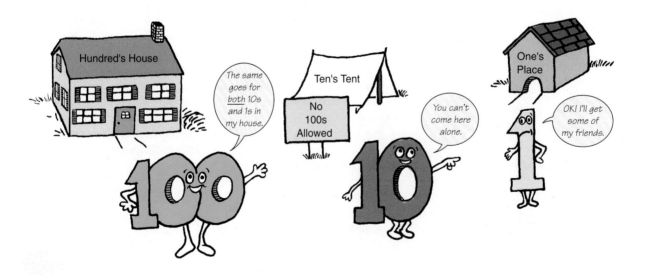

FIGURE 8-2 A bulletin board display for place value.

• *The position of a digit determines the number being represented.* For example, the 2 in 3042 and the 2 in 2403 represent completely different quantities: 2 ones in 3042 and 2 thousands in 2403. Furthermore, the zero plays a similar yet different role in each of these numbers. It has positional value in each case, but it reports the lack of a quantity for that place. Although the notion of zero will continue to be expanded and developed throughout elementary school mathematics, children should experience the role of zero in place value early and often.

In the Hindu-Arabic number system, place value means that any number can be represented using only 10 digits (0–9). Think about the problems of representing numbers without place value! Each number would require a separate and unique symbol. Your memory storage would quickly be exceeded, and you would probably have to use only the few numbers with symbols you could remember. Nevertheless, place value is difficult for some children to grasp. Oral counting or rote recitation of numbers by young children is often interpreted as understanding place value. Yet many children who can count correctly have absolutely no concept of place value. In most cases, the confusion or misunderstanding can be traced to a lack of counting and trading experiences with appropriate materials and the subsequent recording of these results. Early and frequent hands-on counting activities, similar to those described in Chapter 7, are essential prerequisites to meaningful understanding of place value.

Place-value concepts are encountered before starting school. For example, many children distinguish between the one- and two-digit numbers on a channel indicator of a television, a timer for a microwave oven, and house or apartment numbers. Children learn early that apartment numbers 201 and 102 are different.

Modeling—Ungrouped and Pregrouped

Two types of materials help young children develop place value, ungrouped materials and pregrouped materials. Ungrouped materials include beans, cubes, straws or Popsicle sticks, or tongue depressors that children form into groups as shown in Figure 8-3. If there are enough beans to make a group of 10, then those beans can be placed in a cup or bag or glued on a stick. Once these beans are glued on a stick then they can be considered pregrouped materials.

Pregrouped materials are formed into groups before the child uses them and Figure 8-3 also

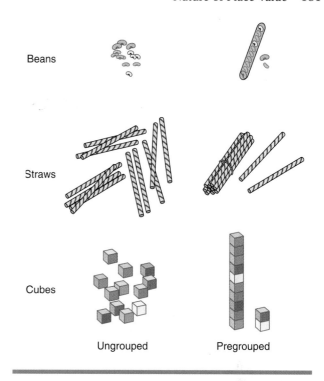

Beans

Straws

Cubes

Ungrouped   Pregrouped

FIGURE 8-3 Ungrouped and pregrouped models for developing place value.

shows three examples of pregrouped materials. Hands-on experience with manipulatives is essential in establishing and developing the concept of place value. Research suggests that instruction should focus on concrete models that are connected to oral descriptions and symbolic representations of the models (Thompson, 2000; Wearne and Hiebert, 1994).

Modeling—Proportional and Nonproportional

Place-value models may be either proportional or not proportional. Base-ten blocks, beans glued in groups of 10 on a stick, and tongue depressors bundled together are proportional models (Figure 8-4). In proportional models the material for 10 is 10 times the size of the material for 1; 100 is 10 times the size of 10, and so on. Measurement provides another proportional model as was shown in the Annenberg videotape *Place Value Centers* where children use interlocking cubes to measure their height and then form groups of 10. Meter sticks, decimeter rods, and centimeter cubes could also be used to model any three-digit number.

Nonproportional models do not maintain any size relationships. Money is a real-world example of a nonproportional model where size relationships are not maintained. For example, 10 pennies are bigger than a dime but are a fair trade in our

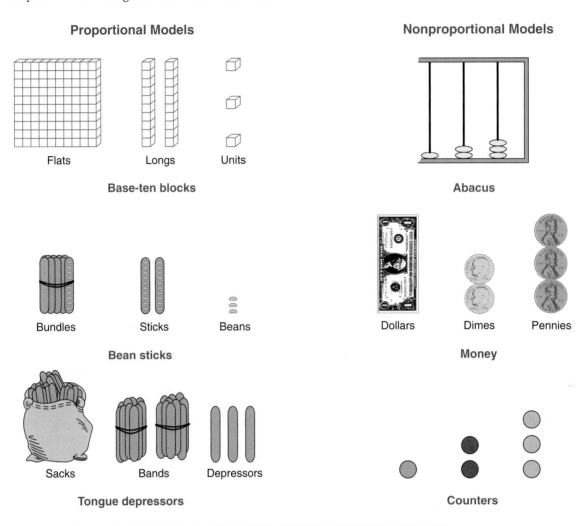

FIGURE 8-4   Place-value models: Proportional models and nonproportional models.

monetary system. Ten dimes are the same value as a dollar, but they are not proportional in size.

Figure 8-4 illustrates some proportional and nonproportional models that are effective in helping students understand not only place value but larger numbers as well. All of the models shown in Figure 8-4 represent the same three-digit number, 123. The value of using different embodiments is that a child is less likely to associate place value with a particular model. In fact, a key instructional goal is to develop concepts to a level that does not depend on any one physical model, instead providing for abstraction of the commonality among all models.

Since nonproportional materials are not related by size, the child must understand the exchange relationship among the pieces. Thus the child must already understand base-ten relationships, and these relationships take time to develop. These ideas introduce children to a level of abstraction based entirely on trading rules. Young students

often focus on size proportionality, which is why they are often willing to trade a dime for one or two pennies, or why they prefer to have a few dimes rather than a dollar bill.

Although both types of embodiments are important and should be represented, proportional models are more concrete, and children need to use and clearly understand them before moving on to nonproportional models.

Of the nonproportional models shown in Figure 8-4, the abacus and the counters are similar. In each model, different-colored beads or counters provide the basis for trading. For example, 10 orange beads (or counters) might be traded for 1 red, 10 red for 1 blue, and so on. Use of a trading mat can help keep the counters in order. The beads on an abacus are arranged in a fixed order. The color distinction is important for the early establishment of proper trades, but it should be dropped as soon as possible so that attention shifts from color of the beads or counters to their position. Only the position of the bead counter has long-range significance.

Grouping or Trading

Children need experience in counting piles of objects; trading for grouped tens, hundreds, and thousands; and talking about the results. The bean sticks and ten-frame thus provide two early models for counting and grouping. As children work with these models, they use these materials (e.g., beans, buttons, cubes, or other counters) to practice counting and grouping. These ungrouped materials provide valuable experience and prepare children for using pregrouped materials. Figure 8-5 shows a transition from an ungrouped pile of beans to grouping by tens to representing that same quantity with pregrouped beans sticks to recording symbols. The transition from 10 beans to 1 stick with 10 beans illustrates how the number 10 is composed of 10 ones.

While ungrouped materials provide practice in counting and grouping, it is tedious and time consuming to count beans and to build models as quantities increase. For example, a large pile of beans is impressive and useful for demonstration, but often not practical for use at individual desks. Pregrouped materials make it easy to build larger numbers.

Trading and grouping by tens provide problem-solving activities that contribute to number sense and provide opportunities for developing mental computation. Asking children to group by tens as they count the larger piles serves several valuable purposes. First, if a child loses count, correction is often easier if these smaller groups have been formed. It is also easier to check for errors by inspecting groups of 10 than to recount the entire pile. The most important purpose of this practice, however, is that it shows children how an unknown quantity can be organized into a form that can be interpreted by inspection. This process of grouping by tens is the framework for place value.

Beginning Place Value (Early Childhood)

A Place to Start

You may have seen some children's errors, such as those shown in Figure 8-6. These examples illustrate confusion involving different aspects of place value. Later errors in computation can often be traced back to a lack of understanding about place value (Whitenack et al., 2004). The importance of place value makes getting a good start essential.

In developing place value and establishing number names, it is far better to skip beyond the teens and start with the larger numbers. Figure 8-6 illustrates that the names for the numbers 11–19 are not consistent with the names for other numbers, even though the symbolization or visual pattern is wholly consistent. This lack of consistency in counting the teen numbers is confusing and children need to explore the vocabulary of larger numbers before the place-value counting patterns are evident. The numbers 11–19 do not exhibit the place-value characteristic in their names that other numbers do. To do so, they would have to be renamed onety-one (1 ten and 1 one), onety-two, . . ., onety-nine, which would make them consistent with larger numbers, such as forty-one, forty-two, . . ., forty-nine. In many other countries, such as Japan, the naming pattern for the numbers 11–19 is consistent with the naming of larger numbers (Yoshikawa, 1994). Vocabulary for counting, naming, and representing numbers is an issue among many countries.

Counting	Becoming confused when counting the teen numbers because of the lack of pattern in the numbers from eleven to nineteen
Bridging the decade or hundred	Making the transition when counting, for example, counting aloud "thirty-eight, thirty-nine, thirty-ten" or writing "38, 39, 3010"
Reversing digits when writing number	For example, writing 52 and 25 and not recognizing any difference in these numbers
Writing numbers that were read aloud	For example, writing "one hundred sixty-four" as 100604

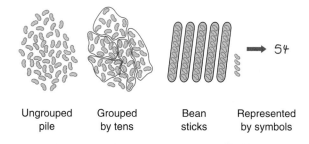

Ungrouped pile   Grouped by tens   Bean sticks   Represented by symbols

FIGURE 8-5 Different stages in developing place value.

FIGURE 8-6 Some common errors related to place value.

What does a number such as 25 mean? The number 25 can be thought of as 25 ones, but it is also composed of 2 tens and 5 ones. It can be decomposed into 1 ten and 15 ones, as well as 5 groups of 5 ones. It is important that children have experiences thinking of numbers in various ways. The ability to compose and decompose numbers in different ways is a reflection of good number sense. For example, when thinking of money, several combinations of coins—such as 25 pennies, 2 dimes and 5 pennies, 5 nickels, or 1 quarter—may be imagined. With certain items, such as eggs, 1 more than 2 dozen and 4 six-packs plus 1 are two different but equivalent representations of the quantity 25 and thus different ways of recomposing or decomposing 25 into other meaningful representations. With metric measures, 25 centimeters might be thought of as 2 decimeters and 5 centimeters; however, it could also be thought of as 0.25 meter. Children with good number sense know when a particular form is useful.

Of course, if place value is to be called on, the tens and ones model is needed. It might use money (2 dimes and 5 pennies) or another model, such as bean sticks. With the bean sticks, 25 could be represented several different ways:

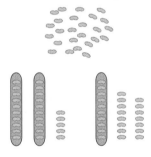

Which way is better? It depends on what is to be done with the 25 beans because there are times when each form may be useful. The grouping at the top, for example, would be easier to divide among several people. Either of the groupings on the bottom would be easier to count.

The notion of representing a quantity with the least number of pieces for a particular model is critical in place value. Establishing its importance at an early stage can eliminate some later errors such as:

Because 10 or more of something (namely, ones) exist on the place-value mat, a trade must be

made. Making the ten-for-one trade results in the least number of pieces and thus 25 becomes the only representation that is meaningful:

Figure 8-7 highlights the advancement from a concrete model to a symbolic representation. The bridges from the physical models to the symbolic representation must be crossed back and forth many times if meaningful learning is to occur. Careful attention must be given to linking modeling with the language. As children become fluent in talking about their models, it will become natural for them to describe 25 in different ways.

Many children reverse the digits of numbers. Although this error is generally caused by carelessness, it may be symptomatic of a disability known as *dyslexia*. In either case, it is important that children understand the consequences of such reversals. Consider, for example, the numbers 25 and 52. The ten-frame (Appendix B) provides a convenient model for representing these two-digit numbers.

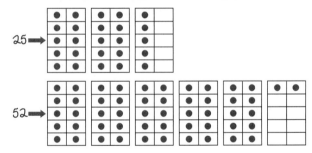

This provides a visual reminder of the physical differences between 25 and 52, which are formed with the same digits but are different because of place value. Children should compare the modeled numbers and talk about them in an effort to better appreciate the magnitude of the differences.

When quantities are grouped by ten, it not only illustrates place value, but it facilitates counting. For example, these two piles show the same number of buttons. One has all of the buttons in a string. The other has recomposed the buttons into groups of tens and ones. Decide how many buttons are in each pile.

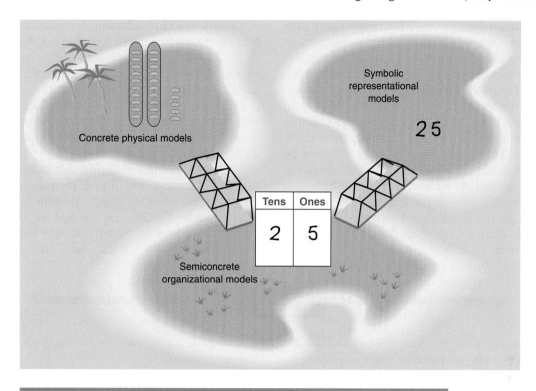

FIGURE 8-7   The idea of place value can help children cross from concrete models of numbers to their symbolic representations.

If you wanted to know how many buttons are in each pile, which arrangement would you use? Explaining which pile and telling why that arrangement was chosen leads to a discussion of how grouping by tens facilitates counting and organizing larger quantities.

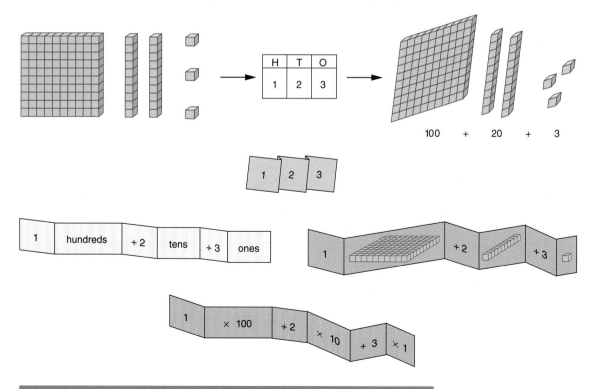

FIGURE 8-8   Connecting models and symbols that reinforce place value.

The base-ten blocks, together with the place-value mat, as shown in Figure 8-8, can be used to model the additive property and illustrate expanded notation for 123. A variety of strips, such as those in Figure 8-8, which connect the base-ten blocks to number symbols in an expanded form, can be used effectively to review key ideas. While 123 is composed of 1 hundred, 2 tens, and 3 ones, if you were dividing the number by 3, it would be easier to think of 123 as 12 tens and 3 ones. Encouraging children to name the same number in different ways promotes number sense.

In the Classroom 8-1 shows two slightly different hundreds charts. One chart goes from 1 to 100, the other from 0 to 99. (Master copies are in Appendix B.) One advantage of the latter chart is that the tens digit in each row is constant, whereas in the 1-to-100 chart the tens digit always changes in the last column. Either hundred chart can be used to explore place value, patterns, mental computation, and algebraic thinking. The Annenberg videotape *Place Value Centers* shows children modeling the tens and ones for numbers that are identified on a hundred chart.

A hundred chart also provides many opportunities for counting and doing mental computation. For example, 43 + 30 can be determined by counting mentally 43, 53, 63, 73 and is a natural by-product of counting by tens on the hundred chart. Furthermore, 43 + 29 can be found by counting

In the Classroom 8-1

OBJECTIVE: Using a hundred chart to explore place value and pattern.

GRADE LEVEL: 3

1	2	3	4	5	6	7	8	9	10
11	12	13	14	15	16	17	18	19	20
21	22	23	24	25	26	27	28	29	30
31	32	33	34	35	36	37	38	39	40
41	42	43	44	45	46	47	48	49	50
51	52	53	54	55	56	57	58	59	60
61	62	63	64	65	66	67	68	69	70
71	72	73	74	75	76	77	78	79	80
81	82	83	84	85	86	87	88	89	90
91	92	93	94	95	96	97	98	99	100

↑ Fifth column

0	1	2	3	4	5	6	7	8	9
10	11	12	13	14	15	16	17	18	19
20	21	22	23	24	25	26	27	28	29
30	31	32	33	34	35	36	37	38	39
40	41	42	43	44	45	46	47	48	49
50	51	52	53	54	55	56	57	58	59
60	61	62	63	64	65	66	67	68	69
70	71	72	73	74	75	76	77	78	79
80	81	82	83	84	85	86	87	88	89
90	91	92	93	94	95	96	97	98	99

▼ Use the hundreds charts to answer these questions:
- What is alike for all the numbers in the fifth column?

- How are the numbers in the fourth and sixth columns alike? Different?

- Tell where you stop, if you start on any square in the first three rows and count forward 10 more squares.

- Start on a different square in the first three rows and count forward 10 more squares. Where did you stop?

- After you have done this several times, tell about a pattern that you found.

▼ Cut out a piece like this [shape] and lay it on the chart.
- What numbers are covered? Tell how you found them.

- Move the piece to a different place, and tell what numbers are covered.

- Do it again with different shapes

  like [shape] and [shape]

▼ Here is only a part of a hundred chart:
- Use what you know about a hundred chart to

- Find *A* _____ *B* _____ *C* _____ *D* _____

- Tell two different ways to find *C*.

- Suppose 46 is replaced by *N*.

- Find *A* _____ *B* _____ *C* _____ *D* _____

43, 53, 63, 73 and then dropping back one to 72. Counting by tens and then dropping back or bumping up illustrate how to adjust numbers and be flexible when using and thinking about numbers.

Consider the following diagram and how patterns and generalizations lead to algebraic thinking:

Patterns from the hundred chart suggest these solutions directly from the hundred chart:

$$A = 46 - 10$$
$$B = 46 + 10 - 1$$
$$C = 46 + 20$$
$$D = 46 + 30 - 1$$

If the diagram is shifted on the hundred chart, then 46 changes to some number N. Although the starting number N has changed, the solutions are similar, as

$$A = N - 10$$
$$B = N + 10 - 1$$
$$C = N + 20$$
$$D = N + 30 - 1$$

Such activities illustrate a variable and the power of patterns in promoting algebraic thinking.

Modeling three-digit numbers provides opportunities to show how the rearrangement of digits impacts a number. Figure 8-9 shows the physical difference between 134, 314, and 413. Looking at the different arrangements show that 413 is about 100 more than 314, and that 134 is more than 100 less than 314. This ability to focus on the lead or "front-end" digits is an important part of number sense.

In the Classroom 8-2 reinforces place value and provides practice in important mental computational skills. Scores are found by counting the darts in each circle, which provides practice counting by ones, tens, and hundreds, and then computing the totals.

FIGURE 8-9 Order of digits makes a difference.

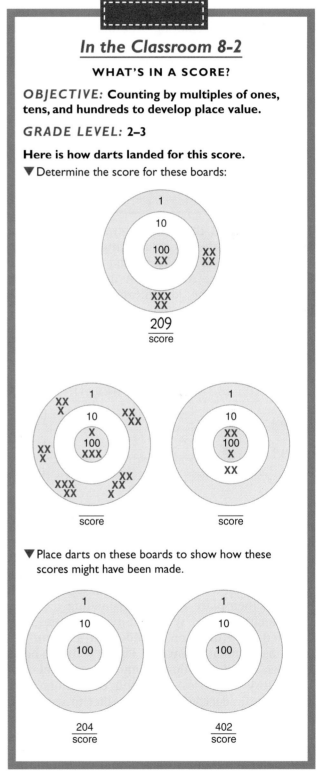

In the Classroom 8-2

WHAT'S IN A SCORE?

OBJECTIVE: Counting by multiples of ones, tens, and hundreds to develop place value.

GRADE LEVEL: 2–3

Here is how darts landed for this score.

▼ Determine the score for these boards:

▼ Place darts on these boards to show how these scores might have been made.

A calculator provides many opportunities to practice and develop important place-value concepts. Wipe Out is a place-value game that involves either addition or subtraction using a calculator. The goal is to change (wipe out) a predetermined digit by subtracting or adding a number. This activity can be made into a competitive game for two people. The players take turns entering a number and naming a specific digit the other player must change to 0.

For example, Kelly enters 431, naming the 3 to be wiped out:

Tanya wipes out the 3 by subtracting 30, which also leaves the other digits unchanged.

A player scores a point for changing the digit to 0 on the first try. A record of the game in table form reinforces the identification of the correct place value:

WIPE OUT RECORD   Name: Tanya

Entered	Wiped Out	Keys Pressed	Display	Score
431	3	−30	401	1
24	4	+6	30	1
849	8	−800	49	1
206	2	−200	6	1

Although Wipe Out or variations of it can be played without a calculator, it is much more exciting with one. Children don't get bogged down with computation. The focus remains on place value. Furthermore, they are often surprised by what happens when they make a place-value error, which increases their place-value understanding.

The challenge of Wipe Out–type activities is illustrated by a question included on a recent national assessment, shown in Figure 8-10. It shows an open-ended question along with examples of satisfactory responses. Although calculators were available, the decision about whether to use a calculator was made by each student; however, more than 60% of the fourth graders made no response or provided an incorrect response. More experiences with Wipe Out–type activities might improve student performance.

Question: Laura wanted to enter the number 8375 into her calculator. By mistake, she entered the number 8275. Without clearing the calculator, how could she correct her mistake?

Satisfactory Responses:

1. 8275 + 100 = 8375

2. She could add 100 more.

3. If she subtracted 100 she could add 200.

FIGURE 8-10 An example from a national assessment test that reinforces the connection between a wipe out–type calculator game and mental computation skills.

Math Links 8.2

*T*here are a number of excellent Web sites that provide opportunities for children to make patterns, practice counting, and develop a better sense about numbers. Here are several:

Go to the Math Forum Web site at http://mathforum.org/mathtools and then go to Math Topics. There you will find a number of K–2 virtual resources related to place value, including Base Blocks, which allows you to explore units, longs, flats, and blocks in an interactive mode, and Place Value, which provides a very fast counter so that children can practice naming digits of very large numbers.

Go to the National Library of Virtual Manipulatives at http://www.matti.usu.edu. There you will find Base Blocks, an Abacus, and Chip Abacus in the K–2 resources. You can use the Base Blocks to provide explorations in several different bases. The Sieve of Eratosthenes provides a hundred chart that can be extended to 1000 and allows for exploring patterns involving multiples, including multiples of 10.

www.wiley.com/college/reys

◀ Extending Place Value

Research reports that many children lack an understanding of the relative sizes of numbers greater than 100 (Payne and Huinker, 1993; Fuson, 2003). This results from many factors, one of which may be the lack of opportunities to model, which helps children develop a visual awareness of the relative sizes of numbers. So a number such as 123 has several different equivalent representations:

One hundred twenty-three
Twelve tens and three ones
100 + 20 + 3
1 (100) + 2 (10) + 3
1 (10^2) + 2 (10) + 3

For large numbers, children can use variations of the models shown in Figure 8-4. For the base-ten blocks, lay another place-value mat to the left of the mat holding hundreds, tens, and ones. This thousands mat holds thousands, ten thousands, and hundred thousands (see Figure 8-11). In addition to these physical models, stories such as those in the Book Nook provide real-world connections to larger numbers.

Figure 8-11 provides another demonstration of how two numbers can have the same digits but be different. How are 2130 and 1032 alike and different? As children engage in discussion to answer this question, their knowledge of place value and their sense of numbers will grow. Using the same digits to represent different numbers helps children appreciate the importance of representing the place values accurately. Although the numbers 2130 and 1032 use the same digits, the models that represent these numbers are dramatically different. Furthermore the symbolic representation of them is different. For example:

Two thousand one hundred thirty is 2130 or in expanded form is 2 (1000) + 1 (100) + 3 (10) or 2 (10^3) + 1 (10^2) + 2(10).

One thousand thirty-two is 1032 or in expanded form is 1 (1000) + 3 (10) + 2 or 1 (10^3) + 3 (10) + 2.

Notice how the language used to describe these expanded notations, namely *ten cubed* and *ten squared* can be linked directly to the base-ten model in Figure 8-11. This type of experience helps develop number sense and alerts children to the importance of the front-end, or lead, digits, which in this case denote thousands.

As the number of digits increases, children should be encouraged to focus on the front-end digits. The front-end digits are used when comparing and ordering numbers, as well as when computing mentally and estimating:

Mental computation   Estimating

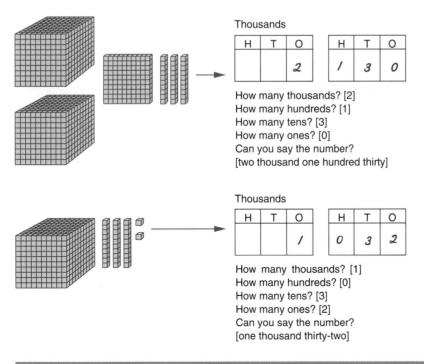

Thousands

H	T	O		H	T	O
		2		1	3	0

How many thousands? [2]
How many hundreds? [1]
How many tens? [3]
How many ones? [0]
Can you say the number?
[two thousand one hundred thirty]

Thousands

H	T	O		H	T	O
		1		0	3	2

How many thousands? [1]
How many hundreds? [0]
How many tens? [3]
How many ones? [2]
Can you say the number?
[one thousand thirty-two]

FIGURE 8-11 Using a thousands mat to demonstrate how two numbers can have the same digits but be different.

The front-end approach can be naturally extended and applied to larger numbers. For example, students could be asked to decide which number is larger when the front-end digits are the same:

And then asked the same question when the back-end digits are the same:

This task helps students compare and order larger numbers.

Try this problem:

Norway has an area of 154780 square miles.

New Mexico has an area of 121593 square miles.

Greece has an area of 50944 square miles.

Why is it easy to tell which has the least area?

Can you tell which is the greatest area by comparing the first front-end digit? the first two front-end digits? the first three front-end digits?

Which has the greatest area?

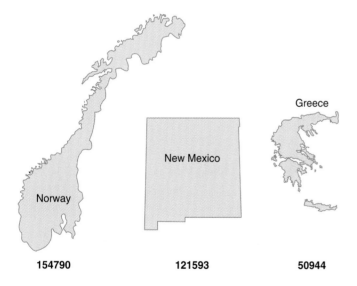

Greece

New Mexico

Norway

154790   **121593**   **50944**

This problem reminds students of the importance of place value when comparing numbers. For example, the front-end approach is used only when the numbers have the same number of digits. It is not needed to compare 125181 square miles with 50944 square miles because the numbers of digits are different.

Counting and Patterns

Practice in skip counting helps decrease bumps in the counting road. Variations of the hundreds charts used in Chapter 7 can be a valuable tool in smoothing out the bumps.

Calculators are also useful in counting and pattern recognition. Seeing each value displayed on the calculator helps students develop important insight into what digits are changing and when. In the Classroom 7-4 provided a calculator counting activity. When children are counting by ones, they observe that the digit on the right (ones place) changes every time they "count," while the next digit (tens place) changes less frequently, and it takes much counting to change the third digit (hundreds place). On the other hand, Figure 8-12 develops an additional understanding of place value by displaying results of counting by ones, tens, hundreds, and thousands.

Calculator counting provides many opportunities to discuss patterns related to place value. Such counting can also contribute to a better grasp of large numbers, thereby helping to develop students' number sense. For example, having students count by ones to 100 and 1000 with the calculator helps them better understand the magnitude of these numbers. By expanding this activity, students will come to realize that it takes about the same amount of time to count to 1000 by ones on a calculator as to count to 1,000,000 by 1000 or to 100 by 0.1 on a calculator.

For example, one fourth grader after doing this calculator counting said, "That means there are as many thousands in one million as ones in one thousand." This is a profound observation—of the type that leads to a better understanding of both place value and large numbers, and it also reflects a growing sense of numbers.

As Figure 8-12 shows, counting on by tens, hundreds, or thousands never changes the ones place; however, when counting by tens, the tens place changes on each count and the next digit (hundreds) changes every 10 counts. Observing these patterns in counting larger and larger numbers helps students recognize place-value properties. In the Classroom 8-3 uses patterns to help students add multiples of 100. Similar exercises should be provided with other powers of 10.

FIGURE 8-12 Calculator counting to illustrate place-value patterns.

In the Classroom 8-3

OBJECTIVE: **Counting by hundreds to develop place value and pattern recognition.**

GRADE LEVEL: **2–3**

▼ Use your calculator or do these mentally.

▼ Begin at the start number and add 100.

▼ Decide which target you will hit.

Start	Rule	Which target?		Guess	Check
20	+100	200	220	_____	_____
35	+100	335	500	_____	_____
41	+100	410	441	_____	_____
86	+100	586	580	_____	_____
97	+100	897	970	_____	_____
169	+100	469	696	_____	_____
123	+100	321	323	_____	_____

Counting back provides similar place-value patterns. The number line below shows how the number line model might be used to count backwards from 2 by threes and tens.

The number line would need to be extended to count back by more tens. Yet the calculator facilitates counting back by threes, tens, and hundreds or whatever, and the resulting values when starting at 2 and counting back by threes, or tens, are shown in Figure 8-13. Place-value patterns resulting from counting back are apparent. Observing these patterns in counting larger and larger (or smaller and smaller) numbers helps students recognize that place-value properties are reflected in both positive and negative integers.

FIGURE 8-13 Counting back to illustrate place value with negative integers.

As you have seen, the hundred chart provides a useful model for counting and pattern recognition related to place value. Activities involving counting with multiples of 10 were illustrated in In the Classroom 8-1. In the Classroom 8-4 shows how similar ideas can be extended to a thousand chart. For example, consider this diagram and the thousand chart in In the Classroom 8-4:

A solution for this diagram requires the use of patterns:

$$A = 430 - 100 - 10$$
$$B = 430 - 100$$
$$C = 430 + 100 + 10$$
$$D = 430 + 200$$

This activity also leads to algebraic thinking when 430 is replaced by any number N. Then

$$A = N - 100 - 10$$
$$B = N - 100$$
$$C = N + 100 + 10$$
$$D = N + 200$$

This activity further develops students' number sense and provides practice in important mental computation skills.

Regrouping and Renaming

Counting suggests many patterns, but one of the most important for young children is observing what happens when we model the number after 9 (or 19, 29, etc.). Trading occurs in every case. The pattern involved in bridging from one decade to another should be recognized and clearly understood by children.

Regrouping and place value are intertwined in later development of computation. Regrouping happens whenever bridging occurs, as from one ten to another (such as 29 to 30) or from one hundred to another (such as 799 to 800). Regrouping or decomposing also happens when 6 tens 7 ones are considered as 5 tens 17 ones, or 245 is thought of as 24 tens 5 ones, or 40 pennies are traded for 4 dimes. The importance of clearly understanding the regrouping (i.e., composing and decomposing) process cannot be overemphasized. Understanding is most likely to develop when children experience this bridging with physical models and practice trading and regrouping.

Whenever trading occurs, there are accompanying changes in how we record the number. Understanding this changed notation requires many experiences with problems involving trading and the related recording process. Figure 8-14 shows how regrouping affects digits and place value.

Figure 8-15 further illustrates the regrouping process with two different models, one proportional

In the Classroom 8-4

THE POWER OF 10 ON THE THOUSAND CHART

OBJECTIVE: Using a thousand chart to identify patterns and skip count by tens and hundreds.

GRADE LEVEL: 2–3

10	20	30	40	50	60	70	80	90	100
110	120	130	140	150	160	170	180	190	200
210	220	230	240	250	260	270	280	290	300
310	320	330	340	350	360	370	380	390	400
410	420	430	440	450	460	470	480	490	500
510	520	530	540	550	560	570	580	590	600
610	620	630	640	650	660	670	680	690	700
710	720	730	740	750	760	770	780	790	800
810	820	830	840	850	860	870	880	890	900
910	920	930	940	950	960	970	980	990	1000

▼ Count by 10:
- Start on any square in the first three rows.
- Count forward 10 squares, and tell where you stopped.
- Start at a different square, and count forward 10 squares.
- After you have done this several times, tell about a pattern that you found.
- Describe a quick way to count "a hundred more" on this thousand chart.

▼ Count by 100:
- Tell how you could use the thousand chart to add 300 to 240.
- Tell how you could use the thousand chart to add 290 to 240.

▼ Connect the charts:
- Tell how using the hundred chart helps you use the thousand chart.

Here is 29¢.   1¢ is added.

Dimes	Pennies		Dimes	Pennies
2	9		2	10

Regrouping is required so a trade is made.

1 Dime   10 Pennies

Dimes	Pennies
3	0

FIGURE 8-14 Nonproportional model illustrating relation between regrouping and place value.

and one nonproportional. Similar models with larger numbers should be used as soon as children have grasped the trading principles involving ones, tens, and hundreds. In fact, this extension process demonstrates the power of mathematical abstraction. Extending to thousands should be done with proportional models to illustrate the dramatic size increase that continues to occur as new places are used. Children soon recognize that it becomes cumbersome to model large numbers with proportional models (see Powers of Ten in Appendix B).

The calculator can be used with very large numbers. Minor variations of In the Classroom 7-6 (such as finding how long a calculator takes to count to one million or one billion) can help students develop a better grasp of large numbers. As the magnitude of numbers increase, physical models of them become more difficult. Yet the need to continue to develop a sense of large numbers is a major goal of school mathematics.

◀ Reading and Writing Numbers

Reading and writing numbers are symbolic activities and should follow much modeling and talking about numbers. The key word is *symbolic*. This recommendation is based on research with young children and alerts us to the danger of a premature

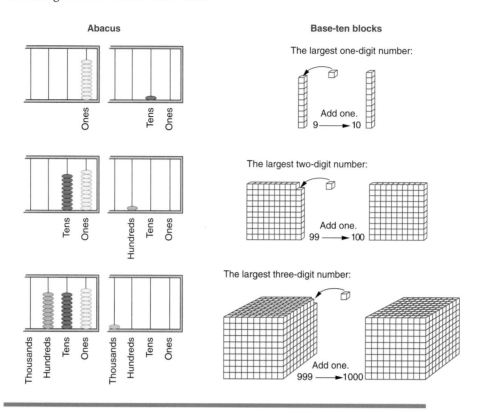

FIGURE 8-15   Nonproportional and proportional models illustrating some relationships between regrouping and place value.

focus on symbols (Payne and Huinker, 1993). A sustained development of number sense should accompany reading and writing numbers. This approach ensures that the symbols the students are writing and reading are meaningful to them.

Consider some ways in which understanding place value helps develop reading and writing numbers. Take the example of the number 123. The places (hundreds, tens, ones) as well as the value of each (1, 2, 3) are easy to identify. The 1 means 1 hundred. The 23 is both 2 tens 3 ones and 23 ones, and 123 is 1 hundred 2 tens 3 ones; 12 tens 3 ones; and 123 ones. These representations are equivalent and may be shown on the place-value mat:

H	T	O
1	2	3

1 hundred 2 tens 3 ones

H	T	O
	12	3

12 tens 3 ones

H	T	O
		123

123 ones

The skill of reading numbers in different ways (and understanding of the grouping that allows

these representations) can be useful in many operations with whole numbers. For example, rereading provides a nice stepping stone to mental computation; more specifically, it leads to multiplying a number by 10:

H	T	O
3	8	0

Reads: 3 hundreds 8 tens 0 ones.
Realizes there are no ones.
Rereads: 38 tens, which is 380.

This idea extends naturally to larger numbers. For example, twenty-three thousand is 23 (1000) or 23,000. Likewise fifty million is 50 (1,000,000) or 50,000,000.

Although it seems logical to write number words as they sound, this procedure can lead to difficulty. If this were done, sixty-one would be incorrectly written as 601 and one hundred twenty-three as 100203. If a child made this mistake, the teacher could use the place-value mat as a model to demonstrate:

Forty-one represents →

Tens	Ones
●● ●●	●
4	1

not this →

Hundreds	Tens	Ones
●● ●●		●
4	0	1

Modeling several numbers on the mat can help clarify this notion.

Similar problems exist in naming and representing larger numbers. Open-ended questions such as those shown in Figure 8-16 encourage children to estimate and think about numbers. As they share their answers and talk about different ways of understanding millions and billions, their number sense grows. Reading books listed in the Book Nook for Children such as *Earth Day-Hooray!* by Stuart Murphy, *The Rajah's Rice: A Mathematical Folktale from India* by Berry, and *Can You Count to a Googol?* by Robert Wells provide real-world examples of larger numbers and provide connections to representing their place value symbolically. *The Wonderful World of Mathematics: A Critically Annotated List of Children's Books in Mathematics* (Thiessen, Matthias, and Smith, 1998) and *Math and Literature: Grades K–1 and 2–3* (Burns and Sheffield, 2004) identify more books to give children additional insight and appreciation of larger numbers.

It is helpful for students to link some of the models to larger numbers. For example, students might begin with a one-cubic-centimeter block. If they then make a cubic-meter box, as illustrated in Figure 8-17, that box will hold one million cubic-centimeter cubes.

Base-ten blocks also can be used to help students make the connection between the concrete model and the symbolic representation, as in Fig-

FIGURE 8-17   Children constructing a cubic-meter box. (Source: Photo by Gene Sutphen.)

ure 8-18. This model helps students mentally "see" that ten thousand is a long piece made up of 10 cubes, where each cube is one thousand. Although this model can be constructed with physical models, children quickly appreciate the power of constructing mental images to represent larger numbers. When students begin to develop an intuitive grasp of larger numbers and begin to use millions and billions intelligently, they are ready to write and read these larger numbers. Place-value mats can be naturally expanded to represent larger numbers:

Billions			Millions			Thousands			Ones		
H	T	O	H	T	O	H	T	O	H	T	O

This provides students an opportunity to generalize the naming of numbers, as the hundreds, tens, ones, applies to not only three-digit numbers, but to larger numbers as well. The only difference is that each block of three digits introduces groupings of thousands, millions, billions, and trillions.

To develop facility in reading large numbers, children need careful instruction and practice in actually naming them aloud. For example, would you read 12,345,678 as "one ten-million two million three hundred-thousand four ten-thousand" and so on? Certainly not! You would use the period names and read it as "twelve million, three

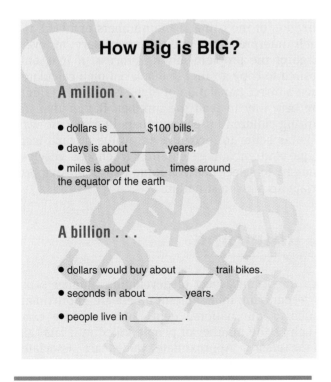

How Big is BIG?

A million . . .

● dollars is _____ $100 bills.

● days is about _____ years.

● miles is about _____ times around the equator of the earth

A billion . . .

● dollars would buy about _____ trail bikes.

● seconds in about _____ years.

● people live in _____ .

FIGURE 8-16   Questions to promote thinking about size of numbers.

The table within the figure:

	One	Hundred	Ten	One	Hundred	Ten	One	Oral
	Million		Thousand					number name
	1000000	100000	10000	1000	100	10	1	Place-value notation
	10^6	10^5	10^4	10^3	10^2	10^1	10^0	Powers of ten notation

FIGURE 8-18   Connecting the symbolic representation of one million with a concrete model.

hundred forty-five thousand, six hundred seventy-eight." This example is a clear application of an organizing strategy: the digits within each period are read as hundreds, tens, and ones, as with "three hundred forty-five thousand." For this reason, children need to think of larger numbers (those of more than three digits) in blocks of three digits.

Recognition and understanding of the hundreds, tens, and ones pattern provide a powerful organizational strategy that can be called on in naming numbers. Only the key terms—ones, tens, and hundreds—along with recognition of the periods for thousands, millions, and billions are needed to name very large numbers.

In many countries, commas are not used to separate blocks of three digits. Instead, for example, the number 2346457 is written as 2 346 457. The blocks of digits remain visible but are separated by spaces rather than commas. Some newspapers, journals, and textbooks in the United States now print numbers this way. This change has instructional implications for both reading and writing numbers. In particular, children must become even more sensitive to the importance of writing numbers clearly and distinctly.

For practice in reading and writing, newspapers provide a rich context to explore numbers of all sizes. Examine a newspaper and highlight all of the numbers reported in headlines and related stories. You may be surprised at the high frequency with which numbers occur. Naming numbers is clearly an important skill. Yet with the widespread use of calculators, a more efficient way to read multidigit numbers is becoming common. For example, 32764 is read as "three two seven six four" and 4.3425 as "four point three four two five." Each of these readings is correct and much easier to say than the respective periods. There is the danger that children will say the digits without any realization of the value of the numbers involved, but such interpretations are not necessary at every stage of the problem-solving process. If it is only desired to copy a number displayed on a calculator, then a direct translation of digits is without a doubt the best way to read the number. Rather than requiring children to read numbers in a specific way, it is far better to recognize the value of each technique and encourage children to choose wisely—namely, to select the technique that is most appropriate for a given situation.

Rounding

An important aspect of developing number sense is recognizing that some numbers are approximate (such as our national debt) and some are exact (such as the number of people killed in a fatal airplane crash). Approximate values are associated with estimation, often involving rounding, and are encountered regularly in our daily lives.

Rounding integrates understanding of approximate values with place value and naming numbers.

Numbers are usually rounded to make them easier to use or because exact values are unknown. How numbers are rounded depends on how they are used. For example, attendance at a major league baseball game may be 54321. Although the attendance could be rounded to the nearest ten (54320) or the nearest hundred (54300), it is more likely to be reported as "about 54000" or "over 50000" or "less than 60000" because these values are convenient and a little easier to comprehend and remember.

As children develop rounding skills, they should come to realize that rounding rules may vary and are not universal. For example, here are two different rules from current textbooks for rounding a number ending in 5:

1. Change the 5 to a 0 and increase the previous digit by 1.

2. Change the 5 to a 0. If the digit preceding the 5 is even, leave it alone. If the digit preceding the 5 is odd, increase it to the next even digit.

In either case, 75 would round to 80; however, 85 would round to 90 using rule 1 and 80 using rule 2. Neither rule is right or best, but this variability across textbooks can confuse children. Checking to make sure students understand the specific rules of rounding that are to be used avoids some of the confusion.

Regardless of the rounding rule used, the precision of the rounded numbers reflects the problem context. For example, a meter stick could serve as a number line. Consider this train of rods, with 7 decimeter rods and 4 centimeter rods:

Is the train closer to 7 or 8 decimeters? [7 decimeters]

Is it closer to 0 or 1 meter? [1 meter]

If you round to the nearest decimeter, then the length is 7 decimeters. If you round to the nearest meter, the length is 1 meter. How numbers are rounded depends on how the values will be used. For example, if you were to cut a strip of cloth to cover this train, it would be foolish to round to the nearest decimeter and cut a length of 7 decimeters; however, a meter of cloth would provide plenty of material to cover the train. Children must think about numbers before rounding them and not just indiscriminately apply rounding rules.

Even in a given context, interpretation of rounded numbers is challenging, as illustrated by this national assessment question:

The length of a dinosaur was reported to have been 80 feet (rounded to the nearest 10 feet). What length other than 80 feet could have been the actual length of the dinosaur?

Any answer from 75 to 85 was scored correct in this open-ended question. (22% of the fourth graders provided a correct answer, 26% answered 90, and 48% gave another number). This performance shows that interpreting a rounded result needs to be carefully addressed.

Base-ten blocks provide a natural method for developing rounding skills with larger numbers. Questions such as these focus attention on the quantity and the idea of *closer to*, which is essential in rounding:

Is this more than three hundred? [yes]

Is this more than four hundred? [no]

Is this closer to three or four hundred? [closer to three hundred]

This model can also be extended to help children become more aware that 350 is halfway between 300 and 400.

A roller coaster model could be used to develop rounding skills. If children understand the number line, the roller coaster provides an effective tool for rounding.

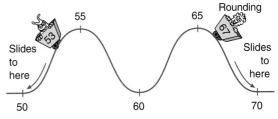

Children know what happens when the coaster stops at certain points. The model also suggests that something special happens at the top: The coaster could roll either way. This observation provides an opportunity to discuss a rule of rounding, such as "if the number ends in 5, you go over the hump to the next valley." In rounding, attention is given to the back-end digit or digits. Children should view rounding as something that not only makes numbers easier to handle but, more important, makes sense.

Perhaps the biggest difficulty related to rounding is knowing whether to round to the nearest ten, hundred, thousand, or whatever. This decision depends on the purpose of rounding and the context of the problem. Consider, for example, the following well-known (to sports fans) situation:

> Carl Furillo (former Major League Baseball player for the Dodgers) had a lifetime batting average of 0.2994 in the major leagues, yet he is not considered a 0.300 hitter.

This suggests that Major League Baseball has a particular procedure for rounding batting averages. Encourage students to explore different ways to round. For example, consider these prices:

How would you round these prices if you wanted to round them to the same number? [to nearest ten]

What would you round these prices to, in deciding how much money is needed to make each purchase? [round up to $25 or $30]

Such real-world situations encourage students to think about both the advantages and consequences of rounding numbers. Meaningful rounding (knowing how much precision is necessary and what to round to) will improve through practice in many different problem contexts.

◀ Cultural Connections

Young children have varying cultural, linguistic, and home experience on which to build mathematics development of numbers. For example, patterns in naming numbers appear throughout Asian languages such as in Japanese, yet in English and Spanish the number names don't always form consistent patterns. Figure 8-19 shows that in English and Spanish the number names from 11 to 20 do not explicitly name the number of tens as do the naming of numbers from 20 and larger. On the other hand, Figure 8-19 shows that in Japan and China the numbers from 10 to 20 clearly name the ten and a related number. In China and Japan, place-value patterns abound. For example, in Japan multiples of ten from 20 to 90 are "(digit)-*ju*"; hundreds from 200 to 900 are "(digit)-*hyaku*"; thousands from 2000 to 9000 are "(digit)-*sen*." These patterns consistently reinforce place value and facilitate naming numbers.

Counting to Ten										
English	One	Two	Three	Four	Five	Six	Seven	Eight	Nine	Ten
Spanish	Uno	Dos	Tres	Cuatro	Cinco	Seis	Siete	Ocho	Nueve	Diez
Chinese	Yi	Er	San	Si	Wu	Liu	Qi	Ba	Jiu	Shi
Japanese	Ichi	Ni	San	Yon, Shi	Go	Roku	Nana, Shichi,	Hachi	Kyuu	Juu, Ju,

Eleven to Twenty										
English	Eleven	Twelve	Thirteen	Fourteen	Fifteen	Sixteen	Seventeen	Eighteen	Nineteen	Twenty
Spanish	Once	Doce	Trece	Catorce	Quince	Diez y seis	Diez y siete	Diez y ocho	Diez y nueve	Veinte
Chinese	Shi yi	Shi er	Shi san	Shi si	Shi wu	Shi liu	Shi qi	Shi ba	Shi jiu	Er shi
Japanese	Ju ichi	Ju ni	Ju san	Ju yon	Ju go	Ju roku	Ju nana	Ju hachi	Ju kyuu	Ni-ju

Some Larger Numbers										
English	Twenty-one	Twenty-two	Twenty-three	Twenty-four	Twenty-five	Fifty	Hundred	Thousand	Ten thousand	Hundred thousand
Spanish	Veinte y uno	Veinte y dos	Veinte y tres	Veinte y cuarto	Veinte y cinco	Cincuenta	Cien	Mil	Dos mil	Cien mil
Chinese	Er shi yi	Er shi er	Er shi san	Er shi si	Er shi wu	Wu shi	Pai	Chien	Wan	Shi wan
Japanese	Ni-ju-ichi	Ni-ju-ni	Ni-ju-san	Ni-ju-yon	Ni-ju-go	Go-ju	Hyaku	Sen	Man	Ju-man

FIGURE 8-19   Counting to 20 in different languages.

Figure 8-20 shows characters used to represent numbers in China. Notice how the larger numbers shown reflect place value and are additive. For example, 751 = 7 (100) + 5 (10) + 1. Whereas 751 written with Chinese characters is 七五一 which literally means seven hundreds, five tens, and one. So if the Chinese characters are known, it is easy to express any Hindu-Arabic number and vice versa (Uy, 2003).

It is also interesting to note that in both Chinese and Japanese four groups of digits are used instead of three. In our number system, the unit changes every multiple of 1000, and we think ones, tens, hundreds and then move to ones, tens, hundreds in the thousands place, then ones, tens, hundreds, in the millions place, and so on. In China and Japan, their number systems are based on ten-thousand, rather than 1000. Thus in Japan 10,000 is called a *"man."* So in the United States, 3000 is read as "three thousand" whereas in Japan 30000 is read *"San-man."*

While mathematical concepts are universal across cultures, the language associated with these cultures is not. For example, in English we name the tens then the ones for two-digit numbers larger than 20, thus 35 is spoken as "thirty-five." In Arabic, numbers are named a bit differently. For example, for a two-digit number, say 45, the number is orally named "five forty." The number 345 is named "three hundred five forty"; 8345 is named "eight thousand three hundred five forty." As larger numbers are named, the digit in the ones place is named before the digit in the tens.

Naming large numbers in the Untied States and the United Kingdom can also become confusing. For example, in both the United States and the United Kingdom a million is a thousand thousands. However a billion in the United States is a thousand million, whereas it is a million million in the United Kingdom. Thus 1,000,000,000,000 is a billion in England but a billion in the United States is 1,000,000,000. These cultural differences in naming numbers underscores the need to know your students well and strive for similar understandings when numbers are named.

◢ A Glance at Where We've Been

Children must have a clear understanding of our number system if they are going to be mathematically literate. They must be able to distinguish the four characteristics of our number system: the role of zero, the additive property of numbers, a base of ten, and place value. Many counting and trading experiences (particularly grouping by tens) are necessary.

As children develop their skills with the aid of various models (such as bean sticks, base-ten blocks, and an abacus), they need to learn how to organize the results in some systematic fashion and record them. Place-value mats serve as a visual reminder of the quantities involved and provide a bridge toward the symbolic representation of larger numbers. Establishing these bridges from the concrete to the abstract is particularly critical in developing place value, whose importance is second to none in all later development of number concepts.

Place-value concepts are developed over many years. Trading plants the seeds early, but recognition of the power and importance of place value is developed, refined, extended, and expanded throughout the study of mathematics. Place-value concepts helps children compose and decompose numbers and begin to recognize equivalent representations. We have seen how place value is reflected in the language and representation in different cultures. While language variations exist, the utilization of place value in these cultures is universal.

Understanding place value is essential to counting and facilitates operating with larger numbers. Place value is not taught and mastered over a few days, weeks, or grades. This means that place value is not completely developed before operations are introduced, because experiences with adding, subtracting, multiplying, and dividing whole numbers develops additional competence and understanding

FIGURE 8-20 Chinese numeration system.

of place-value. Work with decimals in later grades will further extend place-value concepts. For example, systematic work with smaller numbers, such as tenths, hundredths, and thousandths, is based on the same notion of trading and similar patterns in naming numbers result. Thus place-value concepts initiated in the primary grades will be integrated and extended throughout elementary school.

Things to Do: From What You've Read

1. Identify four characteristics of our number system. Select one characteristic and make a visual representation of it.

2. Show how 201 and 120 would be represented with three different place-value models.

3. Distinguish between proportional and nonproportional models. Name an example of each.

4. Tell why trading activities are so important with respect to place value. Describe several materials that could be used for trading.

5. Describe how trading provides opportunities for composing and decomposing numbers.

6. Describe ways in which modeling, reading, and writing numbers can be used to get children actively involved in talking about mathematics and linking concrete materials with their symbolic representations.

7. It has been suggested that centuries, decades, and millenniums can be used to demonstrate some notions of place value. Describe how this could be done.

8. Use your calculator. Enter the largest number possible in the display and name this number. How many digits does it have? Add one to this number and describe what your calculator does.

Things to Do: Going Beyond This Book

IN THE FIELD

1. *Early Number Sense.* Ask a child some questions, such as, What number comes before 17? 30? 200? What number comes after 39? 209?

How many tens are in 40? 47? Try to capture the words students use to describe how they determined their answers. Explain how their answers help you better understand their thinking and their level of number sense.

2. *Checking Place-Value Concepts.* Give a second or third grader some of the following tasks: Write three hundred forty-eight. Write a large number. Name that number. How many tens are in 250? How many hundreds are in one thousand? Explain how the answers to these questions helped you better understand the child's development of place value.

3. *Patterns on a Thousand Chart.* In the Classroom 8-4 provides an extension of the hundred chart. (See Appendix B for other variations.) Show the chart to at least three children (grades 3–5) and say, "Please tell me about some patterns that you see." After each description, say, "Tell me about any other patterns you see." Be sure to allow them time to think and reflect; pattern recognition takes time. Make a list of the patterns for each child and compare their observations.

4. *Models for Large Numbers.* Different models exist for helping children develop a concept of large numbers. Each of the articles (Ellett, 2005; Joslyn, 1990; Thompson, 2000) shows and describes useful physical models. Examine one of these articles and describe the approach taken to help children better understand large numbers.

5. *Understanding Large Numbers.* Select either *Number Sense and Operations* (Burton et al., 1993), *Developing Number Sense in the Middle Grades* (Reys et al., 1991), or *Number SENSE* (McIntosh et al., 1997). Choose an activity that you think would be useful to help students develop a better understanding of large numbers and demonstrate how you would implement the activity.

WITH TECHNOLOGY

6. View the entire Annenberg video *Place Value Centers.* Tell how measurement was used to explore place value. Describe the physical models being used to demonstrate place value. This first-grade lesson focused on two-digit numbers. Tell how these activities might be extended to larger numbers.

7. *The Importance of Number Sense.* View a segment from the videotape series *Number Sense Now!* (Fennell, 1992). Discuss ways in which this tape might help students become more sensitive to the importance and power of number sense.

8. *Standards Exploration.* Check the Number and Operation Standard for pre-K–2 (www.standards-

---

*Additional activities, suggestions, and questions are provided in *Teaching Elementary Mathematics: A Resource for Field Experiences* (Wiley, 2007).

e.nctm.org) for additional explorations of groups of ten and place value. Discuss how the samples of student work influence your thinking of place value.

9. *Counting with a Calculator*. In the Classroom 8-3 provides a structured counting activity that can be facilitated with a calculator. Use this activity as a guide and ask primary-grade students to count by hundreds and predict which results will occur. Ask them to count with the calculator and compare results. Describe any difficulties or discoveries that you observed.

10. If you were able to view the entire *Place Value Centers* video, here are some questions:

    Describe different materials used to develop place value.

    Was trading embedded in all of the materials?

    Choose any of the stations and describe how place value was illustrated.

Note to Instructors: You can find additional resources, learning activities, and black-line masters in this text's accompanying Instructor's Manual, at www.wiley.com/college/reys.

Book Nook for Children

Berry, D. *The Rajah's Rice: A Mathematical Folktale from India*. New York: W.W. Freeman, 1994.

When Chandra, an Indian village girl who bathes the raja's elephants, cures the beasts after they fall ill, the raja offers her jewels as a reward. She refuses, accepting only a measure of rice for the hungry villagers: two grains on the first square of a chessboard, four on the second, and so on, doubling the amount for each subsequent square. Although the amount seems insignificant at first, it grows at an alarming rate, since doubling has little effect on small numbers, but an increasingly enormous effect as the numbers grow larger. The raja's storehouse is soon empty, and he must admit that he cannot fill her seemingly modest request.

Murphy, S. J. *Earth Day—Hooray!* New York: HarperCollins, 2004.

The Maple Street School–Save the Planet Club is having a can drive to recycle aluminum cans. As the club members collect the cans and sort them

into different amounts, the reader will learn about place value. There are activities and games in the back of this book for parents and teachers to use.

Schwartz, D. M. *How Much Is a Million?* New York: Lothrop, Lee & Shepard Books, 1985.

The reader will see how much a million, a billion, a trillion can be. The pictures in the text will let the reader see how these amounts can be.

Schwartz, D. M. *If You Made a Million.* New York: Lothrop, Lee & Shepherd Books, 1989.

Marvelosissimo the Mathematical Magician and his team of cheerful kids (and their multitude of animal friends) take on some jobs. For each job, they'll be paid an appropriate amount of money. But soon the questions arise—what does that much money look like, and how can it be spent, saved, or used to pay off a loan? The fantasy cleverly introduces money from 1 penny to 1 million dollars.

Wells, R. E. *Can You Count to a Googol?* Morton Grove, IL: Albert Whitman, 2000.

This resource book will let children see how our decimal numeration system is developed. Starting with the number 1, the reader will see how our number system can develop many numbers using zeros that will contain the following numbers: billion, trillion, quadrillion, octillion, and finally a googol. Quantities and distances are related to the numbers.

Annotated Resources

Bay-Williams, J. and Martinie, S. *Math and Literature: Grades 6–8*. Sausalito, CA: Math Solutions Publications, 2004.

Bresser, R. *Math and Literature: Grades 4–6*. Sausalito, CA: Math Solutions Publications, 2004.

Burns, M., and Sheffield, S. *Math and Literature: Grades K–1 and 2–3*. Sausalito, CA: Math Solutions Publications 2004. This Math Solutions Publications series identifies children's books and describes specific ways the stories might be linked to a range of mathematical concepts. Although the range of concepts is broad, each book includes stories that promote the development of number sense.

Burns, M. *Math by All Means: Place Value Grade 1–2.* Sausalito, CA: Math Solutions Publications, 1994. Students learn about place value through explorations with grouping, counting, measuring, and graphing. Includes activities from strands of statistics, geometry, and logical reasoning.

Ellett, K. "Making a million meaningful." *Mathematics Teaching in the Middle School*, 10(8) (April 2005), pp. 416–423. Shares many different classroom tested ways to help children better understand the magnitude of a million. Shows some student work and many potential tasks to engage children in exploring a million.

McIntosh, A., Reys, B., Reys, R., and Hope, J. *Simple Effective Number Experiences* (SENSE), *Grades 4–6*. Palo Alto, CA: Dale Seymour, 1997.
These 10-minute activities help students develop a sense of what numbers represent and how to use them by exploring relationships and patterns, encouraging mental computation, recognizing equivalent representations of a number, establishing benchmarks, improving estimation skills, and exploring the idea of reasonableness. Includes activity masters, teacher's notes, and ideas for extending the activities. This series includes a similar book for grades 1–2 and 3–4.

Sowder, J. "Estimation and number sense." In *Handbook of Research on Mathematics Teaching and Learning* (ed. Douglas Grouws). New York: Macmillan, 1992, pp. 371–389.
This article focuses on estimation and distinguishing between estimation and approximation. It includes research on computational estimation, the relationship between number sense and its importance for estimation, and measurement estimation. A section on assessment issues related to estimation is also included as these issues provide unique challenges to educators.

Thompson, I. "Teaching place value in the UK: Time for a reappraisal?" *Educational Review*, 51(3) (November 2000), pp. 291–299.
This article is a critical appraisal of what is traditionally considered to be one of the most important concepts in the teaching and learning of number in primary school: place value. A consideration of the concept from a variety of perspectives suggests that the concept is too sophisticated for many young children to grasp. The conclusion drawn is that there is a need for a reappraisal of the teaching of place value in primary school.

Uy, F. "The Chinese numeration system and place value." *Teaching Children Mathematics*, 9(5) (January 2003), 243–247.
Illustrates the additive and place-value characteristics of Chinese numeration system. Includes several activities that encourage children to record values in expanded form and write equivalent numbers using Chinese characters.

Zaslavsky, C. "The influence of ancient Egypt on Greek and other numeration systems." *Mathematics Teaching in the Middle Grades*, 9(3) (November 2003), pp. 174–176.
Highlights some connections between numerals (hieroglyphics and hieratics) used in ancient Egypt and the symbols in base ten. This discussion is accompanied by activity sheets that allow students to apply some of these ideas.

CHAPTER 9

Operations: Meanings and Basic Facts

◆ Snapshot of a Lesson

Key Ideas

1. Developing familiarity and fluency with addition and subtraction basic facts (with addends 7 or smaller)

2. Recognizing addition/subtraction relationships

Background

This lesson snapshot comes from the video *Window Puzzles,* from Teaching Math: A Video Library, K–4 from Annenberg Media. Produced by WGBH Educational Foundation. ©1995 WGBH. All rights reserved. To view the video, go to http://www.learner.org/resources/series32.html (video #13). Terry Goens, a first-grade teacher at the Martha Fox Elementary School in Belgrade, Montana, engages her students in working in pairs on a number puzzle that involves sums and differences of one-digit numbers.

Ms Goens begins the day's mathematics lesson by reviewing Windows, a puzzle the children worked on the previous week. This is an activity that Ms. Goens uses to engage her students in developing familiarity with basic facts for addition and subtraction. She provides the students with a sample window on the board.

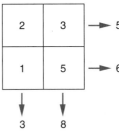

In this activity, the class starts by writing a number in each cell in the window (here, they've put in 2, 3, 1, and 5). Next, they find the row totals (here, 5 and 6) and the column totals (here, 3 and 8) and then they erase the numbers in the window cells and work to find other combinations of numbers that give the same row and column totals.

Ms. Goens asks Sam to describe how he might find other numbers that work for the puzzle.

> **SAM:** Me and Rachel, we know that if four and four would equal eight, then we put those there [*in the cells in the right column*]. And if one and four would equal five we put that there [*put 1 in the top left cell*]. But two and one would equal three [*so put 2 in the bottom left cell*]. And if it was two, and four would equal six [*checking that the bottom row sums to 6, as it should*].
>
> **MS. GOENS:** Okay, were we adding? Is that what we call it? Yes, we call that adding, don't we?

Ms. Goens clears the window by erasing all of the numbers.

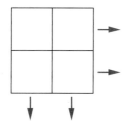

MS. GOENS: Well boys and girls, let's create a window together in class. But I have one rule about putting tiles in these squares. You can put up to seven tiles in these squares. That means you can put seven or less, but you can't go over seven. Okay? Does anyone have a number of tiles that we can put in the first square right here on the top?

The students offer numbers to place inside the four cells of the window. As the children suggest values, Ms. Goens places the corresponding number of tiles in each cell. The following window shows the result.

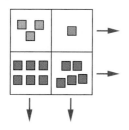

MS. GOENS: What do I do now?

STUDENT: You write in the numbers where the arrows are.

MS. GOENS: And how do I get this number here? [*Points to the top arrow.*]

STUDENT: With the tiles, you don't have to count them if you know the numbers. You can just put the numbers there, the first number up there and which—that first number up there would be four.

Students continue to offer row and column totals resulting in the complete window shown below.

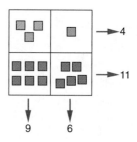

MS. GOENS: Do you think you could create a window at your desk? When you are done with creating your window, I have this recording sheet for you... I want you to write all the different solutions you can come up with if you took all the tiles away and try to get these [*total*] numbers with different tiles.

The teacher removes all the tiles from the window displayed in the front of the class, leaving only the row and column totals. She asks the students to work in pairs to come up with other numbers that will make the puzzle true.

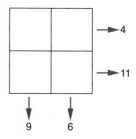

The teacher notes that this is a good lesson for the students because they can work at either the concrete or symbolic levels of understanding—with tiles or with symbols, whichever makes them most comfortable. In order for students to complete the window, given both the column and row totals, they must consider the relationship between addition and subtraction.

As partners work on their own number windows, the teacher spends time with individual students and talks with them about their thinking and problem-solving strategies. The teacher reflects upon her practices and indicates that her own mathematics skills are growing as she listens to the children.

◀ Introduction

The Snapshot of a Lesson incorporates several essential components of a well-planned classroom activity involving computation. First and foremost, it actively involves students in a problem situation

that promotes reasoning and discussion. The problem is accessible to various levels of students. Those who need to count to find sums can use the blocks to find answers. Those who already are working on solidifying their knowledge of basic facts can work at a more abstract level. Note that the window puzzle requires students to think about connections between addition and subtraction because the starting point is the row and column sums, so both operations are required to figure out what numbers could go in the cells. The problem is open-ended because multiple solutions are possible when row and column sums are the starting point.

These components are important in elementary school mathematics lessons, particularly as children develop understanding of the relevance and meaning of computational ideas. An understanding of addition, subtraction, multiplication, and division—and knowledge of the basic number facts for each of these operations—provides a foundation for all later work with computation. To be effective in this later work, children must develop broad concepts for these operations. This development is more likely to happen if each operation is presented through multiple representations using various physical models. Such experiences help children recognize that an operation can be used in several different types of situations. Children also must understand the properties that apply to each operation and the relationships between operations.

Learning the basic number facts is one of the first steps children take as they refine their ideas about each operation. By using these facts, plus an understanding of place value and mathematical properties, a child can perform any addition, subtraction, multiplication, or division with whole numbers. Both understanding the operations and having immediate recall of basic facts are needed for doing pencil-and-paper computations proficiently with all sorts of numbers (whole numbers, fractions, decimals, and percents). But operation sense and basic fact knowledge are just as essential when a calculator is readily available because it is important to monitor the reasonableness of answers obtained by pushing buttons. Operation sense and basic facts also form the building blocks for estimating answers or doing exact computations mentally in many everyday situations where it would be inefficient to use either paper and pencil or a calculator. So, no matter what type of computation a child is doing—paper-and-pencil, calculator, mental exact, or mental estimation—both operation sense and quick recall of the basic number facts are essential.

Figure 9-1 lists the expectations related to operation meanings (for whole numbers) and basic facts that are identified in the Number and Operations Standard from *Principles and Standards for School Mathematics* (NCTM, 2000). We focus on these expectations throughout this chapter. (The other expectations from the Number and Operations Standard are dealt with in Chapters 7, 8, 10, 11, 12, and 13.)

FOCUS QUESTIONS

1. What prerequisites are important prior to engaging students in formal work on the four basic operations?

2. What general sequence of activities helps children develop meaning for the operations?

3. What three distinct types of situations lead to subtraction? What four types of structures lead to multiplication?

4. How should thinking strategies for the basic facts be taught?

5. Describe the key thinking strategies for learning basic facts for addition, for subtraction, for multiplication, and for division.

Math Links 9.1

*T*he full-text version of NCTM's *Principles and Standards for School Mathematics* (PSSM) is available to non-NCTM-members for a 90-day free trial. Visit www.nctm.org to sign up. An all-grades overview of the Number and Operations Standard is provided in PSSM Chapter 3, but you can also click on Pre-K–2, 3–5, or 6–8 for more detailed information by grade level. Access electronic interactive examples tied to the *Standards* (no membership required) by going to http://standards.nctm.org/document/eexamples/index.htm or linking from this book's Web site.

Math Links 9.2

A variety of Web resources for basic facts may be found at NCTM's Illuminations Web site under the Number and Operation Standard. They may be accessed from http://illuminations.nctm.org/swr/index.asp or from this book's Web site. Triangle Flashcards and Multiplication: An Adventure in Number Sense are particularly recommended.

www.wiley.com/college/reys

Helping Children Develop Number Sense and Computational Fluency

Ultimately, the instructional goal is that children not only know how to add, subtract, multiply, and divide, but, more important, know *when* to apply each operation in a problem-solving situation. Children also should be able to recall the basic facts quickly when needed.

Instructional programs from prekindergarten through grade 12 should enable all students to:	Pre-K–2 Expectations All students should:	Grades 3–5 Expectations All students should:
• Understand meanings of operations and how they relate to one another	• Understand various meanings of addition and subtraction of whole numbers and the relationship between the two operations • Understand the effects of adding and subtracting whole numbers • Understand situations that entail multiplication and division, such as equal groupings of objects and sharing equally	• Understand various meanings of multiplication and division • Understand the effects of multiplying and dividing whole numbers • Identify and use relationships between operations, such as division as the inverse of multiplication, to solve problems • Understand and use properties of operations, such as the distributivity of multiplication over division • Describe classes of numbers according to characteristics such as the nature of their factors
• Compute fluently and make reasonable estimates	• Develop and use strategies for whole-number computations, with a focus on addition and subtraction • Develop fluency and basic number combinations for addition and subtraction • Use a variety of methods and tools to compute, including objectives, mental computation, estimation, paper and pencil, and calculators	• Develop fluency with basic number combinations for multiplication and division and use these combinations to mentally compute related problems, such as 30×50 • Develop fluency in adding, subtracting, multiplying, and dividing whole numbers • Develop and use strategies to estimate the results of dividing whole numbers

FIGURE 9-1   Number and Operation Standard with expectations for children in grades prekindergarten–2 and 3–5.

How can teachers help children attain these skills and understandings? Begin by finding out what each child knows. Then capitalize on their knowledge while continuing to build on the number concepts they have already constructed (Kouba and Franklin, 1993). Most children entering school are ready in some ways and not ready in others for formal work on the operations. Four prerequisites for such work seem particularly important: (1) facility with counting, (2) experience with a variety of concrete situations, (3) familiarity with many problem-solving contexts, and (4) experience using language to communicate mathematical ideas.

Facility with Counting

Children use counting to solve problems involving addition, subtraction, multiplication, and division long before they come to school, as research has indicated (Baroody and Standifer, 1993). Any problem with whole numbers can be solved by counting, provided there is sufficient time. Because it is not always efficient to solve problems by counting, children need to be able to use other procedures to cope with more difficult computations. Figure 9-2 illustrates this idea by comparing the counting method with multiplication, which is more efficient.

How many bottles?

We can count —
1, 2, 3, 4, 5, 6

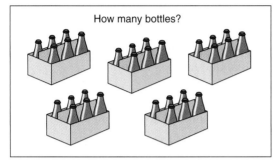

How many bottles?

We could count, but it's more efficient to use a
combination of counting (6 bottles in a carton,
5 cartons) and multiplication — 5 × 6 = 30.

FIGURE 9-2   An example showing the efficiency of
using operations.

Counting nevertheless remains an integral aspect of children's beginning work with the operations. They need to know how to count forward, backward, and how to skip count by twos, threes, and other groups (see Chapter 7). They need to count as they compare and analyze sets and arrays. But they need more than counting to become proficient in computing.

Math Links 9.3

*Y*ou can use electronic manipulatives, such as Number Line Arithmetic and Rectangle Multiplication, to help students visualize their basic facts. Visit http://nlvm.usu.edu/en/nav/vlibrary.html (or link from this book's Web site), then select Number and Operations and scroll through to find these and other useful manipulatives.

www.wiley.com/college/reys

Experience with a Variety of Concrete Situations

Children need to have many experiences in problem situations and in working with physical objects to develop understanding about mathematical operations. Understanding improves if they can relate mathematical facts and symbols to an experience they can visualize. Manipulative materials serve as a referent for later work with the operations, as well as for constructing the basic facts. Materials also provide a link to connect each operation to real-world problem-solving situations. Whenever a child wants to be sure that an answer is correct, materials can be used for confirmation.

Familiarity with Many Problem Contexts

Problem situations are used in mathematics instruction for developing conceptual understanding, teaching higher-level thinking and problem-solving skills, and applying a variety of mathematical ideas. Research indicates the benefits of beginning with problem situations (Fuson, 2003). Word problems require reading, comprehension, representation, and calculation. Children generally have little difficulty with single-step word problems but have more difficulty with multistep, complex problems.

As with other mathematical content, a variety of problem contexts or situations should be used to familiarize students with the four basic operations, continuing all along the way until computational mastery is achieved. Children need to think of mathematics as problem solving—as a means by which they can resolve problems through applying what they know, constructing possible routes to reach solutions, and then verifying that the solutions make sense. Students must realize that mathematics is a tool that has real-life applications. Most children already know that computation is used in everyday life. Mathematics lessons need to be connected to those experiences, but students also need to realize that $6 \times 8 = \square$ or $9 + 2 = \square$ also may be problems—ones that they can solve. They need to have the attitude, "If I don't know an answer, I can work it out."

Experience in Talking and Writing about Mathematical Ideas

Children need to talk and write about mathematics; putting experiences into words helps with making meaning. Both manipulative materials and problems can be vehicles for communicating about mathematics. All early phases of instruction on the operations and basic facts should reflect the important role that language plays in their acquisition. The *Principles and Standards for School Mathematics* (NCTM, 2000) discusses the roles of language in great depth in presenting the recommendations on communication, and thus provides a valuable source of additional information.

The move to symbols is often made too quickly and the use of materials dropped too soon. Instead, the use of materials should precede and then parallel the use of symbols. Early on, children should be manipulating materials as they record symbols. As illustrated in the lesson snapshot that opened this chapter, when children talk and write about what is happening in a given situation, they are helped to see the relationship of the ideas and symbols to their manipulation of materials and of the problem setting.

The oral and written language that children learn as they communicate about what they are doing with materials helps them understand how symbolism is related to mathematical operations. By modeling, talking, and writing, the referent for each symbol is strengthened. Children should begin their work with operations after talking among themselves and with their teacher about a variety of experiences. They need to be encouraged to continue talking about the mathematical ideas they meet as they work with the operations. As soon as feasible, they need to put their ideas on paper—at first by drawings alone; but as soon as they are able to write, children should also be encouraged to write number sentences and narrative explanations of their thinking.

Developing Meanings for the Operations

Children encounter the four basic operations in natural ways when they work with many diverse problem situations. By representing these problem situations (e.g., acting them out, using physical models, or drawing pictures), they develop meanings for addition, subtraction, multiplication, and division. Mastery of basic facts and later computational work with multidigit examples must be based on a clear understanding of the operations.

Thus both computational proficiency and understanding of operations are desired outcomes of mathematics instruction. The following general sequence of activities is appropriate for helping children develop meaning for the four basic operations:

1. Concrete—modeling with materials: Use a variety of verbal problem settings and manipulative materials to act out and model the operation.

2. Semiconcrete—representing with pictures: Provide representations of objects in pictures, diagrams, and drawings to move a step away from the concrete toward symbolic representation.

3. Abstract—representing with symbols: Use symbols (especially numeric expressions and number sentences) to illustrate the operation.

In this way, children move through experiences from the concrete to the semiconcrete to the abstract, linking each to the others.

The four operations are clearly different, but there are important relationships among them that children will come to understand through modeling, pictorial, and symbolic experiences:

- Addition and subtraction are inverse operations; that is, one undoes the other:
$$5 + 8 = 13 \rightarrow 13 - 5 = 8$$

- Multiplication and division are inverse operations:
$$4 \times 6 = 24 \rightarrow 24 \div 4 = 6$$

- Multiplication can be viewed as repeated addition:
$$4 \times 6 \rightarrow 6 + 6 + 6 + 6$$

- Division can be viewed as repeated subtraction:
$$24 \div 4 \rightarrow 24 - 6 - 6 - 6 - 6$$

These relationships can be developed through careful instruction with a variety of different experiences.

Addition and Subtraction

Figure 9-3 illustrates a variety of models (including counters, linking cubes, balance scale, and number line) that can be used to represent addition. Each model depicts the idea that addition means "finding how many in all." The models for addition can also be used for subtraction. Each model can be applied in the three different situations that lead to subtraction.

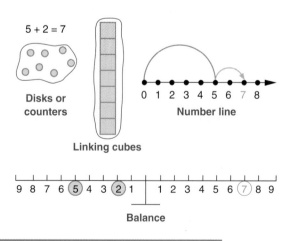

FIGURE 9-3 Some models for addition.

Separation Problems   *Separation,* or take away, involves having one quantity, removing a specified quantity from it, and noting what is left. Research indicates that this subtraction situation is the easiest for children to learn; however, persistent use of the words *take away* results in many children assuming that this is the *only* subtraction situation and leads to misunderstanding of the other two situations. This is why it is important to read a subtraction sentence such as $8 - 3 = 5$ as "8 minus 3 equals 5" rather than "8 take away 3 equals 5." Take away is just one of the three types of subtraction situations.

Peggy had 7 balloons. She gave 4 to other children. How many did she have left?

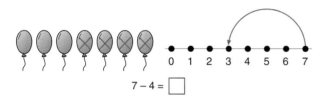

$$7 - 4 = \square$$

Comparison Problems   *Comparison,* or finding the difference, involves having two quantities, matching them one to one, and noting the quantity that is the difference between them. Problems of this type can also be solved by subtraction, even though nothing is being taken away.

Peggy had 7 balloons. Richard had 4 balloons. How many more balloons did Peggy have than Richard?

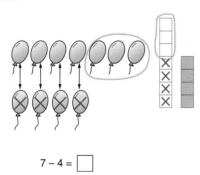

$$7 - 4 = \square$$

Part-Whole Problems   The final type of subtraction situation is known as *part-whole.* In this type of problem, a set of objects can logically be separated into two parts. You know how many are in the entire set and you know how many are in one of the parts. You need to find out how many must be in the remaining part. Nothing is being added or taken away—you simply have a static situation involving parts and a whole.

Peggy had 7 balloons. Four of them were red and the rest were blue. How many were blue?

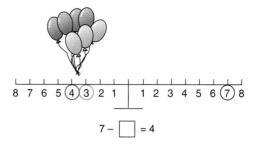

$$7 - \square = 4$$

It is useful to help students recognize that many subtraction problems can also be thought of as "missing-addend" problems because the strategy "think addition" can be used to find the answer. For example, in the preceding problem, you could ask yourself: 4 plus what equals 7?

The importance of providing many varied experiences in which children use physical objects to model or act out examples of each operation cannot be overemphasized. The Snapshot of a Lesson at the beginning of this chapter provided one such experience. It illustrates a task that involves children in thinking about putting two piles of counters together as a lead-in to addition and subtraction. Some children might focus on the concrete, by actually placing chips in the window panes and counting. Other children might be just as comfortable drawing pictures or writing numerals as they work on the puzzle. All students are working toward the goal of being able to relate number sentences (such as $6 + 5 = 11$) with a row or column in the window pane. For students in the earliest stages of understanding, the situation need not be represented by written or spoken symbols. Moving tiles, counting, and thinking about additive and subtractive relationships are the important initial components of the activity. The teacher introduces symbols as a complement to the physical manipulation of objects. Symbols provide a way of recording what's happening with the materials. As work with numbers and operations progresses, the amount of symbolization that the teacher encourages and expects will increase.

Multiplication and Division

The same sequence of experiences used for developing understanding of addition and subtraction—moving from concrete, to pictorial, to symbolic—should also be followed for multiplication and division. However, one important way that multiplication and division problems differ from addition and subtraction problems is that the numbers in the problems represent different sorts of things. For example, consider a problem such as "Andrew has two boxes of trading cards. Each box holds 24 cards. How many cards does he have altogether?" This problem may be written $2 \times 24 = 48$, where the *first factor* (2) tells us how many groups or sets of equal size (here, how many boxes) are being considered, while the *second factor* (24) tells us the size of each set (here, how many cards per set). The third number (48), known as the *product*, indicates the total of all the parts (here, the total number of cards). The old saying "you can't add apples and oranges" points out that in addition and subtraction problems, a common label must be attached to *all* the numbers involved. Apples and oranges can be added only if we relabel all the numbers in the problem with a common label such as "fruit." By contrast, in the trading card problem, the labels for the numbers are all different: in this problem we had boxes (2), cards per box (24), and cards (48).

Math Links 9.4

*I*f you would like to see a variety of lesson plans that provide hand-on experiences and meaningful contexts for developing addition and subtraction concepts, visit NCTM's Illuminations Web site at http://illuminations.nctm.org/ (or link from this book's Web site), then click on Lessons. Do It with Dominoes and Links Away are particularly recommended.

www.wiley.com/college/reys

Figure 9-4 illustrates some of the most commonly used models for illustrating multiplication situations: sets of objects, arrays, and the number line. Research indicates that children do best when they can use various representations for multiplication and division situations and can explain the relationships among those representations (Kouba and Franklin, 1995).

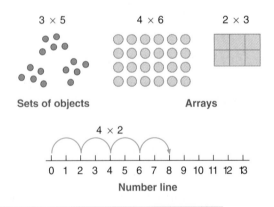

FIGURE 9-4 Commonly used models for multiplication.

Researchers have identified four distinct sorts of multiplicative structures: equal groups, multiplicative comparisons, combinations, and areas/arrays (Greer, 1992). Problems involving the first two of these structures are most common in elementary school, although students should eventually become familiar with all four. The four multiplicative structures are described here to help you, as the teacher, understand and recognize their variety. You are not expected to teach these labels to children, but you should try to ensure that they encounter a broad range of problem situations involving multiplication and division.

Equal-Groups Problems   Equal-groups problems involve the most common type of multiplicative structure, where you are dealing with a certain number of groups, all the same size. When both the number and size of the groups are known (but the total is unknown), the problem can be solved by multiplication. The problem given earlier, about Andrew's trading card collection, is an example of an equal-groups problem. When the total in an equal-groups problem is known, but either the number of groups or the size of the group is unknown, the problem can be solved by division. Two distinct types of division situations can arise, depending on which part is unknown. These two types of division situations are known as measurement and partition division (described later).

Comparison Problems   Comparison problems involve another common multiplicative structure. With comparison problems for subtraction, there were two different sets that needed to be matched one-to-one to decide how much larger one was than the other. In similar fashion, comparision problems with multiplicative structures involve two different sets, but the relationship is not one-to-one. Rather, in multiplicative comparision situations, one set involves multiple copies of the other. An example of a multiplicative comparison situation might be: "Hilary spent $35 on Christmas gifts for her family. Geoff spent 3 times as much. How much did Geoff spend?" In this case, Hilary's expenditures are being compared with Geoff's, and the problem is solved by multiplication. The question does not involve "How much more?" (as it would if the problem involved additive/subtractive comparision). Instead, the structure of the problem involves "How many times as much?" If the problem is changed slightly to include information about how much Geoff spent but to make either Hilary's expenditures unknown or the comparison multiplier unknown, then the problem could be solved by division. Examples of these problem structures are: (a) Hilary spent a certain amount on Christmas gifts for her family, and Geoff spent 3 times as much. If Geoff spent $105, how much did Hilary spend? (b) Hilary spent $35 on Christmas gifts for her family and Geoff spent $105. How many times as much money as Hilary spent did Geoff spend?

Combinations Problems   *Combinations problems* involve still another sort of multiplicative structure. Here the two factors represent the sizes of two different sets and the product indicates how many different pairs of things can be formed, with one member of each pair taken from each of the two sets. For example, consider the number of different sundaes possible with four different ice cream flavors and two toppings, if each sundae can have exactly one ice cream flavor and one topping:

| | **Ice cream flavors** | | | |
	Vanila	Cherry	Mint	Chocolate
Pineapple				
Toppings				
Butterscotch				

Other examples of combination problems are the number of choices for outfits if you have 5 T-shirts and 4 shorts, or the number of different sandwiches possible with 3 choices of meat, 2 choices of cheese, and 2 kinds of bread.

Area and Array Problems   Finally, *area and array problems* also are typical examples of multiplicative structure. The area of any rectangle (in square units) can be found either by covering the rectangle with unit squares and counting them all individually or by multiplying the width of the rectangle (number of rows of unit squares) by the length (number of unit squares in each row). Similarly, in a rectangular array—an arrangement of discrete, countable objects (such as chairs in an auditorium)—the total number of objects can be found by multiplying the number of rows by the number of objects in each row. The array model for multiplication can be especially effective in helping children visualize multiplication. It may serve as a natural extension of children's prior work in making and naming rectangles using tiles, geoboards, or graph paper.

These illustrations show a 2-by-3 or 3-by-2 rectangle.

Tiles   Geoboard   Graph paper

Thus, each rectangle contains six small squares. Asking children to build and name numerous rectangles with various dimensions is a good readiness experience for the concept of multiplication. In the Classroom 9-1 illustrates several experiences designed for this purpose.

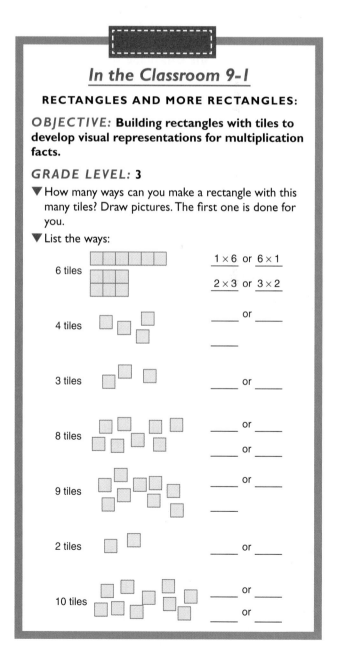

In the Classroom 9-1

RECTANGLES AND MORE RECTANGLES:

OBJECTIVE: **Building rectangles with tiles to develop visual representations for multiplication facts.**

GRADE LEVEL: **3**

▼ How many ways can you make a rectangle with this many tiles? Draw pictures. The first one is done for you.

▼ List the ways:

6 tiles 1×6 or 6×1
            2×3 or 3×2

4 tiles   ____ or ____
            ____

3 tiles   ____ or ____

8 tiles   ____ or ____
            ____

9 tiles   ____ or ____
            ____

2 tiles   ____ or ____

10 tiles   ____ or ____
            ____

Just as sets of objects, the number line, and arrays are useful in presenting multiplication, they can also be useful in presenting division, with the relationship to repeated subtraction frequently shown. For division, however, two different types of situations must be considered: *measurement* and *partition*.

Measurement (repeated subtraction) Problems   In *measurement* (or repeated subtraction) situations, you know how many objects are in each group and you must determine the number of groups.

> Jenny had 12 candies. She gave 3 to each person. How many people got candies?

Here, you can imagine Jenny beginning with 12 candies and making piles of 3 repeatedly until all the candies are gone. She is measuring how many groups of 3 she can make from the original pile of 12.

Person 1   Person 2   Person 3   Person 4

Another measurement subtraction example is measuring how many 2-foot hair ribbons can be made from a 10-foot roll of ribbon. Imagine repeatedly stretching out 2 feet and cutting it off, thus measuring how many hair ribbons you can make.

Partition (sharing) Problems   In *partition* (or sharing) situations, a collection of objects is separated into a given number of equivalent groups and you seek the number in each group. By contrast with measurement situations, here you already know how many groups you want to make, but you don't know how many objects must be put in each group.

> Gil had 15 shells. If he wanted to share them equally among 5 friends, how many should he give to each?

Here imagine Gil passing out the shells to his five friends (one for you, one for you, one for you, etc., and then a second shell to each person, and so on) until they are all distributed, and then checking to see how many each person got.

Friend 1   Friend 2   Friend 3   Friend 4   Friend 5

Partitioning (or sharing) is difficult to show in a diagram, but it is relatively easy for children to act out. Dealing cards for a game is another instance of a partition situation.

It is certainly not necessary for children to learn these terms or to name problems as measurement or partition situations. But it is important for you as a teacher to know about the two types of division situations so you can ensure that your students have opportunities to work with examples of each. It is vital that students be able to identify when a problem situation requires division, and that means being able to recognize both types of situations as involving division.

Mathematical Properties

An understanding of the mathematical properties that pertain to each operation (Table 9-1) is vital to children's understanding of the operation and how to use it. This understanding is not a prerequisite to work with operations, but it must be developed as part of understanding operations.

In elementary school, children are usually not expected to state these properties precisely or identify them by name. Rather, the instructional goal is to help children understand the commutative, associative, distributive, and identity properties and to use them when it is efficient. Table 9-1 gives the meaning of each property, states what children should understand, and provides examples to illustrate how the property can make learning and using the basic facts easier.

Understanding these properties implies knowing when they apply. For example, both addition and multiplication are commutative, but neither subtraction nor division is

$$7 - 3 \text{ is } not \text{ equal to } 3 - 7$$

$$28 \div 7 \text{ is } not \text{ equal to } 7 \div 28$$

Many children have difficulty with the idea of commutativity. They tend to "subtract the

Table 9-1 • Mathematical Properties for Elementary-School Children

Property	Mathematical Language	Child's Language	How It Helps
Commutative	For all numbers a and b: $a + b = b + a$ and $a \times b = b \times a$	If $4 + 7 = 11$, then $7 + 4$ must equal 11, too. If I know 4×7, I also know 7×4.	The number of addition or multiplication facts to be memorized is reduced from 100 to 55
Associative	For all numbers a, b, and c: $(a + b) + c = a + (b + c)$ and $(ab)c = a(bc)$	When I'm adding (or multiplying) three or more numbers, it doesn't matter where I start.	When more than two numbers are being added (or multiplied), combinations that make the task easier can be chosen; for example, $37 \times 5 \times 2$ can be done as $37 \times (5 \times 2)$ or 37×10 rather than $(37 \times 5) \times 2$
Distributive	For all numbers a, b, and c: $a(b + c) = ab + ac$	8×12 is the same as $8 \times 10 + 8 \times 2$. You can split numbers apart to multiply easy pieces, then add $8 \times (10 + 2) = 8 \times 10 + 8 \times 2$	Some of the more difficult basic facts can be split into smaller, easier-to-remember parts; for example, 8×7 is the same as $(8 \times 5) + (8 \times 2)$ or $40 + 16$
Identity	For any whole number a: $a + 0 = a$ and $a \times 1 = a$	0 added to any number is easy; it's just that number. 1 times any number is just that number.	The 19 addition facts involving 0 and the 19 multiplication facts involving 1 can be easily remembered once this property is understood and established

smaller number from the larger" or to "divide the larger number by the smaller" regardless of their order. Care needs to be taken to ensure that they understand why order is important in subtraction (and division).

Overview of Basic Fact Instruction

As children develop concepts of meanings of operations, instruction begins to focus on certain number combinations. These are generally referred to as the *basic facts*:

- *Basic addition facts* each involve two one-digit addends and their sum. There are 100 basic addition facts (from $0 + 0$ up to $9 + 9$; see Figure 9-5). To read off a fact (say, $4 + 9 = 13$), find the first addend (4) along the left side and the second addend (9) along the top. By reading horizontally across the 4-row from the left and vertically down the 9-column from the top, you find the sum (13).

+	0	1	2	3	4	5	6	7	8	9
0	0	1	2	3	4	5	6	7	8	9
1	1	2	3	4	5	6	7	8	9	10
2	2	3	4	5	6	7	8	9	10	11
3	3	4	5	6	7	8	9	10	11	12
4	4	5	6	7	8	9	10	11	12	13
5	5	6	7	8	9	10	11	12	13	14
6	6	7	8	9	10	11	12	13	14	15
7	7	8	9	10	11	12	13	14	15	16
8	8	9	10	11	12	13	14	15	16	17
9	9	10	11	12	13	14	15	16	17	18

FIGURE 9-5   The 100 basic facts for addition.

- *Basic subtraction facts* rely on the inverse relationship of addition and subtraction for their definition. The 100 basic subtraction facts result from the difference between one addend and the sum for all one-digit addends. Thus the 100 subtraction facts are also pictured in Figure 9-5, the same table that pictures the 100 basic addition facts. You read off a basic subtraction fact (say, $13 - 4 = 9$) by finding the box in the 4-row that contains the sum 13, then reading up that column to find the difference (9) at the top of the table. Note that a sentence such as $13 - 2 = 11$ is neither represented in Figure 9-5 nor considered a basic subtraction fact because $2 + 11 = 13$ is not a basic addition fact (since 11 is not a one-digit addend).

- *Basic multiplication facts* each involve two one-digit factors and their product. There are 100 basic multiplication facts (from 0×0 up to 9×9).
- *Basic division facts* rely on the inverse relationship of multiplication and division, but there are only 90 basic division facts. Because division by zero is not possible, there are no facts with zero as the divisor.

Development and mastery of the addition and subtraction facts begins in kindergarten or first grade and continues as multiplication and division facts are developed and practiced in third and fourth grades. Some children, however, have not mastered the facts several years later. Sometimes the problem may be a learning disability that makes it impossible for a child to memorize the facts. Use of a calculator may allow such a child to proceed with learning mathematics. Or, as research by Clark and Kamii (1996) indicates for multiplication, a child may have trouble with multiplication facts because he or she has not developed the ability to think multiplicatively.

More commonly, children's difficulties in mastering basic facts may stem from one (or both) of the following two causes, and in these cases teachers can definitely provide help. First, the underlying numerical understandings may not have been developed. Thus the process of remembering the facts quickly and accurately becomes no more than rote memorization or meaningless manipulation of symbols. As a result, the child has trouble remembering the facts. Second, the skill of fact retrieval itself may not be taught by teachers or understood by children, resulting in inefficient strategies. Teachers can do something about both of these problems by using a three-phase process for helping children learn basic facts:

1. Start where the children are.
2. Build understanding of the basic facts.
3. Focus on how to remember facts.

Start Where the Children Are

Many children come to school knowing some basic facts. For instance, the chances are great that they can say "one and one are two," "two and two are four," and maybe even "five and five are ten." They may know that 2 and 1 more is 3, and that 6 and "nothing more" is still 6. But they probably don't know that $6 + 7 = 13$, nor do they have a clear concept of the meanings of symbols such as + and =.

Similarly, they may know that if you have 3 and take away 2, you have only 1 left. But they might not know the meaning of the symbolism $3 - 2 = 1$ or of the sentence "three minus two equals one." They may be able to figure out that buying three pieces of gum at 5¢ each will cost 15¢, but not know that $3 \times 5 = 15$. They may be able to figure out that eight cookies shared fairly among four children means that each child gets two cookies, but they might not know that $8 \div 4 = 2$.

In other words, young children probably can solve many simple problems involving facts, but they are not likely to be able to either recognize or write the facts. Nor do many children understand that a number sentence such as $4 + 2 = \square$ asks the same question as:

$$\begin{array}{r} 4 \\ +2 \\ \hline \end{array}$$

It is the teacher's task to help children organize what they know, construct more learning to fill in the gaps, and, in the process, develop meaning for basic facts and for the symbolism we can use to represent them.

You need to begin by determining what each child knows, using responses from group discussions, observations of how each child works with materials and with paper-and-pencil activities, and individual interviews. Many teachers use an inventory at the beginning of the year, administered individually to younger children and in a questionnaire format in later grades. The purpose of such an inventory is to discover:

- Whether the children have the concept of an operation (given a story problem involving simple addition, subtraction, multiplication, or division, can they model the situation? solve the problem? explain why their solution makes sense? write a corresponding number sentence? identify the operation they used?)
- What basic facts they understand (given a number fact, can they draw a picture to illustrate it? Or given a picture, can they identify a related number fact?)
- What strategies they use to find the solution to combinations (can they answer the question "How did you know $7 + 9 = 16$?" beyond just saying "I know it"?)
- What basic facts they know fluently (can they answer within about 3 seconds, without stopping to figure them out?)

Teachers use such information to plan instruction. Do some children need more work with manipulative materials to understand what multiplication means? Do some children need help in seeing the relationship of $17 - 8$ and $8 + 9$? Do the children recognize that counting on from a number is quicker than counting all? Which children need practice in order to move beyond counting to mastering the basic facts? You can group children to meet individual needs (as suggested in Chapter 3) and provide activities and direct instruction to fill in the missing links and strengthen understanding and competency.

Build Understanding of the Basic Facts

The emphasis in helping children learn the basic facts should be on aiding them in organizing their thinking and seeing relationships among the facts. Children should develop strategies for remembering the facts before they engage in drill to develop fluency.

Generally, the facts with both addends or both factors greater than 5 are more difficult for most children, but what is difficult for an individual child is really the important point. Although many textbooks, workbooks, and computer programs emphasize practice on the generally difficult facts, many also encourage the child to keep a record of those facts that are difficult for him or her and suggest extra practice on those. The teacher should suggest or reinforce this idea.

How can the basic facts for an operation be organized meaningfully? Many textbooks present facts in small groups (e.g., facts with sums to 6: $0 + 6 = 6$, $1 + 5 = 6$, $2 + 4 = 6$, and so forth). Other textbooks organize the facts in "families" (e.g., facts in the "2-3-5 family" are $3 + 2 = 5$, $2 + 3 = 5$, $5 - 3 = 2$, and $5 - 2 = 3$). Still other textbooks organize the facts by "thinking strategies" (e.g., all facts where 1 is added, or facts involving "doubles" such as $7 + 7$). No particular order for teaching the basic facts has been shown to be superior to any other order. Thus the teacher can use professional judgment about what each group of children needs and can choose whether to use or modify the sequence given in the textbook.

A variety of thinking strategies can be used to recall the answer to any given fact. Thinking strategies are efficient methods for determining answers on the basic facts. The more efficient the strategy, the more quickly the student will be able to construct the correct answer for the sum, difference, product, or quotient of two numbers and, eventually, to develop fluency with the facts so he or she can quickly recall them.

Research has shown that certain thinking strategies help children learn the basic facts (Fuson, 2003). Understanding of the facts develops in a series of stages characterized by the thinking children use. Some of these thinking strategies involve using concrete materials or counting. Others are more mature because a known fact is used to figure out an unknown fact. Teachers want to help children develop these mature, efficient strategies to help them recall facts. The next section on thinking strategies for basic facts provides more detail on how these skills can be developed.

Many children rely heavily on counting—in particular, finger counting—and fail to develop more efficient ways of recalling basic facts. For example, a child might count 4 fingers and then 5 more to solve $4 + 5$. This strategy is perfectly acceptable at first; however, this counting process should not have to be repeated every time $4 + 5$ is encountered. Teachers want the child to move beyond counting on from 4 (which is relatively slow and inefficient), to thinking "$4 + 4 = 8$, so $4 + 5$ is 9" or using some other more efficient strategy. Eventually, the child must be able to recall "$4 + 5 = 9$" quickly and effortlessly. Some children discover efficient fact strategies on their own, but many need explicit instruction. When the teacher is satisfied that the children are familiar with a particular strategy (able to model it with materials and beginning to use it mentally), it is time to practice the strategy.

Math Links 9.5

A variety of drill activities may be found on the Internet at http://www.funbrain.com/kidscenter.html (or link from this book's Web site). For example, you can try games such as Mathcar Racing, Soccer Shootout, Tic Tac Toe Squares, Line Jumper, and Power Football. A variety of operations and levels of difficulty may be selected.

www.wiley.com/college/reys

Focus on How to Remember Facts

Consider this scene: Pairs of children are keying numbers on a calculator and passing it back and forth. Other pairs are seated at a table, some playing a card game and others playing board games. Several are busily typing numbers on computer keyboards. Still others are working individually with flashcards or number triangles. What are they all doing? They could be practicing basic facts.

If children are to become skillful with the algorithms for addition, subtraction, multiplication, and division and proficient at estimation and mental computation, they must know the basic facts with immediate, automatic, recall. The goal is computational fluency and efficiency in problem solving. When should this mastery level be attempted? As soon as children have a good understanding of the meanings of operations and symbols, the process of developing fluency with basic facts can begin. That is, before students start practicing fact retrieval, they should be able to:

- State or write related facts, given one basic fact.
- Explain how they got an answer, or prove that it is correct.
- Solve a fact in two or more ways.

Here are some key principles for basic fact drill:

- Children should attempt to memorize facts only after understanding is attained.
- Children should participate in drill with the intent to develop fluency. Remembering should be emphasized. This is not the time for explanations.
- Drill lessons should be short (5 to 10 minutes) and should be given almost every day. Children should work on only a few facts in a given lesson and should constantly review previously learned facts.
- Children should develop confidence in their ability to remember facts fluently and should be praised for good efforts. Records of their progress should be kept.
- Drill activities should be varied, interesting, challenging, and presented with enthusiasm.

Computer software provides a natural complement to more traditional materials and activities, such as flashcards, games, and audiotaped practice, for establishing the quick recall of basic facts. For example, children may try games found in the Math Links boxes. Most software for fact practice keeps track of the number of exercises attempted and the number answered correctly. Some programs display the time taken to give correct answers, thus encouraging students to compete against their own records for speed as well as mastery. Requiring short response time (within 3 or 4 seconds) is important because it promotes efficient strategies and encourages children to develop fluent recall. Many children enjoy computer software that displays a cumulative record of their individual progress. This feature allows children to diagnose for themselves the basic facts they know and don't know. It also provides a source of motivation

because each student can compete against himself or herself, with the goal of complete mastery always in mind.

When using flashcards for practice, the child should start by going through the entire set and separating the cards into a pack of those known and a pack of those unknown. The known pack should be set aside, so that time can be used efficiently to focus repeatedly on the facts in the unknown pack. The next time the child works with the cards, he or she should again review the cards from both packs, moving any newly learned facts to the known pack and moving any facts that have been forgotten to the unknown pack. Then practice begins again, with the unknown pack. This approach makes progress evident and focuses attention on the facts that really need to be practiced.

Teachers need to take note of whether certain basic addition and multiplication facts occur more (or less) frequently in their elementary school textbook than others. If more difficult facts, or facts involving larger numbers occur less frequently, then students are likely to get less practice with them, even though they might actually need more practice. In some textbooks, facts involving numbers larger than 5 may occur less frequently than facts involving numbers from 2 to 5; and problems involving 0 and 1 may be quite rare. If this is the case, it's important to ensure that more practice is provided with the facts that are not as commonly encountered in the textbook, especially the more difficult facts involving 6 through 9.

Several types of drill-and-practice procedures in the form of games are noted in In the Classroom 9-2. Children of all age groups find such games an enjoyable way to practice what they know. These activities supplement the many other drill-and-practice procedures that you will find in textbooks, journals, computer software, and other sources.

Math Links 9.6

Some basic fact games and puzzles also involve problem solving or require students to use critical thinking to develop a winning strategy. For example, visit http://nlvm.usu.edu/en/nav/vlibrary.html (or link from this book's Web site), then select Number and Operations, and scroll through to find Number Line Bounce, Number Puzzles, and other challenges. Or go to http://illuminations.nctm.org (or link from this book's Web site), then select tools, and scroll through to examine the Product Game and other interesting activities.

www.wiley.com/college/reys

In the Classroom 9-2

GAMES FOR PRACTICING BASIC FACTS

ADDITION BINGO:

OBJECTIVE: Using a bingo game to practice basic addition facts.

GRADE LEVEL: 1–2

▼ Each player needs a different Bingo card and some buttons or macaroni for markers.

9	6	17	11	5
5	8	10	3	7
15	11	Free	13	14
7	9	2	1	12
2	13	11	18	17

The leader needs a pack of cards like these with all possible combinations (basic facts).

▼ It's easy to play:

• The leader draws a card and reads the addends on it.

• Each player covers the sum on his or her Bingo card.

Not all sums are given on each card.

Some sums are given more than once on a Bingo card, but a player may cover only one answer for each pair of addends.

The winner is the first person with 5 markers in a row!

MULTIG

OBJECTIVE: **Using a game to practice basic multiplication facts.**

GRADE LEVEL: 3–4

▼ Use the playing board here or make a larger one on heavy construction paper. Each player needs some buttons, macaroni, or chips for markers.

• Take turns. Spin twice. Multiply the 2 numbers. Find the answer on the board. Put a marker on it.

Don't forget the spinner. You can't play this game without it.

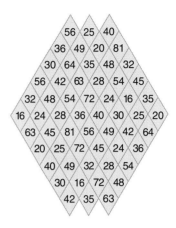

• Score 1 point for each covered ◆ that touches a side or corner of the ◆ you cover.

• If you can't find an uncovered ◆ to cover, you lose your turn.

• Opponents may challenge any time before the next player spins.

• The winner is the player with the most points at the end of 10 rounds.

ZERO WINS:

OBJECTIVE: Using a game to develop number sense and practice addition and subtraction facts.

GRADE LEVEL: 2–3

▼ Make two identical sets of 19 cards with a number from 0 to 18 on each.

▼ Follow these rules:

• After shuffling, the leader deals 4 cards to each player and puts the remaining cards face down in the center of the table.

(continued on next page)

• Players must add or subtract the numbers on their 4 cards so they equal 0. For example, suppose you had these cards:

• With these cards you could write

10 − 6 + 2 − 6 = 0

or

6 + 6 − 10 − 2 = 0

or various other number sentences.

• On each round of play, the players may exchange one card if they wish, and each player takes a turn being first to exchange a card on a round. To make an exchange, the first player draws a card and discards a card, face up. Other players can draw from either the face-down pile or the face-up discard pile.

The first player to get 0 on a round wins the round!

TEST YOUR FACTS:

OBJECTIVE: **Using a variety of activities and puzzles to practice multiplication and division facts.**

GRADE LEVEL: **3–4**

▼ Fill in the empty box:

▼ Complete these five-facts and match them with the clock minutes.

$7 \times 5 = 35$

$2 \times 5 = $ __

$6 \times 5 = $ __

$4 \times 5 = $ __

$5 \times 5 = $ __

▼ Fill in each empty box to make the next number correct:

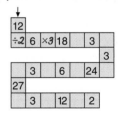

▼ Multiply each number in the middle ring by the number in the center:

Thinking Strategies for Basic Facts

In the following four sections, we discuss thinking strategies for basic facts for addition, subtraction, multiplication, and division and illustrate ways to teach them.

Thinking Strategies for Addition Facts

The 100 basic facts for addition were shown previously in Figure 9-5. These facts should not simply be presented to children to memorize from this completed table; rather, the children should gradually and systematically learn the facts and may fill in or check them off on the table. However, having children examine a completed addition table to look for patterns can be a challenging and educational activity (and can help them learn how to read the table too). For example, you might ask the children questions such as the following:

- What patterns do you see in the table? (They will probably notice that each row or column shows numbers counting up by ones, but they start at different starting points.)
- What is the largest sum? What are its addends? Can you write the addition sentence for this sum?
- Circle all the sums of 5. Why does 5 appear more than once in the table as a sum? Can you write all the addition sentences for this sum?
- What sum appears most often in the table? Can you write all the addition sentences for this sum?

Asking questions like this can help children recognize the orderliness of the basic addition facts. This overview can also help children see their goal as they begin to work on fluency with facts.

Thinking strategies for teaching basic addition facts include commutativity; adding 1, 0, doubles, and near doubles; counting on; combinations to 10; and adding to 10 and beyond. For many facts, more than one strategy is appropriate.

Commutativity   The task of learning the basic addition facts is simplified because of the commutative property. Changing the order of the addends does not affect the sum. Children encounter this idea when they note that putting 2 blue objects and 3 yellow objects together gives the same quantity as putting 3 blue objects and 2 yellow objects together:

In work with the basic addition facts, children will see or write, for example:

$$
\begin{array}{c}
2 \\
+5 \\
\hline
\end{array}
\quad \text{and} \quad
\begin{array}{c}
5 \\
+2 \\
\hline
\end{array}
$$

or

$$2 + 5 = \square \quad \text{and} \quad 5 + 2 = \square$$

Students must realize that the same two numbers have the same sum, no matter which comes first. They need to be able to put this idea into their own words; they do not need to know the term *commutative property*. They need to use the idea as they work with basic facts, not merely parrot a term. A calculator can also help children verify that the order of the addends is irrelevant. Have them key into their calculators combinations such as "5 + 8 =" and "8 + 5 = ." Use a variety of

+	0	1	2	3	4	5	6	7	8	9
0	0	1	2	3	4	5	6	7	8	9
1	1	2	3	4	5	6	7	8	9	10
2	2	3	4	5	6	7	8	9	10	11
3	3	4	5	6	7	8	9	10	11	12
4	4	5	6	7	8	9	10	11	12	13
5	5	6	7	8	9	10	11	12	13	14
6	6	7	8	9	10	11	12	13	14	15
7	7	8	9	10	11	12	13	14	15	16
8	8	9	10	11	12	13	14	15	16	17
9	9	10	11	12	13	14	15	16	17	18

FIGURE 9-6   Addition facts derived by the commutative thinking strategy.

combinations, so the idea that the order does not affect the outcome becomes evident.

Note that Figure 9-6 has exactly the same 45 numbers above and to the right of the diagonal as below and to the left. This mirror image helps you see that the commutative property reduces the number of facts to be learned by 45. Each box below the diagonal can be matched with a box above the diagonal with the same addends and sum. (If there are 100 facts altogether, why are there 55 distinct facts to learn, rather than just 50?)

Adding One and Zero   *Adding one* to a number is easy for most children. In fact, most children learn this idea before they come to school, and they only have to practice the recognition and writing of it rather than develop initial understanding. To reinforce their initial concept, experiences with objects come first, followed by such paper-and-pencil activities as these:

$$5 + 1 = \square$$

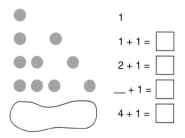

Recognition of the pattern is then encouraged:

The strategy for *adding zero* applies to facts that have zero as one addend. These facts should be learned, through experience, as a generalization: *Zero added to any number does not change the number.* This idea follows from many concrete examples in which children see that any time they add "no more" (zero) they have the same amount. Activities then focus on this pattern:

○	1 + 0 = ☐	0 + 1 = ☐
○○	2 + 0 = ☐	0 + 2 = ☐
○○○	3 + 0 = ☐	0 + 3 = ☐
○○○○	4 + 0 = ☐	0 + 4 = ☐

Although adding zero may seem easy to adults, this is actually one of the hardest strategies for children to learn. Concrete modeling of the situation is tricky because it is difficult to picture adding nothing. Therefore, explicit work on facts involving zero should be postponed until children have mastered some of the other fact strategies.

Adding Doubles and Near Doubles   Doubles are basic facts in which both addends are the same number, such as 4 + 4 or 9 + 9. Most children learn these facts quickly, often parroting them before they come to school. Connecting doubles facts to familiar situations often helps students remember them (e.g., two hands shows 5 + 5 = 10, an egg carton shows 6 + 6 = 12, 2 weeks on a calendar shows 7 + 7 = 14). Students can profit from work with objects followed by drawings:

4 + 4 = ☐   8 + 8 = ☐

Another strategy, *near doubles*, can be used for the facts that are one more or one less than the doubles:

	Think
7 + 8 = ☐	7 + 7 = 14
	So 7 + 8 is one more
	7 + 8 = 15
	Think
7 + 6 = ☐	7 + 7 = 14
	So 7 + 6 is one less
	7 + 6 = 13

The four thinking strategies in the preceding two sections can be used with the addition facts shown in Figure 9-7.

(a) Addition facts derived by the adding one and adding zero strategies

+	0	1	2	3	4	5	6	7	8	9
0	0	1	2	3	4	5	6	7	8	9
1	1	2	3	4	5	6	7	8	9	10
2	2	3								
3	3	4								
4	4	5								
5	5	6								
6	6	7								
7	7	8								
8	8	9								
9	9	10								

(b) Addition facts derived by the adding doubles and near-doubles strategies

+	0	1	2	3	4	5	6	7	8	9
0	0	1								
1	1	2	3							
2		3	4	5						
3			5	6	7					
4				7	8	9				
5					9	10	11			
6						11	12	13		
7							13	14	15	
8								15	16	17
9									17	18

FIGURE 9-7   Addition facts derived by four strategies.

Counting on   The strategy of *counting on* can be used for any addition facts but is most easily used when one of the addends is 1 or 2. To be efficient, it is important to count on from the larger addend. For example,

	Think
2 + 6 = ☐	6 . . . 7 . . . 8
	2 + 6 = 8

Initially, children will probably count all objects in a group, as noted in Chapter 7.

1   2   3   4   5   6 . . .   7   8

They need to learn to start from the larger addend, 6, and count on, 7, 8. (Notice that understanding of the commutative property is assumed.) Often young children will count on but not necessarily from the larger addend. Thus the strategy must be taught to many children using activities such as this one:

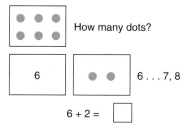

The counting-on strategy can be rather efficiently used with the addition facts noted in Figure 9-8 (where at least one addend is 1 or 2); however, it is *not* efficient to use counting on when both addends are larger than 2 (e.g., for 6 + 8 = 14 or 5 + 8 = 13 or 9 + 8 = 17). Counting on for facts such as these is both slow and prone to error. Unfortunately, some children develop the habit of using counting on all the time and thereby fail to develop more efficient strategies, sometimes still relying on counting on even after they have graduated to middle school or high school. It is important to help students move beyond counting on because fluency (efficiency and accuracy) is extremely important for work with basic facts. When students are slowed down by inefficient strategies for basic fact retrieval, they are often hampered in doing more advanced work in mathematics.

Combinations to 10 The combinations-to-10 facts are those nine pairs of numbers that together make 10: 1 + 9, 2 + 8, 3 + 7, 4 + 6, 5 + 5, 6 + 4, 7 + 3, 8 + 2, and 9 + 1. Note that recognition of the commutative property can reduce this list to just 5 facts (since each of the 9 facts except 5 + 5 has a commutative partner-pair—for example, 8 + 2 and 2 + 8 are pairs, etc.). Of the 9 combinations to 10, 5 have already been mentioned in previous fact strategies (either *counting on* or *doubles*). The "new" facts here are 3 + 7 (with 7 + 3) and 4 + 6 (with 6 + 4). As you will read in Cultural Connections at the end of this chapter, American students have traditionally been less likely than children in certain other countries to really use the combinations-to-10 strategy effectively. This is likely due, in part, to the structure of the English language, though it probably also is a reflection of how little American textbooks have emphasized these facts.

Adding to 10 and Beyond With the strategy of *adding to 10 and beyond*, one addend is broken apart so that one part of it can be used with the other addend to make 10. Then the remaining part of the first addend is added to the 10 to go beyond to the final teen sum. This strategy is used most easily when one of the addends is 8 or 9. However, if children are fluent with combinations to 10, then *adding to 10 and beyond* can be useful in many other situations too. Here is an example:

> Think
>
> 8 + 5 = □   8 + 2 = 10 so I will use 2 from the 5
>
> I'll think of 5 as 2 + 3
>
> 8 + 5 = (8 + 2) + 3 = 10 + 3 = 13

Recognizing that 8 + 2 = 10, the child mentally breaks 5 apart into 2 + 3 (to obtain the desired 2). The 2 is used with the 8 to "add to 10," and the 3 is used to go "beyond." A ten-frame can be helpful in teaching this strategy because it provides a visual image of adding to 10 and going beyond:

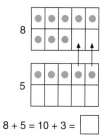

8 + 5 = 10 + 3 = □

The research of Funkhouser (1995) indicates that working with five-frames as a base and then moving to ten-frames may be particularly helpful for children with learning disabilities.

Children must know the combinations to 10 well in order to use the adding-to-10-and-beyond strategy efficiently. They also need to realize how easy it is to add any single digit to 10 to get a number in the teens, without having to count on. They

+	0	1	2	3	4	5	6	7	8	9
0										
1		2	3	4	5	6	7	8	9	10
2		3	4	5	6	7	8	9	10	11
3		4	5							
4		5	6							
5		6	7							
6		7	8							
7		8	9							
8		9	10							
9		10	11							

FIGURE 9-8 Addition facts derived by the counting-on strategy.

+	0	1	2	3	4	5	6	7	8	9
0										
1										10
2									10	11
3								10	11	12
4							10		12	13
5						10			13	14
6					10				14	15
7				10					15	16
8			10	11	12	13	14	15	16	17
9		10	11	12	13	14	15	16	17	18

FIGURE 9-9   Addition facts derived by the combinations-to-10 and adding-to-10 strategy.

+	0	1	2	3	4	5	6	7	8	9
0	0	1	2	3	4	5	6	7	8	9
1	1	2	3	4	5	6	7	8	9	10
2	2	3	4	5	6	7	8	9	10	11
3	3	4	5	6	7	8	9	10	11	12
4	4	5	6	7	8	9	10	11	12	13
5	5	6	7	8	9	10	11	12	13	14
6	6	7	8	9	10	11	12	13	14	15
7	7	8	9	10	11	12	13	14	15	16
8	8	9	10	11	12	13	14	15	16	17
9	9	10	11	12	13	14	15	16	17	18

FIGURE 9-10   Addition facts derived by all thinking strategies for addition.

should be able to respond immediately to questions such as $3 + 10 = ?$, $10 + 7 = ?$, and $9 + 10 = ?$.

The *combinations-to-10* and the *adding-to-10-and-beyond* strategies can be used with the addition facts shown in Figure 9-9.

In many cases, more than one strategy can be used to aid in recalling a fact. This point should be made with children. It encourages them to try different ways of recalling a fact, and it may strengthen their understanding of the relationships involved. Notice from Figure 9-10 that all 100 of the basic facts have been covered (with one or more strategies), once the strategies for adding one, adding zero, adding doubles and near doubles, counting on, combinations to 10, and adding to 10 and beyond have been learned. Children should be encouraged to look for patterns and relationships because almost all of the 100 basic addition facts can be developed from a variety of relationships with other facts.

It also should be noted that children might invent additional strategies of their own, such as the following:

> Think
$6 + 7 = \square$ I know $5 + 5 = 10$
> 6 is $5 + 1$
> 7 is $5 + 2$
> So $10 + 3$
> 13

> Think
$6 + 8 = \square$ I know my doubles!
> Move 1 from the 8 to the 6 to make the problem $7 + 7$
> 14

Encourage students' original ideas!

Thinking Strategies for Subtraction Facts

For each basic addition fact, there is a related subtraction fact. In some mathematics programs, the two operations are taught simultaneously. The relationship between them is then readily emphasized, and learning the basic facts for both operations proceeds as if they were in the same family. Even when they are not taught simultaneously, however, the idea of a fact family is frequently used. Figure 9-11 shows several versions of materials for practicing facts via fact families. Students can practice with fact triangles by covering the number in one corner with their thumb and figuring it out by viewing the other two numbers. In a similar way, they practice with folding fact-family cards by folding one door shut to conceal one number, and figuring it out by viewing the other two numbers. The lesson snapshot at the opening of this chapter provides a clear example of a problem situation in which children work simultaneously on related addition and subtraction facts.

"Think addition" is the major thinking strategy for learning and recalling the subtraction facts. Encourage children to recognize, think about, and use the relationships between addition and subtraction facts. They can find the answers to subtraction facts by thinking about missing addends. For example,

> Think
$15 - 7 = \square$ $7 + \square = 15$
> $7 + 8 = 15$
> So $15 - 7 = 8$

Other strategies for finding subtraction facts also can be taught: subtracting one and zero, doubles, counting back, and counting on.

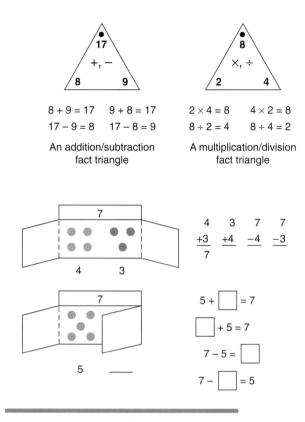

FIGURE 9-11 Examples of fact families.

Subtracting One and Zero Once they have learned strategies for adding 1 and adding 0, most children find it rather easy to learn the related subtraction facts involving 0 and 1. They can profit from work with materials and from observing patterns similar to those used for addition facts.

Doubles The strategy for doubles may need to be taught more explicitly for subtraction facts than for addition facts. It rests on the assumption that children know the doubles for addition. Here is an example:

$$16 - 8 = \square$$

> <u>Think</u>
> $8 + \square = 16$
> $8 + 8 = 16$
> So $16 - 8 = 8$

Counting Back The strategy of counting back is related to counting on in addition. It is most efficient when the number to be subtracted is 1 or 2:

$$9 - 2 = \square$$

> <u>Think</u>
> $9 \ldots 8, 7$
> $9 - 2 = 7$

As for other strategies, use problems and a variety of manipulative materials to help children gain facility in counting back from given numbers.

Counting on The strategy of counting on is used most easily and efficiently when the difference is 1 or 2 (i.e., when it is easy to see that the two numbers involved in the subtraction are quite close together). "Think addition" by counting on:

$$8 - 6 = \square$$

> <u>Think</u>
> $6 \ldots 7, 8$ (that's two numbers that I counted on)
> So $8 - 6 = 2$

Thinking about the counting-on strategy can also be related to thinking about adding on: "How much more would I need?" Children should be encouraged to use known addition facts to reach a solution to the subtraction problem. This is particularly valuable with missing-addend situations, such as $6 + \square = 8$. Research has shown that counting on is a very powerful subtraction strategy for many students (Fuson, 2003).

Thinking Strategies for Multiplication Facts

Multiplication is frequently viewed as a special case of addition in which all the addends are of equal size. The solution to multiplication problems can be attained by adding or counting, but multiplication is used because it is so much quicker.

Instruction on multiplication ideas begins in kindergarten as children develop ideas about groups, numbers, and addition. In grades 1 and 2, children count by twos, fives, tens, and later by other numbers such as threes and fours. These experiences provide a basis for understanding the patterns that occur with the basic multiplication facts. Use of the calculator as described in Chapter 7 can aid teachers in developing ideas about these patterns of multiplication. Using the constant function on calculators, children realize that two sixes equal 12, three sixes equal 18, and so on.

The basic multiplication facts pair two one-digit factors with a product, as shown in Figure 9-12. The basic multiplication facts should not be given to children in the form of a table or chart of facts until they have been meaningfully introduced. Rather, the facts should be developed through problem situations, experiences with manipulative and other materials, and various thinking strategies. The table becomes the end result of this process of developing understanding of operations and facts.

The thinking strategies for multiplication facts provide an efficient way for a child to attain each fact. These strategies include commutativity, skip counting, repeated addition, splitting the product into known parts, multiplying by one and zero, and patterns.

×	0	1	2	3	4	5	6	7	8	9
0	0	0	0	0	0	0	0	0	0	0
1	0	1	2	3	4	5	6	7	8	9
2	0	2	4	6	8	10	12	14	16	18
3	0	3	6	9	12	15	18	21	24	27
4	0	4	8	12	16	20	24	28	32	36
5	0	5	10	15	20	25	30	35	40	45
6	0	6	12	18	24	30	36	42	48	54
7	0	7	14	21	28	35	42	49	56	63
8	0	8	16	24	32	40	48	56	64	72
9	0	9	18	27	36	45	54	63	72	81

FIGURE 9-12   The 100 basic facts for multiplication.

×	0	1	2	3	4	5	6	7	8	9
0										
1										
2			4	6	8	10	12	14	16	18
3			6			15				
4			8			20				
5			10	15	20	25	30	35	40	45
6			12			30				
7			14			35				
8			16			40				
9			18			45				

FIGURE 9-14   Multiplication facts derived by the skip-counting strategy.

Commutativity   Commutativity applies to multiplication just as it does to addition. It is, therefore, a primary strategy for helping students learn the multiplication facts. In the Classroom 9-1 (presented earlier) emphasizes this property. The calculator is also useful in reinforcing the idea. Children can multiply 4 × 6, then 6 × 4, for example, and note that the answer to both is 24. After they have tried many combinations, students should be able to verbalize that the order of the factors is irrelevant. Figure 9-13 (where each box in the upper right can be matched with a corresponding box in the lower left) shows that, as for addition, there really are only 55 multiplication facts to be learned if you recognize the power of commutativity.

Skip Counting   The strategy of skip counting works best for the multiples children know best, twos and fives, but it also may be applied to threes and fours (or other numbers) if children have learned to skip count by them.

Here is an example for 5:

Think

4 × 5 = □   5, 10, 15, 20

4 × 5 = 20

Skip counting around the clock face (as you do when counting minutes after the hour) is a good way to reinforce multiples of 5 by skip counting. The facts that can be established with the skip-counting strategy for twos and fives are noted in Figure 9-14.

Repeated Addition   The strategy of repeated addition can be used most efficiently when one of the factors is less than 5. The child changes the multiplication example to an addition example:

Think

3 × 6 = □   6 + 6 + 6 = 18

3 × 6 = 18

Because this strategy is based on one interpretation of multiplication, children should have had many experiences with objects and materials. Drawings and explorations with a calculator can be used to provide additional experiences to help develop this strategy, as well as the concept for the operation. Figure 9-15 illustrates these ideas. In Figure 9-16, note the facts that can be learned with this strategy.

×	0	1	2	3	4	5	6	7	8	9
0	0	0	0	0	0	0	0	0	0	0
1	0	1	2	3	4	5	6	7	8	9
2	0	2	4	6	8	10	12	14	16	18
3	0	3	6	9	12	15	18	21	24	27
4	0	4	8	12	16	20	24	28	32	36
5	0	5	10	15	20	25	30	35	40	45
6	0	6	12	18	24	30	36	42	48	54
7	0	7	14	21	28	35	42	49	56	63
8	0	8	16	24	32	40	48	56	64	72
9	0	9	18	27	36	45	54	63	72	81

FIGURE 9-13   Multiplication facts derived by the commutative thinking strategy.

Splitting the Product into Known Parts   As children gain assurance with some basic facts, they can use their known facts to derive others. The strategy known as *splitting the product* is based on the distributive property of multiplication. It can be approached in terms of "one more set," "twice as much as a known fact," or "known facts of 5."

Look at these dots:

• Ring sets of 7. How many sets of 7?
• How many dots in all?
    Count them: _7_, ___, ___, ___
    Add them: 7 + 7 + 7 + 7 = □
    Multiply them: 4 × 7 = □
Do these using a calculator:
    3 + 3 + 3 + 3 + 3 =
    5 + 5 + 5 + 5 + 5 =
• Do you know a simpler way? Show it here:

    _____

    _____

FIGURE 9-15   Visualizing multiplication.

• The idea of *one more set* can be used for almost all multiplication facts. If a certain multiple of a number, *N*, is known, the next multiple can be determined by adding the single-digit number, *N*. For example, to find 3 × 5 if doubles are already known, you can think of 2 × 5 (10) and add one more 5 (to get 15). The computation is slightly more difficult if the addition requires renaming (e.g., below, where 8 × 7 is found by adding one more set of 7 to the known fact 7 × 7 = 49):

                    Think
    8 × 7 = □   7 × 7 = 49
                    8 × 7 = 49 + 7 = 56

×	0	1	2	3	4	5	6	7	8	9
0										
1										
2			4	6	8	10	12	14	16	18
3			6	9	12	15	18	21	24	27
4			8	12	16	20	24	28	32	36
5			10	15	20					
6			12	18	24					
7			14	21	28					
8			16	24	32					
9			18	27	36					

FIGURE 9-16   Multiplication facts derived by the repeated addition strategy.

Each fact can be used to help learn the next multiple of either factor. Illustrating this strategy using an array model can be helpful:

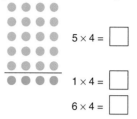

Ask children to name each part of the array and write the multiplication fact for the whole array.

• *Twice as much as a known fact* is a variation of the foregoing strategy. It can be applied to multiples of 4, 6, and 8 because an array with one of these numbers can be split in half. The product is twice as much as each half:

                    Think
    6 × 8 = □   3 × 8 = 24
                    6 × 8 is twice as much, or 24 + 24
                    So, 6 × 8 = 48

Note that some children may have trouble doing the computation mentally when renaming is required to do the doubling by addition. Again, using models helps provide a visual image of this strategy. In this case, children work with already divided arrays.

As they progress, children can divide an array, such as the following; write about each part; and write the multiplication fact for the whole array.

Some options for the array above (6 × 8) might be
    (5 × 8) = 40 and 1 × 8 = 8, so
    6 × 8 = 40 + 8 = 48
or 6 × 4 = 24 and 6 × 8 is twice as much,
    so 6 × 8 = 24 + 24 = 48.

• *Working from known facts of 5* also will aid children. It can be helpful for any problem with large factors but is most useful for multiples of 6 and 8 because both 5 sixes and 5 eights are multiples of 10, so it is rather easy to add on the remaining part without renaming.

×	0	1	2	3	4	5	6	7	8	9
0										
1										
2										
3										
4						24	28	32	36	
5						30	35	40	45	
6					24	30	36	42	48	54
7					28	35	42	49	56	63
8					32	40	48	56	64	72
9					36	45	54	63	72	81

FIGURE 9-17 Multiplication facts derived by the strategy of splitting the product into known parts.

For example, here's how to figure 7×6, if you know $5 \times 6 = 30$.

Think

$7 \times 6 = \square$ $5 \times 6 = 30$

$2 \times 6 = 12$

So 7×6 is $30 + 12$, or 42

The facts that can be solved by splitting the product into known parts are shown in Figure 9-17.

Multiplying by One and Zero The facts with one and zero are generally learned from experience working with multiplication. Children need to be able to generalize that "multiplying by 1 does not change the other number" and that "multiplying by 0 results in a product of 0." Figure 9-18 indicates the facts that can be learned with these strategies.

The preceding strategies account for all the multiplication facts. However, one more strategy can provide help with some difficult facts.

×	0	1	2	3	4	5	6	7	8	9
0	0	0	0	0	0	0	0	0	0	0
1	0	1	2	3	4	5	6	7	8	9
2	0	2								
3	0	3								
4	0	4								
5	0	5								
6	0	6								
7	0	7								
8	0	8								
9	0	9								

FIGURE 9-18 Multiplication facts derived by the strategies for 0 and 1.

Patterns Finding patterns is helpful with several multiplication facts. One of the most useful and interesting patterns concerns nines. Look at the products of the facts involving 9. The digits of the products always sum to 9. Furthermore, the tens digit of each product is always one less than whatever factor was being multiplied times 9. (Why? Think about this.)

$$1 \times 9 = 9 \qquad 0 + 9 = 9$$
$$2 \times 9 = 18 \qquad 1 + 8 = 9$$
$$3 \times 9 = 27 \qquad 2 + 7 = 9$$
$$4 \times 9 = 36 \qquad 3 + 6 = 9$$

The tens digit is 1 less than 4.

The *sum* of the digits of 36 is 9.

So for 5×9,

Think

The tens digit is one less than $5 \rightarrow 4$

The sum of the digits is 9, so $4 + \square = 9 \rightarrow 5$

So, $5 \times 9 = 45$

Now try $7 \times 9 = \square$.

Challenge children to find this and other interesting patterns in a table or chart such as the one in Figure 9-12. They might note, for instance, that the columns (and rows) for 2, 4, 6, and 8 contain all even numbers, although the columns for 1, 3, 5, 7, and 9 alternate even and odd numbers. Why?

You will probably find that children also enjoy various forms of "finger multiplication" (see Figure 9-19), seemingly magical tricks for using finger manipulations to determine basic facts. Actually, though, finger multiplication works because of the patterns that are inherent in the basic fact table.

Thinking Strategies for Division Facts

Teaching division has traditionally taken a large portion of time in elementary school. Now, with the increased use of calculators, many educators advocate reducing the attention accorded to it. Nevertheless, children still need an understanding of the division process and division facts. The facts help them to respond quickly to simple division situations and to understand better the nature of division and its relationship to multiplication.

Just as "think addition" is an important strategy for subtraction, "think multiplication" is the primary thinking strategy to aid children in understanding and recalling the division facts. Division is the inverse of multiplication; that is, in a division problem you are seeking an unknown factor when the product and some other factor are known. The multiplication table (Figure 9-12) illustrates all the division facts; you simply read it

Finger Multiplication for 9-Times Facts Only

1. Hold both hands in front of you with palms facing away.

2. To do 3×9, bend down the third finger from the left.

3. The fingers to the left of the bent finger represent tens. The fingers to the right of the bent finger represent ones. Read off the answer: 2 tens and 7 ones, or 27.

4. To do 5×9, bend down the fifth finger from the left, etc. Try this method for any 9-facts: 1×9 through 10×9.

$$3 \times 9 = 20 + 7 = 27$$

Finger Multiplication for Facts with Factors 6–10 Only

1. Hold both hands in front of you with palms facing you.

2. Think of a multiplication in which both factors are 6 or more (up to 10). For example, you can do anything from 6×6 up to 10×10.

3. For each factor, find the difference from 10.
   - Let's try the example 8×9.
   - For the factor 8, think $10 - 8 = 2$, and bend down 2 fingers on the left hand.
   - For the factor 9, think $10 - 9 = 1$, and bend down 1 finger on the right hand.

4. Look at all fingers that are still up, and count by ten (10, 20, 30, 40, 50, 60, 70).

5. Look at the fingers that are bent down. Multiply the number of fingers bent down on the left hand by the number bent down on the right hand ($2 \times 1 = 2$).

6. So $8 \times 9 = 70 + 2$ or 72.

7. Try this method for any multiplication facts from 6×6 up through 10×10.

$$5 \times 9 = 40 + 5 = 45$$

Multiply 8×9 — Difference between 8 and 10 is 2 (fold down 2 fingers) — Difference between 9 and 10 is 1 (fold down 1 finger)

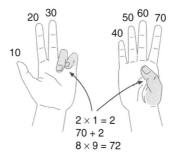

$2 \times 1 = 2$
$70 + 2$
$8 \times 9 = 72$

FIGURE 9-19   Two forms of finger multiplication.

differently. For the division fact $54 \div 9 = \square$, look in the 9-row of the multiplication table for the number 54, then read up that column to find the other factor, 6. Students generally do not learn division facts separately from multiplication facts. Instead, they learn division facts such as $48 \div 6 = 8$ by remembering (and connecting with) multiplication facts such as $6 \times 8 = 48$.

It is important to realize that most division problems, in computations and in real-world prob-

lem situations, do not directly involve a multiplication fact that you have learned. For example, consider the computation $49 \div 6$. There is no basic fact involving 49 and 6. So, what do you do? In this situation most people quickly and automatically mentally review the 6-facts that they know, looking for the facts that come closest to 49 ($6 \times 7 = 42$—too small, $6 \times 8 = 48$—just a little too small, $6 \times 9 = 54$—too big). From this mental review, you can conclude that $49 \div 6 = 8$, with 1 left over. Children need practice in thinking this way (mentally finding the answers to problems involving one-digit divisors and one-digit answers plus remainders).

Just as fact families can be developed for addition and subtraction, they can also be useful for multiplication and division:

$8 \times 4 = 32$

$4 \times 8 = 32$

$32 \div 8 = 4$

$32 \div 4 = 8$

Because of its relationship to multiplication, division can be stated in terms of multiplication:

$$42 \div 6 = \square \qquad \rightarrow \qquad 6 \times \square = 42$$

Thus children must search for the missing factor in the multiplication problem. Because multiplication facts are usually encountered and learned first, children can use what they know to learn the more difficult division facts. Moreover, division is related to subtraction, and division problems can be solved by repeated subtraction (seeing how many times you must subtract to get down to zero):

What's $12 \div 3$?

Since $12 - 3 - 3 - 3 - 3 = 0$ (subtracting 4 3s), then $12 \div 3 = 4$

0 1 2 3 4 5 6 7 8 9 10 11 12

Four threes

It is important for children to recognize that division can be thought of as repeated subtraction, just as multiplication can be thought of as repeated addition. Indeed, when children later encounter division involving multidigit numbers, they will need to understand division as equivalent to repeated subtraction, in order to appreciate why the division algorithm involves repeatedly subtracting.

However, as was mentioned earlier, counting backward is difficult for many children. Skip counting backward (to figure out a division problem mentally) is even more difficult than counting backward by one (to figure out a subtraction problem mentally). Here are two examples of skip counting backward:

Think

$15 \div 3 = \square$ 15 . . . 12, 9, 6, 3, 0

I subtracted 3 five times.

So $15 \div 3 = 5$

Think

$28 \div 7 = \square$ $28 - 7$

$21 - 7$

$14 - 7$ }   4 subtractions

$7 - 7$

0

$28 \div 7 = 4$

A more productive approach is to "think multiplication" (just as it was productive to "think addition" in order to perform subtractions). If you know your multiplication facts, then $35 \div 7 = \square$ is easily figured by thinking "what times 7 is 35?" For facts that are not immediately recognized, splitting the product into known parts is helpful. Obviously, this strategy relies heavily on knowledge of multiplication facts as well as on the ability to keep in mind the component parts.

Think

$35 \div 7 = \square$ I know $2 \times 7 = 14$

I know $3 \times 7 = 21$

$14 + 21 = 35$

$2 + 3 = 5$

So $35 \div 7 = 5$

As with multiplication, work with arrays helps children relate the symbols to the action.

In general, children have little difficulty in dividing by one. But we all need to exercise caution when zero is involved, in division. Dividing zero by some number and dividing some number by zero are very different situations. If you divide 0 by 6 $(0 \div 6)$; the result is 0. Check this by multiplying your answer (6) by your divisor (0): $6 \times 0 = 0$.

But *division by zero is impossible*. For example, to solve $6 \div 0 = \square$ would require a solution so that $6 = \square \times 0$. However, there is no value for $\square$ that would make this sentence true. Therefore, $6 \div 0$ has no solution. A similar difficulty arises if you try to divide zero by itself. That's why *division by zero is undefined* in mathematics. Just as you may have difficulty remembering which is possible, dividing zero by a number or dividing a number by zero, it is likely that children may find this difficult. They will need numerous experiences before they master the idea.

Thinking strategies for division are more difficult for children to learn than are the strategies for the other operations. There is more to remember and regrouping is often necessary. When using skip counting as a division strategy, for instance, the child needs to keep track of the number of times a number is named even as he or she simultaneously struggles to count backward. However, "think multiplication" is an extremely efficient strategy for division, which avoids the difficulties that other division strategies involve. It turns out that being able to recall multiplcation facts quickly and accurately is an essential prerequisite to being able to divide efficiently.

Cultural Connections

Researchers studying how people naturally learn basic addition facts in countries all around the world have noted some fascinating worldwide commonalities, as well as some significant differences. It appears there is a natural learning progression—across all cultures—for single-digit addition and subtraction. All learners very naturally build their later (more sophisticated) addition methods from their earlier methods "by chunking, recognizing and eliminating redundancies, using parts instead of entire methods, and using their knowledge of specific numbers" (Fuson, 2003, p. 73).

The first stages of this natural progression involve different forms of counting—which have already been discussed in Chapter 7. People initially add two piles of objects by counting each separately (1, 2, 3, and 1, 2, 3, 4), and then *counting all* (1, 2, 3, 4, 5, 6, 7). Later, they learn to *count on*—by simply stating the first addend (3), and counting up from there (4, 5, 6, 7). Soon, they learn to *count on* even without objects, keeping track of the numbers by using their fingers or auditory patterns.

In time, people begin to shortcut the counting process of addition by breaking up larger numbers into smaller, easy-to-remember number combinations. For example, they quite naturally begin to use doubles, sums involving one (learned by counting on), and other combinations of small numbers this way. For example, they think of $3 + 4$ as $3 + 3 + 1 = 6 + 1 = 7$.

In many parts of the world—especially Asian countries and some European countries—people progress next—often quite naturally—to the general "make a 10" thinking strategy. This strategy is supported by the languages spoken in many of these countries. As was noted in Cultural Connections in Chapter 7, many languages other than English have teen numbers that transparently contain 10 and some extras; their counting into the teens sounds like "nine, ten, ten-one, ten-two, ten-three" and so forth. By contrast, our two-digit counting prior to 13 (ten, eleven, twelve) reveals

absolutely no connection to ten! Two of the next three numbers (thirteen, fifteen) do suggest a connection to ten, but only if you recognize "teen" as meaning "ten" and if you also recognize the variants of the units words (thir/three, and fif/five). Even for fourteen, and numbers from sixteen up, the connection to ten is not immediately clear, since the word for ten (teen) comes after the word for the number of ones (fourteen, sixteen, seventeen, eighteen, nineteen).

The facts considered "basic" in some countries are not the same as those we call "basic facts" in the United States. For example, basic addition facts in Korea focus on combinations that total 10 or less. This is a reflection of their work with a ten frame and decomposing larger numbers into combinations of 10. Thus $7 + 8$ is not considered a basic fact in Korea, but children there decompose one of the addends to create a basic fact. So, to add 7 and 8, Korean children would think "$7 + 3$ is 10" or "$8 + 2$ is 10," and then—in both cases—they would think "5 more is 15." This approach may seem different to you, but the high levels of performance that Koren children demonstrate is testimony to its effectiveness. With help from textbooks that stress this natural make-a-10 approach, most children in Asian countries are fluent in adding two single-digit numbers by the end of first grade.

Since U.S. and Canadian children are not naturally prompted by the English language to move to the more efficient make-a-10 addition strategy, one might think that American textbooks would attempt to help them along. However, "compared with other countries, the United States has had a very delayed placement of topics in the elementary curriculum" (Fuson, 2003, p. 74). American children often spend almost all of first grade learning addition and subtraction facts with sums below 10. Even in second grade, textbooks often review these simple facts, and many children struggle with learning the facts that sum to numbers higher than 10. It is not at all unusual to find children still counting on in the upper elementary grades.

Interestingly, research conducted in urban and suburban American classrooms, in English and in Spanish, has shown that it is feasible to teach American first graders to think about basic addition facts in a conceptual way, so they can move beyond the limited approach of counting on. The studies showed that the entire range of basic facts were accessible to U.S. first graders, including those who were learning disabled and those with limited English proficiency (Fuson, 2003).

A Glance at Where We've Been

Problem-solving experiences help students develop meaningful skills in computation with whole numbers. In this chapter, we first considered how to help children develop and model meanings for the four basic operations (addition, subtraction, multiplication, and division). Experiences with counting, concrete situations, problem contexts, and talking and writing about mathematical ideas are important. These experiences should move from concrete modeling with materials, to semiconcrete representations with pictures, to abstract representations with symbols. Addition means finding out "how many in all?," but a variety of related situations lead to subtraction (separation, comparision, and part-whole). Multiplication situations include equal-groups, comparision, combinations, and areas/arrays. Measurement (repeated subtraction) and partition (sharing) situations lead to division. Children should learn about mathematical properties at the same time that they are developing their understanding of the basic operations.

In the next part of the chapter we focused on the basic facts for each operation. A variety of thinking strategies for the basic facts for each operation help children move from counting to more mature, efficient ways of developing the facts. Specific suggestions for providing practice and promoting mastery help children master the basic facts for quick recall.

Things to Do: From What You've Read

1. Consider the lesson that opens this chapter. What prerequisites must children have before engaging in this lesson? Why did some students use tiles and others use symbols? How could this lesson be extended to explore other mathematical concepts? Discuss some reasons for using puzzles in learning mathematics.

2. Discuss each of these statements:
   a. When you teach multiplication, you begin preparation for learning division.
   b. Children should not be allowed to count on their fingers when they start addition.
   c. With the wide use of calculators, there is little need for children to attain prompt recall of the basic facts.

3. What properties of addition and multiplication are especially helpful in teaching the basic facts?

4. Describe the thinking strategies a child might use with each of the following computations:

$$8 + 3 = \square \qquad 8 \times 5 = \square \qquad 7 + 8 = \square$$
$$18 \div 3 = \square \qquad 16 - 7 = \square$$

5. For each addition fact strategy (i.e., commutativity, adding one, adding zero, doubles, near doubles, counting on, combinations to 10, adding to 10 and beyond), list three different facts that could use that strategy and explain what a child would think when using that strategy.

6. When is counting back an effective strategy for subtraction? Give an example. Give an example of a fact where counting back is not such an effective strategy, and explain another strategy that would be better to use.

7. Explain why division by zero is considered "undefined" by mathematicians.

8. There are two types of division that arise in real-world problems: measurement (or repeated subtraction) division and fair sharing (or partitive) division.
   a. Write a partitive (or fair sharing) division word problem that would correspond to $24 \div 6$. Draw a picture to illustrate the solution to your problem and in simple language explain why your numerical answer makes sense.
   b. Write a measurement (or repeated subtraction) division word problem that would correspond to $24 \div 6$. Draw a picture to illustrate the solution to your problem and in simple language, explain why your numerical answer makes sense.

Things to Do: Going Beyond This Book

IN THE FIELD

1. Plan an interactive bulletin board to help children learn about one or more thinking strategies for subtraction.

2. Examine a recently published textbook for grades 2, 3, or 4. Analyze how basic facts for the four basic operations are presented in that text. How are the facts grouped? Are thinking strategies presented? If so, how do they compare with the strategies described in this chapter? How would you use this text in teaching basic facts? If you think you would probably want to

supplement the text, explain what sorts of supplementary materials and experiences you would use and why.

3. *Literature Context for Facts.* Find a popular trade book (perhaps from the Book Nook for Children) that would be useful as a motivator for a problem-based lesson revolving around one of the four basic operations (addition, subtraction, multiplication, or division). Identify the operation that the story evokes and write a problem that you might challenge students to work on after hearing the story. If possible, read the story to some children, have them try solving your problem, and analyze their written work for evidence of understanding of the basic operation the story involves.

4. *Timed tests.* Observe children as they take a timed test on basic facts. What behaviors and emotions can you document? How are the results of the test used by the teacher? Talk to at least five children or adults about their memories of timed tests on basic facts. What do they say about their experiences?

5. *Basic Fact Difficulty.* Talk to a fifth- or sixth-grade teacher about what he or she does with students who are not fluent in basic facts. Do they receive special instruction in fact strategies? Do they use calculators routinely for classwork and homework? How many in the class have problems with basic facts? Which facts cause the most difficulties?

6. Use the Basic Addition and Multiplication facts charts, found in Appendix B of your text or in *Teaching Elementary Mathematics: A Resource for Field Experiences,* to assess a child's fluency with the basic facts. Randomly say a fact for the child to answer orally. Use the chart to record his or her responses. You may want to develop some symbols to indicate correctness and quickness of response.

IN YOUR JOURNAL

7. Read the Number Standards for Grades pre-K–2 and 3–5 in the NCTM's *Principles and Standards for School Mathematics* (www.nctm.org). What recommendations are made concerning teaching basic facts? Write a position paper either agreeing with the NCTM's recommendations or taking an opposing position. Clearly explain and defend your position.

---

*Additional activities, suggestions, and questions are provided in *Teaching Elementary Mathematics: A Resource for Field Experiences* (Wiley, 2007).

WITH ADDITIONAL RESOURCES

8. See the activity described in "Problem Solving with Combinations" (English, 1992). How is it related to ideas presented in this chapter?

9. Read the brief research report on "The Empty Number Line in Dutch Second Grade" (Klein, Beishuizen, and Treffers, 2003). The article describes the use of a number line with no zero point shown, as a computational support for children doing multidigit addition and subtraction. What instructional and psychological reasons do the authors give for using the empty number line as a central model for addition and subtraction?

10. Pick a concept or skill from this chapter and compile a brief bibliography of recent articles with research or teaching ideas on the topic.

11. Find the Focus issue on The Magic of Number in the journal *Mathematics Teaching in Middle School.* Read one of the articles and give a written or oral report to your teaching peers.

WITH TECHNOLOGY

12. Find a calculator activity, software package, or game on the Web that focuses on basic facts. Share the ideas you find.

13. Find a computer program that claims to help children learn basic facts and try it out. There are many such programs on the market. Most focus on encouraging development of quick responses, but a few encourage use of thinking strategies. Write a half-page review of the computer program (similar to those published in teacher journals). In your review you should identify the name and publisher of the program, the cost, and the type of hardware required to run it. Explain how the program works. Include answers to the following questions:

- Does the program help children learn strategies for basic facts?
- Does the program keep track of student progress?
- Does the program modify the facts presented to the student according to which ones he or she has gotten right or wrong in the past?
- Do you think the program would be effective in promoting quick recall of facts? Why?
- Do you think children would enjoy using this program? Why?
- How would you use such a program if your classroom had only one or two computers?
- Would you recommend this program to other teachers? Why?

Note to Instructors: You can find additional resources, learning activities, and black-line masters in this text's accompanying Instructor's Manual, at www.wiley.com/college/reys.

Book Nook for Children

Hulme, J. N. *Counting by Kangaroos: A Multiplication Concept Book.* New York: Scientific American Books for Young Readers, 1995.

Multiplication is illustrated using animals from Australia. Groups of three squirrel gliders, four koalas, five bandicoots, . . ., ten wallabys all crowd a house.

Merriam, E. *12 Ways to Get to 11.* New York: Simon & Schuster, 1993.

The book shows how to get to 11 by using different combinations of numbers. Many different pictures are used to show the different combinations of the number 11.

Murphy, S. J. *Spunky Monkeys on Parade.* New York: Harper Collins, 1999.

At the Monkey Day Parade, the reader sees monkeys marching as majorettes, cyclists, tumblers, and band members. They create a spectacle as they move in twos, threes, and fours. This counting book will let the reader see many different ways of counting. There are activities and games for teachers and parents to use at the back of the book.

Sierra, J. *Counting Crocodiles.* Orlando, FL: Gulliver Books, Harcourt Brace, 1997.

A clever monkey, using her counting ability, outwits the hungry crocodiles that stand between her and a banana tree on another island on a sea.

Wakefield, A. *Those Calculating Crows!* New York: Simon & Schuster Books for Young Readers, 1996.

Using different plans to rid crows from invading his corn crop, Farmer Roy tries to scare off the crows. But the crows are crafty. Can they count? This is based on a true story by some hunters.

Annotated Resources

Carpenter, T. P., Fennema, E., Franke, M. L., Levi, L., and Emspon, S. *Children's Mathematics: Cognitively Guided Instruction.* Portsmouth, NH: Heinemann, 1999.

These researchers are among the foremost in the world with respect to studying how story problems can be used to help develop number sense, understanding of operations, basic facts, and computational fluency, through their work known as *cognitively guided instruction (CGI).* They are the originators of the classifications of word problems as described in this chapter, and their work in this arena is explained in detail in their book. The book comes packaged with two CDs: one offers glimpses of CGI classrooms and the other highlights the thinking of individual children.

Fosnot, C. T., and Dolk, M. *Young Mathematicians at Work: Constructing Number Sense, Addition, and Subtraction.* Portsmouth, NH: Heinemann, 2001.

The first in a three-volume set, *Young Mathematicians at Work* focuses on young children between the ages of 4 and 8 as they construct a deep understanding of number and the operations of addition and subtraction. From the work of the Dutch mathematician Hans Freudenthal, the authors define mathematics as "mathematizing"—the activity of structuring, modeling, and interpreting one's "lived world" mathematically. They describe teachers who use rich problematic situations to promote inquiry, problem solving, and construction, and children who raise and pursue their own mathematical ideas. The authors argue for number sense and the development of a repertoire of strategies. Sample lessons on the use of the open number line model show you how to support the development of efficient computation.

Leutzinger, L. P. "Developing thinking strategies for addition facts." *Teaching Children Mathematics,* 6(1) (September 1999), pp. 14–18.

Leutzinger demonstrates activities for primary-grade students to address basic facts like counting on, using doubles, and making 10 with a focus on reasoning and communication. Probability, spatial sense, and money are also discussed.

National Council of Teachers of Mathematics. "The magic of number." Focus Issue of *Mathematics Teaching in Middle School,* 7(8) (April 2002).

This focus issue provides several suggestions for teaching numbers and operations according to the *Standards.*

Schifter, D., Bastable, V., and Russell, S. J. (eds.). *Developing Mathematical Ideas: Numbers and Operations, Part 2, Making Meaning for Operations (Casebook).* Parsippany, NJ: Dale Seymour, 1999.

This collection of 28 stories written by classroom teachers from a variety of school settings offers glimpses into children's thinking about the four basic operations. Each story is short and readable. They all focus on the types of actions and situations modeled by addition, subtraction, multiplication, and division, and the ways that children come to understand these operations for whole numbers and fractions. The stories include transcripts of classroom conversations and samples of student work, as well as teachers' concerns and questions about how they can best help and support children as they grapple with important mathematical understandings.

Trafton, P., and Thiessen, D. *Learning through Problems, Number Sense and Computational Strategies, A Resource for Primary Teachers.* Portsmouth, NH: Heinemann, 1999.

A good book for K–4 teachers who are looking for a better way to use problem solving. Kids can come up with all sorts of ingenious solutions to problems, gaining confidence in working on new problems. The problems focus on simple, everyday situations.

CHAPTER 10

Computation Methods: Calculators, Mental Computation, and Estimation

◆ Snapshot of a Lesson

Key Ideas

1. Show students how to use different computational methods
2. Help students understand estimating and checking whether answers are reasonable

Background

This snapshot is an excerpt from the video *Choose a Method*, from Teaching Math: A Video Library, K–4 from Annenberg Media. Produced by WGBH Educational Foundation. ©1995 WGBH. All rights reserved. To view the video, go to http://www.learner.org/resources/series32.html (video #17). Mary Holden teaches a combined class of fourth and fifth graders in Jeffersontown, Kentucky. She divides her class into three groups, assigning a different task to each group and rotating the students through the groups over a period of several days. One group, called "puzzles and games," works independently on developing tessellating designs, while a second group works on solving problems on computers. The third group meets with the teacher in an exploration activity involving base-ten blocks. This activity involves modeling operations with currency on base-ten manipulatives, which leads into a comparison of methods of computation.

MRS. HOLDEN: Once again today we're going to move back to another idea about these base ten blocks. This is going to be one whole. [*Teacher holds up a flat.*] So, this is a dollar [*the flat*]. What is this? [*Holds up a rod.*] Ten cents. And what is this? [*Holds up a unit.*]

STUDENT: A penny.

MRS. HOLDEN: A penny, okay. Like, for instance, this would be a dollar [*holds up one flat.*] How much is this altogether? [*Holds up one flat, one rod, and one unit.*]

STUDENT: A dollar and eleven cents.

MRS. HOLDEN: A dollar and eleven, okay.

The camera pans to show student-built base 10 structures. Mrs. Holden asks students to consider which student-built structure is "worth" the most. Students estimate the value of their classmates' structures.

CHRIS: Nataya's because it has two dollar bills and a lot of tens, and dimes.

CHRISSY: I think it's Aubrey's because Nataya has a lot of ones in hers and, um, Aubrey's is built mainly of tens and wholes.

STUDENT: I think Andy's would be more than the other ones. There's a lot on the outside. There's mostly tens and wholes.

MRS. HOLDEN: And how much do you think it's worth?

STUDENT: I'd say $3.48.

233

MRS. HOLDEN: Okay. [*Writes "Andy—$3.48" on chalkboard and also writes Nataya—$2.73 and Aubrey—$3.47.*] Okay, let's do the count. Go ahead, and as you trade them in, would you say out loud as you trade them in?

Students are shown in groups of about three, counting their base-10 blocks.

MRS. HOLDEN: Nataya, give me yours. How much is yours worth?

NATAYA: $3.58.

MRS. HOLDEN: Look at the difference. This was our estimate. [*She refers to $2.73 already on board and writes $3.58 next to it.*] Look at the difference—this is our estimate, and this is what it really is. The truth. We were way off with hers, weren't we? Okay. Aubrey's.

AUBREY: $4.20

MRS. HOLDEN: [*Writes $4.20 next to the estimate of $3.47.*] Oh, look at the difference, though. If somebody told you that yours was worth $500.50, would that sound reasonable?

STUDENTS: No.

MRS. HOLDEN: No. Were we close enough to be reasonable?

STUDENTS: Yes.

Mrs. Holden discusses estimation with the students, suggesting that the students round values that are difficult to work with to values that are easier to work with.

MRS. HOLDEN: Is 23 cents, what kind of money is that close to?

STUDENT: A quarter.

MRS. HOLDEN: A quarter. How much money would five quarters be?

STUDENTS: A dollar twenty-five.

MRS. HOLDEN: Is that close to $1.25?

STUDENTS: Yes.

After students become comfortable with the base-10 blocks, Mrs. Holden assigns a particular method of computation to each group member.

MRS. HOLDEN: Okay, you're on paper–pencil, you're on calculator, you're on mental math, and you're on base ten. And, we'll rotate. We'll go around. I'll give you some problems. Slushies are on sale today for 29 cents and you are going to buy everybody that sits at your table one. How many people are at your table?

STUDENT: Four.

MRS. HOLDEN: Four.

Students work independently, using the assigned method of computation. After a few minutes, Mrs. Holden discusses their progress.

MRS. HOLDEN: Now, slushies cost 29 cents and you're buying four of them and it's going to cost 33 cents? What? [*Points to another student.*]

STUDENT 1: A dollar sixteen.

STUDENT 2: I'm totally off. I know that.

STUDENT 3: What did you get?

STUDENT 2: It's totally off. $2.48.

STUDENT 3: I got 47 cents.

MRS. HOLDEN: Does that sound reasonable?

STUDENT 3: Not from what everybody else has been saying.

MRS. HOLDEN: Twenty-nine cents and you're buying four of them?

STUDENT 3: I kind of did like what the problem was on the board. I did it in my mind, and it didn't work.

MRS. HOLDEN: Let's think that through and I'll give you a little trick with the 29 ones. Twenty-nine is hard to work with, isn't it? If you think in your mind, four times 29, it's hard to do, isn't it? What's 29 close to?

STUDENTS: Thirty.

MRS. HOLDEN: Thirty. Then you do what?

STUDENT: You take away a penny from each one.

MRS. HOLDEN: What do you come up with?

STUDENT: A dollar sixteen.

STUDENT: Say you want to equal up 29 times 4, you can use the tens first and then when you're done, you don't count up the tens, you count up the ones.

MRS. HOLDEN: Okay, so like this is a ten, can I use my hands with this? [*Mrs. Holden counts by ten on her fingers.*] 10, 20, is that one of them? 30, 40, is that another one of them? 50, 60, is that another one of them? 70, 80, okay is that all of the tens?

Mrs. Holden and the student discuss a strategy for combining the tens the teacher counted on her fingers and the ones from the original problem. The student adds that 4 times 9 is 36, arriving at a solution of $1.16. Ms. Holden takes advantage of the opportunity to discuss the unique strategy and thanks the student for sharing his way of thinking with the group.

Mrs. Holden takes time at the end of the class to survey her students' opinions on the efficiency of the methods used in the group.

MRS. HOLDEN: Which method do you prefer when you're doing these kinds of problems? What would you rather do? I want to go around the circle and I want everybody to tell me what they think is the best method, paper–pencil, mental math, base 10s, or calculator.

STUDENT: I think it would be pencil and paper.

STUDENT: Calculator.

STUDENT: I think calculator.

STUDENT: I think it would depend. If it's a harder question, it would have to be calculator. But, if it were an easier one, I think it would be a lot easier with mental math.

STUDENT: I think it would be mental math because you can round everything off to something.

STUDENT: I think it would be mental math because if you go to a store when you buy a few things of the same. You're going to expect a reasonable answer. Maybe it will be a little bit more when they ring it up.

MRS. HOLDEN: Okay, did we say that there's any method that's the best method?

STUDENTS: No, not really.

MRS. HOLDEN: No, it depends. Could you all agree on that? That it depends on what you're doing?

MRS. HOLDEN: [*to camera*] I think the best kind of math communication, the best kind of math writing, comes from feeling safe to express that in front of other people and to express wrong turns. And how when somebody makes a wrong turn in their thinking we can correct them again, but that it's safe to say that out loud in front of a group of peers and the teacher so we can get that corrected.

◢ Introduction

Computation has evolved from counting to using such devices as piles of stones or an abacus to using written algorithms. More recently, the calculator has come into wide use, and nothing else has had a greater impact on school mathematics.

Competence with different methods of doing computations is not merely useful; it is essential, and this is reflected in the NCTM's *Principles and Standards for School Mathematics* (see Figure 10-1).

Historically, elementary school mathematics has emphasized written computation far more than other methods. This, together with the fact that learners are more likely to use methods with which they are familiar, means that students often tend to use written computation even when they could use a more efficient method.

As a teacher, you will need to balance your instruction so children learn about a variety of computational methods and learn when to use each:

1. All computation begins with a problem and with the recognition that computation is needed to solve the problem.

2. Certain decisions must be made when doing computation.

Instructional programs should enable all students to:	Pre-K–2 Expectations All students should:	Grades 3–5 Expectations All students should:
Compute fluently and make reasonable estimates	Use a variety of methods and tools to compute, including objects, mental computation, estimation, paper and pencil, and calculators	Select appropriate methods and tools for computing the whole numbers from among mental computation, estimation, calculators, and paper and pencil according to the context and nature of the computation and use the selected method or tool

FIGURE 10-1   Number and Operation Standard with expectations for children in grades prekindergarten–2 and 3–5 to develop operation sense.

3. Estimation is always used to check on the reasonableness of the result.

Math Links 10.1

*T*he full-text electronic version of the standards expectations related to methods of computation is available at the National Council of Teachers of Mathematics at www.nctm.org.

www.wiley.com/college/reys

In Figure 10-2, you can see that the two essential decisions in every computation are, first, deciding on the type of result needed and, second, deciding on the best method for getting that result. The first decision involves the question of whether an estimate is appropriate or an exact answer is needed. The second decision involves such questions as whether a calculator would be helpful, or whether the numbers in the problem make mental computation possible, or whether paper-and-pencil calculation is most appropriate. Thus, your goals when teaching computation will be to help students:

- Develop competence with each of the computational methods.
- Choose a method that is appropriate for the computation at hand.
- Apply the chosen method correctly.
- Use estimation to determine the reasonableness of the result.

In addition, by helping students choose and use computational methods appropriately and effectively, you will also help them develop their number sense.

In this chapter, we begin by discussing some of the issues in deciding how to find the right balance of instructional time devoted to different computational methods. We then consider the use of calculators in computation, and in the process we dispel certain myths about the disadvantages of calculator use. Next we consider how to teach children mental computation, and we discuss the benefits that students derive from using this method. Then we discuss ways of teaching children good strategies for making estimations and how to choose among these strategies. We finish by considering various cultural differences in the choice and use of different computational methods.

Note that we discuss calculators, mental computation, and estimation in this chapter, while written computation is considered extensively in Chapter 11.

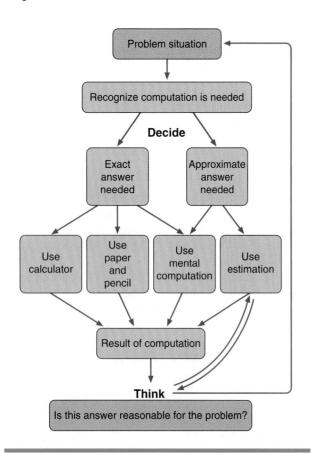

FIGURE 10-2 Computational decisions and methods.

FOCUS QUESTIONS

1. What computational methods should students use?
2. What are some myths and facts about using calculators?
3. What are some strategies for mental computation, and how can teachers encourage mental computation?
4. What are some strategies for computational estimation, and how can teachers encourage estimation?

Balancing Your Instruction

As teachers you need to think about which computational methods are important enough to learn in school and how much time you should devote to each. More than 80% of all mathematical computations in daily life involve mental computation and estimation, rather than written computation. Ironically, research also shows that, in the United

States, 70–90% of the instructional time in elementary school mathematics directed toward computation has focused on written computation (Sowder, 1992).

Many proposals have been made regarding computation, ranging from prohibiting calculator use to eliminating the teaching of written algorithms. Educators have also called for helping children learn to make appropriate choices of computational methods. For example, a report by the National Research Council suggests the following:

> Children should use calculators throughout their school work, just as adults use calculators throughout their lives. More important, children must learn when to use them and when not to do so. They must learn from experience with calculators when to estimate and when to seek an exact answer; how to estimate answers to verify the plausibility of calculator results; and how to solve modest problems mentally when neither pencil nor calculator is convenient. (National Research Council, 1989, p. 47)

Most people recognize the importance of each of the computational methods and suggest that a better balance of instructional time for the computational alternatives is needed than has historically occurred in U.S. elementary schools. What percentage of time should you allot for teaching each method? This remains an open question, though it is clear that the answer depends in part on the developmental levels of the students. Figure 10-3 shows the approximate percentages of instructional time spent on different computational methods in the past (1875 and 1975) and in the present (as of 2000), along with a proposal for a better balance in the future (2025).

The decline in instructional attention to written computation over the years is indisputable; time previously devoted to developing proficiency with tedious written algorithms has become available for other uses. Much of this time has been and can continue to be dedicated to helping students develop their number sense and their ability to select and use other computational methods, including calculators, mental computation, and estimation. Reflecting on your experience and thinking about the future needs of your students will challenge you to develop ways of finding the right balance when you teach computation.

Calculators

The NCTM position statement on calculators recommends that "appropriate calculators should be available to all students at all times." This state-

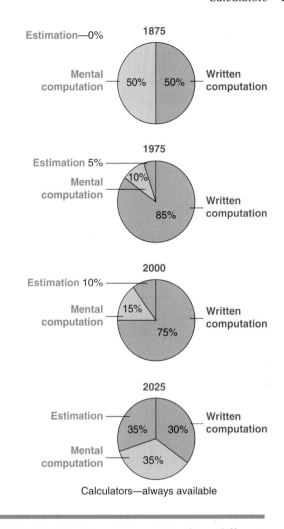

FIGURE 10-3 Time spent on teaching different methods of computation in elementary school in the past, present, and, perhaps, in the future.

ment suggests that as students' mathematical knowledge grows and changes, so does their need for calculators. Children outgrow calculators just as they outgrow shoes. The calculator needs of students in primary grades are different from those of students in intermediate grades and middle school. Electronics companies have responded to these changing needs with fraction calculators, scientific calculators, and graphing calculators.

As a teacher, you need to help students understand how to use calculators appropriately, which includes showing students that not all problems can be solved with a calculator. Also, as with any new tool, you need to give students time to explore with the calculator on their own, and you need to show them how to handle and care for calculators correctly.

In addition, you should communicate with parents so they know you are using calculators in the classroom and so they understand how and why

Dear Parents:

We are using calculators in our second-grade class this year in many different ways. Sometimes we use them to develop skills in counting and recognizing patterns; other times to explore new topics, such as decimals, and often when solving problems that require tedious computations. We believe that a variety of early experiences with calculators will help young children make wise use of calculators both in and out of school.

If you are curious about how we are using calculators, please ask your child to tell you about some things he or she has been doing with this tool. If you have further questions, please let me know.

FIGURE 10-4 A sample note to parents about using calculators in primary grades.

you are using them. Often, a simple note like the one shown in Figure 10-4 is effective.

Math Links 10.2

*T*he National Council of Teachers of Mathematics position paper on Computation, Calculators and Common Sense is available at www.nctm.org.

www.wiley.com/college/reys

Calculators have been used in schools for more than 20 years, but several myths, or incorrect beliefs, about using them persist (which is one reason why communicating with parents is important). In this section, we address these myths as follows:

- *Myth*: Using calculators does not require thinking.

  Fact: Calculators do not think for themselves. Students must still do the thinking.

- *Myth*: Using calculators lowers mathematical achievement.

  Fact: Calculators can raise students' achievement.

- *Myth*: Using calculators always makes computations faster.

  Fact: It is sometimes faster to compute mentally.

- *Myth*: Calculators are useful only for computation.

  Fact: Calculators are also useful as instructional tools.

Using Calculators Requires Thinking

Teachers must make it clear to students (and to parents) that calculators don't think—they only follow instructions. For example, suppose students were using a calculator to solve the following problem:

> One bus holds 32 children. How many buses are needed to hold 1000 children?

Would the calculator decide which keys to press and in what order to press them? Would the calculator interpret the result? Clearly, the answer to both questions is no!

This problem is difficult for elementary students to solve with or without a calculator. To use the calculator effectively, students still must realize that they have to divide 32 into 1000, just as they would have to without a calculator. Then they must decide which calculator buttons to press in which order. And they must still interpret the result (31.25) properly. That is, does the result mean that 31 buses are needed or 32?

As you can see from this problem, calculators don't discourage thinking! In fact, properly used, calculators encourage thinking because they free students from tedious computations (picture using long division here) and give them more time to go through the important problem-solving processes that generally precede, and often follow, the computation.

Using Calculators Can Raise Student Achievement

Research has consistently indicated that the use of "calculators in concert with traditional instruction . . . can improve the average student's basic skills with paper and pencil, both in basic operations and in problem solving" (Hembree and Dessart, 1992). Moreover, "students using calculators possess a better attitude toward mathematics and an especially better self-concept in mathematics." Many parents and some teachers worry that students will become so dependent on calculators that they won't learn to compute. Research shows this is not the case. As a teacher, however, you have to respond to these concerns—not only by showing students how to make effective use of calculators, but also by helping parents overcome their fears.

Calculators Are Not Always the Fastest Way of Doing Computations

As we saw in relation to the bus problem above, calculators can make tedious computations fast and easy. But when it comes to simple calculations, the story is quite different. True, students can use a calculator to compute 2345 × 67 or 34,567 ÷ 89 very quickly; however, calculations such as 4 × 40, 99 + 99 + 99 + 99, $\frac{1}{2} + \frac{1}{4}$, and 1000 × 23 are much quicker to perform mentally than with a calculator, simply because of the time it takes to press the required keys. You can use an activity like the one shown in In the Classroom 10-1 to help children recognize which calculations are more quickly done mentally and which are faster with a calculator.

Calculators Are Useful for More Than Just Doing Computations

The most obvious use of calculators is to calculate, but the process of calculating can reveal many powerful mathematical ideas. For example, calculator counting forward and backward (see In the Classroom 7-4, 7-5, and 8-3) reveals patterns, gives students practice with important skills, and reinforces important knowledge such as basic multiplication and division facts. Older children can use calculators to see patterns such as powers of 10 (10, 100, 1000) and decimals (0.1. 0.01, 0.001).

As a teacher, you should consider using calculators for computation whenever computational skills are not the main focus of instruction. And you should keep in mind that calculators can even be helpful in learning those skills. Clearly, you should not let the use of calculators interfere with the establishment of basic facts, which must remain an important goal of mathematics instruction in the primary grades. Basic facts are natural stepping stones to mental computation and estimation, as well as to the development of number sense over the long term.

In the Classroom 10-1

CALCULATORS VERSUS MENTAL COMPUTATION—WHEN TO USE WHICH

OBJECTIVE: **Help students recognize which types of computations are best done with calculators and which types are best done mentally.**

GRADE LEVEL: **3–5**

▼ Divide the class into pairs of students. In each pair, one student has a calculator and must use it to do computations. The other student doesn't have a calculator and must do computations mentally.

▼ Write computation problems on the board, one at a time.

▼ In each pair, the student who first has an answer raises his or her hand. The other student finishes the computation but doesn't raise his or her hand.

▼ After everyone has finished the computation, ask the students with their hand raised for their answer and whether they used a calculator. If their answer is correct, mark it in the appropriate column of the chart below.

Computation		First and Correct Using a Calculator	First and Correct Using Mental Computation
1.	4 × 100	☐	☐
2.	400 + 50 + 8	☐	☐
3.	99 + 99 + 99 + 99	☐	☐
4.	1000 − 200	☐	☐
5.	50 + 50 + 50 + 50 + 50 + 50	☐	☐
6.	$\frac{1}{2} + \frac{3}{4}$	☐	☐
7.	6300 ÷ 7	☐	☐
8.	10 × 10 × 10 × 10	☐	☐
9.	0.75 + 0.25 + 0.50	☐	☐
10.	$1.00 − $0.25	☐	☐

▼ Write two lists on the board—one list showing the computations that more students did correctly and faster using a calculator, the other list showing the computations that more students did correctly and faster suing mental computation.

▼ Discuss the differences in the two lists.

When is calculator use appropriate? Having students turn the calculator upside down to spell words or use the calculator to check written calculations may help motivate students to use calculators, but the educational value of such activities is questionable. They may communicate the message that a calculator is only for playing games or, even worse, that using a calculator is cheating, that students must do calculations by hand and just use a calculator to check their answers. Research shows that the more teachers use calculators in their classroom, the more they develop creative and productive ways to use them (Sutton and Krueger, 2002). There are two main uses for the calculator in the classroom: as a computational tool and as an instructional tool. A calculator should be used as a *computational tool* when it:

- Facilitates problem solving
- Eases the burden of doing tedious computations
- Focuses attention on meaning
- Removes anxiety about doing computations incorrectly
- Provides motivation and confidence

A calculator should be used as an *instructional tool* when it:

- Facilitates a search for patterns
- Supports concept development
- Promotes number sense
- Encourages creativity and exploration

Calculators also provide a safety net for students having particular difficulties in learning computational procedures. For example, if a learning-disabled student finds it difficult or impossible to use traditional computational procedures, the calculator can provide equity and allow them to engage in problem solving along with other students.

◀ Mental Computation

Mental computation is computation done "all in the head"—that is, without tools such as a calculator or paper and pencil. This is certainly a natural way to do many computations, as shown by the Snapshot of a Lesson at the beginning of this chapter as well as by the fact that many young children develop ways of computing before they are able to write. In fact, research has documented a wide variety of mental computation techniques that children have created on their own and that make sense to them (Fuson, 2003).

Strategies and Techniques for Mental Computation

Mental computation builds on the thinking strategies used to develop basic facts (see Chapter 9) and naturally extends children's mastery of basic facts. Extending basic facts is an early step in developing more powerful strategies and skills in mental computation. Extending basic facts takes different forms. Students might:

- Extend $4 + 5 = 9$ to $40 + 50 = 90$ and $400 + 500 = 900$.
- Use place value in doing a subtraction such as $675 - 200 = 475$ or $675 - 50 = 625$.
- Combine basic facts with place value and recognize that $42 + 16 = 42 + 10 + 6$ and $42 + 10 = 52$ and $52 + 6 = 58$.
- Decompose (break up) numbers to make them easier to handle. For example, to calculate $18 + 17$ the student could decompose 17 into $2 + 15$; thus, $18 + 17 = 18 + 2 + 15$, and $18 + 2 = 20$, and $20 + 15 = 35$. Alternatively, the student could decompose 18 into $10 + 8$ *and* decompose 17 into $10 + 7$; thus, $18 + 17 = 10 + (8 + 7) + 10$, and $8 + 7 = 15$, and $10 + 15 = 25$, and $25 + 10 = 35$. Both solutions use basic facts and place value, while using different ways of decomposing numbers to make them easier to work with mentally.

As you can see from the last two examples above, mental computation is often done by using compatible, or "friendly," numbers. These are numbers that can be combined to make numbers that are easy to compute with, such as 10 (e.g., 8 and 2 are compatible numbers because they add up to 10). Having children work with the ten-frame will help them see how to link different combinations to make 10:

$8 + \_\_ = 10$ $\_\_ + 5 = 10$ $7 + \_\_ = 10$

Using compatible numbers facilitates a mental computation such as $8 + 7 + 22 + 5 + 13$. For example, a student could recognize that, 8 and 22 are compatible numbers ($8 + 22 = 30$, which is 10×3) and that 7 and 13 are compatible too ($7 + 13 = 20$, which is 10×2).

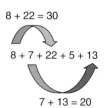

$8 + 22 = 30$

$8 + 7 + 22 + 5 + 13$

$7 + 13 = 20$

Then the student could finish the computation by thinking: $30 + 20 = 50$, and $50 + 5 = 55$.

Another student could do this same computation differently, by thinking: $8 + 7 = 15$, and $15 + 5 = 20$, and $22 + 20 = 42$, and $13 = 10 + 3$, and $42 + 10 = 52$, and $52 + 3 = 55$. There are many other ways of doing this same mental computation, but they all would reflect good number sense and show the importance of fluency with basic facts and with adding 10 or multiples of 10. Understanding the different strategies children use and helping the children understand each other's strategies make the development of mental computation exciting.

The first step in developing proficiency with using compatible numbers is learning to recognize them. Figures 10-5 and 10-6 show one way you can give children practice in this. Such practice also demonstrates that compatible numbers vary and that they can include combinations that add up to 10, 50, or whatever other numbers are easy to work with mentally.

FIGURE 10-5   Find two or more adjacent numbers in a row or column with a sum of 10. (Try to find at least eight different combinations.)

FIGURE 10-6   Find two or more adjacent numbers in a row or column with a sum of 50. (Try to find at least eight different combinations.)

There are many useful strategies for mental computation. Just as teachers can help children develop a repertoire of problem-solving strategies, they also can help children develop a repertoire of mental computation strategies. Figure 10-7 shows

several common strategies for whole-number addition. Chances are, you have used some of these strategies yourself.

Mental computation encourages flexible thinking, promotes number sense, and encourages creative and efficient work with numbers. Consider some of the strategies that children could use to do different types of computations mentally:

- Children could solve a problem in whole-number addition such as $165 + 99$ in different ways. For example,

  "I subtracted 1 from 165 and added it to 99. Then I added 164 plus 100 to get 264."

  "I added 165 plus 100 and got 265, then I subtracted 1 and got 264."

- For multiplication problems such as 4×600 and 4×6000, children could extend the basic multiplication fact $4 \times 6 = 24$ and combine that with their understanding of place value. For example,

  "4×600 is 4×6 hundreds, which is 24 hundreds, or 2400."

  "4×6000 is 4×6 thousands, which is 24 thousands, or 24000."

- And for a division problem such as 1200/4, children could combine place value with extending the basic division fact $12/4 = 3$. For example,

  "1200 is 12 hundreds, so 1200/4 is 12 hundreds/4, or 3 hundreds, or 300."

The strategy of combining basic facts and place-value concepts will suggest different patterns and relationships to students. And by combining mental computation with calculators, students can explore a wide enough range of patterns and relationships to stimulate them to make conjectures and discoveries. For example, students could explore patterns and relationships among multiplications such as 4×6, 4×60, 4×600, and 4×6000, and can tell how the results are alike and how they are different. A slightly different exploration could be used to challenge students to tell why the results are the same: 4×600, 40×60, 400×6, and 4000×0.6. Doing mental computation rewards thoughtful analysis, and it encourages flexible thinking because students see that they can often get the correct results by using very different techniques, as illustrated in Figure 10-8. Each strategy is meaningful to the student using it, even if it seems strange to others. By encouraging children to talk with each other about the different ways they do problems in their heads, you help them learn to think more freely and flexibly. This sharing and explaining is an important

Problem	Strategy	How I Did It
43 + 48	Adding from the left	40 plus 40 is 80, 3 plus 8 is 11, 80 plus 11 is 91
43 + 48	Counting on	I'll count by tens. 48 . . . 58 . . . 68 . . . 78 . . . 88 Then I'll count by ones. 89 . . . 90 . . . 91
43 + 48	Making tens	48 plus 2 is 50, 50 plus 40 is 90, 90 plus 1 more is 91
43 + 48	Doubling	48 plus 48 is 96. Since 43 is 5 less than 48, 96 minus 5 is 91.
43 + 48	Making compatibles	43 and 7 are compatible because they make 50, 50 plus 40 is 90, 90 plus 1 more is 91.
43 + 48	Bridging	I'll break up a number and add the parts. 43 plus 8 is 51, add 40 more is 91

Can you think of any other ways to solve this problem?

FIGURE 10-7 Some common strategies for whole-number addition using mental computation.

part of instructional activities that promote the development of mental computation skills, and it often helps children learn new strategies.

FIGURE 10-8 The volume of the box is 25 × 8 × 20. Each student finds the answer in a different way.

Encouraging Mental Computation

You should make sure that you give students a range of activities that encourage and reward the wide variety of skills they develop when doing mental computation. Rather than have everyone use the same strategy to solve a problem, you should encourage students to use the strategies that make sense to them individually. Here are some things you should encourage children to do:

- Always try mental computation before using paper and pencil or a calculator.
- Use numbers that are easy to work with:

The problem	*One way to think about it*
397 × 4 = ?	400 × 4 = 1600
	3 × 4 = 12
	1600 − 12 = 1588
$6.98 + $7.98 + $9.98 = ?	7 + 8 + 10 = 25
	3 × 2 cents = 6 cents
	$25 − 6 cents = $24.94

- Look for an easy way:

The problem	*One way to think about it*
2 × 3 × 7 × 5 = ?	2 × 3 = 6
	6 × 5 = 30
	30 × 7 = 210

$$6 \times 8 \times 19 \times 0 = ?$$

OR

$2 \times 5 = 10$

$3 \times 7 = 21$

$10 \times 21 = 210$

0 is a factor, which means the product is zero

- Use logical reasoning:

The problem

$$15 \times 120 = ?$$

One way to think about it

That's halfway between 10×120 and 20×120

Halfway between 1200 and 2400 is 1800

OR

That's 10×120 plus half of 10×120

$1200 + 600 = 1800$

- Use knowledge about the number system:

The problem

$$56 - 24 = ?$$

One way to think about it

$50 - 20 = 30$

$6 - 4 = 2$

$30 + 2 = 32$

OR

$54 - 24 = 30$

so $56 - 24 = 32$

Why emphasize mental computation? There are several reasons for helping students develop mental computation skills:

- *Mental computation is very useful.* Adults do more than three-fourths of all their calculations mentally. You should encourage and reward the early development of this practical skill that students will use for the rest of their lives.

- *Mental computation is the most direct and efficient way of doing many calculations.* For example, research has shown that the computation $200 - 5$ is better done mentally than with paper and pencil. Students are more likely to make sensible judgments about the result and less likely to come up with 205 (a common error when writing). In the middle grades, a computation such as $\frac{3}{4} - \frac{1}{2}$ is easier for children to do mentally than by writing (McIntosh et al., 1995).

- *Mental computation is an excellent way to help children develop critical-thinking skills and number sense and to reward creative problem solving.* Students must figure out a strategy and use it. In this process, they become aware that there is more than one way to perform most calculations mentally, and they are encouraged to

seek simple and economical methods that make sense to them.

- *Proficiency in mental computation contributes to increased skill in estimation.* Mental computation is the foundation for estimation because it helps children see alternative algorithms and nonstandard techniques for finding answers.

Mental computation versus written algorithms As we have seen, there are many efficient techniques for mental computation. Moreover, in the process of becoming proficient at mental computation, children gain mathematical insights and develop skills that will serve them well all their life. Unfortunately, however, when children above grade 2 tried mental computation, their dominant strategy was to apply written algorithms mentally (McIntosh et al., 1997). For example, when they were asked to compute $165 + 99$ mentally, a typical response was: "I added 5 plus 9 and got 14. I carried the 1, and 5 plus 9 plus 1 is 15. I carried that 1 and got 2. It's two-six-four, or 264."

Many students think of mental computation this way, as applying written algorithms in their heads. But this notion of mental computation is far different from the kind of mental computation we discuss in this chapter, and applying written algorithms mentally is often difficult and impractical.

A problem is that practice with written computation increases the likelihood that students will try applying written algorithms mentally. This is an international dilemma. In Canada and the United States, for instance, research showed that the range of strategies used for mental computation was far greater than in Japan, but in all three countries the dominant strategy used by students was to apply a written algorithm mentally. The mental application of written algorithms most likely reflects the emphasis given to written algorithms in school; unfortunately, this strategy appears to inhibit the development of flexible and more efficient strategies for mental computation (Reys and Yang, 1998; Shigematsu et al., 1994). As a teacher, you should increase your emphasis on flexible, student-generated strategies that enable students to compute mentally without relying on written algorithms.

Guidelines for developing mental computation skills Here are guidelines you should follow when helping students develop mental computation skills:

- *Encourage students to do computations mentally.* Make it clear that when mental computation is possible, it is not only acceptable but preferable to written computation. Students report that mental computation is not encouraged and is often even discouraged in school (Sowder, 1992). Educators have suggested that when teachers say things like "show your work," students interpret this to mean that mental computation is unacceptable. Thus, instead of quickly and easily computing 1000×945 mentally, students might use paper and pencil, thinking they are required to apply the unnecessary and inefficient written algorithm:

$$
\begin{array}{r}
945 \\
\times\ 1000 \\
\hline
000 \\
000 \\
000 \\
945 \\
\hline
945000
\end{array}
$$

- *Learn which computations students prefer to do mentally.* Research suggests that, when given the choice, students from grade 4 and up prefer to use written computations rather than calculators or mental computation. For example, most fifth graders chose to do 1000×945 with either a calculator or paper and pencil, even though

this computation is most easily done mentally (McIntosh, 2004). This choice typically reflects the student's lack of experience and confidence in doing computations mentally. In the Classroom 10-2 illustrates one way to explore the computational preferences of students with whole numbers, and In the Classroom 10-3 does the same with fractions. If you see that students prefer using a calculator or paper and pencil to do computations that are better done mentally, you can focus on helping them develop mental computation skills that would lead them to change their preferences.

- *Find out if students are applying written algorithms mentally.* Ask students to tell how they did a computation in their heads, so their strategies and thinking become clear to you.

- *Plan to include mental computation systematically and regularly as an integral part of your instruction.* Systematic attention and practice

---

In the Classroom 10-2

HOW WOULD YOU DO IT?

OBJECTIVE: Encourage wise use of computational alternatives.

GRADE LEVEL: 4–5

	In Your Head	With a Calculator	With Paper/ Pencil
60×60	☐	☐	☐
945×1000	☐	☐	☐
450×45	☐	☐	☐
$24 \times 5 \times 2$	☐	☐	☐
$2000\overline{)16000}$	☐	☐	☐
$45\overline{)450}$	☐	☐	☐
4×15	☐	☐	☐
$50 \times 17 \times 2$	☐	☐	☐

Follow Up

▼ Write a computation YOU would solve with a calculator.

▼ Write a computation YOU would solve mentally.

▼ Write a computation YOU would solve with paper and pencil.

In the Classroom 10-3

HOW WOULD YOU DO IT?

OBJECTIVE: Encourage wise use of computational alternatives.

GRADE LEVEL: 4–5

	In Your Head	With a Calculator	With Paper/ Pencil
$\frac{1}{2} + \frac{1}{4}$	☐	☐	☐
$1 - \frac{1}{3}$	☐	☐	☐
$\frac{3}{4} + \frac{3}{4}$	☐	☐	☐
$\frac{1}{5} + \frac{1}{6}$	☐	☐	☐
$\frac{1}{2} + \frac{5}{6}$	☐	☐	☐
$1\frac{1}{2} + 2\frac{3}{4}$	☐	☐	☐
$2 - \frac{3}{4}$	☐	☐	☐
$\frac{1}{2} - \frac{1}{3}$	☐	☐	☐

Follow Up

▼ Write a computation YOU would solve with a calculator.

▼ Write a computation YOU would solve mentally.

▼ Write a computation YOU would solve with paper and pencil.

will improve your students' mental computation skills. You should focus on helping students develop strategies and thinking patterns that make sense to them. Students may develop these strategies and patterns on their own or may adopt ones they have learned from others.

- *Keep practice sessions short, perhaps 10 minutes at a time.* Many teachers use an activity such as Follow Me while children are waiting in line ("3 × 4 + 10 − 4 + 20 . . ." where the teacher calls out "three times four" and the first student in line says "twelve" and the teacher says "plus ten" and the next student says "twenty-two" etc.). Another useful activity is Today's Target, where the date serves as a target that students have to "hit" using specific types of computations (see Figure 10-9). You can vary this activity by changing the target number to something besides a date—for example, you might say, "Today's target is 100," and then ask students to think of different ways to make 100. Or you could vary the questions, for example, by asking them to "use addition and subtraction" or to "do it an unusual way." This type of activity gives students practice with mental computation, and the solutions give you insight into students' thinking—both into the strategies they use and into the level of computational complexity at which they are operating.

- *Develop children's confidence.* Pick numbers that are easy to work with at first (e.g., 3 × 99 or 1/2 of 84), and then increase the difficulty (e.g., 5 × 75 or 2/3 of 96). Working with compatible numbers (see the discussion above) helps children develop confidence at mental computation and improves their number sense.

- *Encourage inventiveness.* There is never just one right way to do any mental computation, but certain ways may be more efficient and interesting than others. Asking students, "How did you do that?" can reveal highly ingenious mental computation strategies. For example, students who computed 60 × 15 mentally reported the following strategies:

    "10 times 60 is 600. 5 times 60 is 300. 600 plus 300 is 900."

    "60 times 10 is 600, and half of 600 is 300, so it is 600 plus 300, or 900."

    "60 is 4 times 15, so that is 4 times 15 times 15. 15 squared is 225, times 4 is 900." (This one was reported by an eighth grader.)

    As we have noted, children often develop their own strategies for mental computation, the power of such self-developed, out-of-school techniques has been documented (Sowder, 1992).

- *Mental computation or estimation?* Make sure children are aware of the difference between estimation (in which answers are approximations) and mental computation (in which answers are exact).

Estimation

Computational estimation is a process of producing answers that are close enough to allow for good decisions without performing elaborate or exact computations. The video *Choosing a Method* nicely illustrates that there are many different real-world situations for using estimation. Computational estimation is typically done mentally. Figure 10-10 illustrates how students can use estimation to monitor their computations at three different points in the process:

- *Before starting exact computation,* students can use estimation to get a general sense of what to expect.

- *While doing computation,* students can use estimation as a check to determine if the computation is moving in the right direction.

- *After completing a computation,* students can use estimation to reflect on their answer and decide if it makes sense.

As children become more aware of these different uses of estimation, they develop a greater respect for its power and view it as an essential part of the total computational process.

Students who are proficient at written computations are not necessarily good estimators.

Today's target is May 24

Try to hit this target by

Adding three numbers	Subtracting one number from another number
Some possible answers	*Some possible answers*
8 + 8 + 8	30 − 6
20 + 2 + 2	25 − 1
10 + 10 + 4	100 − 76

Multiplying two numbers	Using a fraction
Some possible answers	*Some possible answers*
4 × 6	$23\frac{9}{10} + \frac{1}{10}$
8 × 3	$48 × \frac{1}{2}$
24 × 1	$24\frac{1}{2} - \frac{1}{2}$

FIGURE 10-9   Today's target and some ways to hit it.

(a) Before computing

(b) During computing

(c) After computing

FIGURE 10-10 Different times to estimate.

Research suggests that memorizing rules and procedures discourages many students from using estimation (Alajmi, 2004; Reys and Yang, 1998). Good mental computation skills and number sense provide the foundation for the successful development of estimation skills. You can significantly improve students' estimation skills by paying systematic attention to estimation in your instruction. Although some dramatic improvements can occur quickly, the development of good estimation skills is a process that takes years (Sowder, 1992). Thus, students must be given repeated opportunities to estimate.

Learning about estimation gives students their first encounter with an area of mathematics that does not focus on exact answers and yet is a natural part of mathematics. As young children talk about estimation in mathematics, their mathematical vocabulary will expand to include words such as *about, almost, just over,* and *nearly.* As children grow older, they will add words such as *approximate, reasonable,* and *unreasonable* to their vocabulary for describing mathematical answers, as well as phrases such as *in the ballpark* and *close enough.* Becoming comfortable and confident in using language to describe the inexactness found in the real world contributes not only to developing number sense but also to developing better estimation skills.

You should begin by making students aware of what estimation is about, so they acquire a tolerance for error. Estimation involves a different mindset from the mindset that says only an exact answer will do. You have to help children change their exact-answer mindset before beginning to teach specific estimation strategies. This change begins when students recognize that estimation is an essential and practical skill. That's why you must consistently emphasize computational estimation across a range of different problems and along with procedures for exact computation.

Also important is to give students immediate feedback on their estimates, and to not be overly critical initially. Ask students to explain how they obtained their estimates, because such discussion helps clarify procedures and may even suggest new approaches to estimating with a given problem. Make sure students understand that estimation, which produces an approximate answer, is not the same as mental computation, which produces an exact answer.

One of the keys to helping children develop good estimation strategies is encouraging them to be flexible when thinking about numbers. For example, suppose you want students to estimate 418 + 349. One child might think, "400 + 300 is 700, and 49 + 18 is less than 100, so the sum is between 700 and 800." This approach uses the leading, or front-end, digits. Another child might think, "418 is about 400 and 349 is almost 350, so the sum is about 750." This child rounded to numbers that are easy to work with and used number sense to make adjustments.

As with mental computation, it is important that children develop different strategies for estimating different computations. That is, they must learn to think about the problem, the operations, and the numbers involved and not rely on a fixed set of rules to produce an estimate. Many adults think only of rounding when considering estimation; however, as with mental computation, you must help children develop a repertoire of strate-

FIGURE 10-11   Front-end estimation in action.

gies from which they can choose. In the following sections, we discuss some of these strategies.

Front-End Estimation

The front-end strategy for estimation is a basic yet powerful approach that can be used in a variety of situations. Front-end estimation involves checking (1) the leading, or front-end, digit in a number and (2) the place value of that digit. Figure 10-11 shows how front-end digits are used to obtain an initial estimate. The unique advantage of the front-end strategy is that the original problem shows all the numbers that students have to work with. This enables students to reach an estimate quickly and easily. The front-end strategy also encourages students to use number sense as they think about the computations.

You should make sure students understand that a front-end estimate is a lower bound and that students can use the remaining digits to adjust this estimate, as we discuss in the next section.

Adjusting

Number sense has many dimensions, one of which is recognizing when an estimate is a little more or a little less than the exact answer would be. As students develop their estimation skills, it becomes natural for them to refine an initial estimate by adjusting it, or compensating. Students can do this no matter which strategy they used to make their initial estimate.

For example, consider how a student could adjust a front-end estimate of 4000 for the sum 1213 + 2926 + 1578, by thinking: "The answer would be exactly 4000 if all the digits except the front-end ones were zeros. But they're not zeros, so the answer must be more than 4000 . . ." The student could then go on to consider the digits in the hundreds place and raise the estimate accordingly.

FIGURE 10-12   Front-end estimation with adjustment.

Figure 10-12 illustrates how this type of adjusting would work in solving a real-world problem such as deciding if you have enough money to buy lunch. In the Classroom 10-4 presents an activity that will give students practice in using the front-end estimation strategy and then adjusting.

When you teach estimation, be sure students understand that they should adjust estimates regardless of their initial estimation strategy and regardless of the operations involved in the problem.

Compatible Numbers

As in mental computation, using compatible numbers—numbers that go together naturally and are easy to work with mentally—is often helpful in estimation. Figure 10-13 illustrates how compatible numbers can make estimation easier with a variety of different operations.

Using compatible numbers for estimation means rounding the numbers in the problem to numbers that are easier to work with, *given the operations needed to solve the problem*. Notice in Figure 10-13 that 64 and 8 are not compatible for multiplication (64×8 is hard to compute mentally) but are compatible for division (64/8 is easy to compute mentally). Similarly, 60 and 8 are not compatible for division but are compatible for multiplication. Thus, compatibility depends on the operation as well as on the numbers themselves.

The compatible numbers strategy is particularly powerful for division. Children given the problems shown in Figure 10-14, for example, need to be encouraged to think about why 7 and 2800 or 6 and 3000 are compatible numbers for the problem. Asking children to think of "compatible numbers pairs" for different problems in division and to tell why the numbers are compatible will help

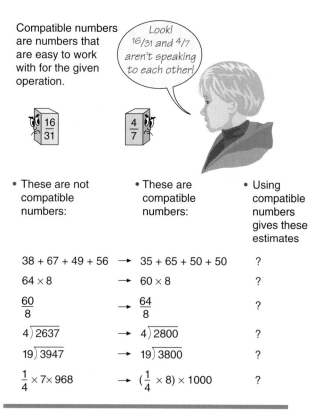

FIGURE 10-13 Compatible numbers for different operations.

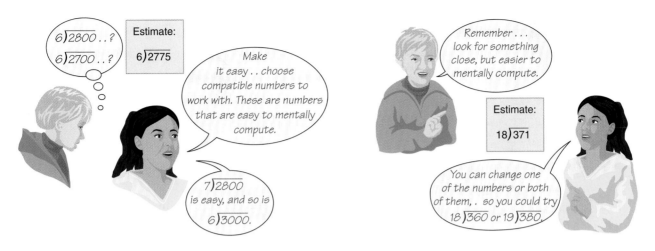

FIGURE 10-14   The compatible numbers strategy for division.

them come up with thoughtful ideas and will give you insight into their number sense. For example, if you ask students to think of some compatible numbers pairs to use in estimating 7029 divided by 23, they might come up with ideas like these:

- 7029 is fairly close to 6900, and 69 is divided evenly by 23, so 23 and 69 are compatible for division. 6900 divided by 23 is 300, which is probably a pretty good estimate.

- 8000 is divided evenly by 20, so 20 and 8000 are compatible for division. 8000 divided by 20 is 400, but 8000 is a lot more than 7029, so the estimate of 400 is probably pretty rough.

- 75 is evenly divided by 25, so 75 and 25 are compatible for division. 7500 divided by 25 is 300, and 7500 is fairly close to 7029, and 25 is close to 23, so an estimate of 300 is probably close.

Compatible numbers are also often used to estimate addition problems. In the following example, the student first used the front-end strategy and then used compatible numbers to adjust the initial estimate:

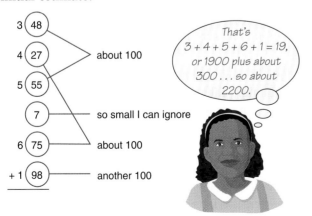

Flexible Rounding

Rounding to get numbers that are easier to work with is a very useful estimation strategy. Rounding is a more sophisticated strategy than front-end estimation because rounding changes, reformulates, or recomposes the numbers in the original problem. When using rounding for estimation, students should use *flexible rounding,* rather than applying rigid rounding rules like those discussed in Chapter 8. Flexible rounding means rounding to numbers that are close but are also compatible. Flexible rounding is appropriate for all operations with all types of numbers, but it is particularly well suited to multiplication. Children should be adept at the process of rounding to compatible numbers. Figure 10-15 shows how students started with the same problem but rounded differently. Notice that each approach produced a different result, but each is a reasonable estimate. It is important for students to know they have the freedom to choose different estimation strategies, but they also need to realize that different strategies produce different estimates. Accepting a range of reasonable estimates, rather than a single best estimate, fosters number sense and encourages students to choose and use their own strategies.

Problems like the one shown in Figure 10-15 need to be accompanied by questions that go beyond asking what the estimate is to encouraging thought about the process—for example:

How did you change the numbers?

Why did you change the numbers?

Children should be encouraged to think of possible substitutions and to reason about which substitutions would be best. The choices illustrated

FIGURE 10-15　Flexible rounding and the different estimates that result.

in the following example lead naturally to such questions as, "Which pair would you choose to make the estimate? Why?"

Also, you should encourage children to adjust estimates that they get by rounding, in order to compensate for how the numbers were rounded. In the following example, the student makes an initial estimate by rounding:

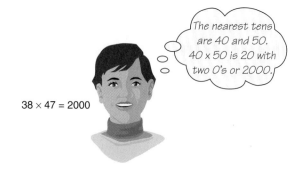

$38 \times 47 = 2000$

Then the student adjusts the initial estimate:

Figure 10-16 shows some other examples. For the first two examples, the rounding procedure clearly indicates whether the result is an underestimate or an overestimate, but the last example is not clear in this regard. Students must think more deeply about the numbers used to produce their estimate.

Problem	Estimate with Rounding	Adjusted Estimate
42 × 61	40 × 60 = 2400	A little more than 2400
39 × 78	40 × 80 = 3200	A little less than 2400
27 × 32	30 × 30 = 900	About 900

FIGURE 10-16　Different ways of estimating products using rounding and then adjusting.

As students become more skillful at mental computation, they become more flexible in their use of rounding to make estimates. They learn to rely more on common sense than on traditional rounding rules, so they can always round to numbers that are easy for them to work with mentally. This means that different people may round the same numbers in a problem differently, depending on what is easiest for them, as we saw in Figure 10-15.

Clustering

The *clustering*, or averaging, strategy uses an average for estimating a sum. Whenever a group of numbers clusters around some value, students can use this two-step process to estimate the sum of all the numbers in the group:

1. Estimate the average value of the numbers—that is, the value that the numbers cluster around.
2. Multiply by the number of numbers in the group.

Figure 10-17 shows two examples of this strategy in action. Questions such as the following can help students understand this strategy:

What value do all the numbers cluster around?

Why is this value the estimated average?

Why is the estimated average multiplied by the number of numbers in the group?

Asking what the estimated total is for a range of problems similar to those in Figure 10-17 will help children become adept at using this strategy.

Clustering is a limited strategy, since it is appropriate only for quickly estimating the sum of a group of numbers that aren't too different from one another (i.e., that cluster around some value). The strength of this strategy is that it eliminates the mental computation involved in adding up a long list of front-end digits or rounded numbers.

Choosing Estimation Strategies

In many cases, different estimation strategies can work for the same problem. The choice of strategies depends mainly on the student, as well as on the specific numbers and operations involved. A challenge for you as the teacher is to help your students become aware of the various estimation strategies and to help them develop confidence in their ability to use any strategy successfully. Here are some useful guidelines for meeting that challenge:

- *Give your students problems that encourage and reward estimation.* For example, you can expect your students to be able to compute 78 + 83 mentally and get an exact answer, but giving them 78342 + 83289 will encourage them to use estimation. As you can see, the idea is to make sure the numbers are messy enough that students will want to estimate the answer, rather than compute an exact answer.

- *Make sure students are not computing exact answers and then rounding to produce estimates.* Research has documented that students frequently use this technique (Sowder, 1992). Unfortunately, this often goes undetected. You should talk with and observe students to see if they are truly estimating.

- *Ask students to tell how they made their estimates.* Individual students often develop unique approaches to estimation. By sharing their different approaches, students develop an appreciation of each other's strategies.

- *Fight the one-right-answer syndrome from the start.* Don't let students fall prey to the "one right" or "best" estimate mentality. This requires helping students realize that several different estimates for the same problem could be equally acceptable. One way to do this is to let students suggest how close to the exact answer an estimate has to be, so all estimates within that range are good estimates. Not only will this counter the idea of one right answer, but it will also generally reveal the students' different estimation strategies and help everyone learn about other strategies. Such experiences help students become more comfortable with the notion that there are several different but correct estimates.

FIGURE 10-17 The clustering strategy for addition.

Over or Under

1. Your car usually gets about 25 miles per gallon on the highway. Your gas tank is about one-quarter full and it is 100 miles to the next gas station. Is this a good time to over- or underestimate your gas mileage?

2. You are talking with a car dealer about buying a car, and you ask about the gas mileage. Do you think the car dealer will over or underestimate the gas mileage of the car?

3. You have $20 to spend on groceries for a group picnic. As you place each item in the grocery cart, is this a good time to over- or underestimate the cost of each item?

4. You are forecasting the lava speed of an active volcano. As the lava is moving down the mountainside toward a town, a decision needs to be made when to evacuate the town. Should you over- or underestimate the speed of the lava?

5. Your plane is scheduled to leave at 4:00 and it usually takes about 1 hour to get to the airport. Should you over- or underestimate the time needed to get to the airport when deciding what time to leave?

FIGURE 10-18   Real-world situations requiring underestimation or overestimation.

• *Encourage students to think of real-world situations that involve making estimates.* Doing this will help students sharpen their critical thinking skills as they decide when to overestimate or underestimate, depending on the situation. Figure 10-18 describes several situations that could encourage such thinking.

The National Research Council underscores the importance of systematically attending to mental computation and estimation in elementary school. The council recommends that students should have opportunities "to develop and use techniques for mental arithmetic and estimation as a means of promoting a deeper number sense" (Kilpatrick et al., 2001).

◀Cultural Connections

For decades, students from Asian countries have excelled at written computation on international mathematics assessments (Lemke et al., 2004), and their performance in mental computation has also been strong. These results reflect the instructional attention given to developing mental and written computation skills throughout elementary school.

In Japan and Taiwan, mental and written computation are an integral part of mathematics programs, but computational estimation has received little attention in their national curricula (Yoshikawa, 1994; Yang, 1995). In fact, estimation is often held in low esteem in Japanese and Taiwanese students because of the emphasis on exact computation. An uncomfortableness in dealing with situations where a range of answers can be correct prompted one Japanese girl to say, "I don't like estimation. I think it is an evil method" (Yoshikawa, 1994). This serves as a reminder of the challenges associated with teaching estimation, not just in Japan or Taiwan, but in many different countries, including the United States.

Beware of assuming that students who are proficient at written computation are also good at estimating; much research shows otherwise. For example, Taiwanese students who showed considerable skill at tedious written computations performed much more poorly at estimating the identical computations (Reys and Yang, 1998), as shown in Table 10-1. Notice that both of the problems in the table involve numbers that are tedious to compute with in writing but that lend themselves well to estimation. That is, 534.6×0.545 is a rather complex computation using a written algorithm, but recognizing that 0.545 is about equal to one-half clearly indicates that the reasonable choice for an estimate is 291.357 (one-half times a number between 500 and 600 is between 250 and 300, so 291.357 is the only reasonable answer of the three choices). Nevertheless, nearly 90% of the Taiwanese students selected 29.1357, and similar results were found among eighth graders in Kuwait (Alajmi, 2004). Clearly, 29.1357 is an unreasonable answer, but it is one that might result by applying the rule "count the digits to the right of the decimal point." The low performance on estimating the sum of two fractions ($12/13 + 7/8$) was similar to the results of the second national assessment of 13-year-olds in the United States. Because both fractions are slightly less than 1, the sum should be less than 2. Yet more than half of the students from both the United States and Taiwan selected either 19 or 21. This is a vivid reminder that teachers must look beneath correct answers to check on students' understanding and their ability to produce reasonable estimates.

Low performance on computational estimation is common across many different countries, including Australia, Kuwait, Japan, Sweden, Taiwan, and the United States (Reys et al., 1999). Much needs to be done in helping children everywhere become competent at estimation. This represents a real opportunity for you to bring about dramatic change in the way your students view estimation and improve their performance.

Table 10-1 • Performance of Taiwanese Sixth Graders on Written Computation and Parallel Estimation Items

Written Computation Items Requiring an Exact Answer		Percentage Correct by Sixth Graders
12/13 + 7/8		61
534.6 × 0.545		61
Estimation Items requiring a correct choice		
Without calculating an exact answer, circle the best estimate for 12/13 + 7/8	A. 1	10
	*B. 2	25
	C. 19	36
	D. 21	16
	E. I don't know	13
This multiplication has been carried out correctly except for placing the decimal point: 534.6 × 0.545 = 291357 Place the decimal point using estimation.	A. 29.1357	87
	*B. 291.357	11
	C. Other Answer	2
* Denotes correct choice		

◢◣ A Glance at Where We've Been

Teachers must help students develop confidence and skill in choosing and using different methods of computation. Thus, teachers must find the right balance in the amount of time they spend on each method.

The NCTM recommends that appropriate calculators should always be available to all students. Teachers must work against myths regarding calculator use and must help students and parents understand that calculators can be very useful tools in elementary mathematics instruction. The important points are these: using a calculator requires thinking; using a calculator can raise student achievement; a calculator is not always the fastest method of computation; the calculator is useful both for computation and as an instructional tool.

Mental computation is a natural way of doing many computations. Mental computation techniques include extending basic facts, using place value, and decomposing numbers, all aimed at mentally computing with compatible numbers. Children often develop their own efficient techniques for mental computation, and it is important for teachers to encourage and reward this. Mental calculation is the most direct and efficient way of doing many calculations, it helps children develop their critical thinking skills and number sense, and it contributes to the development of estimation skills. Teachers must be careful that students do not compute mentally by applying written algorithms in their heads.

Estimation produces an approximate rather than an exact answer. Estimation is useful before, during, and after exact computations, to get a sense of what kind of answer to expect, to check that the computation is moving in the right direction, and to check on the reasonableness of results. Teachers must help children change their exact-answer mindset so they can see the power and usefulness of estimation. Estimation strategies include front-end estimation, using compatible numbers, flexible rounding, and clustering. Regardless of the strategy used, children should learn to adjust their result to get a better estimate. Guidelines for helping children choose and use estimation strategies include giving problems that encourage and reward estimation, making sure students are not computing exact answers and then rounding to produce estimates, getting students to talk about how they made their estimates, helping students overcome the "one-right-answer" syndrome, and encouraging students to think of real-world situations where estimation is needed. Studies across cultures show that students who excel at written computation and mental computation are not necessarily good at estimation.

Things to Do: From What You've Read

1. Here is an actual quote from a fourth grader telling what she thinks her teacher wants:

   "I think she doesn't like us to use mental (computation) because she can't see the writing. And she doesn't like us to use the calculator a whole lot because then we'll get too used to it and we won't want to learn and stuff.... And she likes us to use written (computation) because she can see what we're doing, and if we're having problems she can see what we're doing wrong."

   Suppose you had an opportunity to talk with the student's teacher. What would you tell her teacher?

2. How would you respond to the following statement by a parent? "Calculators should not be used in school, because if students use them, they will never have to think."

3. Look again at Figure 10-3. Decide how you think instructional time devoted to computation should be allocated. Be prepared to defend your proposal.

4. Offer some reasons why student performance on computational estimation is lower in many countries than on written computation?

5. The chapter discusses various uses of the calculator as an instructional tool and as a computational tool. Explain, and give an example of each of them.

6. What do you think are the strongest reasons for encouraging and developing good mental computation skills?

7. A fifth grader described how she computed 7×499 in her head: "I put the 499 on top and the 7 on bottom, then I get 3 and carry the 6 and 9 carry the 6 and 7 times 4 is 28 plus 6 is 34. . . ." Would you say this student was doing mental computation the best way? Explain why. Describe some other strategies she could have used to do this computation mentally.

8. Discuss why it is important for students to develop a tolerance for an acceptable range of answers when doing computational estimation.

9. Discuss why the following is not a good assignment: "I want you to estimate the answers to these problems, then compute the correct answers, and see how far off your estimate was from the correct answer."

10. Explain why adjusting is an integral part of estimating.

11. Figure 10-4 shows a sample note to parents about calculator use in second grade. Prepare a letter to sixth-grade parents telling them that calculators will be used in your class and can be used on homework. Briefly explain why you are encouraging calculator use.

Things to Do: Going Beyond This Book

IN THE FIELD

1. *Do It Mentally*. Ask at least two students to compute $99 + 165$ mentally. Ask them how they did it. Describe the strategies that they used.

2. *About How Much?* Ask several adults to estimate 29×24 and tell how they made their estimate. Describe their strategies and results. Did any of them use the rounding strategies shown in Figure 10-15?

IN YOUR JOURNAL

3. *Computational Methods.* Keep a log of the computational methods (written computation, calculator, mental computation, estimation) that you use for 1 day. Estimate what percentage of your computations made use of each method. In your journal, summarize your results and describe a plan for improving your use of these different computational methods.

4. *Assessing Mental Computation and Estimation.* Select a standardized achievement test. Review the test and determine how much attention is given to assessing mental computation and computational estimation. In your journal, discuss the strengths and weakness of test items that address mental computation or estimation.

WITH ADDITIONAL RESOURCES

5. Read the article "Computation in the Elementary Curriculum: Shifting the Emphasis" (Reys and Reys, 1998). Do you agree or disagree with the authors' proposal for change? Tell why.

6. Review a mental math book (Hope et al., 1987, 1988). Select a lesson and highlight the key ideas for your classmates.

---

*Additional activities, suggestions, and questions are provided in *Teaching Elementary Mathematics: A Resource for Field Experiences* (Wiley, 2007).

7. Read the article "Calculators as Learning Tools for Young Children's Explorations of Number" (Huinker, 2002). Summarize this article and describe an activity that uses the calculator to expand young children's opportunities to explore number concepts.

8. Check the article by Harries and Dobson (1996) or McIntosh et al. (1997) for a summary of different ways students do computations orally and on paper. Do you agree with the summary? Tell why.

WITH TECHNOLOGY

9. View the Annenberg video *Choose a Method* and tell how the teacher brought the notion of reasonable answers into the discussions. Also describe how decomposition was used to promote mental computation.

10. *Calculators and Order of Operations.* Some calculators use arithmetic logic in performing operations. For example, if you entered $3 + 5 \times 4$, the calculator would display $32 = (3 + 5) \times 4$. Other calculators use algebraic logic and would display $23 = 3 + (5 \times 4)$. Explain how you would solve these two problems using each type of calculator: (a) $(253 - 85) \div 4$; (b) $253 - 85 \div 4$.

11. View the entire video *Choose a Method*, and then answer these questions:

   • Did you see students doing mental computation and computational estimation? Describe an example of each.

   • How did the students get compatible numbers to make their computation easier?

   • Do you think the students themselves chose their computational methods? Tell why.

   • If you were doing this lesson, would you do anything differently? Explain.

Note to Instructors: You can find additional resources, learning activities, and black-line masters in this text's accompanying Instructor's Manual, at www.wiley.com/college/reys.

Book Nook for Children

Murphy, S. J. *Coyotes All Around.* New York: HarperCollins, 2003.

Many coyotes try to determine how many roadrunners and other creatures of the desert are in their area. Different coyotes have different methods of counting, but Clever Coyote rounds off and estimates. There are activities and games at the back of the book for parents and teachers to use.

Neuschwander, C. *Amanda Bean's Amazing Dream.* New York: Scholastic, 1998.

This mental computation book shows the reader that Amanda Bean loves to count. She has a dream that helps her realize that being able to multiply will help her count things faster.

Pinczes, E. J., and MacKain, B. *One Hundred Hungry Ants.* Boston, MA: Houghton Mifflin, 1993.

This is a great book for teaching multiplication, division, and grouping strategies. It begins with ants looking for a picnic, but they discover that spending too much time organizing can result in not getting the product! The ants march in one group of 100, two groups of 50, four groups of 25, and so on. Encourage the students to model the ants, draw new patterns, and write a happier ending for the story.

Annotated Resources

Fuson, K. Developing mathematical power in whole number operations. In *A Research Companion to Principles and Standards for School Mathematics* (Eds. J. Kilpatrick, W. G. Martin, and D. Schifter), Reston, VA: NCTM, 2003, pp. 68–94.
A summary of a wide range of research findings related to whole-number work. It addresses computational fluency and research results that provide guidance for teachers developing computational fluency in their students.

Hope, J. A., Leutizinger, L. P., Reys, B. J., and Reys, R. E. *Mental Math in the Primary Grades,* Palo Alto, CA: Dale Seymour, 1988.
This book provides structured activities designed to encourage and promote the development of mental computation. A range of manipulatives and models are used to provide concrete models to facilitate different mental computation strategies.

Huinker, D. "Calculators as learning tools for young children's explorations of number" *Teaching Children Mathematics,* 8(6) (February 2002), pp. 316–321.
Calculators expand opportunities and possibilities to help young children explore ways of representing numbers and number relationships. The article shows how young children can use calculators to investigate number ideas in ways that were previously inaccessible to them.

Markovitz, Z., and Sowder, J. "Developing number sense: An intervention study in grade 7." *Journal for Research in Mathematics Education,* 25 (January 1994), pp. 4–29.

This study demonstrated that students were more likely to use strategies for mental computation and estimation after instructional intervention.

McIntosh, A., Reys, B. J., Reys, R. E.; and Hope, J. *Number Sense: Simple Effective Number Sense Experiences*: *Grades 1–2, 3–4, 4–6, 6–8*. Palo Alto, CA: Dale Seymour, 1997. These 10-minute activities help students develop a sense of what numbers represent and how to use them by exploring relationships and patterns, encouraging mental computation, recognizing equivalent representations of a number, establishing benchmarks, improving estimation skills, and exploring the idea of reasonableness.

Reys, R. E. "Computation versus number sense." *Mathematics Teaching in the Middle Grades,* 4(2) (October 1998), pp. 110–112. Reys offers ways for teachers to research their own students' number sense. Test results from Taiwan are included.

Reys, R. E., and Yang, D. C. "Relationship between computational performance and number sense among sixth and eighth grade students in Taiwan." *Journal for Research in Mathematics Education,* 29(2) (March 1998), pp. 225–237. Shows that student performance on written computation was significantly better than in similar situations that required number sense. The results support looking past the correct answer when testing computation.

Reys, R. E., Reys, B. J., Nohda, N., and Emori, H. "Mental computation performance and strategy use of Japanese students in grades 2, 4, 6, and 8." *Journal for Research in Mathematics Education,* 26(4) (1995), pp. 304–326. Reports results of assessing attitude and computational preferences. Includes examples of assessment questions and performance of Japanese students.

Reys, R. E., Reys, B. J., McIntosh, A.; Emanuelsson, G.; Johansson, B.; and Yang, D. C. "Assessing number sense of students in Australia, Sweden, Taiwan, and the United States." *School Science and Mathematics,* 99(2) (February 1999), pp. 61–70. Provides findings on number sense proficiency of students age 8–14, along with a discussion of number sense and its importance, assessment instruments, and implications for teaching.

CHAPTER 11

Standard and Alternative Computational Algorithms

◆ Snapshot of a Lesson

Key Ideas

1. Children can invent strategies for multidigit computation if they understand how to take numbers apart and put them back together

2. Different children will think of different strategies

3. Children's invented strategies help them develop understanding of multidigit computation

Background

This lesson snapshot comes from the *Investigations in Number, Data, and Space* curriculum, p. 122 of the teacher materials for a lesson entitled "Addition and Subtraction Strategies" in the unit "Putting Together and Taking Apart." Copyright © 1998 by Pearson/Scott Foresman/Addison Wesley Education, Inc. Reprinted by permission. The teacher is leading a whole-class discussion with a group of primary-aged children who have not yet learned any formal processes for doing addition of two-digit numbers.

How Many Buttons?

In this discussion the teacher is recording strategies for solving the following problem:

Kira and Jake were playing Cover-Up. Jake covered 19 buttons, Kira counted 24 buttons that were not covered. How many buttons did they have in all?

[*As students explain their strategies, the teacher records them, then asks students to think about whether they solved the problem in a similar way.*]

SIMON: I added 19 to 24.

TEACHER: How did you do it?

SIMON: I know 24 is 20 plus 4, so I added 20 to 19. That's 39. Then I added the 4. That's 43.

[*The teacher writes*]

$$19 + 20 = 39$$
$$39 + 4 = 43$$

TEACHER: Simon, does this show your strategy? Did anyone else use a way similar to Simon?

LAURA: Well, I added on the 20 by 10s. 19 plus 10 is 29; 29 plus 10 is 39. Then 4 more is 43.

TEACHER: You broke apart the 24 into 10 plus 10 plus 4.

PHOEBE: I did it a little different. I added the 19 to the 24. Like I went 10 plus 9 is 19, so 24 plus 10 is 34, then add the 9 to the 34.

[*The teacher records*]

```
   19 + 24        24 + 10 = 34      34 + 9 = 43
   / \
  10 + 9
```

TEACHER: These strategies are similar. Each person broke apart one of the numbers into smaller numbers—in each case a multiple of 10—that were easier to work with. Any more strategies?

FRANCO: I drew 24 lines in a row. Then I drew 19 and then I counted 19 and 24 and got 43.

[*The teacher draws 24 vertical lines and then 19 vertical lines.*]

TEACHER: Did you count all of them?

FRANCO: Yes.

[*The teacher writes "counted all" under Franco's vertical lines.*]

PAUL: I built towers of 19 cubes and 24 cubes, then I put them together and counted them.

[*The teacher adds "Paul used cubes and counted all" to Franco's strategy.*]

JUANITA: I wrote the problem 19 plus 24 going up and down.

TEACHER: Like this? [*The teacher records the problem using vertical notation.*]

$$\begin{array}{r} 19 \\ +24 \end{array}$$

JUANITA: Well, first I added the 9 and 4 and got 13. Then I added the 2 and 1 and got 3. [*Juanita shows her written work.*]:

$$\begin{array}{r} 19 \\ +24 \\ \hline 313 \end{array}$$

But I knew it couldn't be this high a number. So then I did 30 plus 13 and got 43.

[*The teacher writes*]

$$\begin{array}{r} 19 \\ +24 \\ \hline 30 + 13 = 43 \end{array}$$

JUANITA: You can't put the 13 below the line. It's too big. You have to do something like borrow.

TEACHER: Yes, you have to do something with the 13.

JEFFREY: The 1 goes over here with the other 10s.

TEACHER: Juanita's way works because this helps her remember that this is 30, not 3. [*The teacher points to the tens column.*]

BJORN: I did 10 plus 20 is 30, and then 4 plus 9 is 13, and 30 plus 13 is 43.

[*The teacher records*]

$$10 + 20 = 30$$
$$4 + 9 = 13$$
$$30 + 13 = 43$$

JUANITA: Hey, that's sort of like me!

TEACHER: Juanita's way of solving the problem and Bjorn's way are similar. They just recorded and kept track of their thinking in different ways.

◀ Introduction

For hundreds of years, computational skill with paper-and-pencil procedures, called *algorithms*, has been viewed as an essential component of children's mathematical education. The teaching of computation has become more exciting in the past few years. Instead of teachers merely presenting algorithms, showing children just what to do, step by step by step, the focus has shifted to more attention on what children construct or develop for themselves. Computation has become a problem-solving process, one in which children are encouraged to reason their way to answers, rather than merely memorizing procedures that the teacher says are correct.

This change also means that children can explore alternative algorithms. The algorithms that teachers usually present have been refined over the centuries. They are highly efficient, but they do not necessarily reflect the way children think as they compute. Accuracy and efficiency are still impor-

tant, but efficiency is of lesser importance. The focus is on reasoning and thinking as emphasized in NCTM's *Principles and Standards for School Mathematics* (2000), through the Reasoning and Proof Standard (see Appendix A).

Math Links 11.1

*T*he full-text version of NCTM's *Principles and Standards for School Mathematics* (PSSM) is available to non-NCTM members for a 90-day free trial. Visit www.nctm.org to sign up. An all-grades overview of the Number and Operations Standard is provided in PSSM Chapter 3, but you can also click on Pre-K–2, 3–5, or 6–8 for more detailed information by grade level. Access electronic interactive examples tied to the Standards (no membership required) by going to http://standards.nctm.org/document/eexamples/index.htm or linking from this book's Web site.

www.wiley.com/college/reys

Although calculators are readily available to relieve the burden of computation, the ability to use algorithms is still considered essential. The NCTM *Standards* stress the need for children to be able to choose computational techniques that are appropriate for problems at hand and also to determine whether the answers they obtain are reasonable. As described in the Number and Operations Standard (see Appendix A), students must have access to computational methods that are supported by an understanding of numbers and operations.

A balance between conceptual understanding and computational proficiency is essential for developing computational fluency. To develop such an enhanced ability, revisions in the teaching of computation include the following:

- Fostering a solid understanding of and proficiency with simple calculations
- Abandoning the teaching of tedious calculations using paper-and-pencil algorithms in favor of exploring more mathematics
- Fostering the use of a wide variety of computation and estimation techniques—ranging from quick mental calculation, to paper-and-pencil work, to using calculators or computers—suited to different mathematical settings
- Developing the skills necessary to use appropriate technology and then translating computed results to the problem setting
- Providing students with ways to check the reasonableness of computations (number and algorithmic sense, estimation skills)

Math Links 11.2

A variety of Web resources for whole-number computation, that may be used by teachers and children, may be found at NCTM's Illuminations Web site under the Number and Operation Standard. It may be accessed from http://illuminations.nctm.org/swr/index.asp or from this book's Web site.

www.wiley.com/college/reys

Many parents and some teachers have worried that students will become so dependent on calculators that they will forget how to compute. This concern is not supported by research. Hembree and Dessart (1986) reported from an analysis of many research studies that the use of "calculators in concert with traditional instruction . . . can improve the average student's basic skills with paper and pencil, both in basic operations and in problem solving" (p. 96).

Over the years, educators have developed several models for teaching the algorithms for the 4 basic operations. Underlying the development of these models is the idea that children must be actively involved in constructing their own mathematical learning. Children may be more comfortable using a standard operational algorithm or an alternative variation; the choice is theirs. In this chapter, we emphasize the importance of teaching children to choose an appropriate calculation procedure, depending primarily on whether an exact or approximate answer is needed.

FOCUS QUESTIONS

1. Why are manipulative materials useful in helping children develop understanding of algorithms?
2. How can teachers help children develop the addition algorithm? Do all children need to use the same addition algorithm?
3. What are two standard subtraction algorithms and how did they develop?
4. How does the distributive property support the development of the multiplication algorithm?
5. What is the partial-products algorithm for multiplication, and how is it related to the traditional multiplication algorithm?
6. Why is the traditional division algorithm the most difficult for children to master?

Teaching Algorithms with Understanding

Computational fluency with addition, subtraction, multiplication, and division includes the ability to use various methods for computing and to recognize the relationships among the various methods. This ability requires that children learn the procedures for particular algorithms; however, they must also gain a conceptual understanding that supports this procedural understanding. As teachers focus their instruction on algorithms, they need to support children in gaining "a balance and connection between computational proficiency and conceptual understanding" (NCTM, 2000, p. 35). Two instructional considerations are important in ensuring that children do not just learn algorithmic procedures by rote, but that they learn them with understanding.

Math Links 11.3

*W*orking with electronic manipulatives can help children develop deeper understandings of multiplication and division. Visit http://nlvm.usu.edu/en/nav/vlibrary.html (or link from this book's Web site), then select Number and Operations, and scroll through to see all the choices available. Rectangle Multiplication and Rectangle Division are particularly recommended.

www.wiley.com/college/reys

Using Materials

The use of manipulative materials in developing understanding of the algorithms is essential. Materials form a bridge between the real-life problem situation and the abstract algorithm, helping to forge the recognition that what is written down represents real objects and actions. Children must be given sufficient time to handle the materials and make the transition to pictures and symbols (Thompson, 1991). Unifix cubes, base-ten blocks, rods, Popsicle sticks, beansticks and loose beans, buttons, and myriad other materials, either derived from the problem setting or representative of that setting, help children construct an understanding of when and how an algorithm works.

Using Place Value

Each of the algorithms for whole-number computation is based on place-value ideas, many of which were discussed in Chapter 8. Children need to have a firm understanding of these ideas before they can work effectively with the algorithms. Linking place-value ideas directly with renaming ideas is a necessary step as children explore and develop algorithms for each operation. Providing numerous trading activities is accompanied by renaming activities.

Regroup 138 ones into tens and ones using base-ten blocks:

138 is _____ tens _____ ones

Show 46 with bundles of tens and ones, using Popsicle sticks and rubber bands to bundle them:

46 is _____ tens _____ ones

Rename:

* 7 tens 16 ones = 8 tens _____ ones

Tens	Ones
7	16

T	O
8	6
7̶	1̶6̶

* 35 is 2 tens _____ ones

Tens	Ones
3	5

T	O
2	?
3̶	5̶

* 5 tens 3 ones to show more ones:

Tens	Ones
5	3

T	O
4	13
5̶	3̶

Write:

* 6 tens 5 ones in five different ways
* 37 in all the different ways you can

Don't be surprised at the many different ideas that arise in response to this last activity. Students frequently can handle challenges that you thought were beyond them.

Developing the algorithms that work with multidigit numbers has to evolve from students' understanding of place value, which

> . . . involves building connections between key ideas of place value—such as quantifying sets of objects by grouping by ten and treating the groups as units—and using the structure of the written notation to capture this information about groupings. (Wearne and Hiebert, 1994, p. 273)

 Addition

*F*luency with basic addition is a goal for the pre-K–2 grades, but gaining fluency depends on many diverse experiences in grouping and counting. As children work with multiple objects, they develop a concrete understanding of addition. They move objects together and use a counting strategy to identify the total number of objects. Initially, they may begin by recounting all the objects; later, this strategy often yields to a more efficient strategy of counting on. A closer look at how children make sense of addition reveals a wide variety of estimation and computation strategies.

Suppose you are teaching first grade. After a brief activity to review renaming numbers (e.g., renaming 52 as 5 tens 2 ones and also as 4 tens and 12 ones, and so on), you pose a problem to the children:

Jill and Jeff both collected baseball cards. Jill had 27 cards and Jeff had 35. How many did they have together?

To focus attention on the reasonableness of the answers they will find, you might begin with such questions as:

Would they have more than 50 cards? Why do you think so?

More than 100 cards? Why do you think so?

Then, you might give actual cards (or slips of paper to represent cards) to each group of four or five children, with the direction to figure out an answer, show it on paper, and be ready to tell why it is right. Instead of providing them with cards, you might simply encourage students to use whatever aids they are accustomed to using for math problem solving, such as tiles, base-ten blocks, an abacus, or drawing pictures. At other times, instead of working in groups, the children might be asked to solve the problem individually and to write an explanation of what they did. They need time and repeated opportunities to explore and invent strategies and to make connections between different ways of thinking about or doing the same process. After each group or individual has reached an answer, the whole class may meet to share the ways in which they solved the problem. You might record on the board the essence of each explanation.

- Group 1 counted out 27 cards and counted out 35 cards, and then counted all the cards together, one by one:

$$27 + 35 = 62$$

- Group 2 made 2 piles of 10 cards, with 7 extras and 3 piles of 10 cards, with 5 extras:

2 tens + 7
3 tens + 5
5 tens + 12, which is renamed as 6 tens + 2, or 62

- Group 3 recognized that 20 and 30 make 50, and 7 and 5 make 12:

$$
\begin{array}{r}
20 + 7 \\
+30 + 5 \\
\hline
50 + 12, \text{ or } 62
\end{array}
$$

- Group 4 relied on what Kim's older brother had shown her, first adding $5 + 7$, to get 12, writing the 2 ones and "carrying 1" ten, then adding it to 2 tens and 3 tens to get 6 tens, or 62 altogether. The teacher showed another way to record this way of thinking about the problem.

$$
\begin{array}{r}
\overset{1}{2}7 \\
+35 \\
\hline
62
\end{array}
\qquad
\begin{array}{r}
27 \\
+35 \\
\hline
12 \\
50 \\
\hline
62
\end{array}
$$

- Group 5 did almost the same thing, but because they thought about adding $20 + 30$ before adding 7 and 5, the teacher proposed recording their work a little differently:

$$
\begin{array}{r}
27 \\
+35 \\
\hline
50 \\
12 \\
\hline
62
\end{array}
$$

- Group 6 decided to work with a multiple of ten that is easier to think about, and then compensated. They checked their answer by doing the problem a different way too!

$$
\begin{array}{r}
27 + 3 = 30 \\
+35 - 3 = 32 \\
\hline
62
\end{array}
\qquad
\begin{array}{r}
27 - 5 = 22 \\
+35 + 5 = 40 \\
\hline
62
\end{array}
$$

- Group 7 added $27 + 5 = 32$, and then $32 + 30 = 62$. Some of the students in the class pointed out that you could also think $27 + 30 = 57$, and then $57 + 5 = 62$.

Everyone was sure they were right and could tell why—and they were sure that the other groups were right, too! Is 62 correct just because it is the answer every group reached? "No," retorted a number of children! It is a reasonable answer because 27 is almost 30, and 35 more would make it 65, but 27 is 3 less than 30, so 62 is right. Note that some of the students worked from left to right, as research has indicated children frequently do when constructing their own algorithms (Kamii, Lewis, and Livingston, 1993). Not all children used the manipulative materials, but those who did were able to describe or write an algorithm that modeled what they had done with the materials. Or they used procedures that they had invented outside of school. If children have had frequent opportunities to think about how numbers fit together, and how our base-ten system can help with mental computation, they will be more likely to be flexible in their thinking about computation. For example, In the Classroom 11-1 shows a game that helps students develop the ability to add and subtract 10 and multiples of 10 from any number.

In the Classroom 11-1

CAPTURE 5

OBJECTIVE: **Using a chart game to teach addition and subtraction of multiples of tens and ones.**

GRADE LEVEL: **K–3**

MATERIALS:

1. A chart divided into 100 squares numbered from 1 to 100.
2. A deck of 52 change cards numbered + 1, − 1, + 2, − 2, + 3, − 3, + 5, + 10, − 10, + 20, − 20, + 30, − 30, (each of the these numbers appears 4 times).
3. Student sheets for recording moves.
4. 12 markers of the same color
5. 1 game piece per person or group

How to play

1. Place each marker on any number on the chart.
2. Place your game piece on any number without a marker. That is where you will begin playing.
3. Place the change cards face down.
4. Take 5 cards from the deck of change cards.
5. Spread them on your table in the order in which you want to use them.
6. A number with a minus (−) sign tells you to take steps backwards. A number with a plus (+) sign tells you to go forward.
7. You can use one or more than one card at a time.
8. If your last count is on a marker, capture that marker.
9. You can only use your card or cards once. After you have used them place them face down on a discard pile, and replace them from the change card pile.
10. If your card or cards are not good, replace them with new ones from the deck and reshuffle the deck.
11. If you replace a card or cards you lose your chance to play.
12. Begin the game by placing markers on the squares shown in the chart below.

Activity

1. Jane's game piece was on 9 and she captured a marker on 25. She wrote her equation as:
   9 + 3 + 10 + 2 + 1 = 25. How many spaces did Jane move? Explain how you found this out.

   Rewrite Jane's equation to show how far she moved:
   9 + _____ = 25.

2. Lee's game piece was on 52 and he captured a marker on 85. He wrote his equation as:
   52 + 3 + 20 + 10 = 85. How many spaces did Lee move? Explain how you found this out.

   Rewrite Lee's equation to show how far he moved:
   52 + _____ = 85.

3. Kanye's game piece was on 10 and he captured a marker on 33. He wrote his equation as:
   10 + 20 + 2 + 1 = 33. How many spaces did Kanye move? Explain how you found this out.

   Rewrite Kanye's equation to show how far he moved:
   10 + _____ = 33.

4. Alona's game piece was on 72 and she captured a marker on 59. She wrote her equation as:
   72 − 10 − 1 − 2 = 59. How many spaces did Alona move? Explain how you found this out. Rewrite Alona's equation to show how she moved.

   Rewrite Alona's equation to show how far she moved:
   72 − _____ = 59.

5. Ramona's game piece was on 97 and she captured a marker on 56. She wrote her equation as:
   97 − 30 − 10 − 3 + 2 = 56. How many spaces did Ramona move? Explain how you found this out?

   Rewrite Ramona's equation to show how far she moved: 97 − _____ = 56.

6. Partner with one of your classmates. Now place the 12 markers wherever you want and start a new game of your own.

1	2	3	4	5	6	7	8	9	10
11	12	13	14	15	16	17	18	19	20
21	22	23	24	25	26	27	28	29	30
31	32	33	34	35	36	37	38	39	40
41	42	43	44	45	46	47	48	49	50
51	52	53	54	55	56	57	58	59	60
61	62	63	64	65	66	67	68	69	70
71	72	73	74	75	76	77	78	79	80
81	82	83	84	85	86	87	88	89	90
91	92	93	94	95	96	97	98	99	100

(Source: Adapted from Economopoulos, K., and Russell, S. J. Putting Together and Taking Apart: Addition and Subtraction. A Unit in the *Investigations in Number, Data, and Space Curriculum.* White Plains, NY: Dale Seymour, 1998, pp. 112–117 and pp. 180–184.)

Standard Addition Algorithm

Perhaps it occurred to you when reading p. 261 that some of the procedures the children used were as plausible for mental computation as for paper-and-pencil computation. Children need to recognize this, too, as well as that much addition involving one- and two-digit numbers can and should be done mentally. Lots of activities with re-naming have given these children a good base from which to tackle addition algorithms. Note that only the group that relied on what Kim's brother had told them came up with the standard algorithm:

$$
\begin{array}{r}
^{1} \\
27 \\
+35 \\
\hline
62
\end{array}
\quad
\begin{array}{l}
\textit{Think} \\
\hline
7 + 5 = 12 \\
\text{Write 2 in the ones column} \\
\text{and 1 in the tens column.} \\
2 + 3 + 1 = 6 \text{ tens}
\end{array}
$$

That most students did not use the standard algorithm should not surprise you. That algorithm is the result of centuries of refinement. It is commonly used because it is efficient (requires less writing than some other algorithms), but it is also less obvious. Someone probably needed to tell you about placing the one ten from 12 in the tens column. When students attempt to use the standard algorithm without understanding why it works, they may be more prone to errors than when they do addition in ways that intuitively make sense to them. For this reason it is important for the students to develop this idea from activities such as those in Figure 11-1. Here children experience the "creation and placement of the one" (or regrouping) by trading 10 units for 1 ten using the base-ten blocks.

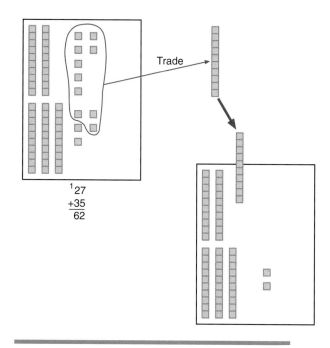

FIGURE 11-1   Base-ten blocks build the ideas of regrouping in the standard addition algorithm.

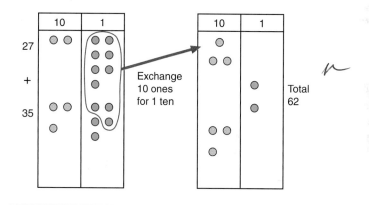

FIGURE 11-2   Use of chips and a place-value mat for modeling the standard addition algorithm.

as in Figure 11-2 provides a natural progression in building the notion of regrouping before introducing the standard algorithm.

Partial-Sum Addition Algorithm

The algorithm used by group 5 (p. 261) is similar to the standard algorithm but less obscure because all the partial sums are shown separately, so there is less chance for errors with regrouping. As group 5 used it, they added from left to right (tens first, then ones), which is more natural than working right to left. But this same partial-sum algorithm works equally well starting with ones, then tens,

---

Math Links 11.4

*P*ractice using electronic base-ten blocks to add whole numbers (or even decimals). See if you can use them to illustrate a variety of problems. Visit http://nlvm.usu.edu/en/nav/vlibrary.html (or link from this book's Web site), then select Number and Operations, and scroll through to see all the variations of base-ten blocks activities available.

www.wiley.com/college/reys

As groups share their different ways of working, children learn from each other. At some point, you will probably want to share the standard algorithm with the children, noting that it is shorter than some of their methods and that this is probably the way that their parents and other adults learned to add. Using chips and a place-value mat and so on (as shown by group 4). The partial-sum algorithm can be used as an alternative algorithm for addition (an end-goal for students) or it can be useful as a transitional algorithm (intermediate step on the way to learning the standard algorithm). Ideally, however, children should be encouraged to work with whichever procedure they find easiest to understand. There is no reason why all children should end up using the same algorithm.

Suppose the next problem posed to the children involved the addition of 13 and 54. Until recently, teachers might have introduced this problem, which does not require regrouping, far earlier than the one involving 27 and 35, which does involve regrouping. Teachers have come to realize, however, that this type of artificial control of problem situations can lead students to misconceptions about the operation and the algorithm. It is more realistic and better pedagogically for them to work, from the outset, on addition computations stemming from problems that involve both regrouping and no regrouping.

The addition of

$$
\begin{array}{c}
437 \\
+25
\end{array}
\quad \text{or} \quad
\begin{array}{c}
437 \\
+521
\end{array}
\quad \text{or} \quad
\begin{array}{c}
254 \\
+283
\end{array}
\quad \text{or} \quad
\begin{array}{c}
672 \\
+188
\end{array}
$$

is simply an extension of the regrouping procedure to the hundreds place. Children need enough experience with numbers with more than two digits so they realize that there are no hidden difficulties; if they had no calculators, they could do the computation. Most practice, however, focuses on two-digit numbers, with which they do need to become proficient.

Adding multiples of 10, 100, and so on is another simpler case. This is an important skill for students to develop, for use both in mental computation and estimation and as a building block in performing written computations:

$$
\begin{array}{c} 4 \\ +2 \end{array}
\qquad
\begin{array}{c} 40 \\ +20 \end{array}
\qquad
\begin{array}{c} 400 \\ +200 \end{array}
$$

As children work with addition (and other operations), they must be encouraged to estimate in order to ascertain whether the answer they reach is approximately correct. Use of *compatible numbers*—numbers that are easy to compute mentally—is a powerful estimation strategy. Some problem-solving activities to practice mental computation and

sharpen estimation skills, as well as deepen understanding of addition algorithms, are found in In the Classroom 11-2.

In the Classroom 11-2
STARTERS

OBJECTIVE: Using compatible numbers to develop mental computation and estimation skills involving addition.

GRADE LEVEL: 1–3

▼ Find each missing digit:

$$
\begin{array}{c} 52 \\ +16 \\ \hline 6\blacksquare \end{array}
\qquad
\begin{array}{c} 29 \\ +36 \\ \hline \blacksquare 5 \end{array}
\qquad
\begin{array}{c} \blacksquare 8 \\ +21 \\ \hline 79 \end{array}
\qquad
\begin{array}{c} 452 \\ +\blacksquare 7 \\ \hline 489 \end{array}
$$

▼ Use only the digits given in the cloud to make a problem with the sum shown:

$$
\begin{array}{c} 4\ 4 \\ +\ 4\ 6 \\ \hline 9\ 0 \end{array} \ (4,6)
\qquad
\begin{array}{c} -\ - \\ +\ \underline{-\ -} \\ 8\ 8 \end{array} \ (3,5)
\qquad
\begin{array}{c} -\ - \\ +\ \underline{-\ -} \\ 7\ 0 \end{array} \ (7,3)
$$

▼ Use 2, 4, 6, and 8 for these problems:
  • Use each digit once to make the smallest sum possible.

$$
\begin{array}{c} \blacksquare\blacksquare \\ +\blacksquare\blacksquare \end{array}
$$

  • Use each digit once to make the largest sum possible.

$$
\begin{array}{c} \blacksquare\blacksquare \\ +\blacksquare\blacksquare \end{array}
$$

  • Use each digit once to make a sum as near 100 as possible.

$$
\begin{array}{c} \blacksquare\blacksquare \\ +\blacksquare\blacksquare \end{array}
$$

▼ Use only these numbers:

| 24 | 40 | 22 | 15 | 31 | 14 |

  • Name two numbers whose sum is 64. _____
  • Name two numbers whose sum is more than 70.

  _____
  • Name two numbers whose sum ends in 8.

  _____
  • Name three numbers whose sum is 93.

  _____

Higher-Decade Addition

Combinations such as 17 + 4 or 47 + 8 or 3 + 28, called *higher-decade combinations*, are used in a strategy sometimes referred to as "adding by endings." Note that the two-digit number may come either before or after the one-digit number.

The need for higher-decade addition arises in many real-life problems; for instance, adding 6¢ tax to a purchase of 89¢. The skill is also necessary in multiplication. The strategy of counting on will probably occur to some children, and it is clearly one way of solving this type of problem, but counting on is not efficient. In the Classroom 11-3 focuses attention on the relationship of 9 + 5, 19 + 5, 29 + 5, and so on.
As a result of this activity, children realize the following:

- In each example, the sum will have a 4 in the ones place because 9 + 5 = 14, and the tens place will always have 1 more ten.

- The sum of 9 + 5 is 4 more than 10, so the sum of 19 + 5 is 4 more than 20 and the sum of 29 + 5 is 4 more than 30.
- For 59 + 5, there will be a 4 in the ones place and 6 (5 + 1) in the tens place.

Children need to learn to perform higher-decade additions automatically, without needing to think about adding ones and then tens and without counting on. Children who have already developed good number sense and facility with basic-fact addition strategies (such as those described in Chapter 9) should have little difficulty thinking through higher-decade addition problems. Looking for patterns such as those in In the Classroom 11-3, and explicitly discussing them with classmates and with the teacher, not only encourages mental computation but also greatly increases the skill of higher-decade addition.

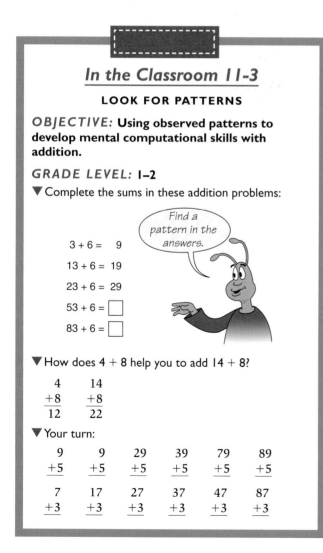

In the Classroom 11-3

LOOK FOR PATTERNS

OBJECTIVE: Using observed patterns to develop mental computational skills with addition.

GRADE LEVEL: 1–2

▼ Complete the sums in these addition problems:

Find a pattern in the answers.

$3 + 6 = 9$

$13 + 6 = 19$

$23 + 6 = 29$

$53 + 6 = \boxed{}$

$83 + 6 = \boxed{}$

▼ How does 4 + 8 help you to add 14 + 8?

```
  4      14
 +8      +8
 ‾‾      ‾‾
 12      22
```

▼ Your turn:

```
  9    9   29   39   79   89
 +5   +5   +5   +5   +5   +5

  7   17   27   37   47   87
 +3   +3   +3   +3   +3   +3
```

◆Subtraction

Like addition, subtraction of multidigit numbers requires prerequisite knowledge of basic facts and of place value. Experiences with trading or regrouping are important to develop the idea that 10 in any place-value column or a number can be traded for 1 in the column to the left, or vice versa. A child who has become comfortable with the idea, for example, that 37 can be thought of as 3-tens-and-7-ones, or as 2-tens-and-17-ones, or as 1-ten-and-27-ones, or just as no tens and 37 ones has developed the flexibility of thought needed to develop strategies for subtraction with meaning. Similarly, prior to learning subtraction algorithms, children benefit from plenty of experiences with problem-solving situations involving subtraction (solved in any way they can).

Standard Subtraction Algorithm

The standard subtraction algorithm taught in the United States for the past 50 or 60 years is the *decomposition algorithm*. It involves a logical process of decomposing or renaming the sum (the number you are subtracting from). In the following example, 9 tens and 1 one is renamed as 8 tens and 11 ones:

Think

$8\,1$
$\cancel{9}\cancel{1}$
-24 11 − 4 = 7 ones
‾‾‾   8 tens −2 tens = 6 tens
67

Children often naturally develop different algorithms for subtraction, just as they do for addition. They may try to work from left to right, and at this point some confusion may begin. But, if they think carefully about the numbers, they may construct alternatives such as the following:

$$\begin{array}{r} 74 \\ -58 \\ \hline 20 \\ -4 \\ \hline 16 \end{array}$$

or

$$\begin{array}{r} 70 + 4 \\ -50 - 8 \\ \hline 20 - 4 = 16 \end{array}$$

or

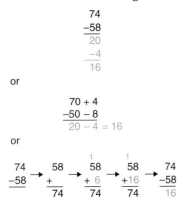

To learn to use algorithms with understanding, children need to connect the steps that are used to solve a problem with manipulatives to the steps in the symbolic solution of the algorithm. Questions that encourage children to focus on the connections between manipulatives and symbols are important. Consider the following example using a problem posed by Rathmell and Trafton (1990, p. 168):

There were 61 children who did not sign up for hot lunch. Of these, 22 went home for lunch. The rest brought a cold lunch. How many brought a cold lunch?

What are we trying to find? (How many brought cold lunch?)

Do you think it will be more or less than 60? (Less, because there are 61 children who didn't have hot lunch, but some of those went home for lunch.)

How many did not sign up for hot lunch? (61)

How many went home? (22)

How can we show this? (Use cubes to model 61, then separate out 22 cubes.)

Let's assume we want to subtract off the ones first.

Are there enough ones to subtract 2 ones? (No.)

How can we get more ones? (We can trade a stick of tens.)

If we trade in a 10 for ones, how many ones do we get? (10)

How many ones do we have now? (11) And how many tens? (5)

How much is 5 tens and 11 ones? (61)

Now are there enough ones to subtract 2? (Yes, we have 11 ones. 11 is more than 2.)

What is 11 − 2? (9)

Now what do we subtract? (the tens)

What is 5 tens minus 2 tens? (3 tens)

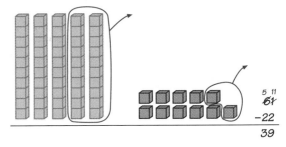

So, if we have 9 ones and 3 tens, how many children are eating a cold lunch? (39)

Does this answer make sense? Why? (Yes, 39 makes sense because it is close to 40. There were about 60 kids who didn't have hot lunch. There were about 20 kids who went home. 60 − 20 = 40. So there should be about 40 kids who brought cold lunch. Because 39 is close to 40, it makes sense.)

Experiences with regrouping from tens to hundreds or in both places are also helpful. In the Classroom 11-4 (Race-to-a-Flat and Give-Away-a-Flat) describes two games played with base-ten blocks that can help develop students' understanding of regrouping for addition or subtraction.

The presence of zeros in the sum demands special attention when the standard algorithm is used. In this example with zero in the ones place only, 50 is renamed as 4 tens and 10 ones:

$$\begin{array}{r} {\scriptstyle 4\ 10} \\ 850 \\ -237 \\ \hline \end{array}$$

When zero appears in the tens place, the problem is slightly more difficult, especially when regroup-

In the Classroom 11-4

RACING WITH BASE-TEN BLOCKS

OBJECTIVE: Develop students' understanding of regrouping for addition or subtraction using base-ten blocks.

GRADE LEVEL: 1–5

NUMBER OF PLAYERS: 2–5

MATERIALS: Base-ten blocks, place-value mat (full-sized paper divided into three columns) for each player, and one pair of dice

PLACE-VALUE MAT

Flats	Longs	Units

RACE-TO-A-FLAT

BEFORE THE GAME BEGINS: Choose one player to be the base-ten "banker."

HOW TO PLAY: Players take turns rolling the dice, adding the numbers on the tops of the two dice, and then asking the banker for that number of units. For example, if you roll a 4 and a 5 as shown on the dice, ask for 9 units.

Place the pieces on your place-value mat. You may never have 10 or more pieces in any portion of your place-value mat. Whenever you can, you must trade units for a long (or longs for a flat). When all the trading is complete, it is the next player's turn to roll the dice, collect units, and trade pieces. The first player to trade up to a flat is the winner.

GIVE-AWAY-A-FLAT

BEFORE THE GAME BEGINS: Choose one player to be the base-ten "banker." Banker distributes one flat to each player who places it in the flats column on her or his place-value mat.

HOW TO PLAY: Players take turns rolling the dice, finding the sum of the numbers on the tops of the two dice, and *giving away* that number of units to the banker. Clearly, trades will have to be made during each player's first turn and possibly again during subsequent turns. The first player to return all of her or his base-ten pieces to the banker is the winner.

QUESTIONS FOR GIVE-AWAY-A-FLAT

1. Is it possible to give away one long with one roll of the dice?
2. Is it possible to give away two longs with one roll of the dice?
3. Can you win the game with one roll of the dice?
4. What is the fewest number of rolls required to give away all of the pieces?
5. What is the most number of rolls required to give away all of the pieces?

VARIATIONS: To challenge fifth and sixth graders, race to a cube (1000) or give away a cube. For games involving larger goals, students can multiply the two dice instead of adding.

---

ing in the ones place is also necessary. Two ways to approach the regrouping (using either one step or two steps) are shown in Figure 11-3.

Math Links 11.5

*P*ractice using electronic base-ten blocks to subtract whole numbers (or even decimals). See if you can use them to illustrate the hot lunch problem. Experiences with problems that require regrouping from hundreds to tens (or even multiple regroupings) are also helpful. Visit http://nlvm.usu.edu/en/nav/vlibrary.html (or link from this book's Web site), then select Number and Operations, and scroll through to see all the variations of base-ten blocks activities available.

www.wiley.com/college/reys

A subtraction involving numbers with more than one zero is generally even more difficult. One alternative is multiple renaming—renaming from hundreds to tens, then renaming again from tens to ones:

$$
\begin{array}{cccc}
& & \overset{9}{}\,\overset{10}{} & \overset{9}{}\,\overset{10}{} \\
& \overset{4}{}\,\overset{10}{} & \overset{4}{}\,\overset{\cancel{10}}{} & \overset{4}{}\,\overset{\cancel{10}}{} \\
500 & 5\cancel{0}0 & 5\cancel{0}\cancel{0} & 5\cancel{0}\cancel{0} \\
-257 & -257 & -257 & -257 \\
\hline
& & & 243
\end{array}
$$

If students learn a procedure like this rotely, without understanding, it is likely that they will make errors but be unable to notice or correct them. Place-value experiences are important in preparing children to cope with these problems. They must clearly understand that 500 can be renamed as 4 hundreds and 10 tens, or as 4 hundreds, 9 tens, and 10 ones. They will then find it easier to recognize

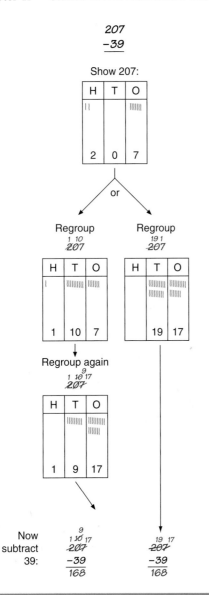

FIGURE 11-3   Place-value representations for the subtraction model.

the need for multiple regrouping when they see multiple zeros and will be able to do all the renaming at once:

$$
\begin{array}{r}
500 \\
-283
\end{array}
\qquad
\begin{array}{r}
^{4\ 9\ 1} \\
5\cancel{0}\cancel{0} \\
-283
\end{array}
\qquad
500 = 4 \text{ hundreds, } 9 \text{ tens, } 10 \text{ ones}
$$

Alternately, if they understand that 500 can be thought of as 50 tens, they can think of renaming it directly as 49 tens and 10 ones. In Figure 11-3, for the problem 207 − 39, 207 can be renamed as 19 tens and 17 ones in one step. The need to do this is not readily recognizable by all children, however; those who need to do the double renaming should be allowed to do so.

Partial-Difference Subtraction Algorithm

A common error made by children who have been taught to subtract without understanding, is to simply do the subtraction in each column separately, always subtracting the smaller number from the larger, without recognizing when regrouping is required. For example, a student might incorrectly write

$$
\begin{array}{r}
523 \\
-385 \\
\hline
262
\end{array}
$$

If your students make this sort of mistake, it's probably important to have them return to modeling some simple problems (such as 23 − 19 or 34 − 15) so they can see why the answers here are not 16 and 21.

However, an interesting correct variation of this approach is the following strategy, which we have named the "partial-difference subtraction algorithm" because it bears some resemblance to the previously mentioned partial-sum addition algorithm. Here, the subtractions in each column can be done in any order—left to right, right to left, or even out of order. You first write down the result of each subtraction, column by column, and then combine those partial-differences to get your final answer. The key is that when the bottom number is larger than the top number, you do not worry about regrouping—instead, you simply make note of how much more needs to be subtracted. For example, when doing 20 − 80, you write −60. (Adults may think of this as "negative 60," but children are more likely to think something like "Starting with 20, I can get to 0 by subtracting 20, but I will still need to subtract 60 more." The second step in the procedure is to combine the partial differences. If a child has developed good number sense for basic subtraction facts and for working with multiples of 10 and 100, it will not be difficult for him or her to do each part of the second step mentally (e.g., doing 200 − 60 = 140 mentally and, finally, 140 − 2 = 138 mentally). Note that the Capture game from In the Classroom 11-1 provides valuable practice in exactly this skill.

Multiplication

Before children tackle multiplication algorithms, they must have a firm grasp of place value, expanded notation, and the distributive property, as well as the basic facts of multiplication. As with the other operations, it is wise to review each of these prerequisites before beginning work with multiplication algorithms. It is also wise to develop situations or problems for which children compute mentally, without concern for the paper-and-pencil forms.

Multiplication with One-Digit Multipliers

Children should be encouraged to talk about their thinking, at the same time that the meaning of multiplication is reinforced with materials:

$$2 \times 14 = 14 + 14$$

Looking at these models, we can see not only that 14 can be represented by one bundle of tens and 4 ones, but also that 2×14 can be represented by *two* bundles of tens and *two* groups of 4 ones. This points out the use of the distributive property:

$$2 \times 14 = 2 \times (10 + 4) = (2 \times 10) + (2 \times 4)$$
$$= 20 + 8 = 28$$

Arrays can also be used to develop meaning and visual images of multiplication:

$$2 \times 14$$

$$2 \times 10 \qquad 2 \times 4$$

Place-value ideas are noted along with materials:

Expanded algorithms can be developed or constructed by the children

14	1 ten	4 ones	14	
× 2	×	2	× 2	
	2 tens	8 ones	8	$2 \times 4 = 8$
			+ 20	$2 \times 10 = 20$
			28	$20 + 8 = 28$

Partial-Products Multiplication Algorithm The partial-products algorithm for multiplication (Figure 11-4) is one form of the expanded algorithm, where all the individual products produced by the multiplication are recorded on separate lines, then summed. Just as the partial-sums algorithm for addition is a useful alternative or transitional algorithm, the partial-products algorithm can be useful for multiplication.

The traditional American multiplication algorithm is a streamlined version of the partial-products algorithm. In the traditional algorithm, some of the partial products are added mentally before writing down their sum. In some cases this traditional method is more efficient (because it requires less writing), but it is not as easy to understand step-by-step and it may be more susceptible to error (because steps are combined and done mentally).

The distributive property helps children understand the relationship between the partial-products algorithm and the traditional algorithm (see Figure 11-4). Whenever students see a multiplication such as 7×124, they should readily think that it could be computed by finding $(7 \times 100) + (7 \times 20) + (7 \times 4)$. Similarly, they can think of 4×59 as $(4 \times 50) + (4 \times 9)$. Or, if the multiplication is to be

$$
\begin{array}{ll}
57 & \\
\times\ 3 & \\
\hline
21 & (3 \times 7) \\
+150 & (3 \times 50) \\
\hline
171 &
\end{array}
\qquad
\begin{array}{ll}
452 & \\
\times\ 7 & \\
\hline
14 & (7 \times 2) \\
350 & (7 \times 50) \\
+2800 & (7 \times 400) \\
\hline
3164 &
\end{array}
$$

$$3 \times 57 = (3 \times 50) + (3 \times 7)$$

$$7 \times 452 = (7 \times 400) + (7 \times 50) + (7 \times 2)$$

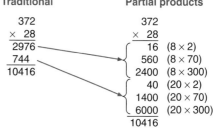

FIGURE 11-4 Multiplication comparing the traditional multiplication algorithm with the partial-products algorithm.

done mentally, they might think of 4×59 as $(4 \times 60) - (4 \times 1)$. In the Classroom 11-5 includes several types of activities that focus on using the distributive property.

In the Classroom 11-5

WHAT'S MISSING?

OBJECTIVE: Using number puzzles to develop estimation skills with multiplication.

GRADE LEVEL: 3–5

▼ Guess the numbers that will go into the circles and boxes.

Write your number and then check it on a calculator. Score 2 points if correct on the first try and 1 point if correct on the second try.

(④ ⑥ ⑦ ⑧   32 48 68 82)

◯ × ☐ = 408   ◯ × ☐ = 272

◯ × ☐ = 476   ◯ × ☐ = 336

◯ × ☐ = 384   ◯ × ☐ = 492

▼ Try these using only 2, 3, and 4. (You may use the same numeral more than once.)

☐☐
× ☐
4 6

☐☐
× ☐
6 6

☐☐
× ☐
8 4

☐☐
× ☐
1 2 6

• Now use only 4, 6, 8, and 9.
• Make the largest product. (Use each numeral only once.)

☐☐☐
×   ☐

• Make the smallest product: (Use each numeral only once.)

☐☐☐
×   ☐

Lattice Multiplication Algorithm   Lattice multiplication is an interesting algorithm, though not many people today are familiar with it. For each multiplication problem, you draw a rectangular lattice of boxes with diagonals drawn from bottom-left to upper-right in each interior square. You write the numbers to be multiplied on the top and right of the rectangle, one digit per square, and the boxes in the lattice help you organize where to write digits of the partial products. Some people really like this method because using the lattice eliminates the need for thinking about place value or for writing lots of zeros. Lattice multiplication is a very old approach. In fact, historians believe it has Hindu origins in India more than 900 years ago, though this method first appeared in print in the 1400s in Italy. In Fig. 11.5 you can see the same multiplication problem (26×368) done with the partial products algorithm (Method A) and with the lattice multiplication algorithm (Method B). Where do you see the answer in Method B? Look at the digits in each column in Method A and compare them with the digits found along each diagonal in Method B. For example, can you see which diagonal in Method B corresponds with each column (ones, tens, hundreds, thousands) in Method A? Can you explain to someone else how Method B works?

Multiplication by 10 and Multiples of 10

The ability to work flexibly with powers of 10 is an important prerequisite to handling multiplication algorithms with understanding. Multiplying by 10 comes easily to most children, and it is readily extended to multiplying by 100 and 1000 as children gain an understanding of larger numbers. Children can be shown a series of examples, after which they are asked to discuss and generalize, noting

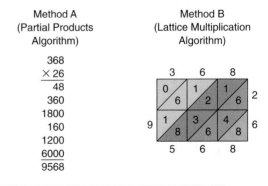

FIGURE 11-5 Comparing partial products multiplication with lattice multiplication.

that, when there is a zero in the ones place, each digit moves one place to the left in the product.

Multiplying by 20, 30, 200, 300, and so on is an extension of multiplying by 10 and 100. Emphasize what happens across examples and generalize from the pattern. For example, have children consider 3×50:

$3 \times 5 = 15$

3×5 tens $= 15$ tens $= 150$

$3 \times 50 = 150$

Then have them consider 4×50:

$4 \times 5 = 20$

4×5 tens $= $ _____ tens $= $ _____

$4 \times 50 = $ _____

A similar sequence can be followed for examples with hundreds, such as 2×300;

$2 \times 3 = 6$

2×3 hundreds $= $ _____ hundreds $= $ _____

$2 \times 300 = $ _____

Multiplication with Zeros

When zeros appear in the factor being multiplied, particular attention needs to be given to the effect on the product or partial product. Many children are prone to ignore the zero. Thus, for 9×306, their answer may (incorrectly) be

$$\begin{array}{r} \overset{5}{306} \\ \times 9 \\ \hline 324 \end{array}$$

When an estimate is made first, children have a way of determining whether their answer is in the ballpark. Writing each partial product separately, rather than attempting to add them mentally, can also help avoid place-value errors due to zeros. In the previous problem, a student might actually write the partial products 54 and 0 and 2700. Use of a place-value chart may also help students understand what the correct procedure must be, as will expanded notation:

Estimate

$$\begin{array}{r} 306 \\ \times 9 \end{array}$$

T	H	T	O
	3	0	6
			9
2	7	5	4

$9 \times 3 = 27$

$9 \times 300 = 2700$

$9 \times 306 = 9 \times (300 + 6)$

$= (9 \times 300) + (9 \times 6)$

$= 2700 + 54$

$= 2754$

Multiplication with Two-Digit Multipliers

When children begin to work with two-digit multipliers, the use of manipulative materials becomes cumbersome. Arrays or grids offer one way to bridge the gap from concrete materials to symbols and they also help illustrate, once again, why the partial-products algorithm makes sense. As shown in Figure 11-6, a grid can also provide entirely new ways of viewing and writing about a multiplication example. Materials such as base-ten blocks can be used to tie this work to previously learned procedures, but increasingly the emphasis will shift to working with symbols, as shown in Figure 11-7. This approach is possible because students already have a conceptual foundation built on the use of materials and on understanding of the distributive property.

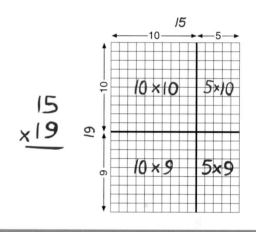

FIGURE 11-6 Use of a grid to solve multiplication with two-digit multiplier.

It is always important for students to connect new ideas to earlier understandings, continually building on a foundation of previous knowledge. Children should see that the process of multiplying by a two- or three-digit number is just an extension of the procedure for multiplying by a one-digit number. Similarly, illustrating this process by using an array is essentially the same no matter what the multiplier. Moreover, in the middle grades, when students begin to learn about symbol manipulation in algebra, they should be able to connect the new idea of multiplying binomials to their prior understanding of multidigit multiplication. In Figure 11-8, the illustration of the "foil" method for multiplying two binomials should look familiar because it is the same as the illustration for multiplying two two-digit numbers together; the simple explanation is that the distributive property governs both of these parallel procedures.

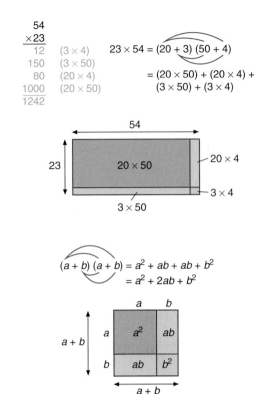

$$54$$
$$\times 23$$

12	(3×4)
150	(3×50)
80	(20×4)
1000	(20×50)
1242	

$$23 \times 54 = (20 + 3)\,(50 + 4)$$
$$= (20 \times 50) + (20 \times 4) +$$
$$(3 \times 50) + (3 \times 4)$$

$$(a + b)\,(a + b) = a^2 + ab + ab + b^2$$
$$= a^2 + 2ab + b^2$$

FIGURE 11-7   Multiplication with two-digit multiplier.

FIGURE 11-8   Extending multiplication ideas to algebra.

Multiplication with Large Numbers

How can we use a calculator to solve computations involving numbers that appear too big for the calculator? As children experiment with using a calculator for multiplication, there will come a time when they overload the calculator. Sometimes the number to be entered contains more digits than the display will show. At other times the factors can be entered, but the product will be too big for the display. For instance, if this example is entered in a four-function calculator, an error message results:

$$2345678$$
$$\times \quad 4003$$

When this happens, children should be encouraged to estimate an answer and then use the distributive property plus mental computation along with the calculator.

Estimate

$4000 \times 2000000 = 8000000000$
$4003 = 4000 + 3$
$\quad\;\; = (4 \times 1000) + 3$

Calculate

$4 \times 2345678 = 9382712$ (with the calculator)
$9382712 \times 1000 = 9382712000$ (mentally)
$3 \times 2345678 = 7037034$

Add

$$7037034$$
$$+\; 9382712000$$

Such examples show how an understanding of multiplication, plus problem-solving skills, can be used with calculators to reach a solution. Use of the calculator, mental computation, and paper-and-pencil recording may be integrated to solve a single problem. This sort of approach reminds us that calculator algorithms differ from the currently used paper-and-pencil algorithms.

Division

The traditional division algorithm is without doubt the most difficult of the algorithms for children to master, for several reasons:

- Computation begins at the left, rather than at the right as for the other operations.

- The algorithm involves not only the basic division facts but also subtraction and multiplication.

- There are several interactions in the algorithm, but their pattern moves from one spot to another.

• Trial quotients, involving estimation, must be used and may not always be successful at the first attempt—or even the second.

Many teachers struggle to teach the long division algorithm, and many children struggle to learn it. Since handheld calculators became readily available more than 30 years ago, making it possible for everyone to calculate answers to division problems quickly and easily, mathematics educators have suggested that too much emphasis on the division algorithm can be a waste of scarce instructional time. As *An Agenda for Action* (NCTM, 1980, p. 6) indicated, about 25 years ago:

> For most students, much of a full year of instruction in mathematics is spent on the division of whole numbers—a massive investment with increasingly limited productive return. . . . For most complex problems, using the calculator for rapid and accurate computation makes a far greater contribution to functional competence in daily life.

On The National Assessment of Educational Progress (NAEP), some exercises are given both with and without the use of calculators. For example, on the fourth NAEP, third graders were given the problem 3)42. When calculators were not used, about 20% of the answers were correct; when calculators were used, about 50% were correct (Lindquist et al., 1988). On one item on the sixth NAEP, students who reported using a calculator scored 82% correct, and those who reported they did not use a calculator scored only 35% (Kenney and Silver, 1997). Even more dramatic were results from the second NAEP (Carpenter et al., 1981). One exercise involving division by a two-digit divisor was given to 9-, 13-, and 17-year-olds. All the 9-year-olds were tested with calculators available (perhaps because they presumably had not yet been taught division with a two-digit divisor). For comparison purposes, some students in each of the two older groups were tested with calculators, while others were tested without calculators. Thirteen-year-olds scored 46% and 17-year-olds scored 50% without calculators. With calculators, their scores rose dramatically, to 82% and 91%, respectively. Fifty percent of the 9-year-olds obtained the correct answer (with calculators available). Considering that half of the 17-year-olds could not perform the division even after years of practice, is it not reasonable to let them use the tool with which they are successful—and which they will use anyway for the rest of their lives?

The NCTM's *Standards* stress that in today's technological society, teachers should rethink how computation is taught and how it is performed. Helping students understand *when* division is appropriate and *how to estimate* answers to division problems is extremely important. In terms of actually performing computations, division with one-digit divisors should be the focus of instruction, followed by some work with two-digit divisors so that students understand how such division is done. Performing more complex division—perhaps any that takes more than 30 seconds to do—with paper and pencil is a thing of the past for adults. Schools should not demand that children spend countless hours mastering an antiquated skill. Teachers can't afford the instructional time for this task. Instead, estimation skills should be used to define the bounds of the quotient, so that the reasonableness of calculator answers can be determined—just as such estimates should be used with division with one-digit divisors and, in fact, with all addition, subtraction, and multiplication.

Division with One-Digit Divisors

It is essential to begin division instruction with real-world problems. The most important thing is for students to develop an understanding of what division is all about. There is no reason for children not to encounter division problems with remainders from the outset of their work with division. Children should be encouraged to use blocks or counters to model division situations and to explain their thinking. The teacher should help students see how their thinking can be clearly and efficiently recorded on paper. Thus learning a paper-and-pencil algorithm essentially turns into learning a way to record what is done concretely.

For example, Burns (1991) posed problems and had third-grade students explain their answers and the methods they used to reach them. One problem called for four children to divide 54 marbles equally. Group 1 counted out 54 cubes (to represent the marbles), divided them into four groups, and wrote:

> We think we get 13 each. We think this because we took the cubes and dealed out them one by one. We had two left. Bryce was sick so we gave the extra to him. (Burns, 1991, p. 16)

Other groups wrote:

> ***Group 2***: We had 54. We gave each person 10 because we thout if there was 40 there would be 4 tens and 14 would be left. Each person gets 3, witch leves 2. Each person gets 13.

> ***Group 3***: We drew 54 marbles and then I numbered them 1, 2, 3, 4, and then we counted the ones and then we knew that each child gets 13 marbles and we lost the other two.

Group 4: I wrote down 54. I took away 12. I got 42. I took another 12 away. I got 30. I took another 12 away. I got 18. I took another 12 away. I got 6. Then I took away 4. I got 2. I chiped each of them into halfs that made 4 halfs. Each person got 13 and a half. (Burns, 1991, pp. 16–17)

Burns noted that, from listening to each others' methods, the children not only heard different approaches to solving division problems, but they also learned that division can be done in a variety of ways. Their teacher might have helped the class see how each of their different explanations could be recorded symbolically in a slightly different way, but always with the same final result. Refer to Figure 11-9 to see how each group's work might be recorded.

FIGURE 11-9   Solutions of groups 1–4.
(Source: Burns (1991)).

Distributive Algorithm   Clearly, there are many ways to figure and record the answer to a division computation, and certain methods are much more efficient than others. Two algorithms have been used for division most frequently; both are effective. The *distributive algorithm* is most common and familiar and is considered the standard division algorithm by most Americans. Consider the problem of sharing $954 among 4 people (refer to Figure 11-10a).

When using the distributive algorithm for this problem, first share as many of the 9 hundreds as possible (8 hundreds can be shared, 2 to each of the 4 people). Record how many were given to each person above (2 hundreds). Record the total number shared below (8 hundreds). Be careful to preserve place value by writing these numbers in the proper columns. "Subtract and bring down"

FIGURE 11-10a-d   Examples of the distributive division algorithm (a) and the subtractive division algorithm (b–d).

and note that you still have 1 hundred and 5 tens to be shared (or 15 tens). Begin the process again, sharing as many of the tens as possible, recording the number for each person above, recording the total shared below, and subtracting to see how much more still remains to be shared. Share 12 of the 15 tens, 3 to each of the 4 people, so write 3 above (in the tens place) and 12 below. Now, "subtract and bring down" again, noting now that you still have 3 tens and 4 ones to be shared (or 34 ones). Once again, share as many as possible, this time writing 8 above and 32 below, and then subtracting. You now have just 2 ones left. Starting with $954, you were able to give $238 to each of 4 people, with $2 left over.

Subtractive Algorithm   The *subtractive algorithm*, although not as familiar as the distributive algorithm, provides an intuitive and straightforward method for helping children learn to divide. This algorithm is easier than the standard algorithm for most children to learn because it is flexible enough to be made to correspond to a wide variety of approaches to thinking about division. Refer to Figure 11-10b for an example of how the subtractive algorithm might be used to solve this same division problem. You have $954 to share among four people. Perhaps begin by giving each person $50. Subtract and see that you still have $754 to share. Obviously, you didn't need to start with such a small share. Now choose to give each person $100. You still have $354 to share. You might give each person $50 again, leaving $154 still to share. You don't have enough to share $50 again, so maybe give each person $30. That leaves $34. Now give each person $8, leaving $2 as remainder. The total each person received was $50 + $100 + $50 + $30 + $8, or $238, the same answer you obtained above with the standard algorithm. The choices made here in using the subtractive algorithm were arbitrary. You might instead have chosen to repeatedly distribute $30, over and over, and in that case the problem would take a long time to complete (see Figure 11-10c). On the other hand, if you were efficient, the solution would look very much like the standard algorithm solution (see Figure 11-10d).

The thinking process used in the subtractive algorithm is also clearly illustrated by the work of groups 2 and 4 in the previous problem involving marbles. Both groups were computing $54 \div 4$. Group 4 began by recognizing that 12 marbles could be shared fairly among four people (three to each). So they first shared just 12 marbles (leaving 42 still to be shared). Then they repeatedly shared 12 more each time (leaving 30, then 18, then 6 still to be shared). Finally, they shared four of those final six, leaving two marbles (which, amusingly, they cut in half to complete the sharing). Because each person was awarded three marbles four distinct times (for a total of 12 marbles), and also was awarded 1 more marble plus $\frac{1}{2}$ marble, the solution can be written $54 \div 4 = 13\frac{1}{2}$. By contrast, group 2 initially thought about sharing 40 of the 54 marbles among the four people (10 to each). That left 14 still to be shared. Those 14 could be distributed 3 per person. Thus each person got 10 + 3 marbles (or 13), and 2 marbles were left over.

In using the subtractive algorithm, the child can choose to subtract off any multiple of the divisor at each step. Although the process may take more or less time, depending on how efficient the thinking is, the answer will be correct no matter how many steps are required. If children are extremely efficient, the subtractive algorithm can look almost exactly like the traditional division algorithm. Thus the subtractive algorithm can serve as a transitional algorithm (a stage on the way to learning to divide using the traditional method), or children may learn it as an alternative algorithm.

Although teachers can help children understand algorithms such as those described previously, they also need to let them explore. As with the other operations, children are likely to develop their own algorithms. Many students will use number sense, reasoning in terms of the numbers involved, as the following examples indicate:

$52 \div 7$ 52 divided by 7 is close to 49 divided by 7, or 7. But there are 3 left over. So the answer is 7 remainder 3.

$85 \div 5$ 20 divided by 5 is 4. There are four 20s in 80, so $80 \div 5$ is 4 times as much as $20 \div 5$. $4 \times 4 = 16$. And then there is one more 5 in 85. So the answer is 17.

$69 \div 4$ 60 + 9. 60 divided by 4 is 15, and 9 divided by 4 is 2, with a remainder of 1. So the answer is 17 remainder 1.

Have you begun to believe that the possibilities for constructing ways to find an answer are myriad? Just when you think you've seen all the possible algorithms, another student will probably come up with a new one. Enjoy this process. Be an explorer right along with the children. But you also have another role. Just because all these algorithms are correct doesn't mean that children never come up with incorrect algorithms. They do.

You need to watch for this possibility—and you need to make children aware of the need to prove that a procedure really works across examples. You also need to be aware of consistent error patterns that crop up in children's work—error patterns that usually indicate some difficulty such as lack of knowledge about place value, or a lack of mastery of some basic facts, or some other misunderstanding. Fortunately, there are sources of information, such as Ashlock (1998), to which you can turn. This source not only helps you identify the patterns but also provides specific suggestions for how to help the child get onto the right track.

As with the other operations, it is important that children work with manipulative materials as well as place-value charts. They need to keep in mind the problem situation and not forget that it is the process of sharing that is of concern, not merely working their way through the algorithm. A variety of experiences, such as those In the Classroom 11-6 and 11-7, may help children gain facility with the division algorithm.

There is evidence from research that students also need to be encouraged to do more reasoning about their work. In particular, middle school students were found to have a difficult time providing written explanations of their reasoning about division problems with remainders (Silver, Shapiro, and Deutsch, 1993). They did not associate "sense-making" with the solution of school mathematics problems. Some students assess their results by spurious criteria, such as whether a number "divides evenly" (Garofalo and Bryant, 1992). Help students become aware of the real-world applications of the mathematics they are learning, but also help them become aware of how reasonable the solution is.

Determining a reasonable answer can be particularly difficult with the division algorithms, but questions can help students make sense of them. A necessary first step in determining a quotient is to estimate the size of the quotient. Consider 839 ÷ 6:

Are there as many as 10 sixes in 839? [Yes, 10 sixes are only 60.]

Are there as many as 100 sixes? [Yes, 100 sixes are 600.]

Are there as many as 200 sixes? [No, 200 sixes are 1200.]

So the quotient is between 100 and 200—and probably closer to 100.

Consider another example, 187 ÷ 3:

Are there enough hundreds that we could divide them into three piles? [No. We have only one hundred.]

In the Classroom 11-6

THE MISSING DIGITS GAME

OBJECTIVE: Using a game to develop logical reasoning and number sense involving division.

GRADE LEVEL: 3–5

▼ Try this game with several friends who have been divided into two teams.

- Teams take turns selecting the leader for a round of the game.

- The leader starts a round by working out a division problem and putting the pattern on the board.

- Players on each team take turns asking about the digits that go in the boxes. For example, a player on Team A might ask if there are any boxes containing 2s; then a player on Team B might ask if there are any containing 7s.

- If a digit appears in the problem, the leader writes it in the appropriate box(es).

- A team scores a point for each box that gets filled in during its turn. If there are no boxes for a digit, the team scores 0 for that turn.

- The winner for the round is the team with the highest score. (If a team guesses the problem before all the boxes are filled in, it wins the round and gets bonus points for the number of boxes that are still empty.)

▼ Play several rounds to determine which team wins the game!

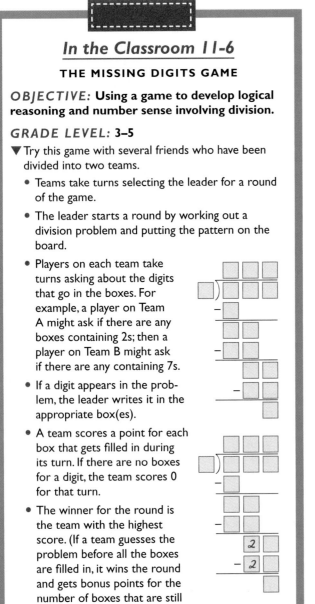

In the Classroom 11-7

MAKING EXAMPLES

OBJECTIVE: Using number puzzles to develop number sense involving division.

GRADE LEVEL: 3–5

▼ Make (and work out) a division example with
- A dividend of 47 and a divisor of 3
- A dividend of 81 and a divisor of 5

▼ Now make (and work out) a division example with
- A quotient of 6 r2
- A quotient of 10 r4
- A quotient of 23 r5

I know I can do this . .

▼ Try these:
- A divisor of 6 and a quotient of 15 r3
- A divisor of 3 and a quotient of 25 r2
- A dividend of 83 and a quotient of 11 r6

Are there enough tens? [Yes, 18 tens—from 1 hundred and 8 tens, and 18 tens ÷ 3 = 6 tens]

So the quotient has two digits [and there are 6 tens].

So you know the answer is between 60 and 70.

Developing the habit of mentally asking these sorts of questions helps students recognize the range for a quotient and mental questions such as these also help students make sense of the division algorithm, while developing valuable estimation skills.

Division with Two-Digit Divisors

Work with two-digit divisors should aim toward helping children understand what the procedure involves but not toward mastery of an algorithm. The calculator does the job of multidigit division for most adults, so there is little reason to have children spend months or years mastering it. Other mathematics is of more importance for children to learn.

The development of division with two-digit divisors proceeds through stages from concrete to abstract, paralleling the work with one-digit divisors. Much practice may be needed with the symbolic form if proficiency is the goal. Use of the calculator is interwoven into the activities, as indicated in In the Classroom 11-8, where the calculator is used to strengthen understanding of the relationships between numbers.

Making Sense of Division with Remainders

Children should encounter division problems involving remainders from the time they begin to work with division ideas (just as they should encounter addition involving regrouping from the outset). It is artificial and counterproductive to begin teaching division with problems that always come out even, saving problems involving remainders for later. As long as problems remain on a concrete level, the concept of remainder is rather easy. Here are some examples of varied situations:

- Pass out 17 candies to 3 children. (Each child receives 5 candies with 2 candies left over. Or, if the candies can be cut into pieces, each child could have 5 candies plus 2/3 of a candy.)
- To make each Valentine's card you need 3 pieces of lace. You have 17 pieces of lace. How many cards can you make? (You can make 5.

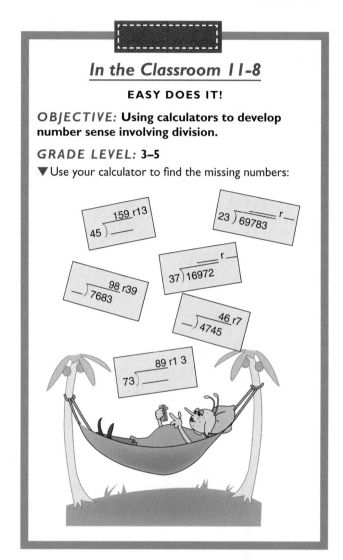

In the Classroom 11-8

EASY DOES IT!

OBJECTIVE: **Using calculators to develop number sense involving division.**

GRADE LEVEL: **3–5**

▼ Use your calculator to find the missing numbers:

$$45\overline{)}\ \ \underline{159}\,r13$$

$$23\overline{)69783}\ \ \underline{}\,r\underline{}$$

$$37\overline{)16972}\ \ \underline{}\,r\underline{}$$

$$\underline{}\overline{)7683}\ \ \underline{98}\,r39$$

$$\underline{}\overline{)4745}\ \ \underline{}46\,r7$$

$$73\overline{)}\ \ \underline{89}\,r1\,3$$

You'll probably have to discard the two extra pieces of lace.)
- If 17 children are going on the class trip and 3 children can ride in each car, how many cars are needed? (You will need 6 cars. With 5 cars you could seat only 15 children, with 2 children still waiting for a ride. With 6 cars, you can seat all 17 children, with 1 seat left over.)
- Separate a class of 17 children into 3 teams. (There can be 5 children on each team, and the 2 children left over can be the scorekeepers, or perhaps you could make two teams of 6 and 1 team of 5.)

Note that the remainder is handled differently in each of these real-world problems. In the candy problem, both the whole number (5) and the remainder 2/3 are reported as parts of the answer. In the Valentine problem, the answer involves only the whole-number part (the remainder must be discarded or ignored). In the class trip problem, the quotient is rounded up because the remainder cannot be ignored (no matter how small). In the team problem, children need to find some other use for the remainder (or they may abandon the attempt to form equal-sized groups if they want everyone to be able to play).

Thus it is important for children to think about and be able to deal with remainders as they appear in real-world problems. With calculators, the results of inexact division are expressed in decimal form, and children need to learn how to interpret the remainder when it is not an integer (see Chapter 13).

Initially, children are taught to write the remainder in one of the following ways:

$$
\begin{array}{r}
2 \\
6\overline{)13} \\
12 \\
\hline
1
\end{array}
\quad \text{with 1 left over}
$$

$$
\begin{array}{r}
5 \\
5\overline{)27} \\
25 \\
\hline
2
\end{array}
\quad \text{remainder 2 (later shortened to R2 or r2)}
$$

It is important to emphasize the real-life situations from which examples arise and to decide whether a "remainder of 2" makes sense in that situation. Activities such as the game in In the Classroom 11-9 provide practice in identifying the remainder.

Calculators can be used to solve problems with remainders, but the correct answer depends on the thinking a child does. Consider this problem:

A bus holds 36 children. If 460 children are being bused to a concert, how many buses do we need?

Research shows this problem to be difficult for children to solve with or without a calculator. An answer of 12 remainder 28 is often reported without a calculator, and 12.777 buses are reported with a calculator. The children seem more intent on producing an answer than on deciding if their answer makes sense. A sensible answer would be 13 buses (12 buses will be full and the last bus will have some empty seats).

◀ Checking

Just as it is important to estimate before computing, it is important to check after computing. Ordinarily, addition and subtraction are used to check each other, as are multiplication and division. Unfortunately, checking does not always achieve its purpose of ascertaining correctness. In fact, if you talk with children as they perform the computational check, you may find that they frequently force the check (i.e., make the results agree without actually performing the computation). Children

In the Classroom 11-9

THE REMAINDER GAME
(FOR 2 TO 4 PLAYERS)

OBJECTIVE: **Using a game to practice mental computation involving division.**

GRADE LEVEL: 3–5

MATERIALS:

- A copy of this gameboard on heavy paper
- Four cards of each numeral 0 to 9
- A counter for each player

GAME RULES:

1. Place the cards face down in a pile.
2. The first player draws a card.
   - For a player's first turn, divide the first number on the board by the number drawn.
   - For a player's additional turns, the dividend is the number on the space where his or her counter landed on the previous turn.
3. Move the counter forward by the number of spaces indicated by the remainder. If the remainder is 0, no move is made.
4. Each of the other players go in turn.
5. To get "home," a player must be able to move the exact number of spaces left. The first person home wins!

need to understand the purpose of checking, as well as what they must do if the solution in the check does not agree with the original solution.

The calculator can serve many other functions, but its use in checking has not been overlooked by teachers. Nevertheless, the calculator should not be used primarily to check paper-and-pencil computation. It insults students to ask them to spend large amounts of time on a paper-and-pencil computation and then use a machine that does the computation instantly. Encourage estimation extensively, both as a means of identifying the ballpark for the answer *and* as a means of ascertaining the correctness of the calculator answer. The words "use your calculator to check" should generally be used only when the calculator is to perform the computation following an estimate.

Choosing Appropriate Methods

As the NCTM *Standards* and the discussion in Chapter 10 make very clear, children must learn to choose an appropriate means of calculating. Sometimes paper and pencil is better; sometimes mental computation is more efficient. Other times use of a calculator is better than either, and sometimes only an estimate is needed. Encouraging students to defend their answers often yields valuable insight into their thinking. Children need to discuss when each method or tool is appropriate, and they need practice in making the choice, followed by more discussion, so that a rationale for their choice is clear. They need to realize that this is a personal decision. A problem that one child chooses to do with a calculator may be done with mental computation by another.

Building Computational Proficiency

Computational fluency with addition, subtraction, multiplication, and division is an important part of mathematics education in the elementary grades; however, "developing fluency requires a balance and connection between conceptual understanding and computational proficiency" (NCTM, 2000, p. 35). Research has demonstrated that extensive practice without understanding is either forgotten or remembered incorrectly (Hiebert, 1999; Kamii and Dominick, 1998). On the other hand, practice is important to help students gain the computational fluency desired. Teachers must carefully provide practice opportunities intertwined with the development and maintenance of conceptual understanding. If students use reasoning, their practice is more likely to help them develop computational fluency.

Many kinds of computer software are available on the market. The challenge is to identify programs that require more than mindless practice with the algorithms. You will find that most programs are typically visually appealing, and they use a variety of characters in a story format; however, few programs involve problem solving or estimation. Some involve the use of games to motivate the child's participation. The question you should ask is whether the software offers advantages over the materials you already have available. Your search for useful computer software must be guided by the mathematics and not by the "bells and whistles" features.

Worksheet activities are available for motivating students to practice their skills with computation. Some worksheets feature a mystery for the students to solve using the answers obtained by completing the computations. In the Classroom 11-10 illustrates one example of this type of worksheet. In this example, the answers to some of the multiplication problems provide clues to identifying the mystery number. The student must organize these clues to help identify the mystery number. While these types of worksheets provide needed practice, overuse can lead to mindless practice rather than actually helping students gain computational fluency.

Cultural Connections

The computational algorithms typically taught in the United States are not universal. In different parts of the world, people have different ways of doing paper-and-pencil computation. If you have children in your classroom who have attended school in other countries or whose parents were educated outside the United States, particularly in Europe or in South America, you may find that confusion may result when those parents attempt to help their children with computation. It helps if you, as the teacher, are well aware of the existence and validity of alternative algorithms. Asking students to explain their methods can help you uncover the reasons for errors that may arise if students confuse the steps from different algorithms. Sometimes you may need to do some careful thinking to figure out how an unfamiliar algorithm works, and why it is valid.

For example, the long division problem $360 \div 8$ is typically taught this way in American schools.

$$
\begin{array}{r}
45 \\
8\overline{)360} \\
32 \\
\hline
40 \\
40 \\
\hline
0
\end{array}
$$

This same computation might look like this in some other countries.

$$
\begin{array}{r}
360 \overline{)8} \\
40 \quad 45 \\
0
\end{array}
$$

In the Classroom 11-10

WHAT NUMBER AM I!

OBJECTIVE: Practice with multiplication to solve a mystery.

GRADE LEVEL: 3–4

▼ **Directions:** Solve each of the multiplication problems. Some of the solutions can help you identify the clues to help you find the mystery number. Circle the answers that are solutions to some of the problems; cross out the other clues. Use the clues to find the mystery number.

1.　15 $\times 9$	2.　51 $\times 21$	3.　63 $\times 24$	4.　68 $\times 21$
5.　77 $\times 21$	6.　18 $\times 15$	7.　22 $\times 14$	8.　69 $\times 66$
9.　18 $\times 9$	10.　72 $\times 9$	11.　88 $\times 18$	12.　34 $\times 31$

Answer	Clue
162	I am less than 100.
189	I am more than 100.
1502	I am an even number.
1071	I am an odd number.
1085	I am divisible by 3.
1308	I am divisible by 4.
280	I am divisible by 5.
647	I am a multiple of 3.
4554	I am a multiple of 5.
1607	I am a multiple of 10.
208	The sum of my digits is an even number.
1428	The sum of my digits is an odd number.

Sometimes this method is known as *Cuban division* because it was particularly noticed in the United States when many Cubans immigrated to Florida in the 1960s, although this same notation is also used in other cultures, including Arabic, Lao, and Vietnamese, and people in the Netherlands and in Poland also use a similar algorithm (Hirigoyen, 1997).

Children schooled in other countries may also use different methods for subtraction. In particular, it is helpful to be familiar with the *equal additions* or *add tens to both* method used in many European and Latin countries. In fact, before the now-standard decomposition algorithm for subtraction gained prominence in this country, the *equal-additions algorithm* was taught here too. The equal-additions algorithm is still taught and used in many other countries around the world (Ron, 1998). In the equal-additions subtraction algorithm, both the sum (the number you are subtracting from) and the known addend (the number you are subtracting) are renamed. In this example, ten is added to each number involved in the subtraction: here 10 ones have been added to the sum (91) and 1 ten has been added to the known addend (24):

$$\begin{array}{r} \overset{1}{9}1 \\ -\underset{3}{2}4 \\ \hline 67 \end{array}$$

Think
11 − 4 = 7 ones
9 tens − 3 tens = 6 tens

This algorithm works because the difference between the numbers (91 and 24) remains the same after both have been increased by the same amount [i.e., 91 − 24 = (91 + 10) − (24 + 10)]. It may help to picture a number line. The distance between 91 and 24 on the number line is what you are finding when you subtract. If you move both numbers up the number line the same amount (10), the distance between them remains the same. The reason for adding 10 to each number (but adding it in different forms) is to make the subtraction possible without any borrowing or regrouping. Although this algorithm may seem strange to many Americans, people who have learned to subtract this way generally find it easy and natural to use. What is important is that individuals understand *what* they are doing and *why* when they learn an algorithm. Research has confirmed that both the decomposition algorithm and the equal-additions algorithm are effective in terms of speed and accuracy when taught meaningfully (Brownell, 1947).

A third subtraction algorithm is used by the Japanese and it also involves doing some addition as part of the procedure for subtracting. To do 531 − 398 using the Japanese method, you first determine the "nines complement" of 398, then add that number to 531, then make an adjustment to get the final answer. The "nines complement" of any number is found by subtracting each of its digits from 9, so the "nines complement" of 398 is 601 (because 999 − 398 = 601). Add 601 to 531, and you get 1132. Remove the 1 from the front (thousands place), and add 1 to the one's place to get 133, and this is the answer to the desired computation: 531 − 398 = 133. (Why does this work? This question is left for you to ponder. Hint: at first you are actually figuring $999 + 531 - 398$. What happens next in the algorithm?)

Many other interesting algorithms are used throughout the world. Recognizing their validity and acknowledging children's rights to use them is important in supporting the cultural backgrounds of all students.

◀▲▶ A Glance at Where We've Been

Although computational skill is viewed as an essential component of children's mathematical achievement, its role in the curriculum and the methods of teaching it are changing. Helping children learn computational algorithms involves encouraging them to reason their own way through problems requiring basic computations. Important prerequisites to developing computational fluency include knowing basic facts, understanding place value, and using manipulative materials and drawings as models. We have provided suggestions for developing the standard (familiar) algorithms for each of the four operations, but also described many transitional and alternative algorithms. The use of calculators has been interwoven with activities that use the algorithms, as well as activities using other materials.

◀▲▶ Things to Do: From What You've Read

1. What prerequisites must a child have in order to succeed in the chapter's opening Snapshot of a Lesson?

2. Consider each example. Describe what a child would think as he or she worked. What questions might you ask to develop or explain the procedure? How could manipulative materials be used?

(a)
$$536$$
$$279$$
$$+\ \ 83$$
$$\overline{\ \ \ \ 8}$$

(b)
$$3\overset{2}{\cancel{4}}\overset{14}{9}$$
$$-1\ 84$$
$$\overline{\ \ \ \ 5}$$

(c)
$$73\overset{14}{\cancel{4}}$$
$$-269$$
$$\overline{\ \ \ 5}$$

(d)
$$\overset{5}{7}9$$
$$\times\ \ 6$$
$$\overline{\ \ \ 4}$$

(e)
$$45$$
$$\times\ \ 3$$
$$\overline{\ 15}$$
$$120$$

(f)
$$38\overline{)291}\ ^{9}$$

3. Explain why we do not recommend spending long periods of time drilling students on the long-division algorithm. What level of facility with division would you be satisfied with? How would you justify this position when parents question your teaching of computational algorithms?

4. Analyze each of the following student-invented algorithms. Do they work all the time? If so, do two more examples using that method. If not, explain why the method does not work.

a. Subtraction—uses missing addend addition

$$
\begin{array}{r} 3452 \\ -1784 \\ \hline \end{array}
\rightarrow
\begin{array}{r} \overset{1}{1784} \\ +\ \ \ \ 8 \\ \hline 3452 \end{array}
\rightarrow
\begin{array}{r} \overset{11}{1784} \\ +\ \ 68 \\ \hline 3452 \end{array}
\rightarrow
\begin{array}{r} \overset{111}{1784} \\ +\ 668 \\ \hline 3452 \end{array}
\rightarrow
\begin{array}{r} \overset{111}{1784} \\ +1668 \\ \hline 3452 \end{array}
$$

b. Subtraction—subtract from 10 when regrouping, then add on

$$
\begin{array}{r} 3452 \\ -1784 \\ \hline 6 \\ +\ \ 2 \end{array}
\rightarrow
\begin{array}{r} \overset{10}{\overset{4}{3}\overset{10}{4}52} \\ -1784 \\ \hline 26 \\ +\ 42 \end{array}
\rightarrow
\begin{array}{r} \overset{10\ 10}{\overset{2\ 3\ 4}{3}452} \\ -1784 \\ \hline 326 \\ +\ 342 \end{array}
\rightarrow
\begin{array}{r} \overset{10\ 10}{\overset{2\ 3\ 4}{3}452} \\ -1784 \\ \hline 1326 \\ +\ 342 \\ \hline 1668 \end{array}
$$

c. Subtraction—work left to right, crossing out when regrouping is needed

$$
\begin{array}{r} 3452 \\ -1784 \\ \hline 2 \end{array}
\rightarrow
\begin{array}{r} 3452 \\ -1784 \\ \hline \overset{1}{2}7 \\ 1 \end{array}
\rightarrow
\begin{array}{r} 3452 \\ -1784 \\ \hline \overset{11}{2}\cancel{7}7 \\ 16 \end{array}
\rightarrow
\begin{array}{r} 3452 \\ -1784 \\ \hline \overset{111}{2}\cancel{7}\cancel{7}8 \\ 166 \end{array}
$$

d. Division—uses distributive property to subtract twice for each multiplication by two-digit divisor

$$
\begin{array}{r}
2058\ \ \text{r}20 \\
23\overline{)47354} \\
\underline{40} \\
7 \\
\underline{6} \\
135 \\
\underline{100} \\
35 \\
\underline{15} \\
204 \\
\underline{160} \\
44 \\
\underline{24} \\
20
\end{array}
$$

5. Sketch a diagram to show how 12×17 can be modeled with an array on grid paper. Relate the model to the partial-products algorithm for 12×17, showing how each of the partial products in the array relates to the model.

6. Hands-on modeling of the traditional division algorithm: Consider a problem such as $798 \div 6$. Model the dividend (798) with base-ten blocks. The divisor (6) tells how many equal-sized piles you want to make. Start by sharing the biggest

blocks possible, and then make trades if necessary. Next, share the next-biggest blocks. Again, make trades if necessary and continue the process until all blocks possible have been shared. Try several other problems such as 458 ÷ 3, 597 ÷ 2, 4782 ÷ 4, and 7365 ÷ 5. After doing several of these problems using just the materials, do them over again and record your findings step by step.

Questions to ask yourself (repeatedly), after sharing cubes or flats or longs or units:

- How many did you put into each pile? (Write this number up top in the appropriate place.)
- How many did you share altogether? (Write this number below.)
- How many do you still have left to be distributed? (Write this number after subtracting.)

7. Consider problems involving subtraction with regrouping, such as 52 − 25, 91 − 79, and 47 − 18. How would you approach these problems if you were teaching second grade? What do you think children need to understand or be able to do before they can start learning subtraction with regrouping?

8. Assume you are a sixth-grade teacher. You notice that several of your students are making the same mistake when multiplying multidigit numbers. When computing 15 × 23 or 173 × 234, they seem to forget to "move over the numbers" on each line. They are writing:

```
      23                   23                234                    234
    ×15    instead       ×15      and      ×173    instead        ×173
    ‾‾‾      of          ‾‾‾       of       ‾‾‾       of           ‾‾‾
    115                  115               707                     707
     23                   23               1638                   1638
    ‾‾‾                  345                234                     234
    138                                    ‾‾‾                    ‾‾‾‾‾
                                          2574                   40482
```

What will you do to help these students? How will you help them correct their mistake?

9. For the problem 4578 ÷ 7, find the quotient by using the subtractive algorithm. Then do the problem again, using at least three more steps or three fewer steps than you used the first time to illustrate the flexible nature of this algorithm.

10. Write two story problems involving 35 ÷ 6 where the answers appropriate for the real world would actually not be the exact answer to the computation ($5\frac{5}{6}$). For your first story problem involving 35 ÷ 6, the appropriate answer should be 5. For your second story problem involving 35 ÷ 6, the appropriate answer should be 6.

11. Examine the games in In the Classroom 11-4 (Race-to-a-Flat and Give-Away-a-Flat). Answer the following questions about Race-to-a-Flat:

a. Can you win a long with one roll of the dice? Can you win two longs with one roll? three longs?

b. Can you win a flat with one roll of the dice?

c. What is the fewest number of rolls you would need to win a flat? the most rolls to win a flat?

d. What is the fewest number of units a player will need to play this game?

e. How many units, longs, and flats should you give each student, so that he or she is sure to have enough pieces to play the game no matter what rolls he or she gets?

Answer the following questions about Give-Away-a-Flat:

a. Is it possible to give away a long with one roll of the dice? two longs?

b. Can you win the game with one roll of the dice?

c. What is the fewest number of rolls required to give away all of the blocks?

d. What is the most number of rolls required to give away all of the blocks?

e. How many units, longs, and flats should you give each student, so he or she is sure to have enough pieces to play the game no matter what rolls he or she gets?

Things to Do: Going Beyond This Book

IN THE FIELD

1. *Computation in the Textbook and Classroom.* Choose a textbook for the grade level of a classroom you can visit and analyze a lesson plan on computation in the teacher's guide. What stages from concrete to abstract are involved in the lesson? Talk to the teacher about how he or she teaches computation. Is the textbook approach supplemented? How? What manipulatives, if any, are used? How?

2. *Addition with Regrouping.* Develop three evaluation items that would assess students' understanding of adding two two-digit numbers with regrouping. Explain why you chose the exam-

---

*Additional activities, suggestions, and questions are provided in *Teaching Elementary Mathematics: A Resource for Field Experiences* (Wiley, 2007).

ples that you did. Try your items with several children and analyze their responses.

3. *Transitional Algorithms.* Ask a classroom teacher if you can spend some time working with a student who is having trouble with paper-and-pencil computation (addition, subtraction, multiplication, or division, depending on age and grade level). See if you can figure out what the child's problem is. You might try helping him or her by suggesting the use of one of the transitional algorithms described in this chapter.

4. Choose two or three third graders and give them a word problem on addition involving two-digit numbers. Encourage them to use at least two different methods to solve it. Evaluate their methods and determine which ones are similar to the ones discussed in this chapter.

IN YOUR JOURNAL

5. Suppose you are a fourth-grade teacher. Following advice from the NCTM *Standards* (2000), you have decided to spend less time this year than in the past on multidigit multiplication and on long division. Instead, you will spend more time on mental computation, number sense, computations embedded in problem situations, and developing students' abilities to recognize and work with patterns and functions (early algebraic thinking). At the upcoming open house for parents, you want to explain to the parents how you have decided to modify your teaching approach and why. You decide that getting them involved with three or four problems as examples may be the best way to help them understand. Identify three problems to present at the open house. Write a brief narrative explaining why you chose each problem and how you would use it with the parents to convince them of the reasonableness of your new approach to teaching mathematics.

6. Some people wonder why it makes sense to encourage students to invent their own computational algorithms, since students are unlikely to discover the standard algorithms on their own. The standard algorithms, which are generally quick and efficient, were refined through centuries of invention and modification. Why not just teach the standard (traditional) algorithms directly to students? Answer this question in your journal—either agreeing or disagreeing that standard algorithms should be taught directly, and providing rationale for your position.

7. Consider the order in which the four operations + × − ÷ have been introduced in this chapter. Do you think the order in which they are taught to students matters? Why or why not? Analyze and write about the relationship among the four operations.

8. "Now that we have calculators, long-division algorithms should be abolished." Write a convincing argument, pro or con.

WITH ADDITIONAL RESOURCES

9. Choose a textbook for grade 3 or 4. Trace the development of multiplication algorithms. How are they introduced? What steps do children go through?

10. Choose a textbook series. Trace the development of division algorithms. What phases of development have been or should be modified because of the use of calculators?

11. Read "Computational Fluency, Algorithms, and Mathematical Proficiency: One Mathematician's Perspective" an article by the noted mathematician, Hyman Bass (2003). Using the five qualities that Dr. Bass considers important in evaluating the usefulness of computational algorithms, write an analysis of the relative usefulness of three multiplication algorithms: the partial products method, the lattice multiplication method, and the traditional method.

12. Go to www.nctm.org (Web site for the National Council of Teachers of Mathematics). Find *Principles and Standards for School Mathematics* (NCTM, 2000). Read the Number Standard for either the pre-K–2 grade-band or the 3–5 grade-band. As you read, think about what recommendations are made concerning teaching computational algorithms. Do you agree with NCTM's recommendations? Or do you take an opposing position? Why? Write a position paper in which you either agree with the NCTM's recommendations or take an opposing position. In either case, clearly explain and defend your point of view.

13. Pick a concept or skill from this chapter and compile a brief bibliography of recent articles containing research or teaching ideas on this topic.

WITH TECHNOLOGY

14. *Drill and Practice Software.* Find a drill-and-practice software program that is available at a local school. Learn to use this program and identify how you might use this software when teaching algorithms such as those developed in this chapter.

15. *Calculators.* In division, the calculator provides a decimal remainder. For example, for $476 \div 23 = 20.69565217$. Describe two different ways you could find the fractional remainder using a simple calculator.

16. *Internet software.* A search of the Internet will identify many Web sites teachers can use to create math worksheets. Find one of these sites and create a worksheet for practicing basic skills. Explain when or if you would recommend use of these worksheets.

Note to Instructors: You can find additional resources, learning activities, and black-line masters in this text's accompanying Instructor's Manual, at www.wiley.com/college/reys.

Book Nook for Children

Anno, M. *Anno's Magic Seeds.* New York: Philomel Books, 1999.

Jack meets a wizard who gives him two magic seeds and instructs him to eat one, which will sustain him for a full year, and to plant the other. The following spring, the plant bears two seeds. Jack eats one and plants the other, as he does for several years until he determines to plant both seeds. The next year he has two plants each bearing two seeds, he eats one seed and plants the other three. Six seeds! As the years go by, he marries, raises a family, plants many crops, endures a flood, and saves enough seeds to feed his family and start planting again.

Murphy, S. J. *Too Many Kangaroo Things To Do.* New York: Harper Collins, 1996.

A kangaroo is getting ready to have a birthday. His friends are planning a surprise party for the kangaroo. The reader will see how to add and multiply many different things that they will have at the party. There are activities and games in the back of the book for teachers and parents to use.

Murphy, S. J. *Divide and Ride.* New York: Harper Collins, 1997.

A group of 11 friends go to a carnival. At the carnival, some of the rides takes two people to a seat and therefore, they must divide themselves for the ride. The book uses different algorithms to show how they divide themselves for the rides, as well as tickets and other carnival activities. There are activities and games to use in the back of the book for teachers and parents to use.

Annotated Resources

Bass, H. "Computational fluency, algorithms, and mathematical proficiency: One mathematician's perspective." *Teaching Children Mathematics,* 9(6) (February 2003), pp. 322–327. A mathematician discusses five qualities that he considers important in evaluating the usefulness of computational algorithms: accuracy, generality, efficiency, ease of accurate use, and transparency. Using these qualities as a guide, he examines some familiar, alternative, and student-invented algorithms. He concludes that "teachers must combine a renewed appreciation of the contributions algorithms make to mathematical proficiency with a design of approaches to teaching and learning that can develop both understanding and skill. They must also appreciate what efficiency affords and respect what it takes to use compact methods sensibly, flexibly, and appropriately" (p. 327).

Burns, M. "Introducing division through problem-solving experiences." *Arithmetic Teacher,* 38 (April 1991), pp. 14–18. Using a problem-solving focus, Burns offers five ways to introduce division to third graders without resorting to an algorithm.

Campbell, P. F. "Connecting instructional practice to student thinking." *Teaching Children Mathematics,* 4 (October 1997), pp. 106–110.
This article explores children's thinking and its interconnection with a teacher's instructional decisions. Students frequently devise problem-solving techniques that are different from an adult's technique.

Carpenter, T. P., Franke, M. L., Jacobs, V. R., Fennema, E., and Empson, S. B. "A longitudinal study of invention and understanding in children's multidigit addition and subtraction." *Journal for Research in Mathematics Education,* 29(1) (January 1998), pp. 3–20.
This three-year study focused on children's development of number concepts. It shows that children can invent addition and subtraction strategies and explores those strategies.

Carroll, W. M., and Porter, D. "Invented strategies can develop meaningful mathematics procedures." *Teaching Children Mathematics,* 3 (March 1997), pp. 370–374.
Carroll and Porter investigate children's invented algorithms for meaningful computation. They assert that most primary students are capable of developing their own solution processes.

Harel, G., and Behr, M. "Ed's strategy for solving division problems." *Arithmetic Teacher,* 39 (November 1991), pp. 38–40.
This article asserts that good teachers build on student's knowledge and honor creative solutions. An example of such a solution from a second grader is demonstrated.

Huiniker, D., Freckman, J. L., and Steinmeyer, M. B. "Subtraction strategies from children's thinking: Moving toward fluency with greater numbers." *Teaching Children Mathematics,* 9(6) (February 2003), pp. 347–353.
Third graders exhibited four different strategies for subtracting of three-digit numbers. Through whole-class discussion, they were encouraged to consider the generalizability of their strategies. The goal of computational instruction should be to help students develop fluency, not simply to encourage them to come up with many strategies.

Kamii, C., Lewis, B. A., and Livingston, S. J. "Primary arithmetic: Children inventing their own procedures." *Arithmetic Teacher,* 41 (December 1993), pp. 200–203.
Kamii presents evidence supporting the idea that primary students can invent their own algorithms and offers suggestions of how to motivate them to do so.

Kouba, V. L., and Franklin, K. "Multiplication and division: Sense making and meaning." In *Research Ideas for the Classroom: Early Childhood Mathematics* (ed. R. J. Jensen). Reston, VA: NCTM, and New York: Macmillan, 1993, pp. 103–126.
This discussion of research shows that instruction should strengthen conceptual understanding of multiplication and division, instead of having students memorize rules. Action research ideas are included.

Morrow, L. J., and Kenney, M. J. (eds.). *The Teaching and Learning of Algorithms in School Mathematics* (1998 Yearbook). Reston, VA: NCTM, 1998.
This NCTM Yearbook addresses questions about teaching and learning algorithms at all school levels of mathematics. Consider potential curricular changes needed to reflect the broadening views about algorithms, especially the importance of algorithms in performance-based assessments. Capsule lessons with alternative algorithms suggest changes for the mathematics curriculum.

Silver, E. A., Shapiro, L. J., and Deutsch, A. "Sense making and the solution of division problems involving remainders: An Examination of middle school students' solution processes and their interpretations of solutions." *Journal for Research in Mathematics Education,* 24 (March 1993), pp. 117–135.
These researchers looked at how middle school students solved division story problems and considered models that helped explain students' difficulty.

Torrence, E. "Learning to think: An American third grader discovers mathematics in Holland." *Teaching Children Mathematics,* 10(2) (October 2003), pp. 90–92.
A mother describes the very different ways her third-grade son made sense of computation when he was enrolled in an American classroom, and when he transferred temporarily to a school in Holland. In America, the children were taught structured approaches to computation, but in Holland they were encouraged to develop methods that made sense to themselves. After this experience, the mother wonders, "Are we systematically teaching American children to be inflexible problem solvers from a very young age by teaching them the arithmetic algorithms so early?"

Thompson, F. "Two-digit addition and subtraction: What works?" *Arithmetic Teacher,* 38 (January 1991), pp. 10–13.
This article focuses on a study of three instructional strategies in second-grade classrooms. Findings of results with proportional materials and nonproportional materials, with pictorial models are discussed. Recommendations for teaching are offered.

Van de Walle, J. A. "Implementing the standards: Redefining computation." *Arithmetic Teacher,* 38 (January 1991), pp. 44–51.
Highlighting the teaching of computation and estimation as suggested by the NCTM *Standards,* the author discusses redefining computation. Specific activities for implementation in K–4 and 5–8 are included.

CHAPTER 12

Fractions and Decimals: Meanings and Operations

Snapshot of a Lesson

Key Idea

Extending students' concept of fractional to include regions with equal area

Background

This snapshot of a lesson is based on the video *Fractions with Geoboards*, from Teaching Math: A Video Library, K–4 from Annenberg Media. Produced by WGBH Educational Foundation ©1995 WGBH. All Rights reserved. To view the video, go to http://www.learner.org/resources/series32.html (video #37). Constance Richardson is a coteacher of a class of 40–50 students in Tucson, Arizona. In this video, the class is examining various ways of representing the halves of a large square on a 5 × 5 geoboard.

MS. RICHARDSON: What do we mean by halves?

After eliciting students' responses such as "two of the same size," "two equal parts," and "two equal lengths," Ms. Richardson asks the students how they would show halves on a geoboard. The students give this example:

They discuss how to tell the two rectangles are equal parts of the large square. One student focuses on the number of pegs, others say they look alike, while others consider the size of the rectangles. Ms. Richardson then asks what they mean by the same size, and this leads to counting the small squares. They establish that the area of each part (the halves) is 8 small squares.

The students' next example involves cutting the square on the diagonal to make two triangles. This leads to an interesting discussion of whether or not the area of each triangle is 8 small squares. Watch the entire video to see how the students establish this.

Ms. Richardson then challenges the students to find as many ways as they can to show halves. One group comes up with this example, saying, "The two parts looked the same." Ms. Richardson has them think about area. They see that each part consists of 6 small squares and two triangles. They

put the two triangles together and see that the two triangles are equivalent to two small squares.

Students come up with several other ways of showing halves of the large square, as illustrated below. Ms. Richardson has the students record their solutions on geopaper (see Appendix B) and then try to convince the class that their solutions do, in fact, show halves.

Introduction

Fractions and decimals have long been a stumbling block for many students. One reason may be that curricula tend to rush to symbolization and operations without developing the strong conceptual understandings that children must have for fractions and decimals. Therefore, much of this chapter is devoted to helping children develop the concepts they need for working with fractions and decimals and for the mathematical processes underlying operations with these numbers.

Figure 12-1 shows the Number and Operations Standard from *Principles and Standards for School Mathematics* (NCTM, 2000) with expectations about fractions and decimals for prekindergarten through grade 5. As the figure indicates, older children should work to develop fluency in the use of fractions and decimals only after they have developed estimation skills and relevant conceptual understandings.

Math Links 12.1

*T*he full-text electronic version of this standard is available at the NCTM's Web site, which you can access from http://www.nctm.org/standards (if you have a membership) or from this book's Web site.

www.wiley.com/college/reys

As you will see, the concepts associated with fractions and decimals are complex; however, two rather simple but powerful ideas—*partitioning* and *equivalence*—can help tie many of the concepts together. Partitioning refers to sharing equally (sharing a cake equally among eight people means partitioning the cake into eight equal portions; sharing six candy bars equally among four people means partitioning six candy bars into four equal portions). Equivalence focuses on different representations of the same amount (three-fourths of a cake is the same amount as six-eighths of that cake, so three-fourths is equivalent to six-eighths). Keep in mind that equivalence is not just a relationship among fractions but also among decimals and fractions. For example, $\frac{1}{2}$, $\frac{5}{10}$, and 0.5 are all equivalent ways of representing the same amount: one-half. Decimals are just another notation for fractions, but fractions can represent any partitioning whereas decimals can represent partitions of only tenths and powers of tenths (hundredths, thousandths, and so on).

In this chapter, the initial concentration on fractions does not imply that the entire study of fractions precede the study of decimals. Teachers can introduce decimal notation after a beginning foundation has been built with fractions. In fact, many operations with decimals are easier than the corresponding operations with fractions and can be taught meaningfully before you finish teaching operations with fractions.

There is some controversy over the importance of studying fractions, since technology uses decimals almost exclusively; however, common fractions are important in daily life and necessary for further study in mathematics, so current recommendations are that the development of computational fluency should include fluency with common fractions (Kilpatrick et al., 2001).

FOCUS QUESTIONS

1. What are three meanings of fractions, and what are models of the part-whole meaning?
2. How can you help children make sense of fractions, and how can you use concrete and pictorial models to develop children's understanding of ordering fractions and equivalent fractions?

Instructional programs from prekindergarten through grade 12 should enable all students to:	Pre-K–2 Expectations All students should:	Grades 3–5 Expectations All students should:
• Understand numbers, ways of representing numbers, relationships among numbers, and number systems	• Connect number words and numerals to the quantities they represent, using various physical models and representations. • Understand and represent commonly used fractions, such as $\frac{1}{4}$, $\frac{1}{3}$, and $\frac{1}{2}$	• Understand the place-value structure of the base-ten number system and be able to represent and compare whole numbers and decimals • Develop an understanding of fractions as parts of unit wholes, as parts of a collection, as locations on number lines, and as divisions of whole numbers • Use models, benchmarks, and equivalent forms to judge the size of fractions • Recognize and generate equivalent forms of commonly used fractions, decimals, and percents
• Understand meanings of operations and how they relate to one another	• Understand various meanings of addition and subtraction	• Understand various meanings of multiplication and division
• Compute fluently and make reasonable estimates		• Develop and use strategies to estimate computations involving fractions and decimals in situations relevant to students' experience • Use visual models, benchmarks, and equivalent forms to add and subtract commonly used fractions and decimals • Use a variety of methods and tools to compute, including objects, mental computation, estimation, paper and pencil, and calculators

FIGURE 12-1   Number and Operations Standard with expectations for children's learning of fractions and decimals in grades prekindergarten–2 and 3–5.

3. Describe how children can use estimation strategies for adding and subtracting by rounding to whole numbers and benchmark numbers to determine reasonableness of answers to fraction and decimal problems.

4. How can models assist the development of children's conceptual understanding of adding, subtracting, multiplying, and dividing fractions or decimals?

Conceptual Development of Fractions

The *Principles and Standards for School Mathematics* (NCTM, 2000) emphasizes that students should be given the opportunity to develop concepts as well as number sense with fractions and decimals. A careful examination of the items on the mathematics assessment of the National Assessment of Educational Progress (NAEP) reveals that concepts and models underlying fractions are not well developed by grade 4. Although older students can relate fractions to pictorial models, they do not realize that these models can be helpful in solving problems (Wearne and Kouba, 2000). Helping students develop the necessary conceptual understandings is better done with a curriculum that emphasizes many representations—physical, pictorial, verbal, real-world, and symbolic—than with more traditional approaches that depend only on rote procedures (Cramer, Post, and DelMas, 2002).

Many materials, such as fraction bars and pattern blocks, are available to assist you in helping children develop concepts about fractions (see Appendix B for paper versions of these commercial materials). Some of the most effective materials, such as construction paper and counters, are commonly found in the classroom.

Math Links 12.2

A variety of electronic resources for fractions and decimals for teachers and children may be found at the NCTM's Illuminations Web site under the Number and Operations Standard. It may be accessed from http://illuminations.nctm.org/ or from this book's Web site.

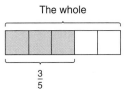

www.wiley.com/college/reys

Mathematics literature can also be very useful in helping children develop concepts for fractions. For example, *The Hershey's Milk Chocolate Fraction Book* (Pallotta and Bolster, 1999) develops the language of fractions. *The Doorbell Rang* (Hutchins, 1987) is excellent for introducing the concept of partitioning.

Three Meanings of Fractions

Three distinct meanings of fractions—part-whole, quotient, and ratio—are found in most elementary mathematics programs, but the focus is usually on the part-whole meaning, with little development of the other two meanings. Ignoring these other meanings may be one source of students' difficulty with fractions.

Part-whole   The part-whole meaning of a fraction indicates that a whole has been partitioned into equal parts—for example, the fraction $\frac{3}{5}$ indicates that a whole has been partitioned into five equal parts and that three of those parts are being considered. This fraction may be shown with a region model:

The whole

$$\frac{3}{5}$$

Quotient   The fraction $\frac{3}{5}$ may also be considered as a quotient, $3 \div 5$. This meaning also indicates partitioning. For example, suppose you had 20 big cookies to share equally among five people. If you gave each person one cookie, then another, and so on until you had distributed all the cookies, you could represent this process mathematically by the quotient $20 \div 5$—each person would get four cookies.

But what if you had just three big cookies and you still wanted to share them equally among five people? Now the quotient would be $3 \div 5$. How much would each person get? Would anyone get a whole cookie? One way to solve this problem would be to use pictures of the cookies, as shown in Figure 12-2. This interpretation of fractions is used when a remainder in a division problem is expressed as a fraction. It is also the interpretation that is needed to change a fraction to a decimal (i.e., $5 \div 8$ is the same as 0.625).

Begin with 3 cookies. Cut each into 5 parts

Each person gets $\frac{1}{5}$ of each cookie.

Thus, each person gets

$$\frac{1}{5} + \frac{1}{5} + \frac{1}{5} \quad \text{or} \quad \frac{3}{5} \quad \text{or} \quad 3 \div 5 = \frac{3}{5}$$

FIGURE 12-2   The quotient interpretation of a fraction.

Math Links 12.3

If you would like to see third and fourth graders solving a problem involving fractions, view "Cookies to Share" (video 36) from the Annenberg series, *Teaching Math: A Video Library K–4*, which you can access from http://www.learner.org/resources/series32.html or from this book's Web site.

www.wiley.com/college/reys

Some Types of Regions

Circle: Easy to see it is a whole; difficult to partition.

Rectangle: Easy to partition; difficult to know if it's a whole.

Triangle: Difficult to partition; difficult to know if it's a whole.

FIGURE 12-3 Types of regions for concrete models.

Ratio The fraction $\frac{3}{5}$ may also represent a ratio—for example, in a class of 6 boys and 10 girls, the ratio of boys to girls is 6 to 10 which is equivalent to $\frac{3}{5}$. That is, for every 3 boys there are 5 girls. What else could be the make up of a class with this ratio?

The ratio interpretation of fractions is conceptually different from the part-whole and quotient interpretations, since it doesn't involve the idea of partitioning. In this chapter, we focus on the part-whole interpretation and bring in the quotient interpretation as relevant (see Chapter 13 for discussion of the ratio interpretation).

Models of the Part-Whole Meaning

Attributes such as region, length, set, and area are useful in modeling the part-whole meaning of a fraction. The region is the most commonly used model for this interpretation of fractions because it is the most concrete and the most easily handled by children. You can also model the quotient interpretation using any of these attributes, but here again the region model is most often used because it is the simplest. Other attributes, such as capacity, volume, and time, also can model the meaning of fractions.

Region In the region model, the region is the whole (the unit), and the parts are *congruent* (same size and shape). The region may be any shape, such as a circle, rectangle, square, or triangle. You should use a variety of shapes when presenting the region model, so that the children do not think that a fraction is always a particular shape—for instance, "part of a pie" (if the region is a circle).

A rectangle is the easiest region for children to draw, and as Figure 12-3 indicates, it is also the easiest region to partition. (Try partitioning each of the shapes shown into three equal parts to see which is easiest.) The circle has the advantage of

being easy to see as a whole, but this does not outweigh the advantages of the rectangle, which we use extensively throughout this chapter.

Length Any unit of length can be partitioned into fractional parts of equal length. Children can begin by folding (partitioning) a long, thin strip of paper into halves, fourths, and so on. Later, you can use length partitioning to represent fractions as points on a number line. For example, as shown in Figure 12-4, you could partition lengths into thirds to help children realize that the number $4\frac{1}{3}$ is $4 + \frac{1}{3}$.

Keep in mind, however, that young children need plenty of prior experience with the number line before they can understand it as a model for fractions. For example, fewer than one-third of fourth graders could identify the point on a number line that represented a given fraction, even when the number line was partitioned into the same number of parts as the fraction indicated (Kloosterman et al., 2004).

Set The set model uses a set of objects as a whole (the unit). This model sometimes causes children difficulty, partly because they have not often considered a set of, say, 12 objects as a unit. In the 1996 NAEP, about three-fourths of fourth-grade students chose the correct region model for a given fraction, whereas only about half chose the correct set model (Wearne and Kouba, 2000). It is encouraging to note that there was a significant improvement on both these tasks from 1996 to 2000 (Kloosterman et al., 2004). Another, more obvious reason why children have difficulty with the set model is that they have

FIGURE 12-4 Length model of $4\frac{1}{3}$.

not had much experience with physically partitioning the objects in a set and sharing them. Instead, they have had the set model presented only abstractly, in terms of numbers—for example, as the idea that 5 pencils in a set of 12 pencils represents the fraction $\frac{5}{12}$.

Without mentioning fractions, you should give children experiences with physically partitioning sets. This will give them a background for both division and fractions. For example, you could ask a student to share 12 toys equally among four children. Later, you should focus on whether a given number of objects can be partitioned equally among a given number of people. For example, you can ask whether 15 toys can be partitioned (shared) equally among:

5 people? [yes]

4 people? [no]

3 people? [yes]

2 people? [no]

Once children develop the understanding to deal with these questions, you can use the set model for fractions (e.g., finding fifths by partitioning the set into five equal parts). Figure 12-5 shows a set of 15 marbles that has been partitioned into five equal parts. Each part is one-fifth of the whole set. From this modeling, children develop the set meaning of fractions and can answer questions such as these:

What is one-fifth of 15? [3]

Two-fifths of 15? [6]

Three-fifths of 15? [9]

Experience of this type allows children to solve many practical problems and prepares them for multiplication of fractions.

Area The area model is a special case of the region model, in which the parts must be equal in area but not necessarily congruent. Before using this model, you must be sure that your students have some idea of when two different shapes have equal areas. This makes the model more appropriate for older children (about third and fourth grade) than for younger ones. The Snapshot of a Lesson at the beginning of this chapter shows students in grades 4 and 5 using the area model for halves.

In the Classroom 12-1 shows examples and nonexamples of three-fourths. It provides a way to assess children's understanding of the different models—region, length, set, and area. Use it first as a self-assessment, and then try it with elementary

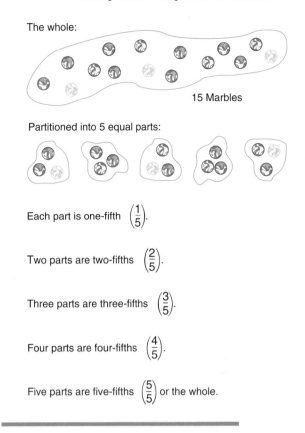

The whole:

15 Marbles

Partitioned into 5 equal parts:

Each part is one-fifth $\left(\frac{1}{5}\right)$.

Two parts are two-fifths $\left(\frac{2}{5}\right)$.

Three parts are three-fifths $\left(\frac{3}{5}\right)$.

Four parts are four-fifths $\left(\frac{4}{5}\right)$.

Five parts are five-fifths $\left(\frac{5}{5}\right)$ or the whole.

FIGURE 12-5 Working with a set model.

students. Which do you expect to be the easiest examples for students? Why?

Making Sense of Fractions

Begin to build children's conceptual understanding of fractions by starting with the simplest meaning and the simplest model: the part-whole meaning and the region model. After you introduce this model and the language and symbols associated with fractions, you can show the children other models of the part-whole (length, set, and area). Students can develop much of this conceptual background in early childhood, but you should be ready to revisit these ideas with students who do not have this background.

Partitioning The important idea in partitioning is the idea of making equal shares by separating a whole into equal parts. The whole is whatever is specified as the unit. At first, you should use a whole that will be obvious to children (e.g., a rectangle). If the whole is a region, then the parts must be equal in size and the same shape; if it is a length, then the parts must be equal lengths; if it is a set, then the parts must have the same number of objects in each, and if it is an area, then the parts must be equal in

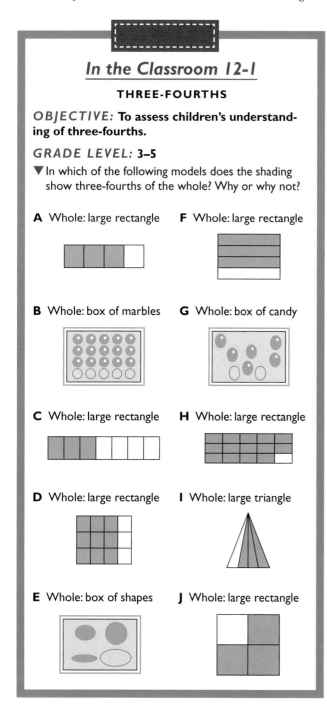

In the Classroom 12-1

THREE-FOURTHS

OBJECTIVE: **To assess children's understanding of three-fourths.**

GRADE LEVEL: 3–5

▼ In which of the following models does the shading show three-fourths of the whole? Why or why not?

A Whole: large rectangle

B Whole: box of marbles

C Whole: large rectangle

D Whole: large rectangle

E Whole: box of shapes

F Whole: large rectangle

G Whole: box of candy

H Whole: large rectangle

I Whole: large triangle

J Whole: large rectangle

area. Whatever the model, children must learn to partition the whole into equal parts and to describe those parts with fractional names.

Let the children do the partitioning. For example, each child could be given a "candy bar" (a piece of paper the size of a large candy bar) to share with a friend. Have them fold the "candy bar" to show how they would share it. Talk about whether a fold like the one sketched here would be a "fair share" for two people.

Move on to sharing equally among 3, 4, 6, and 8 people. For some of the more difficult sharing problems, such as with 5 people, you may want to use a strip of paper that has already been marked. When children become familiar with the process of sharing by partitioning regions into equal parts, describing the parts with words, and counting the parts, move to the other models. Children especially like to share collections of objects (set model)—for example, sharing 12 marbles between two friends is appealing to children because they can share fairly, with each friend getting half the marbles.

Words   As children develop the idea of equal parts, introduce the words *halves, thirds, fourths,* and so on. The words will be familiar to students since they are usually the plural of the ordinal words: third, fourth, etc. This connection can help, but you need to make sure that students hear the "s" and that they connect the word with the number of parts of the whole. Help them make that connection by asking such questions as, "How many fifths make a whole? How many eighths? How many twenty-fourths?" On the NAEP mathematics assessment, only half of the fourth-grade students correctly responded that 4 fourths make a whole (Wearne and Kouba, 2000).

Counting   Once children are familiar with the words for fractional parts, begin counting the parts. This process should not be any more difficult than counting apples, but the children need to know what fractional parts they are counting. In the Classroom 12-2 has a few ideas for getting children to practice counting fractional parts.

Counting the number of parts can lead to questions about ordering and equivalent fractions—for example, Which is more 3 fourths or 5 eighths? How many halves are equal to 4 eighths? Counting fractional parts can also help children see how much more is needed to make a whole. For example, if children have counted to 3 fifths with a model, they can see that 2 more fifths would make the whole. Counting fractional parts can lead to developing improper fractions and mixed numbers. For example, if three children are counting all the fourths they have, the class can hear the third child counting "9 fourths, 10 fourths, . . ." and can see that the three children have 2 wholes and 1 fourth, 2 wholes and 2 fourths, and so on. When they hear "12 fourths," they will see the 3 wholes. This also is a natural introduction to adding and subtracting fractions with like denominators.

After developing the initial ideas of partitioning, the words for fractional parts, and counting parts, you can introduce other fractional models. For example, In the Classroom 12-3 uses a length

In the Classroom 12-2

FRACTION BARS

OBJECTIVE: Develop an understanding of equal sharing and counting fractional parts using fraction bars.

GRADE LEVEL: 3–5

MATERIALS: 4 constructions paper strips (3″ × 9″) of 4 different colors for each child

Preparation of Fraction Bars: **Each child should fold a green strip into "halves," mark the fold with a dark line, and write halves on the back.**

Make fraction bars for thirds, fourths, and sixths in other colors in the same way.

ACTIVITIES:

▼ Ask each child to count the parts on a fourths bar: [one-fourth, two-fourths, . . .]

1, 2, 3, 4   fourths

▼ Ask each to count the parts of another bar.

▼ Ask a pair of children to count the fourths in two bars:

1, 2, 3, 4   5, 6, 7, 8   fourths

▼ Make sure the class sees that 8 fourths is 2 wholes, 6 fourths is 1 whole and 2 fourths, and so on.

▼ Ask a group of 4 students to count all the sixths in their group's sixths-bar.

▼ Challenge all the children to tell how many strips it would take to show 11 sixths or 23 sixths. Let them experiment in groups of 4.

In the Classroom 12-3

SHARING RODS

OBJECTIVE: To investigate sharing rods equally and naming the fractional parts and the amount in each equal part.

GRADE LEVEL: 1–2

MATERIALS: Unifix cubes or other connecting cubes

LAUNCH: Have each child make a unifix rod of 12 cubes and name it the 12-rod. Tell the children that we are going to investigate making halves, thirds, fourths, and sixths from the 12-rod.

QUESTIONS:

1. Have the children "break" their 12-rod into two rods of equal length. (Make 2 shares.) Ask the children: "What is each share (fractional part) called?" [halves] "How many halves make the 12-rod?" [2] "How many cubes in each half?" [6] "What is one-half of a 12?" [6]

2. Have the children make 3 equal shares from their 12-rod. Ask: "What fractional part is one share?" [thirds] "How many thirds make the 12-rod?" [3] "How many cubes in each third?" [4] "What is one-third of 12?" [4]

3. Have the children make 6 equal shares from their 12-rod. Ask: "What fractional part is 1 share?" [sixths] How many sixths make the 12-rod? [6] How many cubes in each sixth? [2] What is one-sixth of 12? [2]

4. Have the children make 4 equal shares from their 12-rod. Ask: "What fractional part is one share?" [fourths] How many fourths make the 12-rod? [4] How many cubes in each fourth? [3] What is one-fourth of 12? [3]

EXTEND

1. Ask the children how many cubes in two-thirds and three-thirds of their 12-rod. Continue with other fractional parts, such as two-fourths and five-sixths.

2. Use other rods, such as a 10-rod (halves and fifths) or a 16-rod (halves, fourths, eighths).

model and connects it to the set model while still using only the fractional words without symbols.

Symbols Symbols and written words should be used together or alternately until students understand the meaning of the symbols.

Using the written fraction symbol is appropriate only after children can name, count, and compare using oral language with facility. . . . Written symbols are developed in the same way as oral language. The

same kind of questioning can be used, but now the model and the oral language are connected with the symbol. (Payne et al., 1990, p. 185)

Connections can be depicted as follows:

Model:

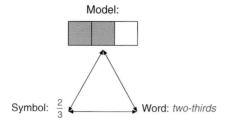

Symbol: $\frac{2}{3}$ Word: *two-thirds*

When children can match the words with the model, it is time to tell them that "$\frac{2}{3}$" is the symbol for *two-thirds*. Then they need many opportunities to make all three kinds of connections between the different representations:

Connection 1. Model and words

Connection 2. Model and symbol

Connection 3. Words and symbol

Textbooks usually concentrate on part of connection 2 (going from a model to a symbol), so you will find plenty of examples of these. However, they often do not go from a symbol to having the students produce the model. Connection 3 requires oral work, so you need to give children opportunities to solve problems and describe the solutions. When you read fractions, be sure to use the fraction words (e.g., "three-fifths"). Children who hear only "3 over 5" often think of two numbers rather than a fractional part.

Drawing a model   Children who have modeled fractions by folding paper or by choosing a picture should also be able to draw a picture of fractional parts. The rectangle is probably the easiest shape to use to show a good approximation of a fractional part. Encourage the children to be as accurate as possible, and do not worry too much about other aspects of their drawings. For example, which of these two drawings would you prefer as a picture of two-thirds?

Bob's work   Marilyn's work

Bob's work is neater than Marilyn's, but he seems to have missed the point that the three parts must be equal. You might help Marilyn be a little neater, but she does seem to have the idea of two-thirds.

Extending the model   Table 12-1 shows a question on the second national mathematics assessment and how children responded to it (Carpenter et al., 1981). Little has changed in the over 25 years since this item was given; the performance level on a

similar question on the 2003 assessment was almost identical for fourth-grade students (age 9). There is no doubt that this model is more complicated than those described in the previous section, since the number of parts (12) is greater than the denominator (3) of the simplest fraction corresponding to it $\left(\frac{1}{3}\right)$. However, this model is useful for introducing equivalent fractions and for teaching children how to order fractions.

Table 12-1 • Results of National Assessment Question Using the Region Model

What fractional part of the figure is shaded?

	Percent Responding	
Responses	Age 9	Age 13
Acceptable responses $\frac{1}{3}, \frac{4}{12}, .33$	20	82
Unacceptable responses $\frac{1}{4}, .25$	5	4
Top 4 or $\frac{4}{8}$	36	6
Other	15	6
I don't know	17	1
No response	7	1

You can also use paper folding to introduce the model in Table 12-1 as well as to introduce equivalent fractions. Give each child a sheet of plain paper to fold into thirds and to shade two-thirds. Then fold the paper in half the other way. Ask how many parts and what kind of parts [6, sixths]. Then ask what part is shaded, and make it clear that both $\frac{2}{3}$ and $\frac{4}{6}$ are correct answers. Tell the children that $\frac{2}{3}$ and $\frac{4}{6}$ are called *equivalent fractions* because they represent the same amount.

Folded into thirds

Folded in half to make sixths

Shaded to show $\frac{2}{3}$ is the same as $\frac{4}{6}$

Move to rectangle models such as the one below. Make certain the students can identify the way the paper was folded in both directions. Have them show thirds and fourths. Then have them identify $\frac{1}{4}$, $\frac{2}{4}$, $\frac{3}{4}$, $\frac{1}{3}$, and $\frac{2}{3}$, as well as $\frac{4}{12}$, and $\frac{8}{12}$. Some children will need to color in the parts on different models to focus their attention on the specific part.

Folded into fourths

Folded into thirds

After doing some more examples and getting more practice with folding paper, children should be ready for drawing. Reinforce the connection between folding and drawing by having the children make a step-by-step record of the folding process on a picture of a rectangle.

Going from a part to a whole   Most students can recognize a simple representation of a fractional part of a whole. However, asking students to figure out a whole when they are shown a fractional part will often reveal that children's understanding of fractions is limited. The following exchange from a fifth-grade classroom illustrates the kind of question you should ask (Mrs. May is the teacher):

MRS. MAY: If I told you that this picture represents three-fifths of a cake, could you draw a picture of the whole cake?

$\frac{3}{5}$ of a cake

ROSA LEE: It sure would be a skinny cake.

CAMILLE: That depends where the two-fifths was cut off.

MRS. MAY: You are both right; you won't be able to tell exactly what the shape of the cake was before it was cut. Let's pretend you can see that it was cut here [*pointing to the right side*]. What do you know?

GILBERT: You have three of the five equal pieces. If we divide this into three equal parts, we know how large one fifth is.

Three parts of the cake

OLAV: Now all you have to do is add the missing two fifths. Rosa Lee, it *is* a skinny cake!

Whole cake

Mrs. May continued the classroom discussion by giving the children other tasks—for example: Given $\frac{2}{7}$ of a stick of licorice (to represent a length) or $\frac{3}{5}$ (12 pieces) of a box of candy (set model), find the whole. Children work independently on several problems and then share their solutions. These types of tasks should also include an improper fraction (e.g., $\frac{8}{5}$) and a mixed number (e.g., $1\frac{2}{3}$), so you can see which students have made sense of fractions greater than one.

The importance of understanding equivalence   As we have discussed, making sense of fractions begins with partitioning and continues with the gradual introduction of words, symbols, and more complicated models and meanings. Before moving to operations with fractions, you must make sure that your students have a firm understanding of equivalence. Children who have worked only with whole numbers are used to describing the number of objects with only one number—for example, if they have counted eight objects, they will say "eight" or write "8" to describe those objects. Fractional parts, however, can be described in many equivalent ways, depending on the denominator—for example, one-half of a pie can be described with "$\frac{1}{2}$" or "$\frac{4}{8}$" (depending on the problem being solved, one name may be more appropriate than another).

Ordering Fractions and Equivalent Fractions

Part of understanding fractions is realizing that they are numbers and therefore can be ordered, added, subtracted, multiplied, and divided. The goal is to have children order fractions and find equivalent fractions symbolically, but you can help children connect the concrete to the symbolic. Not only will this connection help children realize what they are doing when they are ordering and finding equivalent fractions, but it also will give them another context in which to practice relating fractions and the models. Many problems involving ordering capture children's interest because they want to know which is more, which is shorter, which is larger, and so on. Problems about equivalent fractions are central to understanding fractions and being able to operate (add, subtract, multiply, and divide) with them.

Math Links 12.4

A wide variety of electronic fraction manipulatives may be found at the National Library of Virtual Manipulatives for Interactive Mathematics Web site, which you can access from http://nlvm.usu.edu/en/nav/index.html or from this book's Web site.

www.wiley.com/college/reys

Concrete models Children can make concrete models and then use them to order fractions or to find equivalent fractions. For example, fraction bars (see In the Classroom 12-2) are concrete models that children can make and then use to find out which is larger, $\frac{2}{3}$ or $\frac{3}{4}$. They can fold the thirds bar so that it is $\frac{2}{3}$ long and the fourths bar so that it is $\frac{3}{4}$ long and then compare the models to see which is longer.

Fraction bars can also be used as concrete models to find equivalent fractions. For example, by comparing a thirds bar and a sixths bar, children can readily see that $\frac{2}{3}$ is the same as $\frac{4}{6}$. For simplicity, our examples have focused on the rectangle and on paper models. Keep in mind, however, that children need to work with multiple representations. Pattern blocks (see Appendix B) are another model accessible to young children. In the Classroom 12-4 shows how to plan a lesson using pattern blocks for ordering fractions and finding equivalent fractions.

Pictorial models Children can also use pictorial models to order fractions. For example, the accurate scale of the fraction bars in Appendix B lets children compare lengths to decide which is larger, $\frac{7}{9}$ or $\frac{8}{10}$. These bars can also be used to identify equivalent fractions—for instance, children can see that $\frac{1}{2}, \frac{2}{4}, \frac{3}{6}$, $\frac{4}{8}$ and $\frac{6}{12}$ are all the same length and therefore represent the same amount.

You should also make sure that children are able to draw their own pictorial models to represent fractions, so they can solve problems for which no ready-made models are available. For example, suppose you give students this problem: Jacqui ate $\frac{1}{3}$ of the cake. Tom ate $\frac{2}{7}$ of the cake. Who ate more? You could have students approach this problem as follows:

1. Have the children draw two equal-size pictures of the cake, partitioning one into thirds horizontally and the other into sevenths vertically and then shading $\frac{1}{3}$ of one and $\frac{2}{7}$ of the other, as shown on the right:

In the Classroom 12-4

COMPARING MODELS

OBJECTIVE: Use concrete models to represent fractional parts of a whole

GRADE LEVEL: 3–5

MATERIALS NEEDED: Pattern blocks
The four basic shapes of the pattern blocks that you will use are the hexagon, triangle, rhombus, and trapezoid. Each child or pair of children will need multiple copies of each shape.

Let children have a chance to explore by making designs and seeing how they could make the hexagon with the other pieces.

IDEA ONE: Use the hexagon as the whole. What is the size of each of the other places? Use the pieces to show that

$$\frac{2}{6} = \frac{1}{3} \quad \frac{3}{3} = 1 \quad \frac{3}{6} = \frac{1}{2} \quad \frac{2}{3} > \frac{1}{2} \quad 2\frac{2}{3} = \frac{8}{3}$$

IDEA TWO: Use the figure made from two hexagons as the whole.

Use to cover the yellow shape. How many does it take? What fractional part of the whole is the rhombus? What fractional part of the whole is the trapezoid?
Use the shape to show that $\frac{3}{4}$ is greater than $\frac{2}{3}$.

IDEA THREE: Give the shape of a fractional part and have children construct the whole as in the lesson snapshot

If [shape] is $\frac{2}{3}$, what is the whole?

If [shape] is $\frac{3}{4}$, make the whole.

If [shape] is $\frac{1}{5}$, make the whole.

If [shape] is $\frac{2}{5}$, draw the whole.

Show thirds — Jacqui

Show sevenths — Tom

2. Have the children recognize that it is difficult to tell which shaded part is larger.

3. Have the children draw two more equal-size pictures of the cake, but this time partitioning both into thirds horizontally and into sevenths vertically and then again shading $\frac{1}{3}$ of one and $\frac{2}{7}$ of the other, as shown below:

Show both thirds and sevenths

Jacqui   Tom

4. Now the children can see that Jacqui ate 7 pieces and Tom ate 6 pieces, so Jacqui ate more (i.e., $\frac{1}{3}$ is more than $\frac{2}{7}$).

Your students may find other ways to solve the problem, but this is one approach you could have in your repertoire. Also, you can use the picture of the cake partitioned into thirds horizontally and into sevenths vertically to help children understand a symbolic way of comparing fractions, as well as to help them understand a way of adding and subtracting fractions.

Symbolic representation   It is easier to compare two measurements given in the same unit (e.g., 78 meters and 20 meters) than two measurements given in different units (e.g., 83 meters and 231 feet). Similarly, it is easier to compare two fractions that are symbolically represented by the same partitionings (e.g., $\frac{3}{5}$ and $\frac{2}{5}$, where the denominators are the same) than two fractions that are represented by different partitionings (e.g., $\frac{3}{7}$ and $\frac{2}{5}$, where the denominators are different). In mathematics, we often try to deal with difficult cases by changing them into simpler ones. With fractions, making the difficult case with different denominators simpler means expressing each fraction as an equivalent fraction so that both fractions represent the same partitioning—that is, so they have a common denominator.

Now we can see how to use the cake partitioning shown above to compare $\frac{1}{3}$ and $\frac{2}{7}$ by expressing them as equivalent fractions with a common denominator. The rectangle that has been partitioned into both thirds and sevenths is partitioned into 21 parts—that is, into twenty-firsts. Children can easily recognize that $\frac{1}{3}$ is 7 of the 21 parts, or $\frac{7}{21}$, and that $\frac{2}{7}$ is 6 of the 21 parts, or $\frac{6}{21}$. Since $\frac{7}{21}$ is greater $\frac{6}{21}$, $\frac{1}{3}$ is greater than $\frac{2}{7}$.

Students who have considered various models showing equivalent fractional parts such $\frac{2}{3}$ and $\frac{4}{6}$ will be familiar with the concept of equivalent fractions, but they may not have developed many of the skills associated with finding equivalent fractions

symbolically. Finding an equivalent fraction rests on the generalization that both the numerator and denominator of a fraction may be multiplied (or divided) by the same number without changing the value of the fraction. One way to develop this generalization is to start with a paper-folding model and symbolically describe what is happening:

Fold into fourths

Fold in half to make eighths

1. Make a model of $\frac{3}{4}$ by folding a piece of paper in fourths and shading three of the fourths. Write down how many fourths there are (4) and how many are shaded (3). Then fold the paper in half the other way to make eighths.

2. Have the children look at the fourths. Ask what happened to the fourths when the paper was folded in half. You created twice as many equal parts ($2 \times 4 = 8$).

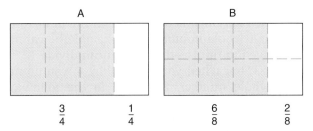

3. Notice that there are also twice as many shaded parts in B ($2 \times 3 = 6$).

4. Express the model symbolically:

$$\frac{2 \times 3}{2 \times 4} = \frac{6}{8}$$

After investigating more examples like this one, children should be able to make the generalization that multiplying the numerator and the denominator by the same number results in an equivalent fraction.

Note that you could also begin with the model of eight parts and describe how to get to four parts by dividing the eight parts by two ($8 \div 2$) and dividing the six shaded parts by two ($6 \div 2$). In this case, you would express the model symbolically as:

$$\frac{6}{8} = \frac{6 \div 2}{8 \div 2} = \frac{3}{4}$$

Examples of this type should lead children to make the generalization that dividing the numerator and denominator by the same number also results in an equivalent fraction.

After students have made these generalizations, that multiplying or dividing the numerator and denominator by the same number yields equivalent fractions, they are ready for exercises such as these:

1. $\frac{2}{3} = \frac{a}{12}$. What is a?

2. $\frac{8}{12} = \frac{4}{b}$. What is b?

In example 1, you need to lead students to ask "What is 3 multiplied by to get 12?" Once they have the answer to that question (4), they should think and write:

$$\frac{2 \times 4}{3 \times 4} = \frac{8}{12}, \text{ so } a \text{ is } 8$$

In example 2, they should realize that 8 was divided by 2 to obtain 4, so 12 also has to be divided by 2:

$$\frac{8 \div 2}{12 \div 2} = \frac{4}{6}, \text{ so } b \text{ is } 6$$

The first example illustrates the type of thinking needed to find a common denominator; the second illustrates the type of thinking needed to simplify many problems. Both show ways to express fractions as equivalent fractions in order to solve a problem.

You should also help children see that they cannot always change a fraction to an equivalent one with a specified denominator (if the numerator must be a whole number). For example, $\frac{5}{12}$ cannot be changed to thirds—that is, you can divide 12 by 4 to get 3, but when you divide 5 by 4, you do not get a whole number. Similarly, in the following problem, c cannot be a whole number (i.e., you cannot change $\frac{2}{3}$ to fifths):

$$\frac{2}{3} = \frac{c}{5}$$

There is no whole number that you can multiply 3 by to get 5. In the Classroom 12-5 will help children focus on whether or not a given fractional part (halves, thirds, etc.) can be changed to a different fractional part.

In the past, there was much emphasis on finding the *least common denominator*. For any two fractions, the product of the denominators always gives a common denominator, but this is not always the least common denominator. For example, a common denominator of $\frac{5}{6}$ and $\frac{3}{4}$ is 6 × 4, or 24, but the least common denominator is 12. The general point is that the least common denominator is the smallest number that can be divided evenly by both denominators (in this case, 12 is the smallest number that can be divided evenly by both 6 and 4). With small denominators, it is often easiest to find the least common denominator by inspection, and children will probably benefit more from that approach than from just learning a routine. In middle school, students can learn to use prime factorization to determine the least common denominator.

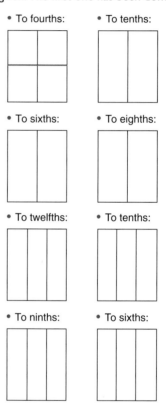

In the Classroom 12-5

CAN YOU DIVIDE IT?

OBJECTIVE: Use an area model to learn how to compare fractions.

GRADE LEVEL: 3–5

Here are a few ideas to start your discussion. After children understand these, have them investigate other fractional parts.

▼ All of these regions have been divided into parts with vertical (up and down) lines. Use horizontal (across) lines to see if you can change the model to the fraction given. The first one has been done.

- To fourths: • To tenths:

- To sixths: • To eighths:

- To twelfths: • To tenths:

- To ninths: • To sixths:

▼ Draw a region divided into fifths by vertical lines. Can you draw horizontal lines to change it to other fractional parts? Which ones? Write a conjecture and explain why you think it is true.

Children who can order fractions symbolically may enjoy the quick and easy game from In the Classroom 12-6. If they have difficulty playing, let them use a concrete or pictorial representation of the fractions. If the game is too easy, use a gameboard with 48 squares and fractions less than $\frac{1}{3}$ that may be expressed as equivalent

In the Classroom 12-6

WHOLE HOG

OBJECTIVE: To compare fractions.

GRADE LEVEL: 3–5

MATERIALS:

- A copy of the H grid.
- Squares of paper
- Markers

▼ Cut 10 squares of paper. Write one of these fractions on each square:

$$\frac{1}{2} \quad \frac{1}{3} \quad \frac{1}{6} \quad \frac{2}{6} \quad \frac{1}{9} \quad \frac{2}{9} \quad \frac{3}{9} \quad \frac{1}{18} \quad \frac{2}{18} \quad \frac{3}{18}$$

GAME RULES:

1. Shuffle the fraction cards and put them in a pile face down.
2. Each player picks a card from the top of the pile and turns it face up.
3. The player with the smaller fraction colors in that fractional part of her or his H.
4. Put both cards at the bottom of the pile.
5. If the player with the smaller fraction cannot color the fractional part shown on the card (because not enough of the H is left uncolored), both players put their cards at the bottom of the pile and pick again.
6. Continue playing until one player colors the whole H. That person is the first to go Whole Hog and loses the game.

▼ Make a new H and play again.

---

fractions with a denominator of 48 [e.g., $\frac{1}{4}(=\frac{12}{48})$ or $\frac{3}{16}(=\frac{9}{48})$].

Benchmarks

Initially, children need to develop facility with friendly fractions such as halves, thirds, and fourths, so they can relate these to fractions that look more intimidating, such as sevenths, elevenths, and twenty-fifths. By building what are referred to as *benchmarks* in *Principles and Standards for School Mathematics* (NCTM, 2000), children will be able to reason with these more difficult fractions. For example, when you consider the following fractions, you can easily see that they are all near one-half:

$$\frac{6}{11} \quad \frac{11}{23} \quad \frac{18}{35} \quad \frac{44}{90} \quad \frac{354}{700} \quad \frac{800}{1605} \quad \frac{100001}{200000}$$

Moreover, you can quickly say which are more than $\frac{1}{2}$ and which are less than $\frac{1}{2}$. Children can build this same intuitive feel for fractions near the benchmark $\frac{1}{2}$ by beginning with smaller numerators and denominators.

Students also need to be able to tell if a fraction is near 0 or near 1. This will let them use the benchmarks 0, $\frac{1}{2}$, and 1 to put in order a set of fractions such as $\frac{13}{25}, \frac{2}{31}, \frac{5}{6}, \frac{4}{11}$, and $\frac{21}{20}$, which would be a time-consuming task if they tried to find a common denominator. Using benchmarks as shown on the following number line makes the task rather easy: $\frac{13}{25}$ is a little more than $\frac{1}{2}$, $\frac{4}{11}$ is a little less than $\frac{1}{2}$, $\frac{2}{31}$ is near zero, $\frac{5}{6}$ is a little less than 1, and $\frac{21}{20}$ is a little more than 1. Thus, the correct order is $\frac{2}{31}, \frac{4}{11}, \frac{13}{25}, \frac{5}{6}, \frac{21}{20}$.

Children can also use benchmarks to check the reasonableness of computations with fractions and to estimate answers. For example, if they know that $\frac{3}{5}$ and $\frac{6}{7}$ are each more than $\frac{1}{2}$, then they know that $\frac{3}{5} + \frac{6}{7}$ is not $\frac{9}{12}$—the sum must be more than 1.

Mixed Numbers and Improper Fractions

Through models, you can lead children naturally into mixed numbers and improper fractions, even as they are learning the initial concepts of fractions. For example, the mixed number $2\frac{1}{4}$ is a natural symbolic representation of the following model:

You can add partitions in the model to show all the fourths, so children can see that the initial counting is 9 fourths, or the improper fraction $\frac{9}{4}$.

This helps them understand that $2\frac{1}{4}$ and $\frac{9}{4}$ are equivalent representations. To help children gain experience with mixed numbers and improper fractions, use models as much as possible and ask them to write *both* types of numbers to represent the models. After children understand this process, they need practice in changing from one form to the other without the use of models. Do not rush to teach them a routine, however, but encourage them to think problems through. In the following example, see if you can follow Cerise's thinking as she considers how to change $8\frac{2}{3}$ to an improper fraction. Note that her thinking depends on understanding that a whole can be equivalently expressed in terms of fractional parts (e.g., five-fifths and six-sixths each make a whole).

Cerise: I know that 1 is 3 thirds.

So I need to figure how many thirds in 8 wholes. That is 8 groups of 3 thirds, which is 24 thirds.

Now, I have to add on the 2 thirds, so it is 26 thirds, or $\frac{26}{3}$.

Children also must be able to think through the opposite process—changing an improper fraction to a mixed number—for example, changing $\frac{17}{6}$ to $2\frac{5}{6}$. In this case, their thinking could go like this: 6 sixths make a whole, so 17 would make 2 wholes, and there would be 5 sixths more. So $\frac{17}{6}$ is $2\frac{5}{6}$. If children understand the quotient meaning of fractions, then students can also think of $\frac{17}{6}$ as $17 \div 6$, which they can calculate as $2\frac{5}{6}$.

Operations with Fractions

The key to helping children understand operations with fractions is to make sure they understand fractions, especially the idea of equivalent fractions. When children are solving problems that involve operations with fractions, be sure the children can use what they know to make sense of the operations. Whenever possible, they should be able to extend to fractions what they know about operations with whole numbers. Keep in mind, however, that some operations with whole numbers do not extend directly to fractions. For example, multiplication of two fractions is not repeated addition as it is with whole numbers. There are other differences too—for instance, when you multiply two positive whole numbers, the product is always larger than either factor; but when you multiply two proper fractions, the product is always less than either factor.

The *NCTM Standards* recommends that students in grades 3–5 have experience estimating sums and differences, using benchmarks and other strategies, and adding and subtracting fractions with pictorial models. For students in middle school, the emphasis is on multiplying and dividing fractions and on symbolic computation.

Children gain a better understanding of operations with fractions if they learn to estimate answers by using whole numbers and benchmarks such as $\frac{1}{2}$. For example, before computing the answer to $3\frac{2}{3} + 4\frac{5}{6}$, they should estimate the answer by considering, first, that the sum must be more than 7 $(3 + 4)$ and, second, that $\frac{2}{3}$ and $\frac{4}{6}$ are each more than $\frac{1}{2}$, so the answer must be more than 8. Developing this type of number and operation sense makes it easier to figure out whether answers to problems are reasonable. Having the conceptual understanding to check answers for reasonableness is also important because many calculators can perform operations with fractions.

Addition and Subtraction

Instead of beginning addition and subtraction of fractions with a symbolic sentence such as $\frac{2}{3} + \frac{1}{4}$, begin with problems that involve joining and separating. Such problems, together with pictorial models, can:

- Help children see that adding and subtracting fractions can solve problems similar to problems involving whole numbers.

- Help children develop an idea of a reasonable answer.

- Help children see why a common denominator is necessary when adding or subtracting.

Use what children know about solving whole-number addition and subtraction word problems to begin examining how to add and subtract fractions. If children understand how to count fractional parts (e.g., 3 sevenths and 2 more sevenths is 5 sevenths) and how to compare two fractions using a pictorial model, they may find their own ways to solve joining and separating problems with fractions.

Look at the word problems in Figure 12-6. Children with a strong conceptual background should be able to solve the first two of these problems. Have them show how they solved each one, encouraging them to tell how the two problems are alike (e.g., both problems involve adding 2 and 1; in problem A, you have to add Cyrilla's 2 apples to Carey's 1 apple, and in problem B, you have to add Cyrilla's 2 fifths of the pie to Carey's 1 fifth). Also, have children draw a picture to illustrate the first two problems, even if they find it quite simple to do so. Then let them try problem C. Discussing how problem C is like the other two problems and how it is different. If the children need help, encourage them to draw a rectangle to represent the cake.

A

Cyrilla ate 2 apples, and Carey ate 1 apple. How many apples did they eat altogether?

B

Cyrilla ate $\frac{2}{5}$ of a pie, and Carey ate $\frac{1}{5}$ of a pie. How much pie did they eat altogether?

C

Cyrilla ate $\frac{2}{3}$ of a cake, and Carey ate $\frac{1}{4}$ of the cake. How much of the cake did they eat altogether?

FIGURE 12-6 Three joining problems.

Children may come up with various ways to approach the problem. If they have drawn pictures to compare fractions, they may draw pictures like these:

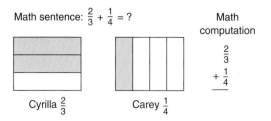

Math sentence: $\frac{2}{3} + \frac{1}{4} = ?$

Math computation

$\frac{2}{3}$

$+ \frac{1}{4}$

Cyrilla $\frac{2}{3}$ Carey $\frac{1}{4}$

Show both portions on each cake:

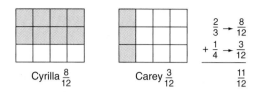

Cyrilla $\frac{8}{12}$ Carey $\frac{3}{12}$

$\frac{2}{3} \rightarrow \frac{8}{12}$

$+ \frac{1}{4} \rightarrow \frac{3}{12}$

$\frac{11}{12}$

Note how the picture above could also be used to see the result if Carey had eaten $\frac{3}{4}$ of a cake and Cyrilla had still eaten $\frac{2}{3}$. The picture shaded differently could show that Carey had eaten $\frac{9}{12}$ of a cake. Together, therefore, they would have eaten $\frac{17}{12}$, or one whole cake and $\frac{5}{12}$ of another.

This highlights the point that, when adding fractions, the whole (the unit) is assumed to be the same. That is, in this example, where Cyrilla ate $\frac{2}{3}$ of a cake and Carey ate $\frac{3}{4}$ of a cake, not only would there have to be two cakes, but the cakes are assumed to be the same size. If Cyrilla ate $\frac{2}{3}$ of a very small cake and Carey ate $\frac{3}{4}$ of a large cake, you would need to know the relative sizes of the cakes before you could determine how much they ate altogether or who ate more.

Adding mixed numbers is no more difficult than adding proper fractions. Children who have made sense of adding proper fractions can put this together with what they know about adding whole numbers to handle a computation such as $5\frac{2}{3} + 3\frac{3}{4}$. Adding the whole numbers gives 8, and adding the fractions gives $\frac{17}{12}$, as we saw above. Putting these together gives $8\frac{17}{12}$, and children can then use their knowledge that $\frac{17}{12}$ is $1\frac{5}{12}$ to express the total as $9\frac{5}{12}$.

You can approach subtracting two proper fractions in the same way that you approached adding. Begin with subtraction problems that involve comparison—for example, you could ask: how much more cake Cyrilla ate than Carey in problem C (Figure 12-6), and you could use the same model to find the answer. Note that knowing how to order fractions is important in real-life situations. In problem C, it would not make sense to ask how much more cake Carey ate than Cyrilla.

Subtracting improper fractions or mixed numbers is often more difficult, partly because children have not worked on changing a mixed number to another mixed number and partly because they lack understanding of regrouping. Using a model such as the fraction bars in Appendix B can help children think about how fraction equivalents are useful for subtracting when regrouping is necessary. For example, the symbolic subtraction problem $6\frac{3}{7} - 2\frac{4}{7}$ requires regrouping $6\frac{3}{7}$ to express it as $5\frac{10}{7}$. You can help children understand this regrouping by getting them to see that

$$1 \text{ is } \tfrac{7}{7}; \text{ so } 6 \text{ is } 5 + \tfrac{7}{7}$$

Thus,

$$6\tfrac{3}{7} \text{ is } 5 + \tfrac{7}{7} + \tfrac{3}{7}, \text{ or } 5\tfrac{10}{7}$$

If children are having difficulty with regrouping fractions, a model like the following can help them see, for example, that $6\frac{3}{7} = 5\frac{10}{7}$

$6\frac{3}{7}$ is 6 wholes plus $\frac{3}{7}$

$6\frac{3}{7}$ is 5 wholes plus $\frac{7}{7}$ plus $\frac{3}{7}$ or $5\frac{10}{7}$

Students often find subtraction more difficult than addition because subtraction often involves more steps. As in addition, students must express the fractions as equivalent fractions with a common denominator. However in subtraction, they may also have to regroup, if the fractional part being subtracted is larger than the other fractional part. Thus, in the previous example $\left(6\frac{3}{7} - 2\frac{4}{7}\right)$, since they cannot subtract $\frac{4}{7}$ from $\frac{3}{7}$, they have to regroup $6\frac{3}{7}$ to $5\frac{10}{7}$.

Students who approach subtraction problems by trying to follow a rule have a great deal of difficulty with problems like $2 - 1\frac{3}{5}$. In contrast, students who have a mental picture of this subtraction and who see that $\frac{2}{5} + \frac{3}{5}$ makes a whole, will be able to think through this problem rather than compute mindlessly. Children who have a firm foundation in understanding fractions will find ways to add and subtract fractions without having to rely solely on the traditional algorithms.

Multiplication

The algorithm for multiplication of fractions is one of the simplest: multiplying the numerators gives the numerator of the product, and multiplying the denominators gives the denominator of the product. Students can learn this algorithm in minutes (and forget it in seconds unless they practice it a great deal); however, learning this algorithm does not give students insight into why it works or when to use it. That is why we suggest teaching multiplication of fractions in a way that helps students understand the meaning of multiplication, helps them get an idea of the size of an answer, and helps them see

why the algorithm works before they are presented with the algorithm itself. Children who have a good background with fractions will often come up with their own methods for multiplying them (Warrington and Kamii, 1999).

In the following sections, we examine three different cases: a whole number times a fraction, a fraction times a whole number, and a fraction times a fraction. In each case, we tie multiplication with fractions to a meaning of multiplication with whole numbers—for example, using the knowledge that 3×4 means three groups of four and that 3×4 is the area of a 3-by-4 rectangle. It is not the purpose here to teach algorithms as it will be in middle school, but to build understanding of the operations.

Whole number times a fraction Begin with a problem like this one:

> You have 3 pans, each with $\frac{4}{5}$ of a pizza. How much pizza do you have?

Ask your students how this problem is like having three bags, each with four marbles. See if this helps them understand the similarity between multiplying whole numbers and multiplying a whole number times a fraction. How do we find three groups of four? We could put out three groups of four marbles and count them. Similarly, to find three groups of $\frac{4}{5}$, we could put out three pans of pizza, each with $\frac{4}{5}$ of a pizza, and count the number of fifths. This approach is shown by a model like the following:

3 groups of 4 is 12

3 groups of 4 fifths is 12 fifths

If we symbolize three groups of four as 3×4, it makes sense to symbolize three groups of $\frac{4}{5}$ as $3 \times \frac{4}{5}$.

Then, we can consider 3×4 as repeated addition:

$$4 + 4 + 4 = 12$$

And we can approach $3 \times \frac{4}{5}$ in the same way:

$$\frac{4}{5} + \frac{4}{5} + \frac{4}{5} = \frac{12}{5}$$

After students have solved problems like this one with pictures, see if they can solve them without pictures, maybe with repeated addition. Be sure to place a strong emphasis on the words. For example, in discussing the problem $5 \times \frac{2}{3}$, have them listen carefully as you read:

$5 \times \frac{2}{3}$ is 5 groups of two-thirds, which is

5 groups of 2, or 10, thirds—which is $\frac{10}{3}$.

Fraction times a whole number   Again, begin with a problem—for example:

You have $\frac{3}{4}$ of a case of 24 bottles. How many bottles do you have?

If children have worked with the set model for fractions, they have the background to solve this problem using physical objects. Now they must move to solving it symbolically and tying it to multiplication.

First, help the children look at why it makes sense to consider this problem a multiplication problem. Ask them: If you had 5 cases with 24 bottles in each, what would you do to find out how many bottles you have? Get them to see that they would multiply 5×24. Similarly, for 20 cases they would multiply 20×24, and for 53 cases they would multiply 53×24. Thus, for $\frac{3}{4}$ of a case they should multiply $\frac{3}{4} \times 24$.

Then have children tell how to find $\frac{3}{4}$ of 24. Lead them to see that they would first partition (or divide) the set into four equal parts (each part would have 6); in other words, first find $\frac{1}{4}$ of 24, which is 6, and then look at 3 of the parts—that is, $\frac{3}{4}$ is three times as many as $\frac{1}{4}$, or $3 \times 6 = 18$. Thus, $\frac{3}{4} \times 24 = 18$. This thinking is summarized below:

Think

$\frac{3}{4} \times 24 = \square$ one-fourth of 24 is 6

three-fourths is 3 times as many, or 3×6

$3 \times 6 = 18$

At first glance, this procedure looks different from the usual algorithm for multiplying numerators and multiplying denominators. First you divide the number in the set (24) by 4 and then multiply that by 3. When you perform the standard algorithm, you multiply first (3×24) and then divide by 4.

Another way to approach this type of problem (fraction times a whole number) is to use the idea of commutativity. That is, point out to the children that $\frac{3}{4} \times 24$ is the same as $24 \times \frac{3}{4}$, so they can multiply using the procedure discussed above (whole number times a fraction). However, children do not readily understand that $\frac{3}{4}$ of a case of 24 is the

same as having 24 groups of $\frac{3}{4}$. Although this approach may be easier, the opportunity to present the "of" meaning of multiplication is lost.

Fraction times a fraction   Consider this problem:

You own $\frac{3}{4}$ of an acre of land, and $\frac{5}{6}$ of this is planted in trees. What part of the acre is planted in trees?

Children need to understand why this is a multiplication problem. Showing them pictures like the ones below may help them see how this problem is related to the area of a rectangle and thus to multiplication. In the first picture, the acre is partitioned into fourths and the amount you own ($\frac{3}{4}$) is shaded.

$\frac{3}{4}$ of an acre (the amount you own)

In the next picture, the acre is partitioned into sixths, with little drawings of trees marking the $\frac{5}{6}$ of your land that is planted in trees. Help the children see that they need to identify the size of each of the small rectangles in order to find what part of the whole acre is planted in trees. Since there are 24 small rectangles, each is $\frac{1}{24}$ of an acre. And since 15 of the small rectangles are planted in trees, $\frac{15}{24}$ of the acre is planted in trees.

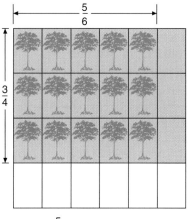

$\frac{5}{6}$ of what you own

Pictures like these can help the children see that the tree-planted rectangle is $\frac{3}{4}$ by $\frac{5}{6}$, so its area is found by multiplying $\frac{3}{4} \times \frac{5}{6}$.

You need to develop this model slowly and only after children have had experience with finding areas of rectangles. After children use a model for problems like this, make a list of fraction-times-fraction products (do not simplify the products). See if the children notice a pattern for multiplying two fractions.

This model can be used with children who have had experience with finding area to help them understand the algorithm for multiplying fractions (multiply the numerators, multiply the denominators). You can refer to the diagrams to show why the procedure works. The acre is partitioned into fourths one way and sixths the other way, so there are $4 \times 6 = 24$ equal parts (24 is the denominator). Trees were planted in three rows of five of these parts, so the numerator is $3 \times 5 = 15$. Symbolically, write

$$\frac{3}{4} \times \frac{5}{6} = \frac{3 \times 5}{4 \times 6} = \frac{15}{24}$$

At this point, return to earlier examples and have the children verify that this algorithm works for those examples also. Make sure the children understand that any whole number can be represented by a fraction (e.g., $6 = \frac{6}{1}$); this will help them see that they can use the algorithm of multiplying numerators and denominators when one of the factors is a whole number.

Division

Consider this problem:

> How many 2-foot hair ribbons can be made from a 10-foot roll of ribbon?

Students should understand that they are being asked to find how many 2-foot pieces (the size of the group) are in the whole, or how many twos are in ten. A picture like this would show them how they might do this in real life:

10-foot roll of ribbon

2-foot ribbon

Students can readily see that the 10-foot roll contains five 2-foot hair ribbons. This is symbolized by $10 \div 2 = 5$.

Now you could modify this picture by marking off $\frac{1}{2}$-foot sections instead of 1-foot sections to show

students how to find the number of $\frac{1}{2}$-foot hair ribbons they could make from this same 10-foot roll (i.e., what is $10 \div \frac{1}{2}$?). The picture would look similar to the one Susie drew when she was finding the number of $\frac{1}{4}$-foot hair ribbons she could make from a 3-foot roll:

3-foot roll of ribbon

$\frac{1}{4}$-foot ribbon

In this problem, we want to know how many one-fourths are in 3, or $3 \div \frac{1}{4} = \square$. Students can see that there are twelve $\frac{1}{4}$-foot ribbons in a 3-foot roll. You should also have students notice that the picture shows that there are 3 groups of 4 (3×4) hair ribbons.

Now ask students how they would draw a picture to find out how many $\frac{3}{4}$-foot pieces there are in a 6-foot roll of ribbon? They should see that, in this case, they would mark off $\frac{3}{4}$-foot lengths, as shown here:

6- foot roll of ribbon

$\frac{3}{4}$-foot

Point out that fourths are marked off first, and then the fourths are grouped by threes. That is, we multiplied by 4 and divided by 3 (or multiplied by $\frac{1}{3}$). When you were in school, you probably learned this as inverting the divisor and then multiplying, as indicated by this symbolic representation:

$$6 \div \frac{3}{4} = \frac{6}{1} \times \frac{4}{3} = \frac{6 \times 4}{1 \times 3} = \frac{24}{3}, \text{ or } 8,$$

In these types of problems, students (even adult students!) often have difficulty with ribbon being left over after they cut as many pieces of the specified length as possible. You can help students understand such cases by posing a problem like this:

> Suppose that you have a 2-foot roll of ribbon and you want to cut as many $\frac{3}{4}$-foot ribbons as you can. You know that you can cut at least two because you can get one from each foot of ribbon. Can you cut three?

Students can approach this problem by looking at this picture.

2-foot roll of ribbon

$\frac{3}{4}$-foot

Students can see that they can cut two $\frac{3}{4}$-foot ribbons (indicated by the two shaded parts) but that the leftover (unshaded) part is not enough for another $\frac{3}{4}$-foot ribbon. Ask them: What part of another can they make? They should see that the unshaded part is $\frac{2}{3}$ of a $\frac{3}{4}$-foot ribbon. From this, children should be able to conclude that they can make $2\frac{2}{3}$ hair ribbons (each $\frac{3}{4}$-foot long).

Doing examples like the last one ($2 \div \frac{3}{4}$) will help children reason through problems in which the divisor is larger than the dividend—for example, how many $\frac{1}{2}$-foot ribbons could be cut from a strip of ribbon that is $\frac{1}{3}$-foot long ($\frac{1}{3} \div \frac{1}{2}$)? Children should recognize that $\frac{1}{2}$ is larger than $\frac{1}{3}$, so they could not cut even one $\frac{1}{2}$-foot ribbon. The question is, what part of a $\frac{1}{2}$-foot ribbon could they cut? Have the children draw a picture to convince themselves that they could cut $\frac{2}{3}$ of a $\frac{1}{2}$-foot ribbon.

In the Classroom 12-7 consists of a few rhymes that incorporate questions about fractions. Even older children like their silliness. Be sure, however, that you balance fanciful activities like this with activities involving situations from students' everyday life. Use the diversity in your class as a resource by making up problems that relate to students' different customs.

Conceptual Development of Decimals

When you introduce decimals, you should relate them to what students already know about common fractions and place value. For ease of discussion, we consider these relationships separately, but you should keep in mind that you will need to weave them together in your teaching. You should also keep in mind that it is important to relate decimals to everyday experiences as well, since context

---

In the Classroom 12-7

A NEW TWIST ON OLD RHYMES

OBJECTIVE: Verifying whether or not computational statements about fractions are true.

GRADE LEVEL: 4–6

▼ Have the students decide if the following rhymes are true and show how they know by using models or drawing pictures.

Humpty Dumpty sat on a wall.
"Wow, I have 45 balloons in all."
The wind blew 2/5 of them to the sky.
"Now, I have 30 balloons, oh my!"

Jack and Jill went up the hill
To fetch a pail of water.
Jack filled $\frac{2}{3}$ without fail.
Jill added $\frac{1}{4}$ to the pail.
And $\frac{11}{12}$ spilled as Jack caught her.

Little Miss Muffet
Sat on a tuffet
And ate $\frac{1}{2}$ of a candy bar.
Along came a spider
And ate $\frac{1}{5}$ right beside her.
The remaining $\frac{1}{10}$ won't go far.

Little Jack Horner
Sat in the corner
Eating a pizza pie
He ate $\frac{1}{2}$ and $\frac{1}{2}$ of the rest
"None left," said he, "I am the best."

▼ Have the students make up their own rhymes using fractions or change these rhymes with other fractions.

will often help students understand the mathematics (Irwin, 2001).

Math Links 12.5

*P*ractice using electronic base-ten blocks to represent decimals. The process is similar to using base-ten blocks to represent whole numbers; however, the values of the blocks now represent decimals. Access this from this book's Web site.

www.wiley.com/college/reys

Relationship to Common Fractions

As we mentioned near the beginning of this chapter, decimals are just another notation for fractions—specifically, for tenths, hundredths, and other powers-of-ten parts of a unit. Thus, basic to understanding decimals is understanding these fractional parts—an understanding that you should build when you are developing the meaning of fractions.

Tenths Before introducing the decimal notation for tenths, review what students should know about tenths from their prior study of fractions. They should know that partitioning a unit into tenths results in 10 equal parts. They also should be able to make the connection between a model of a fraction, the word for the fraction, and the fraction written symbolically. And they should know that 10 tenths make a whole, that 7 tenths is less than a whole, and that 27 tenths is more than a whole.

With this background, children should be ready to learn that, for example, 0.3 is a symbol for $\frac{3}{10}$. You should help children link their knowledge about place value to this new notation (see the discussion in Chapter 8 on place value). You also need to stress that 0.3 and $\frac{3}{10}$ are both said as "three-tenths." Then have them look at a number such as $2\frac{7}{10}$. Show them that this is written 2.7 in the new notation and said as "two and seven-tenths." Point out that the word *and* is said for the decimal point. Saying decimals aloud in this way helps students relate what they know about fractions to decimals. In the Classroom 12-8 shows a quick game that children can play to practice writing in decimal and fraction notation.

Before introducing hundredths, you should make certain that students have made all three connections shown by this triangle (model and symbol, symbol and word, word and model).

In the Classroom 12-8

CAN YOU BEAT THE TOSS?

OBJECTIVE: Write numbers as fractions or decimals.

GRADE LEVEL: 3–5

MATERIALS: Paper and pencil for children; a penny for the teacher

Directions:

▼ The teacher reads a number.

▼ Each child writes the number in either decimal or fraction notation.

▼ Each child receives 1 point if he or she writes the number correctly.

▼ The teacher tosses a coin.

- If it's *heads*, each child who wrote a correct *decimal* receives one point.

- If it's *tails*, each child who wrote a correct *fraction* receives one point.

Suggested Numbers:

two-tenths	one and three-tenths
seven-tenths	twenty-two and five-tenths
five and seven-tenths	thirty-four and no-tenths
eleven and four-tenths	

Challenge Numbers:

sixteen-tenths	five and eleven-tenths

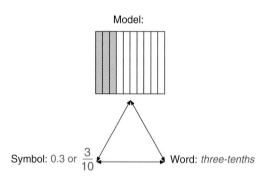

Model:

Symbol: 0.3 or $\frac{3}{10}$ Word: *three-tenths*

Hundredths Give each child multiple copies of the model of hundredths (in Appendix B, the decimal or percent paper contains six copies of the 10 by 10 grid that you can use for this model). Make certain that the children know that the unit (the entire square grid) is one and that each part (each small square) is one hundredth. Ask them to shade $\frac{3}{100}$, $\frac{7}{100}$, $\frac{10}{100}$, and $\frac{21}{100}$ on the model.

Have the children shade the first and second columns on the hundredth model and three more small squares. Ask what part of the whole is covered. Elicit both responses: $\frac{2}{10} + \frac{3}{100}$ as well as $\frac{23}{100}$. Then write the following:

$$\frac{23}{100} = \frac{2}{10} + \frac{3}{100}$$

Now connect the place-value interpretation and the decimal notation 0.23. You can also use the model to show that 0.2 = 0.20. Continue having children make the connections shown in the triangle (i.e., by connecting the model, the symbol, and the word). These two examples are only an introduction to hundredths. You will need to return to models as you continue helping students make sense of hundredths and how they relate to tenths. See Chapter 8 for other models.

Thousandths and other decimals   Older students often do not understand small decimals such as 0.234 or 0.0003, partly because there is less emphasis on these decimals but also because teachers often expect children to generalize from hundredths to all the other places. Most of your work with smaller decimals should be done through the place-value interpretation because the fractions become unwieldy. However, you should make sure children understand that a thousandth is one-tenth of a hundredth and you should develop this understanding by using a model. Students often have difficulty hearing the difference between "thousands" and "thousandths"— careful pronunciation of all the fractional names (tenths, hundredths, thousandths, etc.) is essential.

Writing fractions as decimals   If decimals have been introduced carefully, students should be able to write the fraction notation for any decimal and the decimal notation for any fraction expressed in tenths, hundredths, and so on. For example, they should be able to write $\frac{2}{10}$ and $\frac{23}{100}$ as 0.2 and .23, no matter whether they read the written fractions or hear them read as "two tenths" and "twenty-three hundredths."

However, the fact that students can write fractions as decimals when the fractions are expressed in tenths, hundredths, and so on does not mean that they will be able to write other fractions as decimals. Students try to make sense of the relationship between fractions and decimals, but they often do not have a firm understanding of the quotient meaning of fractions. For example, they do not understand that $\frac{4}{5}$ means $4 \div 5$. To divide 4 by 5, children must know that 4 is equivalent to 4.0 and must be able to divide decimals. If you can help students gain these understandings, they can use a calculator or the traditional algorithm to see that $\frac{4}{5} = 0.8$. Children who also understand equiva-

lent fractions should know that $\frac{4}{5} = \frac{8}{10} = 0.8$. Having children see that both methods lead to the same decimal is important. They can use the method of division to change any fraction to a decimal (or a decimal approximation, if the division doesn't terminate in zeros).

Children can explore many interesting patterns. Some can be investigated with a calculator—for example, the decimal equivalents for ninths:

$$\frac{1}{9} = 0.11111\ldots$$
$$\frac{2}{9} = 0.22222\ldots$$
$$\frac{3}{9} = 0.33333\ldots$$

You should do a few of these calculations by hand to show that the pattern continues forever. If you only use a calculator, students may think that $\frac{1}{9} = 0.11111111$ exactly (i.e., the number of places on their calculator display).

Similarly, you should be looking at the meaning of $\frac{1}{3}$ to help students see that $\frac{1}{3}$ does not exactly equal 0.33, 0.333, or 0.3333. For instance, you can point out that if $\frac{1}{3} = 0.33$, then each of three equal parts of a whole would be 0.33, and thus the whole would be 0.33 + 0.33 + 0.33, or 0.99, which is not one. Similarly, you can show students that $\frac{1}{3}$ does not equal 0.3333 (although this is a closer approximation to $\frac{1}{3}$).

Relationship to Place Value

The place-value interpretation of decimals is most useful for helping children understand computation with decimals. Let's look now at one way to develop this interpretation and consider how to use it in teaching children how to order and round decimals.

What do children know about place value? Consider the number 2463. By third grade, children can identify the places (ones, tens, hundreds, and thousands) and the number in each place (3, 6, 4, and 2). They know, for example, that the four means four hundreds. They also have learned how the places are filled: beginning with ones as a unit, grouping 10 of these to form a new unit (tens), grouping 10 of these to form a new unit (hundreds), and so forth.

In introducing place-value ideas with decimals, again begin with ones as the unit. But instead of grouping by tens, group by one-tenth of the one to form the new unit of tenths. To indicate this new unit in the place-value system, use a decimal point after the ones place. Help students understand that 10 of the tenths make a one (just as 10 of any unit make the next larger unit). They also should be able to identify the tenths place in a number. Be sure to integrate the place-value interpretation of decimals with the interpretation of decimals as fractions.

When introducing hundredths, you should again focus on the place-value interpretation. Given a number such as 51.63, a child should be able to tell what number is in the tenths place and what number is in the hundredths place, as well as the relationships between the places (a hundredth is one-tenth of a tenth, or 10 hundredths is 1 tenth). After you introduce thousandths in a similar way, the children should be able to generalize to any decimal place.

Be sure to read decimals aloud in a way that emphasizes the tie between decimals and fractions. For example, read 24.09 as "twenty-four and 9 hundredths," not as "two four point zero nine" or "twenty-four point oh nine." The words *tenths, hundredths,* and so on help students maintain that tie.

Often, you can use a place-value grid to help students having difficulty with decimals. Consider, for example, this grid for the number 32.43:

T	O	tth	hth
3	2 •	4	3

Point out that the decimal can be seen both as *32 and 43 hundredths* and as *32 and 4 tenths and 3 hundredths.*

These children will also benefit from being asked questions like the ones in Figure 12-7 and organizing their thoughts on a decimal grid.

Children can end up using a grid in as rote a way as a rule unless you continue to help them explain their thinking and relate the grid to the model. It is certainly not enough to fill in zeroes on the grid anywhere there is not a number. It is more important to discuss why, for example, 4.3 is equivalent to 4.30.

Ordering and Rounding Decimals

Children should be able to understand the ordering and rounding of decimals based directly on their understanding of decimals and their ability to order and round whole numbers. For decimals, this understanding must include being able to interpret the decimals in terms of place value and being able to think of, for example, 0.2 as 0.20 or 0.200.

Here is an example of two children discussing which is larger, 23.61 or 23.9?

CARTER: I think that 23.61 is larger because it has more places, just like 2361 is larger than 239.

JEANE: But both of these (23.61 and 23.9) are 23 and some more, so all we have to do is compare the decimal parts.

Write 8 hundredths:

T	O	tth	hth
	•	0	8

Children should realize there are 0 tenths.

What is 29 hundredths?

T	O	tth	hth
	•	2	9

Children should realize there are 2 tenths and 9 hundredths.

What is 29 tenths?

T	O	tth	hth
	2 •	9	

Children should realize this is 2 ones and 9 tenths.

Now look at 4.3 on the grid. How many tens?

T	O	tth	hth
	4 •	3	

Children should realize there are no tens.

Tell the children that we could write a 0 in the tens place, but this is not customary.

How many hundredths?

T	O	tth	hth
	4 •	3	0

Children should realize that 4.3 is equivalent to 4.30.

FIGURE 12-7 Using a decimal grid with place value.

CARTER: Okay, it's not like whole numbers.

JEANE: Well, sort of. We begin with the largest place—the tens are the same, the ones are the same, so we need to look at the tenths. The 9 is larger than the 6, so 23.9 is larger than 23.61.

CARTER: I follow you until that last part. Now you have a 9 and a 61, and 61 is larger.

JEANE: But the 9 is 9 tenths and the 61 is 61 hundredths. Want to look at a model?

CARTER: I get it—I remember the model. Nine tenths is 9 strips, or 90 little squares. It is 90 hundredths, so it is larger.

As you see from this conversation, if children really understand the notation and meaning of decimals, they can figure out ways to compare decimals.

In rounding a decimal such as 24.78 to the nearest tenth, children need to ask themselves the same types of questions as with whole numbers. Children must also understand that 24.7 = 24.70.

Questions	Expected Responses
What "tenths" is 24.78 between?	It's between 24.7 and 24.8 (or 24.70 and 24.80)
Is it nearer 24.7 or 24.8?	It's nearer to 24.80
How will you round it?	To 24.8

Operations with Decimals

One advantage of decimals over fractions is that computation is much easier, since it basically follows the same rules as for whole numbers. In teaching the algorithms for decimals, you should build on the place-value interpretation of decimals and the corresponding whole-number algorithms. Given the wide availability of calculators, it is important that you spend as much time seeing whether answers are reasonable as you spend on the algorithms. Thus, estimation skills are crucial (see Chapter 10).

In the Classroom 12-9 shows an activity that requires estimation skills. Encourage students to use whole numbers that are compatible when trying to answer the questions. You can present questions of this type to students before they learn about decimal computation. For example England's population is about 45 million and Scotland's is about 5 million, so England has about 9 times as many people as Scotland.

Addition and Subtraction

Children who have a good concept of decimals have little trouble extending the whole-number algorithms for addition and subtraction to decimals. They realize that they need to:

- Add or subtract like units (tenths with tenths, hundredths with hundredths, and so forth).
- Regroup in the decimal places as they did with whole numbers.

Difficulty with adding or subtracting decimals arises mainly when the values are given in horizontal format or in terms of a story problem and the decimals are expressed to a different number of places (e.g., 51.23 + 434.7). To deal with this difficulty, have the children first estimate by looking at the wholes (about 480). Some children may need

---

In the Classroom 12-9
WHAT'S YOUR ANSWER:

OBJECTIVE: Use estimations about decimal quantities to answer questions.

GRADE LEVEL: 4–5

▼ Use the data in this table. These are data about the parts of the United Kingdom.

Parts	Area (Thousands of km^2)	Population (Millions)
England	130.422	49.300
N. Ireland	14.144	1.692
Scotland	78.772	5.200
Wales	20.761	3.005

▼ Answer these questions:
- About how much larger in area is England than Scotland? _____
- About how large in area is the United Kingdom? _____
- About what is the population of the United Kingdom? _____
- Do twice as many people live in Wales than live in N. Ireland? _____
- Is England more than six times larger in area than Wales? _____

help in lining up the like units and so may benefit from using a grid:

	H	T	O	tth	hth
		5	1	2	3
+	4	3	4	7	
	4	8	5	9	3

Multiplication and Division

Multiplying and dividing a decimal by a whole number are conceptually easier than multiplying two decimals or dividing a decimal by a decimal. Children can build on this to understand the more sophisticated computation. Begin by having children consider a problem like this:

Six tables are lined up end to end. Each table is 2.3 meters long. How long is the line of tables?

From their previous work with multiplication, students should realize that this is a multiplication problem. Of course, they should also see that they can solve the problem by adding decimals. That is:

$$6 \times 2.3 = 2.3 + 2.3 + 2.3 + 2.3 + 2.3 + 2.3,$$
which equals 13.8

However, just as children moved away from repeated addition to find the product of two whole numbers, they need to do so when multiplying a decimal by a whole number.

Children with a firm understanding of the place-value interpretation of decimals can think about multiplication with decimals in another way. For example: 2.3 is 23 tenths, so 2.3 × 6 is

23 tenths
× 6
138 tenths, which is 13.8

Similarly, for the problem 2.37 × 6, children could realize that 2.37 is 237 hundredths, so:

237 hundredths
× 6
1422 hundredths, which is 14.22

Working with a decimal grid can help students remember that 138 tenths is 13.8. In using this method, you should first have the students decide on a reasonable answer. Ask them: is 6 × 2.37 more than 12? is it as much as 142?

To help students make sense of multiplying a decimal by a decimal, rather than only remembering a rule about counting decimal places, see if they can model this problem: What is the area of a porch that is 3.2 meters by 1.9 meters?

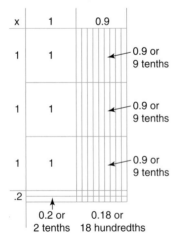

Add the parts:
1 + 1 + 1 = 3
9 tenths + 9 tenths + 9 tenths =
27 tenths or 2.7
Now find the total:
3.
2.7
0.2
0.18
6.08

Students need to discuss whether 6.08 square meters is a reasonable answer. Ask them: What would be the area of a porch that is 3 meters by 2 meters?

Children can use the distributive algorithm for dividing whole numbers to divide a decimal by a whole number. Consider this problem:

A vinegar company distributed 123.2 million liters of vinegar equally among eight customers. How much vinegar did each customer receive?

First, ask for reasonable answers.

Did each customer get more than 10 million liters? [Yes, that would be only 80 million liters.]

Did each get more than 20 million liters? [No, that would be 160 million liters.]

What is an estimate for the answer? [Between 10 and 20 million liters]

Then, talk through the division, as in Figure 12-8:

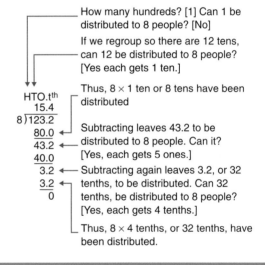

FIGURE 12-8 Talking through division of a decimal by a whole number.

For students in middle school, you will need to develop division of a decimal by a decimal as well as extending the work on multiplying decimals. The development of fluency with multiplication and division of decimals takes more practice than with addition and subtraction, partly because children's understanding of multiplication and division of whole numbers is not as firm as their understanding of addition and subtraction, but also because new rules are needed. You will find a great variation in skill level among children in your class. You might want to begin collecting some challenging activities such as In the Classroom 12-10, as well as games and other practice materials that will help children develop computational fluency with decimals.

In the Classroom 12-10

PLUG-IN PUZZLES

OBJECTIVE: Develop decimal number sense.

GRADE LEVEL: 4–5

▼ Use these decimals to fill in the blanks.

8.3   4.2   5.5   3.1   7.6   6.7

Do each multiplication or division. In the division problems, divide to the hundredths place. Sum the four answers.

____ × ____ = □

____ ÷ 5 = □

____ × ____ = □

____ ÷ 3 = □

Total □

• Can you get a total greater than 50?

• Can you get one greater than 100?

• What is the largest total you can get?

▼ Arrange these four decimals in the blanks so that the sentence is true. (Remember to do the parts in the parentheses first.)

5.13   4.24   3.84   3.16

(____ × 5) + ____ = (4 × ____) + ____

▼ Pick the two decimals from those listed that will make the sentence true.

21.21   42.42   36.36   63.63   27.27

(____ ÷ 7) × 8 = (____ ÷ 9) × 6

Cultural Connections

The Egyptians as early as 3500 B.C. were one of the first cultures in recorded history to make use of fractions. However, in their hieroglyphics, they wrote all fractions as the sum of unit fractions (i.e., fractions with 1 as the numerator). For example, $\frac{3}{4}$ would have been written as $\frac{1}{2} + \frac{1}{4}$, and $\frac{2}{3}$ as $\frac{1}{2} + \frac{1}{6}$. They could do all four operations with fractions using this notation. (And you thought *our* system is cumbersome!)

At grade 4 there are considerable differences among countries with regard to the emphasis placed on fractions (Mullis et al., 2004). Japan expects only half of their fourth-graders to have a firm background in concepts involving fractions; they do little with fractions until about grade 5,

when they expect students to add and subtract fractions with like denominators. The United States expects three-fourths and two-thirds, respectively, of fourth-grade students to have some conceptual background in fractions and experience in adding and subtracting fractions. Other countries, such as Singapore, expect all students to have experiences in both of these areas. If you have students from other countries, you can expect a wide variety of skills and experience in dealing with fractions.

Some countries teach operations with decimals before operations with fractions, while others do the opposite. Many countries use a comma instead of a period for the decimal point, and this, along with the way numbers are displayed on a calculator, is one reason you often see whole numbers written without commas. Some countries say the denominator before they say the numerator. Be alert to these differences; students will adjust to the U.S. system if you are aware of the situation and don't assume that they lack basic understandings.

A Glance at Where We've Been

Three meanings of fractions are part-whole, quotient, and ratio (this chapter focuses on the part-whole meaning). Useful models of the part-whole meaning include such attributes as region, length, set, and area. The region model is the easiest for children to understand, and the rectangle is the easiest type of region. To help children make sense of fractions, begin with the important idea of partitioning (making equal shares) and then introduce words for fractional parts and counting the parts. Help children make connections between words, symbols, and models. Make sure children can figure out a whole from fractional part and that they understand the idea of equivalent fractions. Use concrete models, pictorial models, and symbolic representations to build children's ability to order fractions and find equivalent fractions. Make sure children understand how to use benchmarks for estimating and checking the reasonableness of answers. Use models to develop children's understanding of mixed numbers and improper fractions.

To teach addition and subtraction of fractions, begin with problems and pictorial models that help children (1) see how adding and subtracting fractions can solve problems similar to problems with whole numbers, (2) develop an idea of a reasonable answer, and (3) see why a common denominator is necessary. Teach multiplication of fractions in a way that helps children (1) understand the meaning of multiplication and (2) estimate the size of an answer. In middle school, this will help them see why the algorithm for multiplication works (multiply numerators and denominators). Begin with whole number times a fraction, then fraction times a whole number, and then fraction times a fraction. For division, relate the way partitioning works with whole numbers to the way it works with fractions, using pictorial models.

Help children develop the concept of decimals by relating decimals to common fractions. Emphasize the place-value interpretation of decimals to help children in ordering and rounding decimals and to prepare them for operations with decimals.

Students in different countries learn about fractions and decimals at different grade levels; they also have different ways of writing and saying decimals. Teachers should be aware of these differences so they can deal appropriately with diverse students.

Things to Do: From What You've Read

1. The part-whole meaning of a fraction can be developed with different attributes, such as length and sets. Draw part-whole models for four different attributes to show $\frac{3}{4}$.

2. Illustrate three different meanings of $\frac{3}{4}$.

3. Describe how you can develop the concept of equivalent fractions.

4. What is partitioning? How is it related to division and to fractions?

5. Verify that the last three examples in the Snapshot of a Lesson are halves. Then show six different ways to show fourths (use the geoboard paper in Appendix B; you may want to copy it so you will have a master for geoboard paper when you are teaching).

6. Illustrate how two fractions can be ordered using the pictorial model described on page 297.

7. With pictures, show why $2\frac{3}{5}$ is equivalent to $\frac{13}{5}$; show why $2\frac{3}{5}$ is equivalent to $1\frac{8}{5}$.

8. What is a benchmark for fractions? How are benchmarks used? Propose a problem that could be solved using benchmarks for fractions.

9. How is multiplication of fractions different from multiplication of whole numbers?

10. Describe how decimals and common fractions are alike and different.

11. Give three different exercises in which students are asked to order decimals. Tell why you chose each, that is, what you would expect to learn about children who did these exercises. Tell what you would do if the children encountered difficulties.

12. How would you help children who have difficulty with a problem like this: $25.03 - 8.459$?

Things to Do: Going Beyond This Book

IN THE FIELD

1. Create five story problems that ask children to order and compare fractions. You may want to use one of the books from the Book Nook for Children to set the scene.

2. *Three-Fourths.* Assess at least three children using the tasks from In the Classroom 12-1. Which of the models for fractions were the most difficult for children to understand?

3. Develop a lesson plan to make the transition from a length model to representing length on a number line.

4. Develop two activities for fractions using pattern blocks (see In the Classroom 12-4) that children could do at centers.

5. *Fraction Bars.* Use fraction bars to teach the concept of fractions as parts of a whole.

6. *Can You Beat the Toss?* Play the game from In the Classroom 12-8 with children. Include hundredths if the children are familiar with hundredths. Notice whether some children prefer decimal notation to fraction notation.

IN YOUR JOURNAL

7. Examine an elementary mathematics textbook series to see what models for fractions they use and whether they introduce set models through partitioning.

---

* Additional activities, suggestions, and questions are provided in *Teaching Elementary Mathematics: A Resource for Field Experiences* (Wiley, 2007).

8. Describe how you were taught fractions in elementary school. Did those experiences help you make sense of fractions?

WITH ADDITIONAL RESOURCES

9. Read at least one article listed in the references from *Teaching Children Mathematics* or *Mathematics Teaching in the Middle School*. Describe how the article complements or contradicts the suggestions in this chapter.

10. Read one of the articles about fractions or decimals from *Making Sense of Fractions, Ratios, and Proportions* (NCTM, 2002). Briefly summarize the article; then tell why you selected it and what you learned.

11. Read *Low-Performing Students and Teaching Fractions for Understanding: An International Analysis* (Epsom, 2003). Describe one of the interaction transcripts of the teacher and the two children. What did you learn from thinking about the two children and this interaction?

WITH TECHNOLOGY

12. Experiment with a calculator that has a fraction key. What fraction skills and understandings would be important for children to have if they were to use such calculators?

13. Become familiar with one of the virtual manipulatives for fractions and decimals, described in Math Links 12.4.

14. Watch the video, *Fractions with Geoboards*, summarized in the Snapshot of a Lesson. What are three things from the video you would do if you were the teacher, and what are three things that you would change?

Note to Instructors: You can find additional resources, learning activities, and black-line masters in this text's accompanying Instructor's Manual, at www.wiley.com/college/reys.

Book Nook for Children

Adler, D. A. *Fraction Fun*. New York: Holiday House, 1996.

This book is a basic introduction to fractions using different objects, such as paper plates and pizzas, as the region model. The author extends the models to include money and weight.

Dryk, M. *The Fraction Family Heads West*. Manchaca, TX. Bookaloppy Press, 1997.

The Fraction Family is heading west from Texas during the Gold Rush of 1849. Each family member has a fraction name; for example, Sam's name is $\frac{200}{100}$ and Fern's is $\frac{14}{21}$. The family encounters the Ratio Rascals, who take money from the family, and they have to learn how to deal with the Ratio Rascals. Appropriate when studying equivalent fractions.

Hutchins, P. *The Doorbell Rang*. New York: Greenwillow Books, 1987.

This book is an excellent source to use when introducing the concept of partitioning. Children are challenged to share cookies fairly in what can be an interactive story.

Murphy, S, J. *Jump, Kangaroo, Jump!* New York: HarperCollins, 1999.

This book is about Australian animals planning a field day of events at a camp. Kangaroo and his friends must divide themselves up into different groups for the events that are taking place. There are activities and games in the back of the book for teachers and parents to use.

Pallotta, J., and Bolster, J. *The Hershey's Milk Chocolate Fraction Book*. Needham, MA. Title Wave Press, 1999.

This book uses the whole candy bar, partitioned into various smaller squares, to present problems involving fractional parts. Vocabulary is stressed throughout the book.

Annotated Resources

Edwards, T. G. "Using ancient Egyptian fractions to review fraction concepts. "*Mathematics Teaching in the Middle School*, 10 (5) (December 2004-January 2005), pp. 226–229.
Challenge your students to write fractions in the manner that the Egyptians did. This article contains background information and ideas to use with students that will help them develop a deeper understanding of fractions.

Epsom, S. B. "Low-performing students and teaching fractions for understanding: An interactional analysis." *Journal for Research in Mathematics Education*, 34(4) (July 2003), pp. 305–343.

This is a detailed analysis of the progress of two first-grade students who are learning initial concepts of fractions. The author proposes reasons for the success of these two low-performing students.

Litwiller, B., and Bright, G. (eds.). *Making Sense of Fractions, Ratios, and Proportions: 2002 Yearbook.* Reston, VA: NCTM, 2002.
This yearbook has many articles about helping early childhood, elementary, and middle school students. You will find ties to literature, ways to use manipulatives, and extensions of ideas touched on in this text.

Mack, N. K. "Connecting to develop computational fluency with fractions." *Teaching Children Mathematics,* 10(3) (November 2004), pp. 226–232.
This article tells the story of a teacher who let the students' thinking guide her teaching of adding and subtracting fractions. It includes a sequenced progression of addition and subtraction problems.

Riddle, M., and Rodzwell, B. "Fractions: What happens between kindergarten and the army?" *Teaching Children Mathematics,* 7(4) (December 2000), pp. 202–206.
A group of teachers of different grades look at how their students solve addition and subtraction problems involving fractions and how they used their understandings of fractions; the teachers contrast their students to a group of adults.

Wu, Z. "Multiplying fractions." *Teaching Children Mathematics,* 8(3) (November 2001), pp. 174–178.
This article considers four problems, similar to the ones in the text, to illustrate multiplying fractions.

CHAPTER 13

Ratio, Proportion, and Percent: Meanings and Applications

Snapshot of a Lesson

Key Ideas

1. Developing ratios in a real-world context
2. Engaging in measurement and using equivalent ratios
3. Representing ratios in different ways
4. Connecting them to fractions and decimals

Background

Carey Tuckey is a seventh-grade teacher. She is using the story of *Gulliver's Travels* to introduce ratios. The lesson has children measuring, recording ratios, and then connecting their ratios to fractions and decimals. This excerpt is from the beginning of the lesson which leads to the children's constructing a model of a shirt for Gulliver. This is a transcript of part of a video from the Modeling Middle School Mathematics Project. Go to http://www.mmmproject.org (Modeling Middle School Mathematics) and click on the video matrix.

An excerpt from the video *Body Ratios*

MS. TUCKEY: Who knows the story of *Gulliver's Travels*? Can anybody tell us about *Gulliver's Travels*? Allison?

ALLISON: Well there's this guy and they think he's crazy, but then he goes sailing away and he is on a strange land and he's like really big and these little people, called Lilliputians, they tie him down and they want to make a new shirt for him.

Later in the lesson, the teacher has a student read from the book.

MS. TUCKEY: And Allison, would you read for us what they decided would work in order to measure Gulliver's shirt?

ALLISON: "The seamstresses took my measure. As I lay on the ground one standing at my neck and another at my mid leg with a strong chord extended, that each, held by the hand, while the third measured the length of the cord with a rule of a inch long. Then they measured my right thumb and desired no more, for by a mathematical computation twice around the thumb is once around the wrist and so on, to the neck and the waist. And by the help of my old shirt, which was displayed on the ground before them for a pattern, they fitted me exactly."

MS. TUCKEY: If we knew that the Lilliputians were 6 inches tall, and Jonathan Swift who wrote this said Gulliver was about 6 feet tall. What is the ratio of one Gulliver to a Lilliputian? How many Lilliputians is it going to take to make a Gulliver? Pablo?

PABLO: Um…12.

MS. TUCKEY: And what ratio is that?

PABLO: 1 to 12.

MS. TUCKEY: That means the Lilliputians were pretty tiny compared to Gulliver. I have a little friend here that I found who is exactly $\frac{1}{12}$ of my height. And if we put him down on the ground next to me, can you imagine him having to measure to make a shirt for me? I'm pretty huge compared to him, aren't I?

MS. TUCKEY: The Lilliputians were smart. They had a formula. And their formula used ratios. They said, that twice round the thumb is once round the wrist and so on to the neck and the waist. What did they mean by and so on to the neck and the waist? David what does that mean?

DAVID: Twice around the wrist equals around the neck and twice around the neck equals twice around the waist.

MS. TUCKEY: So we have a ratio, don't we? And if we look at the ratio of thumb to wrist, everybody, how many thumbs did they say it took to make a wrist?

CLASS: Two.

MS. TUCKEY: Do you believe that?

CLASS: No.

MS. TUCKEY: You don't? What we're going to do is see if it is real. In the box on your desk, you have some string and you have some scissors.

The students begin the measuring activity.

MS. TUCKEY: [To the camera] The kids are very skeptical as to whether or not once around your thumb was indeed half of your wrist measurement. When we moved into the first exploration we took string and they used rulers and all kinds of things to verify that ratio. They were very surprised to find out that Mr. Swift did know what he was talking about.

STUDENT: She measured my thumb and then she put it on this [*indicates ruler*], then she measured my wrist and she put it on this [*ruler*] and then we said, since we have to do two times around that's 8, and then 8 times 2 is 16 and then this is 16…almost 16.

Later, the teacher has students share their findings.

MS. TUCKEY: So how many of you found out that the Lilliputians were correct? You were pretty close. Almost all of you. They were pretty smart, weren't they? Let's suppose then that we have a classmate whose thumb measures 5 centimeters. What would we estimate his wrist would measure. Laurie?

LAURIE: 10 centimeters.

MS. TUCKEY: And how did you figure 10 centimeters?

LAURIE: Because if you go twice around your thumb the Lilliputians say it would equal your wrist so twice, 2 times 5 is 10.

MS. TUCKEY: So if we know that the thumb is 5 centimeters and the wrist measures 10 centimeters, how do we say that as a ratio?

CLASS: 5 to 10.

MS. TUCKEY: Would you please take your dry erase boards out and write that ratio two different ways?

The students comply with the teacher's request.

MS. TUCKEY: I'm glad to see that everybody remembered that not only can we write a ratio as a fraction, we can write a ratio using a colon and we can write a ratio using the word to and all of these are read the same way. How is that?

CLASS: 5 to 10.

MS. TUCKEY: Now sometimes we find that it's much easier to compare ratios if we make them into decimals. We know that you can take a fraction and you can easily make into a decimal by doing what? Sara?

SARA: By dividing them.

MS. TUCKEY: Good and are we going to divide 5 by 10 or 10 by 5?

SARA: 5 by 10.

MS. TUCKEY: So if we take 5 divided by 10, what decimal will we end up with?

CLASS: Five-tenths.

MS. TUCKEY: And how do we write that as a decimal?

CLASS: 0.5.

MS. TUCKEY: 0.5 good. Let's see if the Lilliputians knew what they were doing when they were talking about ratios.

We're going to use our string again and we're going to see if one time around our wrist is half of our neck. So is our neck indeed twice our wrist? We're going to do the same thing going from our neck to our waist.

Now, as we measure this time, I'm going to ask you to use centimeters. When we talked about the Lilliputians and Gulliver, we were using inches and feet. But one thing that's nice about ratios is no matter what unit of measure you use, the ratio is going to stay the same.

◆Introduction

"Twice around your thumb is equivalent to once around your wrist."

"Family income this year increased by 10 percent."

"Ian did only half the work Angela did."

"Her salary is three times my salary."

"The cost of living tripled during the last 8 years."

"Your chances of winning the lottery are less than one in a million."

"I can purchase a 12-ounce bottle of soda for $1 or a 16-ounce bottle for $1.50. Which bottle is the better buy?"

Statements like these reflect the fact that much of quantitative thinking is relational. In such thinking, what is important is the multiplicative relationship between numbers, rather than the actual numbers themselves. By emphasizing multiplicative relationships, you will help your students take advantage of the many opportunities to use these relationships in real-world situations. As illustrated by the statements above, these situations often require fluency in ratios, proportions, and percents, as well as fractions and decimals. The NCTM's *Principles and Standards for School Mathematics* (2000) clearly states that students in elementary school and middle school must be able to express appropriate relationships using fractions, ratios, proportions, and percents (see Figure 13-1). In Figure 13-1, note how the expectations in grades 3–5

provides the basis for work on ratios and proportions in grades 6–8.

Math Links 13.1

You can find detailed recommendations and suggestions for helping students develop ratio, proportions, and percents at the Web site of the National Council of Teachers of Mathematics at www.nctm.org.

www.wiley.com/college/reys

Here is an example to get you started thinking about ratios, proportions, and percents. Consider the prices of three carpets:

CARPET SALE

The difference in price between carpet A and carpet B is $9 per square yard, and so is the difference in price between carpet B and carpet C. Yet B is twice as expensive as A while C is three times as expensive and 50 percent more expensive than B. Whether one considers the difference in the prices or the ratio of the prices is essential to relational thinking that we will explore.

Instructional programs from prekindergarten through grade 12 should enable all students to:	Grades 3–5 Expectations All students should:	Grades 6–8 Expectations All students should:
Understand relationships among numbers, compute fluently, and make reasonable estimates	Recognize and generate equivalent forms of commonly used fractions, decimals, and percents	Understand and use ratios and proportions to represent quantitative relationships

FIGURE 13-1   Number and Operations Standard with expectations for children in grades 3–5 and grades 6–8.

FOCUS QUESTIONS

1. How is a ratio different from a proportion?

2. How can teachers use student intuition to develop students' thinking about proportions?

3. Why do students mistakenly use an additive method to find proportions rather than the correct multiplicative method?

4. What models help develop the concept of percents?

Ratios

Ratios involve comparing things. In *Gulliver's Travels,* comparing the distance around the thumb to the distance around the wrist to the distance around the neck illustrated a series of ratios. Some of children's earliest experiences with comparisons involve ratios or rates. For example, if a child pays one dime for three stickers, the rate is three stickers for one dime

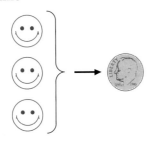

This ratio may be read as "three to one" and recorded as 3 to 1, 3:1, or $\frac{3}{1}$. Any of these forms is acceptable.

We can also form ratios to report the number of stickers to nickels as 3 to 2 or stickers to pennies as 3 to 10:

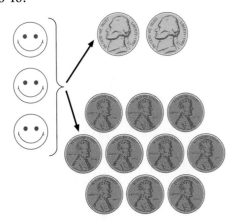

Note that this ratio could also be expressed in reverse, as 10 pennies for every 3 stickers, which we could write as 10 to 3 or as a quotient, $\frac{10}{3}$. You could use the quotient form to help children see that the cost per sticker is more than three pennies,

which illustrates a powerful application of ratios—knowing the cost of multiple items lets us calculate the cost of a single item.

Early experiences with ratios should enable children to think of two related numbers simultaneously. As children use manipulatives such as coins or draw pictures, they should be encouraged to think about ordered pairs of numbers, such as (3 stickers, 10 pennies). The models help link the operation of multiplication directly to ordered pairs and ratios.

Working with facts about money (the number of pennies in a nickel, nickels in a quarter, and so on) gives children natural and meaningful experiences with ratios. In the Classroom 13-1 shows how organizing such facts in a ratio table not only visually displays many ratios, but also helps students realize that a ratio is a multiplicative relationship between two or more numbers in a given order. The ratio table also contains patterns that encourage students to explore relationships, generate formulas, and engage in algebraic thinking.

Prices—for instance, two cans for 99¢, 3 pounds for $1.99, and 88¢ per dozen—provide meaningful contexts for ratios. The money model also lets you naturally extend ratios to more than two numbers—for example, the ordered triple (2, 10, 50) relates 2 quarters, 10 nickels, and 50 pennies. Other real-life examples of ratios are shown in *Each Orange Had 8 Slices: A Counting Book* (Giganti, 1992).

Patterns often lead to ratios. For example, in Figure 13-2 the ratio of red links to green links in chain A is 2 to 3. Extending the chain would reveal a pattern where two red links are followed by three green links, followed by two red links, and so on. Extending chain B would show a different pattern—four red links, followed by six green links, followed by four red links, and so on. In chain B, the ratio of red to green links 4 to 6. Chain C shows how doubling chain A forms a chain with the same ratio of red to green links as chain B (4 to 6). Chains B and C are the same length (10 links),

Chain A—with 2 red links and 3 green links—RRGGG

Chain B—with 4 red links and 6 green links—RRRRGGGGGG

Chain C—with 2 red links and 3 green links—RRGGGRRGGG

FIGURE 13-2   Chains showing equivalent ratios.

In the Classroom 13-1

KNOW YOUR COINS

OBJECTIVE: **Using value of coins in a ratio table to develop patterns and proportions and to examine algebraic relationships.**

GRADE LEVEL: **4–6**

▼ Use a ratio table to help complete these patterns:

Number of coins

Quarters	1	2		4	5	6
Nickels	5	10	15	20		30
Pennies	25	50	75		125	150

▼ Answer these questions and fill in the blank:

- Describe a pattern you found in each row.

- Write a ratio for the number of quarters to nickels. _____

- Write a ratio for the number of nickels to pennies.

  _____

- Write a ratio for the number of quarters to pennies. _____

▼ Try these:

- How many nickels will be needed for 8 quarters?

  _____

  Tell two different ways to decide.

- How many pennies will be needed for 10 quarters?

  _____

  Tell two different ways to decide.

- Give three numbers (not shown in the table) that could go

  in the nickles row _____

  in the pennies row _____

- Give three numbers that could *not* go

  in the nickles row _____

  in the pennies row _____

- How many quarters would you have when the number of quarters plus the number of nickels plus the number of pennies (all in one column of the ratio table) first exceeds $30? _____

So far, we've been discussing the chains in Figure 13-2 from a part-to-part perspective—that is, we've been discussing the ratio of one part of the chain (the red links) to another part of the chain (the green links). Now let's examine these chains from a part-to-whole perspective (see Chapter 12 for use of a part-to-whole model for constructing and interpreting fractions). For example, consider the ratio between the number of red links (the part) and the total number of links (the whole) in each chain. In chain A, this ratio is 2 to 5, whereas it is 4 to 10 in both chains B and C, which shows that these two ratios are also equivalent. Note that we have used the same model to show different ratios, depending on the perspective (part-to-part was 2 to 3 and part-to-whole was 2 to 5). In your instruction, therefore, you must be very clear about what is being compared when discussing ratios.

Children encounter ratios in many different forms: "three video games for a dollar," "twice around," "half as much," and so on. Showing children real-world examples of ratios helps them develop a greater awareness and understanding of ratios and how they work. For instance, you can show children how adjusting recipes can mean working with ratios that involve more than two numbers. Other examples might include a can of mixed nuts with a ratio of cashews to almonds to peanuts of 3:5:10 or a sack of lawn fertilizer where with "8–12–20" printed on it, indicating ratio of the percentages of phosphorus, nitrogen, and potash in the fertilizer. You can also use examples like these to remind students of the order of the numbers in a ratio and the importance of understanding what each number represents—for instance, the ordered pair (5, 25) from ratio table in In the Classroom 13-1 could represent 5 quarters and 25 nickels or 5 nickels and 25 pennies. Ratios have little meaning unless you know what the numbers represent. Using physical models such as those shown in In the Classroom 13-1 and Figure 13-2 helps children learn to make real sense of ratios.

Figure 13-3 shows a ratio table with the ratios between the numbers of wheels on different types

	Number of vehicles					
	1	2	3	4	5	6
Number of wheels on bicycles	2	4	6	8	10	12
Number of wheels on tricycles	3	6	9	12	15	18
Number of wheels on wagons	4	8	12	16	20	24

and each chain has the same number of red links (4) and green links (6). This shows that 2:3 and 4:6 are equivalent ratios (though they make a different pattern).

FIGURE 13-3 Ratio table comparing the number of vehicles with number of wheels for bicycles, tricycles, and wagons.

of vehicles, as well as between the number of vehicles and the number of wheels on those vehicles. The ratio table contains many different patterns and gives children a visual way of understanding different ratios. For example, the table lets children see that the ratio of wheels on bicycles to wheels on tricycles could be expressed as 2:3, 6:9, or 10:15; it also lets them see that the ratio of the number of wagons to the number of wheels on those wagons could be expressed as 1:4, 4:16, or 6:24.

Students are sometimes confused by the different symbols used to write ratios. Linking the symbols to models and promoting class discussion can help minimize this confusion. For example, round chips or cut-out pictures of wheels could be used to model the wheels in Figure 13-3 before children try writing the ratios. And ratio tables help organize the information. After children record the ratios in writing, you can help children talk about the mathematics by guiding them to discuss the information in the table and the situation represented in the ratios. For the ratios in Figure 13-3, for example, you could give children early practice in verbalizing and describing some of the mathematics surrounding the concept of ratio by asking them questions such as the following:

> If I have three bicycles and six wheels, is the ratio three to six or six to three?
>
> If the ratio of bicycles to wheels is four to eight, how many bicycles do I have?
>
> If the ratio of bicycles to wheels is five to ten, how many wheels do I have?
>
> If I have six bicycles, how many wheels are there? What is the ratio of bicycles to wheels?

In addition to understanding that ratios can be constructed in different ways (e.g., part-to-part and part-to-whole), children need to understand that combining ratios is not the same as adding fractions. For example, in Figure 13-4 chain A has 2 blue links and 3 orange links (a ratio of $\frac{2}{3}$), and chain B has 4 blue links and 5 orange links (a ratio of $\frac{4}{5}$). We could join together chains A and B to form chain C, with 6 blue and 8 orange (a ratio of $\frac{6}{8}$). However, the sum of the fractions $\frac{2}{3} + \frac{4}{5}$ is not $\frac{6}{8}$ (it's $1\frac{7}{15}$). Remember that operations, such as addition, can be performed on fractions but not on ratios.

Of course, it is important that you help students understand the equivalence of different representations of ratios (e.g., 2 to 3, 2:3, and $\frac{2}{3}$) and that you help them link these representations to real-world models. But far more important is helping students understand the relationships signified by ratios. Young children with a good understanding of numbers use expressions such as "twice as much" or "half as much" more often than the representations listed above. When children use these expressions, you should take advantage of the opportunity to help them make connections and develop reversible thinking.

Math Links 13.2

Session 8 Rational Numbers and Proportional Reasoning from the Annenberg Learning Math Series provides some excellent examples that you can use to explore part-part interpretation; part-whole interpretation as well as absolute and relative comparisons. You can view this resource at http://www.learner.org/channel/ courses/learningmath/number/session8/index.html

www.wiley.com/college/reys

Proportions

A proportion is a statement that two or more ratios are equal or "the same"—for example, that the ratio 2:3 is the same as the ratio 4:6. Alternatively, you could say that two ratios are proportional (e.g., 2:3 and 4:6) or not proportional (e.g., 2:3 and 4:8). Understanding the relationships in proportions and working with these relationships is termed *proportional reasoning* and has been called the "capstone" of elementary school mathematics (Cramer, Post, and Currier, 1993). To get a sense of what proportional reasoning means, consider the following problem, which is illustrated in Figure 13-5.

A month ago, plant A was 12 cm and plant B was 15 cm tall. Now plant A is 18 cm tall and plant B is 21 cm tall. Which plant grew the most?

Chain A	ratio of blue to orange is 2 to 3 or 2/3
Chain B	ratio of blue to orange is 4 to 5 or 4/5
Chain C	ratio of blue to orange is 2 to 3 or 6/8

FIGURE 13-4 Combining ratios is different than adding fractions.

FIGURE 13-5   Which plant grew the most?

FIGURE 13-6   Comparing prices of hot cross buns in two places.

You could compare the absolute amounts that the plants grew, which might lead you to conclude that the two plants grew equally, since both plants grew 6 cm. Or you could make a multiplicative, or relative, comparison by looking at how much each plant grew in relation to its original height. From this perspective, the plant A grew $\frac{6}{12}$ of its original height, whereas plant B grew just $\frac{6}{15}$ of its original height, which might lead you to conclude that plant A grew more. Of course, both conclusions are correct—they just reflect a different basis of comparison, absolute versus relative. But it is the ability to make comparisons in relative rather than absolute terms that characterizes proportional reasoning, and it is this ability that is the hallmark of the formal operational level of cognitive development in Piaget's system (see Chapter 2).

Now let's look at another example. The two rectangles shown below are similar (i.e., have the same shape) but different sizes.

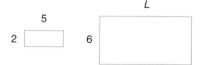

When asked to find the length of the side L, students frequently come up with 9, instead of 15, because they add when they should multiply. That is, they see that the height of the large rectangle is 4 units more than the height of the small rectangle, so they add the same 4 units to the length of the small rectangle to get $L = 9$. Instead, they should find the ratio of the height of the large rectangle to the height of the small rectangle $\left(\frac{6}{2} = 3\right)$ and then multiply the length of the small rectangle by that same ratio to find L ($5 \times 3 = 15$). The fact that the two rectangles are the same shape means that their corresponding sides are in the same ratio—that is, they are in proportion.

Research shows that this type of error reflects students' misconceptions about ratio and proportion and is not simply the result of carelessness (Cramer et al., 1993; Lesh, Post, and Behr, 1998).

These two problems are similar because they both involve comparison of like quantities—plant height to plant height and length of sides to length of sides. But problems where proportional reasoning is needed can also involve comparison of unlike quantities, such as the price comparison shown in Figure 13-6.

With a problem like this, your first task is to help students clarify what the problem is asking. In this case, the question is, which buns are the best buy, which cost less per bun? Next, you have to help students determine a method for approaching the problem. For instance, you could encourage them to construct ratio tables like these:

Number of buns	1	3
Cost		51¢

Number of buns	1	4
Cost		64¢

Alternatively, you could suggest that double number lines (also called two-sided number lines) would be a powerful model:

With either of these models, your goal would be to help students find equivalent ways of representing the cost of a bun at the two stores. Both models let students come up with these equivalent representations:

At store A: 3:51 = 1:17

At store B: 4:64 = 1:16

Thus, at store A a hot cross bun costs 17¢, while at store B a hot cross bun costs 16¢. This means that the best buy is at store B. (Of course, this answer ignores issues such as the quality of the buns, as well as whether to walk a block to save a penny!)

Students will frequently encounter situations involving comparisons of like and unlike quantities, both in problems they are given at school and in their everyday lives. Generally speaking, children have an easier time working with proportions involving unlike quantities, as they are less likely to make the error of adding instead of multiplying.

Note that there is another way to look at the hot cross buns problem, by comparing fractions with common denominators. That is, you can represent the ratios as the quotients $\frac{1}{17}$ and $\frac{1}{16}$, which can be converted into quotients with the common denominator 272 ($16 \times 17 = 272$):

$$\frac{1}{17} = \frac{16}{272} \text{ compared to } \frac{1}{16} = \frac{17}{272}$$

This again shows that store B offers the better buy because you can get 17 buns for $2.72, compared to 16 for the same cost at store A.

Math Links 13.3

*Y*ou can view a range of activities involving proportion—including patterns, ratio tables, rate/time, and similar triangles at The Math Forum Web site at http://mathforum.org/mathtools/cell/m5,7.9.3,ALL,ALL/ These activities emphasize practice rather than the conceptual development of proportional reasoning.

www.wiley.com/college/reys

Now let's examine another problem that requires proportional reasoning:

> Suppose 10 horses need 4 acres of pasture to live comfortably. How many acres would 15 horses need to live comfortably?

Rather than teach students an algorithm for solving a problem like this, you want them to approach it using their intuition or their existing skills. Figure 13-7 shows five student responses to this problem. Many students, like Karen, draw pictures (or use manipulatives); others, like Tom, make a list showing a pattern; some make a ratio table and use their knowledge of equivalent fraction, as Carrie did; and some find a unit rate, as Jose did. Still others may use an incorrect strategy, like Bob.

Note that Bob's approach reflects a misconception that students commonly bring to solving proportion problems: "When in doubt, add" (Miller and Fey, 2000). The concept of proportion is closely linked to multiplication, yet it is often diffi-

KAREN: *Using a picture or a diagram* I drew the picture and then counted the acres to be 6.

TOM: *Using patterns* I noticed:
- 10 horses need 4 acres of pasture . . . so
- 20 horses need 8 acres of pasture

Then I split the difference and got 15 horses need 6 acres of pasture.

CARRIE: *Using a ratio table* I did it this way:

Number of horses	10	15
Number of acres	4	?

I thought 10 is to 4 as 5 is to 2 and 15 is to 6. So they need 6 acres of land

JOSE: *Using a unit rate or density* I thought, 4 divides into 10 two times with a remainder of $\frac{2}{4}$ or $\frac{1}{2}$ So there are $2\frac{1}{2}$ horses per acre. Then I saw how many acres it would take for 15 horses. I divided 15 by $2\frac{1}{2}$. Or $15 \div \frac{5}{2}$ which is the same as $15 \times \frac{2}{5}$. That means that it would be 6 acres.

BOB: *Using an incorrect addition/subtraction strategy* I figured there are six more horses than acres ($10 - 4$). So I subtracted 6 from 15 and the number of acres is 9.

FIGURE 13-7 Methods children use to solve the horse and pasture problem.

cult for students to make the necessary connections. Having students share their solutions—both correct and incorrect—on the board may help them grasp this important idea.

We have considered three different types of problems where proportional reasoning is needed (Kilpatrick et al., 2001; Miller and Fey, 2000). The hot cross buns problem (see Figure 13-6) illustrates *numerical comparison problems*; the horses per acre problem (see Figure 13-7) illustrates *missing*

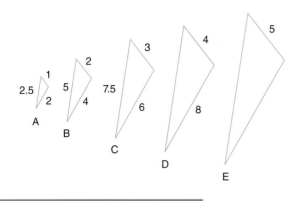

FIGURE 13-8 Some similar triangles.

number problems; and the problem with similar rectangles illustrates *scaling problems*, as does Figure 13-8, which shows a collection of similar triangles and gives children opportunities for examining different patterns.

Help students understand that triangle A is similar to triangle B because the ratios of the sides are equal: 1:2:2.5 = 2:4:5. Likewise, triangles B and C are similar. What about triangles D and E? Ask students: if D is similar to A, what is the length of the longest side of D? Here you have to help students see that a proportion needs to be established, and since there are several similar triangles, there are multiple solutions, each of which produces the same result. For example, you could compare corresponding sides of triangles A and D, where L indicates the longest side of D:

$\frac{1}{4} = \frac{2}{8} = \frac{2.5}{L}$, so L must be 4×2.5, or 10 units.

If you compared triangles B and D, the proportion would be:

$\frac{2}{4} = \frac{4}{8} = \frac{5}{L}$, so L must be double 5, or 10 units.

Now you could ask students: If triangle E is also similar to triangle A, what proportions can be established to find the lengths of its other two sides, where one side is S and the other side is OS? At this point, students should recognize that:

$\frac{1}{5} = \frac{2}{S} = \frac{2.5}{OS}$, so $S = 5 \times 2 = 10$ units and

$OS = 5 \times 2.5 = 12.5$ units.

Once again, comparing different similar triangles would have involved different proportions but the same result. For example, comparing E and B gives this:

$\frac{5}{2} = \frac{S}{4} = \frac{OS}{5}$, so $S = \frac{(4 \times 5)}{2} = 10$ units and

$OS = \frac{(5 \times 5)}{2} = 12.5$ units

Once students have made sense of proportions by solving many problems in a variety of ways, you can introduce them to a more algebraic

method of solving missing number problems. For example, consider the following problem:

> How much will a dozen balloons cost if 3 balloons cost 48¢?

Here are visual models with the double number line for two popular thinking strategies upper elementary children use to solve this problem:

a. By package per price strategy

  3 balloons cost $0.48,

  so 12 balloons is 4 × 3,

  so 4 × $0.48 is $1.92.

b. By unit price strategy

  3 balloons cost $0.48,

  so each balloon is $0.16.

  12 balloons would be 12 × $0.16 or cost $1.92.

Middle grade students will be able to write an algebraic equation in a variety of ways:

$\frac{3}{48} = \frac{12}{\square}$ Thinking $\frac{3 \text{ balloons}}{\$0.48}$ as $\frac{12 \text{ balloons}}{\square}$

  (where the symbol $\square$ is the cost of the balloons)

$\frac{3}{12} = \frac{48}{\square}$ Thinking $\frac{3 \text{ balloons}}{12 \text{ balloons}}$ as $0.48 is to $\square$

$\frac{48}{3} = \frac{\square}{12}$ What would students be thinking in this case?

$\frac{12}{4} = \frac{\square}{48}$ What would students be thinking in this case?

Although students should recognize the equivalence of these statements, they should feel free to use the model or form of their choice.

The pennies–nickels comparisons shown in In the Classroom 13-1 contain many equivalent ratios (1:5 = 2:10, 2:10 = 3:15, and so on). The concept of equivalent ratios is important and can be anchored in different ways. For example, Figure 13-9 shows a table displaying the result of 5 pennies for 1 nickel as $y = 5x$. These tabular data provide opportunities to discover patterns, explore an algebraic relationship, and observe that the ratio of all of these proportions is constant.

Another approach to help students make sense of proportions is to use estimation skills. Think about the following problem.

X	Y
1	5
2	10
3	15
4	20
5	25
6	30
7	35

FIGURE 13-9 Table comparing number of nickels (*X*) to number of pennies (*Y*).

A trout swam 5.8 meters in 3 seconds. At this rate, how far could it travel in 19 seconds?

Students could think:

That's about 6 meters in 3 seconds or 2 meters per second. And 2 meters per second times about 20 seconds would give 40 meters.

Another student could say:

19 seconds is about 6 times the 3 seconds, so approximately 6 meters times 6 would be about 36 meters.

Although each of these estimates is different, each of them is reasonable. This type of estimation thinking is very productive. It should be both encouraged and rewarded. It uses estimation along with ratios to produce ballpark answers. Frequent experiences similar to this one will improve students' judgment, making them less likely to fall victim to unreasonable answers resulting from indiscriminate number crunching. Suppose the student mistakenly set up the proportion:

$$\frac{5.8}{3} = \frac{19}{\square}$$

And then correctly computed that $\square = 9.8$

What mistake did the student make in this proportion? How could he determine that he was making an error in his thinking? What would a correct proportion be? Using estimation to produce a ballpark result might help the student realize that 9.8 is an unreasonable answer and encourage the student to reflect on the procedures used.

Of course, using a double number line model provides a model for a correct ratio, $\frac{3}{5.8} = \frac{19}{\square}$ but also allows the rejection of 9.8 as being an unreasonable answer.

Figure 13-10 shows an item given to fourth graders on a national assessment (Kenney, Lindquist,

A fourth-grade class needs 5 leaves each day to feed its 2 caterpillars. How many leaves would they need each day for 12 caterpillars?

Answer _____

Use drawings, words, or numbers to show how you got your answer.

Correct	Incorrect

FIGURE 13-10 Samples of students' solutions to a problem involving proportion.

and Heffernan, 2002). Examples of two correct and incorrect responses are also shown. The incorrect answers demonstrate how some children considered this an additive rather than multiplicative problem. The overall performance was low, as only 6% of the students gave a correct answer with a correct explanation, and another 7% gave a correct answer without an explanation or made an error using a correct method. The majority (86%) of the fourth graders gave an incorrect response.

Consider using other real-life applications of proportions with which children are familiar, such as the thumb to wrist or other body parts as described in the *Body Ratios* Snapshot of a Lesson. Other real-world applications include recipes, photographs of different sizes, maps, and scale drawings or models. Using a zoom in or out on a computer screen or when photocopying both illustrate proportions between the original and its new image. The concepts of ratio and proportionality can be naturally connected to geometry problems, as similarity is based on proportions. Two figures are similar if their respective sides are in the same ratio (i.e., proportional). Thus all squares are similar, but all rectangles are not. Figure 13-11 shows drawings of similar rectangles. Notice that in each of the five rectangles, the ratio between the vertical side and the horizontal size is constant. For example, in the smallest rectangle, the ratio is 2:6 and the largest rectangle the ratio is 6:18. The rectangles in Figure 13-11b show that a single line passes through the vertex of each of these rectangles, and this demonstrates that the slope of the diagonals (i.e., the ratio of the vertical height to the horizontal length) of each of these rectangles is the same. This is visible from Figures 13-11a and 13-11b. The ratio table shown in Figure 13-11c shows these lengths and the equivalence of each of the ordered pairs shown. The pattern can be extended in the graphs as well as in the ratio table. An examination of these ratios, such as—2:6, 3:9, or 5:15 confirms that each of them is equivalent, and the resulting slope is $\frac{1}{3}$.

(a)

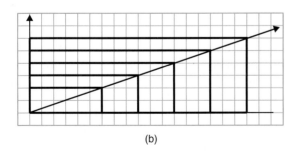

(b)

Length of vertical side	2	3	4	5	6
Length of horizontal side	6	9	12	15	18

(c)

FIGURE 13-11 Drawing similar rectangles and ratio table.

Children's books, such as *Anno's Math Games* (Anno, 1987), provide different yet interesting contexts to explore ratios and proportions and connect them to percent. Other excellent ideas on using literature to explore proportional reasoning are available (Thompson, Austin, and Beckmann, 2002; Martinie and Bay-Williams, 2003).

Math Links 13.4

*T*he PBS Mathline video *Blazing the Trail* provides a lesson that engages students in working with scales on a map as a stepping stone to proportional reasoning. Details on this tape are available at http://www.pbs.org/teachersource/mathline/lessonplans/atmp/blazing/blazing_procedure.shtm

www.wiley.com/college/reys

Percents

You only need to read a newspaper or watch television to be reminded that percent is one of the most widely used mathematical concepts:

Save 23 to 55%
MONEY MARKET CERTIFICATES
14.70% YIELDS
16.07%

Serious crimes drop 5 percent

City Asks For
40% Budget Increase

Wholesale Price Index Up 0.6 Pct.

38 Percent Plunge In Profits

Understanding of percent is taken for granted, although there is plenty of evidence to the contrary. Incorrect usage of percent is common among secondary students and adults. Flagrant errors abound, suggesting that often the most basic ideas are unclear (Gay and Aichele, 1997). For example, about one-third of the 17-year-olds and adults missed the following question on the first national assessment:

If 5% of the students are absent today, then 5 out of how many are absent?

An error on such a fundamental idea suggests they did not know that 100 is the comparison base for percent.

Misconceptions, distortions, and confusion surrounding percent are surprisingly easy to find. Here are some examples:

• "Prices reduced 100%." If this advertisement were correct, the items would be free. Probably, the prices were reduced 50%. If an item that originally cost $400 was on sale for $200, then the ad based the 100% on the sale price, when it should have been based on the original price.

- "Of all doctors interviewed, 75% recommended our product." This type of claim could be an effective advertisement for a company. If, however, the ad said "3 out of the 4 doctors we interviewed recommended our product," the consumer reaction might be different. Percents can often be used to disguise the number involved. Thus they can be misused. Percents allow for easy comparisons because of the common base of 100, but they may appear to represent a larger sample than actually exists.

Discussing the following questions and providing real-life examples can help students develop a number sense for percents:

- Can you eat 50% of a cake?
- Can you eat 100% of a cake?
- Can you eat 150% of a cake?
- Can a price increase 50%?
- Can a price increase 100%?
- Can a price increase 150%?
- Can a price decrease 50%?
- Can a price decrease 100%?
- Can a price decrease 150%?

Ironically, the understanding of percent requires no new skills or concepts beyond those used in mastering fractions, decimals, ratios, and proportions. In fact, percent is not really a mathematical topic, but rather the application of a particular type of notational system. The justification for teaching percent in school mathematics programs rests solely on its social utility. Consequently, percent should be taught and learned in application situations. Because the primary objective is to solve problems involving percent, the use of calculators is appropriate and allows students to focus on the concepts of percents rather than get bogged down in written algorithms. Special function keys such as the percent key and the memory keys also could be introduced.

As is true with decimals and fractions, percents express a relationship between two numbers. Percents are special ratios based on 100 and without a doubt are the most widely used of all ratios. Percent is derived from the Latin words *per centum,* which mean "out of a hundred" or "for every hundred." Thus the origin of percent and its major uses are more closely associated with ratio and proportions than with either decimals or fractions.

When is percent understood? Students understand percent when they can use it in many different ways. For instance, if a child understands 25%, he or she can do the following tasks.

- Find 25% in various contexts:

    Cover 25% of a floor with tiles.

    Determine 25% off the price of a given item.

    Survey 25% of the students in class.

In many such situations, estimates of 25% are not only appropriate but essential.

- Identify characteristics of 25%:

    25% of the milk in a glass is less than half.

    If 25% of the milk in a glass is spilled, then 75% remains.

- Compare and contrast 25% with a range of other percents and numbers such as 5%, 50%, 100%, one-fourth, one-half, and 0.25.

    25% is half as much as 50%, one-fourth as much as 100%, five times as much as 5%, less than one-half, and the same as one-fourth and 25 hundredths.

Early development of percent can be facilitated with literature connections. For example, *The Grizzle Gazette* illustrates percent in several different ways (Murphy, 2003).

Understanding Percents

Percents should be introduced only after students thoroughly understand fractions and decimals and have had experience with ratios and proportions. Percent is not studied extensively in elementary school, although it is typically introduced in fifth or sixth grade.

Initially, students need a variety of experiences with the fundamental concepts of percent, and these experiences should be connected to various concrete models and real-world contexts. Computation applying percent in problem-solving situations is generally reserved for later. Students who understand that percent means parts out of one hundred and have a good pictorial representation of percent are more successful in solving percent problems than those who do not. Research has found that students naturally use benchmarks to make initial judgments about percent situations (Lembke and Reys, 1994). Helping students develop the concepts for common percent benchmarks and their fraction and decimal equivalents—such as 10%, 25%, 33%, 50%, and 75%—helps them apply their percent number sense to problem-solving situations.

Initial instruction should build on familiar models (Gay and Aichele, 1997). A dollar is made up of 100 cents; therefore, it provides a natural connection among percents, fractions, and decimals. For example, 25 cents is $0.25, one-fourth of a dollar, and also 25% of a dollar.

This model should be expanded to illustrate a wide range of percents, such as 50%, 90%, 5%, 100%, 99%, 1%, and 200%.

These percents should be illustrated with a variety of different situations and models. For example, a rope with 100 disks arranged in multiples of 10 in alternating colors shows 50% of each color.

These two rectangular grids also show 50%.

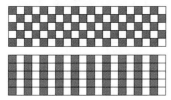

Percent bars can be used to show percent. This bar is showing 75%:

A meterstick provides another easily accessible and effective model. Cover part of the meterstick with blue paper and ask children to estimate the percent of the meterstick that is covered.

Also to remind them of the notion of 100%, be sure to ask: About what percent of the meterstick is not covered with blue paper?

This model allows many different situations (25%, 50%, 1%, and so forth) to be presented and

discussed quickly. Patterns may also emerge as students realize that the sum of the covered and uncovered portions always totals 100%. The percent bars can also be used to show connections between percents and decimals:

Shaded fraction circles (Appendix B) can also be used to provide multiple representations and help students see connections between fractions and percents.

These early experiences with percent should be followed by activities that center on direct translation experiences involving 100. The national assessment data revealed that only 31% of seventh graders could correctly write the decimals 0.42 and 0.9, respectively, as percents. These data are reminders of the fragile nature of students' understanding and the importance of connecting the representation of percents to decimals and fractions. Having students use percent bars, base-ten blocks, or share decimal paper (Appendix B) provides another concrete model for percents and helps students make connections between decimals and percents.

Figure 13-12 illustrates how the same diagram can be represented symbolically by a fraction, a decimal, and a percent. It should be emphasized that each small square represents 1% and the large square represents 100%. Practice activities using this model to convert percents to fractions and decimals, and vice versa, should be plentiful. For example, Figure 13-12 provides a visual reminder that 17% can also be thought of as $17 \times \frac{1}{100}$. Also, 17% can be thought of as $\frac{17}{100}$, so the concept of ratio is reinforced. This approach helps students feel comfortable with different interpretations of percent. Calculators that convert fractions, decimals, and percents are useful when students are discovering patterns and relationships.

The importance of establishing 100 as the base for percent cannot be overemphasized. Also, 50% should be recognized as the fraction $\frac{50}{100}$ or the product $50 \times \frac{1}{100}$. It is also important that students know that an infinite number of equivalent fractions ($\frac{1}{2}$, $\frac{2}{4}$ . . . . . .) also represent 50%.

FIGURE 13-12 Models and symbolizations of 17%.

In the Classroom 13-2 provides a natural means of developing some important ideas in an informal and yet meaningfully structured way. Each of the four activities should further develop children's concept of percent. Activities B, C, and D require some collection and recording of data before reporting the percents. The use of three different base numbers (10 logs, 100 pennies, and 20 chips) helps strengthen the link between ratio and percent. Even though answers on each activity depend on the data recorded, some patterns will emerge. A few questions from the teacher should trigger some stimulating discussion. For example, do the percents in each item total 100%? Why does this happen? Can you think of a time when it would not?

One particularly troublesome aspect of percents involves small percents between 0% and 1%. For example, percent, as in "percent milk fat," is not well understood. A visual representation, as in Figure 13-13, can help show that percent may indeed be less than 1%. Understanding rests on the earlier agreement that each small square represents 1%, which cannot be mentioned too often. As is true with all percents, this percent also can be shown symbolically as a fraction or a decimal. However, it is more important in elementary school to establish the intuitive notion of relative size of small percents than to devote extensive time to the algebraic gymnastics of showing the fraction and decimal equivalents.

Percent:	Fraction:	Decimal:
$\frac{1}{2}$%	$\frac{\frac{1}{2}}{100} = \frac{1}{200}$	.005

FIGURE 13-13   Model and symbolizations of $\frac{1}{2}$%.

Development of percents greater than 100% also is challenging and should be illustrated with models. Once the idea is established that a given region represents 100%, more than one such region can be used to represent percents greater than 100%. For example, 234% could be represented by two completely shaded large squares and a partially shaded one (see Figure 13-14). Using every opportunity to show equivalence of percents, fractions, and decimals helps establish and maintain these relationships.

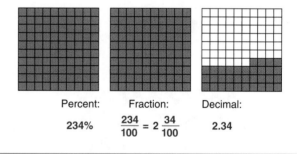

Percent:	Fraction:	Decimal:
234%	$\frac{234}{100} = 2\frac{34}{100}$	2.34

FIGURE 13-14   Model and symbolizations of 234%.

In the Classroom 13-2

USING PERCENTS

OBJECTIVE: Using different models to relate quantities to percents.

GRADE LEVEL: 4–5

A. Color this circle:

- 25% red
- 50% blue

What percent is uncolored? _____

B. Use 3 colors:

- Blue
- Green
- Yellow

Color each log with only one color.

Color all logs.

	Number Colored	Percent Colored
Blue	_____	_____
Green	_____	_____
Yellow	_____	_____

C. Put 100 pennies in a box. Shake the box. Count the number of heads, and fill in the blanks.

	Number	Percent
Heads	_____	_____
Tails	_____	_____

D. Here are 20 poker chips. Count the number of each color.

	Number	Percent
Red	_____	_____
Blue	_____	_____
White	_____	_____

Math Links 13.5

Go to the National Library of Virtual Manipulatives at http://www.matti.usu.edu. There you will find Percentages under the Number & Operations for grades 3–5. This interactive activity provides visual connections using part-whole relationships between equivalent percentages and decimals. Bar and circle graphs provide visual connections between part-whole relationships ranging from 0 to 100.

www.wiley.com/college/reys

Applying Percents

Early experiences with percent should help children establish important benchmarks, such as 0%, 50%, and 100%. Then other benchmarks, such as 10% and 90% should also be examined. Familiarity with benchmarks provides conceptual anchors to use when percents are encountered. Children come to realize that 10% is small, 50% is one-half, and 90% is nearly the entire unit. In the Classroom 13-3 provides opportunities to apply these percents by making visual estimates. In In the Classroom 13-3(A) Al's stack of coins serves as 100% and provides a guage to estimate the others. The notion of 100% is implicit when the glass is full as shown in In the Classroom 13-3(B), whereas a relative comparison is required in In the Classroom 13-3(C). In all of these activities, estimation rather than exact counts should be used to made decisions.

In elementary school, students should solve percent problems meaningfully and avoid rushing toward symbolic methods. Whenever possible, students should be asked to discuss how to solve percent problems mentally, using what they know about common percent benchmarks. Even when a formal method is required, using informal methods first to obtain an estimate promotes sense making and will help students focus on the reasonableness of formal results.

Although percents are regularly encountered in many real-life problem-solving situations, only three basic types of problems involve percents. Several different formal methods can be used to solve percent problems; two methods typically found in elementary and middle school textbooks are equation and ratio, both of which utilize algebraic thinking. The effective use of these methods requires a firm understanding of the concepts of percent and ratio as well as the ability to solve simple equations and proportions. Such skills are developed over a period of several years and need not be rushed.

In the equation method, the following equation is used:

percent × total = part

The two known values are placed in the equation and then students solve the equation for the third, unknown value.

In the ratio method, a (part) is b (percent) of c (total). The variables are set up as equal ratios or a proportion:

$$\frac{b \text{ (percent)}}{100} = \frac{a \text{ (part)}}{c \text{ (total)}}$$

Students place the three known values into the proportion and solve for the fourth, unknown value.

In the Classroom 13-3
ESTIMATING PERCENTS

OBJECTIVE: **Connect benchmarks of 10%, 50%, 90% to physical quantities.**

GRADE LEVEL: **4–5**

A. Al has 100 pennies. Estimate to decide who has about 90 pennies, 50 pennies, and 10 pennies.

Al   Barb   Rustin   Whitney

B. Estimate to decide which of these glasses are closest to 10%, 50%, and 90% full.

C. Estimate to decide in which of these sets are the blue balls closest to 10%, 50%, or 90% of all the balls.

Now let's take a brief look at each of the three types of percent problems and how they may be solved using both informal and formal methods:

• Finding the percent of a given number.

Lucas receives $60 per month for a paper route. Next month he will get a 10% raise. How much will his raise be?

The context of this problem suggests that the raise will be something considerably less than $60. The situation might be solved mentally or modeled as shown in Figure 13-15.

The rectangular array shown in Figure 13-15 is very similar to the percent bar model and can be used to construct several different proportions:

Any of these proportions leads to $R = \$6$. The computation is simple and may disguise the level of difficulty this type of problem presents. Only about one-half of eighth graders were successful at solving this type of problem on the seventh national assessment (Silver and Kenney, 2000).

• Find what percent one number is of another number.

The Cardinals won 15 of their 20 games. What percent did they win?

Intuitively, it is clear that the Cardinals did not win all of their games, so the answer must be less than 100%. Similarly, they won more than half of their games, so it must be more than 50%. The situation could be solved mentally or modeled as shown in Figure 13-16.

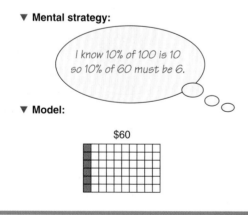

FIGURE 13-15 "How big a raise is 10% of $60?" Use a mental strategy or a model to find a percent of a number.

FIGURE 13-16 "The Cardinals won 15 of their 20 games—what percentage did they win?" Use of mental strategy or model for finding what percent one number is of another number.

Here are two other ways to find the solution:

$P/100\% = 15/20$ or $P/15 = 100\%/20$

Equation method: $P \times 20 = 15$
$P = 15/20 = .75 = 75\%$

The percent bar provides a model to help children construct different proportions that lead to the same result. Once again the computation is easy, but the national assessment provides a reminder of the difficulty students have with percent. For example, 43% of seventh graders correctly answered "30 is what percent of 60?" but only 20% correctly answered "9 is what percent of 225?" (Silver and Kenney, 2000).

• Find the total (100%) when only a percent is known.

The sale price on a coat was $40 and it was marked down 50%. What was its original price?

Common sense suggests that the original price should be more than $40. Guess-and-test is often a very effective strategy in solving this type of problem. For example, if children guess an original price of $60, then the sale price of $30 is too low. Still, they are on the right track, and if they continue this approach, it will eventually lead to the correct price of $80. The problem could be solved mentally or modeled as shown in Figure 13-17.

▼ Mental strategy:

I know
50% is the same as one-half.
If $40 is half of the original price and 40 is half of 80, the original price must be $80.

▼ Model:

Pecent bar

0	50%	100%

0	$40	OP
	Sale price	Original price

FIGURE 13-17 "A coat is on sale for $40 after being marked down 50%—what was the original price?" Use of mental strategy or model for finding the total when only a percent is known.

The percent bar model provides a base for either of these solutions, where *OP* is the original price:

Ratio method: $\dfrac{50\%}{100\%} = \dfrac{\$40}{OP}$ $OP = \$80$

Equation method: 50% of $OP = \$40$

$$OP = \dfrac{\$40}{.50} = \$80$$

Research has shown this type of problem is typically more difficult to solve (Silver and Kenny, 2000). The consistently poor performance on percent problems means that instruction must become more meaningful. If emphasis is placed on a particular method before the problem is thought through and well understood, the result will probably be confusion and poor performance. Instructional emphasis in elementary school must be on thinking aloud and talking about what should be done and what a reasonable answer would be. These teacher-led discussions should occur before any serious efforts are made to solve the problem with pencil and paper. Early emphasis on writing a solution to a percent problem forces many students to operate mechanically (without any conscious thinking) on the numbers to produce an answer.

Students should be encouraged to think quantitatively in solving problems involving percent. Research does not support the teaching of a single method (such as ratio or equation) to solve such problems (Lemke and Reys, 1994). Instruction, therefore, should be flexible and not locked into a single method. You should present a variety of problems involving percent and then follow student leads flexibly toward solutions. Encourage students to verbalize their solutions as they engage in the actual problem-solving process. This verbalization helps clarify what was done (right or wrong). It also encourages them to reflect on the reasonableness of an answer.

This less formal, intuitive approach lacks the structure and security of emphasizing a particular method, but it has several important advantages. In particular, it encourages students to understand the problem in their own minds along with possible solutions and decreases the likelihood of their applying a method blindly.

Cultural Connections

Ratio, proportion, and percent are core elements in mathematics programs in countries throughout the world. International assessments have documented comparatively low performance on items involving proportional thinking, yet the cognitive processes required in developing these concepts is consistent across countries. For example, much of the work done by Piaget involved French children and the levels of thinking he proposed to describe their cognitive development described in Chapter 2 have been documented to apply across different cultures, including the United States. Studies in different countries have also demonstrated that children reflecting high levels of success with proportional thinking are consistently operating at a formal operations level (Kilpatrick et al., 2001).

Percent is a common topic as well and research has demonstrated that children in other countries who are not proficient in computational procedures often reflect a lack of some underlying principles. For example, only about half of the sixth graders tested in Japan correctly reported that 100% of 48 is 48 (Reys, 1993). It is fair to conclude that the topics of ratio, proportion, and percent are challenging to teach and learn regardless of where teachers and children are in the world.

A Glance at Where We've Been

Ratios compare two or more numbers. They take different forms and have many applications; money (pennies for nickels), measurements (12 inches in a foot), consumer purchases (3 for 29¢), scale drawings, and blueprints are but a few. Ratio tables provide an excellent model for exploring patterns involving ratios.

A proportion provides a relationship between two or more ratios. Together with proportion, ratios provide an opportunity to practice many computational skills as well as strengthen problem-solving skills. Proportions provide a way to find answers to problems where the numbers are relational. These relationships may be considered additive (absolute) or multiplicative (relative). Children often apply additive procedures to proportions that require multiplicative thinking, particularly in dealing with like quantities. The ability of children to apply multiplicative thinking or proportional reasoning is an important instructional goal, and is one of the reasons why proportional reasoning has been called the capstone of elementary school mathematics. The use of the double number line is a powerful model for helping children engage in proportional reasoning.

Proportional reasoning is complex, both in terms of the mathematics and of the developmental experiences it requires. Yet it is an important skill for students to gain because it facilitates algebraic thinking. Ratios and proportions also provide a natural means of studying percent, which has a comparison base of 100. Because few mathematical topics have more practical usage than percents, it is essential that meaningful and systematic development of percent be provided. Instruction should use concrete models to support foundational percent concepts. Key among those concepts are benchmarks of 100% and 50% as well as 90%, 10%, and 1%. These benchmarks provide anchors for students to solve a wide range of problems involving percent, and to gauge the reasonableness of their answer.

Things to Do: From What You've Read

1. Give a real-life example of a ratio and a proportion. How could you help children distinguish between them?

2. Describe how estimating the number of heartbeats in an hour or in a lifetime uses ratios. How could you use a calculator or a spreadsheet to solve the problem?

3. Describe how proportions could be used to compare two products: If a 24-ounce can of pears sells for $1.90 and a second 32-ounce can of pears sells for $2.65, which one is the better buy?

4. Describe how you could use a meterstick, graduated in millimeters, to illustrate each of the following percents:
   a. 35%
   b. 3.5%
   c. 0.35%

5. If a dinner bill was $48. Tell how you would estimate a 15% tip. Explain how knowing a way to find 10% of a number mentally would be useful.

6. Rose was making $45,000 per year. She received a 10% raise. Later in the year, the company started losing money and reduced all salaries by 10%, Rose said, "I'm making less money than last year." Is her thinking correct? Tell why.

7. Describe how you would think through a solution to this problem: The population of a city increased from 200,000 to 220,000. What is the percent increase? Demonstrate two different ways to solve the problem.

8. A 35-mm film is in the ratio of 2 to 3. Photographs are usually printed in 4 × 6, 5 × 7, or 8 × 10. While a 4 × 6 print maintains the same 2 to 3 ratio, the others don't—thus larger pictures are made and then cropped. That is why 4 × 6, 5 × 7, and 8 × 10 photographs of the same event are not identical. If a 2 × 3 ratio is used to generate larger pictures, what is the size of the picture that an 8 × 10 must result from? Describe how you might use this real-world application of ratio with a class.

Things to Do: Going Beyond This Book

IN THE FIELD

1. *Finding Out about Proportions.* Ask several fifth or sixth graders this question: "A design is 2 cm wide and 2.4 cm long. If the picture is to be enlarged so that it is 5 cm wide, how long will it be?" Ask them to explain their reasoning and answer. Check to see if students tended to be "adders" (i.e., added 3 cm to the dimensions, thus getting 5 cm wide and 5.4 cm long). If they modeled the solution correctly and used multiplication, report the thinking they used.

2. *Know Your Coins.* In the Classroom 13-1 provides a structured activity for exploring patterns

---

*Additional activities, suggestions, and questions are provided in *Teaching Elementary Mathematics: A Resource for Field Experiences* (Wiley 2007).

and connecting them to ratio. Use this activity as a guide to ask a fifth or sixth grader a series of questions. What patterns seemed to be the strongest? Explain how experiencing this activity would help develop the notion of ratio.

3. *Finding Out about Percents.* Ask fifth or sixth graders some of these questions: What is 50% of $80? What is 100% of 50? What does the % on a milk carton mean? Is it possible to get a raise of 200%? In each question, ask them to explain their thinking. Do you think they have a good understanding of percent? Tell why.

IN YOUR JOURNAL

4. Ratios may be used to determine the best buy. Use local newspaper advertisements to find information and set up ratios to compare prices for different sizes of the same product. Respond in your journal to this question: Can you refute the claim "the larger the quantity, the lower the unit price"?

WITH ADDITIONAL RESOURCES

5. Read the articles "Three balloons for two dollars: Developing proportional reasoning" by Langrall and Swafford (2000), "Proportional reasoning" by Miller and Fey (2000), "Improving middle school teachers' reasoning about proportional reasoning" by Thompson and Bush (2003), "Assessing proportional reasoning" by Bright, Joyner and Wallis (2003), or any article from the *2002 NCTM Yearbook.* Describe instructional suggestions they offer from research to help students better understand proportions.

6. Read the articles, "Our diets may be killing us" by Shannon (1995), "Diet, ratios, proportions: A healthy mix" by Telese and Abete (2002), or "Making sense of percent" by Metz (2003). Describe how you could use ideas like those to make a ratio or percent lesson.

7. Read the articles, "The legend of Paul Bunyan" (Bohl, Oursland, and Fince, 2003) or "Using literature as a vehicle to explore proportional reasoning" (Thompson, Austin, and Beckmann, 2002). Discuss some ways these stories might be used to help students understand ratio and proportion.

WITH TECHNOLOGY

8. If you were able to view the tape *Body Ratios,* here are some questions:

Did the children believe that some of the ratios of body parts discussed in *Gullivers Travels* were true? Do you?

How is ratio used to make connections with fractions and decimals?

Explain how the teacher used estimation to help children deal with some messy ratios.

How could the ratios experienced in this lesson be used to develop proportions?

Note to Instructors: You can find additional resources, learning activities, and black-like masters in this text's accompanying Instructor's Manual, at www.wiley.com/college/reys.

Book Nook for Children

Anno, M. *Anno's Math Games.* New York: Philomel Books, 1987.

Uses proportion to compare the relative numbers of sugar cubes in different-sized containers. A wealth of ideas appear in this book that can be extended to a number of situations; for this reason, it may be desirable to explore one chapter at a time.

Giganti, Jr., P. *Each Orange Had 8 Slices: A Counting Book.* New York: Greenwillow Books, 1992.

If each orange has eight slices and each slice has two seeds, how many seeds are there in all? You can multiply, add, or count your way through the math puzzles hiding in the world all around you.

Murphy, S. J. *The Grizzly Gazette.* New York: Harper Collins, 2003.

The Camp Grizzly is having a parade and must elect a mascot to wear the Grizzly bear outfit. Candidates have started to campaign to wear the outfit. The reader will see how the candidates are keeping track of the daily polls by using percentages in circle graphs. As the last day approaches, each candidate gave a speech and the candidate that won, wrote a new camp cheer and she won with 50% of the vote. There are activities and games in the back of the book for teachers and parents to use.

Swift, J. *Gulliver's Travels* was originally published in 1726.

A number of different adaptations of this masterpiece have been published. Many contemporary versions exist, and the one by James Riordan, published by Oxford University Press in 1998 is excellent. Following Gulliver on the miniature island of Lilliput provides a rich context for discussing and exploring ratio and proportion.

Annotated Resources

Bright, G., Joyner, J., and Wallis, C. "Assessing proportional reasoning." *Mathematics Teaching in the Middle School.* 9 (3) (November 2003), pp. 166–172.
The authors made the point that in order to assess proportional reasoning it is important to provide settings where additive and multiplicative reasoning can be applied—either correctly or incorrectly. Sample items to assess proportional reasoning along with student performance on them (including actually student explanations) are provided.

Langrall, C., and Swafford, J. "Three balloons for two dollars: Developing proportional reasoning." *Mathematics Teaching in the Middle School*, 6(4) (December 2000), pp. 254–261.
Four different levels of strategies students use in developing proportional reasoning are illustrated and discussed. These strategies range from Level 0—Nonproportional reasoning, Level 1—Informal reasoning about proportional situations, Level 2—Quantitative Reasoning, and Level 3—Formal proportional reasoning.

Litwiller, B., and Bright, G. *Making Sense of Fractions, Ratios, and Proportions: 2002 Yearbook.* Reston, VA: National Council of Teachers of Mathematics, 2002.
The book emphasizes that fractions, ratios, and proportion are pivotal concepts in the middle school but that their development and understanding begin in the elementary school. It shows the importance of proportional reasoning as a foundation of many applications of mathematics to real life and as an essential element of more sophisticated mathematics.

Martinie, S., and Bay-Williams, J. "Using literature to engage students in proportional reasoning." *Mathematics Teaching in the Middle School*, 9(3) (November 2003), pp. 142–148.
Three investigations using literature to explore proportionally across the curriculum—including percent, algebra, and measurement—are illustrated. Nine different books that provide opportunities to explore proportional reasoning are annotated.

Metz, M. L. "Making sense of percent." *Mathematics Teaching in the Middle School*, 9(1) (September 2003), pp. 44–45.
Different problem situations involving percent are provided to promote thinking and problem solving. For example: Is it better to buy an item with a 25% discount followed by a 40% discount, or an item with an original discount of 40% followed by a 25% discount?

Miller, J. L., and Fey, J. T. "Proportional reasoning." *Mathematics Teaching in the Middle School,* 5(5) (January 2000), pp. 310–314.
This article looks at strategies to develop proportional reasoning among students and discusses a study to compare proportional reasoning of students in a standards-based program with students in a control group.

Thompson, C., and Bush, W. "Improving middle school teachers' reasoning about proportional reasoning." *Mathematics Teaching in the Middle School*, 8(8) (April 2003), pp. 398–404.
Some challenges of developing proportional reasoning are discussed. Rich sample problems are illustrated along with examples of solutions to them by "proportional thinkers" and "non-proportional thinkers."

Thompson, D., Austin, R., and Beckmann, C. "Using literature as a vehicle to explore proportional reasoning." In *2002 Yearbook Making Sense of Fractions, Ratios, and Proportions* (eds. B. Litwiller and G. Bright), Reston, VA: NCTM, 2002, pp. 130–137.
Annotations on nearly 20 books are included and each book provides interesting context for engaging in problems involving ratio and proportions. Both fiction and nonfiction books are provided.

CHAPTER 14

Algebraic Thinking

Snapshot of a Lesson

Key Ideas

1. To explore and describe growing patterns
2. To encourage students to think algebraically

Background

This is a transcript of part of a video from the Modeling Middle School Mathematics project. Mr. Dauray, a sixth-grade teacher, is using the mathematics program, *Maths in Context* (1996) in a school in Rhode Island. Go to http://www.mmmproject.org (Modeling Middle School Mathematics) and click on the video matrix to view *V Patterns*.

MR. DAURAY: The other day, I come out of my house and . . . I heard this [*sound of geese honking*]. It was a sure sign of fall. Does anybody know what that might be?

JESUS: It would probably be the birds that fly in a pattern, with the V-line. I forgot the name.

STUDENT: Geese.

JESUS: Yeah, geese.

MR. DAURAY: I've got these geese right here. Can someone come up to the board and show me how you might see them flying in the air? Say I had just three geese. Can someone come up and put them on the board?

The students add geese to continue the pattern as shown in the dots below. Then Mr. Dauray explains the notation they will use.

MR. DAURAY: This happens to be the first V. This is number 1, OK, the first V. Another V pattern, this is the second V, we'll call it V2. And then we get this next one, this is the third V pattern. And it looks like this. How many birds are in the first V pattern? Jenny?

JENNY: There are 3 birds in the first V pattern.

After discussing the first three V patterns, the notation, and the number of birds in each, Mr. Dauray has the students work in groups.

MR. DAURAY: I want you to copy this chart, and I want you to extend the chart for a V pattern of 4, 5, and 6. And I want you to tell me what it looks like. Discuss in your groups, what do you think you see happening?

The students talk among themselves about the patterns. One student thinks there is something about two and two-times a number. Watch the video to see how his fellow students help him with his misconception.

Another group focuses on odd numbers. Watch the video to see if you think they justified their conjecture that there would always be an odd number of geese in the V pattern.

We rejoin the video when the class is back as a whole.

MR. DAURAY: Can someone tell me the number of geese that would be in the V number 10, the 10th pattern along?

OSCAR: I got 21.

MR. DAURAY: And how did you find that information?

OSCAR: I multiplied 10×2.

MR. DAURAY: Why did you do that?

OSCAR: Because I was thinking that every time the two extra birds come, they come and then they have a group.... Then I multiplied it by 2 and it comes out to 20, and then I added a 1, the one in the middle, then it came out to 21.

JENNY: What they are saying is that there are two geese in a pair and there are 10 pairs, so he would try and multiply it by 2×10 and then add the leader would be 21.

MR. DAURAY: Does everybody agree? Anybody want to try it out? Let's try it out for a V-number of 15. How many geese would that be?

ASHLEY: In V-pattern number 3, the V means that there are three groups, or three pairs, plus that extra one. So let's say there's 15 pairs in the 15th pattern, plus this one here.

Mr. Dauray continues with larger and larger numbers to see if students were making the generalization of multiplying the V number by 2 and adding 1.

◆ Introduction

Traditionally, children do not begin to study algebra until they have a solid foundation in arithmetic. Thus, many students who have not mastered the basic arithmetic operations never have the opportunity to learn algebra. Research in the latter part of the twentieth century indicated that students in elementary school should receive instruction that prepares them to study algebra. More importantly, it showed that these students built a deeper understanding of arithmetic concepts and skills and became better problem solvers (Carpenter, Franke, and Levi, 2003). The NCTM's *Standards* (2000) call for an increased emphasis on algebra in elementary and middle school and for everyone to study algebra in high school. The NCTM's expectations for pre-K through grade 5 are shown in Figure 14-1 (expectations for grades 6–8 are in Appendix A).

Substitute "algebra" for "mathematics" in the five views of mathematics in Chapter 1, and you will see reasons and ways to include algebra in the elementary school:

1. *Algebra is a study of patterns and relationships.* Patterns and relationships are important in their own right, and studying them leads naturally into algebraic ideas.

2. *Algebra is a way of thinking.* Algebra provides strategies for analyzing representations, modeling situations, generalizing ideas, and justifying statements.

3. *Algebra is an art, characterized by order and internal consistency.* Children who are involved in algebraic thinking gain a better understanding of the underlying structure and properties of mathematics (Carpenter and Levi, 2000).

4. *Algebra is a language that uses carefully defined terms and symbols.* These terms and symbols enhance children's ability to communicate about real-life situations and mathematics itself.

5. *Algebra is a tool.* In the past, many algebra courses presented algebra as a tool. But too often, students only learned the intricacies of the tool, without learning how to use it in any practical or meaningful way. The NCTM's Principles and Standards does not recommend this limited

Instructional programs should enable all students to:	Pre-K–2 Expectations All students should:	Grades 3–5 Expectations All students should:
• Understand patterns, relations, and functions	• Sort, classify, and order objects by size, number, and other properties • Recognize, describe, and extend patterns such as sequences of sounds and shapes or simple numeric patterns and translate from one representation to another • Analyze how both repeating and growing patterns are generated	• Describe, extend, and make generalizations about geometric and numeric patterns • Represent and analyze patterns and functions, using words, tables, and graphs
• Represent and analyze mathematical situations and structures using algebraic symbols	• Illustrate general principles and properties of operations, such as commutativity, using specific numbers • Use concrete, pictorial, and verbal representations to develop an understanding of invented and conventional symbolic notations	• Identify such properties as commutativity, associativity, and distributivity and use them to compute with whole numbers • Represent the idea of a variable as an unknown quantity using a letter or a symbol • Express mathematical relationships using equations
• Use mathematical models to represent and understand quantitative relationships	• Model situations that involve the addition and subtraction of whole numbers, using objects, pictures, and symbols	• Model problem situations with objects and use representations such as graphs, tables, and equations to draw conclusions
• Analyze change in various contexts	• Describe qualitative change, such as a student's growing taller • Describe quantitative change, such as a student's growing 2 inches in 1 year	• Investigate how a change in one variable relates to a change in a second variable • Identify and describe situations with constant or varying rates of change and compare them

FIGURE 14-1   Algebra Standard with expectations for children in grades prekindergarten–2 and 3–5.

approach to algebra, nor is it the approach we will present here. Algebra is a tool, but one that should be meaningful and useful.

Bringing algebra to elementary school does not mean just adding one more topic to a crowded curriculum. It does mean using the mathematics in the curriculum to help children develop algebraic thinking. This chapter begins with a discussion of topics—problems, patterns, and relations—that will be used in the remainder of the chapter to build algebraic thinking. After discussing the algebraic language and symbols appropriate for elementary students, we will look at ways to help children to develop algebraic thinking through modeling, generalizing, and justifying.

Math Links 14.1

The full-text electronic version of the Algebra Standard is available at the NCTM's Web site. Click on pre-K–2, 3–5, or 6–8 to read more about this standard. You can access this from http://www.nctm.org/standards/ (if you have NCTM membership) or from this book's Web site.

www.wiley.com/college/reys

FOCUS QUESTIONS

1. What does algebraic thinking mean for elementary students?

2. How do patterns help children develop algebraic thinking and ideas?

3. How can you encourage algebraic thinking as children solve problems?

4. How can you use children's understanding of relations to help develop the concept of variables?

5. How do modeling, generalizing, and justifying intertwine?

Problems, Patterns, and Relations

The teaching of algebra in elementary school should build on ideas that are an essential part of the curriculum. Problems, patterns, and relations are each an essential part of elementary school mathematics. Throughout this chapter, we will develop these three topics to illustrate ways they tie to algebraic thinking. As you read, you should: work the problems, extend the patterns, answer the questions, and ask yourself how these topics can be used to develop algebraic thinking.

Problems

Both routine and nonroutine types of problems are good topics for developing algebraic concepts and thinking. In this section, we list a few such problems, which we will view from an algebraic perspective later in this chapter.

Routine problems   Routine problems are often considered exercises for practicing computation, but they can also be used to build algebraic understanding. You will find routine problems like these in every textbook:

> Before her birthday, Jane had 8 toy trucks. At her birthday party, she was given some more trucks. That night she counted all her trucks and found she had 15. How many trucks was she given at her party?
>
> Bill had 24 pencils to put in 4 boxes. He put the same number of pencils in each box. How many pencils did he put in each box?
>
> Pat took 4 pails to the beach. She had 3 shovels and 2 rakes in each pail. How many tools did she take to the beach?

Nonroutine problems   Many nonroutine problems, especially look-for-a-pattern problems and number puzzles, lend themselves well to an algebraic approach.

Here are the *look-for-a-pattern problems* that we will use in this chapter:

> *Geese.* The geese problem in the Snapshot of a Lesson at the beginning of this chapter can be solved by examining the numerical pattern of the number of geese in any V-formation. It is the type of problem that can lead to generalization in a very natural way. Young children can solve this problem for a given V-formation by making a table, but algebra is needed to represent the general solution for all V-formations.
>
> *Sidewalk garden.* A family is building a rectangular sidewalk garden surrounded by 1-foot by 1-foot tiles. For a 1-foot by 1-foot garden, they need 8 tiles. For a 1-foot by 2-foot garden, they need 10 tiles. How many tiles do they need for a 1-foot by 8-foot garden?
>
> *Cube painting.* A large cube is made of small cubes. The large cube is 4 small cubes high, 4 small cubes wide, and 4 small cubes deep. The surface of the large cube is to be painted. How many of the small cubes are painted on 6 faces, 5 faces, 4 faces, 3 faces, 2 faces, 1 face, and no face?

Here are the *number puzzles* we will use in this chapter. Try them. Can you explain why each works?

> *Same number.* Pick a number. Add 4. Double. Subtract 6. Divide by 2. Subtract 1. What did you get? Why does it work?
>
> *Calendar.* Choose any 3 consecutive days (e.g., Tuesday, Wednesday, and Thursday) for any 3 consecutive weeks in a month (e.g., July 8–10, 15–17, and 22–24). How can you easily find the sum of all nine dates?

Patterns

Patterns are an important part of mathematics because they help children organize their world and understand mathematics. In Chapter 7, we discussed how you can use patterns to help children think about numbers. Here we will use two types of patterns, repeating and growing, for building algebraic ideas.

Repeating patterns   A repeating pattern has a core element that is repeated over and over. One of the simplest repeating patterns is an alternating pattern such as the following:

This simple pattern raises many questions about how children work with patterns. What color should be used next? This problem is not as easy as it appears, since there can be more than one correct answer. Some children may say that the next color should be red because the pattern is just alternating red and blue (i.e., the core element is a red followed by a blue). Others might say that the next color should be blue because the pattern is a red with one blue, followed by a red with two blues, followed by a red with three blues, and so on (i.e., the core grows by one blue each time it repeats). It is often difficult to get into the minds of children, so having them explain their thinking is crucial. Also, sharing ideas helps children consider alternative ways of looking at patterns. As children become familiar with patterns like this one, they can extend other patterns or make their own patterns.

Research has shown that children should begin recognizing and thinking about patterns by describing and extending patterns with pictorial models, as illustrated by In the Classroom 14-1. As children become able to identify the missing pieces in the patterns, encourage them to look at the patterns in different ways that would lead to different ways of extending the patterns. Ask questions such as "How can you describe this pattern?" or "How can you extend this pattern?" Questions like these help children begin to think algebraically.

Can you see the cores in the repeating patterns below?

Pattern A: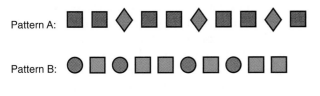

Pattern B: ⬤ ▢ ⬤ ▢ ▢ ⬤ ▢ ⬤ ▢ ▢

Pattern C: ♠ ♣ ♠ ♣ ♣ ♠ ♣ ♠ ♣ ♣ ♠ ♣

In pattern A, the core consists of three elements: two red squares followed by one blue rhombus. This is repeated over and over. In pattern B, the core consists of 5 elements: one pink circle, one green square, one pink circle, two green squares. Do you see that the core in pattern C is the same type as in pattern B?

Research from the mathematics assessment of the National Assessment of Educational Progress (NAEP) indicates that fourth-grade students often have more difficulty identifying a missing element

---

In the Classroom 14-1

THINKING ABOUT PATTERNS

OBJECTIVE: **Recognizing, describing, and extending patterns.**

GRADE LEVEL: **1–2**

▼ Provide children with a variety of patterns like these, asking them questions like:

- How do you describe this pattern?
- What shape (or object) goes in the empty space? Why?
- Are some of these patterns alike? How?

1. What pattern block shape should come next?

2. One of the shapes is missing in this string of shapes. What shape and what color would you insert? Why?

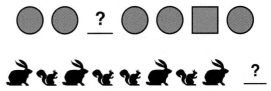

3. What animal should be in the next place? Why?

---

in a pattern (as in Problem 2 from In the Classroom 14-1) than identifying the element that continues the pattern (Kloosterman, 2004). This difficulty may simply be the result of having been asked to continue patterns more often than to fill in missing parts. Be sure to ask children both types of questions.

Math Links 14.2

*W*atch kindergarten children work with patterns on the video *People Patterns* (video 38) from the Annenberg series, *Teaching Math: A Video Library K–4*, which you can access from http://www.learner.org/resources/series32.html or from this book's Web site.

www.wiley.com/college/reys

Growing patterns   The geese problem in the Snapshot of a Lesson involves a growing pattern. You can present such patterns verbally, through pictures only, or with symbols only. Both the geese problem and the sidewalk-garden problem, for example, could be presented just with pictures, and you could ask young to continue the pattern:

Geese problem. What would be the next three pictures (terms 4, 5, and 6)?

Term 1   Term 2   Term 3

Sidewalk-garden problem. The green squares represent the garden, and the blue squares represent the tiles. What would be the next picture (term 4)? Draw pictures to illustrate terms 5 and 6.

Term 1   Term 2   Term 3

You can use pictorial representations like these as powerful links to analyzing number patterns that are growing patterns. Mathematics curricula often include problems where children are asked to continue growing number patterns or sequences of numbers. For example, the geese problem could be symbolized as 1, 3, 5, 7, . . ., and the sidewalk-garden problem could be symbolized as 8, 10, 12, . . . Do you see how these growing patterns differ from repeating patterns? In growing patterns like these, each successive term changes by the same amount from the preceding term (in both the geese problem and the sidewalk-garden problem, this amount is 2). Traditionally, children in elementary school have been given only numerical patterns like these, where the difference between successive terms is some constant amount. However, numerical patterns need not be so simple. Growing patterns, like repeated patterns, can be thought of in different ways, and we need to help children look at different ways in which patterns can grow. For example, consider the numerical patterns below:

Pattern A: 1, 2, 4, . . .

Pattern B: 1, 4, 9, 16, . . .

Pattern C: 1, 1, 2, 3, 5, . . .

In a fourth-grade classroom working with pattern A, Andy suggested that the next number in the sequence is 5. The teacher asked what the next number after 5 would be, and Andy answered 7 (1, 2, 4, 5, 7, . . .). Do you see what Andy may have had in mind? Some children said: "Andy writes two numbers, skips one, and writes the next two," "Andy skips all the threes—3, 6, 9, and all those

3-times numbers," and "Andy adds one, then two, then one, then two." Sue suggested a different pattern from Andy: " I think that the pattern goes 8, 16, and on. It just doubles." Argon said, "I think it goes 1, 2, 4, 6, 9, 12, and so on." Can you figure out what rule Argon was using?

This episode illustrates several key ideas to consider as you work with children. First, do not expect children to see patterns the way you do. It is important to have them explain their thinking. It is also important to have them realize that there is often more than one way to look at a pattern and to explain it.

Pattern B is the sequence of perfect squares, but perhaps you can describe it in a different way. Pattern C is the Fibonacci sequence. The next numbers are 8 and 13 (1, 1, 2, 3, 5, 8, 13, . . .). Can you figure out the number after that? Once you know the rule, it is easy to generate the sequence, but many people (adults as well as children) do not immediately see the rule. Children need practice in recognizing and analyzing patterns before we can start teaching them to represent patterns algebraically.

Relations

We will explore two types of relations that we can use to help children build algebraic concepts and thinking: *properties of numbers* (including relations based on number theory) and *functions*. Another relation—the *equality relation*—underpins both these types of relations as well as all of algebra.

Young children have a good sense of equality in terms of the same size or amount. Even young children know when they do not get a cookie that is the same size as yours, when one block tower is not the same height as another, or when they have three marbles just as you do. However, very few programs build on the idea of equality being "the same as" in size or amount and describing the relationship of two quantities as being the same (equal) or different (unequal). A balance provides a model of how to relate two quantities in this way (Mann, 2004). In the Classroom 14-2 shows some questions that children in primary school can investigate.

Properties of numbers   Table 9-1 in Chapter 9 reviews some of the mathematical properties of numbers (commutative, associative, distributive, and identity). In this chapter, we will discuss how to use number properties and number theory relations to promote algebraic thinking. Here are examples of number theory relations that you could encourage students to explore:

The sum of an odd number and an odd number is even.

In the Classroom 14-2

BALANCE ME

OBJECTIVE: **To explore what balances a balance scale.**

GRADE LEVEL: **1–3**

MATERIALS:

Weights (1–10 ounces or 1–10 washers), or Labeled containers weighing 1–10 units (2 of each)

(Note: You can fill containers with unifix cubes to make weights.)

Balance scale

QUESTIONS TO ASK STUDENTS:

A. I am going to put some weights on each side of the balance. Which will balance?

Left side	Right side
4	4
3	8
2 and 3	5
3 and 4	6
1, 2, and 3	6

B. If I put a 5 weight on the left side, what could I put on the right side to balance it?

C. If I put a 3 weight on one side and a 7 weight on the other side, what would I need to add to the side with the 3 weight to make the scale balance?

D. If I put a 8 weight on the left side and a 2 weight on the right side, can I balance the scale by adding a 6 weight to the left side?

E. I have the scale balanced with a 6 weight on each side. What could I add to each side to keep it balanced?

F. I only have four weights, 3, 4, 5, and 7. Could I put all or some of the weights on the scale to have it balance?

G. Could I balance the scale by using one of each of the 10 different weights?

If a number is divisible by 2 and by 3, then it is divisible by 6.

If the sum of the digits of a number is divisible by 9, then the number is divisible by 9.

Functions   Suppose two sets of numbers are related in such a way that each number in the first set is related to one and only one number in the second set. A function is a way of expressing that relation. Young children can explore ways that functions work in a very informal way. For example, they can explore how the number of boys in a group is related to the number of hands. Begin by having students tell the number of hands of 3, 4, and 10 boys; then write the numbers in a table, as shown below.

Number of boys	3	4	10	6	11	5	11
Number of hands	6	8	20				

Have students complete the table. You want the students to focus on the relationship between the number of boys and the number of hands—that is, to focus on the function. For this reason, it is best not to write the number of boys in order from 1 to 12 in the table, so students cannot easily see the pattern of the number of hands increasing by 2 with each additional boy in the group (see the table below).

Number of boys	1	2	3	4	5	6	7	8	9	10
Number of hands	2	4	6	8	10	12	14			

Another informal way for children to explore functions would be to consider the relationship of the number of girls to the number of triangles as the children make triangles with string below.

Unlike the 1-to-2 relationship of boys to hands, this is a 3-to-1 relationship (3 girls for each triangle). Some children may have difficulty describing this relationship in general terms because it calls for division rather than multiplication. Again, begin by writing the numbers in a table (in this case, it may be useful to write the number of girls in order, to help students see the relationship):

Number of girls	3	6	9	12	15	18	21	24
Number of triangles	1	2	3	4	5	6	7	8

At times, you may want to model relations using a machine that outputs a number for each number input. The challenge for the students is to decide what the machine does and how to describe it. These machines can be simple, such as one that always gives an output of one more than the number input, twice as much as the number input, or two less than the number input. A more complicated machine might relate input and output as shown in the following table, which you can have children complete:

Input	3	5	7			20	53
Output	7	11	15		29	41	

You need to help children focus on the change from the input to the output. Some children will focus only on the change from one input value to the next, but this does not help them understand the input–output relationship. So you need to ask questions like, "Given the input _____, what is the output?" You could also try drawing the table vertically, because children are accustomed to reading right to left. In the Classroom 14-3 shows an activity with a "function machine" that you can modify to suit the level of your students.

Language and Symbols of Algebra

Children can learn the language and symbols associated with algebra as they are learning about numbers. In this brief section, we look only at equality and inequality, variables, and expressions and equations, because these are the ideas that are central to the algebra that is appropriate for elementary students.

Of course, there are many other algebraic terms and symbols, but we will use them only when it is clear from the context what is meant. For example, you probably understood what was meant by the three dots that we used in earlier sections of this chapter to represent the continuation of number sequences (e.g., 1, 4, 9, 16, . . .). When you are helping children learn to think algebraically, you should use algebraic terms and symbols as you would if you were teaching children a foreign language. That is, you should weave the terms and symbols naturally into your discussions, as the teacher did in this chapter's Snapshot of a Lesson. For instance, the teacher used the terms V1, V2, and V3 in a natural manner that made sense to the students.

Math Links 14.3

If you have questions about algebra, turn to "Ask Dr. Math." This service is available from the Math Forum. It can be accessed from http://mathforum.org or from this book's Web site.

www.wiley.com/college/reys

Equality and Inequality

As we have noted, young children understand sharing equally and balancing a scale. Nevertheless, they are baffled by the equal sign (=). It is well known that many children think that the equal sign means "get an answer." For example, many children in grades 1–6 respond that 12 or 17 is the number that should be placed in the box to make the following symbolic sentence true: $8 + 4 = \square + 5$. Research showed that only 5% of students in grades 1–2 and 9% of students in grades 3–4 responded with the correct answer, 7 (Carpenter and Levi, 2000). Typically, children in these grades have not learned what "equals" means and have not learned how to interpret the structure of symbolic sentences. However, after instruction similar to that recommended in this chapter, children's results were greatly improved (66% correct in grades 1–2 and 72% correct in grades 3–4).

Math Links 14.4

A variety of Web resources for algebra that may be used by teachers and children may be found at NCTM's Illuminations Web site under the Algebra Standard. In particular, the balance activity gives students an opportunity to explore equality. You can access this from http://illuminations.nctm.org/ or from this book's Web site.

www.wiley.com/college/reys

In the Classroom 14-3

IN–OUT MACHINE

OBJECTIVE: **To analyze the actions of a function machine.**

GRADE LEVEL: **3–4**

Dr. de Zine invented an in–out machine. The machine adds, subtracts, multiples or divides markings on animals as they go through it. He has kept a record of what happened each day as animals went in and came out of the machine. Your job is to fill in the blanks in his record and to figure out how the machine worked each day.

	IN	OUT
M O N	skunk with 3 stripes	skunk now has 12 stripes
	leopard with 12 spots	leopard now has 48 spots
	zebra with 5 stripes	zebra now has _____ stripes
T U E S	dog with 5 spots	dog now has 15 spots
	cat with 2 stars	cat now has 12 stars
	rabbit with 3 marks	rabbit now has _____ marks
W E D	horse with 12 lines	horse now has 6 lines
	pig with 8 spots	pig now has 4 spots
	cow with 0 spots	cow now has _____ spots
T H U R	elephant with 32 stars	elephant now has 16 stars
	rhino with 24 diamonds	rhino now has 8 diamonds
	hippo with 41 spots	hippo now has _____ spots
F R I	frog with 4 spots	frog now has 11 spots
	toad with 3 spots	toad now has 9 spots
	salamander with _____ stripes	salamander now has 15 stripes

You can help children grasp the meaning of the equal sign (and the unequal sign, ≠) by introducing it in an activity like the one in In the Classroom 14-2. You can tell children that two quantities are equal if the scale balances. Thus, the relationships in part A of In the Classroom 14-2 would be represented as shown on the right.

You can help children use the inequality symbols (< and >) to describe larger or smaller quantities. Children can describe the relationship using words and then use the symbols. For example, they

Left side	Right side	Representation
4	4	4 = 4
3	8	3 ≠ 8
2 and 3	5	2 + 3 = 5
3 and 4	6	3 + 4 ≠ 6
1, 2, and 3	6	1 + 2 + 3 = 6

can say "3 is less than 8" and then write $3 < 8$; similarly, they can say "12 is greater than 4" and then write $12 > 4$.

In everyday life, the equal sign is used in different ways. For example, on a spreadsheet an equal sign signals the computer to do an operation. In the classroom, it is often carelessly used in carrying out a string of operations. Look at this statement:

$$5 + 3 = 8 - 6 = 2 \times 5 = 10 + 14 = 24$$

What does this mean? The equal sign was used to signal steps performing operations. It would be better to use another symbol such as an arrow. Certainly, $5 + 3$ does not equal 24.

Variables

There are three different uses of *variables*, and you should be aware of the differences. The most common use in elementary school is as a *place-holder*—for example, in the sentence $3 + \square = 7$, the box is a placeholder for the number that makes the sentence true. This is no different from using a letter, as in $3 + a = 7$; children easily adjust to using both boxes and letters to represent variables. Variables are also used in *generalizations*—for example, the generalization "any number subtracted from itself is equal to zero" may be represented as $a - a = 0$. In this generalization, the variable a represents any number, in contrast to the single number represented by a variable used as a placeholder.

Variables are also used in *formulas* and in *functions*. For example, the function relating the number of boys (B) to the number of hands (H) could be represented by $H = 2 \times B$, where H and B are the variables. If the value of one variable changes, the value of the other variable also changes.

The following table summarizes these three uses of variables:

Use of Variable	Representation	Characteristics
Placeholder	$3 + a = 7$	Specific value for a
Generalization	$a - a = 0$	All values of a make the sentence true
Function	$H = 2 \times B$	Each value of B produces one and only one value of H

Expressions and Equations

Think of an expression as representing a phrase and an equation as representing a complete sentence. For example, the expression $n + 3$ represents the phrase "three more than n" (or "n plus three" or any other equivalent phrase). The equation $n + 3 = 7$ represents the complete sentence

"three more than n is 7" (or "n plus 3 is 7" or "n plus 3 equals 7" or any other equivalent sentence). Knowing how to represent phrases will help students represent complete sentences. In many elementary programs, an equation such as $n + 3 = 7$ is called an *open sentence* because there is an unknown (often, an open box is used for the variable, rather than a letter, as we discussed in the section on variables). In contrast, the equation $4 + 3 = 7$, which does not have an unknown, is referred to as a *closed sentence*.

Modeling, Generalizing, and Justifying

The NCTM's Algebra Standard calls for students to use mathematical models to represent and understand quantitative relationships, to represent and analyze mathematical situations and structures using algebraic symbols, and to analyze change in various contexts. In this section, we will examine how the processes of modeling, generalizing, and justifying relate to each of these topics in elementary school mathematics.

Routine Problems

The following discussions show how you can use modeling and justifying to help children think algebraically about routine problems. Such problems, however, do not lend themselves to generalizing, because the equations corresponding to those problems contain variables used only as placeholders, not to make general statements about numbers.

Modeling Many elementary mathematics curricula include the use of equations to solve routine problems, but all too often, these curricula fail to emphasize helping children understand where these equations come from and how the equations make mathematical sense. For example, consider this routine problem:

> Before her birthday, Jane had 8 toy trucks. At her birthday party, she was given some more trucks. That night she counted all her trucks and found she had 15. How many trucks was she given at her party?

Young children can model this situation with physical materials (concrete models). For instance, they can put out 8 trucks and keep adding trucks until they reach 15 trucks. (A potential difficulty is that many young children will lose track of how many trucks they have added on and will have to repeat the process many times before they realize that it would be helpful to keep the original 8 trucks separated from the others. Therefore, you should begin modeling routine problems with simpler problems that involve just joining or separating existing groups of materials.) After modeling with physical materials, children can move to drawing pictures (semiabstract models). Often, the purpose of modeling, whether with physical materials or with pictures, is to find an answer. In this case, however, we want to turn children's attention to the idea of representing a situation with an open sentence, or equation (abstract model). Second-grade students who were already familiar with using open sentences to represent problems involving simple joining or separating explained their thinking about this more complicated problem as follows:

> Agnes, who wrote $8 + \square = 15$, explained: "Jane started with 8 trucks. She got some more; some more is a box because we don't know how many she got. She ended up with 15."

> Baylor, who wrote $15 - 8 = \square$, explained: "Jane had 15 trucks after the party. If you took away the ones she had before, you could tell how many she got at the party, and that is what we want to know."

> Candiza, who wrote $15 = 8 + \square$, explained: "I thought about the balance. I put 15 here (pointing to the left side of a make-believe balance) and 8 on the other side. That is sort of like the before and after. I have to change the before side, the 8, to make it equal to the 15. Need to add on to the 8 to make it equal the 15."

> Julian asked Candiza: "Why didn't you take away from the 15 to make it balance?" Couldn't you write $15 - \square = 8$?"

What would you ask Julian? The teacher, who had been working with her students on writing open sentences to model problems, asked Julian what the open box stood for in his sentence. She was satisfied that his sentence made sense to him when he explained it was the number of trucks Jane was given. He said, "Jane had 15, if she gave back those she got (the box), she would have 8. That is what my sentence says."

This type of discussion does not happen the first time students write sentences. Look at the understanding of the problem and the open sentences that this group developed: they understood the structure of both addition and subtraction sentences, the meaning of the equal sign, and that many different sentences could model the same problem.

Now consider another routine problem:

Bill had 24 pencils to put in 4 boxes. He put the same number of pencils in each box. How many pencils did he put in each box?

How would you represent this with an open sentence (an equation)? How would you explain each of the following possibilities:

Sentence A:	$4 \times p = 24$
Sentence B:	$24 \div 4 = p$
Sentence C:	$p + p + p + p = 24$
Sentence D:	$24 - p - p - p - p = 0$

Sentence A focuses on the multiplicative nature of the problem. To understand this sentence, a child would have to understand that it is a sentence of the form $G \times N = T$, where G stands for the number of groups, N stands for the number of items in each group, and T stands for the total number of items. Sentence B also focuses on the multiplicative nature of the problem but puts it in terms of division. Sentences C and D focus on the additive/subtractive nature of the problem. Students writing these sentences were probably thinking: "I have to put p pencils in one group and then in another group and so on until I have 4 groups, so $p + p + p + p$ must equal the 24 pencils.

These two problems and children's responses to them illustrate that different children often look at problems, even routine ones, in different ways. Therefore, you need to be careful about giving tests that ask questions like "what operation would you use to solve this problem?" As the pencil problem shows, there will often be more than one correct answer to such questions.

You should ask children not only to write open sentences that represent problems, but also to write problems that correspond to given open sentences. For example, here are four different problems that correspond to the equation $28 - n = 12$:

> Jennifer had 28 cookies. She gave some to friends for lunch. After lunch, she had 12. How many cookies did she give away at lunch? (separating)

> Jill has 28 books and Amanda has 12. How many more books does Jill have than Amanda? (comparing)

> There are 28 1-ounce weights on the left side of a balance scale and 12 1-ounce weights on the right side. How many 1-ounce weights need to be removed from the left side to balance the scale? (equalizing)

> James has 28 stickers. Twelve of them are blue and the rest are green. How many are green? (part/whole)

Note that these problems differ not only in the objects involved (books, cookies, weights, and stickers), but also in the type of activity involved (separating, comparing, equalizing, and part/whole). You should make sure that your students have experience with writing all four types of problems. Many mathematics programs do not require students to write problems of the equalizing type, but we think they are important because of their close tie to the idea of balancing. They give children another way of understanding abstract representations and help them make sense of equations.

Justifying   Having children justify their answers or their approaches to problems can help them understand the mathematics and gain confidence in their knowledge and skills. You should apply this principle when children are working with open sentences and ask them to justify their solutions. For example, if a student says the solution to the open sentence $35 + a = 51$ is 16, ask, "How do you know?" Note that you should do this even when the solution is correct, as it is in this case. Often, because of time pressure, teachers ask students to justify only when their solutions are incorrect. Think how this could affect a child's confidence!

Figure 14-2 shows some open sentences and how students explain the thinking behind their solutions. Having students explain their thinking is a way to encourage justifying. The students' solutions depend on understanding equality and the abstract representation of the equation. See if you can follow each student's explanation.

Patterns and Pattern Problems

Sometimes, you may ask students directly to describe a growing pattern, and at other times, you may give students a problem whose solution requires them to use a growing pattern. In either case, modeling the pattern with a table showing every term will help students organize their thinking and describe the pattern.

The table below summarizes the information that the students in this chapter's Snapshot of a Lesson found from modeling the geese problem with paper geese and then with pictures.

Geese V-term	1	2	3	4	5	6	...	V
Number of geese (n)	3	5	7	9	11		...	?

The teacher's task would be to help students generalize the pattern so they can represent it symbolically. There are two ways to consider the gen-

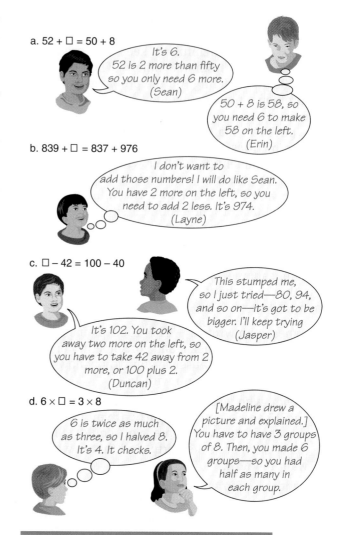

FIGURE 14-2   Explaining solutions to open sentences.

eralization: as a *recursive expression* or as an *explicit equation*.

A recursive expression is an expression that tells how to find the value of a term given the value of the previous term. In the geese problem, it is clear that if you know the value of one term, the value of the next term will be two more (i.e., two geese join the pattern each time). Thus, if you know that there are 101 geese in the pattern, you know that the next step in the pattern would have 103 geese. Symbolically, we could express this as, "if n is the value of one term, then $n + 2$ is the value of the next term. Younger children find the recursive expression easier.

An explicit equation lets you calculate the value of one term given the number of the term. In the geese problem, an explicit equation would let you calculate the number of geese given the number of the V-term. The students in the snapshot expressed this as "double the term number plus one," which can be represented by the equation $n = (2 \times V) + 1$. An equation is a more powerful representation than a recursive expression because you do not need any information about values of previous terms but can calculate the value of any arbitrary term.

Now let's consider the sidewalk-garden problem again. Here is the picture of the "growing garden," which you have already seen, along with a table that models the pattern:

Term	1	2	3	4	5			...	G
Number of tiles	8	10	12	14				...	N

Using the table, young children would find it relatively easy to tell how many tiles would be needed for garden number 6. As in the geese problem, the recursive expression is $n + 2$ (2 more tiles each time); thus, if garden 3 has 12 tiles, garden 4 would have 14 tiles, garden 5 would have 16 tiles, and garden 6 would have 18 tiles. Young children with patience could extend this to tell how many tiles for garden 10 or even, say, garden 33! But what if they wanted to know how many tiles for garden 200? An explicit equation would be more useful.

Look again at the picture of the growing garden above. Note that, no matter how long the garden is, there are three tiles at each end. Also note that the number of tiles above and below the garden are both the same as the term number (G)—that is, in term 2, there are 2 tiles above and 2 tiles below; in term 3, there are 3 tiles above and 3 tiles below; and so on. Thus, we can describe the sum (N) of all the tiles as $N = 3 + 3 + G + G$ (i.e., 3 tiles at one end plus 3 tiles at the other end plus G tiles above plus G tiles below).

If you had students working on this problem, trying to describe the pattern, it would be important to have them explain their thinking. For instance, one might say $N = 6 + (2 \times G)$, another might say $N = (2 \times 3) + (2 \times G)$, and still another might say $N = 2 + 2(G + 2)$. Look at the picture and see if you can tell how these students might explain their thinking to justify their solutions. Of course, the power of algebra would let us show that all these expressions are equivalent, but children will find that out later in their study of algebra. At the elementary levels, the important thing is that they should think about the models and patterns and explain their thinking.

When you show elementary students number patterns that are not in a context such as a problem or a geometric figure, encourage them to explain the rule, either in terms of a recursive expression that relates one term to the next or, possibly, in terms of a closed sentence that expresses the value of one specific term. For example, students presented with the pattern 2, 4, 6, 8, . . . could be encouraged to come up with a recursive expression such as "each number is two more than the previous one" or to come up with a closed sentence such as "the tenth number will be 20." Having students generalize rules like these will wait until middle school.

You can also have students connect repeating patterns to algebraic expressions. Most elementary programs emphasize extending the pattern, filling in missing terms, and doing other activities that help children analyze the overall pattern. Some programs have children describe patterns in terms of the core. For instance, the simple alternating pattern ABABAB . . . is called an AB pattern because AB is the core. You can ask students questions such as, "What is the difference between an ABB and an ABC pattern?" and "Can you give two examples of each?" to help them move to more abstract thinking.

One of the most powerful ways to tie repeating patterns to algebra is to number the terms as you would do for growing patterns. This simple strategy can really help children begin to recognize and generalize the pattern. For example, consider the repeating pattern of geometric shapes in Figure 14-3. Questioning guides student thinking about patterns in a more general way. Ask questions like:

- What shape is the ninth term? the twelfth term? (they are both squares)

- What is the sixteenth term? (a hexagon) How do you know? (starting with term 1, every fourth term is a hexagon—terms 4, 8, 12, 16, and so on)

- What can you say about the terms of all the squares? (they are all multiples of 3)

- How many of each shape are needed to extend the pattern to 20 terms? (7 hexagons, 7 trapezoids, and 6 squares)

Children in the upper elementary grades can begin to describe the terms of all the squares as multiples of 3. They may also see that the hexagons are always two places before the squares and

FIGURE 14-3 Repeating pattern with terms numbered.

the trapezoids are one place before the squares. They can now begin to use symbols to describe their thoughts. The square's place can be described by $3 \times s$, where s represents the number of the squares; thus, the first square ($s = 1$) is in the third place. This means that the place of the hexagons can be described as $(3 \times s) - 2$ (i.e., hexagons are two places before squares); so the first hexagon is in the first place and the second hexagon is in the fourth place. The place of the trapezoids (one place before the squares) can be described by $(3 \times s) - 1$.

Nonroutine Problems

In the Classroom 14-4 shows a generalized version of the cube-painting problem, which we presented earlier in this chapter. This problem involves several different patterns to analyze and describe. The activity can be done with children in grades 5–8, but it is a good one for you and your peers to try as well. Go through the steps of modeling with actual cubes, find a systematic way of counting the painted faces, record your counts in the table, find a general rule for the counts in each column, and justify your generalizations. To see the patterns, you may need to model and count up to a $5 \times 5 \times 5$ cube and visualize the counts for a $6 \times 6 \times 6$ cube. Why does it help to figure out the total number of small cubes in each large cube?

Figure 14-4 shows a number puzzle that also was presented earlier in the chapter. Number puzzles like this can help children think about gener-

---

In the Classroom 14-4

PAINTING CUBES

OBJECTIVE: **Modeling and generalizing.**

GRADE LEVEL: **5–8**

MATERIALS: **Small cubes**

PROBLEM: **If you painted the surface of a large cube made from smaller unit cubes, how many of the smaller cubes would be painted on no (0) face, 1 face, 2 faces, 3 faces, 4 faces, 5 faces, and 6 faces?**

MODEL EACH CUBE: **Fill in the table below for the $1 \times 1 \times 1$ cube. Make a $2 \times 2 \times 2$ cube and refer to it to fill in the table below. Do the same with a $3 \times 3 \times 3$ cube and a $4 \times 4 \times 4$ cube. Some of the numbers have been filled in for you. Why is there no column for 4 faces or 5 faces?**

GENERALIZE: **What pattern do you see? Can you predict the numbers for a $5 \times 5 \times 5$ cube? (You may have to build a model for the $5 \times 5 \times 5$ cube to verify your numbers.) How about for an $N \times N \times N$ cube? Justify your answers.**

Cube Size	Painted Faces					Total
	None	One	Two	Three	Six	Small Cubes
$1 \times 1 \times 1$	0				1	1
$2 \times 2 \times 2$	0			8	0	8
$3 \times 3 \times 3$	1		12			
$4 \times 4 \times 4$						
$5 \times 5 \times 5$					0	125
$N \times N \times N$					0	

Numbers	Modeling Materials	Algebra
	Pick a number:	
11	Call it ◯	Call it *N*
	Add 4:	
11 + 4 = 15	◯ ◯◯◯◯	*N* + 4
2 × 15 = 30	**Double it:**	
	◯ ◯◯◯◯	2 × (*N* + 4) or
	◯ ◯◯◯◯	2*N* + 8
	Subtract 6:	
30 − 6 = 24	◯ ⊗⊗⊗⊗	2*N* + 8 − 6 or
	◯ ⊗⊗◯◯	2*N* + 2
	Divide by 2:	
24 ÷ 2 = 12	◯ ◯	$\dfrac{2N + 2}{2}$ or
	◯ ◯	*N* + 1
	Subtract 1:	
12 − 1 = 11	◯ ⊗	*N* + 1 − 1
	Answer: The original number	
11	◯	*N*

FIGURE 14-4 A number puzzle.

alizing. First, have children do the puzzle with many different numbers chosen by the children. Then let them use materials to model the steps. As they use the materials, you should be able to see whether they have strongly developed concepts about the operations. If you discover, for example, that some children do not know how to model "multiply by two" or "divide by two," then you can reinforce the meanings.

You can move to a symbolic representation of the puzzle, as shown in the third column of Figure 14-4. After the students model the actions with materials, you can ask them to describe the steps using symbols. Notice the concepts they can gain by doing this. For example, they can easily see that

$2 \times (N + 4)$ is equal to $(2 \times N) + 8$ because both of these symbolic representations describe the same model.

Most children love number puzzles of all types, especially puzzles that let them predict a number, such as someone's favorite number. Find puzzles like these and first let children just enjoy them. Then challenge them to figure out how the puzzles work, and ask them to justify their solutions, by using either materials or symbolic representations.

You can also use calendars as a context for number patterns that will engage students in algebraic thinking. Figure 14-5 uses the calendar for September as the context for the calendar number puzzle that we presented earlier. Have younger children look at how the numbers on the calendar change as you go across a row for a week. Also have them look at how the numbers change as you go down a column for a specific day of the week. The children may be able to recognize patterns such as that every other date is an even number or that the date of the next Friday after September 12 is 7 more, or September 19. Have students find the sum of all the numbers in a 3 × 3 square of dates (as shown in Figure 14-5). After finding this sum in several different squares of the same size, students may realize that the sum is always 9 times the number in the center. Older students should be able to see why this is the case. As shown in Figure 14-5, using a letter (*m*) for the number in the center and using expressions with that letter for the numbers in the other squares can help. Note that the sum of the expressions in the nine squares is $9 \times m$. Children in the upper elementary grades should not find it difficult to make this generalization.

Functions

Functions may be treated as patterns, much like the growing patterns modeled in some of the previous tables in this chapter. By making tables and discussing the patterns that students see, you can help students find the general rule (the function) that relates the two quantities. Children will find it easier to do this if the relationship involves only one operation. For example, the rules that describe how the machine works in In the Classroom 14-3 are easy to state for Monday through Thursday, as shown below (*R* is the result, or output, and *I* is the input *I*):

Monday:	$R = I \times 4$
Tuesday:	$R = I + 10$
Wednesday:	$R = I \div 2$
Thursday:	$R = I - 16$

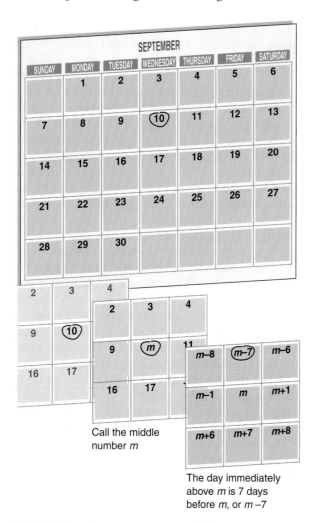

FIGURE 14-5 A pattern in calendars.

What about Friday? Remember the machine does the same thing all day long. Student reactions tend to be like this: "It looks like it added 7 spots to the frog. But that doesn't work for the toad. It's 3 times for the toad." Here are some questions you can ask students to start them on the right track:

• Do the animals have more or fewer spots when they come out than when they went in?" (more)

• Does adding the same number work? (no)

• Does multiplying by the same number work? (no—it's 3 times for the toad, but it's not quite 3 times for the frog and the salamander)

• What if the machine used two operations? What if it multiplied and then added? (let the students try to work with just this hint)

Do not rush the students in their thinking. Later in their study of algebra they will learn specific techniques for solving such problems, but at this point it is important for them to make conjectures and try to verify them.

In recent TIMSS and NAEP assessments, fourth-grade students were asked questions about how pairs of quantities were related. Often, they found a rule that related one pair but not the others. They did not realize that every pair had the same relation and that they were supposed to determine it. Activities like In the Classroom 14-3 are needed to help make children aware of this general idea of expressing patterns in terms of functions.

You should also ask children to "undo" their thinking. For example, when doing In the Classroom 14-3, you would tell children the output (how the animal came out) and ask them to tell how many marks it had going in. Educators call this *reversibility of thinking* (Driscoll, 1999) and look at it as one of the crucial skills for children to develop as they learn to think algebraically.

Functions also are a good way to study change in subject areas other than mathematics. For example, in science lessons, students often collect data about how plants grow or how other natural phenomena change, and the patterns in which such changes occur can often be expressed as functions. Such changes may not always fit a simple rule, but students can model the changes by graphing the data and then look at the graph to see if that helps them determine the rule. In the Classroom 14-5 helps children see the relationship between rules (functions), numerical values of pairs of variables, and graphs.

Connecting equations (the rules), the table of values, and the graphs gives students ways to analyze situations. The questions asking the students to compare the graphs are a first step in having them look at how changing one representation (the rule) changes the other (the graph).

Math Links 14.5

*E*lectronic manipulatives (such as algebraic tiles and graphing) that may be used to build algebraic concepts are available from the National Library of Virtual Manipulatives for Interactive Mathematics Web site, which you can access from http://nlvm.usu.edu/en/nav/index.html or from this book's Web site.

www.wiley.com/college/reys

In the Classroom 14-5

FROM A RULE TO A GRAPH

OBJECTIVE: **To graph a function given a rule.**
To analyze the graphs.

GRADE LEVEL: **4–6 (graphing)**
5–6 (analyzing)

MATERIALS: **Graphing paper**

▼ Make a table of values for each of these rules. Let *x* be 0, 1, 2, 3, 4, and 5.

Rule A
$y = 2x + 1$

Table	
x	*y*
0	1
1	3
2	5
3	7
4	9
5	11

Rule B: $y = x$

Rule C: $y = 2x$

Rule D: $y = 4$

Rule E: $y = 2x + 2$

Rule F: $y = 2x + 4$

Graph

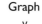

1. Look at the graphs for Rules B and C. How are they alike? How are they different?
2. Look at the graphs for Rules B and D. How are they alike? How are they different?
3. Look at the graphs for Rules C and E. How are they alike? How are they different?
4. How do you think the graph of the rule $y = 2x + 3$ would compare with Rule E and Rule F? Check your conjecture.

Properties of Numbers and Number Theory

Investigating properties such as distributivity and number theory relations such as divisibility rules can help students develop their ability to make and justify generalizations. Students may make conjectures entirely on their own, or you can initiate the process by asking thoughtful questions. Some teachers keep a written record available to the class, showing students conjectures along with the name of the child who stated each conjecture. Students can revisit these conjectures as they gather evidence as to whether or not they are true of all numbers. Remember that only one example is needed to prove that a conjecture is not true for all numbers. Consider, for example, the conjecture "all numbers that are divisible by 2 and by 6 are divisible by 12." Clearly, this conjecture is true for some numbers, such as 12, 24, and 36, each of which is divisible by 2, 6, and 12. However, 18 is divisible by 2 and by 6 but not by 12. Thus, the conjecture is not true for all numbers and is therefore disproved. Disproving conjectures is as important as proving them, and often it is simpler.

Modeling and generalizing Young children use many of the mathematical properties intuitively because "they work." For example, most first-grade students will find 2 + 9 by counting on 2 from 9. Actually, they are using the commutative property for addition, which can be stated like this: for any two numbers, *a* and *b*, *a* + *b* = *b* + *a*. Of course, this language and symbolization is too formal for very young children, but they can justify it by modeling it with concrete objects. Figure 14-6 shows how third- and fourth-grade students used linking cubes to model 8 × 5 = 5 × 8, which is a specific example of

$a \times t = t \times a$ (the commutative property for multiplication), (Carpenter and Levi, 2000).

This figure illustrates a particular case, but the students went on to argue that the model shows that all you have to do is turn one of the array of cubes on its side, so it would work for any array. Does this convince you that the commutative property holds for all whole numbers?

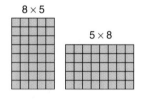

FIGURE 14-6 A model of 8 × 5 = 5 × 8.

The distributive property states that $a \times (b + c) = (a \times b) + (a \times c)$ for any three numbers *a*, *b*, and *c*. Again, students use this property naturally without realizing it. For example, consider a problem that we presented earlier in the chapter:

Pat took 4 pails to the beach. She had 3 shovels and 2 rakes in each pail. How many tools did she take to the beach?

Generally, children approach this problem in one of two ways:

1. They might add the number of shovels and number of rakes (3 + 2) first, to find out the number of tools in each pail, and then multiply the sum by 4. You could represent this by (3 + 2) × 4 or use the commutative property to represent it as 4 × (3 + 2).

2. They might find the total number of shovels (4 × 3) and the total number of rakes (4 × 2) and then add (4 × 3) + (4 × 2).

The fact that both approaches give the same correct answer (20) demonstrates the distributive property—that is, 4 × (3 + 2) = (4 × 3) + (4 × 2). How would you model the distributive property with physical materials? How would you justify the property more generally?

It is important to give children examples illustrating mathematical properties to see if they can generalize those properties. First show them closed sentences and have them verify that the sentences are true; then have them solve similar open sentences; finally, encourage them to make conjectures for generalizing the properties illustrated by the example sentences. Do not expect children to immediately come up with good generalizations; it may help to give them some additional example sentences or to have the students themselves give more examples. Probably, the wording of the children's conjectures will need to be revised; a class discussion about how to word the conjectures so they make sense is important in helping children learn to write mathematically. The following table shows the kinds of closed and open sentences and corresponding generalizations that you can use with students:

Closed Sentences	Open Sentences	Generalizations (Mathematical Properties)
79 + 0 = 79	37 + □ = 37	When you add 0 and any number, you get that number.
0 × 54 = 0	0 × □ = 0	When you multiply any number by 0, you get 0.
33 − 0 = 33	83 − □ = 83	When you subtract 0 from any number, you get that number.
67 − 67 = 0	3456 − □ = 0	When you subtract any number from itself, you get 0.
24 × 1 = 24	1002 × □ = 1002	When you multiply any number times 1, you get that number.

The wording of the generalizations in this table is informal but correct. Children will also use informal wording and you should help them focus on whether or not their wording is clear and correct. For example, if a student says, "When you subtract any number and 0, you get that number," encourage the class to discuss why this is not clear ("subtract any number *and* zero" doesn't make sense).

Mathematical statements that express generalizations about number theory relations are useful for prompting students to justify those generalizations. Three such statements are discussed below:

- *The sum of an odd number and an odd number is even.* As they do with all number statements, children will try specific numbers to see if the generalization is true. This process is important, and you should encourage it. It helps them get comfortable about moving on to making arguments that come closer to justifying the statement for all numbers.

  Figure 14-7 shows a model that children could use to extend their argument from specific examples to a more general justification. One student argued, "Each odd number has a tail when you try to make a rectangle of twos. You can always put two tails (the two odd numbers) together to make a rectangle without a tail."

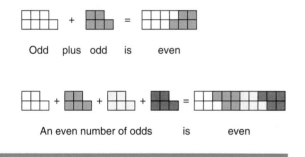

Odd   plus   odd   is   even

An even number of odds   is   even

FIGURE 14-7   Models for summing odd numbers.

- *If a number is divisible by 2 and by 3, then it is divisible by 6.* Check this conjecture with specific numbers. Can you justify it for all numbers?

- *If the sum of the digits of a number is divisible by 9, then the number is divisible by 9.*

  The number 243 is a specific number that you can have children use to test this statement (2 + 4 + 3 = 9, so the sum of the digits is divisible by 9). Use the model for 243 shown in Figure 14-8 that if they shared one of the hundred blocks among 9 people, 1 unit block would be left over. Similarly, 1 unit block would be left over from the other hundred blocks. And the same thing would happen with the ten rods if

Share 243 among 9 people

Here is what is left after the sharing

2   4   3

FIGURE 14-8   Is 243 divisible by 9?

each was shared among 9 people—1 unit block would be left over from each. In sum, 2 unit blocks would be left over from the hundred blocks, 4 unit blocks from the ten rods, plus the three original unit blocks. This makes a total of 9 one blocks left over, which you can clearly share among 9 people. Thus, 243 is divisible by 9.

Justifying   "The arguments that students typically use to justify generalizations fall into three basic categories: appeal to authority, justification by example, and deductive arguments" (Carpenter and Romberg 2004, p. 28). These educators then go on to point out that appealing to authority is really avoiding justification. For example, a student who says, "My teacher told us to divide fractions, you just flip the one after the division sign and multiply" is not providing a mathematical justification for doing so and is not showing an understanding of division of fractions. Children need to learn that, in mathematics as in most subject areas, they should not do something a certain way just because someone tells them to; rather, they need to understand why doing it that way makes sense (or doesn't make sense).

In this chapter, we have mainly focused on justification by examples and by informal explanations (i.e., explanations that aren't as tightly logical as formal deductive arguments). We have encouraged you to have children make models, move on to symbolic representations when they can, and discuss how they arrived at their generalizations. These are important steps in understanding and fully justifying generalizations, and they may be as much as young children can handle.

We close this section by referencing an interview with a second grader, Susie, whose teacher was in a study group investigating how to encourage algebraic thinking (Carpenter and Romberg,

2004). The video in *Powerful Practices* shows how much at ease and confident Susie was, as well as how the interviewer encouraged her to delve deeper, as Susie attempted to justify the generalization $a + b - b = a$.

> Susie initially proposes to justify the conjecture by trying a lot of different examples with different types of numbers. She recognizes that she cannot try all the numbers, and that she cannot be sure the generalization is true for all numbers by trying a few examples. Although at first she cannot come up with a more general method of justification to show that the generalization is true for all numbers, she uses knowledge about subtracting a number from itself and about adding zero to a number as she does the calculations. Her initial strategy of operating on numbers does not depend on the specific numbers she chooses; she actually uses properties appropriate for a more general proof and that is what the interviewer, Ms. L., leads her to see.
>
> She then uses two conjectures that her class has discussed: $b - b = 0$ and $a + 0 = a$. She argues that if these conjectures are true, then her conjecture of $a + b - b = a$ must be true. (Carpenter and Romberg, 2004, pp. 35–36)

Cultural Connections

Algebra has a long history in the development of mathematics. It was not until the nineteenth century, however, that algebra began to be studied in secondary schools around the world. During the twentieth century, algebra became a central subject for any one who expected to advance in their study of mathematics. But only recently has it become a subject that all students in the United States are expected to study; this is in contrast to most other developed countries, where algebra has been a core subject for all students for a long time. In the first half of the twentieth century in the United States, many of the topics included in algebra, such as positive and negative numbers and exponents, were made part of the junior high school curriculum. Now, much of this material is in every middle school curriculum in the United States, as it has long been in other countries. How has that changed what is done in elementary schools?

The recent TIMSS (Mullis et al., 2004) gathered information about which algebraic topics were included in the fourth-grade curricula of the countries that participated in the study. The study looked at six topics: patterns, equality, finding missing numbers in equations, simple equations, finding pairs of numbers related according to a given rule, and finding the rule that related given pairs of numbers. The most commonly included topic across the countries was finding missing numbers in equations, followed by patterns. More countries expected students to find pairs of numbers related by a given rule than to find the rule that related given pairs of numbers.

Fourth-grade students in the United States scored significantly better than the international average in algebra, as they did in all areas but measurement. Students in only six countries (out of 25) performed significantly better than U.S. students, and U.S. students significantly outperformed those of 11 other countries. Of course, this does not tell us what individual students who come to your classroom from other countries will know about algebra. Only careful questioning and listening will tell you what experiences they have had.

A Glance at Where We've Been

The NCTM's Algebra Standard emphasizes patterns and relationships, ways of representing and analyzing mathematical situations using algebraic symbols, the use of models to represent and understand relationships, and the analysis of change in various contexts. These ideas have been blended into this chapter as we have considered problems, patterns, and relations as topics to develop algebraic thinking. These topics occur in all strands of the mathematics curriculum as well as in other subjects. Helping children to think algebraically does not mean adding another topic; it does mean we probably need to teach those areas differently. We can help children develop algebraic concepts and habits of algebraic thinking through questioning, helping students model problems, patterns, and relations, encouraging them to generalize, and expecting them to justify their thinking and statements. We have emphasized the need for teachers to ask questions and provide opportunities for children to discuss and defend their ideas with any of the mathematics they are learning.

Things to Do: From What You've Read

1. Why should algebra be studied in elementary school? How would you describe that algebra?

2. What are topics in the elementary curriculum that can be used to develop algebraic concepts and thinking?

3. What are two common types of patterns? How do they differ? How are they alike? In particular, how are they alike and different in developing algebraic thinking discussed in this chapter?

4. What algebraic language and symbols are essential for elementary school students?

5. What is the difference between an open sentence and a closed sentence?

6. How does representing routine problems promote algebraic thinking?

7. What three processes were used to describe algebraic thinking?

8. What are the different meanings of variable?

9. Complete the cube-painting problem (In the Classroom 14-5).

10. Justify the statement: "The sum of any two even numbers is even."

Things to Do: Going Beyond This Book

IN THE FIELD

1. *Sentences.* Ask students about the truth of mathematical sentences or to solve sentences such as the ones in the chapter that showed initial misunderstandings. What did you learn about students' understanding of equality, mathematical sentences, and justifying?

2. *Relationships.* Create an input–output machine where a child is inside a box and responds to input from number cards that other children insert. Ask the other children to describe on paper how the output value is related to the input value. Collect their descriptions of the relationships. Are they all the same? If they have different descriptions, are those descriptions equivalent?

3. *Algebraic thinking.* Observe an elementary mathematics class where the students are working with patterns. Talk with the children about the patterns they are working with. Can you see evidence of the development of algebraic thinking as they describe how they are thinking about their problems? What ideas could encourage algebraic thinking?

4. *Children's ideas about algebra.* Many students in upper elementary grades have heard the words *algebra* and *variables.* Ask them what they think these words mean. What are their ideas? Do they see these ideas in some of the same ways that were described in this chapter?

IN YOUR JOURNAL

5. Describe your understanding of what algebraic thinking means for elementary students.

6. Describe your understanding of variables. How can you stop children from thinking of a variable as just a placeholder?

7. What was your experience in algebra classes? Do you think that if you had the background recommended in this chapter that it would have been different? Give ways and examples to explain your comments.

8. Describe why equality is an important idea in algebraic thinking.

WITH ADDITIONAL RESOURCES

9. Read one of the articles or chapters described in the annotated resources. Summarize how that article or chapter supports the ideas in this chapter about the development of algebraic thinking.

10. Select an instructional idea in a current textbook series that is listed as an algebra lesson. Briefly summarize the lesson and tell how it supports the ideas or how it is contrary to the ideas in this chapter.

11. Select one of the activities found in the *Navigating through Algebra* series, grades pre-K–2 or grades 3–5. Design a lesson that incorporates the idea. Explain how this lesson will help children's algebraic thinking develop.

WITH TECHNOLOGY

12. Explore the pan balance on the NCTM's Illuminations Web site (Math Links 14.4). You can use this interactive pan balance to "weigh" numeric or algebraic expressions. Develop a lesson plan that would use this activity.

13. Watch one of the mathematics videos from *Powerful Practices* (Carpenter and Romberg, 2004). What ideas are in both the video and this chapter?

Note to Instructors: You can find additional resources, learning activities, and black-line masters in this text's accompanying Instructor's Manual at www.wiley.com/college/reys.

---

*Additional activities, suggestions, and questions are provided in *Teaching Elementary Mathematics: A Resource for Field Experiences* (Wiley, 2007).

Book Nook for Children

Ahlberg, J., and Ahlberg, A. *Each Peach Pear Plum.* Hamondsworth, Middlesex: Penguin Books, 1986.

This is a rhyming book about nursery rhyme characters that can be used to introduce the concept of pattern to pre-K through first graders.

Barry, D. *The Rajah's Rice.* New York: W.H. Freeman, 1994.

A smart peasant girl outsmarts the rajah and ensures the village plenty of food forever after. The rajah agrees to give the girl the rice that would cover his chessboard when he puts one grain on the first square and doubles it for the next square, and then doubles that square, and so on for all sixty-four squares.

Calmenson, S. *Dinner at the Panda Palace.* New York: Harper Collins, 1991.

This book for grades 1 to 3 counts dinner guests as they arrive at the Panda Palace. Each group is one guest larger than the group before. Children can identify the expanding (+1) pattern. They might be challenged to make up a similar story with a different expanding pattern. The class can figure out how many guests it takes to fill the restaurant.

Emberley, B., and Emberley E. *Drummer Hoff.* New York: Simon & Schuster, 1967.

This classic book is written in an increasing pattern style. As each new element is added, the list is repeated from the beginning, with the new element now at the end of the list. Students can model the patterns with manipulatives or label the elements and represent the patterns with symbols (e.g., *a*, *ab*, *abc*, or *abcd*).

Geringer, L. *A Three Hat Day.* New York: Harper & Row, 1987.

A man who loves hats has a collection of 12 different hats. One day he decides to wear three hats and it brings him good luck. The students figure out how many different combinations of three he could make with the hats he has. The book is most appropriate for third and fourth graders.

Martin, B. *Polar Bear, Polar Bear, What Do Your Hear?* New York: Henry Holt, 1991.

This predictable pattern book is a good illustration of patterns for kindergarten and first graders.

Murphy, S. J. *Beep, Beep, Vroom, Vroom!* New York: Harper Collins, 2000.

Kevin keeps his toy cars in a pattern on the shelf. Suddenly, the cars fall from the shelf and Kevin's sister, Molly, puts the cars back on the shelf in a different pattern. This happens again, but this time the pattern is the same as the original. There are activities and games for parents and teachers to use.

Swinburne, S. R. *Lots and Lots of Zebra Stripes.* Honesdale, PA: Boyds Mills Press, 1998.

This book explains with colorful illustrations how patterns encompass our world. The author explains that the patterns can have a purpose or be seasonal.

Annotated Resources

Bay-Willams, J. M. What is algebra in elementary school? *Teaching Children Mathematics*, 8(4) (December 2001), pp. 196–201.
Focuses on the NCTM's Algebra Standard for elementary students. Discusses the importance of understanding card patterns, creation and analysis of color-tile patterns, and the role of teachers in teaching algebra to elementary students.

Cai, J. "Developing algebraic reasoning in the elementary grades." *Teaching Children Mathematics*, 5(4) (December 1998), pp. 225–230.
Emphasis on developing algebraic strategies in the elementary grades can promote the twin goals of mathematical power and algebra for all. This article discusses the use of algebraic strategies in problem solving, opportunities for algebraic reasoning, advantages of cross-cultural studies in mathematics, problem-solving techniques for algebraic expressions, and direct modeling with concrete objects as powerful problem-solving strategies for young children.

Carpenter, T. P., Franke, M. L., and Levi, L. *Thinking Mathematically. Integrating Arithmetic and Algebra in the Elementary School.* Portsmouth, NH: Heinemann, 2003.
This book is essential reading for everyone who is integrating algebra into the elementary curriculum. It includes a more in-depth description of the research and students' thinking on which several of the videos in *Powerful Practices* (Carpenter and Romberg, 2004) are based.

Driscoll, M. *Fostering Algebraic Thinking.* Portsmouth, NH: Heinemann, 1999.
A must read for middle and secondary teachers, it includes ideas and ways to develop algebraic thinking appropriate for all grades. It contains questions to illicit student thinking as well as ways to use algorithms, number sense, and number theory to build algebraic thinking. It has many classroom ideas of ways to encourage generalization and to develop symbol sense.

Mann, R. L. "Balancing act: The truth behind the equals sign." *Teaching Children Mathematics,* 11(2) (September 2004), pp. 65–69.
This article stresses the importance of building meaning for the equal sign, describes students' thinking as they work with a balance, and includes ideas for activities to develop meaning for equality.

National Council of Teachers of Mathematics. *Algebraic Thinking, Grades K–12: Readings from NCTM's School-Based Journals and Other Publications.* Reston, VA: NCTM, 1999.
This book, edited by Moses, provides a multitude of articles designed to help teachers understand the development of algebraic thinking and the types of activities at different grade levels that can foster algebraic thinking in children. A comprehensive collection of 59 specially selected articles defines algebraic thinking, analyzes the algebra curriculum, and supplies many classroom activities dealing with patterns, functions, and technology.

National Council of Teachers of Mathematics. *Navigations— Steering through Principles and Standards: Algebra in Grades PreK–2 and Grades 3–5.* Reston, VA: NCTM, 2001.
These two books make the vision of algebra through the grades a reality. This book series is designed to give teachers ideas, activities, and materials to support the implementation of Algebra standard.

National Council of Teachers of Mathematics. "Algebraic thinking" (focus issue). *Teaching Children Mathematics,* 3(7) (February 1997).
This issue contains many articles that you will find helpful in encouraging students to think algebraically.

Stiff, L. (ed.). *Developing Reasoning in Grades K–12. 1999 Yearbook.* Reston, VA: NCTM, 1999.
Although this book focuses on reasoning, there are several chapters that provide valuable insight to developing algebraic thinking in elementary school. In particular, see the chapters by Russell, Schifter, and Greenes and Findell.

CHAPTER 15

Geometry

◆ Snapshot of a Lesson

Key Idea

To make and identify basic geometric shapes

Background Information

This snapshot is based on the video *Shapes from Squares*, from Teaching Math: A Video Library, K–4 from Annenberg Media. Produced by WGBH Educational Foundation © 1995 WGBH All Rights reserved. To view, go to http://www.learner.org/resources/series32.html (video #20). Mr. Ramirez is a teacher in a bilingual second/third grade classroom in Tucson, Arizona. In the video, the students are investigating what shapes they can make by folding a square.

Mr. Ramirez presents step-by-step directions on folding a 5″ × 5″ construction paper square to his class and then challenges them to work in pairs to find as many shapes as they can by folding only on the crease. [*Before you see what the children did, follow the abbreviated directions below and make the folding square.*]

1. Fold the square in half.
2. Make airplane folds from each corner to the fold line.

| 5 × 5 | First fold | "Airplane" fold | Final: open |

The children then work in pairs at tables. Mr. Ramirez talks with various groups, having the children record their findings, identify the shape, and report the number of sides. One pair made a shape with 5 sides. When Mr. Ramirez asked what the name was, they replied five-a-gon. They called their 6-sided shape a six-a-gon, but one student said six is the same as hex, so it is a hexagon. (Make the hexagon; do you see why the students may not have related it to the hexagon in the pattern blocks? Paper pattern blocks are in Appendix B of this text.)

Hexagon folded from the square   Hexagon from pattern blocks

A boy, we'll call him Antonio, made the shape and recorded it by drawing a sketch.

358

MR. RAMIREZ: What is this shape?

ANTONIO: This is a triangle and this is a triangle [*pointing to the two triangles in his drawing*].

MR. RAMIREZ: So the two triangles make up this shape [*pointing to the whole shape*]. How many sides does it have?

ANTONIO: Five. [*He counts the five, saying the inside line is a side of the triangle.*]

After some discussion and counting sides of other shapes, Antonio persists in counting the inside lines.

MR. RAMIREZ: Let's look at your hand. [*Antonio places his hand flat on the table.*] Where are the sides? [*Antonio points to an edge of his hand. Mr. Ramirez points to line on Antonio's palm. Antonio responds that is a palm, not a side.*]

Mr. Ramirez returns to a folded shape but Antonio persists in counting the inside lines.

MR. RAMIREZ: Open up your paper shape. What is this?

ANTONIO: It is a square.

MR. RAMIREZ: How many sides does it have?

ANTONIO: Four.

MR. RAMIREZ: Why didn't you count these? [*Pointing to the inside lines.*]

ANTONIO: Those are folds.

MR. RAMIREZ: How about this one [*back to the original shape under discussion*].

ANTONIO: Four sides. That other one is a fold.

Mr. Ramirez brings the class back together to share what they had found. He sees this as just one of many opportunities for his students to work with shapes.

◆ Introduction

You may find yourself working with some teachers who respond to geometry in the following ways:

"Oh, I could never do proofs."

"The children don't understand it, so why do it?"

"We do it if we finish everything else first."

There are many reasons for such responses. Some are based on personal experiences such as an unsatisfactory geometry course in high school. Some are based on inappropriate geometry curriculum materials for elementary students that use, for example, an abstract, definitional approach. Some are based on a historical emphasis on computation—even though various professional groups have recommended geometry be included in the curriculum for over a hundred years.

You may find that you are working with teachers who respond like this:

"It amazes me who is good in geometry; it's not always my best arithmetic students."

"What a joy it is to see a child's eyes light up as she discovers. . ."

"Some of my students could work on a geometry problem for hours."

"Geometry gives me an opportunity to work on communication skills and to help children follow instructions."

"The change in the spatial ability of children after they work with geometric shapes always surprises me."

"I love to learn with my students; I never liked geometry before."

Why should you include geometry in elementary school? The previous responses certainly give several reasons including being a mathematics topic that engages children differently both in performance and persistence. It is a natural site to include other skills such as following directions and for reasoning about shapes and their properties. Children can make and verify conjectures about geometric figures. For example, by folding models of isosceles triangles on the line of symmetry, children can see that two sides are congruent and two angles are congruent. It is also a topic that will help you teach many other mathematical topics. For example, many representations are geometric in nature—models for fractions, area model for multiplication, and patterns that lead to algebraic expressions.

The rich cultural connections found in geometry give you a meaningful way to celebrate the diversity of your class. The Book Nook gives only a few examples, but you will have no difficulty in finding resources about geometry in different cultures.

The *Principles and Standards for School Mathematics* (NCTM, 2000) calls for geometry to be an integral part of the mathematics programs of all elementary students in the Geometry Standard (see Figure 15-1). In fact, it is seen as the second most important area in pre-K–2 and in grades 3–5 (see Figure 1-1 in this text). This chapter is organized around the four parts of the standard: properties of two- and three-dimensional shapes, locations and spatial relationships, transformations, and visualization and spatial reasoning. The process standards (reasoning, problem solving, communicating, representing, and connections) play a prominent role in geometry for elementary students.

Instructional programs should enable all students to:	Pre-K–2 Expectations All students should:	Grades: 3–5 Expectations All students should:
Analyze characteristics and properties of two- and three-dimensional geometric shapes and develop mathematical arguments about geometric relationships	• Recognize, name, build, draw, compare, and sort two- and three-dimensional shapes • Describe attributes and parts of two- and three-dimensional shapes • Investigate and predict the results of putting together and taking apart two- and three-dimensional shapes	• Identify, compare, and analyze attributes of two- and three-dimensional shapes and develop vocabulary to describe the attributes • Classify two- and three-dimensional shapes according to their properties and develop definitions of classes of shapes such as triangles and pyramids • Investigate, describe, and reason about the results of subdividing, combining, and transforming shapes • Explore congruence and similarity • Make and test conjectures about geometric properties and relationships and develop logical arguments to justify conclusions
Specify locations and describe spatial relationships using coordinate geometry and other representational systems	• Describe, name, and interpret relative positions in space and apply ideas about relative position • Describe, name, and interpret direction and distance in navigating space and apply ideas about direction and distance • Find and name locations with simple relationships such as "near to" and in coordinate systems such as maps	• Describe location and movement using common language and geometric vocabulary • Make and use coordinate systems to specify locations and to describe paths • Find the distance between points along horizontal and vertical lines of a coordinate system

FIGURE 15-1 Geometry Standard with expectations for children in grades prekindergarten–2 and 3–5. (*Continued on next page*)

Math Links 15.1

*R*ead the text surrounding the Geometry Standard at the pre-K-2, 3–5, or 6–8 grades. You can access this from the NCTM Web site http://www.nctm/org/standards (if you have NCTM membership) or from this book's Web site.

www.wiley.com/college/reys

As you begin this exploration of teaching geometry, you may encounter new ideas. By trying the activities you will begin to extend your knowledge of geometry and of how to help children learn geometry as envisioned in these standards.

FOCUS QUESTIONS

1. Why should the elementary mathematics program include geometry?

2. What should early childhood and elementary students learn about geometric shapes?

3. How do the van Hiele levels guide the development of geometric experiences for elementary children?

4. What types of explorations with geometry help build elementary children's spatial reasoning and visualization skills?

5. What do location and movement have to do with geometry?

Instructional programs should enable all students to:	Pre-K–2 Expectations All students should:	Grades: 3–5 Expectations All students should:
Apply transformations and use symmetry to analyze mathematical situations	• Recognize and apply slides, flips, and turns • Recognize and create shapes that have symmetry	• Predict and describe the results of sliding, flipping, and turning two-dimensional shapes • Describe a motion or a series of motions that will show that two shapes are congruent • Identify and describe line and rotational symmetry in two- and three-dimensional shapes and designs
Use visualization, spatial reasoning, and geometric modeling to solve problems	• Create mental images of geometric shapes using spatial memory and spatial visualization • Recognize and represent shapes from different perspectives • Relate ideas in geometry to ideas in number and measurement • Recognize geometric shapes and structures in the environment and specify their location	• Build and draw geometric objects • Create and describe mental images of objects, patterns, and paths • Identify and build a three-dimensional object from two-dimensional representations of that object • Identify and build a two-dimensional representation of a three-dimensional object • Use geometric models to solve problems in other areas of mathematics, such as number and measurement • Recognize geometric ideas and relationships and apply them to other disciplines and to problems that arise in the classroom or in everyday life

FIGURE 15-1   (*Continued*)

Properties of Two- and Three-Dimensional Shapes

All too often, elementary programs have concentrated on the names of geometric objects and have not helped children develop a deeper understanding of the properties of the objects or the relationships among different geometric objects. Before discussing how to help children learn and use the ideas in the standards, we introduce some of the research on children's learning of these ideas.

The research of the Dutch couple, Dina van Hiele-Geldof and Pierre Marie van Hiele, has provided teachers with guidelines for the growth of geometric understanding and thought (Crowley,

1987). They proposed and studied a model of five levels of understanding (see Figure 15-2). Considering this model, it is not difficult to see why our students do not do well in geometry (Kloosterman et al., 2004). Many of the geometry experiences at the elementary level only require students to be at the visualization level.

In the beginning years, children focus on visual cues—it is a rectangle because it looks like a rectangle. This is much like—it is a dog because it looks like one. Just as very young children can identify many dogs when they see one, children can identify rectangles. Where can they see an object shaped like a rectangle? A door, a book, a tabletop—the examples are plentiful in our world. It is important to help move children beyond Level 0, Visualization. Even in kindergarten, students can begin to look at shapes more critically, such as describing a rectangle as having four sides and

Level	Description	Sample Responses of Children
0 Visualization	Children view a geometric shape as a whole. They do not describe properties of the shape.	Shown a rectangle and asked to identify it, the child may say "It is a rectangle because it looks like a book cover."
1 Analysis	Children recognize the properties of figures. They do not see relations between properties.	A child may say that the rectangle has four sides and square corners.
2 Informal Deduction	Students see relations between properties of a class of shapes.	A student may say that since the angles of a rectangles are right angles, the opposite sides are parallel.
3 Deduction 4 Rigor	Both Level 3 (level at which students can use deduction in an axiomatic system to prove statements) and Level 4 (level at which students see geometry in the abstract) are beyond the scope of most students in middle school. Level 3 is the level at which a proof-oriented high school geometry course is taught.	

FIGURE 15-2 Van Hiele Levels of Understanding Geometry.

square corners. With many experiences that specifically require children to describe the properties of the figures (Level 1, Analysis), they begin to recognize and more carefully describe properties of all rectangles. All rectangles have right angles and equal (congruent) opposite sides. They are not at the level of seeing the relationships among properties. For example, they do not realize that if a quadrilateral has two pairs of parallel sides and one right angle, that it must be a rectangle. It is at Level 2, Informal Deduction, that students establish relationships among properties and among figures. It is at this level that students can classify figures based on the properties and not just on how they look. As students are doing the same activity, you can often see them working at different levels and through questioning you can help them develop a deeper understanding. We will return to these levels throughout this section.

Math Links 15.2

A variety of Web resources for geometry, which may be used by teachers and children, may be found at the NCTM's Illuminations Web site under the Geometry Standard. You can access this from http://illuminations.nctm.org or from this book's Web site.

www.wiley.com/college/reys

Three-Dimensional Shapes

We live in a three-dimensional world that can be represented and described geometrically. We begin with three-dimensional shapes because this is the world of the young child—a world that they can explore in the geometric sense. It is important to begin their geometry explorations from their perspective with familiar three-dimensional objects, such as balls and blocks. They may roll the ball and perhaps try to roll the block. Different experiences help them to describe these solid, three-dimensional shapes. A three-dimensional shape such as a ball is often referred to as a *solid* even though the object may be hollow; we will refer to the shapes as solids in this chapter.

We have chosen to include all the discussion of the three-dimensional shapes, so you can see the development of ideas. It does not mean that we recommend doing all of it before considering two-dimensional shapes. Students need concepts from two-dimensional shapes in order to more completely describe three-dimensional objects.

Models play an important role in all of geometry, but especially in three-dimensional geometry. If wooden or plastic solids are not available, you can make models as suggested later in this section. You and your students should also collect real objects that have particular geometric shapes, including spheres (balls), cylinders (cans), prisms (boxes), and cones, as well as solids that may not have geometric names.

Studying geometric properties of three-dimensional objects also provides an opportunity to emphasize the process goals of geometry. This section is built around some of these processes: describing and sorting, constructing, exploring, and discovering.

Describing and sorting   Children need to be able to describe properties of three-dimensional objects to tell how two or more objects are alike or different geometrically. Describing and sorting are processes that are begun in early childhood and should be continued throughout elementary school. New and more complex properties can be added to children's repertoire. Describing and sorting activities help children develop thinking at Level 0 and lead toward the Level 1 thinking described by the van Hiele model.

In the activities that follow, vocabulary and properties appropriate for beginning, intermediate, and more advanced students are used. Older children who have not been exposed to three-dimensional activities will benefit from activities such as those described in the beginning activities. Their responses, of course, will be more sophisticated.

BEGINNING ACTIVITIES   Children are often taught the names of the geometric shapes, but they do not develop the discriminating power they need to use the names with meaning. In these beginning activities you should build on the children's own vocabulary, adding new words as appropriate. Although the names of the solids can be used, they need not be formally introduced until children have done activities like these. Notice that they are not just asking questions like "mark all the pictures of cones," they require children to describe and to justify their answers.

1. *Who am I?* Put out three objects (such as a ball, a cone, and a box). Describe one of them (it is round all over, it is flat on the bottom, or its sides are all flat). Ask the children which object you are describing and have them tell why it is that object and not one of the others.

2. *Who stacks?* Provide a collection of solids for children in small groups to sort according to which will stack, which will roll, and which will slide. A more sophisticated sorting is one that requires three sets of objects: solids that can be stacked no matter what face is down, solids that can be stacked if placed in some ways but not in other ways, and solids that cannot be stacked in any way.

3. *How are we alike or different?* In a whole-class discussion, hold up two solids such as the following:

Ask children to tell how they are alike or different. For example, children may compare the two solids shown as follows:

> "They are both flat all over."
>
> "One is tall."
>
> "One has bigger sides."
>
> "They both have some square faces."
>
> "They both have six faces."

4. *Who doesn't belong?* For another whole-class activity, put out three solids such as these:

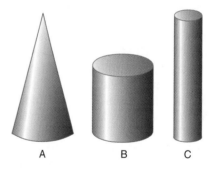

Ask the children which does not belong with the other two. Since there are many ways to solve this problem, be ready to encourage lively discussion. For example, some children may say A doesn't belong because it has a point. Others may say B doesn't belong because it's short, or C doesn't belong because it's skinny or has a smaller bottom.

5. *How many faces do I have?* A *face* is a flat side of a solid object. Have children in small groups count the number of faces on solids of various shapes. Then ask them to collect objects with six faces (boxes, books), with two faces (cans), and with zero faces (balls). You will be surprised at what you find! Some children have difficulty counting the number of faces on many-faced solids. You can help by using tape and numbering them as they count.

INTERMEDIATE ACTIVITIES The following activities introduce the names of some solids and consider sizes (or measure properties) as well as edges, faces, and vertices. The thinking is moving toward Level 1; the vocabulary and ideas are more mathematical than those in the beginning activities.

1. *Edges, vertices, and faces: Who am I?* After introducing the concepts of *edge* (a straight segment formed by two faces) and *vertex* (a point at which three or more edges come together), have children in small groups solve these riddles:

   I am a solid with:

   Eight edges—who am I?

   Six edges and four faces—who am I?

   Five corners—who am I?

   The same number of vertices as faces—who am I?

   No faces (no corners) —who am I?

   One face and no corners—who am I?

2. *Classifying solids.* Introduce each type of solid—cube, cone, pyramid, cylinder, and sphere—by putting out solids that are examples and nonexamples of each type of solid. As illustrated below, show two or three cylinders and two or three solids that are not cylinders. Then have the children select from the third set, which are cylinders and which are not. Since it may be difficult to collect examples of such cylinders, you could use pictures. The important part of this activity is the discussion, having children say why or why not the object is a cylinder. For example, many children think A is too "thin" to be a cylinder. They may be thinking at Level 0—it does not look like one. Whole-class discussions about what is common about all cylinders (a circular cylinder has two faces that are congruent circles joined by a curved surface) can help them move to a higher level of thought.

Cylinders

Not cylinders

Which are cylinders?

3. *Searching for solids.* Make up a set of activity cards that have children in small groups search out solids according to the size and shape of the faces and the length of the edges. The clues you give will depend on the solids you use, but here are some samples to get you started:

   Search for a solid with:

   Exactly two faces that are the same size and shape (*congruent*)

   Exactly three faces that are the same size and shape

   All edges the same length

   Edges of three different lengths

ADVANCED ACTIVITIES These activities focus on the properties of parallel and perpendicular faces and edges as well as more careful definition and classification of the solids. These activities are at Level 1 and use more sophisticated geometric ideas than in the previous activities. They also consider more than one property, leading students to see relationships between properties and helping them move toward Level 2.

1. *Parallel faces.* This activity can be done after parallel lines and parallel faces have been introduced. It consists of questions about real objects and why faces are parallel. A few sample questions that you can use in a whole-class discussion are given here to start you thinking:

   Why are the top and bottom of soup cans parallel?

   Why are shelves of a bookcase parallel to the floor?

   Why are roofs of houses in cold climates usually not parallel to the ground?

   Why is the front side of a milk carton parallel to the backside?

2. *Perpendicular edges.* In the Classroom 15-1 provides clues about particular solids, focusing on perpendicular edges, and asks students to construct the solids from sticks and connectors. See the "stick" models section that follows for a

variety of materials that can be used to model the mystery objects. Students enjoy making up their own mysteries for other students to solve. This experience provides an excellent opportunity to work on developing written descriptions that are clear, precise, and not contradictory.

3. *Right prisms.* This activity introduces the definition of right prisms and how to name prisms. Show examples and nonexamples of right prisms (as in the second of the intermediate activities), and ask students to describe the bases and faces, ultimately encouraging them to come up with the definition of *prism*—a solid that has congruent and parallel bases (top and bottom) joined by rectangular faces. Then have students

in a whole-class activity discuss how prisms are named. See if they can determine a way to distinguish between prisms. For example, if the base is a triangle, it is a triangular prism.

Prisms

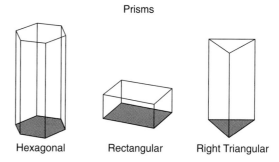

Hexagonal   Rectangular   Right Triangular

Constructing to explore and discover One of the difficulties that children have with three-dimensional geometry is visualizing the solids. It is essential to have models of the solids, but they often are expensive to purchase. There are many ways for children to make three-dimensional models. We have included suggestions of two ways to make "face models" and two ways to make "edge models." Face models (construction-paper tubes and polyhedra shapes) emphasize the faces, while edge models (toothpicks and newspaper) focus on edges. As children are making models, they often discover many properties of solids. However, for some properties they may need structured investigations as suggested here.

FACE MODELS Some of the easiest and most versatile models can be made from heavy construction paper. Figure 15-3 shows how to make open-ended paper tube models of prisms. The top and bottom faces may be added to these models by tracing the top of the tube, cutting out the shape, and taping it to the tube. As this figure suggests, many variations of prisms can be made, and these can be cut (truncated) to create many strange shapes.

Any solid whose faces are all polygons is a polyhedron. Prisms and pyramids are polyhedra (plural of polyhedron), but spheres, cones, and cylinders are not. The exploration, In the Classroom 15-2, deals with a special case of Euler's formula. [Euler's (pronounced "oil-ers") formula relates the number of edges (E), faces (F), and vertices (V) of a polyhedron to each other: $V + F = E + 2$.] In this activity, students investigate the relationship of the number of edges, faces, and vertices in open-ended prisms (called tubes). The formula for these tubes is $V + F = E$. Have your students look for other relationships between two of these variables. For example, they may see that the number of edges is always three times the number of faces (not counting the top and bottom

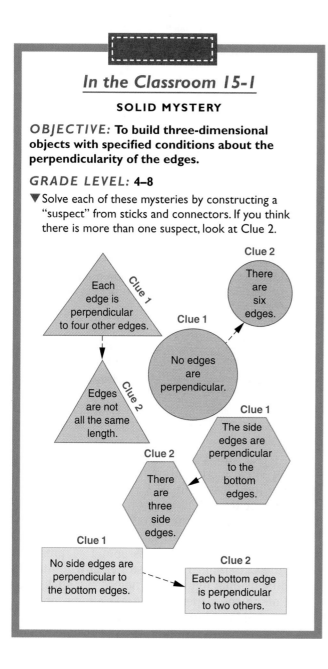

In the Classroom 15-1

SOLID MYSTERY

OBJECTIVE: **To build three-dimensional objects with specified conditions about the perpendicularity of the edges.**

GRADE LEVEL: **4–8**

▼ Solve each of these mysteries by constructing a "suspect" from sticks and connectors. If you think there is more than one suspect, look at Clue 2.

Clue 1 — Each edge is perpendicular to four other edges.

Clue 2 — Edges are not all the same length.

Clue 1 — No edges are perpendicular.

Clue 2 — There are six edges.

Clue 2 — There are three side edges.

Clue 1 — The side edges are perpendicular to the bottom edges.

Clue 1 — No side edges are perpendicular to the bottom edges.

Clue 2 — Each bottom edge is perpendicular to two others.

Use construction paper and masking tape to construct these tubes. Fold and tape each as shown.

• Prism with three congruent faces:

• Six-sided prism:

• Truncated prism:

FIGURE 15-3   Constructing tubes to think about properties of prisms.

---

faces). This is another opportunity to use an algebraic description: $E = 3 \times F$.

Triangular or square grid paper (see Appendix B) can be used to make polyhedra. A challenging activity is to find all the networks consisting of six squares and determine which will fold into cubes. Since there are 35 different networks, this is a good small-group project. If this is too advanced for your students, try using only five squares (12 different networks), and fold into open cubes. Students often do not have the opportunity to work with the triangular grid paper. A larger triangle consisting of four smaller triangles will fold into a triangular pyramid. Can you arrange the four smaller triangles in any other way to make a pyramid? Experiment with other number of triangles.

EDGE MODELS Models can be made from straws, pipe cleaners, toothpicks, or other "sticks" that can be connected with clay or tape. There are also reasonably priced, commercial materials

In the Classroom 15-2

WHAT CAN YOU DISCOVER?

OBJECTIVE: To explore the relationships among the number of vertices, edges, and faces of prisms.

GRADE LEVEL: 4–5

It's easy to complete this table if you've made the tubes in Figure 15-3.

	Tube 1	Tube 2	Tube 3
Faces	3		
Edges			
Vertices			

A. Count the number of faces of Tube 1. (Remember there is no top or bottom, so don't count them.)

B. Count the number of edges of Tube 1. (Don't forget the top and bottom edges.)

C. Repeat A and B for Tube 2.

• Do you see an easy way to tell how many edges if you know the number of faces? _____

• Write your conjecture:_____

_____

D. Count the vertices of Tube 1 and Tube 2.

• Do you see an easy way to tell how many corners if you know the number of faces and edges? _____

• Write your conjecture: _____

_____

Check your conjecture with Tube 3.

---

designed for this purpose. Young children enjoy building stick models from toothpicks and gumdrops. In the Classroom 15-3 uses this stick model to build specific objects given the number of gumdrops (vertices) and the number of edges (toothpicks). If your students need more of a challenge, use the ideas that In the Classroom 15-1 presents.

In the Classroom 15-4 illustrates how to make a three-dimensional figure from newspaper sticks and tape. Rolling the paper tightly takes some practice for some children; however, as with many geometry activities, often you will be surprised at who can do

In the Classroom 15-3

GUMDROPS AND TOOTHPICKS

OBJECTIVE: **To construct three-dimensional figures with given number of edges and faces.**

GRADE LEVEL: **4–6**

MATERIALS: **Gumdrops and toothpicks (about 20 of each for each child). Clay can be substituted for gumdrops.**

LAUNCH: **Explore making three-dimensional shapes with the gumdrops and toothpicks. Here are a few examples. How many gumdrops and toothpicks did each take?**

ACTIVITY: **Now, try some with the given number of gumdrops and toothpicks.**

Three rules to follow:

1. Two gumdrops can be used on each toothpick, one at each end.
2. Toothpicks should only be used to make the outline of a face (no extra ones stuck across the face).
3. The figure should be closed. Imagine it is a container with no openings.

Figure out which ones (A–L) are possible and why. If you can make a shape, tell whether it is a prism, a pyramid, or another shape.

Letter	Gumdrops	Toothpicks	Possible? (Yes or no)	Name of Shape
A	6	9		
B	5	8		
C	8	5		
D	6	10		
E	7	12		
F	8	12		
G	10	15		
H	12	18		
I	8	14		
J	10	3		
K	6	12		
L	5	9		

1. What is your conjecture about the ones that could not be made?
2. Which ones make pyramids? What is the relationship of the number? Using the models, explain why.
3. Which ones make prisms? What is the relationship of the numbers? Using the models, explain why.

this easily. When building three-dimensional objects with newspaper sticks, the children can investigate the rigidity of triangles, squares, or other polygons. They should find that the pyramid built with In the Classroom 15-4 is a rigid structure, but the cube needs bracing to be sturdy.

In the Classroom 15-4

BUILD YOUR OWN PYRAMID

OBJECTIVE: Explore pyramids through construction.

GRADE LEVEL: 5–6

- Follow these easy steps to construct a "stick" pyramid from newspaper. Use masking tape for the connectors.

Step 1: Take three sheets from a newspaper and roll tightly from corner to corner.

Roll

Tape

Step 2: Tape to hold rod.

Step 3: Make several rods and tape together as shown.

Tape

Cut off tails

Step 4: Put them together to make a pyramid.

▼ Your turn:
Use the same method to construct other three-dimensional shapes, such as a cube.

Two-Dimensional Shapes

There are several general things that you should keep in mind as you work with children in extending their knowledge of two-dimensional shapes. Children first recognize shapes in a holistic manner (van Hiele Level 0)—that is, a triangle is a triangle because it looks like a shape that someone has called a triangle. If an equilateral triangle with its base parallel to the bottom of the page is always used, then this shape will be children's image of a triangle. A teacher could not understand why all her first graders were coloring triangles green. Then, she realized that she had only been using the pattern blocks (see Appendix B) and this was their only image of a triangle.

Children should begin to recognize types of shapes through examples and nonexamples, not through definitions. In the Classroom 15-5 gives examples and nonexamples of triangles. Do you see why the different shapes were included? If a child says that C, B, F, or G is a triangle, what property of triangles do you think is being ignored in each case? If a child fails to realize that D is a triangle, what do you think may be the reason?

In the Classroom 15-5

FIND ME

OBJECTIVE: Identify examples and nonexamples of triangles.

GRADE LEVEL: 2–6

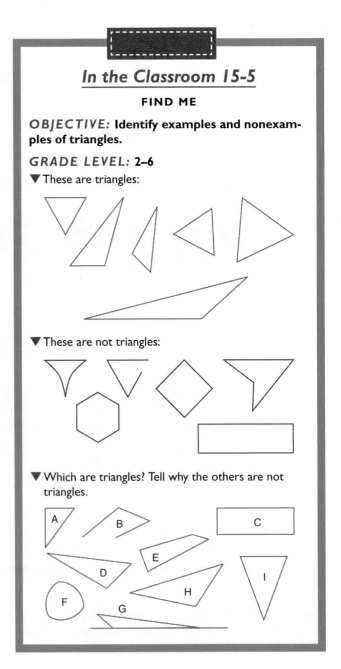

▼ These are triangles:

▼ These are not triangles:

▼ Which are triangles? Tell why the others are not triangles.

Children need to be able to recognize geometric shapes as models for real objects. For example, you might have young children write a "book" about circles. What is shaped like a circle? Let them find examples and draw pictures. Older children can be challenged to tell why certain objects are shaped in a certain way:

Why are walls rectangular?

Why are support braces triangular?

Why are most buttons shaped like a circle?

Why is paper rectangular?

Children also should know the names of common shapes such as triangle, square, rectangle, circle, and parallelogram. They also should be aware of other words that are used with shapes (e.g., children should be able to identify the *center, radius, diameter,* and *circumference* of a circle or the *sides, vertices,* and *angle*s of a polygon). Build vocabulary gradually, tying the new vocabulary to other words. For example, how is a triangle like a tricycle and a tripod? The most important thing with all vocabulary is that, after it is introduced, it is used.

Children are often taught the geometric names without being given much opportunity to explore the properties or to solve problems. A recent national assessment shows that students in the United States know the names of geometric shapes but have difficulty with complex geometric properties (Kloosterman et al., 2004). This section discusses each property separately, but the aim is to have children respond as in Figure 15-4.

Number of sides and corners   One of the first properties children focus on is the number of sides. They readily count the number of sides (line segments) of a shape, unless a shape has many sides. Then they may need to mark the place where they begin counting. Or, as you noticed in the snapshot, children may have difficulty knowing what counts as a side. As you have children participate in activities such as those that follow, they will begin to make many conjectures about shapes and learn vocabulary.

1. *How many sides?* This simple activity uses pattern blocks (see Appendix B). Each child needs only one shape for this activity.

   • Call a number and ask children who have a shape with that number of sides to stand. Call numbers such as two and seven, for which no one will stand.

   • Then have a search for all the different shapes that have three sides, four sides, five sides, six sides, and zero sides (the circle).

Compare these shapes:

They have four sides.
A is a rectangle. B isn't.
A can be folded to match.
They each have corners.
B looks lopsided.

Primary responses

They each have
4 sides and 4
corners.
A is a rectangle.
B is a parallelogram.
A has perpendicular
sides.
B has 2 pairs of
parallel sides: so
does A.
The angles of A are
equal: they are right
angles.
The length of
opposite sides
are equal.
They aren't congruent.

Intermediate responses

All of the above and:
Both are parallelograms.
They have the same
height.
They have the same area,
but they aren't
congruent.
They are convex.
Opposite angles are
equal.
They are not similar.
A has two lines of
symmetry. B has more.
Both have rotational
symmetry.

Middle school responses

FIGURE 15-4 Examples of children's responses that reflect their understanding and relationships between figures.

- Put a sample of each different shape somewhere within view of all children, and call on children to tell how the four-sided shapes differ (some are bigger than others, some are skinny, and some are slanty—accept their everyday words at this point). It is important for them to realize that the number of sides does not determine the shape.

2. *Less is best.* In the Classroom 15-6 provides a more advanced activity in which children put pattern blocks together to make new shapes with as few sides as possible. Two or more children choose three pattern blocks. Watch to see that they are counting the sides of the new shape, not the sides of the pieces. For example, if Marrietta said ten, it is likely that she counted the sides of the pieces.

2. *Can you make _____?* In this challenging activity, children make a figure of a given number of sides on a geoboard. (See Appendix B for a geoboard model.) Give each child a geoboard and one rubber band. Begin by asking them to make simple shapes, and gradually add other conditions. For example:

- Can you make a four-sided figure?
- Can you make a four-sided figure that touches only four pegs?
- Can you make a four-sided figure that touches six pegs?
- Can you make a four-sided figure that has two pegs inside (not touching) it?

Closely related to counting the numbers of sides is counting the number of corners. Children will soon realize that any polygonal figure has the same number of sides as corners if they count both on each shape. The activities suggested for counting the number of sides can be modified for counting corners.

Symmetry Two types of symmetry—line or reflectional symmetry and rotational symmetry—may be used to describe geometric shapes as well as objects in the real world.

To introduce line symmetry, ask children to compare two snowmen:

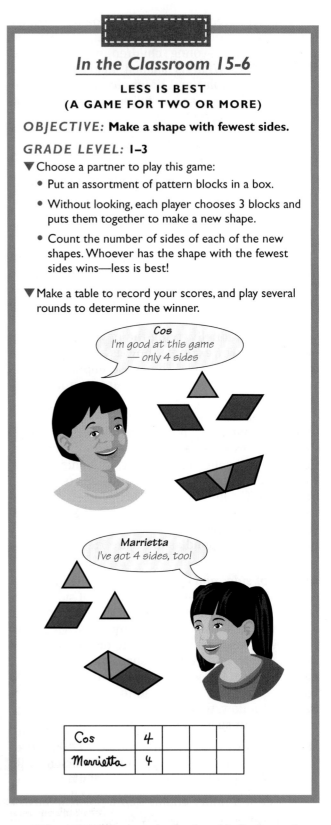

When they say one looks lopsided, show them how they can fold the drawings in the center to see if the sides match. A child's first perception of symmetry is visual. Use this visual perception to help build the idea of folding to match the sides or edges. You may also want the children to explore with mirrors or Miras to bring in the idea of reflection. A figure has line or reflectional symmetry if, when reflected over a line, the resulting image coincides with the original figure.

Have students find the line(s) of symmetry of geometric shapes. Be sure to let them try folding a square (four lines of symmetry), an equilateral triangle (three lines of symmetry), and a circle (an infinite number) to find lines of symmetry before moving to activities such as in In the Classroom 15-7. Older children can often see the lines of symmetry without folding, but some shapes (such as parallelograms) are misleading. Many children say a parallelogram has two lines of symmetry. Try it yourself to see when this is true and when it is false.

Children notice symmetry in things around them. Together, you might make a bulletin board of pictures of things that are symmetric. They also enjoy making symmetric shapes. One way to make a symmetric shape is to fold a piece of paper and cut the folded piece, leaving the fold intact. (Can you figure out how to make a shape with two lines of symmetry?) There are many activities on the computer in which children can investigate symmetry. Battista (2003) describes children's activities and learning about line symmetry using the *Geometer's Sketchpad*.

Lengths of sides Many of the definitions of geometric shapes, as well as classification schemes, depend on the lengths of sides. Help children focus on the length by having them find the shape with the longest side, find the shortest side of a given shape, and measure lengths of sides. In the Classroom 15-8 presents an example of a more advanced activity in which children make shapes on a geoboard according to certain specifications about the lengths of the sides. Try the items yourself and classify each as to whether it is easy, medium, or challenging.

In the Classroom 15-7

HOW MANY LINES?

OBJECTIVE: **Identify lines of symmetry.**

GRADE LEVEL: **4–5**

- Draw the lines of symmetry on each shape.

In the Classroom 15-8

SHOW MY SIDES

OBJECTIVE: **Make shapes with a specified number of congruent sides.**

GRADE LEVEL: **5–8**

▼ Use a geoboard to show these figures:

1. Can you make a 4-sided figure with exactly two equal sides?
2. Can you make a 12-sided figure with all sides equal?
3. Can you make a 3-sided figure with three equal sides?
4. Can you make an 8-sided figure with four sides of one length and the other four of another length?
5. Can you make a 5-sided figure with exactly four equal sides?
6. Can you make a 4-sided figure with two pairs of equal sides that is not a parallelogram?
7. Can you make a 3-sided figure with two equal sides?
8. Can you make a 7-sided figure with no equal sides?

Sizes of angles   There are many ways to examine the angles of geometric figures. A more complete introduction to angles may be found in Chapter 16. Here are some of the properties related to angles that older children may discover:

- The sum of the angles of a triangle is 180 degrees.
- The sum of the angles of a quadrilateral is 360 degrees.
- The base angles of an isosceles triangle are equal.
- Opposite angles of a parallelogram are equal.
- A polygon with more than three sides can have equal sides without having equal angles.
- The angle opposite the longest side of a triangle is the largest.

A guided activity such as the one in In the Classroom 15-9 will help students discover for themselves that the angles of a quadrilateral sum to 360 degrees.

Parallel and perpendicular sides   In addition to examining parallel and perpendicular sides in geometric shapes, children need to be able to identify parallel lines and perpendicular lines in a plane and, later, in space. Two lines in a plane are parallel if they never intersect. (Remember, a line can be extended indefinitely in either direction.) Another useful definition states that two lines are parallel if they are always the same distance (perpendicular distance) apart. Two lines are perpendicular if they intersect at right angles.

In the Classroom 15-9

HOW MANY DEGREES IN A QUADRILATERAL?

OBJECTIVE: To explore the sum of the degrees of the angles in quadrilaterals and triangles.

GRADE LEVEL: 5–8

▼ Try this method for finding the sum of the angles in a quadrilateral:

Trace and cut out.   Tear off the corners.   Put the angles around a point.

Name of shape *parallelogram*

Number of degrees of $A + B + C + D$ ___$360°$___

▼ Use the same method for these quadrilaterals. (Reminder: there are 360 degrees around a point.)

Name of shape _____

Number of degrees _____

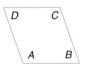

Name of shape _____

Number of degrees _____

Name of shape _____

Number of degrees _____

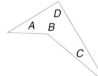

Name of shape _____

Number of degrees _____

▼ Now

- Try some more four-sided figures.
- Try a five-sided figure.

- Try a three-sided figure.
- What do you conclude?

It is important that children recognize perpendicular and parallel lines in the world around them. Have them search for perpendicular and parallel lines in the room. You might start a list together on the board, letting children add to it as they find other examples. Here is a start:

Parallel lines

- Opposite sides of a book
- The horizontal lines in E
- The top and bottom of the chalkboard

Perpendicular lines

- Adjacent edges of a book
- The vertical line and horizontal lines in E
- The edge of the wall and the edge of the floor

You may also have the children identify parallel and perpendicular sides on the pattern blocks. Ask them to find all the pieces that have one pair of perpendicular sides (none), the pieces with more than one pair of perpendicular sides (square), and the pieces with one pair of parallel sides (trapezoid). Use the puzzles in In the Classroom 15-10 to challenge children to arrange pattern blocks to make shapes with a specified number of parallel sides.

Convexity and concavity Often children are exposed only to convex shapes (any polygon with all angles less than 180 degrees). Many of the activities suggested thus far have included concave shapes. When children are making shapes, concave examples will often give interesting variety.

Show children two shapes such as these and have them describe how they are alike and different:

A   B

They will probably express the idea that shape A "comes back" on itself or "caves in" (concave). Introduce the terms *concave* and *convex*. After children classify shapes as convex or concave, you might have them investigate questions such as the following:

Can you draw a four-sided (five-sided, six-sided, seven-sided) figure that is concave?

Can you draw a five-sided (six-sided, seven-sided) figure that is concave in two places (or that has two angles greater than 180 degrees)?

Can you draw a six-sided (seven-sided, eight-sided) figure that is concave in three places?

In the Classroom 15-10
PIEZLES

OBJECTIVE: To build shapes with parallel sides.

MATERIALS: Pattern blocks

GRADE LEVEL: 4–5

▼ Solve these *piezles* (puzzles) using pattern blocks. Draw a sketch of the shape you made.

1. Use two different pieces: make a shape with
   - Exactly 2 pairs of parallel sides.
   - Exactly 1 pair of parallel sides.
   - No parallel sides.

2. Use three different pieces; make a shape with
   - Exactly 3 pairs of parallel sides.
   - Exactly 2 pairs of parallel sides.
   - Exactly 1 pair of parallel sides.
   - No parallel sides.

3. What is the largest number of pairs of parallel sides of a shape you can make from
   - 2 pieces?
   - 3 pieces?
   - 4 pieces?

4. Can you put all the pieces together to make a shape with no parallel sides?

It is challenging to try these exercises with *Logo* on the computer because the turtle turns the external angles of shapes. Have the children keep a record of the steps it takes to make each figure.

Altitude The altitude (or height) of a geometric shape depends on what is specified as the base. Identifying and measuring the altitude is essential in finding the area of geometric figures. In the Classroom 15-11 is designed to help children realize that a geometric object has different heights or altitudes. After students do this with the triangular model, have them draw a triangle on paper and again measure each side and each altitude.

Classification schemes What makes a parallelogram a parallelogram? When is a rhombus a square? What is a regular polygon? When students begin to understand the defining properties of two-dimensional shapes, they are moving into van Hiele Level 2. We take a brief look at classifying triangles, quadrilaterals, and polygons and some of the defining properties.

In the Classroom 15-11

WHAT'S MY ALTITUDE?

OBJECTIVE: Identifying and measuring the altitude of a triangle.

GRADE LEVEL: 4–5

▼ Make a triangle from a stiff piece of paper. Cut a strip 2 cm by 20 cm. Mark off segments of 9 cm, 4 cm, and 7 cm and label them A, B, and C, respectively. Fold and tape as shown:

I. Set the triangle on side *A*. This is the base.
  • How long is the base? _____
  • What is the altitude? _____
  • How long is the altitude? _____

2. Set the triangle on side *B*. This is the base now.
  • How long is the base? _____
  • What is the altitude? _____
  • How long is the altitude? _____

3. Set the triangle on side *C*. This is the base now.
  • How long is the base? _____
  • What is the altitude? _____
  • How long is the altitude? _____

TRIANGLES   Triangles are classified either by sides or by angles:

By Sides	By Angles
Equilateral three congruent sides	**Acute** all angles less than 90 degrees
Isosceles at least two congruent sides	**Right** one angle equal to 90 degrees
Scalene no sides congruent	**Obtuse** one angle greater than 90 degrees

After children have learned to identify triangles by sides and by angles, the two classification schemes may be put together. For example, can you make an isosceles, right triangle? a scalene, obtuse triangle? an equilateral, right triangle?

What defines a triangle? Here are some definitions that students wrote.

  a. A triangle has three sides.
  b. A triangle has three sides and three angles.
  c. A triangle is a polygon with three sides.

Although all three statements are true, only the last defines the triangle. Can you think of a figure that has three sides and is not a triangle? How about an example of b that is not a triangle?

QUADRILATERALS   There are many special names for quadrilaterals. Common names are parallelograms, rectangles, squares, rhombuses, trapezoids, and kites. These classes of quadrilaterals are not disjoint; one shape may fall into several categories. For example, a rectangle is also a parallelogram. This type of classifying process is more difficult for children than partitioning the whole set into disjoint classes, as is the case of classifying triangles by lengths of sides. It requires more than just recognizing examples of figures; it requires understanding the defining properties. For example, a parallelogram is a quadrilateral with two pairs of parallel sides. Assuming you know that a quadrilateral is a four-sided, closed, simple figure, can you identify which of the following are parallelograms? What other names do they have?

You are correct; they all are parallelograms. Thus a square, a rhombus, and a rectangle are all special types of parallelograms.

Discuss these questions with a peer. A *rhombus* is a parallelogram with all sides congruent. Does that mean that a square is a rhombus? Why? A *rectangle* is a parallelogram with right angles. Does that mean a square is a rectangle? Why?

How do you begin to teach such relationships? Children must first begin to verbalize many properties of the figure. For example, they must be able to describe a square:

As a closed, four-sided figure (property 1),

With opposite sides parallel (property 2),

All right angles (property 3), and

All sides congruent (property 4).

Properties 1 and 2 make it a parallelogram; properties 1, 2, and 3 make it a rectangle; properties 1, 2, and 4 make it a rhombus; properties 1, 2, 3, and 4 make it a square. In the Classroom 15-12 helps students with this idea.

In the Classroom 15-12

CLASSIFY ME

OBJECTIVE: **Classifying and naming quadrilaterals.**

GRADE LEVEL: **4–5**

▼ Mark each of the figures with a

   1. if it is a quadrilateral,

   2. if it has two pairs of parallel sides,

   3. if it has all right angles,

   4. if it has all congruent sides.

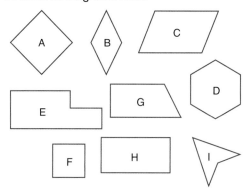

- Any figure marked 1 and 2 is a _____
- Any figure marked 1, 2, and 3 is a rectangle as well as a _____
- Any figure marked 1, 2, and 4 is a _____ as well as a _____
- Any figure marked 1, 2, 3, and 4 is a _____ and a _____ as well as a square.

POLYGONS Polygons are named according to the number of sides:

   3 sides: triangles

   4 sides: quadrilaterals

   5 sides: pentagons

   6 sides: hexagons

   7 sides: heptagons

   8 sides: octagons

   9 sides: nonagons

   10 sides: decagons

This classification scheme is not difficult, but often children are shown only regular polygons. Thus, among the shapes shown here, a child sees only the first as a hexagon, instead of realizing they are all hexagons.

Children should be encouraged to think of real objects that are shaped like these. A fun hunt for children at any age is to find different-shaped polygons in their neighborhood. If the children live in a rural area, have them draw all the different-shaped pentagons they see (the sides of many roofed buildings). Buildings in cities often use wonderful geometric shapes.

The names *heptagon, nonagon,* and *decagon* are not widely used, so in doing activities you may have to remind children of these names. In the Classroom 15-13 uses the names as well as other properties; students are asked to see shapes within other shapes, a task that is difficult for some. The geometric design paper in Appendix B may be used for similar searches.

In the Classroom 15-13

CAN YOU FIND IT?

OBJECTIVE: **Shade polygons with given properties.**

GRADE LEVEL: **5–8**

▼ See if you can find each of these in the design. Fill in the shape, and mark it with the matching letter.

   A. triangle—isosceles

   B. triangle—scalene

   C. quadrilateral—not symmetric

   D. quadrilateral—4 lines of symmetry

   E. pentagon—concave

   F. pentagon—convex

   G. hexagon—exactly 2 pairs of parallel sides

   H. hexagon—symmetric

   I. heptagon (7 sides)—symmetric

   J. heptagon—not symmetric

   K. octagon

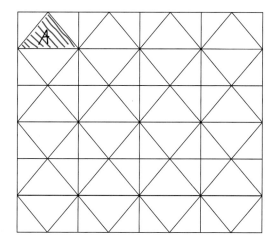

Locations and Spatial Relationships

Typically geometry in elementary school focuses on shapes. Yet, another part of geometry deals with locations and movements that describe direction, distance, and position. Where are you? Are you above or below the floor? Are you in front of or behind your desk? Are you between the cabinet and the computer? Where would you be if you moved five steps forward? Starting at your desk, how far from your desk will you be if you move five steps forward and three steps backward?

Examining locations and movements gives children a way to describe their world and give order to their surroundings. It also provides an opportunity to build mathematical concepts such as that of positive and negative numbers (forward and backward) and skills connected to other subjects, such as map skills. Give students opportunities to move by describing directions and distances traveled and where they must identify positions of an object through several movements. You might begin by taping to the floor of the classroom a map of several city blocks, as in Figure 15-5. Ask students to describe the directions and the distances in blocks between specific locations, such as between the school and home. Have the students describe a set of directions from home to school where they would use the crosswalks provided at stoplights and stop signs. Have the students describe a set of directions from school to the playground.

Later, students can formalize their navigational thinking by examining a coordinate system as in Figure 15-6. The coordinate system in Figure 15-6 uses all four quadrants. Although many programs do not introduce negative numbers in early childhood, this is a natural way to use them for children. You may want to begin with only the positive quadrant, similar to map grids. Tie movement and location together. For example, describe a movement and ask for a location: If I am at point (3, 1) and move 2 spaces, where could I be? (Many answers.) Describe two locations (3, 2) and (5, 6) and ask what movements would take you from one point to the other. (Again, many answers.)

The number line is a representation that involves location and can be used to represent movements on a line rather than in two dimensions. Movements like move forward five steps and back three steps can be represented on the number line. Suppose you begin at 0, where would you end? The number line below shows this movement:

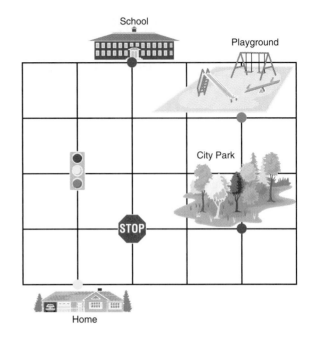

FIGURE 15-5 Map of locations.

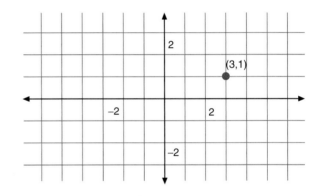

FIGURE 15-6 Coordinate system for describing spatial relationships.

There are three parts to problems like this: the beginning point, the movement, and the ending point. Knowing any two, you can figure out the other. The movement, however, could occur in many ways. For example, suppose you begin at 2 and end at 8, what are ways you could have moved? The shortest movement is forward 6, but consider forward 4, back 3, forward 5, back 4, and so forth. Will you get there? How many separate movements will it take? How far would you have moved in all?

Logo programs and other software for computers offer a wide variety of activities for children to explore movement and location. In *Logo*, an angle is considered as a turn and a figure is a path created as the turtle travels with its pen. With only a few simple commands (FD for <u>F</u>orwar<u>D</u>, BK for <u>B</u>ac<u>K</u>, RT for <u>R</u>igh<u>T</u>, etc.), children can begin drawing pictures and hypothesizing about geometric figures. An important feature of *Logo* is the angle that is created when the turtle is instructed to turn. Figure 15-7 shows some turtle commands and the resulting figure that is drawn. What is the measure of the angle the turtle needs to turn in order to create an equilateral triangle where each of the angles is 60 degrees?

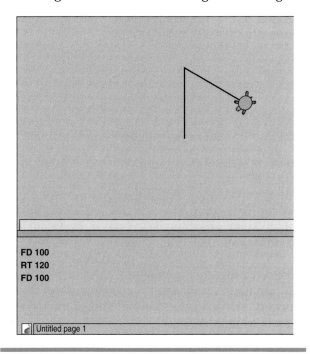

FD 100
RT 120
FD 100

Untitled page 1

FIGURE 15-7   *Logo* commands: instructing the turtle to begin to create an equilateral triangle.

Have children in the early grades begin exploring *Logo* through the *Logo* simulation, Turtle Pond, at the NCTM's Illuminations Web site at the iMath Investigations. In this activity students are to move the turtle to the pond. It helps to first have students actually walk the path described in the instructions to get the sense that the turtle is turning through the exterior angles of the object being drawn.

Math Links 15.3

<u>Y</u>ou can find an electronic *Logo* turtle at the NCTM Web site in the electronic examples section. For pre-K–2, look for example 4.3. You can access this from http://standards.nctm.org/document/eexamples or from this book's Web site.

www.wiley.com/college/reys

Children love to plot points on a coordinate system and connect the dots to make pictures. This certainly is one way to have them practice plotting points, but then it is a rather low-level activity. It is more challenging if they draw a picture and create their own directions. There are many problem-solving activities that involve coordinates and geometric shapes. In the Classroom 15-14 has challenging problems involving shapes and changing shapes. If you are teaching younger children, then consider having them draw shapes with given descriptions related to the coordinate grid. For example, you may ask them to draw a rectangle in the first quadrant (the one with all positive coordinates) with one vertex at (3, 2) and the length of the longer sides is 4 and shorter sides is 3.

In the Classroom 15-14

SHAPES ON A GRID

OBJECTIVE: **To explore various shapes on a coordinate grid.**

GRADE LEVEL: **4–6**

MATERIALS: **Grid paper (see Appendix B)**

LAUNCH: **Use these as a problem of the day (or week). Have students share the different solutions. Only rule: the vertices must be on the grid.**

1. Two vertices of a square are (2, 0) and (4, 2). What are the other two vertices? (3 solutions)

2. Two vertices of a right triangle are (0, 0) and (3, 0). What could be the third vertex? How many possibilities are there? Give at least 5 examples.

3. Parallelogram *ABCD* has vertices at (0,0), (0,4), and (1,3). What are the coordinates of the fourth vertex shown in the picture. Find other parallelograms with these three vertices. Give the fourth vertex.

4. The octagon below is in a 3-by-3 grid. What other octagons can you draw in a gird this size. Remember: the vertices must be on the grid.

    Which of your octogons are

    a. symmetric?

    b. convex?

    Which has

    a. the largest area?

    b. the largest perimeter?

Transformations

Geometry is often studied in terms of patterns. Think of wallpaper patterns or look at the three border patterns in Figure 15-8. What basic design is repeated? How is the basic design moved? Describe the moves in your own words. Did you use words such as turn, slide, or flip?

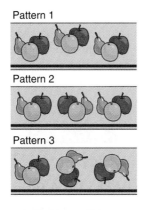

FIGURE 15-8 Wallpaper borders.

The NCTM *Standards* call for students to become familiar with the three geometric transformations: slide (translation), turn (rotation), and flip (reflection) illustrated in Figure 15-9. Research (Jacobson and Lehrer, 2000) points to the crucial role of the teacher when children are investigating transformations. If students are asked to make conjectures and justify their thinking, they develop a deeper understanding of the transformations. For example, older children may be asked to investigate what one motion would be the same as two flips over parallel lines, first over line *m* and then over line *l*:

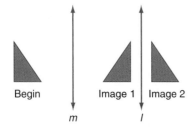

What if the lines are not parallel? What if the lines are perpendicular? What if you first flipped it over line *l* and then over line *m*?

Some questions about transformations can be answered just by looking, but for others children

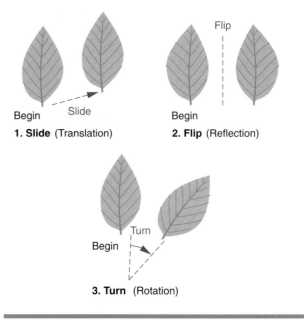

FIGURE 15-9 Motions for determining congruence.

will need to develop techniques. For example, children can fold on a line of reflection as they have done on lines of symmetry to see if the image is a reflection over that line. They can trace and turn or slide shapes to see the rotation or the slide. Computer programs such as the *Geometer's Sketchpad* provide a way even for elementary school children to investigate many of the characteristics of transformations.

Congruence Two shapes are said to be *congruent* if they have the same size and the same shape. Young children grasp this idea when they see that one shape can be made to fit exactly on the other. If the two shapes are line segments, they are congruent if they have the same length. If the two shapes are two-dimensional and they are congruent, then they have the same area. The converse is not true. Two shapes with the same area may not be congruent. Children have difficulty with this concept, and many middle school students would respond that the parallelogram shown here is congruent to the rectangle:

This difficulty may be more a function of the word *congruence* than of the concept. Young children have little difficulty identifying figures with the same shape and size, such as with these two right triangles. They can cut the shapes out and show that one fits exactly on top of the other to demonstrate the idea. Thus the task becomes one of asking young children to match figures to see if they are the same size and shape and gradually introducing and using the word *congruence.*

Congruence is often investigated through transformations. If two shapes are congruent, they can be made to fit by one or more of the three motions. What motion or motions could you use to move one of the triangles above onto the other? In terms of transformations, why are the rectangle and parallelogram shown above not congruent?

Similarity   Another type of transformation is that of enlargement (or reduction). You have probably used these terms when using a copy machine. What happens to a triangle on a sheet of paper when you reduce or enlarge it by a certain percentage? We say the two triangles are similar.

Similar is a word used in everyday language to mean alike in some way. In mathematics it has a special meaning: two figures are *similar* if corresponding angles are equal and corresponding sides are in the same ratio. We have also used the same shape to mean, for example, they are all rectangles. But not all rectangles are similar. So part of your task in teaching similarity will be to refine the intuitive notions about similarity to fit the mathematical definition stated above.

This definition is too formal for a beginning. Instead, you can begin by using a geoboard and geopaper. Children can make a design on the geoboard and transfer it to smaller geopaper, or they can copy designs from one size of graph paper to another. Older students can explore doubling, tripling, etc. the lengths of the sides of geometric shapes to see what affect this has on the perimeter and area on the electronic geoboard (see Math Links 15.4). After students have been introduced to ratio, they can investigate similarity in a more rigorous way. (Similar triangles are discussed in Chapter 13 as an example of proportions.)

Math Links 15.4

A variety of electronic geometry manipulatives may be found at the National Library of Virtual Manipulatives for Interactive Mathematics Web site, which you can access from http://nlvm.usu.edu/en/nav/index.html or from this book's Web site.

www.wiley.com/college/reys

Visualization and Spatial Reasoning

The last part of the NCTM *Geometry Standard* considers the role of visualizing, spatial reasoning, and modeling to solve problems. If you have been doing the activities in this chapter thus far, you probably have been using all three of these processes. Geometric modeling using number lines, coordinate grids, and rectangular arrays for multiplication have been used throughout the book. In this section we consider several aspects of visualization and spatial reasoning that we have not emphasized in the previous discussions.

Using Geometric Instructional Tools

Research shows that the use of physical materials including paper models, plastic or wooden geometric shapes, geoboards, and solids can be helpful in developing geometric representations but they must be used wisely (Clements, 2004). Although we have illustrated much of this chapter with the use of physical materials, we have only done a little with the expectation in the *Standards* of putting together (combining) and taking apart (subdividing) shapes. The ability to see shapes rearranged to make other shapes or seeing shapes within shapes is important to develop. The more that students work with materials to do this, the more ways they have to visualize geometric shapes and properties.

The opening snapshot used simple paper folding to make shapes from a square. The tangram puzzle (see Appendix B) provides pieces for endless explorations of ways to put the shapes together to make animals, figures, and other shapes. Children love to make designs and fill in pictures with the pattern blocks. All of these types of activities are a beginning, but students need to be encouraged

In the Classroom 15-15

SHAPE MAKER

OBJECTIVE: **To make shapes with given characteristics.**

GRADE LEVEL: **3–5**

MATERIALS: **These pattern blocks**

▼ Use as many of the blocks as you need. Record your answers with drawings showing the blocks used.

1. How many different ways can you make the hexagon?

2. Can you make a triangle with 2 pieces? with 3 pieces? with 4 pieces? with 5 pieces? 6 pieces?

3. Can you find two different ways to make a triangle with 4 pieces?

4. Make a rhombus using one hexagon and other pieces.

5. Make a convex hexagon using one hexagon and other pieces. Find another way.

6. Make a concave hexagon using one hexagon and other pieces. Find another way.

7. Make a nonregular hexagon (all sides are not congruent) with 3 pieces, with 4 pieces, with 5 pieces, with 6 pieces.

8. Make a large triangle only using the green triangles. How many did it take?

9. Make a larger rhombus only using the blue rhombuses. How many did it take?

10. Make a larger trapezoid only using the red trapezoids? How many did it take?

11. You cannot make a larger hexagon only using yellow hexagons. Can you explain why?

to take these activities further—to make predictions, to investigate various ways to make the same shape, to describe the pictures they make with geometric terms, to make shapes with given properties. In the Classroom 15-15 uses the pattern blocks (Appendix B) to present some problems of combining shapes to make other shapes.

Math Links 15.5

*Y*ou can access an electronic Tangram Puzzle, which allows children to develop their visualization skills as they use the puzzle pieces to create and cover various figures, from the Math Forum Web site, http://mathforum.org/trscavo/tangrams/contents.html, or from this book's Web site.

www.wiley.com/college/reys

Pictures or diagrams also are important tools. Can you imagine learning what a rectangle is without seeing examples? You should think about this if you have students who have visual difficulties. What can you do to help those students with pictures and diagrams? Think about using models they can feel with raised interior lines (a piece of string glued). It is not only these students who have difficulty; many students see diagrams and pictures differently than intended. It is important to have them create their own pictures and diagrams from work with the physical materials.

Computers have provided a tool that opens up many possibilities for many students. Students who have trouble moving the pattern blocks into place and recording their work can often use one of the shape-making computer programs. Computers also allow students to create many more examples of shapes they are trying to explore. For example, the exploration of altitude and bases (In the Classroom 15-11) is with only one triangle. On a computer, students could extend this to many examples and realize that to find the area of a triangle it does not matter which side is the base. Many of the textbooks you will be using will have special computer programs; see what is available in your school to use.

Using Mental Images

Although you can help children learn geometric ideas by using physical materials, you also need to help them develop visual images of geometric shapes. As your students mature, you can help them manipulate these images in their minds. For example, visualize a rectangle that is longer than it is wide. Now turn it (in your mind) to the right 90 degrees. What does it look like now? Draw a line from the top right corner to the middle of the bottom side. What two figures did you create?

One of the classic tasks to encourage developing mental images is to cover up most of the shape and reveal it slowly, asking students to predict what shape is covered. See the example below. There are questions to get you started, but let children come up with what they think it is before you ask them these specific questions.

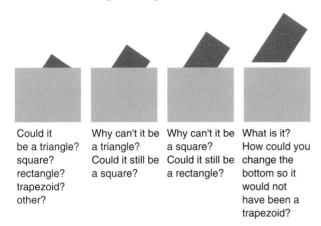

| Could it be a triangle? square? rectangle? trapezoid? other? | Why can't it be a triangle? Could it still be a square? | Why can't it be a square? Could it still be a rectangle? | What is it? How could you change the bottom so it would not have been a trapezoid? |

Visualizing two-dimensional patterns that can be folded to make three-dimensional patterns is an important aspect of geometric thinking. In the process, you may visualize the folding, or you may use spatial reasoning to help you decide. For example, imagine trying to fold an open cube (no top face) from five connected squares. Which of the configurations in Figure 15-10 could be folded into an open cube? Which would be the bottom square? Being able to make these visual manipulations mentally is enhanced by experience in doing such manipulations physically.

Visualizing three-dimensional objects from different perspectives is another aspect of geometry. What happens if you view a solid from different perspectives? Pretend you are a fish, swimming below a pyramid that is sitting on top of the water. You can see the entire bottom of the pyramid. What do you see? Begin with putting the children in easy locations where they see only one face and then move to ones that show more than one face. Pretend you are a bird and you are looking down on the point of a (square) pyramid. Can you describe what it would look like? Then have children put out solids and ask them to draw what they see from different views (down, under, directly in front, front when the solid is turned to see two faces).

FIGURE 15-10 Which figure can be folded into the shape of the open box?

Students need to work with models to help them make these mental images. Young children can begin with the basic solids and describing the faces. Make imprints in play dough (homemade works great) of the faces of wooden geometric solids. Have children match each solid with a face. The faces can be traced instead of making imprints, but younger children can work easily with imprints.

One way to help students see shapes from different perspectives is to look at structures built with cubes. Have students build a structure with cubes and then draw the different faces on square grid paper. There are several variations of this task. Give the children the drawings of the faces and see if they can construct the building. Or, have the children draw the structure using the isometric paper as shown below. (A master sheet of isometric paper can be found in Appendix B.)

Front

Another visualization task involves cross sections of solids. Cutting paper tubes (see Figure 15-3) helps children to see the cross sections. Use other objects that can be cut (e.g., oranges, carrots shaped in cones, or zucchini shaped in different solids), you can help the children see the cross sections. The next time you eat cheese, cut some small cubes of cheese and then try slicing each cube so the slice shows different geometric shapes. Can you slice the cube to see a triangle? A different triangle? How can you slice the cube to make a rectangle that is not a square? Try a pentagon and a hexagon.

Cultural Connections

Geometry opens the doors to many cultures. Literally, a search on the Web for doors from other countries can be an exciting adventure. We found African doors from the thirteenth century, including a beautifully carved wooden door with an intricate geometric pattern around the edge and a pitcher of wheat in the center. Mexican doors often had many rectangular panels, some plain and some decorated with geometric designs; Chinese doors had elaborate screen designs. Of course, the doors of every country differ by the period they were made, the availability of materials, and the socioeconomic status of the owners. Have you ever thought about what cultures did not have doors? What cultures have doors that are not rectangular? Why are most doors rectangular? What geometry do you see in the doors in your neighborhood?

Cultures have their own designs for their arts and crafts—quilts, rugs, pottery, jewelry—the list is endless. Many of these designs at some period in any culture's history are geometric. Homes and other structures also have distinctive geometric properties. In the United States, homes are some variation of rectangular prisms with roofs that are a mixture of triangular prisms. Look around your neighborhood or in house magazines for homes that are made up of rectangular prisms.

In the nineteenth century, Orson Squire Fowler claimed that octagonal houses were the most economical (less siding material for the same area of floor space) and healthiest (more windows and ventilation). Although he promoted his idea through several books and his own designs, there are only a handful of octagonal buildings. What other shapes are used for the structure of buildings or roofs? A classic article (Zaslavsky, 1989) looks at round houses.

Geometry has played different roles in schools of other countries. The French curriculum concentrates more on geometry in middle grades than we do, but does much less before that time. "Although there are 11 geometry topics in the TIMSS fourth-grade mathematics assessment, their inclusion in participants' curriculum varies more widely than any other strand, as does the percentage of students taught each of the topics" (Mullis et al., 2004, p. 213). Most of the topics are included in other grades, mainly in higher grades.

While in the United States we have spent the majority of the time in elementary school teaching geometric vocabulary, the curriculum in Japan expects students to learn the vocabulary naturally as they use it in solving geometric problems. Realize that the geometric vocabulary in many countries is more closely aligned with other words. For example, tri (from triangle) is a variation of *tres* (Spanish) or *trois* (French), Also the names of many geometric shapes are often descriptive. In English, this would be like using "six-sides" for hexagons.

In the diverse classrooms of today, you will find students with many different backgrounds. The visual nature of geometry helps you accommodate these differences in many of the geometric activities.

A Glance at Where We've Been

Geometry is a topic that is often neglected in elementary school, yet it has many benefits for children if it is presented in an intuitive, informal manner. This chapter presented a variety of sample activities that provide this type of informal experience. The discussion of three-dimensional shapes included ways to have children describe and sort solids as well as ways to make three-dimensional models. The discussion of the two-dimensional shapes focused on properties of shapes. It emphasized moving from simple recognition of geometric shapes (van Hiele Level 0) to the higher levels.

Geometry is used to help us represent the space in which we live and to describe the movements and the relationships between objects in space. Ideas were presented for young children and more formal ideas using a coordinate system. Geometric transformations also can be used to describe our world and to solve problems. Building children's visual skills and reasoning is an important aspect of geometry. The ultimate aim is to be able to use geometry to solve problems and to appreciate the geometry in the world around you.

This chapter touched on only a few things you can do to help children build concepts and skills in geometry, as well as only a few ways to present problems and apply geometry. There are many other fascinating topics and activities that you can use. Begin collecting and using these in your teaching.

Things to Do: From What You've Read

1. Name three properties of solids that children should learn at each of these levels: beginning, intermediate, and advanced.

2. Explain how the children's answers in Figure 15-4 differ from primary to intermediate. What more is shown by the middle school students.

3. Describe different geometry ideas that you find in the cover of *Helping Children Learn Mathematics*.

4. Give the reason for including each example and nonexample of a triangle in In the Classroom 15-6.

5. Design a sorting activity for intermediate students based on one of the ideas in the beginning activities with solids.

6. Explain how quadrilaterals can be classified. Why are squares a type of rectangle? How could rectangles be defined so that squares would not be rectangles?

7. Complete the activity in In the Classroom 15-8. Build a list of at least 10 objects in the world around you that have lines of symmetry.

8. What are the three geometric transformations that leave shapes unchanged except for position and location?

9. Do one of the challenging activities from In the Classroom 15-11, 15-14, or 15-15.

Things to Do: Going Beyond This Book

IN THE FIELD

1. *Symmetry.* Find an art project that deals with symmetry for elementary students. Ask some elementary-aged students to do this project. Reflect on the usefulness of this project in helping students understand symmetry.

2. Design an investigative lesson for one of the properties of angles of triangles or quadrilaterals listed in the section on angles. Look at Chapter 3 for structure of an investigative lesson plan. Try it with students and record their reactions.

3. *Solid Activity.* Try with children one of the three-dimensional activities described in the section on describing and classifying objects.

4. *Classifying.* In the Classroom 15-6 provides examples and nonexamples of triangles. Ask young children to tell which of the mixed examples are not triangles and to justify their selections. Or use In the Classroom 15-13 with older children to see what they understand about the classification of quadrilaterals.

5. *Compare Shapes.* Interview a range of students from K to 8, asking them to compare the two shapes in Figure 15-4. Compare their responses with those in the text.

6. *3-D.* In the Classroom 15-4 is one of the activities with building three-dimensional shapes. As you try this with children, observe which shapes children make and whether they can tell the number of edges and vertices. Can they make shapes with a given number of edges and vertices?

7. *Number of Sides.* In the Classroom 15-7 is a game for younger children, and In the Classroom 15-9 has challenging puzzles. Try one of these with students and observe how they react to games or puzzles.

IN YOUR JOURNAL

8. Give four reasons why geometry should be included in an elementary mathematics program. Explain, in your own words, what one of these reasons means to you.

9. Defend spending time in a classroom constructing models of solids.

10. A fellow teacher says that he cannot start to teach any geometry until the students know all the terms and definitions and that his fifth graders just cannot learn them, so he does not do any geometry. What misconceptions about teaching geometry does this teacher hold?

11. Read about the use of geometry in everyday life in another country or culture. Describe how it is different and how you could use this information in your teaching.

12. Look at the geometry in a textbook at a given grade level. Make a list of the activities from this chapter that would complement the text.

WITH ADDITIONAL RESOURCES

13. Read one of the children's books annotated in the Book Nook. Describe how you would use the book in teaching geometry.

14. Review the recent issues of *Teaching Children Mathematics* for an idea for teaching geometry at the elementary level. Describe how this idea can support the development of geometric thinking.

15. Read an article about geometry in other cultures (see suggestions in the annotated references). Design a lesson using the material from the article.

---

*Additional activities, suggestions, or questions are provided in *Teaching Elementary Mathematics: A Resource for Field Experiences* (Wiley, 2007).

WITH TECHNOLOGY

16. Write a lesson plan for children to use the Turtle Pond activity from the iMath activities of NCTM's Illuminations Web site. (See Math Link 15.3)

17. Explore drawing geometric shapes in *Geometer's Sketchpad*. What happens as you drag the shape around? How could this software be used with elementary students?

18. Read the article by Battista that is annotated in the references. Design an activity in which elementary students could explore symmetry.

19. Choose one of the geometric materials from the Virtual Manipulatives for Interactive Mathematics (see Math Links 15.4). Teach one of your peers to use the material and together design an activity for children.

Note to Instructors: You can find additional resources, learning activities, and block-line masters in this text's accompanying Instructor's Manual at www.wiley.com/college/reys.

Book Nook for Children

Ayture-Scheele, Z. *Beautiful Origami*. New York: Sterling, 1990.

Lots of beautiful animals in this book, as the title implies. The photographs help you figure out the steps. There are books on origami appropriate for any age.

Burns, M. *The Greedy Triangle*. New York: Scholastic, 1994.

This story is about a shape that wants to be another shape. A shapeshifter turns the triangle into another shape, but the triangle still is not happy. This continues until the triangle realizes that he really wants to be a triangle. There are activities for children, parents, and teachers.

Flournoy, V. *The Patchwork Quilt*. New York: Four Winds Press, 1991.

Tanya loves listening to her grandmother talk about the quilt she is making from pieces of colorful fabric from the family clothes. When Grandma becomes ill, Tanya decides to finish Grandma's masterpiece with the help of her family. This book can lead to discussions about different shapes used in the quilt pieces.

Friendman, A. *A Cloak for the Dreamer*. New York: Scholastic, 1994.

A tailor has been asked by the archduke to make new clothes for a very important journey that he will take. The tailor asks his sons, Ivan, Alex, and Misha to help in making the clothes. The tailor is concerned when Misha, the dreamer, uses geometric shapes in his tailoring designs. There are extended activities to use in the classroom.

Grifalconi, A. *The Village of Round and Square Houses*. New York: Little, Brown, and Company 1986.

Based on a true story of how people in Central Africa live in a village called Tos in Cameroon. The women live in round houses and the men live in square houses. A young girl listens to her grandmother as she tells the story of a volcano erupting and burning everything but one round house and one square house.

Hoban, T. *Spirals, Curves, Fanshapes and Lines*. New York: Greenwillow Books, 1992.

Intriguing shapes—spirals, curves, fanshapes, and lines—are all around. This book helps to heighten children's attention to the geometry in their own world.

Isaacson, P. M. *Round Buildings, Square Buildings, and Buildings That Wiggle Like a Fish*. New York: Knopf, 1988.

This book uses a poetic approach to focus children's visualization of some famous buildings in different ways. The Taj Mahal is "made of marble the color of cream"; a stone church is "like an old monk gathered up in his robes"; and windows are "pathways to the spirit of a building."

Jonas, A. *Reflections*. New York: Greenwillow Books, 1987.

This unusual children's book helps establish the basic concepts of symmetry. It allows students to examine images in a variety of ways—read the book, turn it upside down, and in every full-color picture there is another picture reflected.

Murphy, S. J. *Let's Fly a Kite*. New York: Harper Collins, 2000.

Bob and Hannah go to the beach with their babysitter, Laura. Laura teaches them how to make and fly a kite. They learn about symmetry when constructing the kite. There are activities and games for teachers and parents.

Rau, D. M. *A Star in My Orange: Looking for Nature's Shapes*. Brookfield, CT: Milford Press, 2002.

This beautiful book for young children contains many pictures of geometry in nature. There are suggestions for other explorations.

Tompert, A. *Grandfather Tang's Story.* New York: Crown, 1990.

A tangram adventure in which the animals change into different animals. Just rearrange the seven tangram pieces to form a rabbit, a dog, a squirrel, a hawk, and a crocodile. Using the tangram pattern (see Appendix B in this text) children can explore different shapes.

Annotated Resources

Alejandre, S., and Moore, V. "Technology as a tool in the Primary Classroom." *Teaching Children Mathematics,* 10(2) (September 2003), pp. 16–18.
A kindergarten teacher combines literature, pattern blocks, paper-and-pencil recordings, and a computer program for a rich study of shapes. In so doing, she thought about questions whose answers helped her students to build richer understandings.

Barkley, C. A., and Cruz, S. "Geometry through beadwork designs." *Teaching Children Mathematics,* 7(7) (February 2001), pp. 362–367.
The authors present a geometry lesson using beadwork based on the levels of the van Hieles. Interwoven are stories of different cultures and study of transformations.

Battista, M. "Computer technologies and teaching geometry through problem solving." In (eds. F. K. Lester and R. I. Charles) *Teaching Mathematics through Problem Solving: Prekindergarten–Grade 6.* Reston, VA: NCTM, 2003.
This chapter considers how computer software and carefully sequenced problems can assist students' reasoning and constructing increasingly sophisticated and abstract geometric concepts.

Bradley, C. "Making a Navajo blanket design with Logo." *Arithmetic Teacher,* 40(10) (May 1993), pp. 520–523.
In this activity students design a Navajo blanket with geoboards and then develop a *Logo* program to produce the design.

Confer, C. *Math by All Means: Geometry Grade 2.* Sausalito, CA: Math Solutions, 1994.
Students develop an understanding of spatial relationships and learn mathematical terminology to describe their discoveries. They also examine and create quilt patterns.

Frederick, B., and Williams, N. "Thinking geometrically: Totally tessellated." *Teaching Children Mathematics,* 10(8) (March 2004), p. 358.
A brief article that describes a teacher's use of a Web site focused on tessellations. Fifth graders explore the history, art, and geometry of tessellations.

Lehrer, R., and Curtis, C. L. "Why are some solids perfect? Conjectures and experiments by third graders." *Teaching Children Mathematics,* 6(6) (January 2000), pp. 324–329.
In an exploration activity students identify characteristics and develop a precise definition to classify the five Platonic solids.

Lipka, J., Wildfeuer, S., Wahlberg, N., George, M., and Ezran, D. R. "Elastic geometry and storyknifing: A Yup'ik Eskimo example." *Teaching Children Mathematics,* 7(7) (February 2000), pp. 337–343.
Introduces elastic geometry, or topology, in an elementary classroom through the study of connecting the intuitive, visual, and spatial components of storyknifing and other activities.

National Council of Teachers of Mathematics (NCTM). *Navigating through Geometry in Prekindergarten–Grade 2, Grades 3–5, and Grades 6–8* (with CD-ROM). Reston, VA: NCTM, 2002.
These three books contain geometry lessons built on the NCTM *Standards.* You will find many extensions of the ideas presented in this text in usable form for the different grade levels.

Paznokas, L. S. "Teaching mathematics through cultural quilting." *Teaching Children Mathematics,* 9(6) (January 2003), pp. 250–256.
This article gives examples and history of Hawaiian, Freedom, Hopi, Ozark, and Civil War quilts. Lesson ideas as well as an extensive bibliography are included.

Zaslavsky, C. "People who live in round houses." *Arithmetic Teacher,* 37(1) (September 1989), pp. 18–21.
This article considers why some people live in round houses and the geometry involved. Contains activities and information that can easily be used in the classroom.

CHAPTER 16

Measurement

Snapshot of a Lesson

Key Idea

To apply area concepts and skills to a practical situation

Background Information

This snapshot is based on the video *Pencil Box Staining*, from Teaching Math: A Video Library, K–4 from Annenberg Media. Produced by WGBH Educational Foundation © 1995 WGBH All Rights reserved. To view, go to http://www.learner.org/resources/series32.html (video#27). Mr. Levy is a teacher of fourth-grade students in Lexington, Massachusetts. In this video, each member of the class has made a wooden pencil box. The task today is to determine how much stain is needed to cover all the boxes.

MR. LEVY: This is an example of our boxes we are making. This one has been stained on the inside and outside. If I go to the hardware store and say, "We need some stain," what is Mr. Cuttingham going to ask?

DANNY: Did you measure what you are staining?

MR. LEVY: Right, and here is the chart to tell us the amount of stain:

1 pint	About 25 square feet	$6.30
1 quart	About 50 square feet	$8.40
1 gallon	About 200 square feet	$28.60

After introducing the problem, Mr. Levy has the students work in groups of 4. Each student in a group is assigned a specific role (measurer, recorder, calculator, director); together they are to figure out how much stain is needed.

(We have provided a glimpse into what is happening in four of the groups. If you watch the video you will get a more thorough understanding of the groups at work.)

GROUP 1: We should begin with the big pieces. Do we know if any are the same size? Mr. Levy, do we need to find how much for our box or all the boxes? [*After Mr. Levy asks the student who posed the last question what she thinks, she realizes that the stain was for all the boxes so they need to find out the total area for 26 boxes. They then begin the task.*]

GROUP 2: This is $\frac{1}{2}$ inch—OK, that is 0.5—and 0.5 × 9 is 4.5. [*Later, we see this group adding the areas of all the rectangles.*] The total is 162 square inches. Oh no, we need square feet. Do we have to do it again? [*They figure out they can divide 162 by 144. Using calculators, they find this is about 1.1 square feet. They conclude that 26 boxes would be about 28.6 square feet.*]

GROUP 3: [*This group made a model of 1 square foot and covered the model with the pieces to get an estimate of the area.*]

GROUP 4: [*This group made one large rectangle (as nearly as possible) from all the pieces, and found the area of that rectangle and doubled it since they were staining both sides.*]

After the students had worked, Mr. Levy gathers the class together to report their findings. He records the findings of the groups who had completed the task on the board:

65 sq. ft	1 pt 1 qt	$14.70
29 sq. ft (28.6 rounded)	1 qt	$8.40
39 sq. ft	1 qt	$8.40
86 sq. ft	2 qt	$16.80

MR. LEVY: What in the world am I going to tell Mr. Cuttingham?

The group that answered 39 square feet realized they had figured stain for only one side, so they doubled their answer to 78 feet, the amount to 2 quarts, and the price to $16.80.

Mr. Levy asked the students how they could resolve this. One student answered they could do it together the next day. Another suggested he buy 1 quart to stain one side and see if they needed more for staining the next day.

If you were the teacher, what would you do the next day?

Introduction

The Snapshot of a Lesson provides a glance into a fourth-grade classroom learning about measurement. What experiences should the children have before this lesson? How do you help children have these experiences? What concepts and skills are important for the children to learn? Before examining these and other questions, consider why measurement should be included in school mathematics.

Stop and think about how you have used numbers in the past few days. Did you tell someone how long it took you to drive to school, how many calories are in a piece of chocolate cake, how far it is to the nearest store, or how many cups of coffee you drank? All of these are measurements. Measurement is the topic from the elementary mathematics curriculum that is used the most directly in students' daily lives. Measurement is one of the 10 standards in the *Principles and Standards for School Mathematics* (NCTM, 2000) because of its power to help students see the usefulness of mathematics in everyday life.

Another reason is that measurement can be used in teaching other topics in mathematics. It is apparent that children need many mathematical skills to help them with measuring. For example, they may count the number of grams it takes to balance an object on a scale, multiply to find a volume, divide to change minutes to hours, subtract to see how close an estimate was to the actual amount, or add to find the perimeter of a triangle.

To report the number of units, children may use whole numbers, common fractions, decimals, or negative numbers.

Although not quite as apparent, measurement can also help children learn about other areas of mathematics. Many of the numeration models are based on measurement. For example, the number line is based on length. One model for multiplication is the area of a rectangle. Also, there are concepts and procedures that underlie both measurement and number ideas. As shown in Figure 16-1, measuring to the nearest unit is similar to rounding to a given unit. Thus measurement ideas may be used to complement numerical ideas.

Not only is measurement useful in everyday life, but it also is useful in other areas of the curriculum. If you are trying to connect mathematics with other subjects, consider the ways that measurement is used in art, music, science, social studies, and language arts. Much of the practice with measurement skills could be accomplished as you teach these other subjects.

Another reason measurement is an important part of the mathematics curriculum is not so much mathematical as pedagogical. Measurement is an effective way to engage many types of students some of whom you may have difficulty reaching through other topics. They often see the usefulness of the task as it relates to them personally. Think about the Snapshot of a Lesson at the beginning of this chapter. Were you fortunate enough to have such lively math classes when you were in fourth grade?

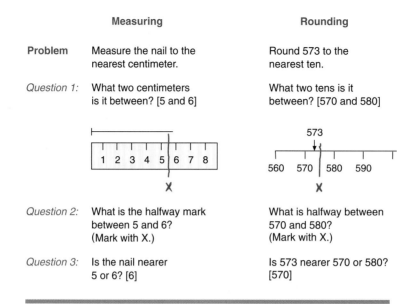

	Measuring	Rounding
Problem	Measure the nail to the nearest centimeter.	Round 573 to the nearest ten.
Question 1:	What two centimeters is it between? [5 and 6]	What two tens is it between? [570 and 580]
Question 2:	What is the halfway mark between 5 and 6? (Mark with X.)	What is halfway between 570 and 580? (Mark with X.)
Question 3:	Is the nail nearer 5 or 6? [6]	Is 573 nearer 570 or 580? [570]

FIGURE 16-1 The similarity between measuring and rounding.

Research from international studies has often shown that measurement is a strand on which U.S. students perform less well than their counterparts in other countries. This was also true for fourth-grade students on the TIMSS 2003 assessment being the only strand which U.S. students were not above the international average. Through the years, the data from the mathematics assessments of the National Assessment of Educational Progress (**NAEP**) have given reason for concern about students' performance on measurement items. As you read about these results in this chapter, think about your responsibility to help students develop better understanding of measurement and measuring skills.

In summary, measurement should be an integral part of the mathematics curriculum for several important reasons:

- It provides many applications to everyday life.
- It can be used to help learn other mathematics.
- It can be related to other areas of the school curriculum.
- It engages students in learning.

The NCTM *Principles and Standards* (2000) call for measurement to be a continuing part of the mathematics program, rather than being presented in a few isolated lessons (Figure 16-2). The first measurement statement concentrates on the conceptual understanding of the attributes, units, and processes of measurement and the second statement focuses on techniques and skills. This chapter integrates both of these as it considers the process of measurement that depends both on concepts and skills.

Math Links 16.1

*T*he full-text electronic version of the Measurement Standard is available at the NCTM's Web site. If you have NCTM membership, you can access from http://standards.nctm.org/documents. or from this book's Web site.

www.wiley.com/college/reys

FOCUS QUESTIONS

1. Why should measurement be included throughout the elementary mathematics curriculum?

2. What is the measurement process and why is it important?

3. Why are concepts related to the unit of measurement important to develop?

4. How is measuring one attribute (e.g., length) like measuring another attribute (e.g., area)?

5. How can you use estimation to strengthen measurement skills?

Instructional programs should enable all students to:	Pre-K–2 Expectations All students should:	Grades 3–5 Expectations All students should:
Understand measurable attributes of objects and the units, systems, and processes of measurement	• Recognize the attributes of length, volume, weight, area, and time • Compare and order objects according to these attributes • Understand how to measure using nonstandard and standard units • Select an appropriate unit and tool for the attribute being measured	• Understand such attributes as length, area, weight, volume, and size of angle and select the appropriate type of unit for measuring each attribute • Understand the need for measuring with standard units, and become familiar with standard units in the customary and metric systems • Carry out simple unit conversions, such as from centimeters to meters, within a system of measurement • Understand that measurements are approximations and understand how differences in units affect precision • Explore what happens to measurements of a two-dimensional shape such as its perimeter and area when the shape is changed in some way
Apply appropriate techniques, tools, and formulas to determine measurements	• Measure with multiple copies of units of the same size, such as paper clips laid end to end • Use repetition of a single unit to measure something larger than the unit, for instance, measuring the length of a room with a single meterstick • Use tools to measure • Develop common referents for measures to make comparisons and estimates	• Develop strategies for estimating the perimeters, areas, and volumes of irregular shapes • Select and apply appropriate standard units and tools to measure length, area, volume, weight, time, temperatures, and the size of angles • Select and use benchmarks to estimate measurements • Develop, understand, and use formulas to find the area of rectangles and related triangles and parallelograms • Develop strategies to determine the surface areas and volumes of rectangular solids

FIGURE 16-2   Measurement Standard with some expectations for children in grades prekindergarten–2 and 3–5.

The Measurement Process

Much of the research about how children measure and think about measurement has focused on children's conceptual development. However, there have also been classroom studies (Lehrer, 2003) that shed light on what students can do when given the opportunity. Wilson and Osborne (1988, p. 109) gave the following recommendations:

- Children must measure frequently and often, preferably on real problems rather than on textbook exercises.

- Children must develop estimation skills with measurement in order to develop common referents and as an early application of number sense.

- Children should encounter activity-oriented measurement situations by doing and experimenting rather than by passively observing. The activities should encourage discussion to stimulate the refinement and testing of ideas and concepts.

- Instructional planning should emphasize the important ideas of measurement that transfer or work across measurement systems.

In the discussion that follows, look for these four characteristics in the suggestions and activities. More importantly, keep these four recommendations in mind as you plan instruction.

Measurement is a process by which a number is assigned to an attribute of an object or event. Length, capacity, weight/mass, area, volume, time, and temperature are the measurable attributes considered in most elementary mathematics programs. Although each of these attributes is different, the process of measuring is common to all of these attributes. The following outline, based on the measuring process, can be used to plan instruction:

I Identify the attribute by comparing objects
  A. Perceptually
  B. Directly
  C. Indirectly through a reference
II Choose a unit
  A. Nonstandard
  B. Standard
III Compare the object to the unit
IV Find the number of units
  A. Counting
  B. Using instruments

C. Using formulas
V Report the number of units

If a new attribute is being introduced, cycle through steps: first focus on comparison, then use nonstandard units and counting, the next time use standard units and counting, and finally introduce instruments or formulas. This cycling may take place over several years for the first attributes studied, but after several attributes have been introduced, the time spent on the cycle can and should be shortened.

Math Links 16.2

A variety of Web resources for measurement, which may be used by teachers and children, may be found at the NCTM's Illuminations Web site. You can access this site at http://illuminations.nctm.org/index.asp or from this book's Web site.

www.wiley.com/college/reys

Identifying Attributes

To measure with understanding, children should know what attribute they are measuring. Consider for yourself the attribute of attitude. What are you actually measuring? Because the attribute being measured is not fully understood, scores on attitude tests are often difficult to interpret. For young children, measuring the area of an object also can be difficult if they do not understand the concept of area. Older children, who have difficulty measuring an angle, often do not have a solid understanding of an angle. Thus one of your first tasks is to build an understanding of measurable attributes.

Three types of comparisons can build understanding of attributes: comparing two objects perceptually (they look the same or they look different), comparing two objects directly (they are placed next to each other), and comparing two objects indirectly (a third object is used to compare objects). As children make these types of comparisons, not only are they gaining an understanding of the particular attribute and the associated vocabulary, but they are also learning procedures that will help them in assigning a number to a measurement. We consider each attribute commonly found in elementary mathematics programs because of the importance of having children participate in such comparison experiences for each attribute. As you read, see if you can tell the differences among the three types of comparison and how each can be used to develop an understanding of that attribute.

Length Length is one of the most easily perceived attributes of objects. Very young children have some concept of length and some vocabulary associated with it; however, they often have what adults may consider misconceptions about length. For example, they may say that a belt is shorter when it is curled up than when it is straight. These misconceptions disappear as children develop cognitively and are involved in constructive experiences. In the Classroom 16-1, 16-2, and 16-3 illustrate comparison activities that are appropriate for early childhood from preschool through grades 1 and 2.

In the Classroom 16-1 involves comparisons made perceptually and is designed to be done with your whole class or a small group. In the beginning of this activity, all irrelevant perceptual attributes have been masked (i.e., the objects are the same except for length). This allows children to build the concept of length as an attribute of long, thin things. Note that you do not ask which is longer, but allow the children to tell you what they

---

In the Classroom 16-1

PERCEPTUAL COMPARISON OF LENGTHS

OBJECTIVE: **Compare lengths of physical objects perceptually.**

GRADE LEVEL: **K–1**

MATERIALS: **Collections of long, thin objects such as rods, spaghetti, pencils, and crayons**

DESCRIPTION:

(a)

(b)

▼ Hold up two long objects and one short object.
- Ask children to tell which is different.
- Use vocabulary of *shorter, taller,* and *longer.*
- Repeat with other objects that differ *only* on the length and are obviously different in length.

▼ Hold up a long pencil and a short crayon.
- Ask how they are different. Expect answers such as color, type of object, paper wrapper, eraser.
- If no one says the crayon is shorter or the pencil is longer ask "which is longer?"

In the Classroom 16-2

DIRECT COMPARISON OF LENGTH

OBJECTIVE: **Compare lengths of physical objects directly.**

GRADE LEVEL: **K–1**

MATERIALS: **A box of long, thin objects and three sheets of construction paper (labeled shorter, same, longer)**

LAUNCH: **Present the class with a problem by holding up two pencils that look like they are the same length. Ask the students which is longer? You should have some disagreement. Have a child compare the lengths by putting the pencils upright on a table.**

baseline

After children have had the opportunity to compare objects directly (their height with a partner, the length of two shoes, etc.) using a baseline, set up the following center.

CENTER: **Place the box of objects at a center and choose one object to be the reference. Place it on the sheet labeled same. Have the students sort the other objects as shown below.**

Shorter (if possible)	Same	Longer

Students can then change the reference object and re-sort.

GEAR DOWN: **Work with individual students to help them with the words and with the idea of a baseline. Have them verify their sort by showing you why they placed an object in that category. First ask about an object they placed correctly.**

GEAR UP: **Challenge the students to pick a reference object so one category will have no objects. See if they can generalize that if they choose the shortest (longest) object, that there will be no objects in the shorter (longer) category.**

In the Classroom 16-3

INDIRECT COMPARISON OF LENGTH

OBJECTIVE: **To indirectly compare two objects on length.**

GRADE LEVEL: **2–3**

MATERIALS: **String or connecting links, index cards, tape, and objects in the room selected for children to represent**

DESCRIPTION: **Choose two lengths that are about the same on objects that cannot easily be moved to compare directly. For example, the height of your desk with the width of your desk. Ask the children which is longer, and let them pose a solution of how they can tell.**

▼ Discuss the ways they propose and then show them how you would use the links (or string) to represent each of the lengths and then compare.

▼ After this discussion and demonstration, give each pair of children a string and have them represent one of the objects you have marked.

▼ Make a "graph" of all the lengths for easy comparison.

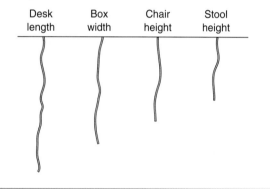

| Desk length | Box width | Chair height | Stool height |

observe and know. In the second part of this activity, objects that differ on many attributes (color, function, etc.) are used, but the focus remains on length. You can assess how your students are answering these questions. Do they focus on length? Do they know the vocabulary associated with length? You may need to gear down for some students who have not had the opportunity to learn the vocabulary (especially shorter) by asking more questions and letting students learn from each other. You can gear up by asking questions about a set of three to five objects: which object is the longest, which object is the shortest, or what object is shorter than the longest object?

In the Classroom 16-2 is designed to be used at learning centers after introducing the procedure of placing two objects side by side on a common baseline (comparing directly). Present a problem of comparing two objects that are not perceptually different in length. Ask children which object is longer and how they can justify their answer. If no one suggests putting the two objects side by side on a baseline, do so. This activity may be extended to seriating objects by length (i.e., arranging them from shortest to tallest). Seriating could be another center for students who need challenging. For the young child, this task is more difficult because multiple comparisons must be made. Later, when children are using rulers, they are comparing two lengths—the object to the ruler.

In the Classroom 16-3 presents the problem of indirectly comparing two objects when they cannot be placed side by side. Children must represent the lengths to help them make the comparison. Notice that in launching this activity the students are presented with a problem to solve. For example, which is longer the height of the teacher's desk or the width of the door? Children can represent the height of the desk and the width of the desk with string or connecting link chains. They can then directly compare the strings or link chain to determine which object is longer. Later, a ruler will be used to represent length and the objects will be compared indirectly using numbers.

Through activities such as these, children begin to develop an understanding of length as an attribute of long, thin objects; however, length is used in other ways. For example, length is the distance around your waist. Young children can use string to compare their waists or to compare their wrists with their ankles. In the Classroom 16-4 is an activity appropriate for older children in which they estimate the distance around a can and the height of a can, and then check their conjecture by comparing the lengths with a representation (a piece of string).

The *distance* between two points is also measured by length. In this case, words such as *nearer* and *farther* may be used when comparing two distances. Distance is often more difficult to perceive than the length of a long, thin object, so it should be introduced later. There is also other vocabulary associated with length such as *higher* and *lower* as well as the superlatives of all these words.

Perimeter—the distance around a region—is a special type of length. Children should be given the opportunity to measure the distance around a region with string or a measuring tape if they are familiar with a ruler. Later, they can add the lengths of the various sides of the region to find the perimeter. There are many everyday examples of problems that require finding the perimeter such as

In the Classroom 16-4

COMPARING HEIGHT AND CIRCUMFERENCE

OBJECTIVE: Compare the distance around an object with its height.

GRADE LEVEL: 3–4

MATERIALS: Cans of various sizes (at least one for each pair of students) and string. Label the cans and make a recording sheet as suggested below. (If you cannot find cans, roll construction paper to represent cans of various sizes.)

A   B   C   D   E

LAUNCH: Ask students, showing them a can, which they think is longer: The distance around the can or the height of the can. Students are often surprised about the comparison. Have them verify their conjecture by using string to mark each of the distances.

ACTIVITY: Have pairs of children work together. They should first decide which is longer (the distance around or the height) by looking and then verify their guess by measuring each with a piece of string. Have them record their guess and verification on a chart like the following:

Can	My Eyes Said	The String Showed
A	height	distance around
B		
C		
D		

DISCUSSION: Which cans were obvious? Which cans fooled your eyes?

Math Links 16.3

*A*n electronic manipulative that provides experience with length allows children to plan and produce instructions for moving a ladybug along a path. The children must estimate distances in order to hide a ladybug under a leaf, draw rectangles of different sizes, and complete mazes. You can access from http://standards.nctm.org/documents or from this book's Web site.

www.wiley.com/college/reys

Capacity   Capacity is considered the attribute that tells "how much can a three-dimensional container hold." Although perceptual comparisons can be made between two containers, young children often make the comparisons based on length (height) rather than on capacity. When asked which holds more—a tall container or a short container—most children will choose the taller container even if the shorter one may actually hold more. Thus it is probably best to begin the study of capacity by using direct comparisons.

Some type of filler is needed to make direct comparisons. Water and sand are perhaps messy but easy for even preschool children to use. Given a variety of containers, they can fill one and pour it into the other to see which holds more. After children have experimented with direct comparison (filling one and pouring it into another container), activities involving perceptual comparisons are possible. For example, children greatly enjoy guessing contests in which they guess which container holds more, and then you can check the results together. Figure 16-3 displays a possible comparison.

FIGURE 16-3   Which container holds more seeds? Tell why you think the one you chose holds more.

finding the distance around a bulletin board to determine how much border is needed or how far it is around a city block or around a track on a field. *Circumference* is a special word for the distance around a circle.

Indirect comparisons are used when two containers cannot be compared perceptually or directly. For example, suppose you have two containers with small openings that make it difficult to pour from one into another. By pouring each into a pair of identical large-mouth containers, the capacities can be compared. Note that this activity is similar to what you do when you use graduated cylinders in a science lab to identify amounts of liquid.

Weight/Mass   Weight and mass are different: mass is the amount of a substance and weight is the pull of gravity on that substance. On Earth, in contrast to on the moon, the two attributes are about equal. For example, if you weighed 120 pounds on Earth, you would weigh about 20 pounds on the moon. The same comparison words are used with children for both attributes.

The weight/mass of two objects are compared perceptually by feel by lifting the two objects. Children should be given a variety of pairs of objects (one of which is much heavier than the other) and asked to hold one in each hand. Children often think that a larger object weighs more. These children need opportunities to compare small and heavy with large and light objects. Children should learn that to find which is heavier, they must do more than look at the object. An easy way to provide this experience is by having children compare two identical containers with lids (such as cottage-cheese containers), but filled with different amounts of objects. For example, you could put 3 washers in one container and 14 washers in the other.

If you cannot feel the difference between the weights/masses of two objects, you need a balance scale to assist in the comparison. To introduce the balance, choose two objects that differ greatly in weight so children can see that the heavier object "goes down" on the balance. Figure 16-4 shows that even though one rock is larger, it is not the heavier of the two rocks.

FIGURE 16-4   Use a balance to show which rock weighs more.

Many activities may be set up for children to compare the weights of two objects. One challenging activity is to compare five identical containers, with lids secured and filled with different amounts of objects and to put them in order from lightest to heaviest. If the masses are not perceptually different, then this task requires multiple comparisons on the balance.

Indirect comparisons are not necessary until units of weight are introduced because, whenever each of two objects could be compared to a third on the balance, it would be much simpler to compare the two directly.

Area   Area is an attribute of plane regions that can be compared by sight (perceptually) if the differences are large enough and the shapes similar enough. You can modify the length activity (In the Classroom 16-1) for area. Begin with three sheets of construction paper, two of which are the same size and one that is larger. Ask the children which is different and to describe the difference. They will say that one is "bigger." Begin to build the vocabulary: this region is "larger in area."

The first direct comparisons should be made with two regions, one of which fits within the other. This is simple for students, so begin to challenge them to compare regions like A, B, and C. If the regions can be cut out, it is fairly easy to compare regions B and C by placing one on top of the other. It is more difficult to compare either B or C with A. When children have some idea of *conservation of area*—that a region can be cut and rearranged without changing the area—this experience can be meaningful. However, you will be surprised at the solutions that young children will propose; they are often more perceptive than older students who often rely on formulas.

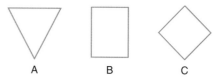

If objects cannot be moved to place one on top of the other, children can trace the objects and use these representations to make an indirect comparison. Chose two objects in the room that are about the same area and cannot be moved. For example, the electric switch cover and the door handle plate.

To help children understand that regions can be rearranged and not affect the area many experiences with geometry activities are helpful. Notice that in In the Classroom 16-5 children are asked to discuss the area of the shapes; this type of discussion helps focus on the objective of comparing

FIGURE 16-5   How many blocks will fill the box?

In the Classroom 16-5

ARE WE THE SAME SIZE?

OBJECTIVE: **To indirectly compare areas.**

GRADE LEVEL: **2–3**

MATERIALS: **Cut out the four right, isosceles triangles below.**

Are We the Same Size?

1. Draw a line to show how you placed two triangles to make each of the shapes A, B, and C.

    A.   B.   C.

2. Which of shapes A, B, or C looks the smallest to you? Explain to your classmates why each shape actually is the same size in terms of area. What is different?

3. What shapes can you make from three of the triangles? Draw a sketch of each.

4. What is the area (use the triangle as the unit) of each shape you made? What would be the area if the unit was the square shown in B above?

shapes indirectly using the right triangles as a representation to help make the comparisons. Although this activity was designed for younger children, it is appropriate for children in upper elementary who have not had such experiences.

Volume If volume is considered as "how much space a three-dimensional object takes up," then it is difficult to make anything but perceptual comparisons before units are introduced. Thus volume should receive little attention until fourth or fifth grade. However, because of the close connection between volume and capacity, some background can be provided for young children if containers are filled with nonliquids, such as blocks, balls, or other objects. Figure 16-5 uses blocks to fill a box allowing for the units counted to make volume comparisons with other boxes. Challenge your students to see if they can figure out how many cubes it would take without filling the entire box. Experiences like this are essential to help children make sense of volume formulas.

Angle Students are not often given the opportunity to compare angles before they are taught to measure them with a protractor. If an angle is considered a turning (such as the clock hands), then even young children can compare perceptually two angles (the amount of turning). Young children can also compare angles directly by comparing the amount of space the turn would make. Look at the direct comparison of these two angles:

Students can move to comparing the angles indirectly, but tracing one and then comparing the tracing with the other angle. Later, they will use an instrument such as a protractor to make these comparisons.

Temperature You can certainly sense (perceptual) great differences in temperatures. Before introducing thermometers, you can have children compare to see which of two objects is colder (or warmer). You can also talk about things (or times) that are hot or cold; however, there are few other comparisons you can make without an instrument (thermometer).

Time Time is a very abstract attribute; like temperature, it is not an attribute of objects that can be seen. There are two attributes of events (rather than of objects) that can be measured: *time of occurrence* and *length of duration.* You can begin describing the time of occurrence: we went to the gym yesterday, we have rug time in the morning, or we collected fall leaves in October. Young children need to develop the vocabulary of days, months, and seasons of the year. They also need to hear occurrences described in hours and minutes: school begins at 9 o'clock, you eat lunch at 12 o'clock, or you have 30 minutes to play. A lot of this learning takes place naturally if children are made aware of time. Look for opportunities in all your teaching to use this type of vocabulary.

Children can tell which of two events takes longer (duration) if their lengths are greatly different. Does it take longer to brush your teeth or read a story? If the events are similar in duration, children can tell which lasts longer if they both begin at the same time (note the similarity to deciding which object is longer when both are placed on a baseline). You can think of many contests that use this idea: who won the race, whose paper plane flew longer, whose eyes were shut longer, or who hopped for a longer time.

Other attributes   There are many other measurable attributes appropriate for middle grade students; for example, speed and density. An interactive way to look at speed is found in the activity referenced in Math Links 16.4.

Math Links 16.4

A three-part electronic lesson plan for middle grade students, Competing Coasters, may be viewed at the NCTM Web site, which you can access from this book's Web site. In these lessons, children use the Internet to learn about roller coasters from around the country. They predict which one is faster, higher, and takes longer. Then they compare their estimates with actual data. You can access it from http://standards.nctm.org/documents or from this book's Web site.

www.wiley.com/college/reys

Choosing a Unit

After children have begun to develop a firm concept of an attribute through comparison activities, it is important to help them move through the remaining steps of the measurement process (steps II–V). To answer the question, "How long is the pencil?" you can say, "It's longer than my thumb" or "It's shorter than my arm." These are relative statements that give a range of possibilities for length but do not do an accurate job of describing it. To be accurate, you need to compare the pencil to a unit. You can use a nonstandard unit such as a paper clip and report that the pencil is 7 paper clips long, or you can use a standard unit and report that it is 16 centimeters long. First you must

choose a unit. In so doing, you consider all the concepts listed below.

These concepts develop over time. A single activity as described for each concept will not suffice; you need to include similar activities. Look for opportunities within any measurement activity, whether it is with nonstandard, customary, or metric units to help children develop these eight concepts. Children will learn these concepts as they proceed through the other steps of the measurement process.

1. *A measurement must include both a number and the unit.* How many times do you remember a teacher telling you to be certain to write inches? Probably because you were only measuring in inches, you did not see why this was necessary. When children measure the same object with many different nonstandard units, they are more likely to see the need to report the unit. Having children measure the length of a book with paper strips, erasers, or cubes, or weigh an object with washers, pennies, or paper clips, is the type of task that will encourage younger children to write (or draw) the unit. In the Classroom 16-6 provides an activity that encourages children to focus on the importance of reporting the unit.

2. *Two measurements may be easily compared if the same unit is used.* This may be an obvious concept to you, but comparing the results of measuring with different units will shed light on children's understandings. Young children often rely on only numbers to make comparisons. For example, if one pencil is 6 blue strips long and another pencil is 2 red strips long, some children will say that the pencil that measures 6 is longer. They may not have yet reached the stage where they can coordinate the number with a unit. Students with special needs will need more experiences of measuring the same object with different units to realize that different numbers may occur if different units are used.

If students realize that it is easy to compare sizes if the same unit is used, they will understand the need to convert to the same unit when comparing measurements such as 3.4 meters with 1459 millimeters or when comparing $\frac{4}{5}$ with $\frac{2}{3}$.

3. *One unit may be more appropriate than another to measure an object.* The size of the unit chosen depends on the size of the object and on the degree of accuracy desired. If children are allowed to choose the unit rather than always being told what unit, the idea of the unit's size depending on the size of the object develops naturally. To encourage this

In the Classroom 16-6

MEASURING LENGTH
WITH ARBITRARY UNITS

OBJECTIVE: **To measure lengths with different arbitrary units; to compare those measurements.**

GRADE LEVEL: **2–3**

MATERIALS: **Erasers, paper clips, books, boxes, and other objects that can be used as arbitrary units of measure**

DESCRIPTION:

▼ Give each pair of children an arbitrary unit and the name of what they are to measure.

▼ Have the children record their measurements at a place everyone can see. Observe to see whether they record the unit (if they do not, it will lead to the discussion below).

▼ Ask children to use the information about the lengths to compare the lengths of the different objects.

▼ Ask children why the unit is necessary. Ask the children which comparisons are easy to make (ones measured with the same unit) and what they can tell about those made with different units.

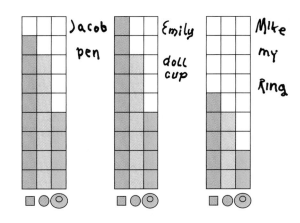

FIGURE 16-6   Children's graphs of weights of objects.

concept, ask questions such as "Should you use the edge of a book or a paper clip to find out how tall the door is? Should you use a thimble or a coffee mug to find out how much water the big bucket will hold? Should you use a paper clip or a pencil to find out the length of the book?"

4. *There is an inverse relationship between the number of units and the size of the unit.* When measuring the same object with three different units, children soon realize that the larger the unit, the fewer are required. For example, you could ask each child to weigh an object with pennies, washers, and cubes. If each child makes a graph of the results, a pattern becomes apparent when all the graphs are compared. As depicted in Figure 16-6, it always takes more cubes than washers to weigh each object. So cubes are lighter than washers.

5. *Standard units are needed to communicate effectively.* Many concepts about units can be developed with nonstandard units. At the same time, you will be teaching procedures of measuring with units (e.g., how to line up units, use a balance, cover a region, keep track of how many units). However, at

some point children need to learn about standard units. Standard units are either customary (e.g., inch, pint, pound) or metric (e.g., meter, liter, gram). Unfortunately, in the United States both types of units are used. It is clear from the recent national assessments that children have a better understanding of customary units (Kloosterman et al., 2004).

Stories and activities that demonstrate the difficulty in communicating sizes when there is no standard of measurement are one way to present the necessity of a standard unit. The classic story retold in *How Big Is a Foot?* (Myller, 1991) is an interesting and amusing source to use in helping children see the necessity for a standard unit. Another enjoyable activity for children is making a recipe of powdered drink such as lemonade, using a very large cup for the water and a very small spoon for the powder. (Be sure to have enough of the powder so the children can make it tasty.)

6. *A smaller unit gives a more exact measurement.* All measurements are approximate. If children do a lot of measuring of real objects, they are reporting approximate measurements, but perhaps without being fully aware of it. A practice of saying "about 6 inches," "more than 6 inches," or "between 6 and 7 inches" helps develop this idea.

To set up the need for a more precise measurement, give one child a strip of paper that is 27 centimeters long and another child, sitting across the room, a strip that is 29 centimeters long. Give each child decimeter (10 centimeters) strips with which to measure the paper. After they report the measurement, ask the class which strip is longer (no fair comparing the strips directly). Next, have them measure with centimeters. Discuss with the class why a smaller unit was needed.

7. *Units may be combined or subdivided to make other units.* When students are given the experience of making their own instruments, they often combine units (say inches) to make a larger unit (feet). Seldom are they given the opportunity to subdivide units to make smaller units. This can be done by folding to make fractional parts of a length unit or by using fractional parts of square units when covering areas.

8. *Units must match the attribute that is being measured.* Length is measured with a length unit, area with a square (or other shape that will cover the region) unit, and volume with a cubic unit that "fills" the same space. That is, we compare the object to be measured to a unit of the same type. Children often say the area is so many inches because they have only learned to use the length of the sides to calculate area. They have missed the concept of square units in the rush to formulas.

Comparing an Object to a Unit and Finding the Number of Units

In the section on identifying attributes, we considered ways that children could compare two objects on a specified attribute. Measuring with units is very similar to this. Instead of comparing two objects, you compare an object with a unit and find how many units would be equal to that object. In measuring area, for example, you can compare a region to a square unit and find how many of these square units cover the region. There are three techniques that are used to find the number of the units. The first is counting units; this may be done by merely counting the units or by using addition or multiplication to assist in that counting. The second is using an instrument such as a ruler that tells the number of units. Lastly, there are formulas that produce the number of units.

Counting units Length is the first attribute that most children measure. The beginning point should be with multiple copies of a nonstandard unit that are put end to end long enough to represent the object they are measuring. From previous experiences with direct comparisons of two objects, children should know when the lengths are the same. However some children do not understand that they need to line up the units in a straight line with no gaps and no overlaps. Do not expect too much precision with young children, but keep encouraging this skill. Give your students problems to solve, "how long is your desk in strips?" Observe to see how they are lining up the strips. Students with special needs and all students enjoy measuring with units that connect, such as connecting cubes or links. These

are good units because they are easy to handle and line up without gaps or overlaps.

Later, children can take one unit and move it along the object (an *iteration*). This more advanced skill is needed for proper use of a ruler when measuring objects longer than the ruler. It is a skill that should not be pushed too early. If you find that children cannot move the unit and mark the end, then postpone this skill until later.

If children have been measuring with nonstandard units, then using standard units should be easy. They will have a good understanding of the process of measuring, so the purpose should be to give them a feel for the standard unit. We have illustrated this with the decimeter because it is a good length for young children to handle.

Give each child a paper strip that is 10 centimeters (1 decimeter) by 2 centimeters. Strips can easily be cut from a 4″ × 6″ index card, or you could use 10-rods from a Cuisenaire set. Here are some simple ways to have children compare, estimate, or construct to develop a mental image of a decimeter:

- *Decimeter list-up.* (Comparing to a decimeter) Pose the problem for children to find something that is the same length as a decimeter. Put a list on the board of objects children find. Also have each child find a decimeter length on his or her hand. Perhaps it is from the tip of the thumb to the wrist. This is a handy reference.

- *Decimeter hold-up.* (Estimating a decimeter length) Pair the children and have one child try to hold two forefingers one decimeter apart, vertically, horizontally, and obliquely. The partner should check each time; then roles should be reversed. Or you could have them try to write their name or draw a picture that is one decimeter long.

- *Decimeter stack-up.* (Constructing a decimeter length) Set up centers with pennies, chips, clips, beans, cubes, and the like. At one center, children stack the chips 1 decimeter high. At another center they make a line of chips 1 decimeter long.

After children are somewhat familiar with the length of a decimeter, they can begin to measure with decimeters. A good way to begin is by asking them to estimate the lengths of objects and then measure. As children are measuring with decimeter strips, they (and you) should notice that putting down strip after strip is not the easiest way to measure. Have them tape their strips together, end-to-end, alternating colors.

Now they have a "decimeter ruler," except they still have to count the units. After they have done some counting, see if anyone suggests numbering the strips. This activity helps children understand how rulers are made and that they are counting units.

| 1 | 2 | 3 | 4 | 5 | 6 | 7 | 8 | 9 | 10 | 11 | 12 |

Once children are familiar with the decimeter measurement of small objects, the next stage is measuring something very long. Have each child make a 10-decimeter ruler. Tell the children that this unit is called a *meter* and is used to measure longer distances. Activities similar to those suggested with decimeters will help them become familiar with meters. New units should be related either by combining or subdividing the units children have already used to help them understand the new unit and to assist them in making conversions from one unit to another.

Children become familiar with standard units through comparing, estimating, and constructing. As they measure with that unit they will also gain an understanding of it. It is also important that not too many standard units are introduced at one time, that the unit is not too small or too large for a child of that age to handle, and that the numbers generated are not too large. Table 16-1 is a guide to the most common standard units used in elementary school and approximate grade levels at which it is appropriate to introduce them. Although, we have only concentrated on length and only on a few units, these ideas can be generalized to many of the other attributes. Think about how you could introduce a square inch, a liter, a pound, or a square centimeter.

Table 16-1 • Standard Units for Elementary Students (with Approximate Grade Level)

Attribute	Metric Units	Customary Units
Length	Decimeter (1–2) Centimeter (2–3) Meter (2–3) Millimeter (3–4) Kilometer (4–5)	Inch (1–2) Foot (2–3) Yard (2–3) Mile (4–5)
Weight	Kilogram (2–3) Gram (4–5)	Ounce (2–3) Pound (2–3)
Capacity	Liter (1–2) Milliliter (4–5)	Quart (2–3) Cup (1–2) Gallon (2–3)
Area	Square centimeter (4–5) Square meter (5–6)	Square inch (4–5) Square foot (4–5) Square yard (4–5)
Volume	Cubic centimeter (5–6) Cubic meter (5–6)	Cubic inch (5–6) Cubic foot (5–6) Cubic yard (5–6)
Temperature	Celsius degree (2–3)	Fahrenheit degree (2–3)
Time		Hour (1–2) Minute (1–2) Second (3–4) Day (K–1) Week (1–2) Month (K–1)

Using instruments   Instruments are used to measure some attributes. In elementary school, the more common instruments are rulers, scales, graduated containers, thermometers, protractors, and clocks. Other attributes (such as area and volume) are assigned a measurement by the use of a formula after an instrument has been used to measure some dimensions. Later, other attributes are derived from measurements of more than one attribute (e.g., speed is derived from distance and time).

Much of the emphasis in the elementary curriculum is on instruments and formulas, and some children encounter difficulty with both. One probable source of difficulty is that the children do not understand what they are measuring and what it means to measure. The activities and suggestions presented so far in this chapter have dealt with building this understanding. Here we will look at some common problems students with special needs have with particular instruments and some ways to assist in developing the appropriate skills.

RULER   A ruler automatically counts the number of units, but children must realize what unit they are using and line up the ruler properly. Children focus on the unit being used if the scale on the ruler has only that unit. For example, if the unit is centimeters, choose a ruler marked only in centimeters, not in centimeters and millimeters. Or, if the unit is inches, choose a ruler without the markings of fourths or eighths.

It is important that children measure real objects with the ruler. Make certain that you include activities in which children measure objects longer than one ruler. Can they move the ruler (iterate), and do they have the addition skills to add the units? For example, suppose the children have a 25-centimeter ruler and they are going to measure something that is 43 centimeters long. Can they add 25 and 18? Of course, they could use counting or techniques that rely on their place value and counting background: 25, 35, 36, 37, . . ., 43. Let them try; they will surprise you if they are given a problem to solve. Your role is to ask questions to assist them.

Older children may have difficulty in measuring to the nearest fourth, eighth, or sixteenth of a unit. One cause of this difficulty may be the smallness of the unit (there is more room for error), but more probably it is their lack of confidence and understanding of fractions, their lack of understanding of the unit (fourths), and their lack of consciousness of how to measure to the nearest unit. In measuring to a unit, they tend to decide by simply looking at the nearest larger unit. The example previously given in Figure 16-1 shows how to make this process more explicit. The rulers in Appendix B marked in halves, fourths, and eighths provide a good intermediate step before moving to a standard ruler marked in sixteenths. It also is helpful to emphasize the units by asking, "What two units is the nail between—two-fourths and three-fourths or three-fourths and four-fourths?" Children must be able to answer this question before deciding which it is nearer. A firm foundation of fractions and fractional parts of lengths helps with measuring to the nearest unit.

Figure 16-7 illustrates an item for using a ruler similar to a question that has appeared in various versions of NAEP. What do you think was the most common answer of fourth-grade students? Most said the segment was 5 inches long.

Children begin counting with one, so it is natural that they often begin measuring at one. Activities like making a ruler and seeing that the 1 is placed at the end of the first unit are helpful. If children are having difficulty, return to directly comparing the object with the ruler (use a baseline as described in the section on direct comparison). You also could use separate units or just mark the inches on the segment and count the units.

Although we have emphasized difficulties that some children have in learning to use a ruler, do not be discouraged. Children love to use rulers, and overall they do quite well with them. Make certain you have children not only measuring objects but also constructing line segments or objects of a given length. Research shows that children have more difficulty drawing a line segment of a given length than in measuring. Part of this difficulty may be the lack of experience.

SCALED INSTRUMENTS Instruments such as bathroom scales, graduated cylinders, and thermometers are easy to read if they are digital or if each unit is marked. They cause children some trouble when each unit is not marked. On national assessments, students have always had difficulty reading thermometers on which the markings represent 2 degrees. Over half of the fourth-grade students on the sixth national mathematics assessment chose an option based on thinking the marking represented one rather than two units (Kenney and Kouba, 1997).

One way to help children become more aware of the markings on a scale is to have them make their own instruments. They can make graphs, for example, using different scales, or they can mark their own graduated cylinders. In the Classroom 16-7 gives instructions on how to make the "cylinder." Children can make such a measurement instrument and then use it to measure the amounts other containers hold. Note that this activity is also good practice for finding multiples of a number; in this case, children are working with multiples of six since it took six spoons to fill the small container.

CLOCKS The ordinary dial clock or analog watch is one of the most complicated instruments to read—and yet it is often one of the first to be taught. Not only are there two or more ways to read the scale on a clock (hour, minute, and second), but also the hands (indicators of the measures) move in a circular fashion. Children who easily read linear scales (rulers, for example) may be confused by this circular arrangement. There is no set age at which children appear ready to learn how to tell time; you will often notice a wide range of ability within a class. The following list of skills associated with telling time is not necessarily in the order in which children may develop them:

- Identify the hour hand and the minute hand and the direction they move.
- Orally tell time by the hour (noting that the minute hand is on the 12) and move the hands of a clock to show the hourly times.
- Identify the hour that a time is "after" (e.g., it's after 4 o'clock).
- Count by fives to tell time to the nearest 5 minutes and report it orally (e.g., as 4 o'clock and 20 minutes after).

How long is this segment?

FIGURE 16-7 Assessing understanding of a ruler.

	NOW	2 hr., 20 min. LATER
	_____ : _____	_____ : _____
	NOW	15 min. BEFORE
	_____ : _____	_____ : _____
	NOW	5 hr. LATER
	_____ : _____	_____ : _____
	NOW	20 min. BEFORE
	_____ : _____	_____ : _____

FIGURE 16-8   Time problems.

ing to read a regular clock, a child learns the relationship of the minutes and hours and has a model to use in solving such problems. If all clocks were digital, teachers would need to spend less time on how to read time but more on how our time system works.

To integrate math and history, an interdisciplinary unit on the history of time and clocks could prove to be interesting to older students. Students might enjoy seeing how the measurement of time has evolved through the years. Students could make sand clocks, sundials, or other primitive instruments (Branley, 1993).

PROTRACTORS   The protractor often is a difficult instrument for students who do not understand angles. The most common protractors have two scales on them so that students first have to make a decision of which scale they are using. Young children who have been asked to compare angles, especially to the benchmark of a right angle, have less trouble with the protractor scales because they already know whether the angle is greater or less than 90°. Estimating sizes of angles (it is about half of a right angle or 45°, it is about a five-minute turn or 1/3 of a right turn or 30°) will also help students make sense of the protractor.

Using formulas   Formulas for area, perimeter, volume, and surface area are usually introduced in the upper grades. Although formulas are necessary in many measurement situations, they should not take the place of careful development of measurement attributes and the measuring process. The skill of using formulas should be developed, but not at the expense of helping students build meaning for the formulas.

- Count on by ones from multiples of 5 to tell time to the nearest minute (e.g., 25, 26, 27).
- Identify the hour that a time is "before" (e.g., it's before 10) and count by fives and ones to tell about how many minutes before the hour.
- Write the time in digital notation (4:20).
- Match the time on a digital clock to an analog clock.

These skills need to be developed over a long period of time, and children need to have clocks with movable hands. Encourage parents or caregivers to help you teach telling time.

You can begin problem solving with young children if they have clocks or watches. For example, as soon as children can tell time on the hour, you can ask questions such as, "What time will it be in 2 hours?" As the children become more familiar with the clock, you can give more challenging questions such as the ones in Figure 16-8.

Although reading digital clocks is easier than reading analog clocks, solving problems in Figure 16-8 is more difficult with a digital clock. In learn-

Before considering area formulas, students should be given the opportunity to compare areas of regions with and without units. Comparing areas without the aid of units have been discussed by placing one region on top of the other and by cutting one region in order to make the comparison as described in learning about the attribute.

When introducing units of area, provide students with experiences in covering a region with a variety of types of units—squares, triangles, and rectangles. To find the area of a region, they should count the number of units. Covering many different shapes helps students see the need to approximate and to use smaller units. For example, this region was first covered by one size of squares and then by smaller squares in order to more adequately report its area.

RECTANGLE The formula for the area of a rectangle is often the first formula children encounter. Use of the rectangle is appropriate because it can be developed easily, building on models that children may have used for multiplication. Figure 16-9 shows a sequence of steps that can be used to develop instructional activities that lead to the formula for the area of a rectangle, $A = b \times a$ (where A is area, b is base, and a is altitude). This form of the formula generalizes to other polygons better than $A = l \times w$.

When children measure with square units, the base and altitude may not be an exact number of units. You may have them begin by estimating how many squares it would take to cover the shape. Later, you can develop the idea of using smaller units or fractional parts of the unit.

6 units

4 units

Think

It takes $4 \times 6 = 24$ and about 2 more squares, so the area is 26 square units.

You should not teach the steps as listed in Figure 16-9. It is given as an outline to help you sequence experiences and assess students' understandings. Although some of the steps could be combined into a single activity, step 3 should not be done until children have the experiences listed in step 1 or 2. In addition, problems may arise

---

Developing the Formula for the Area of a Rectangle

Prerequisites:
- Identifies rectangle
- Compares areas directly
- Assigns a measurement by covering with units
- Models multiplication as an array

Step 1: Covering with Nonstandard Units
- Reviews covering of a rectangle with units
- Develops finding the area by multiplying the number of rows by the number in each row

Step 2: Covering with Standard Units
- Uses standard square units such as square centimeters or square inches
- Continues to find area by multiplying the number of rows by the number in each row

Step 3: Shortcut to Covering
- Develops a shortcut to covering the entire rectangle by showing that it is only necessary to see how many rows and how many in each row

Step 4: Shorter Shortcut
- Marks how many squares could fit across and down
- Continues to multiply to find the area

Step 5: Identifying Base and Altitude
- a
- b
- Identifies base and altitude of rectangles (begins with cut-outs of rectangles and measures their bases and altitudes)

Step 6: Formula for Area
- 4
- 8
- Measures base and altitude
- Tells the number of squares across the base and down the altitude
- Multiplies the number of rows (altitude) by the number in each row (base) to give the number of square units
- Uses the formula $A = a \times b$

Step 7: Applying Formula to Real Objects
- Practices finding the areas of regions and of real objects

FIGURE 16-9 One sequence for developing the area formula for a rectangle.

---

when children are doing step 7 if they have not had prior experience in covering real objects.

One difficulty that children often have with the area of a rectangle is that they may learn, by rote, that the area is the length times the width (or base times altitude) but not develop the underlying concepts. Thus, when they are faced with finding the area of a square, they run into difficulty. (It has no side that is longer than the others!)

We have concentrated on the formula for the rectangle because it can be used to develop the formulas for other common shapes as described below. See if you can visually make the connections between the shapes.

PARALLELOGRAM Every parallelogram can easily be transformed into a rectangle as shown here. Students do not have difficulty seeing this: however, they often use the side of the parallelogram instead of the altitude. They need experiences in measuring (and marking) the altitudes on parallelograms. Students with special needs may need to cut out copies of parallelograms and stand it up to see the altitude (measuring from the top to the "floor" much like you measure your height)

TRIANGLE Every triangle is half of a parallelogram. Before students are introduced to the formula for the area of a triangle, they should experiment with all types of triangles. Have each student cut out two congruent triangles and make a four-sided figure. After sharing their results, they should follow the argument below that the area of a triangle is half the area of the parallelogram.

TRAPEZOID Two congruent trapezoids can be put together to make a parallelogram. As with the triangles, have students experiment with a variety of trapezoids. See if they can generalize to give the formula.

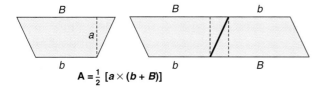

After learning how to use these formulas, children need experiences like those in In the Classroom 16-8 in which they cut the shapes into different smaller shapes for which they can use area formulas that they know. There are many different ways to subdivide the shapes. If you try this with students, have them show the different ways they subdivided the shapes.

Reporting Measurements

This last step in the measurement process requires the students to tell both the number and the unit. The attributes that we have discussed in this chapter are continuous, in contrast to the discrete attribute of numeracy (number of objects in a set). To tell the measurement of a set of objects, we use the exact number. However, the measure of a continuous attribute is the nearest number to the actual measure using that specified unit. In essence, we have treated these attributes as being represented by discrete units. However, even young children realize that the length of a pencil is not exactly 6 inches. We encourage you to think about saying about 6 inches or between 6 and 7 inches. If a more precise measurement is needed, then subdivide the original unit into smaller parts. We might report the length as $6\frac{1}{2}$ inches, or another length as 4 feet 5 inches. Later, students will study precision and error of measurements.

◆Comparing Measurements

Solving problems involving measurements often involve a comparison or an arithmetic operation. In so doing, it may be necessary to change from one unit to another (*conversion*), which relies on the *equivalence* relationship between the two units.

In this section, we examine equivalences and conversions within the customary or the metric system. Students need to become conversant in each system and not rely on converting between systems. However, if they have benchmarks for the different units in each system and how they are related, they will make more sense of the units. For example, they should realize that a liter is a little more than a quart, a meter is a little longer than a yard, or an inch is a little more than 2 centimeters.

Equivalences

As you introduce new standard units, you should relate them to others. For example, suppose you are introducing the millimeter, you should relate it to a centimeter by showing that it is smaller and that it is one-tenth of a centimeter.

After using different units, children should learn certain equivalences. Some of these, such as 7 days = 1 week, 60 minutes = 1 hour, and 12 inches = 1 foot, should become known through repeated use. Children need to know that they are expected to know other equivalences. Look at your state guidelines to know which are expected of your students.

Although children are no longer required to memorize long tables of equivalences, you should expect them to know the ones that are commonly used. The task is easier with the metric system because of the standard prefixes and tens relationship between units, as indicated in Table 16-2. The table shows the relationship between metric measurements of different units of length, capacity, and mass (or weight). For example, the meter (m) is the base unit for length. A kilometer (km) is 1000 times as long as a meter. A decimeter (dm) is one-tenth of a meter.

Children need to be able to use a table of equivalences. This involves several skills, which are illustrated in the questions that follow this table:

Unit	Equivalent
1 day	24 hours
1 hour	60 minutes
1 minute	60 seconds

How many hours in a day? (This answer only requires reading the table.)

What part of a day is 1 hour? (This answer involves knowledge of fractional relations of the units in the table.)

How many seconds are in an hour? (This answer involves conversion of units in the table.)

Area and volume equivalences can be difficult for many children because they are often derived from the linear equivalences. For example, knowing that 1 m = 10 dm allows you to derive 1 m² = 100 dm² and 1 m³ = 1000 dm³. In the Classroom 16-9 illustrates these relationships for

Table 16-2 • Most Commonly Used Metric Units

	Kilo (k)	Hecto (h)	Deka (da)		Deci (d)	Centi (c)	Milli (m)
	1000	100	10	Base Unit	0.1	0.01	0.001
Length	Kilometer (km)			Meter (m)		Centimeter (cm)	Millimeter (mm)
Capacity				Liter (l)			Milliliter (ml)
Mass	Kilogram (kg)			Gram (g)			

area. In the snapshot, the fourth graders who had measured in inches found that if they knew that 144 square inches was equivalent to a square foot, they did not have to measure again in feet.

In the Classroom 16-9

SOLVING CONVERSION PROBLEMS WITH SQUARE UNITS

OBJECTIVE: Determine the equivalents between dm² and m²

GRADE LEVEL: 4–5

▼ Ask students how many square decimeters (dm²) are in 1 square meter (m²). A representation of the relationship is shown below.

1 dm²

1 m²

▼ Show that each row would have 10 squares and there would be 10 rows. So 1 m² = 100 dm².

10 × 10 = 100 squares

▼ Use sketches and the model above to answer the following questions.
  • Conrad has a piece of cloth that is 3 m² or 3 m × 1 m. How many dm² is that?
  • Maria has a blanket that is 15 dm × 10 dm. How many m² is it?

Conversions

To change from one unit to another, children must know the equivalence or relation between the two units. By itself, however, this information is not sufficient to make conversions. Let's look at an example of a class discussion.

MR. BANE: It seems that several of you are stumped on the assignment. Devon, please read the first exercise and let's look at it together.

DEVON: *Blank dm equals 5 m.*

[Mr. Bane writes on the board: _____ dm = 5 m.]

MR. BANE: Who can tell me what we are looking for?

GEORGE: How many decimeters there are in 5 meters.

MR. BANE: What do you know about decimeters and meters?

ALANA: A decimeter is about this big and a meter is about this big.

MR. BANE: Could everyone see Alana's hands? Which unit is larger, the meter or the decimeter?(Meter)…. Right, so will it take more or less than 5 decimeters to make 5 meters?

KARINA: It'll take more. It takes 10 decimeters to make 1 meter.

[Mr. Bane draws this on the board:]

1 m

1 dm

MR. BANE: If 1 meter is 10 decimeters, then what would 5 meters be?

DEVON: I see, it's 5 groups of the 10 decimeters or 50 decimeters.

MR. BANE: Good. Let's try another:

20 cm = _____ dm

LEON: Centimeters are smaller, takes more of them to measure something; so it won't be as many as 20.

MR. BANE: Good. We know our answer must be less than 20.

RANDY: Let's draw a picture like this. Oh, there's no use drawing in all 20 marks. We know 10 centimeters makes 1 decimeter. So we want to know how many tens in 20.

MR. BANE: Right, in this case we can just look at the picture and see that it is 2 decimeters. But what if it was 184 centimeters?

DAVE: We still need to know how many tens in 184—we divide.

JIM: There are 18 decimeters.

MR. BANE: What about the 4 left over?

PAULA: Those are centimeters. We have 18 full decimeters and 4 leftover centimeters.

MR. BANE: Let's write that down:

$$184 \text{ cm} = 18 \text{ dm } 4 \text{ cm}$$

Okay. Try some on your own, and I'll help you if you have questions.

This discussion points out many good techniques to use in developing conversions. First, Mr. Bane had the children decide whether their answer would be larger or smaller than the number given. This relies on children knowing the relative sizes of the units and understanding that the smaller the unit, the more it takes to represent the attribute. Second, Mr. Bane tried to have the children visualize the relationship between the units. Third, he related the operation to be used to their understanding of what multiplication and division mean.

Estimating Measurements

Estimating is the mental process of arriving at a measurement without the aid of measuring instruments. There are many reasons to include estimating in the development of measurement. For one, it helps reinforce the size of units and the relationships among units. For another, it is a practical application—think of all the times you want to know approximately how long, how heavy, or how much something holds.

There are two main types of estimation. In the most common type, the attribute and object are named and the measurement is unknown. For example, about how long is your arm? In the other type, the measurement is known and the object is to be chosen. For example, what piece of furniture in your room is about 1 meter long? By keeping the two classes of estimation in mind, you can expand your repertoire of estimation activities. Identify these two types in the activities in In the Classroom 16-10.

Several common strategies can be used with either type of estimation. You can help children develop these strategies by talking through the various methods that different children use to make estimations and by presenting the following strategies.

What is the height of the door?

Using a referent: *I am about 6 feet, so the door must be about 7 feet.*

Chunking: *I know it is a yard to the knob, another yard to here, so a little more than 2 yards.*

Unitizing: *Each cylinder block is about 8 inches. There are 10 blocks, so about 80 inches.*

1. One strategy is to *compare to a referent*. If you know that you are 1 meter 70 centimeters tall, then you can estimate the height of a child who comes up to your waist. Or, if you have to choose a board that is 2 meters long, you will have some idea of the size. The NCTM *Standards* call for developing common referents or benchmarks to help in estimating measurements. As suggested previously, it is helpful to have a referent for each of the units.

2. Another strategy is that of *chunking*. In this process, you break the object into subparts and estimate each part. For example, you want to know about how far you walked from your home to the library and the store and then back to your home. If you know that from your home to the library is about 1 mile, that it's about that same distance from the library to the store, and twice as far from the store back to your home, you walked about 4 miles altogether.

3. A strategy related to chunking is *unitizing*. In this case, you estimate one part and see how many parts are in the whole. For example, someone asks you to cut a piece of string that is about 3 meters long. You estimate 1 meter and take three of these.

When including estimation in your program, you should try to make it a natural part of measurement activities.

1. Encourage children to see if they can tell about how long or heavy the object is before they measure it.

2. Look for ways to include estimation in other subject areas:

   About how far did you jump?

   What size paper do you need for your art project?

   About how long will it take you to read the book?

3. Plan estimating activities for their own sake or use brief ones as daily openers for several weeks throughout the year. In the Classroom 16-10 presents some ideas to get you started. Once you begin thinking about the things in your room, you will be able to come up with a lot of variations.

In the Classroom 16-10

OBJECTIVE: **Estimate measurements of objects and compare measurements with those of other objects.**

GRADE LEVEL: **3–5**

About how many centimeters long?

	Estimate	Measure
Little finger	————	————
Nose	————	————
Foot	————	————

A   B   C

Which holds about 2 cups?

Make a decimeter

Draw a snake that you think is a decimeter long.

Draw a tree that you think is a decimeter high.

CONTEST FOR WEDNESDAY

About how much does the wonderful watermelon weigh?

Name	Guess
————	————
————	————

Winner gets the largest piece at Ho-Ho's picnic.

Guess which of the boxes will hold 60 sugar cubes. ▱

x   y   z

About how many squares?

The floor ————

Your desk ————

The bulletin board ————

We'll collect your estimates on Friday.

HUNT   HUNT

There is something in the room that weighs a kilogram.

Can you find it?

One thing to remember: do not call an estimate right or wrong. Help children develop ways to make better estimates, but do not discourage them. Let them check their estimates by measuring. They will know whether they were close or not. You may be surprised to find out who are the good estimators in your class.

Connecting Attributes

Activities involving two attributes can help children see how the attributes are related or how one attribute does not depend on the other. For example, by doubling the dimensions of a rectangle, children may see how the area is changed. By examining figures with the same area but different shape, children may see that area is independent of shape. We have included some sample activities with suggestions for other variations or extensions.

Area and Shape

In the Classroom 16-11 encourages children in grades 2 through 4 to investigate the different shapes they can make using two to four squares. Younger children enjoy this activity using square tiles. For older children, extend this activity to more squares and place the restrictions that the squares must have touching sides (not corners) and that two shapes are the same if one is a reflection or rotation (see Chapter 15) of the other. A challenging variation is to use triangular grid paper (see Appendix B) rather than the square grid paper. Make certain with all of these that the students can make the generalization: the shapes are the same area but different in shapes. In the upper grades, they should explore similar shapes with different areas.

Volume and Shape

An activity such as the one In the Classroom 16-12 can be done with cubes. Not only does this activity look at the generalization that shapes with the same volume may be of different shapes, it also ties the investigation to number theory (primes and composites).

Perimeter and Area

Children are often confused about perimeter and area. This confusion may be caused partly by a lack of understanding of area and partly by premature introduction of the formulas. Many activities can help children see that a figure with a given perimeter may have many different areas. In the Classroom 16-13 is a sample of this type of activity. Children also should realize that figures with the same area can have different perimeters. You can modify In the Classroom 16-11 by asking the perimeter of each of the shapes or by challenging students to take five squares and see what shape they can make that has the largest perimeter or the smallest perimeter. The electronic geoboard (see Math Links 16.5) will allow students to make a shape and then check the area and the perimeter. For example, have students explore and record (see geoboard paper in Appendix B) the areas and perimeters of

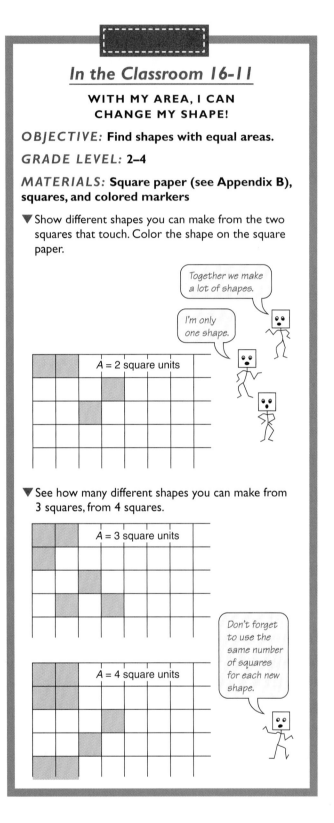

In the Classroom 16-11

WITH MY AREA, I CAN CHANGE MY SHAPE!

OBJECTIVE: **Find shapes with equal areas.**

GRADE LEVEL: **2–4**

MATERIALS: **Square paper (see Appendix B), squares, and colored markers**

▼ Show different shapes you can make from the two squares that touch. Color the shape on the square paper.

Together we make a lot of shapes.

I'm only one shape.

A = 2 square units

▼ See how many different shapes you can make from 3 squares, from 4 squares.

A = 3 square units

A = 4 square units

Don't forget to use the same number of squares for each new shape.

various shapes, then choose an area (say 6 squares) and see how many shapes with different perimeters they can make. What shape has the largest perimeter? What shape had the smallest perimeter?

In the Classroom 16-12

SAME VOLUME, DIFFERENT SHAPE

OBJECTIVE: **Exploring the different shapes of solids that can be made with a given volume.**

GRADE LEVEL: **5–8**

MATERIALS: **Cubes**

I'm 8 cubes—8 by 1 by 1.
My volume is
8 square units.

I'm 8 cubes—2 by 2 by 2.
My volume is
8 square units, too!

▼ See how many different rectangular solids you can make with 12 cubes. Record the dimensions and volume of each.

▼ Now use 2, 3, 4, ..., 17, 18 cubes

▼ How many different solids can you make if the number of cubes is
- prime? _____
- a product of two primes? _____
- a perfect square? _____

▼ How many different solids can you make with 24 cubes? _____

In the Classroom 16-13

DO YOU KNOW HOW TO CONNECT PERIMETER AND AREA?

OBJECTIVE: **Explore different areas that can be made from a given perimeter.**

GRADE LEVEL: **5–8**

MATERIALS: **Centimeter grid (Appendix B) and pencil**

▼ How many different rectangles can you make with a perimeter of 16 cm? Find the area of each.

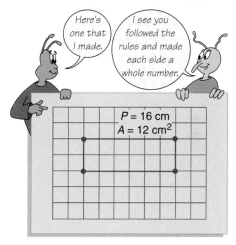

Here's one that I made.

I see you followed the rules and made each side a whole number.

$P = 16$ cm
$A = 12$ cm^2

▼ With three other students, try each of the following perimeters: 8 cm, 9 cm, 10 cm, 11 cm, 12 cm, and 13 cm. Make a table of the number of different rectangles you can make from each perimeter.

▼ How many different rectangles do you think you could make if the perimeter were 52 cm? What is your conjecture?

Math Links 16.5

*T*he virtual electronic manipulatives site has an electronic geoboard. Become skillful in handling it. It has been referenced in the Connecting Attributes (Perimeter and Area) section. Try one of the suggestions there. You can access this from http://nlvm.usu.edu/en/nav/index.html or from this book's Web site.

www.wiley.com/college/reys

Volume and Surface Area

Just as the area of a figure does not depend on the perimeter, the volume does not depend on the surface area. The experiment in In the Classroom 16-14 looks at the relation of lateral surface area to volume. You can vary this activity by having children fold the papers into thirds (sixths) to make prisms or make cylinders (a long, thin one and a short, fat one). In middle school, after developing the formula for a rectangular solid, students could calculate the volume of each of the tubes in In the Classroom 16-14.

◆ Cultural Connections

Most of the world uses the metric system, so it is important for you to understand and prepare your students to live in this world. Certainly if you

In the Classroom 16-14

WHAT IS THE CONNECTION BETWEEN VOLUME AND AREA?

OBJECTIVE: Exploring the volume of prisms and cylinders with the same lateral area.

GRADE LEVEL: 5–8

MATERIALS: Construction paper (9 in. by 12 in.), tape, and dry filler

▼ Use construction paper to make two tubes:

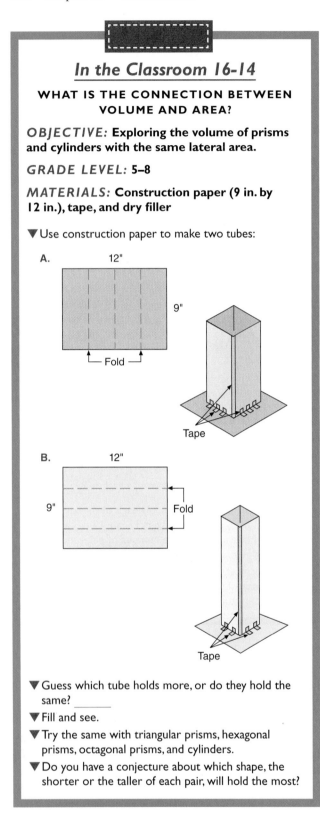

A.   12"

9"

Fold

Tape

B.   12"

9"

Fold

Tape

▼ Guess which tube holds more, or do they hold the same? _____

▼ Fill and see.

▼ Try the same with triangular prisms, hexagonal prisms, octagonal prisms, and cylinders.

▼ Do you have a conjecture about which shape, the shorter or the taller of each pair, will hold the most?

cludes, "the fourth-grade mathematics curriculum included a strong emphasis on measurement topics in many countries." However, that does not mean that all students have had the opportunity to learn many of the measurement concepts and skills and to apply these to realistic situations.

Children may be interested in learning about measurement in the past. Do you know that mouthfuls, jacks, and pottles were all measures of capacity? (a mouthful was used to sell honey or oil, and a jigger was two mouthfuls, a jack was two jiggers, a jill was two jacks, a cup was two jills, a pint was two cups, and a pottle was 8 cups or two quarts). Students also learned about hogsheads, perches, firkins, links, chains, and many more units and their relationships. Measurement was crucial to trade and educated people had to know how to buy and sell. Today, many of our purchases come packaged and premeasured.

Looking at old textbooks will introduce you to what we used in the United States; however, investigating units that are still in use in other countries will broaden your knowledge of other cultures. The Web site, Units of Measurement, (http://www.unc.edu/ ∼ rowlett/units/) contains all the units mentioned in the previous paragraph along with many other units as well as systems of measurement such as "how big is a hat." If you have students using a particular word for a measurement, this is a source to find out what it means. Other countries sell more things by weight. For example, you may buy eggs by weight rather than by the dozen.

In your teaching, it is important to relate measurement activities to different cultures. The article *Freedom Quilts* (Neumann, 2005) is one example of applying measurement and geometry in a way that shows how quilts were used by Africans to communicate messages about escape routes. As you teach social studies, keep in mind how you can include measurement ideas about the topics your students are learning. The suggestions in the cultural connections in the geometry chapter can often be designed to include measurement activities.

◆▲ A Glance at Where We've Been

have students from other countries, our customary system of measurement will be strange to them. The TIMSS survey (Mullis et al., 2004, p. 217) con-

Measuring is a process that may be used when determining the size of many attributes. The measurement process consists of identifying the attribute, choosing a unit, comparing the object being measured to that unit, finding the number of units, and reporting the number of units. To help children understand the attribute, we suggest comparing two objects on that attribute: perceptually, directly, and indirectly. In selecting a unit, there are eight concepts that need to be developed over time. Comparing an object to a unit entails finding the number of units that would represent the object on the attribute in question. For example, comparing a pencil to an inch and finding out how many inches the pencil is in length. Children may first assign a number by counting and later by using instruments or formulas. Other suggested ways to help children learn about measuring are estimating sizes of objects, finding equivalent measurements, and relating two attributes.

By including measuring in your classroom, you have the opportunity to show how mathematics is practical, to develop other mathematical ideas, to relate mathematics to other topics, and to make mathematics meaningful for many children.

Things to Do: From What You've Read

1. What are the five steps in the measurement process?

2. What attributes, units, and instruments are included in most elementary mathematics programs?

3. Explain how you will include estimation throughout your measurement activities and why this will be helpful for children.

4. Why should you include measurement in your mathematics program? Choose one reason and give examples of how measurement fulfills that reason.

5. What concepts related to units need to be developed as children have experiences with measurements?

6. List three difficulties children have with measuring instruments.

7. Why do students need to be able to convert from one unit to another?

8. Show how you would find the areas of each of the figures in In the Classroom 16-8.

9. Give three examples of connections that can be made between different attributes.

Things to Do: Going Beyond This Book

IN THE FIELD

1. *Mesauring Length with Arbitrary Units. Develop and teach the lesson described in In the Classroom 16-6. What ideas about units of measurement do children grasp?

2. *Comparing Height and Circumference. Try the activity in In the Classroom 16-4 with students. What did students learn? Modify this activity to show how to approximate the circumference of a can and try it with upper level students.

3. *Connections. Try the activities in In the Classroom 16-13 or 16-14 with students. Describe your experience, including whether the children could make the connections expected.

IN YOUR JOURNAL

4. You have a child in your class who physically cannot handle a ruler. What would you do in this situation? Give at least two solutions.

5. Describe a set of activities that you could use to introduce a centimeter, a pound, a liter, or a square inch.

6. Design an activity card that investigates a fixed area and varying perimeters (e.g., a fixed area of four square units made with four square tiles and find the different perimeters). Include the answer to the investigation.

7. For a grade level of your choice, design five estimation activities that include both types of estimation (estimating measurement for a known object and choosing an object that fits a known measurement).

8. Outline a series of steps for developing the volume formula for rectangular solids, similar to those for developing the area formula for a rectangle.

9. Keep a record of how many times you used measurement in a week. Classify them as to whether you made an estimate, used an instrument, or calculated the measurement.

*Additional activities, suggestions, or questions are provided in *Teaching Elementary Mathematics: A Resource for Field Experiences*(Wiley, 2007).

WITH ADDITIONAL RESOURCES

10. Check the scope-and-sequence chart of a textbook series to see how the introduction of units corresponds to Table 16-1.

11. Read an article about measurement from the journal *Teaching Children Mathematics* or *Mathematics Teaching in the Middle School*. Briefly summarize the article and describe how you would use it in teaching.

12. Read the article by J. Dwyer "Ordering Rectangles: Which is Bigger?" How would you have ordered the rectangles? What did you learn about children's understanding of "bigger?"

13. Examine upper level textbooks to see how they introduce the formula for the area of a rectangle. Contrast this with the sequence suggested in Figure 16-9.

WITH TECHNOLOGY

14. Watch the video, *Pencil Box Staining*, used in the snapshot. A similar problem may be found on Master 16–4, Paint Problem, in the *Helping Children Learn Mathematics Instructor's Manual* (available at the Wiley Book Companion site). What strategies did the students use to find the area?

15. Look at the Math Links 2. Go to the tools and investigate the volume tool (called cubes). How would you use this in your teaching?

16. Go to Math Links 4 and watch the video that shows another practical application for measurement. How does this video compare with the snapshot one? Which do you think, if you were teaching in the upper grades, you would use.

Note to Instructors: You can find additional resources, learning activities, and black-line masters in this text's accompanying Instructor's manual at www.wiley.com/college/reys.

Book Nook for Children

Branley, F. M. *Keeping Time: From the Beginning and into the 21st Century*. Boston: Houghton Mifflin, 1993.

Early timekeepers were the sun, moon, and stars. Directions for making ancient timekeepers such as the sundial, candle clock, water clock, and sand clock are given. Mechanical clocks are introduced and the need for more accuracy is discussed. An index and bibliography of other books on time for young and more advanced readers are included.

Hightower, S. *Twelve Snails to One Lizard: A Tale of Mischief and Measurement*. New York: Simon & Schuster Books for Young Readers, 1997.

Animals introduce measurement facts in a delightful book for young children. A break in the dam sets the need for nonstandard and standard measurements. This book succeeds in introducing customary length measures and the relationships among such measures in a humorous way.

Lionni, L. *Inch by Inch*. New York: Morrow/Avon, 1995.

This classic book is about an inchworm that convinces a hungry robin that he is useful for measuring the robin's tail. The robin spreads the word about the inchworm to other birds about being measured. Unless the inchworm measures the nightingale's song, the nightingale will eat the inchworm. The inchworm measures far, far away as the nightingale sings.

Myller, R. *How Big Is a Foot?* New York: Dell Publishing, 1991.

This humorous tale about nonstandard measures in which a king decides to have a bed made for the queen as a surprise for her birthday. The large king marks off the dimensions for the proposed bed with his feet. Unfortunately, when the bed is delivered it is the wrong size. The apprentice who made the bed solves the problem from his jail cell.

Murphy, S. J. *Room for Ripley*. New York: Harper Collins, 1999.

Carlos visited a pet store to buy his favorite type of fish, a guppy. His sister Ana shows Carlos how to set up a home for his guppy using different types of liquid measurements. Carlos decides to buy another guppy, which prompts him to add more water to the fish bowl using different liquid measures. There are activities and games for teachers and parents to use.

Schwartz, D. M. *Millions to Measure*. New York: Harper Collins, 2003.

Marvelosissimo the Magician explains the difference between nonstandard and standard unit of measures and how different cultures of the past used to measure using nonstandard units. In the back of the book, the author talks about measuring and the metric system for the reader.

Annotated Resources

Austin, R. A., Thompson, D. R., and Beckmann, C. E. "Exploring measurement concepts through literature: Natural links across disciplines." *Mathematics Teaching in the Middle School,* 10(4) (December 2004-January 2005), pp. 218–234.

Along with suggested ways to connect measurement with other disciplines through literature, an extensive annotated reference list is provided. Many of these are appropriate for younger students as well as upper elementary students.

Burns, M. *Measuring Up!: Experiments, Puzzles, and Games Exploring Measurement.* New York: Atheneum Books for Young Readers, 1995.

Activities that would appeal to many children are provided in this book. For example, optical illusions, interesting animals, unique measuring tools, as well as the height of the tallest person in the NBA are provided throughout this book. Topics that are included are length, quantity, weight, temperature, and volume.

Mann, R. "Responses to the pattern-block-quilts problem." *Teaching Children Mathematics,* 11(1) (August 2004), pp. 28–35.

Students' solutions to a problem of deciding which of two quilts are discussed. First they try to determine which is larger by looking and then they use pattern blocks to cover each quilt.

Moss, J., and Caswell, B. "Building percent dolls: Connecting linear measurement to learning ration and proportion." *Mathematics Teaching in the Middle School,* 10 (2) (September 2004), pp. 68–74.

A good illustration of how measurement can be used to help students learn other mathematics. These fifth–sixth grade students participated in a unit that looked at their own body measurements, related it to percent, and to making a proportional doll.

Moyer-Packenham, P. S. "A mathematical measurement mystery." *Teaching Children Mathematics,* 11(2) (September 2004), pp. 54–61.

Young children investigate the size of the school furniture and playground equipment that would be suitable for their size. The students use both nonstandard and standard units for length measurement. The unit concludes with the students still wondering why a school has such giant furniture and playground equipment.

Neumann, M. D. "Freedom quilts." *Teaching Children Mathematics,* 11(6) (February 2005), pp. 317–321.

This is a fascinating account of how quilt patterns were used for communication in the Underground Railroad. If students are making quilts for communication, they will be considering length and area.

Outhred, L. N., and Mitchelmore, M. C. "Young children's intuitive understanding of rectangular area measurement." *Journal for Research in Mathematics Education,* 3(2) (March 2000), pp. 144–154.

This article focuses on the strategies young children use to solve rectangular covering tasks before they have been taught area measurement. Children's solution strategies were classified into five developmental levels, and the researchers suggest that children sequentially learn four principles underlying rectangular covering. The analysis emphasizes the importance of understanding the relationship between the size of the unit and the dimensions of the rectangle in learning about rectangular covering, clarifying the role of multiplication, and identifying the significance of conceptual understanding of length measurement.

CHAPTER 17

Data Analysis, Statistics, and Probability

Snapshot of a Lesson

Key Ideas

1. Calculating the measures of central tendency: the mode, median, and mean

2. Calculating a measure of variation: the range

3. Using the calculations to rank the data for meaningful interpretation

4. Students using data to support their conclusions

Background

This snapshot takes you into an eighth-grade classroom with teacher Amy Doherty. Amy is using the *MathScape* curriculum in her class, and has introduced the concepts of mode, median, mean, and range in previous lessons. Students have also had a chance to work with all of the measures previous to this lesson. The students have been given the data from three basketball games to analyze. Their task is to prepare a letter to the basketball coach nominating the Most Valuable Player (MVP) based on these data. This is a transcript of part of a video from the Modeling Middle School Mathematics project. Go to http://www.mmmproject.org (Modeling Middle School Mathematics) and click on the video matrix.

An excerpt from the video *Looking behind the Numbers*

MS. DOHERTY: Okay, now that you've all calculated the statistics for each of the basketball players, let's put it up here on the board. So for player B, can someone list the scores for us?

STUDENT: The high score was 21. The median was 18. The mean was 17. The mode was 18 and the range was 8.

MS. DOHERTY: Now, for player C.

STUDENT: The high score was 25, the median was 16, the mean was 18, the mode was 14, and the range was 14.

MS. DOHERTY: Now that we've calculated all of the statistical measures, we're going to use this information to compare the three basketball players and find out who is the best player. So what I'd like you to do is on the next sheet we're going to rank the players according to the different statistical measures. Which player had the best score, the highest score? Grecia?

	High Score	Median	Mean	Mode	Range
Player A	20	13	14	12	9
Player B	21	18	17	18	8
Player C	25	16	18	14	14

GRECIA: Player C and he had 25.

MS. DOHERTY: Okay, and who was second best?

GRECIA: Player B, he had 21.

MS. DOHERTY: Okay, third best?

GRECIA: Player A, he had 20.

MS. DOHERTY: Okay, now what I would like you to do with your partners is to rank the rest of the measures. So rank by median score, by mean score, by the mode, and by the range. Take a minute to do that with your partners.

STUDENT: I have player C first.

STUDENT: And the second best would be player B with 17.

MS. DOHERTY: Okay, let's fill in the rest of this chart. For the median, who had the best (ranking) median, Amy?

AMY: B 18?

The Students continue with the activity.

MS. DOHERTY: Okay, now for the mode, Gregor?

GREGOR: B had 18?

MS. DOHERTY: Yup.

GREGOR: C had 14. And A had 12.

MS. DOHERTY: Okay the last one we need to rank is the range. Jackie?

JACKIE: The best was C 14, the second best was A with 9 and the third best was B 8.

MS. DOHERTY: Why do we have so many hands up? Derrick?

DERRICK: Because the best score is supposed to be B with 8 and A with 9 and C with 14.

MS. DOHERTY: How come?

DERRICK: On the range you want the lowest, because that means that they are the most consistent and they score around the same number of points a game.

◆ Introduction

Data analysis, statistics, and probability provide a meaningful context for promoting problem solving and critical thinking, communication, developing number sense, and applying computation. The study of these topics supports a problem-solving or investigative approach to learning and doing mathematics. As a result, statistics and probability are now highly visible topics in elementary school mathematics programs. The shift of attention to these areas has been dramatic and reflects the growing importance of analyzing data in our daily lives.

Increased attention to data analysis, statistics, and probability in elementary mathematics programs has increased student performance in these areas. For example, the National Assessment of Educational Progress (NAEP) indicates that although there are areas that still need improvement, student performances in data analysis, statistics, and probability have continually increased from the fifth assessment through the eighth (Kloosterman and Lester, 2004; Kenney and Silver, 1997).

Let's look at some reasons for including the study of data analysis, statistics, and probability in elementary school.

- *Children encounter ideas of statistics and probability outside of school every day.*

Radio, television, newspapers, and the Internet bombard us with information. For example, news reports present national economic and social statistics, opinion polls, weather reports, and medical, business, and financial data.

The current demand for information-processing skills is much greater than it was 25 years ago, and technological advances will place a far greater premium on such skills in the years ahead. Many consumer and business decisions are based on market research and sales projections; however, statistics about issues or the quality of commercial products can be misleading to the public. If these data are to be understood and used widely, every educated person must be able to process such information effectively and efficiently. An intelligent consumer, who is able to make informed decisions, must be able to understand and use statistics and probability.

The data students encounter outside of school are often presented in a graphical, statistical, or probabilistic form:

Graphical. Which company holds the majority of the global soccer sales?

Global Soccer Sales by Company

Statistical. The mean player salary of one professional baseball team in 2006 was over $3,000,000 a year.

Probabilistic. The probability of rain today is 0.35.

• *Math Forum*

Each of these statements needs to be understood if meaningful interpretations are to be made.

The context and format of the way such information is presented vary greatly, but correct interpretation of the information often requires the application of mathematics. Consider, for example, the mathematical concepts involved in weather reports (decimals, percents, and probability), public opinion polls (sampling techniques and errors of measurement), advertising claims (hypothesis testing), and monthly government reports involving unemployment, inflation, and energy supplies (percents, prediction, and extrapolation).

• *Data analysis, statistics, and probability provide connections to other mathematics topics or school subjects.*

The study of data provides an excellent opportunity for curriculum integration. For example, each day kindergarten children create a picture graph with their photos to show who is present and absent. In doing so, they practice basic counting skills. Third graders may estimate the number of candies in single-serving packages and graph their estimates. After counting the actual number of candies, a second graph may be created, displaying the actual number of candies in each package. The children are able to compare their estimates with the actual results. Fourth graders measure the height of each student in the class, and then students find the mean, median, mode, and range so they can better understand and summarize their data. As sixth graders conduct a probability simulation with dice, they use fractions, decimals, and percents to report their results.

Statistics and probability are also easily integrated into other school subjects. For example, second graders might use graphs in reading to keep track of numbers and types of books they have read. Fifth-grade students conducting a science experiment on rolling a car down ramps of various heights may calculate the mean distance for the number of trials at each height. In social studies, graphs and charts are frequently used to display information about populations or geographic areas. In physical education class, students may graph pretest data from physical fitness tests and compare it with posttest results at the end of the year. First graders reading folk tales in language arts may develop a chart listing which events from the stories are possible and which are impossible. Effective teachers must look for ways to make data analysis an integral part of the elementary and middle school curriculum.

• *Data analysis, statistics, and probability provide opportunities for computational activity in a meaningful context.*

Data are not merely numbers but numbers with a context. The number 12 in the absence of a context carries no information, but saying that a baby weighed 12 pounds at birth makes it easy to comment about its size! Data provide many opportunities to think, use, understand, and interpret numbers, rather than simply carrying out arithmetic operations. Using data helps further develop number sense. Working with real data requires judgment in choosing methods and interpreting results. Thus statistics and probability are not taught in elementary school for their own sake but because they provide an effective way to develop quantitative understanding and mathematical thinking.

• *Data analysis, statistics, and probability provide opportunities for developing critical thinking skills.*

When students learn how to design and carry out experiments that utilize data analysis and probability, they develop skills to help them answer questions that often involve uncertainty, and they draw conclusions based on their interpretations of the data. As students learn how to approach situations statistically, they can face up to prejudices, think more consistently about arguments, and justify their thinking with numerical information (Burns, 2000). This approach has applications in many areas of our lives—social and political. For example, the snapshot requires students to make thoughtful analysis of the data in determining the MVP.

Data analysis, statistics, and probability should not be viewed or treated in isolation. Their study provides numerous opportunities to review and apply much mathematics in a variety of real-world situations. For example, whole numbers, fractions, decimals, percents, ratios, and proportion are essential ideas for understanding a wide variety of situations. Many computational skills are reviewed and polished as they are applied in graphing or doing statistics and probability.

Math Links 17.1

*T*he full-text electronic version of the Data Analysis and Probability standards is available at the NCTM's Web site at www.nctm.org.

www.wiley.com/college/reys

The content standard titled Data Analysis and Probability, in the NCTM *Standards* (2000), highlights key expectations (see Figure 17-1). As you can see from this standard, the study of data analysis, statistics, and probability should engage students actively. Students need to be involved in asking questions, collecting data, organizing and displaying their data, making conjectures, and reporting their results.

In this chapter you will consider how to involve students with statistics, which includes using data collection, display, and analysis as well as probability, which allows a prediction of what is likely to happen and how often it might occur.

Instructional programs from prekindergarten through grade 12 should enable all students to:	Pre-K–2 Expectations All students should:	Grades 3–5 Expectations All students should:
• Formulate questions that can be addressed with data and collect, organize, and display relevant data to answer them	• Pose questions and gather data about themselves and their surroundings • Sort and classify objects according to their attributes and organize data about the objects • Represent data using concrete objects, pictures, and graphs	• Design investigations to address a question and consider how data-collection methods affect the nature of the data set • Collect data using observations, surveys, and experiments • Represent data using tables and graphs such as line plots, bar graphs, and line graphs • Recognize the differences in representing categorical and numerical data
• Select and use appropriate statistical methods to analyze data	• Describe parts of the data and the set of data as a whole to determine what the data show	• Describe the shape and important features of a set of data and compare related data sets, with an emphasis on how the data are distributed • Use measures of center, focusing on the median, and understand what each does and does not indicate about the data set • Compare different representations of the same data and evaluate how well each representation shows important aspects of the data
• Develop and evaluate inferences and predictions that are based on data	• Discuss events related to students' experiences as likely or unlikely	• Propose and justify conclusions and predictions that are based on data and design studies to further investigate the conclusions or predictions
• Understand and apply basic concepts of probability		• Describe events as likely or unlikely and discuss the degree of likelihood using such words as certain, equally likely, and impossible • Predict the probability of outcomes of simple experiments and test the predictions • Understand that the measure of the likelihood of an event can be represented by a number from 0 to 1

FIGURE 17-1   Data Analysis and Probability Standard with expectations for children's learning in grades prekindergarten–2 and 3–5.

1. How do data analysis, statistics, and probability help children develop critical thinking skills?

2. How can you help children develop skills in analyzing data?

3. What descriptive statistics are appropriate to introduce in the elementary grades? What are some examples of ways they can be introduced?

4. What are some common misconceptions young students have about probability?

Data Analysis

A statistical investigation typically is completed in several steps, which includes (1) posing a question and collecting data to answer the question, (2) displaying the collected data, and (3) analyzing and communicating results.

Posing a Question and Collecting Data

Begin with a good question or problem that interests students, a problem for which the answer is not immediately obvious, and one that also clearly gives students a reason for gathering, analyzing, and presenting data. Allow students to brainstorm questions they would like to answer or problems they have observed. There is a real benefit to having students identify their own questions or problems, for they will take ownership of the investigation and their motivation will be high (Bohan et al., 1995). Questions may come from a variety of sources on many different topics. In the Classroom 17-1 gives a few examples. These ideas may be shared with children to help them brainstorm the kind of questions they might ask as they plan their survey.

Once a suitable question has been identified, students will need to plan how to collect the data needed to answer the question. Communication skills are very important during this stage. To be successful, students must be able to develop clear survey questions and logical steps for their experiments or simulations. They must communicate with others to negotiate the details of the investigation. They must find a clear and efficient method of recording their data. Students may collect data from surveys, experiments, and simulations, all of which typically involve counting or measuring. Data may be recorded in a variety of ways, such as using tally marks or placing information in a table. Computer spreadsheets may also be used for recording data.

In the Classroom 17-1

LET'S FIND OUT

OBJECTIVE: Planning and conducting a survey.

GRADE LEVEL: 4–5

STEPS:

1. Think of a question you would like to answer. Here are some ideas to get you started.

   - **Questions about ourselves:** Who can whistle a tune? How far can we throw a softball? What is our class's typical height, eye color, shoe size, number in family, amount of allowance, pets . . .?

   - **Question about opinions or feelings:** How do you feel about fractions? Does life exist on other planets? What should be done about pollutions? What country do you want to study in social studies? What is your favorite television show, song, book, sport, color, food . . .?

   - **Questions about the world:** Which month has the most birthdays? What is the most popular color of car in the school parking lot? Which brand of cookie has the most chocolate chips? How many paper towels do we use in one day? What is the effect of fertilizer on bean plant growth? What type of paper airplane will fly the farthest?

   My Question: _____

   _____

2. Plan the survey by answering these questions.
   a. Where or from whom will I collect the data?
   b. How will I collect the data?
   c. How much data will I collect?
   d. When will I collect the data?
   e. How will I record the data as I collect them?
   f. What else do I need to do before I start collecting data?

3. Collect your data!

Surveys

Survey data result from collecting information. These data may range from a national public opinion poll or observing cars pass the window, to simply tallying the ages of students in a class. The actual data used depends on student interest and maturity, but survey data collected by students provides a freshness that increases student interest and sustains persistence in related problem-solving activities. Computer software is also available that allows students to design a survey and have the persons surveyed enter their responses directly into the computer. Once the data have been collected, the program can display results in a table or in several types of graphs.

Each question from In the Classroom 17-1 gives students an opportunity to collect data themselves. In order to sharpen data-collecting techniques, students may consider the following questions:

- What questions will this survey answer?
- Where should I conduct my survey?
- When should I conduct the survey?

Why is it important for students to think about these questions before conducting their survey? In planning a survey, students are required to refine and polish their questions to get whatever information they are seeking, which in itself is an important and valuable experience. A host of other idea starters are available (Bright et al., 2003; Lindquist et al., 1992; Zawojewski et al., 1991).

Experiments

Experiments may be somewhat more advanced than surveys. When students conduct experiments, in addition to using observation and recording skills, they often incorporate the use of the scientific method. For example, students may design an experiment to measure the effect of applying different types of fertilizer on plant growth or compare flight times of different paper airplanes. They may try to determine which brand of tissue is the most absorbent. Students may play a spinner game to determine if it is fair to all players.

Simulations

Although a simulation is similar to an experiment, random number tables or devices such as coins, dice, spinners, or computer programs are also used to model real-world occurrences. Students may start with a probability question such as "If I flip a coin 20 times, how many times will it land on heads?" Then they carry out the simulation and record data as they are generated.

Sampling is another method of data collection that students can simulate. In statistics, the whole group you are studying is called the *population*. In real-life data collection, there are times when it is impossible or impractical to collect data from a complete population. A *sample* is a subset of a population. Samples are often collected to learn more about public health issues or the public's buying habits, or to predict election results. It is important

for students to realize that the use of a particular sample may make a survey biased and to discuss ways to reduce bias. For example, consider some students surveying the students in their room in order to purchase some new games to be used during recess. The population to be surveyed is Ms. Smith's fifth-grade class; however, if the students interview only the girls in the class (a sample), their results will probably not reflect the wishes of both boys and girls. Students to be interviewed could be randomly selected by drawing names out of a hat, which would more likely reflect the total population.

Researchers have developed methods of collecting samples so they may learn more about a population that would be impossible to survey completely. For example, when wildlife biologists want to count the number and types of fish in a lake, they use a mark-recapture technique. The biologist captures a number of fish, counts them, marks them, and releases them. More samples are collected, and the number of marked fish in the sample are compared in a ratio to the unmarked fish in the sample. The biologist may then use the data from the samples collected to estimate the total population of fish and the ratio of marked and unmarked fish. These techniques and how they can be simulated with elementary and middle school students using beans, crackers, or games are explained further in Morita (1999), and Quinn and Wiest (1999).

Displaying Data

After data have been collected, graphs are often used to display data and help others digest the results. A *graph* is a type of diagram that may be used to visually present or illustrate data. At the elementary and middle school levels, students frequently encounter and create real, picture, bar, and circle graphs. As they move through school, the types of graphs they read and create increase and become more complex. Tables, tallies, or pictures are also sometimes used to present data. Knowledge related to constructing and interpreting various types of graphs is an important part of mathematics instruction and should begin in the primary grades. Children gain competence with age and experience. The National Assessment of Educational Progress (NAEP) shows that more than 50% of fourth-grade students can read and use tables, picture graphs, and bar graphs, as well as over 80% of eighth-grade students (Kloosterman and Lester, 2004).

For young children, initial work with data means they begin by working with concrete objects in their environment. Collecting and counting objects, sorting them into categories, and then displaying them in an organized fashion is a good introduction. For example, children may each bring a favorite book and then collaborate to organize their collection. A *real graph* or concrete graph is developed as the actual books are arranged in rows. As students work with their "data," they also practice counting skills. Older students may work with larger collections of objects, and by grouping the objects into groups of tens, place value may be reinforced. You must also find ways to help children move from the concrete, real-graph representations to more symbolic representations.

An example of an early experience is to sort real fruit. First, ask each child to choose one piece of his or her favorite fruit from a basket and position this piece of fruit on a table, as shown in Figure 17-2a. The resulting rows of fruit represent the children's preferences in a concrete fashion as a real graph. Next, ask each child to draw the fruit he or she chose on an index card, then have the children use the cards to build a picture-bar graph, as in Figure 17-2b. Although this graph is a less concrete means of showing the information, most children still find it a meaningful way to represent their preferences. Finally, this same information can be expressed more symbolically in the bar graph in Figure 17-2c. Children can also be given blank paper and encouraged to organize and report their data on the page in a way that makes sense to them. In this way, children learn to communicate their information in ways that are meaningful both to themselves and others (Folkson, 1996).

Regardless of how the data are presented, pertinent questions can be asked to encourage thought-ful interpretation of the graphs. Such questions might include the following:

What do you notice about the graph?

How many children prefer apples?

What is the favorite fruit?

How many different fruits are shown?

How many children contributed to the graph?

These types of questions result naturally from the data and provide valuable opportunities for students to ask as well as answer questions.

Math Links 17.2

There are a number of excellent Web sites that provide opportunities for children to collect data via simulations and graph their results. Here are several:
Go to the

- Math Forum Web site at http://mathforum.org/mathtools and then go to Math Topics for All Courses. Under Data Analysis you will find a number of applets (Bar Graph Sorter and Circle Graph) at different grade levels that are applets for use in generating data to graph.

- National Library of Virtual Manipulatives at http://www.matti.usu.edu. There you will find a number of tools that help to build different graphs, such as Bar charts, Pie Chart, and Histogram.

- National Council of Teachers of Mathematics Illuminations Web site http://illuminations. nctm.org/ and go to tools to find an array of applets, such as Bar Grapher, Circle Grapher Histogram Tool, that allow children to create their own graphs.

www.wiley.com/college/reys

Quick and Easy Graphing Methods

For elementary school children, the process of constructing a graph helps them learn about its critical features and is a valuable activity; however, some graphs are more difficult to create than others, and construction may develop into a lengthy process. If the main purpose of visually displaying the data is simply to learn more about the data and easily examine results, several alternatives exist to having students create complete publication-quality graphs by hand. By using some of the materials illustrated in Figure 17-3, data may be displayed immediately as they are being collected. These quick graphs called "sketch graphs" or "working graphs" can be created quickly and provide a visual repre-

FIGURE 17-2 One method for introducing graphs.

sentation of the shape of the data. They should be clear, but they may not be neat. Sketch graphs don't require labels or titles and don't require time-consuming attention to construction. Sketch graphs may be made with concrete materials or with paper and pencil.

Favorite Color

(a) Connecting cubes or blocks

Did you watch TV last night?

(b) Counters in an ice tray

How much do you like winter?

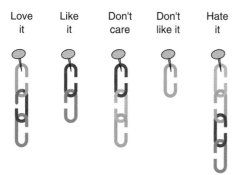

(c) Plastic links or paper clips

How may candies in the jar?

(d) Self-stick notes

FIGURE 17-3 Quick and easy graphing materials.

Computer graphing programs are available that are simple enough for even young children to use (see Math Links 17.3 for a variety of programs for all ages). As an added benefit, once the data have been entered, students can quickly and easily see their data displayed and printed in more than one type of graph or with a different scale. The graphing calculator is another tool that may be used for making graphs. Graphing calculators designed for middle grades allow students to create picture graphs, bar graphs, and pie graphs.

Plots

A *plot* is another type of graph used to visually display data. In recent years, plots have been used frequently in magazines and newspapers because they provide efficient ways of showing information, as well as comparing different sets of data. Some plots, such as line plots and stem-and-leaf plots, are quick and easy to make and can be used as sketch graphs to get an initial look at the shape of the data.

Line plots A line plot may be used to quickly display numerical data with a small range. The range and distribution of the data may be clearly seen in the display. Line plots may be successfully used at all levels. Young children can more easily create a line plot than a bar graph, and older students will enjoy the quick feedback they receive when sketching a line plot. When creating line plots, the data should be plotted with the same scale. This allows for a quick visual interpretation of the data when attempting to identify trends in the data.

Suppose that at a class party, some third-grade students receive candy in single-serving packages. The children open the packs and someone suggests they count to see how many candies they each received. The class begins counting, and soon each child begins calling out his or her total. You write the totals on the chalkboard as they are called out:

17, 19, 21, 20, 15, 18, 22, 17, 20, 18, 17, 18, 22, 17, 20

Discussion continues as students try to draw conclusions from the data. You suggest putting the data into a line graph so it will be easier to see and understand. The children notice that the smallest value is 15 and the largest is 22, so they direct you to draw a horizontal number line beginning with 15 and ending with 22. Next, an *x* is placed above each number to mark its frequency in the set of data. Figure 17-4 shows the completed line plot. The students are easily able to see that 17 occurred most often, followed by 18 and 20. The student who had only 15 in the package felt cheated, and

FIGURE 17-4 Line plot of number of candies per package.

FIGURE 17-5 Stem-and-leaf plot of number of candies per package.

those who had 22 felt lucky. The class talked about why there might not always be the same amount in each package.

Stem-and-leaf plots A stem-and-leaf plot is another quick way to display data and provides a quite different representation than when the data are arranged in a line plot or bar graph. It works best with data that span several decades, since the plot is usually organized by tens. This plot is a little more abstract than the line plot, but it may be used successfully with students in the intermediate grades.

It is often useful to display data in more than one way. Consider the candy data just displayed in a line plot and arrange it in a stem-and-leaf plot (Figure 17-5). To begin, divide each value into tens and ones. The tens become the "stem," and the ones will be the "leaves." Notice that the data fall into two decades, the tens and twenties. A vertical line is drawn with the tens values (1 and 2) on the left of the line. The ones values are placed on the right side, evenly spaced and in numerical order from lowest to highest for each "leaf." By examining the plot, it is easy to see that 17 occurred most often in this set of data. From this arrangement you can also see that more packages contained candy amounts in the tens than in the twenties. Now all those students who had 20 or more feel lucky.

Stem-and-leaf plots may also be used to compare two sets of data in the same plot. In the intermediate grades, students can successfully compare more than one data set. Suppose you wanted to explore some questions related to the height of students in a fourth-grade class. Comparing the heights of the boys and girls will generate some interesting discussion. Questions such as "Which group is tallest?" and "Which group has the most variability?" are naturals. After some conjectures have been made, it is time to have students meas-

ure their heights and begin to analyze those data. Here are some steps that lead to stem-and-leaf plots. The heights of the 27 fourth-grade students (15 girls and 12 boys) are reported in centimeters in the following table:

Boys				Girls			
118	132	135	137	122	155	114	125
120	125	147	129	155	137	136	137
133	148	153	125	134	130	133	145
				148	148	147	

Rather than use a traditional frequency distribution, the values are organized in a stem-and-leaf plot, shown in Figure 17-6. The stem represents the hundreds and tens places of the data on student height, and the leaves represent the ones place. Thus, in the bottom row of Figure 17-6, 8 | 11 | 4 means one girl has a height of 114 cm and one boy is 118 cm tall. The stem-and-leaf plot preserves the individual measures while revealing the general shape of the organized data. Thus it presents all of the information, in this case for both groups, and provides a clear visual picture of it.

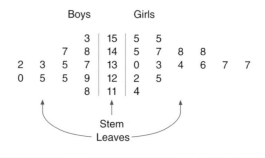

FIGURE 17-6 Stem-and-leaf plot of heights of boys and girls.

In addition to the quick graphs and plots mentioned previously, students should also be involved with graphs that require more construction time and effort.

Box plots A *box plot* (also called a box-and-whisker plot) summarizes data and provides a visual means of showing variability—the spread of the data. The box plot shown in Figure 17-7 is comparing the heights of girls to boys. The median is a key reference point; we will talk more about the median in the next section. The lower hinge, or lower quartile, is the median of the lower half of the data, and the upper hinge, or upper quartile, is the median of the upper half of the data. These are found by computing the medians of the data in the lower and upper halves, respectively. The midspread is a measure of variability and is the difference between the upper and lower quartiles. In Figure 17-7, the midspread for the boys is 17 ($142 - 125$) and that for the girls is 18 ($148 - 130$). The smallest and largest heights represent the lower extreme and the upper extreme. The lines (also called "whiskers") extending from the top of the upper quartile to the maximum value and then from the bottom of the lower quartile to the minimum value provide another visual indication of variability.

The box plot shows many things. For example, it shows the median height for the girls is greater than that for the boys. Although the groups have about the same midspread, the boys are a bit more evenly distributed throughout the box than are the girls. (Why? Because the median of the boys is closer to the middle of the box than is the median of the girls.) The box plot is derived naturally from a stem-and-leaf plot or line plot. The box plot shows many important characteristics of a group visually and, when two or more groups are shown on the same graph, it allows comparisons to be made easily. Since each section represents 25% of the data, multiplicative comparisons can be made. For example, about 75% of the girls are taller than about 50% of the boys (the median for the boys and the lower quartile for the girls are about the same height). The box plot is an appropriate display for middle school students to construct. It provides a nice connection to descriptive statistics such as median and range. In addition, many standardized test results are reported as box plots, so this is an important kind of graph for teachers to understand even if they don't teach it. Finally, box plots allow two groups with unequal amounts of data to be compared to each other since both sets are converted to fractional representations and are shown on the box plot.

Picture Graphs

In *picture graphs,* data are represented by pictures. For example, children may graph pictures of their favorite food or the pets they own. A picture can represent one object (Figure 17-8) or several (Figure 17-9). To properly interpret picture graphs, children must know how much each object represents. Research shows that students often ignore such coding information when interpreting graphs (Bright and Hoeffner, 1993; Friel, Bright, and Curcio, 1997; Curcio and Bright, 2001).

Math Links 17.3

*A*uthentic statistical data may be collected by children. Census data together with a wide range of statistics-related resources, population, and weather is available from the U.S. Census Bureau Web site www.census.gov.

www.wiley.com/college/reys

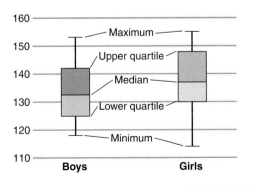

FIGURE 17-7   Box plots for heights of boys and girls.

FIGURE 17-8   A picture graph in which each picture represents one object.

Estimated school retention rates in the United States, 1982 to 2000

Each figure represents 10 persons:

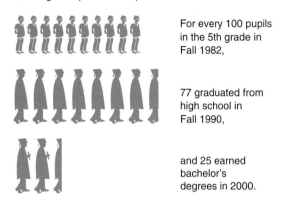

For every 100 pupils in the 5th grade in Fall 1982,

77 graduated from high school in Fall 1990,

and 25 earned bachelor's degrees in 2000.

FIGURE 17-9   A picture graph in which each picture represents several objects.   (From surveys, estimates, and projections of the National Center for Education Statistics).

Bar Graphs

Bar graphs are used mostly for discrete or separate and distinct data; the bars represent these data. For example, they might graph the number of children's birthdays in each month or the number of students who travel to school by bus, car, or foot. Figure 17-2 showed that values can be read from the axis. Figure 17-10 shows that other times the values are reported directly on the graph. Bar graphs are often used for quick visual comparisons of categories of data and are appropriate for all ages.

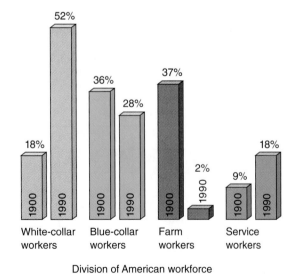

FIGURE 17-10   A bar graph with values shown directly on the bars.

Histograms

Although a *histogram* looks like a bar graph (Figure 17-11), there are some key differences that discriminate the two from each other. A histogram is used with continuous data, not discrete data. Therefore the data are represented with connected bars, each representing an interval. Any data that falls within that interval appears in the bar. If a student uses the Internet for 22 hours, their data point is located between 20 and 29.99 hours. The interval includes all of the numbers up to, but not including the maximum value of the interval. Therefore, individual data points may not be distinguishable from reading a histogram as they would be in a bar graph. Histograms are more appropriate for middle grades students, although many younger children draw them mistakenly when attempting to create bar graphs.

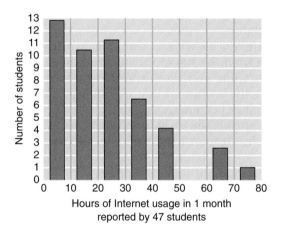

FIGURE 17-11   A histogram showing students' hours of Internet usage in 1 month.

Pie Graphs

A *pie graph* is a circle representing the whole, with wedges reporting percents of the whole, as illustrated in Figure 17-12. The pie graph is popular because it is easy to interpret; however, it has major limitations in that it represents only a fixed moment in time, and it cannot exceed 100 percent. For example, students may graph how they spend their weekly allowance or the favorite colors of the class. While students in the upper elementary grades can read and interpret pie graphs, effective construction may require the use of fractions, percents, proportions, and measurement of angles. Pie graph construction is more appropriate for middle

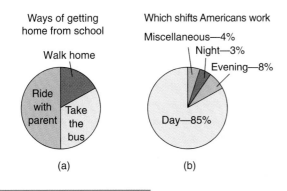

Ways of getting
home from school

Walk home

Ride
with
parent

Take
the
bus

(a)

Which shifts Americans work

Miscellaneous—4%

Night—3%

Evening—8%

Day—85%

(b)

FIGURE 17-12 Pie graphs.

school students; however, there is an effective, concrete method of connecting pie graphs to bar graphs, which elementary students may successfully complete.

As illustrated with the line and stem-and-leaf plots, showing the same data in different displays can be both useful and effective. For example, the data shown in the bar graph in Figure 17-2 can be easily shown in a pie graph. Cubes of different colors to match the fruits could be strung together as shown here equidistance apart:

Then the string can be placed in a circle:

This experience helps make a connection between bar and pie graphs. It also provides a natural context for fractions and percents. For example, the pie graph suggests that $\frac{1}{4}$ of the fruits are oranges.

This model can be extended by placing a meter tape, or a 100-centimeter strip of paper marked with similar units, around the circle of blocks to form concentric circles, as shown in Figure 17-13a. Comparing the sections suggested by the different groups of colored blocks with the markers on the strip or meter tape will identify percents that can be easily read.

As a more concrete visualization, 20 children can be arranged in a circle, and the "wedges" of a circle graph duplicated with string, as illustrated in Figure 17-13b. Both of the models in Figure 17-13 make it easy to estimate or read the percents and conclude, for example, that more than 50% of the children chose apples or bananas.

Similar observations might have been made directly from the bar graph in Figure 17-2, but conclusions involving fractions and percents are much more obvious from the pie graph. Technology applications, such as spreadsheets, are also useful tools that allow students to create bar graphs and pie graphs of the data. The process of moving from a bar graph to a pie graph provides different perspectives for the same set of data, and research suggests that developing such multiple perspectives helps promote greater understanding (Shaughnessy, 1992).

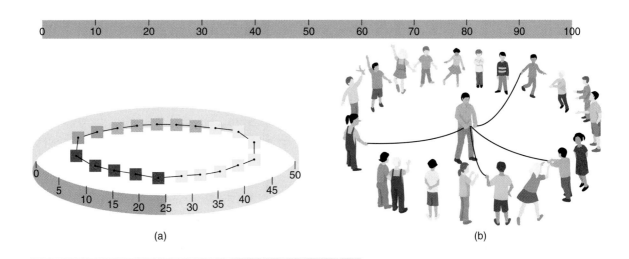

(a)

(b)

FIGURE 17-13 Models for interpreting circle graph data.

Line Graphs

Line graphs are effective for showing trends over time. In line graphs, points on a grid are used to represent continuous or uninterrupted data. Each axis is clearly labeled, so the data shown can be interpreted properly. A wide variety of line graphs exist and are used, but three basic assumptions are inherent:

1. The data are continuous rather than discrete. This means that the data are grouped along a continuous scale and cannot be "counted."

2. Data can occur between points with continuous data. Because of this, the line can also be used to interpret values between plotted data.

3. Change is accurately represented with linear functions (i.e., by lines) rather than some other curve.

As Figure 17-14 shows, line graphs are particularly good for showing variations or changes over time, such as hours of daylight, temperatures, rainfall, and so on. For example, students could graph plant growth in a science experiment. Line graphs are also an effective visual means of comparing several sets of data, as illustrated in Figure 17-15. Constructing or interpreting line graphs requires students to examine both horizontal and vertical axes, which is good preparation for coordinates. Line graphs are used most often at the middle school level.

FIGURE 17-14   A line graph of a single set of varying data.

Graphical Roundup

Each of these graphs deserves instructional attention as students examine ways to display their data. Children need experience constructing them and interpreting information that is represented. In the children's book *The Best Vacation Ever* (Murphy, 1997), a little girl collects and displays data for her family so they can plan a vacation. In the Classroom 17-2 gives students ideas to think about when planning to display a collection of data.

Level of school completed by persons 25 years old and over in United States, 1940 to 2000

 Fewer than 5 years of elementary school

— — 4 years of high school or more

•••• 4 or more years of college

FIGURE 17-15   A line graph comparing several sets of data.

In the Classroom 17-2

SHARING DATA

OBJECTIVE: **Develop techniques for handling data.**

GRADE LEVEL: **4–5**

GETTING STARTED:

- Collect some data
- Before sharing our data we need to agree on some things:

Before Graphing:

- Shall we start with a sketch graph?
- What kind of graph will best display our data?
- Can we show our data in more than one way?
- How shall we label our graph?

Before Reporting Results:

- What questions can we answer with our data?
- Who might be interested in our results?
- How will we report our findings?

▼ Why do these questions need to be answered before graphing and planning our report?

▼ Name two other important questions that need to be answered before beginning.

1. _____

2. _____

Type of Graph	Characteristics
Real	Used by young children
	Actual objects are placed on a graph
Line plot	Provides a quick way to examine the shape and variation or spread of data
	Gives a bar-graph-like representation
Stem-and-Leaf plot	Efficient way to show detailed data
	Provides similar visual patterns as a bar graph but more detailed information
	Uses stem-and-leaf coding that needs to be understood
	Technology has facilitated its use
Picture	Frequently encountered in newspapers and reports
	Generally easy to use and interpret but visuals may be misleading
	Codes/keys which accompany graph need to be understood
Bar	Mostly used for discrete data
	Frequently encountered in newspapers and reports
	Easy to interpret
	Uses scales/codes that need to be understood
Histogram	Used for continuous data, data grouped in intervals
	Similar to bar graph, but individual data are not visible
	Effective to display data with a large range but limited values
Pie	Frequently encountered in newspapers and reports
	Shows fractional parts, which are based on a whole or 100%
	Easy to use and interpret
	Difficult to construct by hand, easy with technology
Line	Frequently encountered in newspapers and reports
	Used for continuous data
	Effective to show patterns, trends, comparisons, and change over time
	Uses vertical and horizontal scales that need to be understood
	Provides good readiness for coordinate graphs
Box plot	Provides useful information about the variability of data
	Requires knowledge of range, median, and quartiles to interpret
	Can be used to compare two data sets with unequal amounts of data
	Technology has facilitated its use

FIGURE 17-16 Characteristics of graphs.

The availability of graphing calculators and graphing programs allows for easy construction of a variety of graphs. This availability of different graphs via technology places a greater premium on interpreting and understanding the graphs that are so easily produced. As children become familiar with different graphs, they should recognize some characteristics associated with them. Figure 17-16 highlights specific characteristics of graphs that are encountered in elementary and middle school. The focus here is not on memorizing characteristics of these graphs, but rather on becoming aware that each type has strengths. The selection of a particular graph should capitalize on these strengths, while recognizing any of its limitations. Figure 17-17 shows graphical complexity, and a suggested progression for introducing different types of graphs (Friel et al., 2001, p. 147). Again, memorizing this information is not the intent. Instead, be aware of how some graphs, due to their complexity, are better understood at different levels, which includes students' ability to read and interpret a graph versus creating the graph.

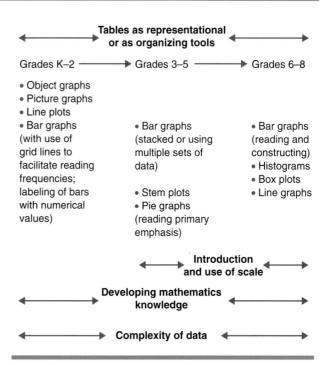

FIGURE 17-17 Graph/display complexity: suggested progress for introduction of types of graphs (includes both reading and constructing graphs).

Analyzing and Communicating Results

Data Sense

Once data have been collected and displayed, they should be examined and analyzed. Just as children develop a knowledge about numbers or number sense, they can also develop knowledge about statistics or *data sense*. Data sense is gradually developed as students pose questions, collect data, construct graphs, and interpret them in a variety of contexts. Students with data sense are able to determine how data should be analyzed. They are able to read and evaluate statistical information being presented, such as material presented by the media. Students also display data sense when they are able to use statistical language when reasoning about data. The goal is for students to develop both procedural knowledge (how to construct a graph or calculate a statistic) and conceptual knowledge (understanding what a graph or statistic is communicating) (Friel, 1998).

Analysis

One way to analyze data is through the use of questions. As in the opening Snapshot of a Lesson, students should be encouraged to examine their results and discuss questions that may be answered by the data. There are three levels of graph comprehension, which progress from lower-level to higher-level questions. Your goal should be to teach students to move beyond lower-level thinking and to ask and answer higher-level questions.

- *Reading the data.* The student is able to answer specific questions for which the answer is prominently displayed. For example, "Which player averaged the most points?"

- *Reading between the data.* The student is able to find relationships in the data such as comparison, and is able to operate on the data. For example, " How many players had a median less than their mean?"

- *Reading beyond the data.* The student is able to predict or make inferences. For example, "Which player had the greatest range? The smallest range? What do these numbers tell you about the player?"

Data may also be analyzed by describing the shape of the data in the graph. Corwin and Friel (1990) suggest first having students use informal language such as "clumps, holes, and spread out"

to describe features of the data. You may want to create a Word Wall or visible word list for students to refer to when describing data. Second, students should attempt to develop theories about why the data look the way they do. This second step encourages students to read beyond the data.

Another beneficial graphical analysis task is to give students mystery graphs that are missing some of their labels and have students predict what the data might be. For example, groups of students may have each measured a body part such as arms, legs, or distance around heads. A graph that contains measurements from 18 to 24 inches is displayed. Students would be asked to hypothesize which body parts might be illustrated on the graph. This activity also reinforces the importance of using labels on graphs.

A variation of the mystery graph activity involves the use of a graphing calculator and a calculator-based laboratory (CBL). With a CBL motion detector, graphs may be created to show movements. Students may be given a CBL graph, and the challenge is to move so they can duplicate the graph. For example, Figure 17-18 shows the graphs of three different people walking. Time is shown on the horizontal axis and the distance from a motion detector is shown on the vertical axis. Examine Parts a, b, and c, and decide which of these graphs shows movement toward the motion detector. Part c is different because, instead of showing continuous movement away or toward, it shows a person leaving and then returning. These sorts of activities encourage students to consider the axes of the graphs and think carefully about how data are placed on a graph.

Misleading Graphs

Another important component in developing data sense is the ability to critically examine graphs and correctly interpret the data presented. "Although viewing data graphically allows the reader to see the trend of the data easily, the choice of scaling along the x- and y-axis could influence their interpretation of the data" (Harper, 2004, p. 341). Sometimes even simple graphs may be misleading. For example, consider the graph shown in Figure 17-19.

(a)   (b)   (c)

FIGURE 17-18 Graphs showing distance and time.

Eighth graders were asked to explain why this graph was misleading.

Although the captions in the graph indicate that the amount of trash has doubled in two decades, the visual elements reflect a doubling of both the width and height to produce a figure whose area is four times greater and a volume that is actually eight times greater. People may focus on the visual graph and ignore the numerical data that accompany the graph. In fact, less than 10% of eighth graders identified the critical problem associated with the graph in Figure 17-19 which suggests that instructional attention needs to be given to helping children examine graphs with a careful and suspicious eye.

Graphs may also be deceptive in other ways. For example, the graph in Figure 17-20a reports changes in allowances for three children. It shows that Ann's allowance was doubled, Bill's tripled, and Chris's increased by one-half. Based on this information, Bill may be feeling philanthropic and Chris complaining of hard times. What is wrong with the graph? Technically, it is correct, but it doesn't tell the entire story because the original allowances were not the same.

Let's look at the data:

	Original Allowance	Size of Increase	Amount of Increase	New Allowance
Ann	$6.00	Double	$6.00	$12.00
Bill	$3.00	Triple	$6.00	$9.00
Chris	$8.00	Half	$4.00	$12.00

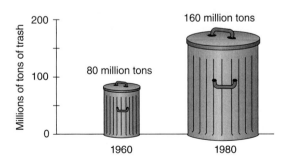

The United States is producing more trash.

The pictograph shown above is misleading. Explain why.

Answer: _Both the width and the_
height have been doubled.

FIGURE 17-19 Eighth-grade national assessment question on interpreting graphs.

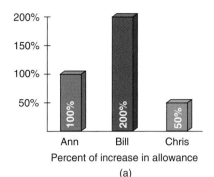

Percent of increase in allowance

(a)

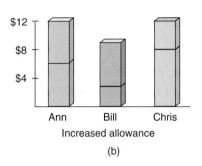

Increased allowance

(b)

FIGURE 17-20 Example of distortion of data in graphs.

As Figure 17-20b shows, a graph with a vertical axis labeled differently reflects the situation more accurately. These different graphs of the same data demonstrate how graphs can distort and sometimes misrepresent information. Developing a healthy skepticism of graphical displays is an important part of developing graphing skills. Harper (2004) suggests having students construct misleading graphs and then discussing the message being conveyed by the graphs. This can help students develop a better sense of misleading or inaccurate graphs, and what to look for when analyzing a display. According to Harper, students are more likely to notice scaling features but, "They are not as keen to observe pictorial embellishments or consider the source of the graph" (p. 343).

Communicating Results

Once data have been collected, displayed, and analyzed, it is appropriate for students to communicate their findings. Just as in problem solving, students should be encouraged to look back at their results. Communication can help students clarify their ideas during this process. For example, students might complete regular journal entries throughout their project. It is also useful to have large- or small-group discussions about the data.

Research supports having students go through a writing process when analyzing data, similar to one used in language arts (Friel, Mokros, and Russell, 1992). First, the students are involved in planning or prewriting. Second, a rough draft is created. Third, students revise their work, and finally the work is published and shared with others. Students could craft business letters to a company or group who would be interested in the data and mail them, similar to the task in the Snapshot of a Lesson. This is an opportunity to integrate across subject areas.

It is valuable for students to learn to communicate their results with others. Their final presentation may include oral or written communication or both. They must learn to report clearly the answers to their original questions and hypotheses and select the most appropriate way to communicate their findings in a graphic format or by using other statistical measures. Some projects may be interesting to share with local media. The presentation may be for other classmates; however, a presentation for someone outside of the classroom can be particularly meaningful. For example, one class calculated the area of classrooms in their building and compared the average area of the fifth-grade classrooms to the sixth-grade classrooms. Their findings were presented to the principal, who made room assignments for the building (Scavo and Petraroja, 1998). Another group of students collected data to find out which school lunches were the most and least popular. Once their findings were collected and displayed, they presented their findings to the director of food services, who planned the monthly menus.

◆Descriptive Statistics

Another way to analyze data is to use descriptive statistics. So much information exists today that it must often be simplified or reduced in ways other than by graphs. The organization and summarization of data is called *descriptive statistics.* Descriptive statistics are in common use. They are introduced in the primary grades through data collection and graphs, and then extended with further exploration and practice activities in the intermediate and middle school grades. Here are some familiar examples:

> "Most children in the fifth grade are 10 years old."

> "The median family income is $45,250."

> "The average temperature today was 29°F."

Each of these statements uses a number to summarize what is typical for a current situation or condition. Two of the most common types of descriptive statistics include measures of variation and measures of central tendency. For each of the descriptive statistics that follow, we provide a concrete example using cubes and an example using numbers. For some children, manipulating the physical model not only helps them understand the formula but also promotes retention.

Measure of Variation: Range

The *range* is a simple measure that is used to describe the variation of a set of data or how spread out the data are. The variation in a data set is easily examined in a line plot or graph. Figure 17-21 shows the ages of five children—2, 3, 7, 9, and 9—illustrated with cubes. Students may find the range by comparing the maximum value to see how much greater it is than the minimum value. The maximum is 7 more than the minimum. Thus the range is calculated by subtracting the minimum value in the spread from the maximum value. For the age data, subtract 2 from 9 to get a range of 7. Once the range has been introduced in the elementary grades, middle school students often learn to measure variability with variance or standard deviations.

Measures of Central Tendency or Averages

The word *average* is a popular statistical term that many children have heard. It is used to report such things as average temperature, average family income, test averages, batting averages, and average life expectancy.

Any number that is used to describe the center or middle of a set of values is called an *average* of

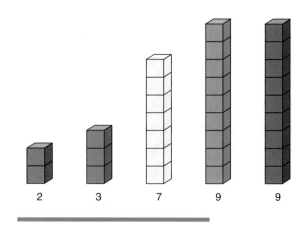

FIGURE 17-21   Ages of children.

those values. Many different averages exist, but three—mode, median, and mean—are commonly encountered in elementary and middle school. Simply being able to state the algorithm for finding these statistics is not enough. To support the development of data sense, each of these should be developed meaningfully through concrete activities before introducing computation. Such experiences provide greater conceptual knowledge or understanding of the concept of average. Spreadsheets and software programs provide explorations that allow middle school students to investigate what happens to various descriptive statistics when different values are used (Wilson and Kraft, 1995).

Mode   The *mode* is the value that occurs most frequently in a collection of data. Using concrete materials such as cubes, the mode is easily identified as the tower height that occurs most often. In Figure 17-21 it is easy to see that 9 is the mode because it occurs twice, while the other values only occur one time each. In graphical terms, this is also the largest portion; the tallest column in a bar graph, for example. In Figure 17-22a, the most frequently occurring test score is 90 (it occurred twice), so the mode is 90. The mode is a versatile average in that it may be used with both numeric and nonnumeric data, also called categorical data. The mode is easy to find and is affected very little by extreme scores. Young children are often interested in which item on the graph received the most votes. Therefore, their initial experience with average begins with mode. The children are comfortable using the mathematical term, *mode*, as the teacher introduces it to them.

Students' ages within a class provide an excellent application of mode, because within a given class, a large number of children are the "same" age. Businesses also frequently rely on the mode to select merchandise. Suppose, for example, that you own a shoe store. The mean and/or median size of shoe you sell has no practical value for restocking, but the modal shoe size holds clear implications because you want to stock the sizes most people wear. In some cases, a data set will have multiple values that occur most frequently. For example, if a class of students is asked how old they are, and there are nine students who are 10 and nine students who are 11, and no age occurs more then nine times, then the data set has two modes. In the case of two, the set is considered to be bimodal; three modes is called trimodal, and so on.

Median   The *median* is another type of average that can easily be identified without the need for computation. It is used with numeric data only and is the middle value in a data set of ordered data. The median divides the data into two equal subsets. Thus the same number of values are above as below the median. The median is easy to illustrate. Look again at the children's ages in Figure 17-21. Before looking for the median, the data must be ordered. For example, these towers are arranged smallest to largest. Once that has been done, the outside towers can be removed, one at a time, until the middle value remains. It is easy to see that the middle age or median tower is 7 years. Reference to a highway median will remind students that a median in statistics is a middle position. Notice that the median is not the middle of the range of data because data aren't always spread symmetrically over the range. One way of visually representing this is to provide children a strip of grid paper that has exactly as many boxes as data values. Have them put each ordered data point into a box and fold the strip in half. The median is the fold. In the children's age example, the median simply tells us that there are as many children in the group from ages 2–7 as there are in the group containing ages 7–9.

The median too, can be modeled with numbers. For example, consider the five test scores shown on cards in Figure 17-22a. Ordering them from lowest to highest, as in Figure 17-22b, provides practice in using greater than, less than, and ordering skills. To find the middle score, or median, simply remove the highest and lowest cards simultaneously, as shown in Figures 17-22c and 17-22d. Continue this process until the middle card remains. This score, 88, is the median.

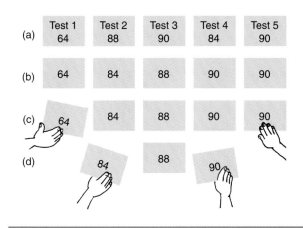

FIGURE 17-22   Model for finding the median of five test scores.

There are five scores in Figure 17-22. Suppose a sixth score of 17 was made. Ordering the six test scores, as shown in Figure 17-23a, could make a new arrangement. Again, remove the highest and lowest cards simultaneously until two cards remain. In this case, as shown in Figure 17-23b the median is the middle point between these two scores, or 86. If you add together the two remaining cards and divide them by 2, you will obtain the median as well $(84 + 88)/2 = 86$.

Mean The *mean* is called the arithmetic average because it is determined by adding all the values involved and dividing by the number of addends. The mean is the most difficult to compute, although it can be understood by children beginning in the upper elementary grades. It is used with numeric data only. When people talk about finding the average of a set of data, they are often referring to calculating the mean. It is important that children realize the mean is not the only type of average.

Simply being able to state or use the algorithm does not indicate understanding of the mean. Difficulties in interpreting the mean were shown on a national assessment. Figure 17-24 shows a question that required eighth graders to determine what data would be reasonable for a given mean. Less than 40% answered all four choices correctly. These assessment results illustrate that many middle grade

students are able to calculate averages when asked to do so, but the depth of their understanding of the concept of average is shallow.

Providing conceptual interpretations for the mean helps develop understanding of average. Say that four students have 9, 5, 3, and 7 trading cards. The cubes in Figure 17-25a show the number of cards each child has. The first interpretation involves the concept of equal distribution or sharing, an idea very familiar to students. In this interpretation, the mean is identified as the number that describes the data if each piece of data was "evened out" or the same as all others. People often think of this as what is typical for the data. If children are asked to even out or share the cards so that each student has a fair or equal share of cards, this evening-out process produces a mean of six cards per student (Figure 17-25b). As students gain experience and become comfortable with the equal distribution interpretation, they also begin to realize that with large data sets, such as whole-class data, trying to share equally becomes cumbersome. Students often discover the add-then-divide algorithm on their own, or you can introduce it with concrete materials. The mean also could have been determined by computing:

$$\text{mean} = \frac{9+5+3+7}{4} = \frac{24}{4} = 6$$

(a) | 17 | 64 | 84 | 88 | 90 | 90 |

(b) | | 84 | 88 | |

FIGURE 17-23 Model for finding the median of six test scores.

Akira read from a book on Monday, Tuesday, and Wednesday. He read an average of 10 pages per day. Circle whether each of the following is possible or not possible.

	Possible	Not Possible		Pages Read		
				Monday	Tuesday	Wednesday
A	A	(A)	(a)	4 pages	4 pages	2 pages
B	(B)	B	(b)	9 pages	10 pages	11 pages
C	(C)	C	(c)	5 pages	10 pages	15 pages
D	D	(D)	(d)	10 pages	15 pages	20 pages

FIGURE 17-24 Eighth-grade national assessment question on interpreting an average (correct responses are circled).

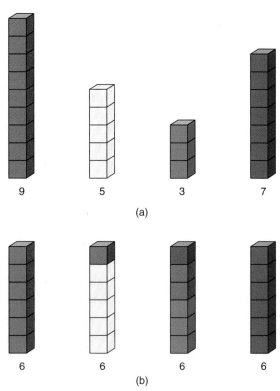

9   5   3   7

(a)

6   6   6   6

(b)

FIGURE 17-25 Equal distribution or sharing model for the mean.

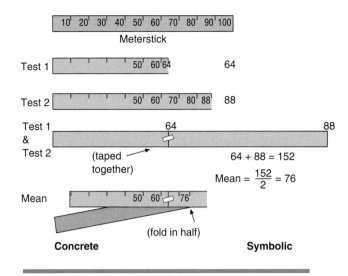

FIGURE 17-26 Model for finding the mean using lengths of adding machine tape to indicate test scores.

Figure 17-26 shows a way to model the add-then-divide algorithm for the mean. Test scores are returned to children on pieces of adding machine tape, and the length of each strip is determined by the score (i.e., a score of 88 is 88 cm long and a score of 64 is 64 cm long). Scores can be physically compared using the tapes (e.g., it is clear that the score on Test 2 was higher). To show the mean score, simply tape the two strips of paper together (add) and then fold the resulting strip in half (divide by 2). It also illustrates the effect of a test score of zero when the fold number on the tape is increased by one. Using this example, the three test scores would be 88, 64, and 0. The length of the tape is still 152 cm. But, if we fold the tape into thirds, rather than in half, the length of the strip is a little over 50 cm. Therefore, the mean test score

dropped over 25 points! This technique is appealing and enlightening.

Not all data sets divide evenly, and once students are comfortable with the concept of evening out, they can discuss what to do with remainders, which makes a natural connection to decimals. They can also discuss how some data cannot be divided and some averages that are calculated are not realistic. For example, in one data set the mean indicated that the average number of children per family was 2.5. Children will be quick to point out that you can't have five-tenths or one-half of a child.

These types of experiences help students understand some fundamental notions related to the mean; namely, that the mean must be somewhere between the values averaged and that it is the typical value or balancing point for a set of data.

Choosing Averages

As students use averages, they must be aware of how averages are influenced by data. For example, in Figure 17-22 the mean for 5 tests is 83 and the median is 88. When the extremely low score of 17 is included in Figure 17-23, the mean drops greatly (from 83 to 72) but the median changes only slightly (from 88 to 86). One negative characteristic of the mean is that its value is affected by extreme scores.

Grasp of average is a powerful tool in estimation and problem solving. Problems such as the one in Figure 17-27 provide opportunities to apply averages and estimation in everyday situations.

Finding the mean, median, and mode for the same data can generate discussion about when certain averages should be used. You can use In the Classroom 17-3 to allow children to calculate averages with concrete materials or numbers and

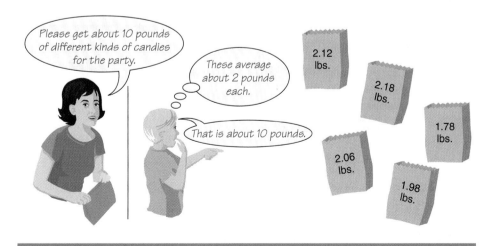

FIGURE 17-27 Example problem for developing averaging and estimating skills.

to discuss how one might select a particular average to describe the data. For another example, look at In the Classroom 17-4. Calculating the mean, median, and mode provides practice in computational skills. More important, however, is deciding which of these averages to report. The median salary of $500,000 or the modal salary of $480,000 seems more representative than the mean salary of $1,030,000. If salary negotiations were taking place, the players might cite one average and the owners a very different average. Discussing which averages are appropriate for what purpose helps students better understand why different ones exist and are used. Once children have collected their own data, they should determine which averages to calculate and report. For an amusing example of this type of activity see the children's book *What Do You Mean by "Average"?* (James, 1978), where Jill is running for student council. To convince the school she will best represent them, she decides to show she is the most average person in the school.

Each of the averages can be modeled and developed in ways that are appealing, interesting, and meaningful. No new mathematics is required, yet learning about averages provides a vehicle for applying many mathematical concepts and skills that students are developing.

Care must be taken to ensure that statistics is viewed as more than a series of skills or techniques. For example, finding an average is an important skill that should be developed; however, the teaching of statistics must not stop with the "how to." Rather, it must raise questions such as, "When is an average useful?"

For example, the ice cream survey in Figure17-8 reports that eight students like chocolate, five like vanilla, and three like strawberry. This picture graph clearly and accurately shows student ice cream preferences. These preferences are an example of non-numeric data, or categorical data. A mean or median of these data could be computed but would be inappropriate. In fact, a mean or median is meaningless for these data! Before any statistics are com-

In the Classroom 17-3

PEANUTS

OBJECTIVE: Choosing the best average.

GRADE LEVEL: 4–8

Suppose you have opened some Nutty Bars to check the company's claim of an "average" of 8 peanuts per bar. Here is what you found after opening 10 bars.

Bar	1st	2nd	3rd	4th	5th	6th	7th	8th	9th	10th
Number of Peanuts	5	8	8	8	11	7	8	6	6	6

▼ Create some different sketch graphs so you can examine the shape of the data. Which graph would the company probably use to promote their product? Why?

▼ Calculate the averages. You may use counters such as beans and grid paper to represent the peanuts if you wish.

- What is the mean number of nuts?
- What is the median number of nuts?
- What is the modal number of nuts?
- Which average did the company probably use? Why?

▼ Write at least three questions that can be answered by your graphs and statistics.

1. _____

2. _____

2. _____

In the Classroom 17-4

WHAT'S THE AVERAGE?

OBJECTIVE: **To calculate mean, median, and mode in deciding which average is most appropriate to use for a particular purpose.**

GRADE LEVEL: 4–8

$380,000	600,000
420,000	740,000
480,000	2,700,000
480,000	3,500,000
480,000	
520,000	

Here are yearly salaries of one profesional basketball team!

- What is the mean salary for the team? _____
- What is the median salary? _____
- What is the mode? _____
▼ Decide on the best average to report for the team:

_____
- Why is your choice better than other averages?

_____
▼ Surf the Internet and find some different salaries. Find and report the averages.

puted, challenge students to decide what questions are to be answered and discuss what statistics, if any, are needed to answer them. Nonnumeric data such as ice cream flavors are better analyzed with frequency tables or graphs. If an average is desired, the mode would be the appropriate average to use.

Additional questions might include "Why should the average be reported?" "What average is most appropriate?" "Why?" "What degree of precision is needed?" These questions are essential and must be asked regularly. This sort of discussion will support students as they develop their data sense. The teaching of statistics in elementary school must aim higher than skill development.

Students should know how to get a statistic, but they must also know what they have gotten.

Math Links 17.4

*T*o view a middle school lesson where students are collecting data and determining averages, you can view *Trashketball* from Modeling Middle School Mathematics at http://www.mmmproject.org/homeS.htm and click on video matrix to find this video.

◆ Probability

In daily conversations, it is common to speak of events in terms of their chances of occurring. *Probability* is used to predict the chance of something happening. The terms *chance* and *probability* are often applied to those situations where the outcome cannot completely be determined in advance. Here are some examples of common probabilistic statements:

"The chance of rain today is 40%."

"The Cardinals are a 3-to-1 favorite to win."

"The probability of an accident on the job is less than 1 in 100."

"The patient has a 50–50 chance of recovering."

"If I study, I will probably pass the test."

"I am sure we will have a test Friday."

"We will have milk in the cafeteria today."

The first four statements are commonly heard and relate directly to probability. The last three illustrate a subtle but frequent use of probability in many everyday situations. In all of these cases, the utilitarian role of probability makes it an important basic skill. One way to increase students' awareness of the use of probability is to have them make a daily or weekly list of probability statements they have seen (in newspapers, magazines, or on television) or heard (on radio and television).

The grade-level expectations shown in Figure 17-1 illustrate how probability is intertwined with data analysis and statistics. "Often times, probability is addressed as a subset of concepts addressed within statistics and little connections is made between data analysis, descriptive statistics, and probability in school mathematics. Some of the most powerful and useful ways to use probability involve making sense of a statistic derived from samples" (Stohl, 2005, p. 350.) In fact, according to the NCTM *Standards* (2000), ideas from probability serve as a foundation for the collection, description, and interpretation of data. Probability will not and should not be learned from formal definitions; rather, the presentation of varied examples and activities helps illustrate and clarify important concepts. In the early grades, the treatment of probability should be informal. At all stages of instruction, though, you must use correct language to describe what is happening. This language serves as a model for children as they begin developing probability concepts and simultaneously add new probabilistic terms to their vocabulary. Let's look at appropriate ways for elementary students to experience some key concepts and terms.

Probability of an Event

Look at these statements that involve probability:

The probability of tossing a head is $\frac{1}{2}$.

The probability of rolling a four on a standard six-sided die is $\frac{1}{6}$.

The probability of having a birthday on February 30 is 0.

In these examples, tossing a head, rolling a four, and having a birthday on February 30 are *events,* or *outcomes.* Probability assigns a number (from zero to one) to an event. The more likely an event is to occur, the larger the number assigned to it, and so the probability is 1.0 when something is certain to happen. These numbers are commonly assigned percents, as well. For example, the probability of students in an elementary class having been born is 1, or 100%. On the other hand, the probability of something impossible happening is zero, or 0%. For example, the probability of students in the class having been born on February 30 is zero. Therefore, all probabilities lie between zero and one, or 0% and 100%. Through the grades, students should be able to move from situations in which the probability of an event can be determined to situations in which sampling and simulations help them quantify the likelihood of an uncertain outcome. Students will also move from fractions to decimals and percents in later grades.

Long before children are ready to calculate probabilities of specific events, it is important that terms such as *certain, uncertain, impossible, likely,*

and *unlikely* be introduced and discussed. Most students, even in primary grades, are familiar with the terms *impossible* and *certain* and can give meaningful examples. Although *likely* and *unlikely* are less familiar and require more careful development, using activities such as In the Classroom 17-5 with children provides a good start. As each card is sorted, an explanation or argument for placing it in the specific box should be given. This rationale is essential in refining and developing a clear understanding of these important terms.

An excellent extension at the bottom of In the Classroom 17-5 is to have students write statements to be sorted into the same categories. Each

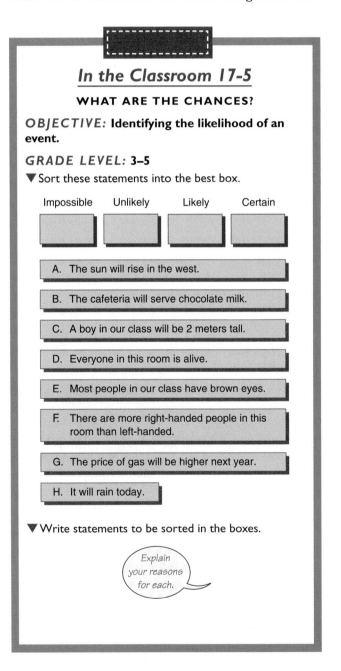

In the Classroom 17-5

WHAT ARE THE CHANCES?

OBJECTIVE: Identifying the likelihood of an event.

GRADE LEVEL: 3–5

▼ Sort these statements into the best box.

Impossible	Unlikely	Likely	Certain

A. The sun will rise in the west.

B. The cafeteria will serve chocolate milk.

C. A boy in our class will be 2 meters tall.

D. Everyone in this room is alive.

E. Most people in our class have brown eyes.

F. There are more right-handed people in this room than left-handed.

G. The price of gas will be higher next year.

H. It will rain today.

▼ Write statements to be sorted in the boxes.

Explain your reasons for each.

student should write several original statements and then exchange papers so that someone else classifies them. Once these general probabilistic terms become familiar, more specific probabilities can be determined.

The activities from In the Classroom 17-6 ask students to determine the likelihood of a particular event. Experiments involving blocks, spinners, dice, and coins are often used to introduce probability concepts and notation. Students should be given many opportunities to create and explore activities that ask them to answer questions about the likelihood of events, using the vocabulary of probability.

Sample space is a fundamental concept that must be established or at least understood before the probabilities of specific events can be deter-mined. The sample space for a probability problem represents all possible outcomes.

Another suggestion to help children think about what outcomes are possible for a particular event is to have students examine some common probabilistic situations: (1) If I flip a coin: will it land heads up, on its edge, tails up, or just float in the air? (2) If I drop a glass: will it hit and break, float in the air, or hit but not break? In each case, have the students discuss whether the event could happen. Consider, for example, the situation in which a coin is tossed. Some children may realize that a coin will not land on its edge, nor will it float. Thus only two outcomes can happen, and these possible outcomes comprise the sample space. Having children create their own events and determine possible outcomes is also a beneficial experience.

Once the sample space is known, the calculation of specific probabilities usually follows naturally. When a coin is flipped, as described in Table 17-1, the probability of a head is the number of ways a head can occur divided by the total number of outcomes (head or tail). Specific probabilities rest heavily on fractions, which provide a direct and convenient means of reporting and interpreting probabilities.

Discussion of possible outcomes helps identify the sample space and clarify notions of probability. Using the example of an equally likely spinner, students can be questioned about the probability of events occurring. Questions along these lines might get the discussion started:

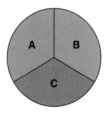

Can the spinner stop in region D?

Can the spinner stop on a line?

The first outcome is impossible. Even though the second outcome is unlikely, it can happen, and a plan of action should be specified if it does. (Maybe you spin again.) See Appendix B for spinner masters.

Consider the sample space for tossing cups, as shown in In the Classroom 17-7. Is a cup equally likely to land on its top, its side, or its bottom? Without additional information, it would be difficult to decide. In the Classroom 17-7 provides

---

In the Classroom 17-6

WHAT'S MORE LIKELY?

OBJECTIVE: Determine the likelihood of an event.

GRADE LEVEL: 4–5

ACTIVITY ONE:

1. If you put four red blocks in a paper bag, can you be sure what color block you will pull out? Why or why not?

2. If you put a green block in the bag with the red blocks, can you be sure what color block you will pull out? Why or why not? Try this experiment. Record your results.

3. If you put three green blocks in a bag with seven red blocks, is one color more likely to be pulled out? Why or why not? Try this experiment. Record your results.

4. Try a blocks-in-a-bag experiment of your own. Record your results.

ACTIVITY TWO:

▼ Mary flipped a coin four times. It came up heads four times. She flipped the coin a fifth time. What is she likely to get on the fifth flip of the coin?

  a. Heads

  b. Tails

  c. It is equally likely to be heads or tails.

▼ Explain your answer. How could you test your idea? Try your experiment and record your results.

Table 17-1 • Sample Spaces of Some Events and Their Probabilities

Questions	Sample Space	Number of Successes	Probability
What is the probability of getting a head on a single toss of a coin?	H, T	1	$\frac{1}{2}$
What is the probability of getting two heads when two coins are tossed?	HH, HT TH, TT	1	$\frac{1}{4}$
What is the probability of getting a five on a single roll of a die?	1, 2, 3, 4 5, 6	1	$\frac{1}{6}$
What is the probability of drawing a spade from a deck of 52 playing cards?	52 cards	13	$\frac{13}{52}$ or $\frac{1}{4}$
If each letter of the alphabet is written on a piece of paper, what is the probability of drawing a vowel?	26 letters of the alphabet	5 (a, e, i, o, u)	$\frac{5}{26}$

suggestions for a possible start. In addition to helping children decide which outcomes are more or less likely, this exploration may lead to more precise statements.

In the Classroom 17-8 involves collecting data, graphing results, and exploring patterns. It uses several valuable ideas of probability, including sample space and probability of an event, in a natural and interesting setting. As children are involved in this process, they are developing and practicing basic facts, as was shown earlier in Chapter 9. Such an activity further illustrates how mathematical topics are interrelated and how important connections can be made.

Once you have tried In the Classroom 17-8 with children, another perspective can be obtained by examining Table 17-2, which summarizes the results when two dice are added (a) and multiplied (b). One diagonal of Table 17-2a shows all the ways that a sum of 7 can be obtained. Table 17-2a also shows the different ways that each of the other sums can result. Is the sum of two dice more likely to be even or odd? An examination of Table 17-2a shows that the even sums will occur 18 out of 36 times, or half the time.

Table 17-2 • Results of Operations with Two Dice

+	1	2	3	4	5	6
1	2	3	4	5	6	7
2	3	4	5	6	7	8
3	4	5	6	7	8	9
4	5	6	7	8	9	10
5	6	7	8	9	10	11
6	7	8	9	10	11	12
a						

×	1	2	3	4	5	6
1	1	2	3	4	5	6
2	2	4	6	8	10	12
3	3	6	9	12	15	18
4	4	8	12	16	20	24
5	5	10	15	20	25	30
6	6	12	18	24	30	36
b						

In the Classroom 17-7

WHAT'S THE PROBABILITY?

OBJECTIVE: Collect data to decide more or less likely outcomes and determine experimental probabilities.

GRADE LEVEL: 4–6

- Toss a cup to see how it lands:

- Before you toss it again, circle how you think it will land:

- Toss your cup 20 more times, and tally how it lands!

Bottom	Top	Side

- I have decided that _____ is most likely.
- I have decided that _____ is least likely.

▼ Here are some results from tossing the cup:

A. | 2 | 0 | 3 | B. | 15 | 10 | 25 |

C. | 32 | 17 | 51 |

- Is it possible that all these tallies are results of tossing the same cup? _____ Explain.
- Which of these tables would you feel best about using? _____ Explain.

DECISION TIME:

The probability of landing on the side is about _____.

In the Classroom 17-8

ROLLING AND RECORDING

OBJECTIVE: Conducting a probability experiment.

GRADE LEVEL: 4–8

▼ Try this:
1. Choose a partner, and each of you make a chart like the one shown. Predict which sum of two dice will come up most often.
2. Each of you take turns rolling two dice.
3. On a turn, find the sum of the spots on the two dice, and place a tally mark in that column on your chart.
4. Continue rolling and recording until one of you has 10 tally marks in one column. Compare your prediction with the actual result.

PUTTING IT TOGETHER:

- Why doesn't the chart need a ones column? A thirteens column?
- In which column did you or your partner reach 10?
- Compare your results, and tell how they are similar. Different.
- Tell why you would expect more sums of 7 than 2.
- Complete the following. "I would expect about the same number of sums of 4 as . . ."
- Would you expect to get about the same number of even sums as odd sums? Tell why.

EXTENDING THIS ACTIVITY:

Suppose you multiplied the numbers on the dice instead of adding them.

- How would the values along the top of the chart change?
- How many values (i.e., different products) would be needed?
- Which values would be least likely?
- Would you expect to get about the same number of even values as odd values? Tell why?

Is the product of two dice more likely to be even or odd? The shaded cells in Table 17-2b show that the even products are much more likely. In fact, an even product would be expected to occur 27 times out of 36, or three-fourths of the time. Analyzing and discussing why this happens helps connect probability to properties and relationships between numbers and operations.

Randomness

Randomness is an important concept underlying all learning in probability. When something is random, it means that it is not influenced by any factors other than chance. In the Classroom 17-9 could be used to build on In the Classroom 17-5 and provides an opportunity to discuss randomness in a specific context. Here students are encouraged to think about events based on their classmates and decide about where these events would be placed on a probability number line that shows 0 and 1. Here are some starter questions:

Why is it important that the "name will be randomly picked"?

Should the names be seen by the person doing the drawing?

In the Classroom 17-9

ARE YOU A WINNER?

OBJECTIVE: **Explore the concept of randomness.**

GRADE LEVEL: **4–8**

Our class is having a drawing. Each person gets to place their name in the drawing one time. One name will be randomly picked, and that person will be the winner.

▼ Read each of the following statements.

▼ Think about the people in our class.

▼ Then, check the number line below and decide about where the following statements should be placed:

   A. The winner will be left-handed.

   B. The winner will be a girl.

   C. The winner will be someone in our class.

   D. The number of letters in the first name of the winner will be less than the number of letters in their last name.

   E. The winner's first name will begin with a vowel.

   F. The winner will wear glasses.

   G. You will be the winner.

   H. The winner will be wearing socks.

   I. You will not be the winner.

0   .5 or $\frac{1}{2}$ 1
Impossible   Certain
                                   to happen

Would it matter if some people wrote their names on large pieces of paper and others on small pieces of paper?

If the names are seen or if people don't all write their names on the same size of paper, the drawing might not be random. When this happens, some people would have an advantage and the notions of *fair* and *unfair* become important.

The term *fair* is often used in describing a situation. For example, to say "a fair coin" or "fair dice" makes it clear that no inherent biases exist that would affect randomness. A person may be asked to toss (not scoot) a die to ensure that one face is not favored. If Ping-Pong balls are drawn from a bowl, it is important that the balls be thoroughly mixed and the person doing the drawing be blindfolded to ensure both randomness and fairness. The children's book *No Fair!* (Holtzman, 1997) describes two children who are trying to determine when activities such as drawing an item from a bag are fair.

Discussions on the consequences of unfairness and absence of randomness should be a regular part of developing probability. For example, would it be fair if two dice are rolled and player A wins if the product is even and player B wins if the product is odd? Table 17-2b shows that A will win much more than B, so this game is not fair. On the other hand, if the game is based on the sum of two dice (Table 17-2a), each player has an equal chance of winning and the game is fair. Suppose you modify the sum-of-two-dice game to play with three players:

Player A wins if the sum is 1, 2, 3, or 4.

Player B wins if the sum is 5, 6, 7, or 8.

Player C wins if the sum is 9, 10, 11, or 12.

Is this game fair for each of the players? Does each player have the same chance of winning? An analysis of Table 17-2a suggests that Player B will win more often than either of the other players. As children explore this game, you might challenge them to tell how the game might be modified to make it fair for everyone.

Independence of Events

Independence of events is an important concept in probability, but one that does not develop naturally from intuition. If two events are independent, one event in no way affects the outcome of the other. Thus if a coin is tossed, lands heads, and then is tossed again, it is still equally likely to land heads or tails. This sounds simple enough, but consider this question: Suppose four consecutive sixes have occurred on four rolls of a fair die. What is the probability of getting a six on the next roll?

A majority of middle grade students miss this question. Many students suggest that the die had a "memory," and things would "even out." Most did not conclude that the probability was unchanged, regardless of what had already happened. If an event has occurred a number of times in a row, most people falsely presume that the "law of averages" makes it unlikely that the event will occur on the next trial. The same thing happens when a coin is flipped multiple times, generating a string of the same outcomes. If the coin lands heads four times in a row, it has an equally likely chance of landing heads or tails on the fifth flip. This basic misunderstanding contradicts the notion of independence of certain events. Research suggests that experiences exploring independence should be encountered in middle school (Jones et al., 1999; Tarr, 1997; Tarr and Jones, 1997; Watson, 1995).

Having children collect data and discuss the results can help dispel some of this erroneous thinking. "Working with real data allows students to appreciate the difference between empirical phenomena and probabilistic models; it shows them the usefulness of these models in explaining, predicting and controlling a variety of real phenomena beyond pure games of chance" (Batanero and Sanchez, 2005, p. 262). When you use In the Classroom 17-10 with children, different students will produce different results, yet the answers to the questions will be very similar. Why? Because these events, the rolls of a die, are independent of one another.

Tossing a coin and recording the outcomes in sequence will likely generate some long runs of an occurrence, even though each outcome is independent of the others. Although the probability of a head is $\frac{1}{2}$, children might flip a coin 10 times and get eight, nine, or even ten heads in a row. Consider this record of 20 tosses of a coin:

T T T T T H T H H H H T T H H T H H H H

There are two sequences of four consecutive heads and one of five consecutive tails. Overall, 11 heads appeared. Such analysis and discussion helps children understand that things don't even out on each flip. As the number of flips gets very large, however, the ratio of heads to the total number of flips will get closer and closer to the theoretical expected value of $\frac{1}{2}$. This latter point is very important, but it often baffles elementary students.

In the Classroom 17-10

CAN YOU MAKE PREDICTIONS?

OBJECTIVE: Identifying independence of events.

GRADE LEVEL: 4–6

▼ Roll a die six times and record the results:

1	2	3	4	5	6

- Did each face appear once? _____
- Does knowing what happened on the first roll help predict the second? _____ the third? _____

▼ Roll a die 24 times and record the results.

1	2	3	4	5	6	7	8	9	10	11	12

13 14 15 16 17 18 19 20 21 22 23 24

- Did each face appear once? _____
- The same number of times? _____
- What face appeared most? _____
- Does this mean the die is unfair? _____
- Does this record tell you what will occur on the next roll? _____

Using simulation programs to repeat an event many times helps children better understand the notion of the expression, *in the long run.*

There are, of course, times when one event may depend on another. For example, suppose you wanted to roll two dice and obtain a sum of 8. If a 1 is shown on the first die, it is impossible to get a sum of 8. This leads toward notions of *conditional probability.*

Instruction is needed to develop the necessary techniques to solve simple probability problems. There are other more complicated situations for which probabilities are difficult to calculate. What is the probability of the New York Mets winning the World Series? Of a woman being elected president? Such questions do not lend themselves to simple solutions, but experts can approximate their probabilities. Regardless of who determines the numerical probabilities, the knowledge and interpretative skills developed in simpler probability situations can be successfully applied.

Math Links 17.5

*T*here are a number of excellent Web sites that provide opportunities for children to simulate many trials with dice and spinners, and to integrate them into lessons:

Go to the

- Math Forum Web site at http://mathforum.org/mathtools and then go to Math Topics. Under Probability and Statistics you will find lessons focusing on various models, including randomness and probability models. A number of applets (Bar Graph Sorter and Circle Graph) for different grade levels are available.

- National Library of Virtual Manipulatives at http://www.matti.usu.edu. There you will find a number of tools that help to simulate different probability models (Spinners, Coin Tossing, Box Model, and Histogram).

- National Council of Teachers of Mathematics Illuminations web site http://illuminations.nctm.org/ to find an array of lessons and tools, such as an Adjustable Spinner and Random Drawing Tool that allow children to gather data via simulations.

www.wiley.com/college/reys

Misconceptions about Probability

"If one intends to develop by instruction a strong, correct, coherent, formal, and intuitive background for probabilistic reasoning, one has to cope with a large variety of misunderstandings, misconceptions, biases and emotional tendencies" (Fischbein, Nello, and Marino, 1991, p. 547). Young children often hold common misconceptions about various aspects of probability. For example, they make predictions based on preference, such as their favorite color or number. They also hold biases against certain numbers, believing, for example, that it may be hardest to throw a 6 on a die. Young children are not surprised by extremely unlikely events and do not search for underlying causes. They may expect all outcomes in an experiment to be equally likely. It is also difficult for many children to make inferences from data.

So do not be surprised when your own students reflect misconceptions in probability. The more opportunities you give them to explore a variety of probability notions through hands-on activities, the better they will be able to develop and evaluate inferences and predictions that are based on data and apply basic concepts of probability.

Cultural Connections

Several previous chapters have discussed the success of the Asian nations on the Trends in International Mathematics and Science Study (TIMSS). Many of these nations have shown success in mathematics overall and high performance in computation in particular. However, an analysis by strand shows some shockingly different results, especially in data analysis and probability.

The TIMSS 2003 mathematics test was designed to test fourth and eighth graders in five content areas. The "Data" portion of the test enables reporting over four topics of data analysis and probability: (1) data collection and organization of data, (2) representing data, (3) interpretation of data, and (4) probability and uncertainty (Mullis et al., 2004). All four areas were tested in the eighth grade, however, probability was not included on the fourth-grade test.

The five top scoring nations on the TIMSS 2003 eighth-grade test were Singapore, the Republic of Korea, Hong Kong, Chinese Taipei, and Japan. All five nations scored significantly higher than the international average scale score. However, four of these nations' scores in data (Japan excluded) were not only their lowest, but the scores in some cases were significantly lower than the next closest strand. The United States, on the other hand, scored the highest in data, 17 points higher than any other area in eighth grade.

Based on the reported use of the curriculum, many nations were not emphasizing data analysis and probability in their curricula. This lack of emphasis is highlighted in Mullis et al. (2004), "with 95% of students across countries having been taught the TIMSS number topics (strand) by eighth grade. This was followed by measurement (78%), geometry (69%), algebra (66%), and data (46%)" (p. 189). In eighth grade, the top five nations ranged from 6 to 59% of the data strand covered, while the United States averaged 83%. Because data is not a key component of curricula in many parts of the world, students are scoring significantly lower on questions related to data.

Why is the United States spending more time on data and scoring much higher? Jones et al. (1999) suggest the release of the NCTM *Standards* in 1989, emphasizing data and probability, as well as the amount of research that has been done in the last 15 years looking at student thinking in both areas. As a result, many mathematics curricula materials in the United States are devoting more attention to data analysis, statistics, and probability.

A Glance at Where We've Been

Data analysis, statistics, and probability provide an opportunity for students to develop problem-solving and critical thinking skills as well as to make connections to other mathematical topics and school subjects. Students engage in the process of data analysis by posing questions that are meaningful to them, collecting the data to answer the questions, and displaying the data in a way that helps others understand and interpret the results. Teachers and students pose questions about the data together, extend students' abilities to analyze their results, and communicate their findings in a way that represents the data in a truthful manner.

In the elementary and early middle school years, students are exposed to many types of graphs: line plots, stem-and-leaf plots, picture graphs, bar graphs, histograms, pie graphs, line graphs, and box plots. Graphing calculators and other technological tools and programs allow students opportunities to experiment with different ways of displaying data, therefore developing multiple perspectives for the same set of data. This helps promote data sense.

Students in the elementary grades learn to analyze data using descriptive statistics, especially measures of variation and central tendency—mean, median, and mode. The goal is to understand fundamental notions related to these statistics and to be able to choose averages that are most appropriate and describe the data in meaningful ways.

Probabilistic thinking develops in elementary students through a variety of hands-on activities and experiments that challenge their intuitive notions of what is fair and unfair. It is important that children know the probability of an event ranges between 0 and 1, and be able to calculate the probability of events. The ability to use the language of probability is an important skill in our daily lives, and it can be explored in many ways that help build excitement for learning mathematics.

Things to Do: From What You've Read

1. Here are the results on three tests: 68, 78, 88. What are the mean and the median? Explain why the mode is of little value. What score would be needed on the next test to get an average of 81? Describe two different ways you could determine this score.

2. Arrange interlocking cubes together in lengths of 3, 6, 6, and 9.
   a. Describe how you could use the blocks to find the mean, median, and mode.
   b. Suppose you introduce another length of 10 cubes. Has the mean changed? the median? the mode?

3. Answer each of the following questions, and tell why you answered as you did.
   a. Is it possible for a set of data to have more than one mode? Give an example.
   b. Is it easier to find the median of 25 or 24 student scores?
   c. Could the mean be as large as the largest value in a set of data? Tell how.

4. Describe the differences between a bar graph and a histogram.

5. Describe two activities that could be used to discuss probabilities of zero and one.

6. Ten cards are marked 0, 1, 2, 3, . . ., 9 and placed face down. If the cards are shuffled and then one card is drawn, tell why the following statements are true:
   a. The sample space has 10 events.
   b. The probability of drawing the 6 is 1/10.
   c. The probability of drawing the 3 is the same as the probability of drawing the 7.

7. Many state lotteries advertise with a slogan, "If you don't play, you can't win." Does that mean if you do play, you will win? Explain.

8. At the end of the Snapshot of a Lesson (p. 415), Derrick says "On the range you want the lowest, because that means they are the most consistent and they score about the same number of points a game." Do you agree? Is this a good generalization? Would you expect that players with very little playing time have a large or small range? Explain.

9. If a lottery consists of picking 6 numbers from the numbers 1 through 45, which group of 6 numbers would you pick? Explain your choice.
   a. 1, 2, 3, 4, 5, 6
   b. 3, 10, 17, 21, 35, 43
   c. both are equally likely to win

10. In the opening snapshot Derrick argued that the range would be a good statistic to use in selecting the Most Valuable Player. Make a case to support his recommendation. How might a case against his argument be made?

Things to Do: Going Beyond This Book

IN THE FIELD

1. *Use In the Classroom 17-1 with a small group of children as they plan and conduct a survey. Describe how it went.

2. Examine the graphs shown by Sakshaug (2000). Use these graphs and questions with some children and compare your results with those reported by Sakshaug and Wohlhuter (2001).

3. *Use In the Classroom 17-2 with some children in grades 4–8. Which key features of various graphs and statistics did you discuss with the children? How did you guide the children to create higher-level questions?

4. *Select a middle school student and use In the Classroom 17-6 to guide some questions related to probability. What did you learn about the child's thinking?

5. Examine the scope-and-sequence chart for an elementary textbook series used in your school. At what level is graphing first introduced? What kinds of graphing skills are highlighted? What important statistical topics are included? At what levels are they taught? Do the same for probability.

6. What would you say to a principal who accused you of allowing your students to "play games" when they were conducting dice experiments?

WITH ADDITIONAL RESOURCES

7. Review the NCTM books *Making Sense of Data* (Lindquist et al., 1992) and *Dealing with Data and Chance* (Zawojewski et al., 1991). Select an activity. Decide where and how you would use it in teaching a lesson.

8. Examine one of the NCTM's *Navigations Series* books for Data Analysis and Probability (preK–2, Sheffield et al., 2002; 3–5, Chapin et al., 2002; 6–8 probability, Bright, Frierson, et al., 2003; or 6–8 data analysis, Bright, Brewer, et al., 2003) and present one of the grade appropriate activities to a group of students. Discuss what happpened.

9. Examine newspapers or magazines. Start a file of graphs students can examine. Make a list of the different kinds of graphs used. Select a few and tell why you think a particular graph (e.g.,

picture graph, pie graph, bar graph) was used in each situation.

10. Games are fun and can help develop a better understanding of probability. Play the game Montana Red Dog, described in *Dealing with Data and Chance* (Zawojewski et al., 1991), play one of the games from "Fair Games, Unfair Games" (Bright, Harvey, and Wheeler, 1981), *What Are My Chances?* (Shulte and Choate, 1996), or the "Cover Up Game" from *Chance Encounters: Probability in Games and Simulation* (Brutlag, 1996). Identify some of the mathematics learned in these games. Tell how you might use these games with students.

11. Read one of the research articles related to probability or statistics listed in Jones (2005), Bright and Hoeffner (1993), or Friel et al. (2001). Discuss the nature of the research. Also identify an instructional idea or activity suggested by the research that you think would be effective in helping children learn a particular concept.

WITH TECHNOLOGY

12. Use technology such as spreadsheet, graphing, or survey software or a graphing calculator to display and analyze data. Evaluate how these tools might be used with children. Better yet, try it out with children and then evaluate.

13. Check the Web for the NCTM's *Illuminations* activities. Look for an activity that can be used in helping elementary children understand probabilty. If you can, try this activity with some students.

Note to Instructors: You can find additional resources, learning activities, and black-line masters in this text's accompanying Instructor's Manual at www.com/college/reys.

---

*Additional activities, suggestions, and questions are provided in *Teaching Elementary Mathematics: A Resource for Field Experiences* (Wiley 2007).

Book Nook for Children

Arnold, C. *Charts and Graphs: Fun, Facts, and Activities*. New York: Franklin Watts, 1984.

Photographs and drawings are used to illustrate real-world applications and examples using pie, bar, and line graphs and pictographs. Illustrations are colorful and interesting and provide a multicultural focus for the book. The glossary is written in terms children can understand and is helpful in comparing various ways of presenting information.

Cushman, J. *Do You Wanna Bet? Your Chance to Find Out about Probability.* New York: Clarion Books, 1991.

Whether flipping coins to decide what television program to watch or analyzing which events are "certain," "impossible," or "maybe," Danny and Brian become involved in everyday situations, both in and out of school, that involve probability. Several important probability concepts are woven into an interesting story line.

Holtzman, C. *No Fair!* New York: Scholastic, 1997.

When Kristy and David cannot agree on which game to play, David brings out a bag of marbles and says they can play Kristy's game if she chooses a blue marble, but Kristy objects when she learns that only one marble was blue.

James, E. *What Do You Mean by "Average"? Means, Medians, and Modes.* New York: Lothrop, Lee & Shepard Books, 1978.

The plans of Jill's student council campaign to appeal to the "average" student lead to an exploration of means, medians, and modes. Other concepts defined and explored include ranges, sampling, random sampling, weighting a sample, and universe. How to collect and tabulate data and how to transform them into percentages and graphs are also presented.

Mori, T. *Socrates and the Three Pigs.* New York: Philomel Books, 1986.

Socrates, a wolf, and his friend Pythagoras, a frog, must figure out how to capture a succulent pig for Xanthippe, Socrates' hungry wife. This unusual book tackles the complicated problems of probability and combinatorial analysis through a series of diagrams showing all possibilities in determining in which of five houses one of the pigs could be found. The intent of this book is to introduce a sophisticated topic in an intuitive manner that leads to understanding through patterns and counting.

Murphy, S. J. *The Best Vacation Ever.* New York: Harper Collins, 1997.

This entry in the MathStart series demonstrates that collecting data and tabulating results can help the decision-making process. A girl with an active, overscheduled family puts math to work to coordinate a family expedition. She uses charts to plot her family's preferences.

Srivastava, J. J. *Averages.* New York: Crowell, 1975.

Averages—mode, median, and mean—are introduced in an easily read text that is complemented by humorous illustrations. This clever book encourages children to try the interesting activities that are clearly illustrated within it.

Annotated Resources

Bright, G. W., Brewer, W., McClain, K., and Mooney, E. S. *Navigating through Data Analysis in Grades 6 through 8.* Reston, VA: NCTM, 2003.

Bright, G. W., Frierson, D., Jr., Tarr, J. E.; and Thomas, C. *Navigating through Probability in Grades 6 through 8.* Reston, VA: NCTM, 2003.

Chapin, S., Koziol, A., MacPherson, J., and Rezba, C. *Navigating through Data Analysis and Probability in Grades 3 through 5.* Reston , VA: NCTM, 2002.

Each of these books in the *Navigation* series provides a wide range of activities to help children develop fundamental concepts of data representation and probability. The accompanying CD-ROM provides grade level appropriate applets that engage children in a range of simulations and tools for representing data.

Friel, S. "Teaching statistics: What's average?" In *The Teaching and Learning of Algorithms in School Mathematics, 1998 Yearbook* (ed. L. J. Morrow). Reston, VA: NCTM, 1998, pp. 208–217.

This article discusses strategies for building conceptual and procedural understandings in teaching mean, median, and mode. Developing "data sense" includes a consideration of the "when and why" of the use of the representations and statistics.

Quinn, R., and Wiest, L. "Reinventing Scrabble with middle school students." *Mathematics Teaching in the Middle School,* 5 (December 1999), pp. 210–213.

Students use the Scrabble game to explore frequency distribution and other topics as they work cooperatively to collect, analyze, and interpret data.

Sakshaug, L E. "Which graph is which?" *Teaching Children Mathematics,* 6 (March 2000), pp. 454–455.

Ideas for engaging elementary children in graphing. Problem posed.

Sakshaug, L E., and Wohlhuter, K. A. "Responses to the Which Graph Is Which? problem." *Teaching Children Mathematics,* 7 (February 2001), pp. 350–353.

Responses to the problem in the previous citation are presented.

Zawojewski, J. S., Brooks, G., Dinkelkamp, L., Goldberg, E., Goldberg, H., Hyde, A., Jackson, T., Landau, M., Martin, H., Nowakowski, J., Paull, S., Shulte, A., Wagreich, P., and Wilmot, B. *Dealing with Data and Chance.* Reston, VA: NCTM, 1991.

This book considers daily experiences with data and chance as it addresses the role of both in middle school mathematic, grades 5–8. Activities are presented to help naturally build data and chance abilities with students.

References

Abrams, J., and Ferguson, J. "Teaching students from many nations." *Educational Leadership*, 62(4) (December 2004/January 2005), pp. 64–67.

Alajmi, A. *Eighth Grade Kuwaiti Students' Performance in Recognizing Reasonable Answers and Strategies They Use to Determine Reasonable Answers.* Unpublished doctoral dissertation, University of Missouri–Columbia, 2004.

Alejandre, S., and Moore, V. "Technology as a tool in the primary classroom." *Teaching Children Mathematics*, 10(2) (September 2003), pp. 16–18.

Akers, J., Battista, M., Godrow, A., Clements, H. D, & Sarama, J. "Halves and Symmetry", *Investigations in Number, Data, and Space: Grade 2*. Menlo Park, CA: Dale Seymour Publications, 1996.

Ameis, J. A. "Stories invite children to solve mathematical problems." *Teaching Children Mathematics*, 8(5) (January 2002), p. 260.

Andrews, A., and Trafton, P. R. *Little Kids—Powerful Problem Solvers: Math Stories from a Kindergarten Classroom.* Portsmouth, NH: Heinemann, 2002.

Ansel, E., and Doerr, H. "NAEP findings regarding gender: Achievement, affect, and instructional experiences." In *Results from the Seventh Mathematics Assessment of the National Assessment of Educational Progress* (eds. E. A. Silver and P. A. Kenney). Reston, VA: NCTM, 2000, pp. 73–106.

Anthony, G. J., and Walsh, M. "Zero: A 'none' number." *Teaching Children Mathematics*, 11(1) (August 2004), 38–42.

Arbaugh, F., Brown, C., Lynch, K., and McGraw, R. "Students' ability to construct responses (1992–2000): Findings from short and extended constructed-response items." In *Results and Interpretations of the 1990 through 2000 Mathematics Assessments of the National Assessment of Educational Progress* (eds. P. Kloosterman and F. K. Lester, Jr.). Reston, VA: NCTM, 2004.

Artzt, A. F., and Newman, C. M. *How to Use Cooperative Learning in the Mathematics Class.* Reston, VA: NCTM, 1990.

Ashlock, R. B. *Error Patterns in Computation*, 7th Ed. New York: Merrill, 1998.

Austin, R. A., Thompson, D. R., and Beckmann, C. E. "Exploring measurement concepts through literature: Natural links across disciplines." *Mathematics Teaching in the Middle School*, 10(4) (December 2004–January 2005), pp. 218–234.

Azzolino, A. "Writing as a tool for teaching mathematics: The silent revolution." In *Teaching and Learning Mathematics in the 1990s*, 1990 Yearbook of the National Council of Teachers of Mathematics (eds. T. J. Cooney and C. R. Hirsch). Reston, VA: NCTM, 1990, pp. 92–100.

Badger, E. "More than testing." *Arithmetic Teacher*, 39(9) (May 1992), pp. 7–11.

Baratta-Lorton, M. *Mathematics Their Way*. Palo Alto, CA: Addison-Wesley, 1976.

Barkley, C. A., and Cruz, S. "Geometry through beadwork designs." *Teaching Children Mathematics*, 7(7) (February 2001), pp. 362–367.

Baroody, A. J., and Standifer, D. J. "Addition and subtraction in the primary grades." In *Research Ideas for the Classroom: Early Childhood Mathematics* (ed. R. J. Jensen). Reston, VA: NCTM and New York: Macmillan, 1993, pp. 72–102.

Bass, H. "Computational fluency, algorithms, and mathematical proficiency: One mathematician's perspective." *Teaching Children Mathematics*, 9(6) (February 2003), pp. 322–327.

Batanero, C., and Sanchez, E. "What is the nature of high school students' conceptions and misconceptions about probability?" In *Exploring Probability in School: Challenges for Teaching and Learning* (ed. G. A. Jones). The Netherlands: Kluwer Academic, 2005, pp. 241–266.

Battista, M. T. "Calculators and computers: tools for mathematical exploration and empowerment." In *Putting Research into Practice in the Elementary Grades* (ed. D. L. Chambers). Reston, VA: NCTM, 2002, pp. 272–278.

Battista, M. T. "Computer technologies and teaching geometry through problem solving." In *Teaching Mathematics Through Problem Solving: Prekindergarten–grade 6* (eds. F. K. Lester, Jr., and R. I. Charles). Reston, VA: NCTM, 2003, pp. 229–238.

Bay-Williams, J. "What is algebra in elementary school?" *Teaching Children Mathematics*, 8(4) (December 2001), pp. 196–201.

Bay-Williams, J., and Martinie, S. *Math and Literature: Grades 6–8*. Sausalito, CA: Math Solutions, 2004.

Bell, M., et. al. *Everyday Mathematics, Sixth Grade Teacher's Lesson Guide (Vol. 1)* and *Level 3, Volume 1-Student Math Journal*. Chicago, IL: SRA/McGraw Hill, 2004.

Beyer, A. "Assessing students' performance: Using observations, reflections, and other methods." In *Assessment in the Mathematics Classroom*, 1993 Yearbook of the National Council of Teachers of Mathematics (ed. N. Webb). Reston, VA: NCTM, 1993, pp. 111–120.

Bishop, A. J. "What values do you teach when you teach mathematics?" *Teaching Children Mathematics*, 7(6) (February 2001), pp. 346–370.

Bohan, H., Irby, B., and Vogel, D. "Problem solving: Dealing with data in the elementary school." *Teaching Children Mathematics*, 1(5) (January 1995), pp. 256–260.

Bohl, D., Oursland, M., and Finco, K. "The legend of Paul Bunyan." *Mathematics Teaching in the Middle School*, 8(8) (April 2003), pp. 441–448.

Boling, A. N. "They don't like math? Well, let's do something." *Arithmetic Teacher*, 38(7) (March 1991), pp. 17–19.

Bradley, C. "Making a Navajo blanket design with Logo." *Arithmetic Teacher*, 40(10) (May 1993), pp. 520–523.

Bransford, J. D., Brown, A. L., and Cocking, R. R. (eds.) *How People Learn: Brian, Mind, Experience, and School*. National Research Council. Washington, DC: National Academy Press, 1999.

Bredekamp, S., and Copple, C. (eds.) *Developmentally Appropriate Practice in Early Childhood Programs*. Revised edition. Washington, DC: National Association for the Education of Young Children, 1997.

Bresser, R. *Math and Literature: Grades 4–6*. Sausalito, CA: Math Solutions, 2004.

Bright, G. W., Harvey, J. G., and Wheeler, M. M. "Fair games, unfair games." In *Teaching Statistics and Probability*, 1981 Yearbook of the National Council of Teachers of Mathematics (ed. A. Shulte). Reston, VA: NCTM, 1981, pp. 49–59.

Bright, G. W. "Understanding children's reasoning". *Teaching Children Mathematics*, 3(1) (September 1996), pp. 18–22.

Bright, G. W., and Hoeffner, K. "Measurement, probability, statistics and graphing." In *Research Ideas for the Classroom: Middle Grades Mathematics* (ed. D. T. Owens). Reston, VA: NCTM and New York: Macmillan, 1993, pp. 78–98.

Bright, G. W., Brewer, W., McClain, K., and Mooney, E. S. *Navigating through Data Analysis in Grades 6 through 8*. Reston, VA: NCTM, 2003.

Bright, G. W., Frierson, D., Jr., Tarr, J. E., and Thomas, C. *Navigating through Probability in Grades 6 through 8*. Reston, VA: NCTM, 2003.

Bright, G., Joyner, J., and Wallis, C. "Assessing proportional reasoning." *Mathematics Teaching in the Middle School*, 9(3) (November 2003), pp. 166–172,

Brodesky, A., Gross, F., McTigue, A., and Tierney, C. "Planning strategies for students with special needs: A professional development activity." *Teaching Children Mathematics*, 11(3) (October 2004), pp. 146–154.

Brown, S. I., and Walter, M. I. *The Art of Problem Posing* (2nd Ed.). Hillsdale, NJ: Lawrence Erlbaum, 1990.

Brownell, W. A. "Psychological considerations in the learning and the teaching of arithmetic." In *The Teaching of Arithmetic*, Tenth Yearbook of the National Council of Teachers of Mathematics (ed. W. D. Reeves). Reston, VA: NCTM, 1935, pp. 1–31.

Brownell, W. A., and Chazal, C. B. "The effects of premature drill in third-grade arithmetic." *Journal of Educational Research*, 29(1) (September 1935), pp. 17–28.

Brownell, W. A. "An experiment on 'borrowing' in third-grade arithmetic." *Journal of Educational Research*, 41(3) (November 1947), pp. 161–171.

Bruner, J. *Actual Minds, Possible Worlds*. Cambridge, MA.: Harvard University Press, 1986.

Brutlag, D. *Chance Encounters: Probability in Games and Simulation*. Palo Alto, CA: Creative, 1996.

Burke, M., and Curcio, F. (eds.) *Learning Mathematics for a New Century*, 2000 Yearbook of the National Council of Teachers of Mathematics. Reston, VA: NCTM, 2000.

Burns, M. "The role of questioning." *Arithmetic Teacher*, 32(6) (February 1985), pp. 14–16.

Burns, M. "Introducing division through problem-solving experiences." *Arithmetic Teacher*, 38(8) (April 1991), pp. 14–18.

Burns, M. *Math by All Means: Place Value Grade 1–2*. Sausalito, CA: Math Solutions, 1994.

Burns, M. *Measuring Up!: Experiments, Puzzles, and Games Exploring Measurement*. New York: Atheneum Books for Young Readers, 1995.

Burns, M. *50 Problem-Solving Lessons: Grade 1–6*. Sausalito, CA: Marilyn Burns Education Associates, New York: White Plains, 1996.

Burns, M. "What I learned from teaching second grade." *Teaching Children Mathematics*, 3(3) (November 1996), pp. 127–134.

Burns, M. *Mathematics: Assessing Understanding, Grades K–6* (Video). Vernon Hills, IL: ETA/Cuisenaire Company.

Burns, M. *About Teaching Mathematics: A K–8 Resource*. Sausalito, CA: Math Solutions, 2000.

Burns, M., and Sheffield, S. *Math and Literature: Grades K–1 and 2–3*, Sausalito, CA: Math Solutions, 2004.

Burton, G., Mills, A., Lennon, C., and Parker, C. *Number Sense and Operations*. Reston, VA: NCTM, 1993.

Bush, W. S. *Mathematics Assessment: Cases and Discussion Questions for Grades K–5*. Reston, VA: NCTM, 2001.

Cai, J. "Developing algebraic reasoning in the elementary grades." *Teaching Children Mathematics*, 5(4) (December 1998), pp. 225–230.

Caine, R., and Caine, G. "Reinventing schools through brain-based learning." *Educational Leadership*, 52(7) (April 1995), pp. 43–47.

Campbell, P. F. "Connecting instructional practice to student thinking." *Teaching Children Mathematics*, 4(2) (October 1997), pp. 106–110.

Campbell, P. F., and Rowan, T. E. "Teacher questions + student language + diversity = mathematical power." In *Multicultural and Gender Equity in the Mathematics Classroom: The Gift of Diversity*, 1997 Yearbook of the National Council of Teachers of Mathematics (eds. K. Trentacosta and M. J. Kenney). Reston, VA: NCTM, 1997, pp. 60–70.

Carpenter, T. P., and Levi, L. "Building a foundation for learning algebra in the elementary grades." In *Brief*, 1(2) (Fall 2000), pp. 1–8.

Carpenter, T. P., and Romberg, T. A. *Powerful Practices in Mathematics and Science*. Madison, WI: The Board of Regents of the University of Wisconsin System, 2004.

Carpenter, T. P., Corbitt, M. K., Kepner, H. S., Jr., Lindquist, M. M., and Reys, R. E. *Results from the Second Mathematics Assessment of the National Assessment of Educational Progress*. Reston, VA: NCTM, 1981.

Carpenter, T. P., Franke, M. L., Jacobs, V. R., Fennema, E., and Empson, S. B. "A longitudinal study of invention and understanding in children's multidigit addition and subtraction." *Journal for Research in Mathematics Education*, 29(1) (1998), pp. 3–20.

Carpenter, T. P., Franke, M. L., and Levi, L. *Thinking Mathematically: Integrating Arithmetic and Algebra in the Elementary School*. Portsmouth, NH: Heinemann, 2003.

Carroll, W. M., and Porter, D. "Invented strategies can develop meaningful mathematics procedures." *Teaching Children Mathematics*, 3(7) (March 1997), pp. 370–374.

Cavanagh, M., Dacey, L., Findell, C., Greenes, C., Jensen-Sheffield, L., and Small, M. *Navigating through Number and Operations in Prekindergarten–Grade 2*, Reston, VA: NCTM, 2004.

Chambers, D. L. "Improving instruction by listening to children." *Teaching Children Mathematics*, 1(6) (February 1995), pp. 378–380.

Chapin, S., Koziol, A., MacPherson, J., and Rezba, C. *Navigating through Data Analysis and Probability in Grades 3 through 5*. Reston, VA: NCTM, 2002.

Charles, R. I., Lester, F. K., Jr., and O'Daffer, P. *How to Evaluate Progress in Problem Solving*. Reston, VA: NCTM, 1987.

Charles, R. I., Lester, F. K., Jr., and Lambdin, D. V. *Problem Solving Experiences: Making Sense of Mathematics.* (Grades 3–8). Parsippany, NJ: Dale Seymour, 2005.

Ciochine, J. G., and Polivka, G. "The missing link? Writing in mathematics class!" *Mathematics Teaching in the Middle School,* 2(5) (March–April 1997), pp. 316–320.

Clark, F. B., and Kamii, C. "Identification of multiplicative thinking in children in grades 1–5." *Journal for Research in Mathematics Education,* 27(1) (January 1996), pp. 41–51.

Clarke, D. J. "Activating assessment alternatives in mathematics." *Arithmetic Teacher,* 39(6) (February 1992), pp. 24–29.

Clements, L. L. "A model for understanding, using, and connecting representations." *Teaching Children Mathematics,* 11(2) (September 2004), pp. 97–101.

Clements, D. H., and McMillen, S. "Rethinking 'concrete' manipulatives." *Teaching Children Mathematics,* 2(5) (January 1996), pp. 270–279.

Clements, D. H. "(Mis?)constructing constructivism." *Teaching Children Mathematics,* 4(4) (December 1997), pp. 198–200.

Clements, D. H. "Subitizing: What is it? Why teach it?" *Teaching Children Mathematics* 5(7) (March 1999a), pp. 400–405.

Clements, D. H. "The effective use of computers with young children." In *Mathematics in the Early Years.* Reston, VA: NCTM, 1999b.

Clements, D. H. "Teaching and learning geometry." In *A Research Companion to Principles and Standards for School Mathematics* (eds. J. Kilpatrick, W. G. Martin, and D. Schifter). Reston, VA: NCTM, 2000, pp. 151–178.

Coburn, T., Bushey, B., Holton, L., Latozas, D., Mortimer, D., and Shotwell, D. *Patterns.* Reston, VA: NCTM, 1992.

Collinson, J. "Using performance assessment to determine mathematical dispositions." *Arithmetic Teacher,* 39(6) (February 1992), pp. 40–47.

Confer, C. *Math by All Means: Geometry Grade 2.* Sausalito, CA: Math Solutions, 1994.

Cooney, T. J., Sanchez, W. B., and Ice, N. F. "Interpreting teacher's movement toward reform in mathematics assessment." *Mathematics Educator,* 11(1) (Winter 2001), pp. 10–14.

Copley, J. *Mathematics in the Early Years.* Reston, VA: NCTM, 1999.

Corwin, R., and Friel, S. *Used Numbers–Statistics: Prediction and Sampling,* Grades 5–6. Menlo Park, CA.: Dale Seymour, 1990.

Countryman, J. *Writing to Learn Mathematics: Strategies That Work.* Portsmouth, NH: Heinemann, 1992.

Cramer, K., Post, T., and Currier, S. "Learning and teaching ratio and proportion: Research implications." In *Research Ideas for the Classroom: Middle Grades Mathematics* (ed. D. T. Owens). Reston, VA: NCTM, 1993, pp. 159–178.

Cramer, K. A., Post, T. R., and DelMas, R. C. "Initial fraction learning by fourth and fifth grade students: A comparison of the effects of using commercial curricula with the effects of using the Rational Number Project curriculum." *Journal for Research in Mathematics Education,* 33(2) (March 2002), pp. 111–144.

Cross, L., and Hynes, M. C. "Assessing mathematics learning for students with learning differences." *Arithmetic Teacher,* 41(7) (March 1994), pp. 371–377.

Crowley, M. L. "The van Hiele model of the development of geometric thought." In *Learning and Teaching Geometry, K–12,* 1987 Yearbook of the National Council of Teachers of Mathematics (ed. M. M. Lindquist). Reston, VA: NCTM, 1987, pp. 1–16.

Crown, W. "Using technology to enhance a problem-based approach to teaching: What will and will not work." In *Teaching Mathematics through Problem Solving: Prekindergarten–Grade 6.* (ed. F. K. Lester, Jr.). Reston, VA: NCTM, 2003, pp. 217–228.

Cuoco, A. A. (ed.). *The Roles of Representation in School Mathematics,* 2001 Yearbook of the National Council of Teachers of Mathematics. Reston, VA: NCTM, 2001.

Davidson, N. *Cooperative Learning in Mathematics: A Handbook for Teachers.* Reading, MA: Addison-Wesley, 1990.

Dehaene, S. *The Number Sense: How the Mind Creates Mathematics.* New York: Getty Center for Education in the Arts, 2000.

De La Cruz, Y. "Reversing the trend: Latino families in real partnerships with schools." *Teaching Children Mathematics,* 5(5) (January 1999), pp. 296–300.

Desoete, A., Roeyers, H., and Buysse, A. "Metacognition and mathematical problem solving in grade 3." *Journal of Learning Disabilities,* 34(5) (September–October 2001), pp. 435–439.

Dienes, Z. P. *Building Up Mathematics.* London: Hutchinson Education, 1960.

Diezmann, C., Thornton, C., and Watters, J. "Addressing the needs of exceptional students through problem solving." In *Teaching Mathematics through Problem Solving: Prekindergarten–*

Grade 6 (ed. F. K. Lester, Jr.). Reston, VA: NCTM, 2003, pp. 169–182.

Driscoll, M. J. "Diagnosis: Taking the mathematical pulse." In *Research within Research: Elementary School Mathematics*. Reston, VA: NCTM, 1981.

Driscoll, M. J. *Fostering Algebraic Thinking*. Portsmouth, NH: Heinemann, 1999.

Ducolon, C. K. "Quality literature as a springboard to problem solving." *Teaching Children Mathematics*, 6(7) (March 2000), pp. 442–447.

Dwyer, J. "Ordering rectangles: Which is bigger?" In *Teaching Mathematics through Problem Solving: Prekindergarten–Grade 6* (eds. F. K. Lester, Jr., and R. I. Charles). Reston, VA: NCTM, 2003, pp. 143–147.

Ebeling, D., Deschenes, C., and Sprague, J. *Adapting Curriculum and Instruction in Inclusive Classrooms: Staff Development Kit*. Bloomington, IN: Institute for the Study of Developmental Disabilities, 1994.

Economopoulos, K., and Russell, S. J. "Putting together and taking apart: addition and subtraction." A unit in the *Investigations in Number, Data, Space Curriculum*. White Plains, NY: Dale Seymour, 1998.

Economopoulos, K., Tierney, C., and Russell, S. J. *Investigations in Number, Data, and Space: Arrays and Shares*. Glenview, IL: Pearson Education, Inc. 2004.

Edwards, T. G. "Using ancient Egyptian fractions to review fraction concepts. "*Mathematics Teaching in the Middle School*, 10(5) (December 2004–January 2005), pp. 226–229.

Ellett, K. "Making a million meaningful, "*Mathematics Teaching in the Middle School*, 10(8) (April 2005), pp. 416–423.

Ellington, A. J. "A meta-analysis of the effects of calculators on students' achievement and attitude levels in precollege mathematics classes." *Journal for Research in Mathematics Education*, 34(5) (November 2003) pp. 433–463.

Elliott, P. (ed.). *Communicating in Mathematics: K–12 and Beyond*, 1996 Yearbook of the National Council of Teachers of Mathematics. Reston, VA: NCTM, 1996.

English, L. "Problem solving with combinations." *Arithmetic Teacher*, 40(2) (October 1992), pp. 72–77.

Epsom, S. B. "Low-performing students and teaching fractions for understanding: An interactional analysis." *Journal for Research in Mathematics Education*, 34(4) (July 2003), pp. 305–343.

Erickson, D. "Percentages and Cuisenaire rods." *Mathematics Teacher*, 83(3) (November 1990), pp. 648–654.

Evertson, C., Emmer, E., and Brophy, J. "Predictors of effective teaching in junior high mathematics classrooms." *Journal for Research in Mathematics Education*, 11 (May 1980), pp. 167–178.

Farivar, S., and Webb, N. M. "Helping and getting help—Essential skills for effective group problem solving." *Arithmetic Teacher*, 41(9) (May 1994), pp. 521–525.

Fennell, F. *Number Sense Now!* Reston, VA: NCTM. 1992.

Fennell, F., Ferrini-Mundy, J., Ginsburg, H., Greenes, C., Murphy, S., and Tate, W. *Silver Burdett Ginn Mathematics, Grade 4, Volume 1*. Parsippany, NJ: Silver Burdett Ginn, 1998.

Fennema, E., Peterson, P. L., Carpenter, T. P., and Lubinski, C. "Teacher attributions and beliefs about girls, boys and mathematics." *Educational Studies in Mathematics*, 21(1) (February 1990), pp. 55–69.

Fischbein, E., Nello, M. S., and Marino, M. S. "Factors affecting probabilistic judgments in children and adolescents." *Educational Studies in Mathematics*, 22(6) (December 1991), pp. 523–549.

Fitzgerald, W. M., and Bouck, M. K. "Models of instruction." In *Research Ideas for the Classroom: Middle Grades Mathematics* (ed. D. T. Owens). Reston, VA: NCTM, and New York: Macmillan, 1993, pp. 244–258.

Folkson, S. "Meaningful communication among children: Data collection." In *Communication in Mathematics*, 1996 Yearbook of the National Council of Teachers of Mathematics (ed. P. Elliott). Reston, VA: NCTM, 1996, pp. 29–34.

Ford, M. I. "The writing process: A strategy for problem solvers." *Arithmetic Teacher*, 38(3) (November 1990), pp. 35–38.

Fosnot, C. T., and Dolk, M. *Young Mathematicians at Work: Constructing Number Sense, Addition, and Subtraction*. Portsmouth, NH: Heinemann, 2001.

Franke, M. L., and Carey, D. A. "Young children's perceptions of mathematics in problem-solving environments." *Journal for Research in Mathematics Education*, 28(1) (January 1997), pp. 8–25.

Frederick, B., and Williams, N. "Thinking geometrically: Totally tessellated." *Teaching Children Mathematics*, 10(8) (March 2004), p. 358.

Friel, S., "Teaching statistics: What's average?" In *The Teaching and Learning of Algorithms in School Mathematics*, 1998 Yearbook of the

National Council of Teachers of Mathematics (ed. L. J. Morrow). Reston, VA: NCTM, 1998, pp. 208–217.

Friel, S., Mokros, J., and Russell, S. J. *Used Numbers—Middles, Means, and In-Betweens, Grades 5, 6*. Palo Alto, CA: Dale Seymour, 1992.

Friel, S., Bright, G., and Curcio, F. "Understanding students' understanding of graphs." *Mathematics Teaching in the Middle School*, 3(3) (November–December 1997), pp. 224–227.

Friel, S., Curcio, F., and Bright, G. Making sense of graphs. *Journal for Research in Mathematics Education*, 32(2) (March 2001), pp. 124–157.

Funkhouser, C. "Developing number sense and basic computational skills in students with special needs." *School Science and Mathematics*, 95(5) (May 1995), pp. 236–239.

Fuson, K. Developing mathematical power in whole number operations, In *A Research Companion to Principles and Standards for School Mathematics* (eds. J. Kilpatrick, W. G. Martin, and D. Schifter). Reston, VA: NCTM, 2003, pp. 68–94.

Gallenstein, N. "Creative discovery through classification." *Teaching Children Mathematics*, 11(2) (September 2004) pp. 103–108.

Garofalo, J., and Bryant, J. "Assessing reasonableness: Some observations and suggestions." *Arithmetic Teacher,* 40(4) (December 1992), pp. 210–212.

Gay, S., and Aichele, D. B. "Middle school students' understanding of number sense related to percent." *School Science and Mathematics*, 97(1) (January 1997), pp. 27–36.

Ginsburg, H. P., and Baron, J. "Cognition: Young children's construction of mathematics." In *Research Ideas for the Classroom: Early Childhood Mathematics* (ed. R. J. Jensen). Reston, VA: NCTM, and New York: Macmillan, 1993, pp. 3–21.

Glanfield, F., Stenmark, J. K., and Bush, W. S. *Mathematics Assessment: A Practical Handbook for Grades K–2*. Reston, VA: NCTM, 2001.

Good, T. L., and Brophy, J. E. *Looking in Classrooms*, New York: Longmans, 2003 (4th ed.).

Greer, B. Multiplication and Division as Models of Situations. In *Handbook of Research on Mathematics Teaching and Learning* (ed. Douglas A. Grouws). New York: Macmillan, 1992, pp. 276–295.

Grouws, D., Smith, M., Schwan, M., and Sztajn, P. "The preparation and teaching practices of United States mathematics teachers: Grades 4 and 8." In *Results and Interpretations of the 1990 through 2000 Mathematics Assessments of the National Assessment of Educational Progress* (ed. P. Kloosterman and F. K. Lester, Jr.). Reston, VA: NCTM, 2004, pp. 221–268.

Groves, S. "Calculators, computation and number sense: Some examples from the calculators in primary mathematics project." In *Beyond Written Computation* (eds. A. McIntosh and L. Sparrow). Perth, Western Australia: Mathematics, Science & Technology Education Center, 2000, pp. 64–76.

Haberman, M. (1991). The pedagogy of poverty versus good teaching. *Phi Delta Kappan, 73*, pp. 290–294.

Harel, G., and Behr, M. "Ed's strategy for solving division problems." *Arithmetic Teacher,* 39(3) (November 1991), pp. 38–40.

Harper, S. "Students' interpretations of misleading graphs." *Mathematics Teaching in the Middle School,* 9(6) (February 2004), pp. 340–343.

Harries, T., and Dobson, A. "Oral and written methods of calculation." *Mathematics Teaching,* 154 (March 1996), pp. 32–35.

Harrington, A. "Understanding then doing: Doing then understanding." *Mathematics Teaching,* 177(4) (December 2001), pp. 10–12.

Hart, L. E., and Walker, J. "The role of affect in teaching and learning mathematics." In *Research Ideas for the Classroom: Middle Grades Mathematics* (ed. D. T. Owens). Reston, VA: NCTM, and New York: Macmillan, 1993, pp. 22–38.

Hartweg, K. "Solutions to the decorative plate hanging problem." *Teaching Children Mathematics*, 10(5) (December 2004–January 2005), pp. 280–284.

Hembree, R., and Dessart, D. J. "Effects of hand-held calculators in precollege mathematics education: A meta-analysis." *Journal for Research in Mathematics Education,* 17(2) (March 1986), pp. 83–99.

Hembree, R., and Dessart, D. J. "Research on calculators in mathematics education." In *Calculators in Mathematics Education*, 1992 Yearbook of the National Council of Teachers of Mathematics (ed. J. Fey). Reston, VA: NCTM, 1992, pp. 23–32.

Henrion, C. *Women in Mathematics: The Addition of Difference*. Bloomington, IN: Indiana University Press, 1998.

Herrell, A. L. *Fifty Strategies for Teaching English Language Learners*. Upper Saddle River, NJ: Merrill, 2000.

Hiebert, J. "Signposts for teaching mathematics through problem solving." In *Teaching Mathematics through Problem Solving: Prekindergarten–*

Grade 6 (eds. R. I. Charles and F. K. Lester, Jr.). Reston, VA: NCTM, 2003a, pp. 53–61.

Hiebert, J. "What research says about the NCTM Standards." In *A Research Companion to Principles and Standards for School Mathematics* (eds. J. Kilpatrick, W. G. Martin, and D. Schifter). Reston, VA: NCTM, 2003b, pp. 5–23.

Hiebert, J. "Relationships between Research and the NCTM Standards." *Journal for Research in Mathematics Education, 30* (January 1999), pp. 3–19.

Hiebert, J., and Carpenter, T. P. "Learning and teaching with understanding." In *Handbook of Research on Mathematics Teaching and Learning* (ed. D. Grouws). New York: Macmillan, 1992, pp. 65–97.

Hiebert, J., Carpenter, T. P., Fennema, E., Fuson, K., Wearne, D., Murray, H., Olivier, A., and Human, P. *Making Sense: Teaching and Learning Mathematics with Understanding*. Portsmouth, NH: Heinemann, 1997.

Hiebert, J., Carpenter, T. P., Fuson, K., Murray, A., Oliver P. H., and Wearne, D. *Designing Classrooms for Learning Mathematics with Understanding*. Portsmouth, NH: Heinemann Educational Books, 1997.

Hildebrand, C., Ludeman, C. J., and Mullin, J. "Integrating mathematics with problem solving using the mathematician's chair." *Teaching Children Mathematics*, 5(7) (March 1999), pp. 434–441.

Hirigoyen, H. "Dialectal variations in the language of mathematics: A source for multicultural experiences." In *Multicultural and Gender Equity in the Mathematics Classroom: The Gift of Diversity*, 1997 Yearbook of the National Council of Teachers of Mathematics (ed. J. Trentacosta). Reston, VA: NCTM, 1997.

Holloway, J. "Closing the minority achievement gap in math." *Educational Leadership*, 61(5) (February 2004), pp. 84–86.

Hope, J. A., Reys, B. J., and Reys, R. E. *Mental Math in the Middle Grades*. Palo Alto, CA: Dale Seymour, 1987.

Hope, J. A., Leutzinger, L., Reys, B. J., and Reys, R. E. *Mental Math in the Primary Grades*. Palo Alto, CA: Dale Seymour, 1987.

Houghton Mifflin. *Mathematics, Grade 6*. Boston, MA: Houghton Mifflin, 2002.

House, P. (ed.). *Connecting Mathematics across the Curriculum*, 1995 Yearbook of the National Council of Teachers of Mathematics. Reston, VA: NCTM, 1995.

Huinker, D. "Calculators as learning tools for young children's explorations of numbers." *Teaching Children Mathematics*, 8(6) (February 2002), pp. 316–321.

Huinker, D., Freckman, J. L., and Steinmeyer, M. B. "Subtraction strategies from children's thinking: Moving toward fluency with greater numbers." *Teaching Children Mathematics*, 9(6) (February 2003), pp. 347–353.

Hulme, J. N. *Counting by Kangaroos: A Multiplication Concept Book*. New York: Scientific American Books for Young Readers, 1995.

Hutchins, P. *The Doorbell Rang*. New York; Green Willow Books, 1986.

Irwin, K. C. "Using everyday knowledge of decimals to enhance understanding." *Journal for Research in Mathematics Education*, 32(4) (July 2001), pp. 399–420.

Jacobson, C., and Lehrer, R. "Teacher appropriation and student learning of geometry through design." *Journal for Research in Mathematics Education*, 31 1(1) (January 2000), pp. 71–88.

Jitendra, A. "Teaching students math problem-solving through graphic representations." *Teaching Exceptional Children*. Arlington, VA: Council for Exceptional Children.

Jones, G. A. (ed.) *Exploring Probability in School: Challenges for Teaching and Learning*. Dordrecht, The Netherlands: Kluwer Academic, 2005.

Jones, G. A., Langrall, C. W., Thornton, C., and Mogill, A. T. Students' probabilistic thinking in instruction. *Journal for Research in Mathematics Education*, 30(5) (November 1999), pp. 487–519.

Joslyn, R. E. "Using concrete models to teach large number concepts." *Arithmetic Teacher*, 38 (March–April 2002), pp. 34–39.

Kabiri, M. S., and Smith, N. L. "Turning traditional textbook problems into open-ended problems." *Mathematics Teaching in the Middle School*, 9(3) (November 2003), pp. 186–192.

Kamii, C., and Lewis, B. A. "Achievement tests in primary mathematics: Perpetuating lower-order thinking." *Arithmetic Teacher*, 38(9) (May 1991), pp. 4–9.

Kamii, C., and Dominick, A. "The harmful effects of algorithms in grades 1–4." In *The Teaching and Learning of Algorithms in School Mathematics*, 1998 Yearbook of the National Council of Teachers of Mathematics (eds. L. J. Morrow and M. J. Kenney). Reston, VA: NCTM, 1998, pp. 130–140.

Kamii, C., Lewis, B. A., and Livingston, S. J. "Primary arithmetic: Children inventing their own procedures." *Arithmetic Teacher*, 41(4) (December 1993), pp. 200–203.

Karp, K. and Howell, P. "Building Responsibility for Learning in Students with Special Needs." *Teaching Children Mathematics*, 11(3), (October 2004), pp. 118–126.

Kazemi, E., and Stipek, D. "Promoting conceptual thinking in four upper-elementary mathematics classrooms." *Elementary School Journal* 102(1) (September 2001), pp. 59–80.

Kenney, P. A., and Kouba, V. L. "What do students know about measurement." In *Results and from the Sixth Mathematics Assessment of the National Assessment of Educational Progress* (eds. P. A. Kenney and E. A. Silver). Reston, VA: NCTM, 1997, pp. 141–163.

Kenney, P. A., and Silver, E. A. "Student self-assessment in mathematics." In Norman L. Webb and Auhur F. Coxford (eds.) *Assessment in the Mathematics Classroom*, 1993 Yearbook, pp. 229–238, Reston, VA: National Council of Teachers of Mathematics.

Kenney, P. A., and Silver, E. A. (eds.). *Results from the Sixth Mathematics Assessment of the National Assessment of Educational Progress*. Reston, VA: NCTM, 1997.

Kenney, P., Lindquist, M., & Heffernan, C. "Butterflies and caterpillars: Multiplicative and proportional reasoning in the early grades" In *Making Sense of Fractions, Ratios, and Proportions* (eds. B. Litwiller & G. Bright). Reston, VA: National Council of Teachers of Mathematics, 2002.

Kilpatrick, J., Swafford, J., and Findell, B. (eds.) *Adding It Up: Helping Children Learn Mathematics*, Washington, DC: National Academy Press, 2001.

Kilpatrick, J., Martin, G., and Schifter, D. (eds.) *Research Companion to Principles and Standards for School Mathematics*. Reston, VA: NCTM, 2003.

Klein, A. S., Beishuizen, M., and Treffers, A. "The empty number line in Dutch second grade." In *Lessons Learned from Research* (eds. J. Sowder and B. Schappelle). Reston, VA: NCTM, 2002, pp. 41–43.

Kloosterman, P. W., and Lester, F. K., Jr. (eds.). *Results and Intrepretations of the 1990 through 2000 Mathematics Assessment of the National Assessment of Educational Progress*. Reston, VA: NCTM, 2004.

Kloosterman, P., Warfield, J., Wearne, D., Koc, Y., Martin, G., and Strutchens, M. "Fourth-grade students' knowledge of mathematics and perceptions of learning mathematics." In *Results and Interpretations of the 1990 through 2000 Mathematics Assessments of the Educational Progress* (eds. P. Kloosterman and F. K. Lester, Jr.). Reston, VA: NCTM, 2004, pp. 71–103.

Koehler, M. S., and Grouws, D. A. "Mathematics teaching practices and their effects." In *Handbook of Research on Mathematics Teaching and Learning* (ed. D. Grouws). New York: Macmillan, 1992, pp. 115–126.

Koontz, T. *Multicultural and Gender Equity in the Mathematics Classroom: The Gift of Diversity*. Reston, VA: NCTM, 1997.

Kostelnik, M., Soderman, A., and Whiren, A. *Developmentally Appropriate Curriculum: Best Practices in Early Childhood Education*. 3rd Ed. Upper Saddle River, NJ: Pearson Education, 2004.

Kouba, V. L., and Franklin, K. "Multiplication and division: Sense making and meaning." In *Research Ideas for the Classroom: Early Childhood Mathematics* (ed. R. J. Jensen). Reston, VA: NCTM, and New York: Macmillan, 1993, pp. 103–126.

Kouba, V. L., and Franklin, K. "Research into practice: Multiplication and division: Sense making and meaning." *Teaching Children Mathematics*, 1(9) (May 1995), pp. 574–577.

Kroll, D. L., Masingila, J. O., and Mau, S. T. "Cooperative problem solving: But what about grading?" *Arithmetic Teacher*, 39(6) (February 1992), pp. 17–23.

Kuhs, T. M. *Measure for Measure: Using Portfolios in K–8 Mathematics*. Portsmouth, NH: Heinemann, 1997.

Labinowicz, E. *Learning from Children: New Beginnings for Teaching Numerical Thinking*. Menlo Park, CA: Addison-Wesley, 1985.

Lambdin, D. V., and Walker, V. L. "Planning for classroom portfolio assessment." *Arithmetic Teacher*, 41(6) (February 1994), pp. 318–324.

Lambdin, D. V., Kehle, P. E., and Preston, R. V. (eds.). *Emphasis on Assessment: Readings from NCTM's School-Based Journals*. Reston, VA: NCTM, 1996.

Lampert, M. *Teaching Problems and the Problems of Teaching*. New Haven, CT: Yale University Press, 2001.

Langrall, C., and Swafford, J. "Three balloons for two dollars: Developing proportional reasoning." *Mathematics Teaching in the Middle School*, 6(4) (December 2000), pp. 254–261.

Lappan, G. "What do we have and where do we go from here?" *Arithmetic Teacher*, 40(9) (May 1993), pp. 524–526.

Lappan, G., Fey, J., Fitzgerald, W., Friel, S., and Phillips, E. *Getting to Know Connected Mathematics: A Guide to the Connected Mathematics Curriculum.* White Plains, NY: Dale Seymour, 1996.

Lehrer, R. "Developing understanding in measurement." In *A Research Companion to Principles and Standards for School Mathematics* (eds. J. Kilpatrick, W. G. Martin, and D. Schifter). Reston, VA: NCTM, 2003, pp. 179–192.

Lehrer, R., and Curtis, C. L. "Why are some solids perfect? Conjectures and experiments by third graders." *Teaching Children Mathematics,* 6(6) (January 2000), pp. 324–329.

Leinhardt, G., Putnam, R. T., Stein, M. K., and Baxter, J. "Where subject knowledge matters." In *Advances in Research on Teaching: Teachers' Subject Matter Knowledge and Classroom Instruction Volume 2* (ed. J. Brophy) Greenwich, CT: JAI Press, 1991.

Lembke, L. O., and Reys, B. J. "The development of and interaction between intuitive and school-taught ideas about percent." *Journal for Research in Mathematics Education,* 25(3) (May 1994), pp. 237–259.

Lemke, M., Sen, A., Pahlke, E., Partelow, L., Miller, D., Williams, T., Kastberg, D., and Jocelyn, L. *International Outcomes of Learning in Mathematics Literacy and Problem Solving: PISA 2003 Results from the U. S. Perspective.* Washington, DC: National Center for Education Statistics, 2004.

Lesh, R., and Landau, M. *Acquisition of Mathematical Concepts and Processes,* New York: Academic Press, 1983.

Lesh, R., Post, T., and Behr, M. "Proportional reasoning." In *Number Concepts and Operations in the Middle Grades* (eds. J. Hiebert and M. Behr). Reston, VA: National Council of Teachers of Mathematics, 1998, pp. 93–118.

Lester, F. K., Jr., and Charles, R. I. *Teaching Mathematics through Problem Solving: Prekindergarten–Grade 6.* Reston, VA: NCTM, 2003.

Leutzinger, L. P. "Developing thinking strategies for addition facts." *Teaching Children Mathematics,* 6(1) (September 1999), pp. 14–18.

Levin, B., Berger, D., and Cave, L. "Where did you go this summer?" *Teaching Children Mathematics,* 8(1) (September 2001), pp. 18–20.

Lindquist, M. M., "Assessing through questioning." *Arithmetic Teacher,* 35(5) (January 1988), pp. 16–18.

Lindquist, M. M., Brown, C. A., Carpenter, T. P., Kouba, V. L., Silver, E. A., and Swafford, J. O. *Results from the Fourth Mathematics Assessment of the National Assessment of Educational Progress.* Reston, VA: NCTM, 1988.

Lindquist, M., Lauquire, J., Gardner, A., and Shekaramiz, S. *Making Sense of Data.* Reston, VA: NCTM, 1992.

Lipka, J., Wildfeuer, S., Wahlberg, N., George, M., and Ezran, D. R. "Elastic geometry and storyknifing: A Yup'ik Eskimo example." *Teaching Children Mathematics,* 7(7) (February 2000), pp. 337–343.

Litwiller, B., and Bright, G. (eds.) *Making Sense of Fractions, Ratios, and Proportions,* 2002 Yearbook of the National Council of Teachers of Mathematics. Reston, VA: National Council of Teachers of Mathematics, 2002.

Long, M. J., and Ben-Hur, M. "Informing learning through the clinical interview." *Arithmetic Teacher,* 38(6) (February 1991), pp. 44–46.

Losq, C. "Number concepts and special needs students: The power of ten-frame tiles." *Teaching Children Mathematics,* 11(6) (February 2005), pp. 310–314.

Lubienski, S. T., McGraw, R., and Strutchens, M. "NAEP findings regarding gender: Mathematics achievement, student affect, and learning practices." In *Results and Interpretations of the 1990 through 2000 Mathematics Assessments of the National Assessment of Educational Progress.* Reston, VA: NCTM, 2004, pp. 305–336.

Lubinski, C., and Otto, A. D. "Meaningful mathematical representations and early algebraic reasoning." *Teaching Children Mathematics,* 9(2) (October 2002), pp. 76–80.

Ma, L. *Knowing and Teaching Elementary Mathematics: Teachers' Understanding of Fundamental Mathematics in China and the United States.* Mahwah, N. J: Lawrence Erlbaum, 1999.

Mack, N. K. "Connecting to develop computational fluency with fractions." *Teaching Children Mathematics,* 10(3) (November 2004), pp. 226–232.

Mann, R. L. "Responses to the pattern-block-quilts problem." *Teaching Children Mathematics,* 11(1) (August 2004), pp. 28–35.

Mann, R. L. "Balancing act: The truth behind the equals sign." *Teaching Children Mathematics,* 11(2) (September 2004), pp. 65–69.

Markovitz, Z., and Sowder, J. "Developing number sense: An intervention study in grade 7." *Journal for Research in Mathematics Education,* 25(1) (January 1994), pp. 4–29.

Martinie, S., and Bay-Williams, J. "Using literature to engage students in proportional reasoning."

Mathematics Teaching in the Middle School, 9(3) (November 2003), pp. 142–148.

Marzano, R., Pickering, D., and Pollock, J. *Classroom Instruction that Works.* Alexandria, VA: ASCD, 2001.

Mathematical Sciences Education Board. *Measuring Up: Prototypes for Mathematics Assessment.* Washington, DC: National Academy Press, 1993.

McClain, K., and Cobb, P. "An analysis of development of sociomathematical norms in one first-grade classroom." *Journal for Research in Mathematics Education,* 32(3) (May 2001), pp. 236–266.

McGivney-Burelle, J. M. "Connecting the dots: Network problems that foster mathematical reasoning." *Teaching Children Mathematics,* 11(5) (December 2004–January 2005), pp. 272–277.

McIntosh, A., and Sparrow, L. *Beyond written computation,* Perth, Western Australia: MASTEC, Edith Cowan University, 2004.

McIntosh, A., Reys, B. J., and Reyes, R. E. "A proposed framework for examining basic number sense." *For the Learning of Mathematics,* 12(3) November 1992, pp. 2–8.

McIntosh, A., Reys, B. J., and Reys, R. E. "Mental computation performance in Australia, Japan and the United States." *Educational Studies in Mathematics,* 29(3) (October 1995), pp. 237–258.

McIntosh, A., Reys, B. J., Reys, R. E., and Hope, J. *Number Sense: Simple Effective Number Sense Experiences: Grades 1–2, 3–4, 4–6, 6–8.* Palo Alto, CA: Dale Seymour, 1997.

Metz, M. L. "Making sense of percent." *Mathematics Teaching in the Middle School,* 9(1) (September 2003), pp. 44–45.

Mewborn, D. "Teaching, teachers' knowledge, and their professional development." In *A Research Companion to Principles and Standards for School Mathematics* (eds. J. Kilpatrick, W. G. Martin, and D. Schifter). Reston, VA: NCTM, 2003.

Midgett, C., and Trafton, P. R. "Learning through problems: A powerful approach to teaching mathematics." *Teaching Children Mathematics,* 7(9) (May 2001), p. 532.

Miller, J. L., and Fey, J. T. "Proportional reasoning." *Mathematics Teaching in the Middle School,* 5(5), (January 2000), pp. 310–314.

Miller, P. C., and Endo, H. "Understanding and meeting the needs of ESL students." *Phi Delta Kappan,* 85(10) (June 2004), pp. 786–791.

Mills, H., O'Keefe, T., and Whitin, D. *Mathematics in the Making: Authoring Ideas in Primary Classrooms.* Portsmouth, NH: Heinemann, 1996.

Mokros, J., Russell, S. J., and Economopoulos, K. *Beyond Arithmetic: Changing Mathematics in the Elementary Classroom.* Palo Alto, CA: Dale Seymour, 1995.

Moon, C. J. "Connecting learning and teaching through assessment." *Arithmetic Teacher,* 41(1) (September 1993), pp. 13–15.

Moon, J., and Schulman, L. *Finding the Connections: Linking Assessment, Instruction, and Curriculum in Elementary Mathematics.* Portsmouth, NH: Heinemann, 1995.

Morita, J. "Capture and recapture your students' interest in statistics." *Mathematics Teaching in the Middle School,* 4(6) (March 1999), pp. 412–418.

Morrow, L. J., and Kenney, M. J. (eds.). *The Teaching and Learning of Algorithms in School Mathematics,* 1998 Yearbook of the National Council of Teachers of Mathematics. Reston, VA: NCTM, 1998.

Moses, B., Bjork, E., and Goldenberg, E. P. "Beyond problem solving: Problem posing." In *Teaching and Learning Mathematics in the 1990s.* 1990 Yearbook of the National Council of Teachers of Mathematics (ed. T. J. Cooney). Reston, VA: NCTM, 1990, pp. 82–91.

Moskal, B. "An assessment model for the mathematics classroom." *Mathematics Teaching in the Middle School* 6(3) (November 2000), pp. 192–194.

Moss, J., and Caswell, B. "Building percent dolls: Connecting linear measurement to learning ration and proportion." *Mathematics Teaching in the Middle School,* 10(2) (September 2004), pp. 68–74.

Moyer-Packenham, P. S. "A mathematical measurement mystery," *Teaching Children Mathematics,* 11(2) (September 2004), pp. 54–61.

Mullis, I. V. S., Martin, M. O., Gonzalez, E. J., and Chrostowski, S. J. *TIMSS 2003 International Mathematics Report.* Boston, MA: TIMSS and PIRLS International Study Center, 2004.

Mumme, J. *Portfolio Assessment in Mathematics.* Santa Barbara, CA: Regents of the University of California, 1990.

Mumme, J., and Shepherd, N. "Implementing the standards: Communication in mathematics." *Arithmetic Teacher,* 38(1) (September 1990), pp. 18–22.

National Center for Educational Statistics. *Pursuing Excellence: A Study of U.S. Eighth-Grade Mathe-*

matics and Science Teaching, Learning, Curriculum, and Achievement in International Context. Washington, DC, 1996.

National Council of Teachers of Mathematics. *An Agenda for Action.* Reston, VA: NCTM, 1980.

National Council of Teachers of Mathematics. *Curriculum and Evaluation Standards for School Mathematics.* Reston, VA: NCTM, 1989.

National Council of Teachers of Mathematics. *Professional Standards for Teachers of Mathematics.* Reston, VA: NCTM, 1991.

National Council of Teachers of Mathematics. *Assessment Standards for School Mathematics.* Reston, VA: NCTM, 1995.

National Council of Teachers of Mathematics. *Teaching Children Mathematics Focus Issue: Algebraic Thinking,* 3(7) (February 1997).

National Council of Teachers of Mathematics. *Algebraic Thinking, Grades K–12: Readings from NCTM's School-Based Journals and Other Publications.* Reston, VA: NCTM, 1999a.

National Council of Teachers of Mathematics. *Mathematics Teaching in the Middle School Focus Issue: Data and Chance in the Middle School Curriculum* 4(7) (March 1999b).

National Council of Teachers of Mathematics. *Principles and Standards for School Mathematics.* Reston, VA: NCTM, 2000.

National Council of Teachers of Mathematics. *Navigations—Steering through Principles and Standards: Algebra in Grades Pre-K–2 and Grades 3–5.* Reston, VA: NCTM, 2001.

National Council of Teachers of Mathematics. *Navigating through Geometry in Prekindergarten–Grade 2, Grades 3–5, and Grades 6–8.* Reston, VA: NCTM, 2002a.

National Council of Teachers of Mathematics, *Mathematics Teaching in Middle School Focus Issue: The Magic of Number,* 7(8), (April 2002b).

National Research Council. Everybody Counts: A Report to the Nation on the Future of Mathematics Education, Washington, DC: National Research Council, 1989.

National Research Council. *How People Learn: Brain, Mind, Experience, and School.* Washington, D.C.: National Academy Press, 1999.

National Research Council. *Adding It Up: Helping Children Learn Mathematics.* Washington, D.C.: National Academy Press, 2001.

National Research Council, *Helping Children Learn Mathematics.* Washington, D.C.: National Academy Press, 2002.

Neumann, M. D. "Freedom quilts." *Teaching Children Mathematics,* 11(6) February 2005, pp. 317–321.

Neuschwander, C. *Amanda Bean's Amazing Dream.* New York: Scholastic, 1998.

O'Brien, T. C., and Moss, A. C. "On the keeping of several things in mind." *Teaching Children Mathematics,* 6(2) (October 1999), pp. 118–122.

Outhred, L. N., and Mitchelmore, M. C. "Young children's intuitive understanding of rectangular area measurement." *Journal for Research in Mathematics Education,* 3(2) (March 2000), pp. 144–154.

Paulson, F. L., Paulson, P. R., and Meyer, C. A. "What makes a portfolio a portfolio?" *Educational Leadership,* 48(5) (February 1991), pp. 60–63.

Payne, J. N., and Huinker, D. M. "Early number and numeration." In *Research Ideas for the Classroom: Early Childhood Mathematics* (ed. R. J. Jensen). Reston, VA: NCTM, and New York: Macmillan, 1993, pp. 43–70.

Payne, J. N., Towsley, A. N., and Huinker, D. M. "Fractions and decimals." In *Mathematics for the Young Child* (ed. J. N. Payne). Reston, VA: NCTM, 1990, pp. 175–200.

Payne, R. *A Framework for Understanding Poverty.* Highlands: TX, aha! Process Inc., 1996.

Paznokas, L. S. "Teaching mathematics through cultural quilting." *Teaching Children Mathematics,* 9(6) (January 2003), pp. 250–256. *Mathematics,* 9(4), (December 2002), pp. 196–201.

Perry, J. A., and Adkins, S. L. "It's not just notation: Valuing children's representations." *Teaching Children Mathematics.* September 2002, pp. 196–201.

Pfenning, N. *Chances Are . . . : Making Probability & Statistics Fun to Learn & Easy to Teach.* Waco, TX: Prufrock Press, 1997.

Piaget, J. *To Understand Is to Invent.* New York: Grossman, 1972.

Polya, G. *How to Solve It.* Princeton, NJ: Princeton University Press, 1973 (1945, 1957). Worth, IL: Creative.

Pursuing Excellence: A Study of Eighth-Grade Mathematics and Science Teaching, Learning, Curriculum, and Achievement in International Context. Washington, DC, 1996.

Quinn, R., and Wiest, L. "Reinventing scrabble with middle school students." *Mathematics Teaching in the Middle School,* 5(4) (December 1999), pp. 210–213.

Ramos, L., and Lambating, J. "Risk taking: Gender differences and educational opportunity."

School Science and Mathematics, 96(2) (February 1996), pp. 94–98.

Rathmell, E. C. "Planning for instruction involves focusing on children's thinking." *Arithmetic Teacher*, 41(6) (February 1994), pp. 290–291.

Rathmell, E., and Trafton, P. "Whole number computation." In *Mathematics for the Young Child* (ed. J. N. Payne). Reston, VA: NCTM, 1990, pp. 153–172.

Renga, S., and Dalla, L. "Affect: A critical component of mathematical learning in early childhood." In *Research Ideas for the Classroom: Early Childhood Mathematics* (ed. R. J. Jensen). Reston, VA: NCTM, and New York: Macmillan, 1993, pp. 22–39.

Reys, B. J., and Barger, R. "Mental computation: Issues from the United States perspective." In *Computational Alternatives for the 21st Century: Cross Cultural Perspectives from Japan and the United States* (eds. R. E. Reys and N. Nohda). Reston, VA: NCTM, 1994, pp. 31–47.

Reys, B. J., and Long, V. M. "Teacher as architect of mathematical tasks." *Teaching Children Mathematics*, 1(5) (January 1995), pp. 296–299.

Reys, B. J., and Reys, R. E. "Computation in the elementary curriculum: Shifting the emphasis." *Teaching Children Mathematics*, 5(4) (December 1998), pp. 236–241.

Reys, B. J., Barger, R., Bruckheimer, M., Dougherty, B., Hope, J., Lembke, L., Markovitz, A., Parnas, A., Reehm, S., Sturdevant, R., and Weber, M. *Developing Number Sense in the Middle Grades*. Reston, VA: NCTM, 1991.

Reys, B. J., Reys, R., and Chavez, O. "Why textbooks matter." *Educational Leadership*, 61(5) (February 2004), pp. 61–66.

Reys, R. E. "Computation versus number sense." *Mathematics Teaching in the Middle Grades*, 4(2) (October 1998), pp. 110–112.

Reys, R. E., and Yang, D. C. "Relationship between computational performance and number sense among sixth and eighth grade students in Taiwan." *Journal for Research in Mathematics Education*, 29(2) (March 1998), pp. 225–237.

Reys, R. E., and Reys, B. J. "Estimation in the mathematics curriculum: A progress report." In *Beyond Written Computation* (eds. A. McIntosh and L. Sparrow). Perth, Western Australia: Mathematics, Science & Technology Education Center, 2004, pp. 101–113.

Reys, R. E., Reys, B. J., Nohda, N., and Emori, H. "Mental computation performance and strategy use of Japanese students in Grades 2, 4, 6, and 8." *Journal for Research in Mathematics Education*, 26(4) (July 1995), pp. 304–326.

Reys, R. E., Reys, B. J., McIntosh, A., Emanuelsson, G., Johansson, B., and Yang, D. C. "Assessing number sense of students in Australia, Sweden, Taiwan, and the United States." *School Science and Mathematics*, 99(2) (February 1999), pp. 61–70.

Reys, R., Reys, B., Lapan, R., Holliday, G., and Wasman, D. "Assessing the impact of *Standards*-based middle grades mathematics curriculum materials on student achievement." *Journal for Research in Mathematics Education*, 34(1) (January 2003), pp. 74–95.

Riddle, M., and Rodzwell, B. "Fractions: What happens between kindergarten and the army?" *Teaching Children Mathematics*, 7(4) (December 2000), pp. 202–206.

Romberg, T. A. *Reform in School Mathematics and Authentic Assessment*. Albany, NY: SUNY Press, 1995.

Romberg, T. A., and Wilson, L. "Alignment of tests with the standards." *Arithmetic Teacher*, 40(1) (September 1992), pp. 18–24.

Ron, P. "My family taught me this way." In *The Teaching and Learning of Algorithms in School Mathematics*, 1998 Yearbook of the National Council of Teachers of Mathematics (eds. L. J. Morrow and M. J. Kenney). Reston, VA: NCTM, 1998, pp. 115–119.

Ross, J., McDougall, D., Hogaboam-Gray, A., and LeSage, A. "A survey measuring elementary teachers' implementation of standards-based mathematics teaching." *Journal for Research in Mathematics Education*, 34(4) (July 2003), pp. 344–363.

Ross, R., and Kurtz, R. "Making manipulatives work: A strategy for success." *Arithmetic Teacher*, 40(5) (January 1993), pp. 254–257.

Rubenstein, R. N. "Communication strategies to support preservice mathematics teachers from diverse backgrounds." In *Multicultural and Gender Equity in the Mathematics Classroom: The Gift of Diversity*, 1997 Yearbook of the National Council of Teachers of Mathematics (ed. J. Trentacosta). Reston, VA: NCTM, 1997, pp. 214–221.

Russell, S. J. *Kindergarten, Investigations in Number, Data, and Space*. Cambridge, MA: Dale Seymour, 1997.

Russell, S. J. "Mathematical reasoning in the elementary grades." In *Developing Mathematical Reasoning in Grades K–12* (ed. L. V. Stiff). Reston, VA: NCTM, 1999, p. 1–12.

Russell, S. J. *Investigations in Number, Data, and Space: Kindergarten.* Glenview, IL: Pearson Education, Inc. 2004.

Russell, S. J., Corwin, R., and Economopoulos, K. *Investigations in Number, Data, and Space: Does It Walk, Crawl, or Swim?* Glenview, IL: Pearson Education, Inc. 2004.

Sakshaug, L. E. "Which graph is which?" *Teaching Children Mathematics*, 6(7) (March 2000), pp. 454–455.

Sakshaug, L. E., and Wohlhuter, K. A. "Responses to the Which Graph Is Which? problem." *Teaching Children Mathematics*, 7(6) (February 2001), pp. 350–353, 394–400.

Sandburg, C. *Carl Sandburg Harvest Poems 1910–1960.* New York: Harcourt, Brace, and World, 1960.

Sanford, S. "Assessing measurement in the primary classroom." In *Assessment in the Mathematics Classroom*, 1993 Yearbook of the National Council of Teachers of Mathematics (ed. N. Webb). Reston, VA: NCTM, 1993.

Scavo, T. R., and Petraroja, B. "Adventures in statistics." *Teaching Children Mathematics*, 4(7) (March 1998), pp. 394–400.

Scheibelhut, C. "I do and I understand, I reflect and I improve." *Teaching Children Mathematics*, 1(4) (December 1994), pp. 242–246.

Schifter, D. *What's Happening in Math Class? Envisioning New Practices through Teacher Narratives.* New York: Teachers College Press, 1996.

Sgroi, L. A., Gropper, N., Kilker, M. T., Rambusch, N. M., and Semonite, B. "Assessing young children's mathematical understandings." *Teaching Children Mathematics*, 1(5) (January 1995), pp. 275–277.

Shannon, B. K. "Our diets may be killing us." *Mathematics Teaching in the Middle School*, 1(6) (April–May 1995), pp. 376–382.

Shaughnessy, M. J. "Research in probability and statistics: Reflections and directions." In *Handbook of Research on Mathematics Teaching and Learning* (ed. D. Grouws). New York: Macmillan, 1992, pp. 495–514.

Sheffield, L. J., Cavanaugh, M., Dacey, L., Findel, C. R., Greenes, C. E., and Small, M. *Navigating through Data Analysis and Probability in Prekindergarten through Grade 2.* Reston, VA: NCTM, 2002.

Shigematsu, S., Iwasaki, H., and Koyama, M. "Mental computation: Evaluation, curriculum and instructional issues from the Japanese perspective." In *Computational Alternatives for the 21st Century: Cross Cultural Perspectives from Japan and the United States* (eds. R. E. Reys and N. Nohda). Reston, VA: NCTM, 1994, pp. 19–30.

Shimizu, Y. "Problem solving as a vehicle for teaching mathematics: A Japanese perspective." In *Teaching Mathematics through Problem Solving: Prekindergarten–Grade 6* (eds. F. K. Lester, Jr., and R. I. Charles). Reston, VA: NCTM, 2003, pp. 205–214.

Shulte, A. P., and Choate, S. A. *What Are My Chances?* Palo Alto, CA: Creative, 1996.

Silbey, R. "What is in the daily news? Problem-solving opportunities." *Teaching Children Mathematics*, 5(7) (March 1999), pp. 390–394.

Silver, E., and Kenny, P. A. (eds.). *Results from the Seventh Mathematics Assessment of the National Assessment of Educational Progress*, Reston, VA: National Council of Teachers of Mathematics, 2000.

Silver, E. A., Shapiro, L. J., and Deutsch, A. "Sense making and the solution of division problems involving remainders: An examination of middle school students' solution processes and their interpretations of solutions." *Journal for Research in Mathematics Education*, 24(2) (March 1993), pp. 117–135.

Smith, N. L., Lambdin, D. V., Lindquist, M. M. & Reys, R. E. *Teaching Elementary Mathematics: A Resource for Field Experiences.* Hoboken: Wiley, 2007.

Sowder, J. "Estimation and number sense." In *Handbook of Research on Mathematics Teaching and, Learning* (ed. D. Grouws). New York: Macmillan, 1992, pp. 371–389.

Sowell, E. J. "Effects of manipulative materials in mathematics instruction." *Journal for Research in Mathematics Education*, 20(5) (November 1989), pp. 498–505.

Spangler, D. A. "Assessing students' beliefs about mathematics." *Arithmetic Teacher*, 40(3) (November 1992), pp. 148–152.

Spicer, J. "Mathematics of world cultures = a world of possibilities." *Eisenhower National Clearinghouse Focus*, January 2005, pp. 8–10

Stanic, G. M. A., and Kilpatrick, J. (eds). *A History of School Mathematics, Volumes 1 and 2.* Reston, VA: NCTM, 2003.

Steele, D. "Learning mathematical language in the zone of proximal development." *Teaching Children Mathematics*, 4(1) (September 1999), pp. 38–42.

Stenmark, J. K. (ed.). *Mathematics Assessment: Myths, Models, Good Questions, and Practical Suggestions.* Reston, VA: NCTM, 1991.

Stenmark, J. K., and Bush, W. S. *Mathematics Assessment: A Practical Handbook for Grades 3–5.* Reston, VA: NCTM, 2001.

Stiff, L. V. (ed.). *Developing Mathematical Reasoning in Grades K–12,* 1999 Yearbook of the National Council of Teachers of Mathematics. Reston, VA: NCTM, 1999.

Stiggins, R. J. "Assessment crisis: The absense of assessment for learning." *Phi Delta Kappan,* 83(10) (June 2002), pp. 758–765.

Stigler, J. W., and Hiebert, J. *The Teaching Gap: Best Ideas from the World's Teachers for Improving Education in the Classroom.* New York: The Free Press, 1999.

Stohl, H., "Probability in teacher education and development." In *Exploring Probability in School: Challenges for Teaching and Learning* (ed. G. A. Jones). The Netherlands: Kluwer Academic, 2005, pp. 241–266.

Strutchens, M., Lubienski, S. T., McGraw, R., and Westbrook, S., "NAEP findings regarding race and ethnicity: Students' performance, school experiences, attitudes, and beliefs, and family influences." In *Results and Interpretations of the 1990 through 2000 Mathematics Assessments of the National Assessment of Educational Progress* (eds. P. Kloosterman and F. K. Lester, Jr.). Reston, VA: NCTM, 2004, pp. 169–304.

Stylianou, D., Kenney, P. A., Silver, E. A., and Alacaci, C. "Gaining insight into students' thinking through assessment tasks." *Mathematics Teaching in the Middle School,* 6(2) (October 2000), pp. 136–143.

Sullivan, P., and Clarke, D. "Catering to all abilities through 'good questions.'" *Arithmetic Teacher,* 39(2) (October 1991), pp. 14–18.

Sutton, J., and Krueger, A. (eds.) *ED Thoughts: What We Know about Mathematics Teaching and Learning,* Aurora, CO: McRel, 2002.

Suydam, M. N. "Planning for mathematics instructions." In *Mathematics for the Young Child* (ed. J. N. Payne). Reston, VA: NCTM, 1990.

Suydam, M. N., and Weaver, J. F. *Using Research: A Key to Elementary School Mathematics.* Columbus, OH: ERIC Clearinghouse for Science, Mathematics and Environmental Education, 1981.

Tarr, J. E. "Using middle school students' thinking in conditional probability and independence to inform instruction." (Doctoral dissertation, Illinois State University, 1997). *Dissertation Abstracts International,* 49, Z5005.

Tarr, J. E., and Jones, G. A. "A framework for assessing middle school students' thinking in conditional probability and independence." *Mathematics Education Research Journal,* 9, (1997), pp. 39–59.

Tayeh, C., and Britton, B. "Make it 36." *Teaching Children Mathematics,* 11(4) (February 2005), pp. 330–331.

Telese, J. A., and Abete, J. "Diet, ratios, proportions: A healthy mix." *Mathematics Teaching in the Middle School,* 8(1) (September 2002), pp. 8–13.

Thiessen, D., Matthias, M., and Smith, J. *The Wonderful World of Mathematics: A Critically Annotated List of Children's Books in Mathematics.* Reston, VA: NCTM, 1998.

Third International Mathematics and Science Study (TIMSS). *U.S. National Research Center Report No.7,* East Lansing, MI: TIMSS U.S. National Research Center, Michigan State University, December 1996.

Thompson, C., and Bush, W. "Improving middle school teachers' reasoning about proportional reasoning." *Mathematics Teaching in the Middle School,* 8(8) (April 2003), pp. 398–404.

Thompson, D., Austin, R., and Beckmann, C. "Using literature as a vehicle to explore proportional reasoning." In *Making Sense of Fractions, Ratios, and Proportions,* 2002 Yearbook of the National Council of Teachers of Mathematics (eds. B. Litwiller and G. Bright). Reston, VA: NCTM, pp. 130–137.

Thompson, F. "Two-digit addition and subtraction: What works?" *Arithmetic Teacher,* 38(5) (January 1991), pp. 10–13.

Thompson, I. "Teaching place value in the UK: Time for a reappraisal?" *Educational Review,* 51(3) (November 2000), pp. 291–299.

Thompson, P. W. "Research into practice: Concrete materials and teaching for mathematical understanding." *Arithmetic Teacher,* 41(9) (May 1994), pp. 556–558.

Thornton, C. A., and Wilson, S. J. "Classroom organization and models of instruction." In *Research Ideas for the Classroom: Early Childhood Mathematics* (ed. R. J. Jensen). Reston, VA: NCTM, and New York: Macmillan, 1993, pp. 269–293.

TIMS Elementary Mathematics Curriculum Project. *Math Trailblazers* (Student guide, Grade 5). Dubuque, IA: Kendall/Hunt, 1998.

Torrence, E. "Learning to think: An American third grader discovers mathematics in Holland." *Teaching Children Mathematics,* 10(2) (October 2003), pp. 90–92.

Trafton, P., and Thiessen, D. *Learning through Problems, Number Sense and Computational*

Strategies, A Resource for Primary Teachers. Portsmouth, NH: Heinemann, 1999.

Turner, P. *Among the Odds and Evens. A Tale of Adventure.* New York: Scholastic, 1999.

United States Department of Education. *Condition of Education.* Washington DC: U.S. Dept. of Education, Office of Educational Research and Improvement, National Center for Education Statistics, 2005.

University of Chicago School Mathematics Project. *Everyday Mathematics: Teacher's Reference Manual (Grades K–3).* Chicago, IL: Everyday Learning Corporation, 2001.

University of Chicago School Mathematics Project. *Everyday Mathematics: Teacher's Reference Manual Grades 4–6.* Chicago, IL: SRA/McGraw-Hill, 2002.

University of Chicago School Mathematics Project. *Everyday Mathematics: Level 3, Volume 1—Student Math Journal.* Chicago, IL: SRM/McGraw-Hill, 2004.

University of Chicago School Mathematics Project. *Everyday Mathematics: Level 3, Teacher's Lesson Guide.* Chicago, IL: SRA/McGraw-Hill, 2004.

University of Chicago School Mathematics Project. *Everyday Mathematics, Third Grade, Volume 1.* Chicago, IL: SRA/McGraw-Hill, 2004.

University of Chicago School Mathematics Project. *Everyday Mathematics, Sixth Grade Teacher's Lesson Guide, Volume 1.* Chicago, IL: SRA/McGraw-Hill, 2004.

Uy, F. "The Chinese numeration system and place value." *Teaching Children Mathematics,* 9(5) (January 2003), pp. 243–247.

Vaac, N. N. "Implement the professional standards for teaching mathematics: Questioning in the mathematics classroom." *Arithmetic Teacher,* 41(2) (October 1993), pp. 88–91.

Vacc, N. N. "Planning for instruction: Barriers to mathematics discussion." *Arithmetic Teacher,* 41(6) (February 1994), pp. 339–341.

Van de Walle, J. A. "Implementing the standards: Redefining computation." *Arithmetic Teacher,* 38(5) (January 1991), pp. 44–51.

Van Zoest, L. E., and Enyart, A. "Discourse of course: Encouraging genuine mathematical conversations." *Mathematics Teaching in the Middle School,* 4(3) (1998), pp. 150–157.

Wagreich, P., et al. *Math Trailblazers.* TIMS Elementary Mathematics Curriculum Project, The University of Illinois at Chicago, Dubuque, IA: Kendall/Hunt, 1997.

Warrington, M. A., and Kamii, C. Multiplication with fractions: A Piagetian constructivist ap-

proach. *Mathematics Teaching in the Middle School,* 3(4) (February 1998), pp. 339–343.

Washburne, C. "Mental age and the arithmetic curriculum: A summary of the committee of seven grade placement investigation to date." *Journal of Educational Research,* 23(3) (March 1931), pp. 210–231.

Watson, J. "Conditional probability: Its place in mathematics curriculum." *Mathematics Teacher,* 88(1) (January 1995), pp. 12–17.

Wearne, D., and Hiebert, J. "Place value and addition and subtraction." *Arithmetic Teacher,* 41(5) (January 1994), pp. 272–274.

Wearne, D., and Kouba, V. L. "Rational number properties and operations." In *Results from the Seventh Mathematics Assessment of the National Assessment of Educational Progress* (eds. E. A. Silver and P. A. Kenny). Reston, VA: NCTM, 2000.

Webb, N. L. (ed.) *Assessment in the Mathematics Classroom,* 1993 Yearbook of the National Council of Teachers of Mathematics Reston, VA: NCTM, 1993.

Weinberg, S. "Going beyond ten black dots." *Teaching Children Mathematics,* 2(7) (March 1996), pp. 432–435.

Weiss, I., and Pasley, J. "What is high-quality instruction?" *Educational Leadership,* 61(5) (February 2004), pp. 24–28.

Wenglinsky, H. *Does it Compute? The Relationship Between Educational Technology and Student Achievement in Mathematics.* Princeton, NJ: ETS Research Report, 1998.

Wheatley, G. H., and Wheatley, C. L. "How shall we teach column addition? Some evidence." *Arithmetic Teacher,* 25(4) (January 1978), pp. 18–19.

Whitenack, J., Knipping, N., Noringer, S., and Underwood, G. "Facilitating children's conceptions of tens and ones: The classroom teacher's important role." In *Beyond Written Computation* (eds. A. McIntosh and L. Sparrow). Perth, Western Australia: Mathematics, Science & Technology Education Center, 2004, pp. 40–50.

Whitin, D. J. "Building a mathematical community through problem posing." In *Perspectives on the Teaching of Mathematics.* 2004 Yearbook of the National Council of Teachers of Mathematics (ed. R. N. Rubenstein). Reston, VA: NCTM, 2004, pp. 129–140.

Whitin, D. J., and Wilde, S. *Read Any Good Math Lately? Children's Books for Mathematical Learning, K–6.* Portsmouth, NH: Heinemann, 1992.

Whitin, D., Mills, H. and O'Keefe, T. "Exploring subject areas with a counting book" *Teaching Children Mathematics*, 1(2) (November 1994), pp. 170–174.

Whitin, P. "Promoting problem-posing explorations." *Teaching Children Mathematics*, 11(2) (November 2004), pp. 180–186.

Wickett, M. "Serving up number sense and problem solving: Dinner at the panda palace." *Teaching Children Mathematics*, 3(9) (May 1997), pp. 476–480.

Wilde, S. "Learning to write about mathematics." *Arithmetic Teacher,* 38(6) (February 1991), pp. 38–43.

Wilson, L. D. "High stakes testing in mathematics." In *Handbook of Research in Mathematics Education* (ed. F. K. Lester, Jr.). Greenwich, CT: Information Age Publishing, in press.

Wilson, M. R., and Kraft, C. M. "Exploring mean, median and mode with a spreadsheet." *Mathematics Teaching in the Middle School,* 1(6) (September–October 1995), pp. 490–495.

Wilson, P. S., and Osborne, A. "Foundational ideas in teaching about measure." In *Teaching Mathematics in Grades K–8* (ed. T. R. Post). Toronto: Allyn and Bacon, 1988, pp. 78–110.

Wood, T., and Sellers, P. "Assessment of a problem-centered mathematics program: Third grade." *Journal for Research in Mathematics Education,* 27(3) (May 1996), pp. 337–353.

Wu, Z. "Multiplying fractions." *Teaching Children Mathematics,* 8(3) (November 2001), pp. 174–178.

Yang, D. C. Number sense performance and strategies possessed by sixth and eighth grade students in Taiwan, Unpublished doctoral dissertation, University of Missouri-Columbia, 1995.

Yoshikawa, S. "Computational estimation: Curriculum and instructional issues from the Japanese perspective." In *Computational Alternatives for the 21st Century: Cross Cultural Perspectives from Japan and the United States* (eds. R. E. Reys and N. Nohda). Reston, VA: NCTM, 1994, pp. 51–62.

Zaccaro, E. *Challenge Math for the Elementary and Middle School Student.* Bellevue, IA: Hickory Grove Press, 2000.

Zaslavsky, C. "People who live in round houses. "*Arithmetic Teacher,* 37(1) (September 1989), pp. 18–21.

Zaslavsky, C. "Symmetry in American folk art." *Arithmetic Teacher,* 38(1) (September 1990), pp. 6–13.

Zaslavsky, C. "Developing number sense: What can other cultures tell us?" *Teaching Children Mathematics*, 7(6) (February 2001), pp. 312–319.

Zaslavsky, C. "The influence of ancient Egypt on Greek and other numeration systems." *Mathematics Teaching in the Middle Grades,* 9(3) (November 2003), pp. 174–176.

A

Standards and Expectations National Council of Teachers of Mathematics, 2000

Number and Operations

Standard	Pre-K–2	Grades 3–5	Grades 6–8
Instructional programs from prekindergarten through grade 12 should enable all students to—	**EXPECTATIONS** In prekindergarten through grade 2 all students should—	**EXPECTATIONS** In grades 3–5 all students should—	**EXPECTATIONS** In grades 6–8 all students should—
Understand numbers, ways of representing numbers, relationships among numbers, and number systems	• count with understanding and recognize "how many" in sets of objects; • use multiple models to develop initial understandings of place value and the base-ten number system; • develop understanding of the relative position and magnitude of whole numbers and of ordinal and cardinal numbers and their connections; • develop a sense of whole numbers and represent and use them in flexible ways, including relating, composing, and decomposing numbers; • connect number words and numerals to the quantities they represent, using various physical models and representations; • understand and represent commonly used fractions, such as $\frac{1}{4}$, $\frac{1}{3}$, and $\frac{1}{2}$.	• understand the place-value structure of the base-ten number system and be able to represent and compare whole numbers and decimals; • recognize equivalent representations for the same number and generate them by decomposing and composing numbers; • develop understanding of fractions as parts of unit wholes, as parts of a collection, as locations on number lines, and as divisions of whole numbers; • use models, benchmarks, and equivalent forms to judge the size of fractions; • recognize and generate equivalent forms of commonly used fractions, decimals, and percents; • explore numbers less than 0 by extending the number line and through familiar applications; • describe classes of numbers according to characteristics such as the nature of their factors.	• work flexibly with fractions, decimals, and percents to solve problems; • compare and order fractions, decimals, and percents efficiently and find their approximate locations on a number line; • develop meaning for percents greater than 100 and less than 1; • understand and use ratios and proportions to represent quantitative relationships; • develop an understanding of large numbers and recognize and appropriately use exponential, scientific, and calculator notation; • use factors, multiples, prime factorization, and relatively prime numbers to solve problems; • develop meaning for integers and represent and compare quantities with them.
Understand meanings of operations and how they relate to one another	• understand various meanings of addition and subtraction of whole numbers and the relationship between the two operations; • understand the effects of adding and subtracting whole numbers; • understand situations that entail multiplication and division, such as equal groupings of objects and sharing equally.	• understand various meanings of multiplication and division; • understand the effects of multiplying and dividing whole numbers; • identify and use relationships between operations, such as division as the inverse of multiplication, to solve problems; • understand and use properties of operations, such as the distributivity of multiplication over addition.	• understand the meaning and effects of arithmetic operations with fractions, decimals, and integers; • use the associative and commutative properties of addition and multiplication and the distributive property of multiplication over addition to simplify computations with integers, fractions, and decimals; • understand and use the inverse relationships of addition and subtraction, multiplication and division, and squaring and finding square roots to simplify computations and solve problems.
Compute fluently and make reasonable estimates	• develop and use strategies for whole-number computations, with a focus on addition and subtraction; • develop fluency with basic number combinations for addition and subtraction; • use a variety of methods and tools to compute, including objects, mental computation, estimation, paper and pencil, and calculators.	• develop fluency with basic number combinations for multiplication and division and use these combinations to mentally compute related problems, such as 30×50; • develop fluency in adding, subtracting, multiplying, and dividing whole numbers; • develop and use strategies to estimate the results of whole-number computations and to judge the reasonableness of such results; • develop and use strategies to estimate computations involving fractions and decimals in situations relevant to students' experience; • use visual models, benchmarks, and equivalent forms to add and subtract commonly used fractions and decimals; • select appropriate methods and tools for computing with whole numbers from among mental computation, estimation, calculators, and paper and pencil according to the context and nature of the computation	• select appropriate methods and tools for computing with fractions and decimals from among mental computation, estimation, calculators or computers, and paper and pencil, depending on the situation, and apply the selected methods; • develop and analyze algorithms for computing with fractions, decimals, and integers and develop fluency in their use; • develop and use strategies to estimate the results of rational-number computations and judge the reasonableness of the results; • develop, analyze, and explain methods for solving problems involving proportions, such as scaling and finding equivalent ratios.

Table of Standards and Expectations. Reprinted with permission from *Principles and Standards for School Mathematics*, copyright by the National Council of Teachers of Mathematics. All rights reserved.

Algebra

Standard	Pre-K–2	Grades 3–5	Grades 6–8
Instructional programs from prekindergarten through grade 12 should enable all students to—	***EXPECTATIONS*** In prekindergarten through grade 2 all students should—	***EXPECTATIONS*** In grades 3–5 all students should—	***EXPECTATIONS*** In grades 6–8 all students should—
Understand patterns, relations, and functions	• sort, classify, and order objects by size, number, and other properties; • recognize, describe, and extend patterns such as sequences of sounds and shapes or simple numeric patterns and translate from one representation to another; • analyze how both repeating and growing patterns are generated.	• describe, extend, and make generalizations about geometric and numeric patterns; • represent and analyze patterns and functions, using words, tables, and graphs.	• represent, analyze, and generalize a variety of patterns with tables, graphs, words, and, when possible, symbolic rules; • relate and compare different forms of representation for a relationship; • identify functions as linear or nonlinear and contrast their properties from tables, graphs, or equations.
Represent and analyze mathematical situations and structures using algebraic symbols	• illustrate general principles and properties of operations, such as commutativity, using specific numbers; • use concrete, pictorial, and verbal representations to develop an understanding of invented and conventional symbolic notations.	• identify such properties as commutativity, associativity, and distributivity and use them to compute with whole numbers; • represent the idea of a variable as an unknown quantity using a letter or symbol; • express mathematical relationships using equations.	• develop an initial conceptual understanding of different uses of variables; • explore relationships between symbolic expressions and graphs of lines, paying particular attention to the meaning of intercept and slope; • use symbolic algebra to represent situations and to solve problems, especially those that involve linear relationships; • recognize and generate equivalent forms for simple algebraic expressions and solve linear equations.
Use mathematical models to represent and understand quantitative relationships	• model situations that involve the addition and subtraction of whole numbers, using objects, pictures, and symbols.	• model problem situations with objects and use representations such as graphs, tables, and equations to draw conclusions.	• model and solve contextualized problems using various representations, such as graphs, tables, and equations.
Analyze change in various contexts	• describe qualitative change, such as a student's growing taller; • describe quantitative change, such as a student's growing two inches in one year.	• investigate how a change in one variable relates to a change in a second variable; • identify and describe situations with constant or varying rates of change and compare them.	• use graphs to analyze the nature of changes in quantities in linear relationships.

Table of Standards and Expectations. Reprinted with permission from *Principles and Standards for School Mathematics*, copyright by the National Council of Teachers of Mathematics. All rights reserved.

Geometry

Standard	Pre-K–2	Grades 3–5	Grades 6–8
Instructional programs from prekindergarten through grade 12 should enable all students to—	**EXPECTATIONS** In prekindergarten through grade 2 all students should—	**EXPECTATIONS** In grades 3–5 all students should—	**EXPECTATIONS** In grades 6–8 all students should—
Analyze characteristics and properties of two- and three-dimensional geometric shapes and develop mathematical arguments about geometric relationships	• recognize, name, build, draw, compare, and sort two- and three-dimensional shapes; • describe attributes and parts of two- and three-dimensional shapes; • investigate and predict the results of putting together and taking apart two- and three-dimensional shapes.	• identify, compare, and analyze attributes of two- and three-dimensional shapes and develop vocabulary to describe the attributes; • classify two- and three-dimensional shapes according to their properties and develop definitions of classes of shapes such as triangles and pyramids; • investigate, describe, and reason about the results of subdividing, combining, and transforming shapes; • explore congruence and similarity; • make and test conjectures about geometric properties and relationships and develop logical arguments to justify conclusions.	• precisely describe, classify, and understand relationships among types of two- and three-dimensional objects using their defining properties; • understand relationships among the angles, side lengths, perimeters, areas, and volumes of similar objects; • create and critique inductive and deductive arguments concerning geometric ideas and relationships, such as congruence, similarity, and the Pythagorean relationship.
Specify locations and describe spatial relationships using coordinate geometry and other representational systems	• describe, name, and interpret relative positions in space and apply ideas about relative position; • describe, name, and interpret direction and distance in navigating space and apply ideas about direction and distance; • find and name locations with simple relationships such as "near to" and in coordinate systems such as maps.	• describe location and movement using common language and geometric vocabulary; • make and use coordinate systems to specify locations and to describe paths; • find the distance between points along horizontal and vertical lines of a coordinate system.	• use coordinate geometry to represent and examine the properties of geometric shapes; • use coordinate geometry to examine special geometric shapes, such as regular polygons or those with pairs of parallel or perpendicular sides.
Apply transformations and use symmetry to analyze mathematical situations	• recognize and apply slides, flips, and turns; • recognize and create shapes that have symmetry.	• predict and describe the results of sliding, flipping, and turning two-dimensional shapes; • describe a motion or a series of motions that will show that two shapes are congruent; • identify and describe line and rotational symmetry in two- and three-dimensional shapes and designs.	• describe sizes, positions, and orientations of shapes under informal transformations such as flips, turns, slides, and scaling; • examine the congruence, similarity, and line or rotational symmetry of objects using transformations.
Use visualization, spatial reasoning, and geometric modeling to solve problems	• create mental images of geometric shapes using spatial memory and spatial visualization; • recognize and represent shapes from different perspectives; • relate ideas in geometry to ideas in number and measurement; • recognize geometric shapes and structures in the environment and specify their location.	• build and draw geometric objects; • create and describe mental images of objects, patterns, and paths; • identify and build a three-dimensional object from two-dimensional representations of that object; • identify and build a two-dimensional representation of a three-dimensional object; • use geometric models to solve problems in other areas of mathematics, such as number and measurement; • recognize geometric ideas and relationships and apply them to other disciplines and to problems that arise in the classroom or in everyday life.	• draw geometric objects with specified properties, such as side lengths or angle measures; • use two-dimensional representations of three-dimensional objects to visualize and solve problems such as those involving surface area and volume; • use visual tools such as networks to represent and solve problems; • use geometric models to represent and explain numerical and algebraic relationships; • recognize and apply geometric ideas and relationships in areas outside the mathematical classroom, such as art, science, and everyday life.

Table of Standards and Expectations. Reprinted with permission from *Principles and Standards for School Mathematics*, copyright by the National Council of Teachers of Mathematics. All rights reserved.

Measurement

Standard	Pre-K–2	Grades 3–5	Grades 6–8
Instructional programs from prekindergarten through grade 12 should enable all students to—	**EXPECTATIONS** In prekindergarten through grade 2 all students should—	**EXPECTATIONS** In grades 3–5 all students should—	**EXPECTATIONS** In grades 6–8 all students should—
Understand measurable attributes of objects and the units, systems, and processes of measurement	• recognize the attributes of length, volume, weight, area, and time; • compare and order objects according to these attributes; • understand how to measure using nonstandard and standard units; • select an appropriate unit and tool for the attribute being measured.	• understand such attributes as length, area, weight, volume, and size of angle and select the appropriate type of unit for measuring each attribute; • understand the need for measuring with standard units and become familiar with standard units in the customary and metric systems; • carry out simple unit conversions, such as from centimeters to meters, within a system of measurement; • understand that measurements are approximations and understand how differences in units affect precision; • explore what happens to measurements of a two-dimensional shape such as its perimeter and area when the shape is changed in some way.	• understand both metric and customary systems of measurement; • understand relationships among units and convert from one unit to another within the same system; • understand, select, and use units of appropriate size and type to measure angles, perimeter, area, surface area, and volume.
Apply appropriate techniques, tools, and formulas to determine measurements	• measure with multiple copies of units of the same size, such as paper clips laid end to end; • use repetition of a single unit to measure something larger than the unit, for instance, measuring the length of a room with a single meterstick; • use tools to measure; • develop common referents for measures to make comparisons and estimates.	• develop strategies for estimating the perimeters, areas, and volumes of irregular shapes; • select and apply appropriate standard units and tools to measure length, area, volume, weight, time, temperature, and the size of angles; • select and use benchmarks to estimate measurements; • develop, understand, and use formulas to find the area of rectangles and related triangles and parallelograms; • develop strategies to determine the surface areas and volumes of rectangular solids.	• use common benchmarks to select appropriate methods for estimating measurements; • select and apply techniques and tools to accurately find length, area, volume, and angle measures to appropriate levels of precision; • develop and use formulas to determine the circumference of circles and the area of triangles, parallelograms, trapezoids, and circles and develop strategies to find the areas of more complex shapes; • develop strategies to determine the surface area and volume of selected prisms, pyramids, and cylinders; • solve problems involving scale factors, using ratio and proportion; • solve simple problems involving rates and derived measurements for such attributes as velocity and density.

Table of Standards and Expectations. Reprinted with permission from *Principles and Standards for School Mathematics*, copyright by the National Council of Teachers of Mathematics. All rights reserved.

Data Analysis and Probability

Standard	Pre-K–2	Grades 3–5	Grades 6–8
Instructional programs from prekindergarten through grade 12 should enable all students to—	**EXPECTATIONS** In prekindergarten through grade 2 all students should—	**EXPECTATIONS** In grades 3–5 all students should—	**EXPECTATIONS** In grades 6–8 all students should—
Formulate questions that can be addressed with data and collect, organize, and display relevant data to answer them	• pose questions and gather data about themselves and their surroundings; • sort and classify objects according to their attributes and organize data about the objects; • represent data using concrete objects, pictures, and graphs.	• design investigations to address a question and consider how data-collection methods affect the nature of the data set; • collect data using observations, surveys, and experiments; • represent data using tables and graphs such as line plots, bar graphs, and line graphs; • recognize the differences in representing categorical and numerical data.	• formulate questions, design studies, and collect data about a characteristic shared by two populations or different characteristics within one population; • select, create, and use appropriate graphical representations of data, including histograms, box plots, and scatterplots.
Select and use appropriate statistical methods to analyze data	• describe parts of the data and the set of data as a whole to determine what the data show.	• describe the shape and important features of a set of data and compare related data sets, with an emphasis on how the data are distributed; • use measures of center, focusing on the median, and understand what each does and does not indicate about the data set; • compare different representations of the same data and evaluate how well each representation shows important aspects of the data.	• find, use, and interpret measures of center and spread, including mean and interquartile range; • discuss and understand the correspondence between data sets and their graphical representations, especially histograms, stem-and-leaf plots, box plots, and scatterplots.
Develop and evaluate inferences and predictions that are based on data	• discuss events related to students' experiences as likely or unlikely.	• propose and justify conclusions and predictions that are based on data and design studies to further investigate the conclusions or predictions.	• use observations about differences between two or more samples to make conjectures about the populations from which the samples were taken; • make conjectures about possible relationships between two characteristics of a sample on the basis of scatterplots of the data and approximate lines of fit; • use conjectures to formulate new questions and plan new studies to answer them.
Understand and apply basic concepts of probability		• describe events as likely or unlikely and discuss the degree of likelihood using such words as *certain*, *equally likely*, and *impossible*; • predict the probability of outcomes of simple experiments and test the predictions; • understand that the measure of the likelihood of an event can be represented by a number from 0 to 1.	• understand and use appropriate terminology to describe complementary and mutually exclusive events; • use proportionality and a basic understanding of probability to make and test conjectures about the results of experiments and simulations; • compute probabilities for simple compound events, using such methods as organized lists, tree diagrams, and area methods.

Table of Standards and Expectations. Reprinted with permission from *Principles and Standards for School Mathematics*, copyright by the National Council of Teachers of Mathematics. All rights reserved.

Problem Solving

Standard
Instructional programs from prekindergarten through grade 12 should enable all students to—

- Build new mathematical knowledge through problem solving
- Solve problems that arise in mathematics and in other contexts
- Apply and adapt a variety of appropriate strategies to solve problems
- Monitor and reflect on the process of mathematical problem solving

Reasoning and Proof

Standard
Instructional programs from prekindergarten through grade 12 should enable all students to—

- Recognize reasoning and proof as fundamental aspects of mathematics
- Make and investigate mathematical conjectures
- Develop and evaluate mathematical arguments and proofs
- Select and use various types of reasoning and methods of proof

Communication

Standard
Instructional programs from prekindergarten through grade 12 should enable all students to—

- Organize and consolidate their mathematical thinking through communication
- Communicate their mathematical thinking coherently and clearly to peers, teachers, and others
- Analyze and evaluate the mathematical thinking and strategies of others
- Use the language of mathematics to express mathematical ideas precisely

Connections

Standard
Instructional programs from prekindergarten through grade 12 should enable all students to—

- Recognize and use connections among mathematical ideas
- Understand how mathematical ideas interconnect and build on one another to produce a coherent whole
- Recognize and apply mathematics in contexts outside of mathematics

Representation

Standard
Instructional programs from prekindergarten through grade 12 should enable all students to—

- Create and use representations to organize, record, and communicate mathematical ideas
- Select, apply, and translate among mathematical representations to solve problems
- Use representations to model and interpret physical, social, and mathematical phenomena

Table of Standards and Expectations. Reprinted with permission from *Principles and Standards for School Mathematics*, copyright by the National Council of Teachers of Mathematics. All rights reserved.

INDEX

Masters

B-1 Attribute Pieces

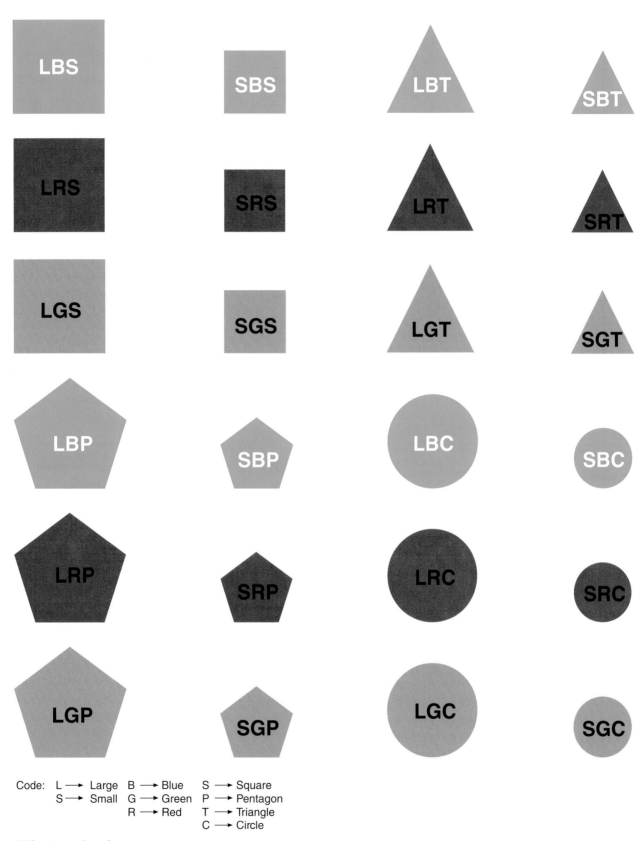

Code: L → Large   B → Blue   S → Square
       S → Small   G → Green   P → Pentagon
                   R → Red   T → Triangle
                              C → Circle

LBS = Large Blue Square

Reys et al., *Helping Children Learn Mathematics*, 8E, copyright © 2007 by John Wiley & Sons, Inc.

B–2 Cuisenaire Rods

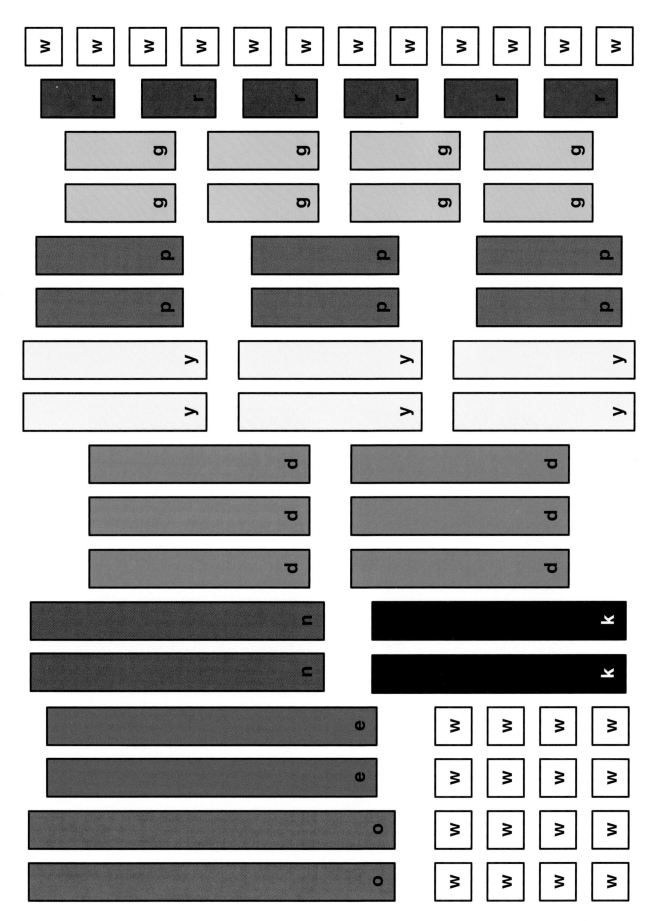

Reys et al., *Helping Children Learn Mathematics*, 8E, copyright © 2007 by John Wiley & Sons, Inc.

B–3 Base 10 Blocks

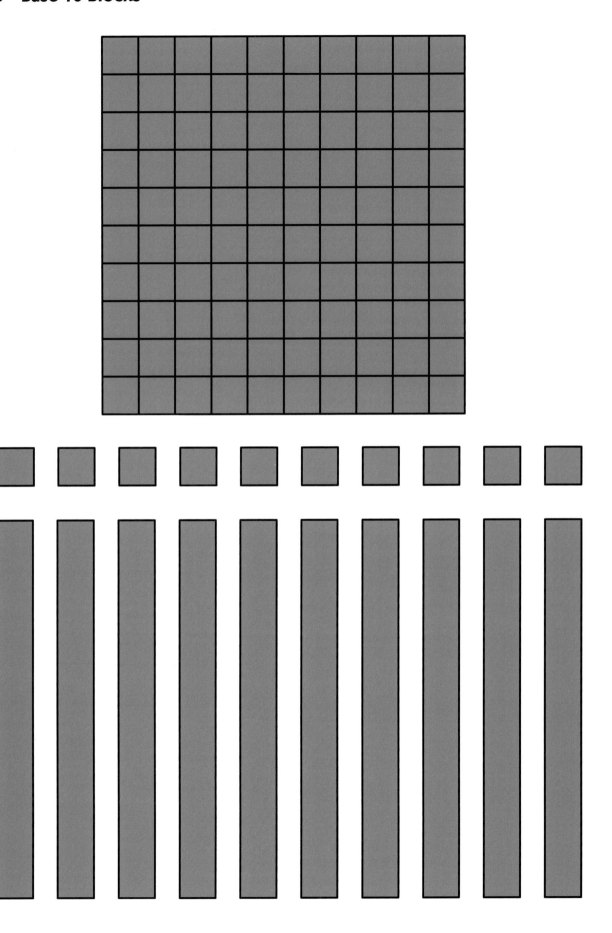

Reys et al., *Helping Children Learn Mathematics*, 8E, copyright © 2007 by John Wiley & Sons, Inc.

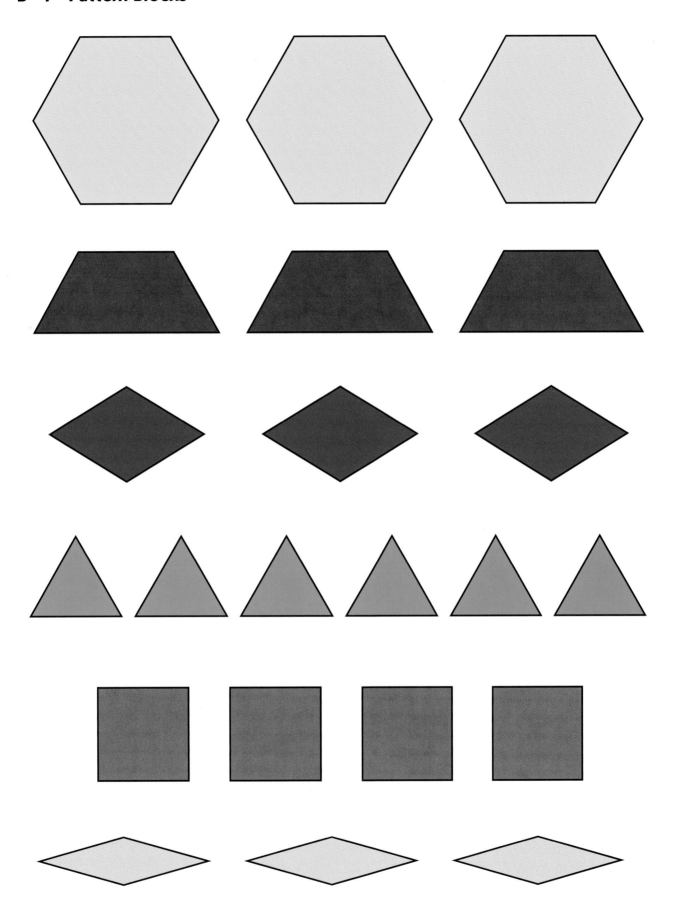

Reys et al., *Helping Children Learn Mathematics*, 8E, copyright © 2007 by John Wiley & Sons, Inc.

B–5   Five and Ten Frames

Reys et al., *Helping Children Learn Mathematics,* 8E, copyright © 2007 by John Wiley & Sons, Inc.

B–6   Hundred Charts

1	2	3	4	5	6	7	8	9	10
11	12	13	14	15	16	17	18	19	20
21	22	23	24	25	26	27	28	29	30
31	32	33	34	35	36	37	38	39	40
41	42	43	44	45	46	47	48	49	50
51	52	53	54	55	56	57	58	59	60
61	62	63	64	65	66	67	68	69	70
71	72	73	74	75	76	77	78	79	80
81	82	83	84	85	86	87	88	89	90
91	92	93	94	95	96	97	98	99	100

0	1	2	3	4	5	6	7	8	9
10	11	12	13	14	15	16	17	18	19
20	21	22	23	24	25	26	27	28	29
30	31	32	33	34	35	36	37	38	39
40	41	42	43	44	45	46	47	48	49
50	51	52	53	54	55	56	57	58	59
60	61	62	63	64	65	66	67	68	69
70	71	72	73	74	75	76	77	78	79
80	81	82	83	84	85	86	87	88	89
90	91	92	93	94	95	96	97	98	99

Reys et al., *Helping Children Learn Mathematics*, 8E, copyright © 2007 by John Wiley & Sons, Inc.

B-7 Variations of Hundreds Charts

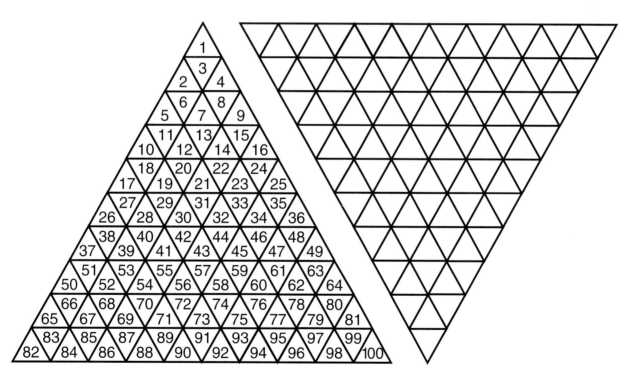

B-8 Basic Addition and Multiplication Facts

+	0	1	2	3	4	5	6	7	8	9
0	0	1	2	3	4	5	6	7	8	9
1	1	2	3	4	5	6	7	8	9	10
2	2	3	4	5	6	7	8	9	10	11
3	3	4	5	6	7	8	9	10	11	12
4	4	5	6	7	8	9	10	11	12	13
5	5	6	7	8	9	10	11	12	13	14
6	6	7	8	9	10	11	12	13	14	15
7	7	8	9	10	11	12	13	14	15	16
8	8	9	10	11	12	13	14	15	16	17
9	9	10	11	12	13	14	15	16	17	18

- ☐ Commutativity
- ☐ Using 0 and 1
- ☐ Doubles, Doubles + or −1
- ☐ Counting On (1,2,3)
- ☐ Adding to 10

X	0	1	2	3	4	5	6	7	8	9
0	0	0	0	0	0	0	0	0	0	0
1	0	1	2	3	4	5	6	7	8	9
2	0	2	4	6	8	10	12	14	16	18
3	0	3	6	9	12	15	18	21	24	27
4	0	4	8	12	16	20	24	28	32	36
5	0	5	10	15	20	25	30	35	40	45
6	0	6	12	18	24	30	36	42	48	54
7	0	7	14	21	28	35	42	49	56	63
8	0	8	16	24	32	40	48	56	64	72
9	0	9	18	27	36	45	54	63	72	81

- ☐ Commutativity
- ☐ Using 0 and 1
- ☐ Skip Counting
- ☐ Repeated Addition
- ☐ Splitting Product into Known Parts
- ☐ Patterns

Reys et al., *Helping Children Learn Mathematics*, 8E, copyright © 2007 by John Wiley & Sons, Inc.

4	9
3	8
2	7
1	6
0	5

Reys et al., *Helping Children Learn Mathematics*, 8E, copyright © 2007 by John Wiley & Sons, Inc.

B–10 Powers of Ten

1   10   100

1000

10000

Reys et al., *Helping Children Learn Mathematics*, 8E, copyright © 2007 by John Wiley & Sons, Inc.

B-11   Decimal or Percent Paper

Reys et al., *Helping Children Learn Mathematics*, 8E, copyright © 2007 by John Wiley & Sons, Inc.

B–12   Fraction Bars

one	1										
halves	$\frac{1}{2}$						$\frac{2}{2}$				
thirds	$\frac{1}{3}$				$\frac{2}{3}$				$\frac{3}{3}$		
fourths	$\frac{1}{4}$			$\frac{2}{4}$			$\frac{3}{4}$			$\frac{4}{4}$	
fifths	$\frac{1}{5}$		$\frac{2}{5}$		$\frac{3}{5}$		$\frac{4}{5}$		$\frac{5}{5}$		
sixths	$\frac{1}{6}$		$\frac{2}{6}$		$\frac{3}{6}$	$\frac{4}{6}$		$\frac{5}{6}$		$\frac{6}{6}$	
eighths	$\frac{1}{8}$	$\frac{2}{8}$	$\frac{3}{8}$	$\frac{4}{8}$	$\frac{5}{8}$	$\frac{6}{8}$	$\frac{7}{8}$	$\frac{8}{8}$			
ninths	$\frac{1}{9}$	$\frac{2}{9}$	$\frac{3}{9}$	$\frac{4}{9}$	$\frac{5}{9}$	$\frac{6}{9}$	$\frac{7}{9}$	$\frac{8}{9}$	$\frac{9}{9}$		
tenths	$\frac{1}{10}$	$\frac{2}{10}$	$\frac{3}{10}$	$\frac{4}{10}$	$\frac{5}{10}$	$\frac{6}{10}$	$\frac{7}{10}$	$\frac{8}{10}$	$\frac{9}{10}$	$\frac{10}{10}$	
twelfths	$\frac{1}{12}$	$\frac{2}{12}$	$\frac{3}{12}$	$\frac{4}{12}$	$\frac{5}{12}$	$\frac{6}{12}$	$\frac{7}{12}$	$\frac{8}{12}$	$\frac{9}{12}$	$\frac{10}{12}$	$\frac{11}{12}$	$\frac{12}{12}$

Reys et al., *Helping Children Learn Mathematics*, 8E, copyright © 2007 by John Wiley & Sons, Inc.

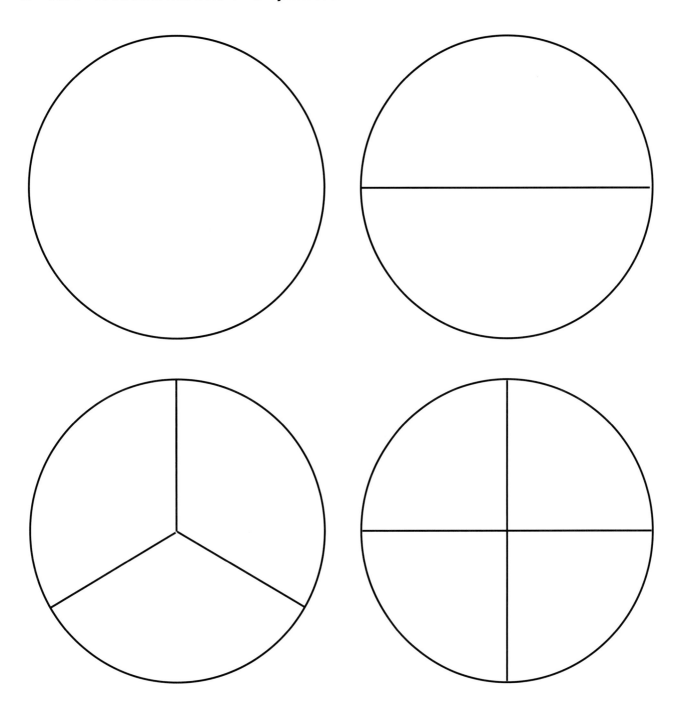

Reys et al., *Helping Children Learn Mathematics*, 8E, copyright © 2007 by John Wiley & Sons, Inc.

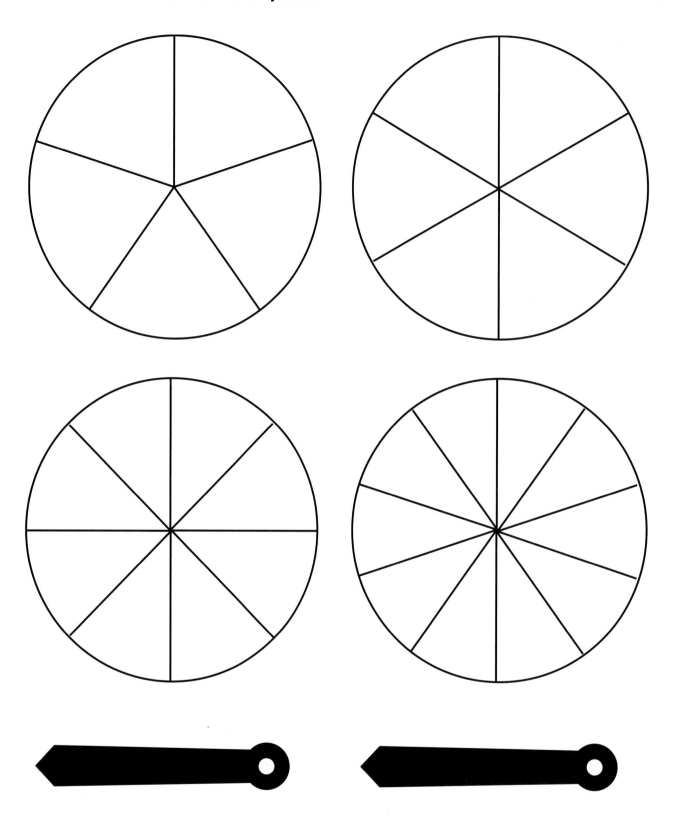

Reys et al., *Helping Children Learn Mathematics*, 8E, copyright © 2007 by John Wiley & Sons, Inc.

B–14 Rulers

Primary inch ruler

Half-inch ruler

Fourth-inch ruler

Eighth-inch ruler

Primary centimeter ruler

Millimeter ruler

Reys et al., *Helping Children Learn Mathematics*, 8E, copyright © 2007 by John Wiley & Sons, Inc.

B–15   Geoboard Template

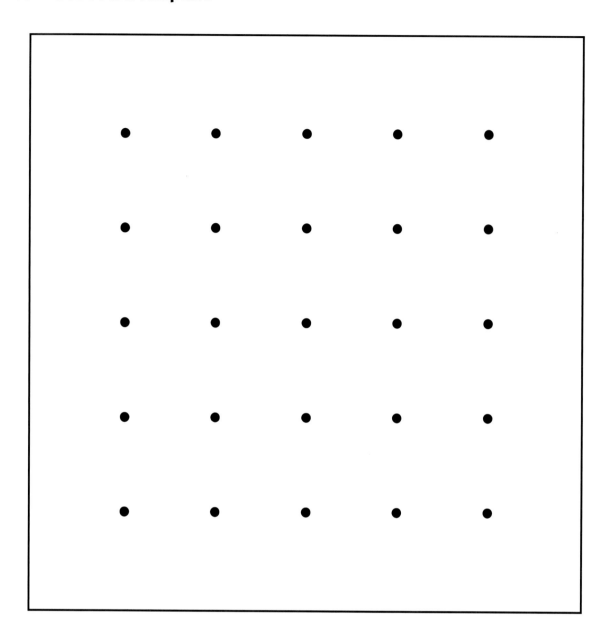

Reys et al., *Helping Children Learn Mathematics,* 8E, copyright © 2007 by John Wiley & Sons, Inc.

B-16 Geoboard Recording Paper

Reys et al., *Helping Children Learn Mathematics*, 8E, copyright © 2007 by John Wiley & Sons, Inc.

B-17 Centimeter Dot Paper

Reys et al., *Helping Children Learn Mathematics*, 8E, copyright © 2007 by John Wiley & Sons, Inc.

B-18 Isometric Paper

Reys et al., *Helping Children Learn Mathematics*, 8E, copyright © 2007 by John Wiley & Sons, Inc.

B–19 Centimeter Grid Paper

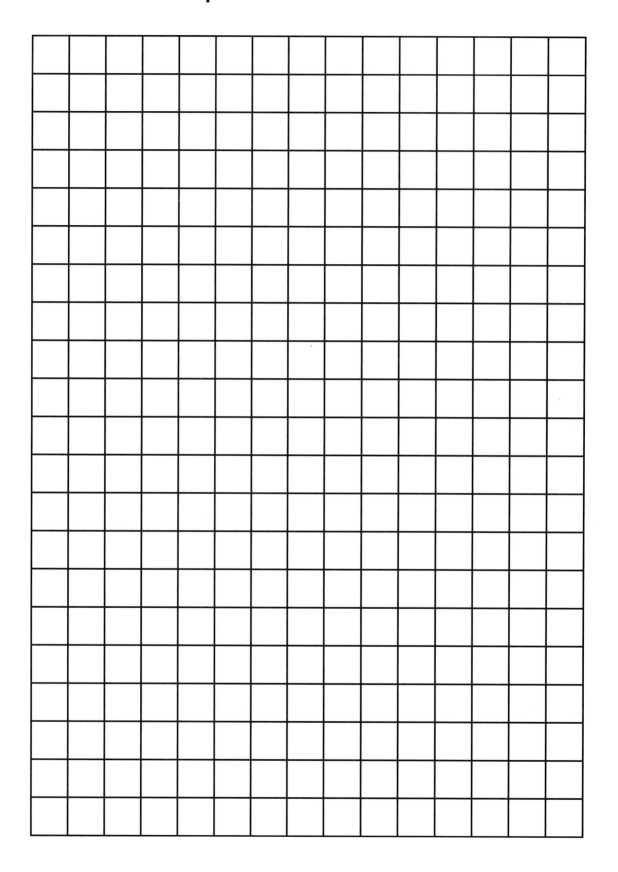

Reys et al., *Helping Children Learn Mathematics*, 8E, copyright © 2007 by John Wiley & Sons, Inc.

B–20 Inch Grid Paper

Reys et al., *Helping Children Learn Mathematics*, 8E, copyright © 2007 by John Wiley & Sons, Inc.

Reys et al., *Helping Children Learn Mathematics*, 8E, copyright © 2007 by John Wiley & Sons, Inc.

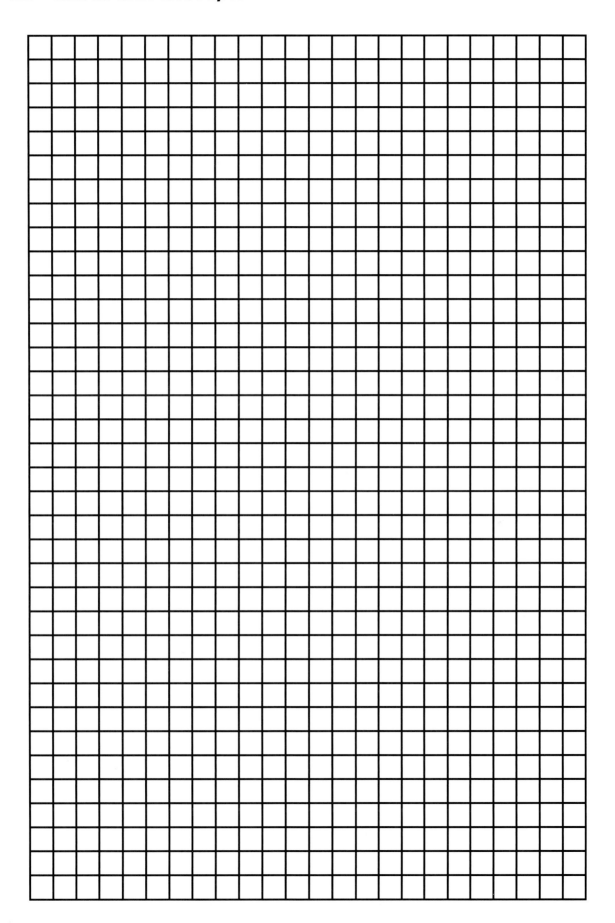

Reys et al., *Helping Children Learn Mathematics*, 8E, copyright © 2007 by John Wiley & Sons, Inc.

B−23 **Geometric Design Paper**

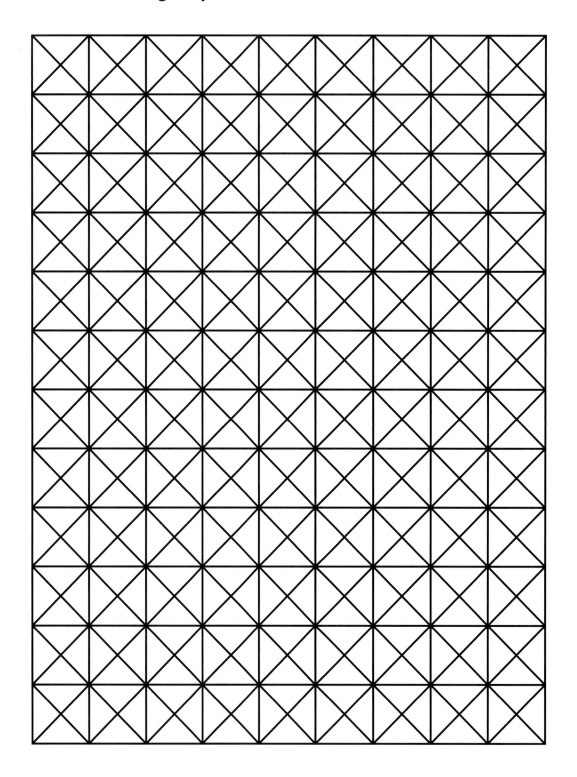

Reys et al., *Helping Children Learn Mathematics*, 8E, copyright © 2007 by John Wiley & Sons, Inc.

B-24 Equilateral Triangle Paper

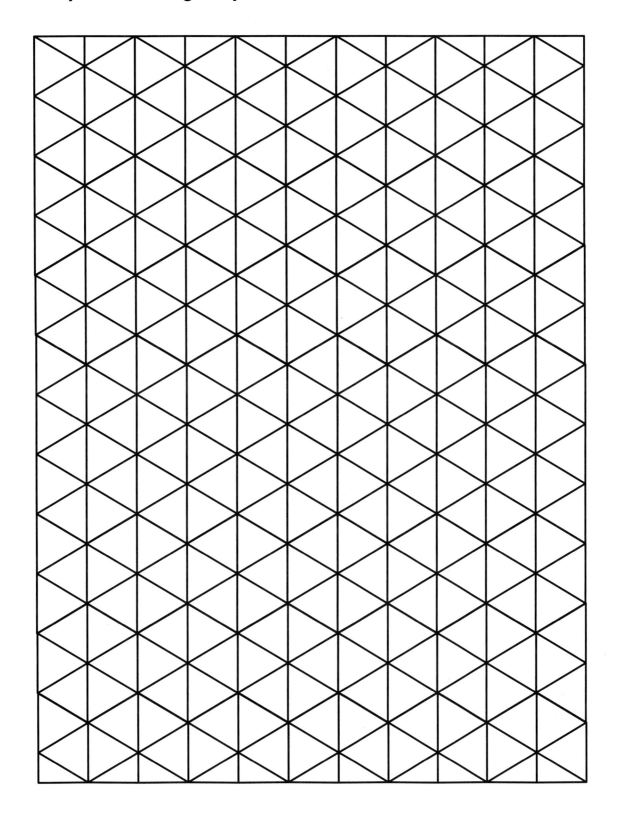

Reys et al., *Helping Children Learn Mathematics*, 8E, copyright © 2007 by John Wiley & Sons, Inc.

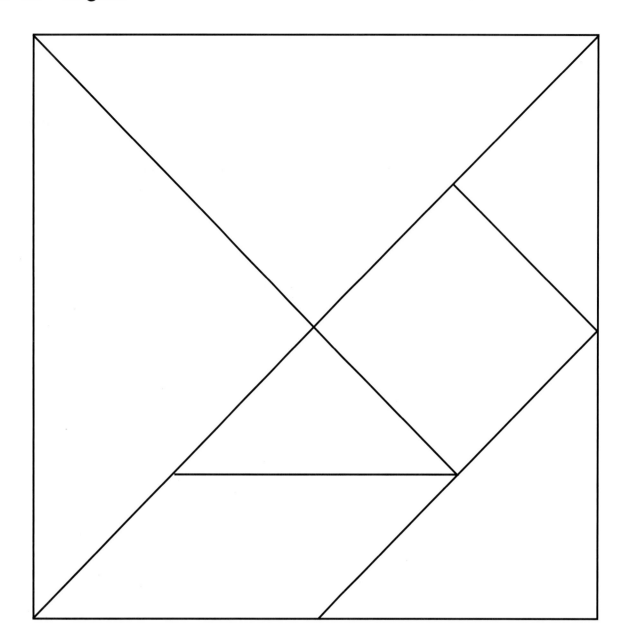

Reys et al., *Helping Children Learn Mathematics*, 8E, copyright © 2007 by John Wiley & Sons, Inc.